ASVAB®

The Armed Services Vocational Aptitude Battery

2007 Edition

ASVAB®

THE ARMED SERVICES VOCATIONAL APTITUDE BATTERY

2007 Edition

PUBLISHING

New York • Chicago

This publication is designed to provide accurate and authoritative information in regard to the subject matter covered. It is sold with the understanding that the publisher is not engaged in rendering legal, accounting, or other professional service. If legal advice or other expert assistance is required, the services of a competent professional should be sought.

Editorial Director: Jennifer Farthing
Editor: Cynthia C. Yazbek
Production Artist: Renée Mitchell
Cover Designer: Carly Schnur

Published by Kaplan Publishing, a division of Kaplan, Inc.
888 Seventh Ave.
New York, NY 10106

Printed in the United States of America

June 2006
10 9 8 7 6 5 4 3 2 1

ISBN 13: 978-1-4195-4208-4
ISBN 10:   1-4195-4208-7

Kaplan Publishing books are available at special quantity discounts to use for sales promotions, employee premiums, or educational purposes. Please call our Special Sales Department to order or for more information at 800-621-9621, ext. 4444, e-mail kaplanpubsales@kaplan.com, or write to Kaplan Publishing, 30 South Wacker Drive, Suite 2500, Chicago, IL 60606-7481.

TABLE OF CONTENTS

Part Three: Review of Technical ASVAB Subtests

Part Four: ASVAB Practice Tests

How To Read Your ASVAB Scores

AVAILABLE ONLINE

FOR ANY TEST CHANGES OR LATE-BREAKING DEVELOPMENTS

kaptest.com/publishing

The material in this book is up-to-date at the time of publication. However, the College Board and Educational Testing Service (ETS) may have instituted changes in the test after this book was published. Be sure to carefully read the materials you receive when you register for the test. If there are any important late-breaking developments—or any changes or corrections to the Kaplan test preparation materials in this book—we will post that information online at **kaptest.com/publishing**.

FEEDBACK AND COMMENTS

kaplansurveys.com/books

We'd love to hear your comments and suggestions about this book. We invite you to fill out our online survey form at **kaplansurveys.com/books**. Your feedback is extremely helpful as we continue to develop high-quality resources to meet your needs.

This book provides you with everything you need to ace the ASVAB. We've included this section with some tips on how to make sure you make the most of your prep time.

Step One: Familiarize Yourself with the ASVAB

The first chapter of this book, The ASVAB Challenge, covers the basics of the test: what's on it, who it's for, and the various formats it appears in. Once you get a sense of what's on the test, you're ready to get a sense of yourself as a test taker. Additionally, the first chapter gives you Kaplan's exclusive test-taking strategies. Read this chapter carefully to learn Kaplan's proven methods for increasing your score on this challenging exam.

Step Two: Take the Diagnostic Test (Practice Test I)

This book contains three simulated full-length ASVAB tests with explanations. We've designed this book to allow you to take one of these tests early in your preparation and get a sense of where you're scoring now, and what score you're shooting for on test day. As you work through your diagnostic exam, pay especially close attention to the areas you perform best in. Particular attention should be given to the two math and the two verbal sections, which form the AFQT, or qualifying part of this armed services exam (more on the AFQT in chapter 1). These areas of strength will provide you with the bulk of your points on the actual exam. Also make note of your problem areas. You will need to shore up your knowledge in your problem areas to maximize your performance on the test.

With a clear sense of your strengths and weaknesses, you will be ready to tackle the content chapters that form the bulk of this book.

Step Three: Work Through the Material So That You Reinforce Strengths and Shore Up Weaknesses

Each content chapter focuses on a specific subject as it is tested on the ASVAB. Based on your performance on the Diagnostic Test, you should have a good sense of which areas you are strongest in, and which areas need the most reinforcement. Each chapter includes quizzes to help you test yourself on the content just covered.

Develop a study plan that devotes roughly equal time to all of the chapters. Aim to complete all the content two weeks prior to your exam date. The last two weeks should be spent working through the second and third practice tests and reviewing your notes.

Step Four: Conclude Your Preparation with Practice Tests II and III

Your preparation with this book should conclude with the second and third simulated full-length ASVAB tests. After completing these exams, work through the explanations that follow them. Be sure to review the explanations for questions you got right as well as for those you got wrong. This will serve as a good review of the wide range of topics covered on the exam. After completing the exams, continue to refer to the content chapters to make sure you are familiar with everything we cover in this book.

Use this game plan to prepare for test day. Then, right before the exam, relax. You can rest easier because you're ready for the ASVAB. With some hard work and a little forward thinking, you're going to get a great score!

Part One

GETTING STARTED

CHAPTER ONE

The ASVAB Challenge

If you've purchased this book, we assume you are considering taking the ASVAB (short for Armed Services Vocational Aptitude Battery). People take the ASVAB for many different reasons, and at different stages in their career decision-making process. And depending on why and how you are taking the ASVAB, you may want to read certain sections of this book more carefully than others.

Many students take the ASVAB in high school or vocational school, because it's offered for free and, even if they aren't considering a career in the United States Armed Forces, it can give them valuable feedback on where their aptitudes presently lie, as well as where they stack up, percentage-wise, against others considering the same career. If you are taking the ASVAB this way and also think that you may want to enlist in the U.S. Armed Services, you will want to make sure to do well on the AFQT (Armed Forces Qualifying Test), which we'll discuss in a bit.

Others take the ASVAB after high school because they have recently considered a career in the military. If you didn't take the ASVAB in high school or elsewhere, and are between the ages of 17 and 35, you can still take the ASVAB for free by simply walking into a recruiting station and asking to take the test. Those of you who are considering taking the test this way should spend some serious study time beforehand figuring out what type of military career you want to pursue, and what subtests of the ASVAB you will need to do well on to assure that you qualify for the position you seek.

THE ASVAB IS NOT AN IQ TEST!

The ASVAB does not purport to measure *intelligence*. The battery of tests is supposed to measure an individual's aptitude to be trained in specific jobs. But it's not an *aptitude* test either, because you can improve your score on the ASVAB greatly by studying this book. What the ASVAB truly measures is your ability and preparedness to take the ASVAB, nothing more or less.

This book won't give you all the answers to the test. The truth is that you probably already have many of the answers rattling around somewhere in your head. But this book can help you understand what will be expected of you on test day and give you strategies for handling the very toughest questions on the test. It can also offer a solid review of those subjects that may not be your areas of strength, but that you are willing to study now in order to increase your military career options.

WHAT IS THE ASVAB?

There are presently four versions of the ASVAB. The first version is Form 18/19, or *student version* of the ASVAB, which is the paper-based test commonly given to over a million high school and vocational school students each year. The ASVAB is administered once or twice a year at almost 15,000 high schools and postsecondary schools in the United States. The second version of the ASVAB, Forms 20–22, is known as the *production version*. This version is given by the Armed Forces for enlistment purposes only. While the questions on the two versions are different, they are designed to be of equal difficulty. The third version is the CAT-ASVAB, which is a computerized version of the Forms 20–22 ASVAB. We'll discuss the pros and cons of taking the computerized test in a bit, but for now just know that, like the other two versions, the computerized version is supposed to be of equal difficulty and yield the same scores. As of this writing, prospective enlistees have their choice as to whether to take either the paper or computerized version of the Forms 20–22 ASVAB, but that may change. Any of these three ASVABs may be used for enlistment in the U.S. Armed Forces.

Finally, a fourth "shortened" version of the ASVAB has been offered in secondary and post-secondary schools since 2002. This shortened test contains only five subtests (the two math and two verbal tests, and the General Science test) and takes about two hours to administer, rather than the 3.5 hours that it takes to administer the full-length ASVAB. For this reason many schools are finding the shortened version easier to administer, and the shortened ASVAB is becoming increasingly popular. Students who take the shortened ASVAB, like students who take the full-length ASVAB, will get an AFQT score that determines their eligibility in the different branches of the Armed Forces. If they then decide to enlist, they can then take a computerized "merge" test of the subtests that they did not take on the shortened student ASVAB.

FIND OUT WHICH KIND OF ASVAB YOU ARE TAKING

If you are taking a school-administered version of the ASVAB, make sure you know whether you are taking the full-length version or the shortened version. If you are taking the shortened version, there are several sections of this book that you won't need to study at this point!

The full-length ASVAB is made up of up to nine sections, depending on which version of the test you take. The paper version of the ASVAB at the time of this writing does not include an "Assembling Objects" subtest, but that may soon change. The CAT-ASVAB does. The order in which the subtests are administered on the ASVAB never varies, and is as follows:

Subtest	Questions	Time limit (minutes)	What's tested
General Science (GS)	25	11	Knowledge of general concepts from life, earth, and physical sciences
Arithmetic Reasoning (AR)	30	36	The ability to answer word problems that involve basic arithmetic calculations
Word Knowledge (WK)	35	11	The ability to recognize synonyms of words
Paragraph Comprehension (PC)	15	13	The ability to answer questions based on short passages (of 30-120 words)
Auto & Shop Information (AS)*	25	11	Knowledge of automobiles, tools, and shop terminology
Mathematics Knowledge (MK)	25	24	Knowledge of math concepts, including applied arithmetic, algebra, and geometry
Mechanical Comprehension (MC)	25	19	Knowledge of basic mechanical and physical principles
Electronics Information (EI)	20	9	Knowledge of electronic principles and terminology, and basic electronic circuitry
Assembling Objects** (AO)	16	9	The ability to interpret diagrams showing spatial relationships and understand how objects are connected

* Note: At the time of the writing, on the CAT-ASVAB this subtest has been split into two separate subtests.

** Note: At the time of the writing, this subtest is given only on the CAT-ASVAB.

WHAT IS THE AFQT?

Your score on the AFQT, or the Armed Forces Qualifying Test, determines your eligibility in all branches of the Armed Services. You'll get a better chance to know all the subtests that make up the ASVAB when you take the practice ASVAB that follows this chapter. But first, because it plays such a crucial role in whether you qualify for the Armed Forces in the first place, you need to understand what the AFQT is all about. The ASVAB does not have an "overall" score. When someone talks about getting a score of, say, a 75 or 80 on the ASVAB, he or she is really talking about the AFQT score, not the overall ASVAB score.

NOT ALL QUESTIONS ARE WORTH THE SAME

ASVAB questions are weighted. Harder questions result in more points than easy ones. There is no particular order of difficulty on the ASVAB subtests. In other words, easy and difficult questions can appear in any order on any subtest.

The AFQT score is derived from your performance on just the verbal and math subtests of the ASVAB, or to be more specific: Word Knowledge, Paragraph Comprehension, Arithmetic Reasoning, and Mathematics Knowledge. You should also realize that your verbal sections are doubly counted, while the math sections are only counted once. Scoring on the AFQT is a rather complicated affair, so let's break it down piece by piece.

The military determines your AFQT score by first adding your Word Knowledge and Paragraph Comprehension scores together to get your "Verbal Expression" or "VE" score. The formula to derive the AFQT "raw Score" is 2VE + AR (Arithmetic Reasoning) + MK (Mathematics Knowledge) = AFQT score. This raw score is then converted to a scaled score which is then converted to a percentile score (it's rather complicated, we know). The percentile score that is your final AFQT score tells you how well you did on the AFQT compared to other test takers. Thus, someone who scores a 50 on the AFQT scores in the 50th percentile, i.e., has a score better than 50 percent of all ASVAB test-takers. (See "How to Read Your ASVAB Scores" at the back of the book.)

So it's your percentile score on the AFQT that determines your eligibility in the Armed Forces. As a general rule, anyone who scores lower than the 30th percentile will not be allowed into any branch of the Armed Forces.

In order to join the **Air Force**, one needs a minimum AFQT score of 40. Those who hold a GED rather than a regular high school diploma have a tougher time getting accepted. The Air Force will accept about one percent per year from non-high school diploma holders, and these candidates must achieve at least a 50 AFQT score even to be considered.

Army recruits must score at least 31 on the AFQT, with no more than ten percent per year being high school dropouts. GED holders must score a 50 percent or better to be eligible (although waivers are possible).

Marine Corps recruits must score at least 32, with no more than five percent being high school dropouts. GED holders must score at least 50 on the AFQT (although waivers are possible).

Navy recruits must score at least 31. Between five and ten percent per year can be high school dropouts, but they also must score a minimum of 50. Additionally, high school dropouts must be at least 19 years of age, and show a proven work history. Female applicants to the Navy must also score at least a 50, because of the limited availability of female accommodations on Navy vessels.

Like the Air Force, **Coast Guard** recruits must also score at least 40 points on the AFQT. A waiver is possible if a recruit's ASVAB "line scores" qualify them for a specific job, and the recruit is willing to enlist in that job. Line scores are composite scores based on various groupings of subtest scores; for instance, someone who wants to qualify for a skilled technical position in the military needs to get a high "Skilled Technician" (ST) line score, which is a composite score derived as follows: ST = GS (General Science) + VE (Verbal Expression) + MK (Mathematics Knowledge) + MC (Mechanical Comprehension). For the very few who will be allowed to enlist in the Coast Guard with a GED, the minimum AFQT score is 50.

RETAKING THE ASVAB

ASVAB results are valid for two years. After taking an initial ASVAB Test (any school-administered ASVAB doesn't count as an initial test), one may retake the ASVAB after 30 days. After the retest, one must wait at least six months before taking the test again. The military services use the latest ASVAB scores, not the highest, for service and job qualifications, so if you are going to retake the ASVAB, make sure you have prepared well to top your previous score.

While each of the services has its own policies governing when or if a retest will be given, in general a retest is not allowed for the mere purpose of improving your scores (unless the overall score is below the minimum acceptable by that service). In the Army and Air Force, if one scores high enough to qualify, then he or she is only allowed to retest if something unusual happened during the test, and there is substantial evidence to show that the score(s) do not reflect the applicant's true potential. An example would be a high school honor student who accidentally mismarked the answer sheet, resulting in an extremely low score. The fact that the individual is an honor student would be evidence that the low score is below their actual potential.

In the Navy, a retest can be authorized only if the following two conditions are met:

(1) There is evidence of substantial improvement in education or language ability, such as earning a high school diploma or GED, or completion of the Navy Functional Skills Course, since the last ASVAB was taken; and

(2) There is a positive reason for the retest, such as to qualify for a specific job program.

THE COMPUTERIZED TEST VERSUS THE PAPER TEST

Computer-adaptive testing, or CAT for short, has recently become a staple among big test-givers. The GRE, GMAT, and other high-stakes exams now require all test takers to take CAT versions of their tests. Computer-adaptive testing is really just a fancy way of saying that the difficulty of the questions you get on the test adapts based on your performance up to that point.

For example, the first question you receive on any particular CAT-ASVAB subtest will be of medium difficulty. If you answer it correctly, the next question you get will be pulled from a bank of above-average difficulty questions. If you get the question wrong, your next question will be of a lower difficulty level. This process is repeated throughout the test, so that the test can more precisely zero in on your exact performance level on the exam.

We've already noted that on the paper version of the ASVAB, harder questions are worth more than easier questions. This is also true, only more so, on the CAT-ASVAB. If you can do well early on while taking a CAT-ASVAB subtest, thus ensuring that the level of difficulty of the questions you are answering is above average, you will get a high score on that subtest even if you get several of the later questions wrong. If you get several questions wrong in a row at the start of a CAT-ASVAB subtest, for the rest of that subtest you will get a lot of softball questions, and even if you get all of these questions right, you may never be able to get out of the hole that you dug for yourself at the start of the test and get to the point where you are answering the tough questions that lead to a high score.

NO DISTRACTIONS

One advantage of taking the CAT-ASVAB is that it gives you the chance to work methodically on one question at a time with no other questions there to distract you.

Studies have shown that, overall, people perform the same on the ASVAB whether they take the paper or CAT version of the test. There are, however, some individuals who will tend to do better on one version of the test than the other. If you do have a choice as to which version of the test you will take, here are some of the advantages and disadvantages of taking the CAT versus the paper test

Advantages of Taking the CAT-ASVAB

- The length of time of many of the subtests has been reduced, and the number of questions that you are required to answer has been reduced even more.
- The test can be scored immediately. You will know how well you did as soon as you finish the test.
- Test administration is very flexible, so you don't have to wait for the next scheduled test date to take the test.
- There's no chance of losing points by filling out your answer sheet incorrectly.

Disadvantages of Taking the CAT-ASVAB

- You cannot skip around on this test; you must answer the questions one at a time in the order the computer gives them to you.
- If you realize later that you answered a question incorrectly, you cannot go back and change your answer.
- You can't cross off an answer choice and never look at it again, so you'll have to use your scrap paper to keep track of the answers you've eliminated.

KAPLAN'S CAT STRATEGIES

If you are taking the CAT-ASVAB, applying certain CAT-specific strategies will have a direct, positive impact on your score:

- At the beginning of the section, each question you get right or wrong will rapidly move the computer's estimate of your score up or down. A key strategy for doing well on the CAT is to get the computer's estimate of your score up to where you are handling the hard questions. Thus it pays to spend more time on those early questions, double-checking each answer before you confirm it. Getting to the hard questions as soon as possible can only help your final score.

- As you progress through the middle part of a section, try to avoid getting several questions in a row wrong, as this can sink you score on the CAT. If you know that the previous question you answered was a blind guess, spend a little extra time trying to get the next one right.

- The CAT does not allow you to skip questions. So if you are given a question you cannot answer, you'll have to guess. Guess intelligently and strategically by eliminating any answer choices that you know are wrong and choosing from those remaining.

- Don't get rattled if you see difficult questions. It just means that you are doing well. Keep it up!

- At the end of the section, you will be penalized more heavily for not getting to a question than for answering it wrong. So if you only have a minute left and several questions remaining, you should guess at random rather than leave anything unanswered.

GENERAL ASVAB TEST-TAKING STRATEGIES

This book is broken into chapters that offer specific test-taking strategies for dealing with each of the subtests, particularly those subtests that constitute the AFQT. But there are some general strategies that will help you no matter what subtest you are taking.

Always Answer Every Question

There is no guessing penalty on the ASVAB. This means that it is absolutely in your interest to guess on every question on every subtest of the ASVAB! Even if you have to make a completely blind guess, you have a 25 percent chance of picking the correct answer.

THE ASVAB IS HIGHLY PREDICTABLE

The key to success on the ASVAB is knowing what to expect. The format—which includes the directions, the types of questions, and even the traps that the test maker places among the answer choices—is remarkably similar from test to test. One of the easiest things you can do to improve your performance on the ASVAB is to understand the test format before you take the test.

Take Charge of Each Subtest

Above we described strategies for taking charge of each subtest when you are taking the CAT-ASVAB. We have a different approach for taking charge of each subtest when you are taking the paper version of the ASVAB. The most important way to take control of the paper ASVAB is to realize the following: Although you are not allowed to work on other subtests while taking a particular section, you are allowed to skip around within each subtest of the ASVAB. High scorers know this. They move through each subtest efficiently. They don't dwell on any one question, even a hard one, until they've tried every question at least once.

The key is to be systematic. When you run into a tough question, circle it in your test booklet and skip it for the time being. You can go back to it later after you've answered the questions you know you can answer. On a second look, questions that gave you trouble on the first round can turn out to be much easier than you thought.

Take Advantage of the Multiple-Choice Format

As noted, every ASVAB question comes with four answer choices, so you have a 25 percent chance of getting the correct answer just by guessing blindly. If you know that one of the four answer choices cannot be right and eliminate it accordingly, you now have a 33 percent chance of getting the correct answer. Remove one more wrong answer choice, and your chance of getting the question right is now 50-50. Finally, if you can get rid of one more wrong answer, bingo! By the process of elimination, you have found the correct answer. On certain ASVAB questions, you will find that using the process of elimination on wrong answer choices is just as effective a way of getting to the correct answer as spotting the correct answer the straightforward way.

Another thing you have to realize is that there are different levels of incorrectness among the wrong answer choices. Some wrong answer choices will be easy to eliminate, whereas others are deliberately put into the test because they are tempting distracters. We will discuss in other parts of this book how to avoid those tempting distracters, particularly as they appear in the all-important verbal subtests of the ASVAB.

But let's get back to those easy eliminators. Often, even if you are completely confused by a question, you can still make a solid guess by eliminating any "odd men out." By this we mean that you're probably on solid ground if you eliminate answer choices that run counter to the other three answer choices. Here's an example of what we mean. We have cleverly replaced the actual text of a Mathematics Knowledge question with gibberish so you will have to rely on the "odd man out" strategy of eliminating likely wrong answer choices. From there we dare you to make your best guess.

> EXAMPLE

Solve for y : Blah, blah, blah, a number here, a number there, more text, a funny looking equation, etc.

(A) $y = -\dfrac{1}{3}$

(B) $y = \dfrac{1}{4}$

(C) $y = \dfrac{1}{2}$

(D) $y = 2$

Which answer choice could you most easily eliminate here? We hope you got rid of choice (A). It's the only negative number here, and the number itself seems a bit off too, given that the other numbers are all related to 2. Some people might also get rid of (D) here, as the only non-fraction of the bunch, and in this case they would be right as well. As is so happens, the correct answer to this question, had we given you the actual question rather than gibberish, was (C), although if you guessed something else other than (A), we still give you credit just for guessing.

Although we came up with a math question to illustrate this concept of eliminating oddball answer choices, it can be effective on the other subtests as well. Of course, the point of the book is to assure you that on test day no question will look like gibberish to you. Our point here is simply that if you keep your wits about you, you can often make a good stab at coming up with the answer, even if you are confused by the question.

USE YOUR SCRAP PAPER

No matter what version of the test you take, you will be given scrap paper to work on. Please use it, especially on those math sections. You will get exactly no credit for doing the math in your head. The rule here is a good one to apply to the rest of your military career: It's better to be safe than sorry!

GETTING READY FOR THE ASVAB

You should be ready now to take your first ASVAB practice test. As you take this test, and as you work your way through the rest of this book, pay especially close attention to the questions you get wrong and to the techniques we describe in this book for getting these types of questions right. You've made the right move in deciding to prepare for the ASVAB. It is a highly coachable test, and we aim to give you the tools you need to score high on the ASVAB and qualify for the military career of your dreams.

ASVAB Diagnostic Test: Practice Test I

DIRECTIONS FOR THE ASVAB DIAGNOSTIC TEST

This diagnostic test is intended as a tool to help guide you in your ASVAB preparation. Ideally, you should take this test before you go through the review lessons in this book. This test will give you a good idea of the kind of questions you can expect, and can help you identify your areas of strength and weakness. Take the test under timed conditions. If you run out of time before you finish any given section, be sure to fill in all the blanks on your answer sheet, as there's no guessing penalty on the ASVAB. Good luck!

ANSWER SHEET

Part 1: General Science (GS)

1 Ⓐ Ⓑ Ⓒ Ⓓ	6 Ⓐ Ⓑ Ⓒ Ⓓ	11 Ⓐ Ⓑ Ⓒ Ⓓ	16 Ⓐ Ⓑ Ⓒ Ⓓ	21 Ⓐ Ⓑ Ⓒ Ⓓ
2 Ⓐ Ⓑ Ⓒ Ⓓ	7 Ⓐ Ⓑ Ⓒ Ⓓ	12 Ⓐ Ⓑ Ⓒ Ⓓ	17 Ⓐ Ⓑ Ⓒ Ⓓ	22 Ⓐ Ⓑ Ⓒ Ⓓ
3 Ⓐ Ⓑ Ⓒ Ⓓ	8 Ⓐ Ⓑ Ⓒ Ⓓ	13 Ⓐ Ⓑ Ⓒ Ⓓ	18 Ⓐ Ⓑ Ⓒ Ⓓ	23 Ⓐ Ⓑ Ⓒ Ⓓ
4 Ⓐ Ⓑ Ⓒ Ⓓ	9 Ⓐ Ⓑ Ⓒ Ⓓ	14 Ⓐ Ⓑ Ⓒ Ⓓ	19 Ⓐ Ⓑ Ⓒ Ⓓ	24 Ⓐ Ⓑ Ⓒ Ⓓ
5 Ⓐ Ⓑ Ⓒ Ⓓ	10 Ⓐ Ⓑ Ⓒ Ⓓ	15 Ⓐ Ⓑ Ⓒ Ⓓ	20 Ⓐ Ⓑ Ⓒ Ⓓ	25 Ⓐ Ⓑ Ⓒ Ⓓ

Part 2: Arithmetic Reasoning (AR)

1 Ⓐ Ⓑ Ⓒ Ⓓ	7 Ⓐ Ⓑ Ⓒ Ⓓ	13 Ⓐ Ⓑ Ⓒ Ⓓ	19 Ⓐ Ⓑ Ⓒ Ⓓ	25 Ⓐ Ⓑ Ⓒ Ⓓ
2 Ⓐ Ⓑ Ⓒ Ⓓ	8 Ⓐ Ⓑ Ⓒ Ⓓ	14 Ⓐ Ⓑ Ⓒ Ⓓ	20 Ⓐ Ⓑ Ⓒ Ⓓ	26 Ⓐ Ⓑ Ⓒ Ⓓ
3 Ⓐ Ⓑ Ⓒ Ⓓ	9 Ⓐ Ⓑ Ⓒ Ⓓ	15 Ⓐ Ⓑ Ⓒ Ⓓ	21 Ⓐ Ⓑ Ⓒ Ⓓ	27 Ⓐ Ⓑ Ⓒ Ⓓ
4 Ⓐ Ⓑ Ⓒ Ⓓ	10 Ⓐ Ⓑ Ⓒ Ⓓ	16 Ⓐ Ⓑ Ⓒ Ⓓ	22 Ⓐ Ⓑ Ⓒ Ⓓ	28 Ⓐ Ⓑ Ⓒ Ⓓ
5 Ⓐ Ⓑ Ⓒ Ⓓ	11 Ⓐ Ⓑ Ⓒ Ⓓ	17 Ⓐ Ⓑ Ⓒ Ⓓ	23 Ⓐ Ⓑ Ⓒ Ⓓ	29 Ⓐ Ⓑ Ⓒ Ⓓ
6 Ⓐ Ⓑ Ⓒ Ⓓ	12 Ⓐ Ⓑ Ⓒ Ⓓ	18 Ⓐ Ⓑ Ⓒ Ⓓ	24 Ⓐ Ⓑ Ⓒ Ⓓ	30 Ⓐ Ⓑ Ⓒ Ⓓ

Part 3: Word Knowledge (WK)

1 Ⓐ Ⓑ Ⓒ Ⓓ	8 Ⓐ Ⓑ Ⓒ Ⓓ	15 Ⓐ Ⓑ Ⓒ Ⓓ	22 Ⓐ Ⓑ Ⓒ Ⓓ	29 Ⓐ Ⓑ Ⓒ Ⓓ
2 Ⓐ Ⓑ Ⓒ Ⓓ	9 Ⓐ Ⓑ Ⓒ Ⓓ	16 Ⓐ Ⓑ Ⓒ Ⓓ	23 Ⓐ Ⓑ Ⓒ Ⓓ	30 Ⓐ Ⓑ Ⓒ Ⓓ
3 Ⓐ Ⓑ Ⓒ Ⓓ	10 Ⓐ Ⓑ Ⓒ Ⓓ	17 Ⓐ Ⓑ Ⓒ Ⓓ	24 Ⓐ Ⓑ Ⓒ Ⓓ	31 Ⓐ Ⓑ Ⓒ Ⓓ
4 Ⓐ Ⓑ Ⓒ Ⓓ	11 Ⓐ Ⓑ Ⓒ Ⓓ	18 Ⓐ Ⓑ Ⓒ Ⓓ	25 Ⓐ Ⓑ Ⓒ Ⓓ	32 Ⓐ Ⓑ Ⓒ Ⓓ
5 Ⓐ Ⓑ Ⓒ Ⓓ	12 Ⓐ Ⓑ Ⓒ Ⓓ	19 Ⓐ Ⓑ Ⓒ Ⓓ	26 Ⓐ Ⓑ Ⓒ Ⓓ	33 Ⓐ Ⓑ Ⓒ Ⓓ
6 Ⓐ Ⓑ Ⓒ Ⓓ	13 Ⓐ Ⓑ Ⓒ Ⓓ	20 Ⓐ Ⓑ Ⓒ Ⓓ	27 Ⓐ Ⓑ Ⓒ Ⓓ	34 Ⓐ Ⓑ Ⓒ Ⓓ
7 Ⓐ Ⓑ Ⓒ Ⓓ	14 Ⓐ Ⓑ Ⓒ Ⓓ	21 Ⓐ Ⓑ Ⓒ Ⓓ	28 Ⓐ Ⓑ Ⓒ Ⓓ	35 Ⓐ Ⓑ Ⓒ Ⓓ

Part 4: Paragraph Comprehension (PC)

1 Ⓐ Ⓑ Ⓒ Ⓓ	4 Ⓐ Ⓑ Ⓒ Ⓓ	7 Ⓐ Ⓑ Ⓒ Ⓓ	10 Ⓐ Ⓑ Ⓒ Ⓓ	13 Ⓐ Ⓑ Ⓒ Ⓓ
2 Ⓐ Ⓑ Ⓒ Ⓓ	5 Ⓐ Ⓑ Ⓒ Ⓓ	8 Ⓐ Ⓑ Ⓒ Ⓓ	11 Ⓐ Ⓑ Ⓒ Ⓓ	14 Ⓐ Ⓑ Ⓒ Ⓓ
3 Ⓐ Ⓑ Ⓒ Ⓓ	6 Ⓐ Ⓑ Ⓒ Ⓓ	9 Ⓐ Ⓑ Ⓒ Ⓓ	12 Ⓐ Ⓑ Ⓒ Ⓓ	15 Ⓐ Ⓑ Ⓒ Ⓓ

Part 5: Automotive and Shop Information (AS)

1 Ⓐ Ⓑ Ⓒ Ⓓ	6 Ⓐ Ⓑ Ⓒ Ⓓ	11 Ⓐ Ⓑ Ⓒ Ⓓ	16 Ⓐ Ⓑ Ⓒ Ⓓ	21 Ⓐ Ⓑ Ⓒ Ⓓ
2 Ⓐ Ⓑ Ⓒ Ⓓ	7 Ⓐ Ⓑ Ⓒ Ⓓ	12 Ⓐ Ⓑ Ⓒ Ⓓ	17 Ⓐ Ⓑ Ⓒ Ⓓ	22 Ⓐ Ⓑ Ⓒ Ⓓ
3 Ⓐ Ⓑ Ⓒ Ⓓ	8 Ⓐ Ⓑ Ⓒ Ⓓ	13 Ⓐ Ⓑ Ⓒ Ⓓ	18 Ⓐ Ⓑ Ⓒ Ⓓ	23 Ⓐ Ⓑ Ⓒ Ⓓ
4 Ⓐ Ⓑ Ⓒ Ⓓ	9 Ⓐ Ⓑ Ⓒ Ⓓ	14 Ⓐ Ⓑ Ⓒ Ⓓ	19 Ⓐ Ⓑ Ⓒ Ⓓ	24 Ⓐ Ⓑ Ⓒ Ⓓ
5 Ⓐ Ⓑ Ⓒ Ⓓ	10 Ⓐ Ⓑ Ⓒ Ⓓ	15 Ⓐ Ⓑ Ⓒ Ⓓ	20 Ⓐ Ⓑ Ⓒ Ⓓ	25 Ⓐ Ⓑ Ⓒ Ⓓ

ANSWER SHEET

Part 6: Mathematics Knowledge (MK)

1 Ⓐ Ⓑ Ⓒ Ⓓ	6 Ⓐ Ⓑ Ⓒ Ⓓ	11 Ⓐ Ⓑ Ⓒ Ⓓ	16 Ⓐ Ⓑ Ⓒ Ⓓ	21 Ⓐ Ⓑ Ⓒ Ⓓ
2 Ⓐ Ⓑ Ⓒ Ⓓ	7 Ⓐ Ⓑ Ⓒ Ⓓ	12 Ⓐ Ⓑ Ⓒ Ⓓ	17 Ⓐ Ⓑ Ⓒ Ⓓ	22 Ⓐ Ⓑ Ⓒ Ⓓ
3 Ⓐ Ⓑ Ⓒ Ⓓ	8 Ⓐ Ⓑ Ⓒ Ⓓ	13 Ⓐ Ⓑ Ⓒ Ⓓ	18 Ⓐ Ⓑ Ⓒ Ⓓ	23 Ⓐ Ⓑ Ⓒ Ⓓ
4 Ⓐ Ⓑ Ⓒ Ⓓ	9 Ⓐ Ⓑ Ⓒ Ⓓ	14 Ⓐ Ⓑ Ⓒ Ⓓ	19 Ⓐ Ⓑ Ⓒ Ⓓ	24 Ⓐ Ⓑ Ⓒ Ⓓ
5 Ⓐ Ⓑ Ⓒ Ⓓ	10 Ⓐ Ⓑ Ⓒ Ⓓ	15 Ⓐ Ⓑ Ⓒ Ⓓ	20 Ⓐ Ⓑ Ⓒ Ⓓ	25 Ⓐ Ⓑ Ⓒ Ⓓ

Part 7: Mechanical Comprehension (MC)

1 Ⓐ Ⓑ Ⓒ Ⓓ	6 Ⓐ Ⓑ Ⓒ Ⓓ	11 Ⓐ Ⓑ Ⓒ Ⓓ	16 Ⓐ Ⓑ Ⓒ Ⓓ	21 Ⓐ Ⓑ Ⓒ Ⓓ
2 Ⓐ Ⓑ Ⓒ Ⓓ	7 Ⓐ Ⓑ Ⓒ Ⓓ	12 Ⓐ Ⓑ Ⓒ Ⓓ	17 Ⓐ Ⓑ Ⓒ Ⓓ	22 Ⓐ Ⓑ Ⓒ Ⓓ
3 Ⓐ Ⓑ Ⓒ Ⓓ	8 Ⓐ Ⓑ Ⓒ Ⓓ	13 Ⓐ Ⓑ Ⓒ Ⓓ	18 Ⓐ Ⓑ Ⓒ Ⓓ	23 Ⓐ Ⓑ Ⓒ Ⓓ
4 Ⓐ Ⓑ Ⓒ Ⓓ	9 Ⓐ Ⓑ Ⓒ Ⓓ	14 Ⓐ Ⓑ Ⓒ Ⓓ	19 Ⓐ Ⓑ Ⓒ Ⓓ	24 Ⓐ Ⓑ Ⓒ Ⓓ
5 Ⓐ Ⓑ Ⓒ Ⓓ	10 Ⓐ Ⓑ Ⓒ Ⓓ	15 Ⓐ Ⓑ Ⓒ Ⓓ	20 Ⓐ Ⓑ Ⓒ Ⓓ	25 Ⓐ Ⓑ Ⓒ Ⓓ

Part 8: Electronics Information (EI)

1 Ⓐ Ⓑ Ⓒ Ⓓ	5 Ⓐ Ⓑ Ⓒ Ⓓ	9 Ⓐ Ⓑ Ⓒ Ⓓ	13 Ⓐ Ⓑ Ⓒ Ⓓ	17 Ⓐ Ⓑ Ⓒ Ⓓ
2 Ⓐ Ⓑ Ⓒ Ⓓ	6 Ⓐ Ⓑ Ⓒ Ⓓ	10 Ⓐ Ⓑ Ⓒ Ⓓ	14 Ⓐ Ⓑ Ⓒ Ⓓ	18 Ⓐ Ⓑ Ⓒ Ⓓ
3 Ⓐ Ⓑ Ⓒ Ⓓ	7 Ⓐ Ⓑ Ⓒ Ⓓ	11 Ⓐ Ⓑ Ⓒ Ⓓ	15 Ⓐ Ⓑ Ⓒ Ⓓ	19 Ⓐ Ⓑ Ⓒ Ⓓ
4 Ⓐ Ⓑ Ⓒ Ⓓ	8 Ⓐ Ⓑ Ⓒ Ⓓ	12 Ⓐ Ⓑ Ⓒ Ⓓ	16 Ⓐ Ⓑ Ⓒ Ⓓ	20 Ⓐ Ⓑ Ⓒ Ⓓ

Part 9: Assembling Objects (AO)

1 Ⓐ Ⓑ Ⓒ Ⓓ	5 Ⓐ Ⓑ Ⓒ Ⓓ	9 Ⓐ Ⓑ Ⓒ Ⓓ	13 Ⓐ Ⓑ Ⓒ Ⓓ
2 Ⓐ Ⓑ Ⓒ Ⓓ	6 Ⓐ Ⓑ Ⓒ Ⓓ	10 Ⓐ Ⓑ Ⓒ Ⓓ	14 Ⓐ Ⓑ Ⓒ Ⓓ
3 Ⓐ Ⓑ Ⓒ Ⓓ	7 Ⓐ Ⓑ Ⓒ Ⓓ	11 Ⓐ Ⓑ Ⓒ Ⓓ	15 Ⓐ Ⓑ Ⓒ Ⓓ
4 Ⓐ Ⓑ Ⓒ Ⓓ	8 Ⓐ Ⓑ Ⓒ Ⓓ	12 Ⓐ Ⓑ Ⓒ Ⓓ	16 Ⓐ Ⓑ Ⓒ Ⓓ

PART 1: GENERAL SCIENCE (GS)

Time: 11 minutes; 25 questions

<u>Directions:</u> In this section, you will be tested on your knowledge of concepts in science generally reviewed in high school. For each question, select the best answer and mark the corresponding oval on your answer sheet.

1. One should not stare directly at the sun because doing so can seriously damage the eye's
   - (A) cornea
   - (B) iris
   - (C) lens
   - (D) retina

2. On a Fahrenheit thermometer the boiling point of water at sea level is
   - (A) 100°
   - (B) 180°
   - (C) 212°
   - (D) 373°

3. The process by which plants convert carbon dioxide and water into sugar and oxygen is called
   - (A) decomposition
   - (B) photosynthesis
   - (C) oxidation
   - (D) respiration

4. In electricity, a unit of resistance is called a(n)
   - (A) ampere
   - (B) ohm
   - (C) volt
   - (D) watt

5. Which of the following depicts a chemical process?
   - (A) Helium is combined with neon.
   - (B) Iron forms rust.
   - (C) Water causes soil erosion.
   - (D) Ice melts.

6. Goiter is caused by a lack of
   - (A) iodine
   - (B) iron
   - (C) protein
   - (D) vitamin K

7. Blood enters the right atrium of the heart from the
   - (A) aorta
   - (B) left ventricle
   - (C) pulmonary vein
   - (D) vena cava

8. Which of the following substances has the highest pH?
   - (A) ammonia
   - (B) battery acid
   - (C) isopropyl alcohol
   - (D) water

9. Insulin is created in the body's
   - (A) adrenal glands
   - (B) kidneys
   - (C) pancreas
   - (D) thymus

10. Which of the following is NOT caused by a virus?

    (A) measles
    (B) mumps
    (C) rabies
    (D) typhus

11. If two brown-eyed parents have a blue-eyed child, the probability that their next child will have blue eyes is

    (A) zero
    (B) 1 in 2
    (C) 1 in 3
    (D) 1 in 4

12. Which of the following is a sedimentary rock?

    (A) granite
    (B) marble
    (C) shale
    (D) slate

13. Which of the following planets does not have an orbiting moon?

    (A) Venus
    (B) Mars
    (C) Saturn
    (D) Neptune

14. The process by which the sun heats the earth is known as

    (A) conduction
    (B) convection
    (C) radiation
    (D) refraction

15. Which of the following foods is the best source of iron?

    (A) cabbage
    (B) spinach
    (C) lima beans
    (D) turnips

16. During a lunar eclipse

    (A) the moon lies between the earth and sun
    (B) the sun lies between the moon and earth
    (C) the earth lies between the moon and sun
    (D) none of the above

17. A sphygmomanometer is used to measure

    (A) blood pressure
    (B) bone density
    (C) metabolism
    (D) muscle mass

18. The climate with the shortest growing season would be in the

    (A) grasslands
    (B) deciduous forest
    (C) tropical forest
    (D) taiga

19. Vitamin B3 is also known as

    (A) ascorbic acid
    (B) biotin
    (C) folic acid
    (D) niacin

20. The major portion of an atom's mass consists of

    (A) neutrons and protons
    (B) electrons and protons
    (C) electrons and neutrons
    (D) neutrons and positrons

GO ON TO THE NEXT PAGE

21. Which of the following is NOT an example of an arthropod?

    (A) crab
    (B) centipede
    (C) sea horse
    (D) spider

22. Which of the following is NOT a metallic alloy?

    (A) tin
    (B) bronze
    (C) pewter
    (D) steel

23. Over the course of 24 hours

    (A) the earth rotates 360 degrees around the sun
    (B) the moon rotates 360 degrees around the earth
    (C) the earth rotates 360 degrees about its axis
    (D) the moon rotates 360 degrees about its axis

24. Which of the following kingdoms is considered the most primitive?

    (A) Fungi
    (B) Protista
    (C) Monera
    (D) Plantae

25. Which of the following is the phylum that includes man?

    (A) Animalia
    (B) Chordata
    (C) Mammalia
    (D) Primata

STOP. IF YOU FINISH BEFORE THE TIME IS UP, YOU MAY CHECK OVER YOUR WORK ON THIS PART ONLY.

PART 2: ARITHMETIC REASONING (AR)

Time: 36 minutes; 30 questions

<u>Directions:</u> In this section, you are tested on your ability to use arithmetic. For each question, select the best answer and mark the corresponding oval on your answer sheet.

1. John bought a camera on sale that normally costs $160. If the price was reduced 20 percent during the sale, what was the sale price of the camera?

   (A) $120
   (B) $124
   (C) $128
   (D) $140

2. A subway car passes 3 stations every 10 minutes. At this rate, how many stations will it pass in one hour?

   (A) 15
   (B) 18
   (C) 20
   (D) 30

3. On a certain map, $\frac{3}{4}$ inch represents one mile. What distance, in miles, is represented by $1\frac{3}{4}$ inches?

   (A) $1\frac{1}{2}$
   (B) $2\frac{1}{3}$
   (C) $2\frac{1}{2}$
   (D) $5\frac{1}{4}$

4. A certain box contains baseballs and golf balls. If the ratio of baseballs to golf balls is 2 : 3 and there are 30 baseballs in the box, how many golf balls are in the box?

   (A) 18
   (B) 20
   (C) 36
   (D) 45

5. Four people shared a taxi to the airport. The fare was $36.00, and they gave the driver a tip equal to 25 percent of the fare. If they equally shared the cost of the fare and tip, how much did each person pay?

   (A) $9.75
   (B) $10.25
   (C) $10.75
   (D) $11.25

6. If a car travels $\frac{1}{100}$ of a kilometer each second, how many kilometers does it travel in an hour?

   (A) 36
   (B) 60
   (C) 72
   (D) 100

GO ON TO THE NEXT PAGE

7. What is the fifth term in this series:

   6.5; 13.75; 21; 28.25; _____?

   (A) 35.25
   (B) 35.50
   (C) 36.50
   (D) 36.75

8. Ms. Smith drove a total of 700 miles on a business trip. If her car averaged 35 miles per gallon of gasoline and gasoline cost $1.25 per gallon, what was the cost in dollars of the gasoline for the trip?

   (A) $20.00
   (B) $24.00
   (C) $25.00
   (D) $40.00

9. After eating 25 percent of the jelly beans, Brett had 72 left. How many jelly beans did Brett have originally?

   (A) 90
   (B) 94
   (C) 95
   (D) 96

10. A student finishes the first half of an exam in $\frac{2}{3}$ the time it takes him to finish the second half. If the entire exam takes him an hour, how many minutes does he spend on the first half of the exam?

    (A) 20
    (B) 24
    (C) 27
    (D) 36

11. A 25-ounce solution is 20 percent alcohol. If 50 ounces of water are added to it, what percent of the new solution is alcohol?

    (A) $6\frac{2}{3}\%$

    (B) $7\frac{1}{2}\%$

    (C) 10%

    (D) $13\frac{1}{3}\%$

12. Marty has exactly 5 blue pens, 6 black pens, and 4 red pens in his knapsack. If he pulls out one pen at random from his knapsack, what is the probability that the pen is either red or black?

    (A) $\frac{2}{3}$

    (B) $\frac{3}{5}$

    (C) $\frac{2}{5}$

    (D) $\frac{1}{3}$

13. From 1980 through 1990, the population of Country X increased by 100 percent. From 1990 to 2000, the population increased by 50 percent. What was the combined increase for the period 1980–2000?

    (A) 150%
    (B) $166\frac{2}{3}\%$
    (C) 175%
    (D) 200%

GO ON TO THE NEXT PAGE

14. If a man earns $200 for his first 40 hours of work in a week and then is paid one-and-one-half times his regular rate for any additional hours, how many hours must he work to make $230 in a week?

    (A) 43
    (B) 44
    (C) 45
    (D) 46

15. If 50 percent of x is 150, what is 75 percent of x?

    (A) 225
    (B) 250
    (C) 275
    (D) 300

16. The total fare for two adults and 3 children on an excursion boat is $14. If each child's fare is one half of each adult's fare, what is the adult fare?

    (A) $2.00
    (B) $3.00
    (C) $3.50
    (D) $4.00

17. A rectangular picture that is 4 inches wide and 6 inches long is enlarged so that it is 10 inches long without changing the width. What is the perimeter, in inches, of the enlarged picture?

    (A) 20
    (B) 24
    (C) 28
    (D) 40

18. A painter charges $12 an hour while his son charges $6 an hour. If the father and son worked the same amount of time together on a job, how many hours did each of them work if their combined charge for their labor was $108?

    (A) 6
    (B) 9
    (C) 12
    (D) 18

Name	Weight in pounds
Chris	150
Anne	153
Malcolm	154
Paul	157
Sam	151

19. What is the average weight, in pounds, of the five people whose weights are listed in the table above?

    (A) 153
    (B) $153\frac{1}{2}$
    (C) 154
    (D) 155

GO ON TO THE NEXT PAGE

KAPLAN

20. At garage *A*, it costs $8.75 to park a car for the first hour and $1.25 for each additional hour. At garage *B*, it costs $5.50 to park a car for the first hour and $2.50 for each additional hour. What is the difference between the cost of parking a car for 5 hours at garage *A* and parking it for the same length of time at garage *B* ?

    (A) $2.25
    (B) $1.75
    (C) $1.50
    (D) $1.25

21. Jan types at an average rate of 12 pages per hour. At that rate, how long will it take Jan to type 100 pages?

    (A) 8 hours and 10 minutes
    (B) 8 hours and 15 minutes
    (C) 8 hours and 20 minutes
    (D) 8 hours and 30 minutes

22. Two large sodas contain the same amount as three medium sodas. Two medium sodas contain the same amount as three small sodas. How many small sodas contain the same amount as 8 large sodas?

    (A) 24
    (B) 18
    (C) 16
    (D) 12

23. If each digit 5 is replaced with the digit 7, how much will 258,546 be increased?

    (A) 2,020
    (B) 2,200
    (C) 20,020
    (D) 20,200

24. Michael bought $2\frac{1}{4}$ pounds of lumber at $4.00 per pound. If a 7% sales tax was added, how much did Michael pay?

    (A) $9.63
    (B) $9.98
    (C) $10.70
    (D) $11.77

25. The ratio of $3\frac{1}{4}$ to $5\frac{1}{4}$ is equivalent to the ratio of

    (A) 3 to 5
    (B) 4 to 7
    (C) 8 to 13
    (D) 13 to 21

26. A cat is fed $\frac{3}{8}$ of a pound of cat food every day. For how many days will 72 pounds of this cat food feed the cat?

    (A) 160
    (B) 172
    (C) 180
    (D) 192

27. After spending $\frac{5}{12}$ of his salary, a man has $420 left. What is his salary?

    (A) 175
    (B) 245
    (C) 720
    (D) 1,008

28. A stock decreases in value by 20 percent. By what percent must the stock price increase to reach its former value?

    (A) 15%
    (B) 20%
    (C) 25%
    (D) 40%

29. Joan can shovel a certain driveway in 50 minutes. If Mary can shovel the same driveway in 20 minutes, how long will it take them, to the nearest minute, to shovel the driveway if they work together?

    (A) 12
    (B) 13
    (C) 14
    (D) 15

30. June's weekly salary is $70 less than Kelly's, which is $50 more than Eileen's. If Eileen earns $280 per week, how much does June earn per week?

    (A) $160
    (B) $260
    (C) $280
    (D) $300

STOP. IF YOU FINISH BEFORE THE TIME IS UP, YOU MAY CHECK OVER YOUR WORK ON THIS PART ONLY.

PART 3. WORD KNOWLEDGE (WK)

Time: 11 minutes; 35 questions

<u>Directions</u>: In this section, you are tested on the meaning of words. Each of the following questions has an underlined word. Select the answer that most nearly means the same as the underlined word and mark the corresponding oval on your answer sheet.

1. <u>Noble</u> most nearly means

   (A) comely
   (B) loose
   (C) majestic
   (D) lackadaisical

2. Couples often have to <u>concede</u> to survive.

   (A) leave
   (B) compromise
   (C) yell
   (D) create

3. <u>Goad</u> most nearly means

   (A) listen
   (B) taunt
   (C) pacify
   (D) ignore

4. Teenagers at the mall love to roam in a <u>herd</u>.

   (A) jacket
   (B) line
   (C) pack
   (D) ratio

5. For an EMT, panicking in an emergency is not a <u>viable</u> response.

   (A) total
   (B) collective
   (C) lucid
   (D) reasonable

6. <u>Judicious</u> most nearly means

   (A) accessible
   (B) cold
   (C) fair
   (D) talkative

7. <u>Hesitating</u> in a time of crisis can often lead to failure.

   (A) broadening
   (B) creating
   (C) leaving
   (D) pausing

8. Applicants who insist on <u>falsifying</u> information ruin the process for everyone.

   (A) fabricating
   (B) listing
   (C) furthering
   (D) taking on

9. <u>Hollow</u> most nearly means

   (A) dangerous
   (B) potent
   (C) empty
   (D) superb

10. <u>Coax</u> most nearly means

    (A) advise
    (B) trade
    (C) plead
    (D) grace

GO ON TO THE NEXT PAGE

11. The <u>monotonous</u> speech left them all feeling sleepy.

    (A) telling
    (B) boring
    (C) caustic
    (D) hilarious

12. A student's <u>consternation</u> may be due to bad teachers.

    (A) desires
    (B) inability
    (C) confusion
    (D) behavior

13. With the holidays approaching, Dave looked forward to a <u>savory</u> feast or two.

    (A) tasty
    (B) guilty
    (C) heroic
    (D) skimpy

14. A man of some <u>renown</u>, the Mayor walked with his chest puffed out.

    (A) size
    (B) fame
    (C) confusion
    (D) toil

15. <u>Raconteur</u> most nearly means

    (A) believer
    (B) storyteller
    (C) standout
    (D) pedant

16. She felt that nothing could really <u>quench</u> her curiosity.

    (A) justify
    (B) break
    (C) illuminate
    (D) satisfy

17. The committee was <u>polarized</u> on the issue.

    (A) split
    (B) disgusted
    (C) grateful
    (D) cold

18. The need to be <u>exact</u> was clear to everyone.

    (A) after the fact
    (B) cautious
    (C) precise
    (D) barren

19. Drucker surveyed the <u>terrain</u> before him for water.

    (A) oversight
    (B) landscape
    (C) river
    (D) goal

20. <u>Terminal</u> most nearly means

    (A) easy
    (B) glittering
    (C) busy
    (D) final

GO ON TO THE NEXT PAGE

21. <u>Augment</u> most nearly means

    (A) craft
    (B) end
    (C) throw away
    (D) enhance

22. She knocked over a lamp with an <u>involuntary</u> spasm.

    (A) accidental
    (B) basic
    (C) listless
    (D) helpful

23. The other owners accused the brothers of <u>collusion</u>.

    (A) coalition
    (B) secret agreement
    (C) hoping
    (D) pretending

24. The mongoose shows great <u>tenacity</u> in the face of danger.

    (A) fear
    (B) candor
    (C) determination
    (D) speed

25. <u>Tactile</u> most nearly means

    (A) ghastly
    (B) easy
    (C) patient
    (D) tangible

26. No one could <u>portend</u> where they would all end up in five years.

    (A) fake
    (B) lose
    (C) predict
    (D) edit

27. <u>Germinate</u> most nearly means

    (A) seed
    (B) oppress
    (C) adulate
    (D) foster

28. <u>Restore</u> most nearly means

    (A) trip up
    (B) invigorate
    (C) care for
    (D) toughen

29. <u>Filament</u> most nearly means

    (A) horse
    (B) triage
    (C) nightmare
    (D) thread

30. Whatever the original intent, the focus has clearly <u>mutated</u> at this point.

    (A) disappeared
    (B) reiterated
    (C) altered
    (D) intensified

31. To be elected president, one must be a calm, yet still <u>dynamic</u> figure.

    (A) reassuring
    (B) exciting
    (C) manic
    (D) terrible

32. <u>Congeal</u> most nearly means

    (A) fade
    (B) swirl
    (C) harden
    (D) undulate

33. <u>Reconnoiter</u> most nearly means

    (A) advance
    (B) posit
    (C) grade
    (D) scout

34. Whether one can <u>accrue</u> enough money to live is always the question.

    (A) accumulate
    (B) acquiesce
    (C) trap
    (D) magnify

35. His <u>innate</u> ability to make the correct turn was amazing.

    (A) unsure
    (B) discussed
    (C) creative
    (D) natural

STOP. IF YOU FINISH BEFORE THE TIME IS UP, YOU MAY CHECK OVER YOUR WORK ON THIS PART ONLY.

PART 4. PARAGRAPH COMPREHENSION (PC)

Time: 13 minutes; 15 questions

<u>Directions</u>: This section contains paragraphs followed by incomplete statements or questions. Read the paragraph and select the answer that best completes the statements or answers the questions that follow, and mark the corresponding oval on your answer sheet.

The first detective stories, written by Edgar Allan Poe and Arthur Conan Doyle, emerged in the mid-nineteenth century, at a time when there was enormous public interest in science. The newspapers of the day continually publicized the latest scientific discoveries, and scientists were acclaimed as the heroes of the age. Poe and Conan Doyle shared this fascination with the methodical, logical approach used by scientists in their experiments, and instilled their detective heroes with outstanding powers of scientific reasoning.

1. The main idea of this passage is

    (A) science fiction was not popular among 19th century readers
    (B) scientific progress made its way into the fiction of the time
    (C) newspapers detailed detective work each day
    (D) the first detective stories were written by scientists

Children have an amazing talent for learning vocabulary. Between the ages of one and seventeen, the average child learns the meaning of about 80,000 words—about 14 per day. Dictionaries and traditional classroom vocabulary lessons only account for part of this knowledge growth. More important are individuals' reading habits and their dialogues with people whose vocabularies are larger than their own. Reading shows students how words are used in sentences. Conversation offers students the chance to ask questions about the language.

2. According to the passage, reading is valuable to students because

    (A) children learn differently than adults
    (B) words used in stories are generally harder
    (C) reading provides vocabulary clues within sentences
    (D) vocabulary is learned mostly through conversation

The first truly American art movement was formed by a group of landscape painters that emerged in the early nineteenth century called the Hudson River School. The first works in this style were created by Thomas Cole, Thomas Doughty, and Asher Durand, a trio of painters who worked during the 1820s in the Hudson River Valley and surrounding locations. Heavily influenced by European artists, these painters set out to convey the remoteness and splendor of the American wilderness. The strongly patriotic tone of their paintings caught the spirit of the times, and within a generation the movement had grown to include landscape painters from all over the United States.

3. Which of the following best tells what this passage is about?

   (A) the history of the Hudson River School of painters

   (B) American art movements of the nineteenth century

   (C) how American landscape painters were influenced by European painters

   (D) the artistic origins of nationalism in the United States

The question of whether a child's personality is the result of genetic material inherited from the parents or the nurturing and environment provided by the parents is a perennial subject of debate. While no one would deny that environment and upbringing play a limited role, the genetic traits that a child inherits provide some sort of basic blueprint for who, and what, that child becomes. After all, if one plants tomatoes, _____.

4. Which of the following best completes this passage?

   (A) one must tend them carefully, in order to gather good vegetables

   (B) one had better choose the variety and location with equal care

   (C) one will eventually get tomatoes, but probably not good tomatoes

   (D) one must expect tomatoes to grow, not cucumbers or daffodils

GO ON TO THE NEXT PAGE

Questions 5 and 6 refer to the following passage.

The painter Georgia O'Keeffe was born in Wisconsin in 1887, and grew up on her family's farm. At seventeen she decided she wanted to be an artist and left the farm for schools in Chicago and New York, but she never lost her bond with the land. Like most painters, O'Keeffe painted the things that were most important to her, and nearly all her works are portrayals of nature. O'Keeffe became famous when her paintings were discovered in New York by the photographer Alfred Stieglitz, whom she married in 1924. During a visit to New Mexico in 1929, O'Keeffe was so moved by the bleak landscape and broad skies of the Western desert that she began to paint its images.

5. In this context, the word *bleak* most nearly means

    (A) empty
    (B) moody
    (C) cold
    (D) vivid

6. Georgia O'Keeffe's work generally shows

    (A) an ability to paint something complex accurately
    (B) her love for Alfred Stieglitz
    (C) her desire for fame
    (D) her love of the natural land

The four brightest moons of Jupiter were the first objects in the solar system discovered with the use of the telescope. This proof played a central role in Galileo's famous argument in support of the Copernican model of the solar system, in which the planets are described as revolving around the Sun. For several hundred years, scientific understanding of these moons was slow to develop. But spectacular close-up photographs sent back by the 1979 Voyager missions forever changed our perception of these moons.

7. Which best describes the Copernican model of the solar system?

    (A) Planets move counterclockwise as they rotate.
    (B) The sun and other planets revolve around the earth.
    (C) The planets move in orbit around the sun.
    (D) The four brightest moons of Jupiter used to be planets.

GO ON TO THE NEXT PAGE

As the sky opened up and sun at last rushed into the room, Toby smiled knowing that the game would proceed as planned. It had to, if only because his father would be there and it might be the last opportunity he would have to see Toby play. Now the birds began to appear here and there. Toby got out his baseball glove and ball and waited for his dad to arrive to take him to the game.

8. The mood of the character in the passage is

   (A) sad
   (B) careless
   (C) uneasy
   (D) eager

A human body can survive without water for several days and without food for as many as several weeks. If breathing stops for as little as three to six minutes, however, death is likely. All animals require a constant supply of oxygen to the body tissues, and especially to the heart or brain. In the human body, the respiratory and circulatory systems perform this function by delivering oxygen to the blood, which then transports it to tissues throughout the body. Respiration in large animals involves more than just breathing in oxygen. It is a complex process that delivers oxygen while eliminating carbon dioxide produced by cells.

9. Which bodily function, according to the passage, is least essential to the immediate survival of the average human being?

   (A) eating
   (B) drinking
   (C) breathing
   (D) excretion

The media is really out of control. When the press gets a story, it seems that within minutes they have produced flashy moving graphics and sound effects to entice viewers and garner ratings. Real facts and unbiased coverage of an issue are totally abandoned in exchange for an overly sentimental or one-sided story that too often distorts the truth. Viewers need to learn to recognize real reporting from the junk on nearly every television channel these days.

10. The author would be most likely to agree with which of the following?

    (A) Newspapers should have more editorials.
    (B) Flashy graphics add substance to television news reporting.
    (C) Objective news reporting is a dying art.
    (D) Television news anchors are valuable sources of information.

The poems of the earliest Greeks, like those of other ancient societies, consisted of magical charms, mysterious predictions, prayers, and traditional songs of work and war. These poems were intended to be sung or recited, not written down, since they were created before the Greeks began to use writing for literary purposes. The different forms of early Greek poetry all had something in common: They described the way of life of the Greek people. Poetry expressed ideas and feelings that were shared by everyone in a community—their folktales, their memories of historical events, and their religious speculation.

11. Early Greek poetry was which of the following?

    (A) mainly an oral form
    (B) a departure from poetic traditions in other societies
    (C) widely thought to be an act of the gods
    (D) usually about lost love and sadness

GO ON TO THE NEXT PAGE

In computer design, the effectiveness of a program generally depends on the ability of the programmer. Still, remarkable progress has been made in the development of artificial intelligence. This progress has scientists wondering whether it will eventually be possible to develop a computer capable of intelligent thought. When a computer defeated Garry Kasparov, considered by many the greatest chess player of all time, it was taken to be a vindication of the claims of the strongest supporters of artificial intelligence. Despite this accomplishment, others argue that while computers may imitate the human mind, they will never possess the capacity for true intelligence.

12. The main idea of this passage is

    (A) computers can never learn to think

    (B) chess is a game in which computers are superior

    (C) great strides have been made in artificial intelligence

    (D) artificial intelligence is a scientific miracle

Questions 13 and 14 refer to the following passage.

Coral reefs are created over the course of hundreds or even thousands of years. The main architect in coral reef formation is the stony coral, a relative of the sea anemone that lives in tropical climates and secretes a skeleton of almost pure calcium carbonate. Its partner is the green alga, a tiny unicellular plant that lives within the tissues of the coral. The two organisms form a mutually beneficial relationship, with the algae consuming carbon dioxide given off by the corals, and the corals thriving on the abundant oxygen produced photosynthetically by the algae.

When the coral dies, its skeleton is left, and other organisms grow on top of it. Over the years the shear mass of coral skeletons together with those of associated organisms combines to form the petrified underwater forest that divers find so fascinating.

13. Which of the following best describes what this passage is about?

    (A) the varieties of animal life that live in coral reefs

    (B) the formation of coral reefs

    (C) the life and death cycles of coral reefs

    (D) the physical beauty of coral reefs

14. The relationship between the coral and the algae is best described as

    (A) parasitic

    (B) competitive

    (C) predatory

    (D) cooperative

GO ON TO THE NEXT PAGE

For do-it-yourself types, the cost of getting regular oil changes seems unnecessary. After all, the steps are fairly easy as long as you are safe. First, make sure that the car is stationary and on a level surface. Always use the emergency brake to ensure that the car does not roll on top of you. Next, locate the drain plug for the oil under the engine. Remember to place the oil drain pan under the plug before you start. When it is drained fully, wipe off the drain plug and the plug opening and then replace the drain plug. Next, simply place your funnel in the engine and pour in new oil. Be sure to return the oil cap when you're done. Finally, run the engine for a minute, and then check the dipstick to see if you need more oil in your engine.

15. After draining the old oil from the engine, you should

    (A) replace the oil cap
    (B) run the engine for a moment and check the dipstick
    (C) wipe off and replace the drain plug
    (D) engage the emergency brake

STOP. IF YOU FINISH BEFORE THE TIME IS UP, YOU MAY CHECK OVER YOUR WORK ON THIS PART ONLY.

PART 5. AUTOMOTIVE AND SHOP INFORMATION (AS)

Time: 11 minutes; 25 questions

<u>Directions</u>: In this section, you will be tested on your knowledge of automotive and shop basics. For each question, select the best answer and mark the corresponding oval on your answer sheet.

1. High-intensity ultraviolet light is generated during _____.

   (A) stick welding
   (B) MIG welding
   (C) soldering
   (D) A and B

2. Most drill bits are made to cut when

   (A) rotated to the right when looking from the top
   (B) rotated to the left when looking from the top
   (C) rotated to the right when looking from the bottom
   (D) none of the above

3. Detergents in motor oil are designed to

   (A) suspend contaminants in the oil
   (B) dissolve contaminants in the oil
   (C) allow contaminants to settle at the bottom of the crankcase
   (D) none of the above

4. The "W" in 10W-30 motor oil stands for

   (A) weather
   (B) weight
   (C) warm
   (D) winter

5. A DOHC V-8 engine would have a total of _____ camshafts.

   (A) two
   (B) three
   (C) four
   (D) eight

6. Carpenters would clean up large holes in wood using a

   (A) smoothing file
   (B) bastard file
   (C) round rasp
   (D) flat rasp

7. Cutting torches use a mixture of _____ and _____ to produce a high-temperature flame.

   (A) nitrogen : acetylene
   (B) nitrogen : oxygen
   (C) acetylene : helium
   (D) acetylene : oxygen

8. All cars are currently being built with _____ electrical systems.

   (A) direct current
   (B) alternating current
   (C) negative ground
   (D) both A and C are correct

9. As lead-acid batteries discharge, their electrolyte gradually turns to

   (A) sulphuric acid
   (B) water
   (C) lead peroxide
   (D) none of the above

10. A loss of compression in an engine cylinder can be caused by all of the following EXCEPT:

    (A) worn engine bearings
    (B) worn piston rings/cylinder wall
    (C) burned valves
    (D) blown head gasket

11. Telescoping gauges are made to be used in conjunction with

    (A) inside micrometers
    (B) depth micrometers
    (C) feeler gauges
    (D) outside micrometers

12. Dial calipers are capable of measuring

    (A) outside diameter
    (B) inside diameter
    (C) depth
    (D) all of the above

13. A carpenter would use a _____ with a miter box.

    (A) rip saw
    (B) crosscut saw
    (C) coping saw
    (D) back saw

14. Engine temperature is controlled by the

    (A) electrical system
    (B) water pump
    (C) radiator
    (D) thermostat

15. The bore of an engine is

    (A) the radius of the cylinder
    (B) the diameter of the cylinder
    (C) the distance between TDC and BDC
    (D) none of the above

16. The three elements needed to initiate combustion are

    (A) air, light, and fuel
    (B) air, fuel, and an ignition source
    (C) air, compression, and an ignition source
    (D) air, heat, and compression

17. A four-cylinder engine's firing order always starts with cylinder number

    (A) 1
    (B) 2
    (C) 4
    (D) 8

18. _____ cylinders will fire in one revolution of a six-cylinder engine.

    (A) two
    (B) three
    (C) four
    (D) eight

GO ON TO THE NEXT PAGE

19. Which of the following is the LEAST likely to be found in a mechanic's tool box?

    (A) ball-peen hammer
    (B) dead blow hammer
    (C) claw hammer
    (D) rubber mallet

20. Most solders are an alloy of _____ and _____.

    (A) tin : copper
    (B) tin : lead
    (C) copper : lead
    (D) brass : copper

21. A lead-acid battery has lead plates immersed in electrolyte composed of _____ and water.

    (A) citric acid
    (B) hydrochloric acid
    (C) carbolic acid
    (D) sulphuric acid

22. The starter motor's drive gear engages with the engine's

    (A) flywheel ring gear
    (B) crankshaft
    (C) vibration damper
    (D) timing chain

23. Increasing the diameter of a vehicle's wheels will make its speedometer read

    (A) slower
    (B) faster
    (C) the same
    (D) none of the above

24. When going around a corner, a vehicle's outside wheels will turn _____ the inside wheels.

    (A) slower than
    (B) the same speed as
    (C) faster than
    (D) none of the above

25. With disk brakes, the _____ rotates with the vehicle's wheels.

    (A) brake rotor
    (B) brake caliper
    (C) brake drum
    (D) wheel cylinder

STOP. IF YOU FINISH BEFORE THE TIME IS UP, YOU MAY CHECK OVER YOUR WORK ON THIS PART ONLY.

PART 6: MATHEMATICS KNOWLEDGE (MK)

Time: 24 minutes; 25 questions

<u>Directions</u>: In this section, you will be tested on your knowledge of basic mathematics. For each question, select the best answer and mark the corresponding oval on your answer sheet.

1. If 48 is divided by 0.08, the result is

   (A) 0.06
   (B) 0.6
   (C) 60
   (D) 600

2. If the number 9,899,399 is increased by 2,082, the result will be

   (A) 9,901,481
   (B) 9,901,471
   (C) 9,902,481
   (D) 9,902,471

3. The cube of 9 is

   (A) 27
   (B) 81
   (C) 243
   (D) 729

4. What is the value of $(-ab)(a)$ when $a = -2$ and $b = 3$?

   (A) −12
   (B) −6
   (C) 6
   (D) 12

5. $(x - 4)(x - 4) =$

   (A) $x^2 + 8x - 16$
   (B) $x^2 - 8x - 16$
   (C) $x^2 - 8x + 16$
   (D) $x^2 - 16x + 8$

6. $0.123 \times 10^4 =$

   (A) 12.3
   (B) 123
   (C) 1,234
   (D) 1,230

7. $\sqrt{100} - \sqrt{64} =$

   (A) 2
   (B) 4
   (C) 6
   (D) 8

8. Circle O above has a diameter of 6, an area of b square units, and a circumference of c units. What is the value of $b + c$?

   (A) 9π
   (B) 15π
   (C) 18π
   (D) 42π

GO ON TO THE NEXT PAGE

9. A bag contains 8 white, 4 red, 7 green, and 5 blue marbles. Eight marbles are withdrawn at random. How many of the withdrawn marbles are white if the chance of drawing a white marble is now 1 in 4?

(A) 3
(B) 4
(C) 5
(D) 6

10. Liza has 40 less than 3 times the number of books that Janice has. If B is equal to the number of books that Janice has, which of the following expressions shows the number of books that Liza and Janice have together?

(A) $3B - 40$
(B) $3B + 40$
(C) $4B - 40$
(D) $4B + 40$

11. If the perimeter of a square is 32 meters, then what is the area of the square, in square meters?

(A) 16
(B) 32
(C) 48
(D) 64

12. If $x \neq 0$, then $\dfrac{6x^6}{2x^2} =$

(A) $4x^4$
(B) $4x^3$
(C) $3x^4$
(D) $3x^3$

13. A number is considered "blue" if the sum of its digits is equal to the product of its digits. Which of the following is "blue"?

(A) 111
(B) 220
(C) 321
(D) 422

14. If $x = \dfrac{1}{8}$, what is the value of y when $\dfrac{2}{x} = \dfrac{y}{4}$?

(A) $\dfrac{1}{4}$
(B) 4
(C) 16
(D) 64

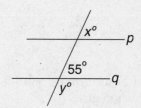

15. If line p above is parallel to line q, what is the value of $x + y$?

(A) 90
(B) 110
(C) 125
(D) 180

16. If $3ab = 6$, what is the value of a in terms of b ?

(A) $\dfrac{2}{b}$
(B) $\dfrac{2}{b^2}$
(C) $2b$
(D) $2b^2$

GO ON TO THE NEXT PAGE

17. For what value of y is $4(y - 1) = 2(y + 2)$

    (A) 0
    (B) 2
    (C) 4
    (D) 6

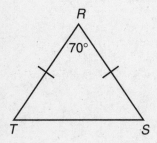

18. In triangle *RST* above, if $RS = RT$, what is the degree measure of angle *S*?

    (A) 40
    (B) 55
    (C) 70
    (D) cannot be determined from the information given

19. When *D* is divided by 15, the result is 6 with a remainder of 2. What is the remainder when *D* is divided by 6?

    (A) 0
    (B) 2
    (C) 3
    (D) 4

20. If the average of 7 consecutive even numbers is 24, then the largest number is

    (A) 26
    (B) 28
    (C) 30
    (D) 34

21. A box that has dimensions of 2 inches by 3 inches by 4 inches has a total surface area of

    (A) 24 square inches
    (B) 26 square inches
    (C) 48 square inches
    (D) 52 square inches

22. If $100 \div x = 10n$, then which of the following is equal to nx?

    (A) 10
    (B) $10x$
    (C) 100
    (D) $10xn$

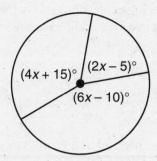

23. In the figure above, what is the value of x?

    (A) 15
    (B) 30
    (C) 55
    (D) 70

GO ON TO THE NEXT PAGE

24. If $7! = 7 \times 6 \times 5 \times 4 \times 3 \times 2 \times 1$, then $5! =$

    (A) 15
    (B) 75
    (C) 120
    (D) 125

25. Melissa took $5n$ photographs on a certain
    trip. If she gives n photographs to each of her
    3 friends, how many photographs will she
    have left?

    (A) $2n$
    (B) $3n$
    (C) $4n - 3$
    (D) $4n + 3$

STOP. IF YOU FINISH BEFORE THE TIME IS UP, YOU MAY
CHECK OVER YOUR WORK ON THIS PART ONLY.

PART 7: MECHANICAL COMPREHENSION (MC)

Time: 19 minutes; 25 questions

<u>Directions:</u> In this section, you will be tested on your knowledge of mechanics and basic physics. Select the best answer for each question and mark the corresponding oval on your answer sheet.

1. Torque is

   (A) a twisting force
   (B) the same as horsepower
   (C) a push or pull
   (D) Both B and C are correct.

2. Speed is different from velocity because

   (A) speed is a scalar quantity, and velocity is a vector quantity
   (B) velocity involves speed and direction
   (C) speed only expresses a magnitude
   (D) All of the above are correct.

3. A larger mass requires _____ force to achieve the same acceleration rate.

   (A) less
   (B) more
   (C) the same
   (D) none of the above

4. All of the following statements about force are true EXCEPT:

   (A) force is a scalar quantity
   (B) force is a push or pull
   (C) greater force results in greater acceleration
   (D) smaller masses require less force to achieve the same acceleration as larger masses

5. An object at rest

   (A) has no forces acting on it
   (B) is not subject to the law of gravity
   (C) has no net force acting on it
   (D) has no mass

6. A hockey puck sliding on the ice

   (A) has no net force acting on it
   (B) would slide forever if the rink was long enough
   (C) has speed, but not velocity
   (D) has a coefficient of kinetic friction

7. An astronaut has less _____ when in outer space.

   (A) weight
   (B) mass
   (C) velocity
   (D) speed

8. All of the following statements about weight are true EXCEPT:

   (A) weight increases closer to earth's surface
   (B) weight is not dependent on mass
   (C) weight is greater on planets with greater mass
   (D) weight varies from location to location

9. While attempting to push a heavy box across the floor

   (A) the amount of force required to start the box sliding is more than that required to keep it sliding
   (B) pushing on the box without moving it results in no work being done
   (C) the coefficient of static friction is dependent on the nature of the surface the box is resting on
   (D) all of the above

GO ON TO THE NEXT PAGE

10. A man pushes on a 1,000 kg car that is stuck in the ditch. He pushes for 10 minutes without moving it. How much work has the man done?

    (A) none
    (B) more than he would have done if he hadn't pushed at all
    (C) the same amount as when two men pushed and didn't move it
    (D) Both A and C are correct.

11. A policeman fires a handgun during target practice. His weapon recoils slightly as he fires because

    (A) for every action, there is an equal but opposite reaction
    (B) the bullet exerts a smaller force on the gun than the gun exerts on the bullet
    (C) the policeman slipped as the gun was fired
    (D) none of the above

12. In order to apply more torque to a bolt, a mechanic would

    (A) use a longer wrench
    (B) apply more force to the wrench
    (C) Both A and B are correct.
    (D) Neither A nor B are correct.

13. A vehicle travels at a constant speed on the highway. It can be said that

    (A) its acceleration rate is zero
    (B) the net forces acting on the vehicle are zero
    (C) the force applied by the vehicle's drive wheels is equal and opposite to the forces that act to slow the vehicle
    (D) All of the above are correct.

14. An astronaut is on a "space walk" and pushes away from his spaceship. Which of the following statements about this event is true?

    (A) the spaceship will not accelerate, because its mass is too great
    (B) the astronaut will accelerate at the same rate as the spaceship
    (C) the astronaut will accelerate at a higher rate because his mass is less than that of the spaceship
    (D) the spaceship will accelerate at twice the rate of the astronaut

15. Meters per second is a measure of

    (A) acceleration
    (B) speed
    (C) gravity
    (D) all of the above

16. Vector quantities express

    (A) magnitude
    (B) direction
    (C) Both A and B are correct.
    (D) Neither A nor B are correct.

17. If a vehicle accelerates from a standstill at a rate of $1 \frac{m}{s^2}$, its velocity after 10 seconds will be

    (A) $0.10 \frac{m}{s}$
    (B) $0.10 \frac{m}{s^2}$
    (C) $10 \frac{m}{s}$
    (D) $10 \frac{m}{s^2}$

GO ON TO THE NEXT PAGE

18. Horsepower is a measure of

    (A) work
    (B) force
    (C) the rate that work is done
    (D) the rate of change in the force applied to an object

19. The energy of movement is known as

    (A) potential energy
    (B) chemical energy
    (C) electromotive energy
    (D) kinetic energy

20. One pound of force is applied to move an object a distance of one foot. _____ of work has been done.

    (A) 1 foot-pound
    (B) 1 watt
    (C) 1 joule
    (D) Both B and C are correct.

21. All of the following statements about energy are true EXCEPT:

    (A) energy cannot be created
    (B) the amount of energy in the universe is slowly diminishing
    (C) energy cannot be destroyed
    (D) energy can be converted from one form into another

22. Raising an object higher from the ground will increase its

    (A) potential energy
    (B) kinetic energy
    (C) momentum
    (D) inertia

23. When gasoline is burned in an internal combustion engine, _____ energy is converted into heat energy.

    (A) kinetic
    (B) electrical
    (C) mechanical
    (D) none of the above

24. Efficiency of a machine is determined by

    (A) how much horsepower it can produce
    (B) how much energy it consumes
    (C) how much of the source energy is converted into usable energy
    (D) how long the machine can operate at full output

25. In order to hit a baseball further, the player must

    (A) hit the ball with more force
    (B) make contact with the ball for a longer period of time
    (C) Both A and B are correct.
    (D) Neither A nor B are correct.

STOP. IF YOU FINISH BEFORE THE TIME IS UP, YOU MAY CHECK OVER YOUR WORK ON THIS PART ONLY.

PART 8: ELECTRONICS INFORMATION (EI)

Time: 9 minutes; 20 questions

Directions: In this section, you will be tested on your knowledge of electronics basics. For each question, select the best answer and mark the corresponding oval on your answer sheet.

1. A load

   (A) has very low resistance and conducts current throughout the circuit
   (B) is a device that converts electrical energy into heat, light, or motion
   (C) is a voltage source
   (D) switches electrical current off and on

2. Household appliances are built to operate on

   (A) alternating current
   (B) direct current
   (C) Both A and B are correct.
   (D) Neither A nor B are correct.

3. Hertz is a unit of measurement that describes

   (A) frequency
   (B) the number of cycles per second of alternating current
   (C) the cost per day for a rental car
   (D) Both A and B are correct.

4. There are two types of variable resistors, the _____ and the potentiometer.

   (A) diode
   (B) rheostat
   (C) thermostat
   (D) capacitor

5. An "earth ground" in residential wiring is

   (A) buried conduit
   (B) a copper rod driven into the ground
   (C) made to protect occupants from electrical shock
   (D) All of the above are correct.

6. A negative-ground electrical system in an automobile means that

   (A) the battery's negative post is connected to the fuse box
   (B) the battery's negative post is connected to the chassis
   (C) the battery's negative post is connected to its positive post
   (D) the battery's negative post is connected to an earth ground

7. _____ voltage drops occur at higher resistances.

   (A) higher
   (B) lower
   (C) zero
   (D) None of the above.

8. According to Kirchoff's Law, the sum of the voltage drops in a circuit are equal to the

   (A) circuit resistance
   (B) the current flow in the circuit
   (C) applied voltage
   (D) All of the above are correct.

9. All of the following are properties of a closed circuit EXCEPT

    (A) an ohmmeter will measure less than infinite resistance in the circuit
    (B) the circuit will have infinite resistance
    (C) current will flow
    (D) the circuit has continuity

10. When resistance in a circuit goes up, current flow

    (A) drops
    (B) rises
    (C) stays the same
    (D) none of the above

11. Increasing the voltage in a circuit and keeping resistance the same will result in

    (A) increased current flow
    (B) decreased current flow
    (C) current flow staying the same
    (D) zero current flow

12. A switch that is turned "off" is

    (A) an open circuit
    (B) an infinite resistance
    (C) Both A and B are correct.
    (D) Neither A nor B are correct.

13. Capacitive reactance decreases as electrical frequency

    (A) decreases
    (B) increases
    (C) varies
    (D) gets closer to DC

14. All of the following statements about capacitors are true EXCEPT:

    (A) capacitors can store an electrical charge
    (B) capacitance is measured in farads
    (C) capacitors will block DC, but allow AC to flow
    (D) capacitors are made of two insulators with a conductor between them

15. The magnetic field in a coil of wire can be made stronger by

    (A) increasing the number of turns of wire in the coil
    (B) increasing the current flowing through the coil
    (C) inserting an iron core into the middle of the coil
    (D) all of the above

16. Whenever current passes through a resistance, _____ is generated.

    (A) voltage
    (B) capacitance
    (C) heat
    (D) light

17. A zener diode is different from a diode because

    (A) it will "break down" at a certain voltage and conduct current in both directions
    (B) its resistance varies with temperature
    (C) it blocks electrical current in both directions
    (D) it can supply voltage to a circuit

GO ON TO THE NEXT PAGE

18. When current passes through a diode, the diode is

   (A) reverse-biased
   (B) forward-biased
   (C) open
   (D) grounded

19. Transistors are turned on and off by voltages applied to their

   (A) collector
   (B) emitter
   (C) base
   (D) cathode

20. Capacitors connected in parallel

   (A) handle more voltage
   (B) produce more capacitance
   (C) produce higher WVDC rating
   (D) produce less capacitance

STOP. IF YOU FINISH BEFORE THE TIME IS UP, YOU MAY CHECK OVER YOUR WORK ON THIS PART ONLY.

PART 9. ASSEMBLING OBJECTS (AO)

Time: 9 minutes; 16 questions

<u>Directions:</u> In this section, you will be tested on your ability to construct or connect a series of objects. For each question, select the best answer and mark the corresponding oval on your answer sheet.

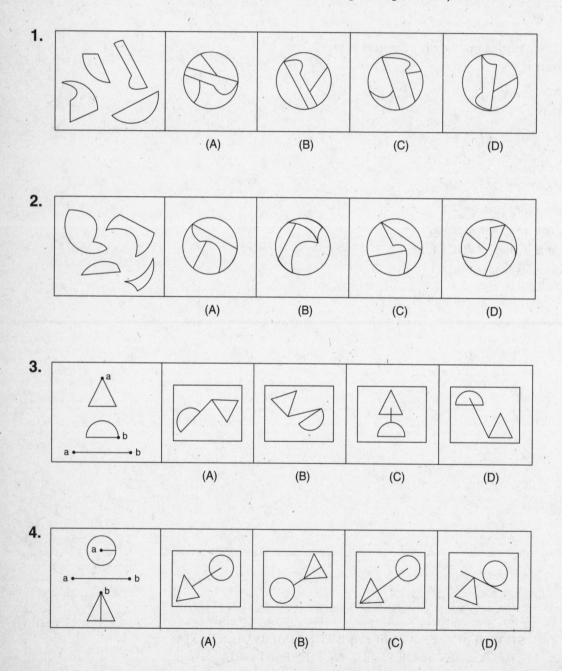

GO ON TO THE NEXT PAGE

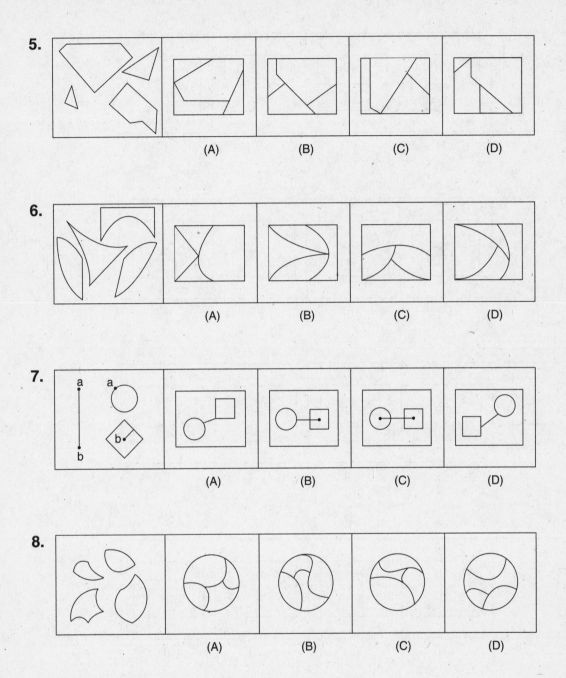

5. (A) (B) (C) (D)

6. (A) (B) (C) (D)

7. (A) (B) (C) (D)

8. (A) (B) (C) (D)

9.

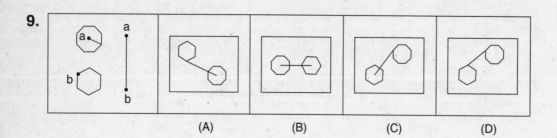

(A)   (B)   (C)   (D)

10.

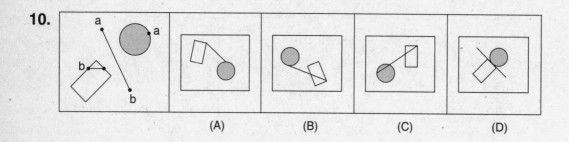

(A)   (B)   (C)   (D)

11.

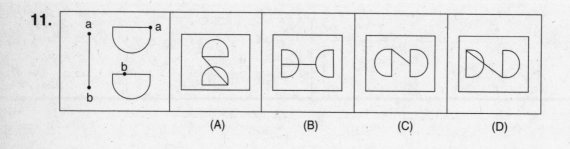

(A)   (B)   (C)   (D)

12.

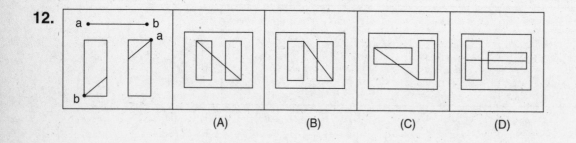

(A)   (B)   (C)   (D)

GO ON TO THE NEXT PAGE

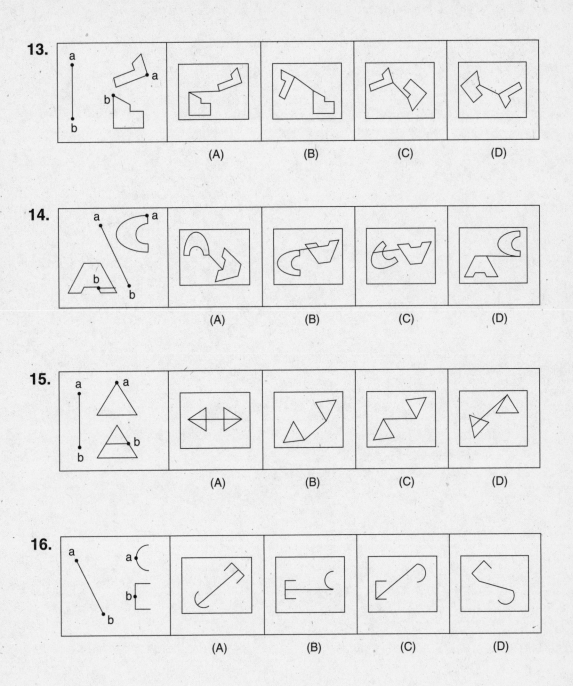

STOP! END OF TEST.

ASVAB Practice Test I
Answers and
Explanations

ANSWER KEY

General Science	Arithmetic Reasoning	Word Knowledge	Paragraph Comprehension	Auto and Shop Information
1. D	1. C	1. C	1. B	1. D
2. C	2. B	2. B	2. C	2. A
3. B	3. B	3. B	3. A	3. A
4. B	4. D	4. C	4. D	4. D
5. B	5. D	5. D	5. A	5. C
6. A	6. A	6. C	6. D	6. C
7. D	7. B	7. D	7. C	7. D
8. A	8. C	8. A	8. D	8. D
9. C	9. D	9. C	9. A	9. B
10. D	10. B	10. C	10. C	10. A
11. D	11. A	11. B	11. A	11. D
12. C	12. A	12. C	12. C	12. D
13. A	13. D	13. A	13. B	13. D
14. C	14. B	14. B	14. D	14. D
15. B	15. A	15. B	15. C	15. B
16. C	16. D	16. D		16. B
17. A	17. C	17. A		17. A
18. D	18. A	18. C		18. B
19. D	19. A	19. B		19. C
20. A	20. B	20. D		20. B
21. C	21. C	21. D		21. D
22. A	22. B	22. A		22. A
23. C	23. D	23. B		23. A
24. C	24. A	24. C		24. C
25. B	25. D	25. D		25. A
	26. D	26. C		
	27. C	27. A		
	28. C	28. B		
	29. C	29. D		
	30. B	30. C		
		31. B		
		32. C		
		33. D		
		34. A		
		35. D		

ANSWER KEY

Mathematics Knowledge	Mechanical Comprehension	Electronics Information	Assembling Objects
1. D	1. A	1. B	1. B
2. A	2. D	2. A	2. B
3. D	3. B	3. D	3. A
4. A	4. A	4. B	4. C
5. C	5. C	5. D	5. D
6. D	6. D	6. B	6. B
7. A	7. A	7. A	7. B
8. B	8. B	8. C	8. A
9. B	9. D	9. B	9. A
10. C	10. D	10. A	10. B
11. D	11. A	11. A	11. C
12. C	12. C	12. C	12. A
13. C	13. D	13. B	13. B
14. D	14. C	14. D	14. B
15. D	15. B	15. D	15. D
16. A	16. C	16. C	16. A
17. C	17. C	17. A	
18. B	18. C	18. B	
19. B	19. D	19. C	
20. C	20. A	20. B	
21. D	21. B		
22. A	22. A		
23. B	23. D		
24. C	24. C		
25. A	25. C		

GENERAL SCIENCE ANSWERS AND EXPLANATIONS

1. D

Staring directly at the sun can cause permanent damage to the eye's delicate retina.

2. C

On a Fahrenheit thermometer the boiling point of water at sea level is 212°. 100° is the degrees Celsius boiling point, and 373° is the degrees Kelvin boiling point.

3. B

The process by which plants convert carbon dioxide and water into sugar and oxygen is called photosynthesis. The reverse process, by which animals convert oxygen and sugars into carbon dioxide and water, is called respiration.

4. B

In electricity, a unit of resistance is called an ohm. An ampere is a unit of electric current, a volt is a unit of electromotive force, and a watt is a unit of power equal to 1 joule per second.

5. B

Iron forms rust when water (or an even better electrolyte) turns iron and oxygen into iron oxide (Fe_2O_3), a chemical process. Helium and neon are both inert, so they do not react chemically. Water causing soil erosion may or may not incur a chemical change, and ice melting does not alter the chemistry of H_2O.

6. A

Goiter is caused by a lack of iodine.

7. D

Blood enters the right atrium of the heart from the vena cava.

8. A

For a substance to have a high pH, it should be a base, or alkaline. A pH of 7 is neutral, like water; a pH of less than 7 is acidic; and a pH of greater than 7 is a base. Of the substances listed, only ammonia is a base.

9. C

Insulin is created in the body's pancreas.

10. D

Typhus is a bacterial disease often transmitted by body lice. Measles, the mumps, and rabies are all viral infections.

11. D

If two brown-eyed parents have a blue-eyed child, the probability that their next child will have blue eyes is 1 in 4. The blue-eyed gene (b) is recessive to the brown-eyed gene (B), so if both parents have brown eyes and one of the children has blue eyes, both parents carry the recessive blue-eyed gene (Bb), and thus the chances of any more of their children being blue-eyed (bb) is 1 in 4.

12. C

Shale, which derives from clay sediments, is an example of a sedimentary rock.

13. A

Of the planets in the solar system, only Venus and Mercury do not have any moons.

14. C

The process by which the sun heats the earth is known as radiation.

15. B

Among vegetables, spinach provides the best source of iron.

16. C

A lunar eclipse happens when the moon passes through the earth's shadow. During a lunar eclipse, the earth lies between the moon and sun.

17. A

A sphygmomanometer is used to measure blood pressure.

18. D

Of the climates listed, the one with the shortest growing season is the taiga, which is characterized by long, severe winters, summers with thawing subsoil, and organisms such as conifers and moose predominating.

19. D

Vitamin B_3 is also known as niacin.

20. A

The major portion of an atom's mass consists of neutrons and protons. Electrons, positrons, neutrinos, and other subatomic particles have practically negligible masses.

21. C

Arthropods represent a large phylum of the animal kingdom characterized by chitinous exoskeletons, segmented bodies, and jointed legs. Examples include crabs, centipedes, and spiders, but not the sea horse, which belongs to the phylum Echinodermata.

22. A

Tin is a pure element, and thus is not a metallic alloy.

23. C

Over the course of 24 hours the earth rotates 360 degrees about its axis.

24. C

The Monera kingdom is considered the most primitive kingdom because its organisms are prokaryotic—that is, their cells lack nuclei.

25. B

The phylum that includes man is called Chordata, meaning vertebrate animals.

ARITHMETIC REASONING ANSWERS AND EXPLANATIONS

1. C

This question asks you to determine the sale price of a camera that normally sells at $160 and is discounted 20%. To solve, determine what 20% of $160 equals. Rewrite 20% as a decimal. 20% = 0.20. So 20% of $160 = 0.20 × $160 = $32. The sale price of the camera would be $160 − $32 = $128, choice (C).

2. B

Since there are 60 minutes in an hour, the subway will pass $\frac{60}{10}$ or 6 times as many stations in 1 hour as it passes in 10 minutes. In 10 minutes it passes 3 stations, so in 60 minutes it must pass 6 × 3 or 18 stations.

3. B

In this question, the ratio is implied: for every $\frac{3}{4}$ inch of map there is 1 real mile, so the ratio of inches to the miles they represent is always $\frac{3}{4}$ to 1. Therefore, we can set up the proportion:

$$\frac{\text{Number of inches}}{\text{Number of miles}} = \frac{\frac{3}{4}}{1} = \frac{3}{4}$$

Now $1\frac{3}{4}$ inches = $\frac{7}{4}$ inches.

Set up a proportion:

$$\frac{\frac{7}{4}\text{ inches}}{\text{Number of miles}} = \frac{3}{4}$$

Cross-multiply:

$\frac{7}{4}(4) = 3$ (Number of miles)

$7 = 3$ (Number of miles)

$\frac{7}{3}$ = Number of miles

or $2\frac{1}{3}$ = Number of miles

4. D

We can express the ratio of baseballs to golf balls as $\frac{2}{3}$. Since we know the number of baseballs, we can set up a proportion: $\frac{2}{3} = \frac{30}{x}$, where x is the number of golf balls. To solve, we cross multiply to get $2x = 90$, or $x = 45$.

5. D

The total cost of the taxi ride equals $36 + (25% of $36), or $36 + ($\frac{1}{4}$ × $36) = $36 + $9 = $45. If four people split the cost equally, then each person paid $\frac{\$45}{4}$, or $11.25 each.

6. A

Find the number of seconds in an hour, and then multiply this by the distance the car is traveling each second. There are 60 seconds in a minute and 60 minutes in one hour; therefore, there are 60 × 60, or 3,600, seconds in an hour. In one second the car travels $\frac{1}{100}$ kilometers; in one hour the car will travel $3,600 × \frac{1}{100}$, or 36 kilometers.

7. B

When given a sequence like the one in this question, look for the relationship between the numbers. The first two terms are 6.5 and 13.75. Subtract the smaller term from the larger one, and you see that 6.5 + 7.25 = 13.75. The same is true of the next two terms: 13.75 + 7.25 = 21. The same applies to the next two terms 21 + 7.25 = 28.25. So the next term in the sequence would be 28.25 + 7.25 = 35.50, choice (B).

8. C

If Ms. Smith's car averages 35 miles per gallon, she can go 35 miles on 1 gallon. To go 700 miles she will need $\frac{700}{35}$, or 20 gallons of gasoline. The price of gasoline was \$1.25 per gallon, so she spent $20 \times$ \$1.25, or \$25, for her trip.

9. D

Be careful with a question like this one. You're given the percent decrease (25%) and the *new* number (72), and you're asked to reconstruct the original number. Don't just take 25% of 72 and add it on. That 25% is based not on the new number, 72, but on the original number—the number you're looking for. The best way to do a problem like this is to set up an equation:

(Original number) − (25% of Original number) = New number

$$x - 0.25x = 72$$
$$0.75x = 72$$
$$x = 96$$

10. B

The time it takes to complete the entire exam is the sum of the time spent on the first half of the exam and the time spent on the second half. We know the time spent on the first half is $\frac{2}{3}$ of the time spent on the second half. If S represents the time spent on the second half, then the total time spent is $\frac{2}{3}S + S$ or $\frac{5}{3}S$. We know this total time is one hour, or 60 minutes. So we can set up a simple equation and solve for S.

$$\frac{5}{3}S = 60$$
$$\frac{3}{5} \times \frac{5}{3}S = \frac{3}{5} \times 60$$
$$S = 36$$

So the second half takes 36 minutes. The first half takes $\frac{2}{3}$ of this, or 24 minutes. You could also find the first half by subtracting 36 minutes from the total time, 60 minutes.

11. A

You're asked what percent of the new solution is alcohol. The *part* is the number of ounces of alcohol; the *whole* is the total number of ounces of the new solution. There were 25 ounces originally. Then 50 ounces were added, so there are 75 ounces of new solution. How many ounces are alcohol? 20% of the original 25-ounce solution was alcohol. 20% is $\frac{1}{5}$, so $\frac{1}{5}$ of 25, or 5 ounces are alcohol. Now you can find the percent of alcohol in the new solution:

$$\% \text{ alcohol} = \frac{\text{alcohol}}{\text{total solution}} \times 100\%$$
$$= \frac{5}{75} \times 100\%$$
$$= \frac{20}{3}\% = 6\frac{2}{3}\%$$

12. A

To find probability, determine the number of desired outcomes and divide that by the number of possible outcomes. The probability formula looks like this:

$$\text{Probability} = \frac{\#\text{ of desired outcomes}}{\#\text{ of possible outcomes}}$$

In this case, Marty is pulling one pen at random from his knapsack, and we want to determine the probability that the pen is either red or black. There are 5 blue pens, 6 black pens, and 4 red pens in the knapsack. Let's return to the probability formula:

$$\text{Probability} = \frac{\#\text{ of desired outcomes}}{\#\text{ of possible outcomes}} .$$

$$= \frac{\text{Number of red} + \text{black pens}}{\text{Number of red} + \text{black} + \text{blue pens}}$$

$$= \frac{4 + 6}{4 + 6 + 5} = \frac{10}{15} = \frac{2}{3}.$$

(A) is correct.

13. D

Be careful with combined percent increase. You generally cannot just add the two percents, because they're generally percents of different bases. In this instance, the 100% increase is based on the 1980 population, but the 50% increase is based on the larger 1990 population. If you just added 100% and 50% to get 150%, you fell into the testmaker's trap.

The best way to do a problem like this one is to pick a number for the original whole and just see what happens. And, as usual, the best number to pick here is 100. (That may be a small number for the population of a city, but verisimilitude is not important—all that matters is the math.)

If the 1980 population was 100, then a 100% increase would put the 1990 population at 200. And a 50% increase over 200 would be 200 + 100 = 300.

Since the population went from 100 to 300, that's a percent increase of 200%.

$$\frac{300 - 100}{100} \times 100\% = \frac{200}{100} \times 100\%$$

14. B

To learn the man's overtime rate of pay, we have to figure out his regular rate of pay. Divide the amount of money made, $200, by the time it took to make it, 40 hours. $200 ÷ 40 hours = $5 per hour. That is the normal rate. The man is paid $1\frac{1}{2}$ times his regular rate during overtime, so when working more than 40 hours he makes $\frac{3}{2} \times \$5$ per hour = $7.50 per hour. Now we can figure out how long it takes the man to make $230. It takes him 40 hours to make the first $200. The last $30 are made at the overtime rate. Since it takes the man one hour to make $7.50 at this rate, we can figure out the number of extra hours by dividing $30 by $7.50 per hour. $30 ÷ $7.50 per hour = 4 hours. The total time needed is 40 hours plus 4 hours, or 44 hours.

15. A

The calculations aren't too bad on this one. The most important thing to keep in mind is that you're solving for 75% of x and not for x. First, we are told that 50% of x is 150. That means that half of x is 150, and that x is 300. So 75% of $x = 0.75 \times 300 = 225$. (A) is correct.

16. D

This is a question where backsolving (working with your answer choices) can save you a lot of time. Let's start with choice (B) and see if it works. If (B) is correct, an adult's ticket would cost $3.00, and a child's ticket would cost $1.50. The total fare we are looking for was for two adults and three children. If an adult's fare were $3.00, that total fare would be 2($3.00) + 3($1.50) = $6.00 + $4.50 = $10.50. That's too low since the question states that the total fare is $14.00.

Now see what happens if an adult fare were more expensive. If (D) were correct, an adult's ticket would cost $4.00 and a child's ticket would cost $2.00. The total fare would equal 2($4.00) + 3($2.00) = $8.00 + $6.00 = $14.00. That's the total fare we're looking for, so (D) is correct.

17. C

The original rectangle was 4 inches by 6 inches. It was lengthened to 10 inches with the width remaining at 4 inches. The perimeter of a rectangle can be found by adding twice the length to twice the width (or by adding up each of the four sides). So the perimeter would be 4 + 10 + 4 + 10 = 28, choice (C).

18. A

When the painter and his son work together, they charge the sum of their hourly rates, $12 + $6, or $18 per hour. Their bill equals the product of this combined rate and the number of hours they worked. Therefore $108 must equal $18 per hour times the number of hours they worked. We need to divide $108 by $18 per hour to find the number of hours. $108 ÷ $18 = 6.

19. A

To find the average, add the weights and divide by the number of people.

$$\text{Average} = \frac{150 + 153 + 154 + 157 + 151}{5}$$

$$= \frac{765}{5}$$

$$= 153.$$

20. B

We need to compute the cost of parking a car for 5 hours at each garage. Since the two garages have a split-rate system of charging, the cost for the first hour is different from the cost of each remaining hour.

The first hour at garage A costs $8.75

The next 4 hours cost 4 × $1.25 = $5.00

The total cost for parking at garage A = $8.75 + 5.00 = $13.75

The first hour at garage B costs $5.50

The next 4 hours cost 4 × $2.50 = $10.00

The total cost for parking at garage B = $5.50 + $10.00 = $15.50

So the difference in cost = $15.50 − $13.75 = $1.75, (B).

21. C

Set up a proportion:

$$\frac{12 \text{ pages}}{1 \text{ hour}} = \frac{100 \text{ pages}}{x \text{ hours}}$$

$$12x = 100$$

$$x = \frac{100}{12} = 8\frac{1}{3}$$

One-third of an hour is $\frac{1}{3}$ of 60 minutes, or 20 minutes. So $8\frac{1}{3}$ hours is 8 hours and 20 minutes.

22. B

This problem sets up relationships between large, medium and small sodas—two large sodas are equal to three medium sodas, and two medium sodas are equal to three small sodas. How many small sodas equal 8 large sodas? Well, 2 larges equal 3 mediums, so 12 mediums must equal 4 × 2 or 8 large sodas. You now can find how many small sodas represent 12 mediums. Since 2 mediums are the same as 3 small sodas, 12 mediums must equal 6 × 3 or 18 small sodas.

23. D

If you change each digit 5 into a 7 in the number 258,546, the new number would be 278,746. The difference between these two numbers would be 278,746 − 258,546 = 20,200. Choice (D) is correct.

24. A

Since 1 pound of lumber costs $4.00, $2\frac{1}{4}$ pounds of lumber cost 2.25 × $4.00 = $9.00.

Then you need to add 7% sales tax to $9.00. Find 7% of $9.00 by multiplying 0.07 × $9.00 = $0.63.

Add $0.63 to $9.00 to get $9.63, choice (A).

25. D

We are asked which of five ratios is equivalent to the ratio of $3\frac{1}{4}$ to $5\frac{1}{4}$. Since the ratios in the answer choices are expressed in whole numbers, turn this ratio into whole numbers:

$$3\frac{1}{4} : 5\frac{1}{4} = \frac{13}{4} : \frac{21}{4} = \frac{\frac{13}{4}}{\frac{21}{4}} = \frac{13}{4} \times \frac{4}{21} \text{ or } 13:21.$$

26. D

This is just another disguised division problem. Divide 72 by $\frac{3}{8}$ and you get:

$$72 \div \frac{3}{8} = 72 \times \frac{8}{3} = 24 \times 8 = 192.$$

27. C

You can save valuable time by estimating on this one. Pay special attention to how much you have left and how much you've already spent. If a man spent $\frac{5}{12}$ of his salary and was left with \$420, that means that he had $\frac{7}{12}$ left, and if the man's salary is x dollars, then $\frac{7}{12}x = \$420$. That means that \$420 is a little more than half of his salary. So his salary would be a little less than 2(\$420) = \$840. Choice (C), \$720 is a little less than \$840. So (C) works perfectly, and it's the correct answer here.

28. C

The key to this question is that while the value of the stock decreases and increases by the same *amount*, it doesn't decrease and increase by the same *percent*. When the stock first decreases, that amount of change is part of a larger whole. If the stock were to increase to its former value, that same amount of change would be a larger percent of a smaller whole.

Pick a number for the original value of the stock, such as \$100. (Since it's easy to take percents of 100, it's usually best to choose 100.) The 20% decrease represents \$20, so the stock decreases to a value of \$80. Now in order for the stock to reach the value of \$100 again, there must be a \$20 increase. What percent of \$80 is \$20? It's $\frac{\$20}{\$80} \times 100\%$, or $\frac{1}{4} \times 100\%$, or 25%.

29. C

Joan can shovel the whole driveway in 50 minutes, so each minute she does $\frac{1}{50}$ of the driveway. Mary can shovel the whole driveway in 20 minutes; in each minute she does $\frac{1}{20}$ of the driveway. In one minute they do:

$$\frac{1}{50} + \frac{1}{20} = \frac{2}{100} + \frac{5}{100} = \frac{7}{100}$$

If they do $\frac{7}{100}$ of the driveway in one minute, they do the entire driveway in $\frac{100}{7}$ minutes. (If you do $\frac{1}{2}$ of a job in 1 minute, you do the whole job in the reciprocal of $\frac{1}{2}$, or 2 minutes.) So all that remains is to round $\frac{100}{7}$ off to the nearest integer. Since $\frac{100}{7} = 14\frac{2}{7}$, $\frac{100}{7}$ is approximately 14. It takes about 14 minutes for both of them to shovel the driveway.

30. B

Pay attention to your calculations on this one. Proceed carefully, one step at a time, and you're sure to get to the answer they're asking for. We're told that Eileen earns \$280 per week. Kelly earns \$50 more than Eileen, so Kelly earns \$280 + \$50 = \$330 per week. June's salary is \$70 less than Kelly's, so June earns \$330 – \$70 = \$260 per week, and (B) is correct.

WORD KNOWLEDGE ANSWERS AND EXPLANATIONS

1. C

Noble means *appearing in a majestic or royal fashion*, therefore choice (C) is correct.

2. B

In this sentence, *concede* refers to a couple's relationship. The intimation is that to succeed, couples need to work together. Of the answer choices, only (B), *compromise*, is a way of working together. By using the context of the given sentence, you could have gotten this answer without knowing the exact meaning of the original word.

3. B

The verb form of *goad* means *to provoke* or *coerce*. Of the answer choices, only (B), *taunt*, is a word that means provoke.

4. C

Using the word *herd* to mean a group being referred to as *a conforming mass*, the correct answer choice is (C), *pack*.

5. D

If you know that an EMT is a rescue technician, then you may grasp the idea that panic is not allowed. *Viable* then can be said to mean rendering something *capable of survival or success*. Of the answer choices given, (C) may seem acceptable. But *lucid* means clear. What we're looking for is a word meaning *acceptable*. Only (D), *reasonable*, works.

6. C

Judicious means *possessing or displaying good judgment*, or in other words, being *fair*.

7. D

Hesitating is a word you probably have seen many times. It can mean different things in different situations. Here it means *to be reluctant or indecisive*. But among the answer choices available, the only possible correct answer is (D), *pausing*.

8. A

You probably know the root word "false" as meaning wrong, or in reference to a lie. The textbook definition is *to misrepresent*. Looking at the possible answer choices, choice (A), *fabricating*, which means "making up," is the best possible answer.

9. C

The word *hollow* means *lacking a center* or *empty*.

10. C

The verb *to coax* means *to try to persuade*. Of the answer choices, only (C), *plead*, approaches being correct.

11. B

The root of the word given, *monotonous*, is "mono" meaning "one." Something *monotone* is in one flat speed and is completely lacking in variety. *Boring* would be another way to say this.

12. C

The big word *consternation* means *unthinkable dismay or frustration*. Of the answer choices, only (C), *confusion*, has this same meaning.

13. A

Savory in reference to food means *appetizing to taste*. Choice (A), *tasty*, is the best answer.

14. B

Renown means *a person or thing that is wildly famous*. In the case of the mayor, *fame* is the word we are looking for.

15. B

A *raconteur* is someone who tells stories. The word even sounds a little like "recount." Choice (B) is correct.

16. D

To *quench* something is to *sate* or *satisfy* it.

17. A

The word *polarized* has the same root as "polar." Think of "polar opposites" and you will be on the right track. In this case, choice (A), *split*, is closest in meaning to *polarized*.

18. C

Exact means *precise* or *specific*. Choice (C) is the correct answer.

19. B

Terrain comes from the root "terra-" or "earth." So of the answer choices, only *river* and *landscape* would be appropriate. *Landscape* is the ground in view. Thus, choice (B) is correct.

20. D

Terminal means *relating to an end, limit or boundary*. Choice (D), *final*, is most similar in meaning.

21. D

Augment means *to enhance something already developed*.

22. A

Something *involuntary* is something done *without plan or accidentally*. Answer choice (A) is correct.

23. B

The noun *collusion* refers to *an agreement of an illicit or secret nature*.

24. C

Tenacity means showing *persistence and determination*. A mongoose is a fierce animal whose ability to stay aggressive even against bigger foes is legendary. Of the answer choices, (C), *determination*, is the best answer.

25. D

Tactile means *relating to the sense of touch*. Of the answer choices, (D), *tangible*, is the most similar in meaning to the original word.

26. C

To *portend* is to make a *prediction*.

27. A

To *germinate* means to *sprout, seed, or bud*. Choice (A) is correct.

28. B

Restore has the prefix "re-", meaning *again*. Thus, restore means *bring back something which had been lost*. Of the choices given, both (B) and (D) refer to affecting change on something. But of the two, only (B), *invigorate*, means to renew.

29. D

A *filament* is any *thread or string which is very thin*.

30. C

Mutate is a word you've probably seen before. Comic books often have mutated characters (like the Hulk or Godzilla). The word means *something that has changed from its original state*. Of the choices given, (C), *altered*, is the best choice.

31. B

The adjective *dynamic* means *constantly changing* or *exciting*.

32. C

Congeal means to *solidify, coagulate, or harden*. Choice (C) is correct.

33. D

To *reconnoiter* means to *make a preliminary inspection*, or *see before others*. Of the answer choices, only (D), *scout*, really means the same thing as the given word.

34. A

The verb *accrue* means to *accumulate over time as a result of growth*.

35. D

Something referred to as *innate* is something *which is seen as inherent or natural*. The word even somewhat looks like the root of *natural*. Answer choice (D) is the best answer.

PARAGRAPH COMPREHENSION ANSWERS AND EXPLANATIONS

1. B

This is a main idea question which can be answered by asking "Is this what the author believes?" Choice (B) answers this well, whereas choice (C) cites a detail that helps answer the question "Why does the author believe this?" Choice (A) is not mentioned in the passage. The author states that science was extremely popular in the nineteenth century, which implies that science fiction was as well, but no direct information is given about the popularity of science fiction. Choice (D) is incorrect because there is no mention of Poe and Doyle being scientists.

2. C

The answer to a detail question such as this will be a paraphrase of what you find in the passage. We are told that reading shows students how words are used in sentences, so (C) is correct. (A) is incorrect because adults are never mentioned. (B) also was not stated in the passage. (D) does not answer the question and is not necessarily true based on the information given.

3. A

Wrong answers on main idea questions are often too broad or too specific. (B) is too broad because the passage is not about all American art movements, only the Hudson River School movement. (C) is too specific because the influence of European painters is just one detail mentioned while (A), the history of the Hudson River School painters, is being described. (D) is incorrect because nationalism is not the focus of the passage.

4. D

Careful tending, discussed in (A), relates to nurture or upbringing, which the author doesn't consider that important. Devoting equal care to variety and location, (B), would illustrate that nature and nurture are equally important. Choice (C), which

discusses getting tomatoes but not necessarily good tomatoes, is close but no cigar. The issue of quality discussed in choice (C) comes out of nowhere, and thus (C) cannot be the correct answer to this inference question. (D) does a much better job of illustrating that certain outcomes are genetically impossible.

5. A

It is important on vocabulary-in-context questions not to rely on your vocabulary knowledge alone of the word in question, but instead to choose an answer that best represents how the word is being used in the paragraph. *Bleak* can be used to mean *cold*, choice (C), or *depressing*, which might make choice (B) seem appealing. But only choice (A) does not alter the meaning of the sentence when plugged in; "the empty landscape and broad skies." Predicting an answer would have eliminated (D).

6. D

Since the answer to a detail question can be found in the text, the clause "nearly all her works are portrayals of nature" would direct you to choice (D). Choices (A), (B) and (C) all state things that were never mentioned in the passage, a characteristic typical of wrong answer choices to detail questions.

7. C

The text states that the Copernican model of the solar system describes that planets are revolving around the sun, choice (C). This is contradicted by choice (B). (A) and (D) are not mentioned.

8. D

Toby is smiling while he waits for his father, already holding his baseball glove and ball. He is eager, choice (D), to get to the game. Choice (A) is distracting since it is sad that it might be the last game that Toby's father will be able to attend, but the descriptive language of the passage supports eagerness and not sadness: the sun rushes into the room, now the birds are appearing. Toby is smiling, so there is no evidence of him being uneasy, choice (C). He is anxiously waiting for his father, which contradicts his being careless, choice (B).

9. A

Since the body can survive without food longer than it can survive without drinking (B) or breathing (C), eating is the least essential to survival. Choice (A) is correct. (D) is incorrect because excretion is not mentioned in the passage.

10. C

For inference questions you should read the entire passage and it is often best to attack each answer choice and eliminate those that do not follow from the passage. (B) clearly contradicts the author's words. The author is not likely to agree that news anchors are valuable sources of information, choice (D), but that only "real reporters" are. (A) goes beyond the scope of the passage, and may or may not be true based on what you have read. The correct answer will be something that must be true based on what's given, like choice (C).

11. A

This is a detail question, which means that you can look up the answer in the text. The poems "were intended to be sung or recited, not written down," so they were mainly an oral form, choice (A). (B) contradicts the passage which states that Greek poetry was like those of other societies. (C) and (D) are not mentioned.

12. C

The correct choice for a main idea question will express what the author believes. The passage states that remarkable progress has been made in artificial intelligence, so choice (C) is correct. While the author discusses the difference of opinion between those who believe that there will eventually be a computer capable of intelligent thought and those who do not, he does not assert the truth of either statement, so choice (A) is incorrect. Be wary of answers such as (D) which use extreme language. Chess is not the main focus of the passage, so choice (B) is incorrect.

13. B

This is a main idea question, so either the correct answer will make so much sense you will want to pick it, or you can eliminate wrong answer choices because they are too broad or too specific, or otherwise don't properly describe the passage. Here the correct answer choice does make a lot of sense. The passage describes how coral reefs are created, so choice (B), the formation of coral reefs, describes the passage well. Choice (A) is out because "varieties" of animal life are nowhere described. (C) is wrong because "death cycles" of coral reefs are never touched upon. And (D) is far too narrow; there's only the barest reference in the passage to "the physical beauty" of coral reefs.

14. D

For this detail question, you just want to pick the answer choice that best paraphrases the relationship between the coral and algae as described in the passage. The passage states that the "two organisms form a mutually beneficial relationship;" in other words, the relationship is cooperative, choice (D).

15. C

For correct sequence questions, look up the answer in the text. According to the passage, when the engine is fully drained, you should wipe off the drain plug and replace it, choice (C).

AUTO AND SHOP INFORMATION ANSWERS AND EXPLANATIONS

1. D

Soldering does not produce the electric arc that welding does. Welders must cover all exposed skin with protective clothing and wear face shields with light filters for protection.

2. A

The vast majority of drill bits are made to cut while rotating in a clockwise direction (as viewed from above). These are known as *right hand* drill bits.

3. A

Oil cannot function alone as motor oil, so petroleum engineers combine it with a chemical additive package that enhances the performance of the oil. Some of the additives in the package that combine with the base oil include detergents, antioxidants, and viscosity improvers. Their purpose is to remove unwanted contaminants. Detergents do this by *suspending* contaminants.

4. D

The "W" in 10W-30 signifies that it is *winter-rated* oil.

5. C

A double overhead cam arrangement puts two camshafts into each cylinder head, and makes it so one cam operates the exhaust valves in that head, and the other operates all the intake valves. Each set of two is contained into one camshaft. Thus, four camshafts is the correct answer.

6. C

Carpenters would use a round rasp for cleaning out holes in wood. Round rasps are useful for cleaning up holes, where a flat rasp would be used to smooth flat surfaces.

7. D

Using an oxyacetylene cutting torch involves the burning of oxygen and acetylene to produce a flame that is hot enough to melt steel.

8. D

Automotive electrical systems are designed to utilize direct current (DC) as well as to send that current from the coil winding through the ignition module and back to the battery through the vehicle ground circuit. Therefore, answer choice (D) is correct.

9. B

As the lead-acid battery discharges, the sulphuric acid in the electrolyte is reduced to water. The lead plates then become lead sulphate. Charging the battery restores the chemical composition of the lead plates and the electrolyte.

10. A

A loss of compression can be caused by worn piston rings or cylinder walls, burned valves, or a blown head gasket. But worn engine bearings do not affect the engine's compression. Thus, the correct answer is (A).

11. D

Telescoping gauges can be used to measure inside diameter by fitting snugly in a hole, and then measuring the diameter with an outside micrometer. Telescoping gauges are especially handy when measuring small holes that an inside micrometer could not fit into.

12. D

A dial caliper is a measuring tool that can measure inside diameter, outside diameter, and depth, just like the vernier caliper. The dial caliper enhances the vernier scale with a large dial face and pointer that makes reading easy.

13. D

A back saw is normally used for making fine cuts, so it has 14 to 16 teeth per inch. Back saws can be used with a miter box for making even cuts at specific angles.

14. D

The thermostat controls engine temperature by allowing coolant to flow into the radiator when the coolant temperature rises above a certain level.

15. B

The cylinder *bore* is the diameter of the cylinder.

16. B

A specific mixture of air and fuel plus an ignition source to get the whole thing going is required for combustion.

17. A

The firing order for four-cylinder engines is 1-3-4-2. Therefore, (A) is the answer.

18. B

It takes two full revolutions of the crankshaft to complete one cycle of events in a four-stroke cycle engine. This means that all of the cylinders in the engine must complete a power stroke in two revolutions of the crankshaft. So in *one* revolution, only three cylinders will fire. Thus, the correct answer is (B).

19. C

Claw hammers are a more specialized tool often preferred by carpenters. Their purpose is two-fold. The hammer head has two ends: One drives nails and the other removes them. This is the tool least likely to be found in a mechanic's tool box.

20. B

Most solder is an alloy of lead and tin. The percentages of each metal in the solder will vary depending on the desired properties of the solder, i.e., melting point.

21. D

An automobile battery, or lead-acid battery, is made up of lead plates immersed in an electrolyte made up of sulphuric acid and water.

22. A

Moving the ignition switch to the "start" position sends an electrical current to the starter solenoid. This engages the starter drive gear onto the engine's ring gear, which is located on the flywheel.

23. A

By increasing the diameter of your vehicle's wheels, you will make the distance traveled per rotation greater, thereby slowing down the reading of the speedometer, which is calibrated to record the same amount of rotation as before.

24. C

The drive axle incorporates a differential, which allows the left and right wheel to turn at different speeds as the vehicle goes around a corner. The outside wheels have a greater distance to travel due to inertia, and will turn faster.

25. A

It is the brake rotor attached to the wheel that rotates. Then the brake caliper clamps to slow the car wheels down.

MATHEMATICS KNOWLEDGE ANSWERS AND EXPLANATIONS

1. D

A question like this one tests your ability to play with decimals. $\frac{48}{0.08}$ is the same as $\frac{4,800}{8} = 600$. (D) is correct. When dividing by a decimal, be sure to move the decimal place the same number of spaces for both numbers.

2. A

Be careful with your number-crunching here. $9,899,399 + 2,082 = 9,901,481$, choice (A)

3. D

The cube of a number is that number multiplied by itself three times. So the cube of 9 would be $9 \times 9 \times 9 = 729$, choice (D).

4. A

Plug in the values for a and b and remember your order of operations when working through your calculations. When $a = -2$ and $b = 3$,

$$(-ab)(a) = [-(-2) \times 3]\ (-2)$$
$$= (2 \times 3)\ (-2)$$
$$= (6) \times (-2) = -12, \text{ choice (A)}.$$

5. C

This is a classic product of two binomials. Remember to FOIL, and you're good to go.

$$(x - 4)\ (x - 4)$$
$$= (x)(x) + (x)\ (-4) + (-4)(x) + (-4)(-4)$$
$$= x^2 - 4x - 4x + 16$$
$$= x^2 - 8x + 16.$$

Choice (C) is correct.

6. D

$10^4 = 10,000$. So $0.123 \times 10^4 = 0.123 \times 10,000 = 1,230$, choice (D).

7. A

Know your perfect squares. $\sqrt{100} = 10$ and $\sqrt{64} = 8$. So $\sqrt{100} - \sqrt{64} = 10 - 8$, choice (A).

8. B

Given a diameter of 6, the radius must equal $\frac{1}{2}$ of 6, or 3. Next, the circumference $= 2\pi r = 2\pi(3) = 6\pi$. The area $= \pi r^2 = \pi(3^2) = 9\pi$. Summing these two we get: $9\pi + 6\pi = 15\pi$.

9. B

To find the probability of something occurring, divide the number of desired outcomes by the number of total outcomes. In the example of the bag of marbles, you begin with $8 + 4 + 7 + 5 = 24$ marbles, and draw out 8, leaving you with 16 marbles. Out of those 16 marbles, 4 must be white since the chance of drawing a white marble is now $\frac{4}{16}$ or $\frac{1}{4}$. If you are left with 4 white marbles, you must have already withdrawn 4 white marbles. (B) is correct.

10. C

If B is equal to the number of books that Janice has, and we know that Liza has 40 less than 3 times the number of books that Janice has, Liza has $3B - 40$ books, and Janice has B books. Together they have $4B - 40$ books, choice (C).

11. D

The perimeter of a square is $4s$ where s is the length of a side. If a square has a perimeter of 32, then it has a side length of 8. The area of the square is $s^2 = 8^2 = 64$, choice (D).

12. C

You can simplify this expression as follows:

$\dfrac{6x^6}{2x^2} = \dfrac{6}{2}\left(\dfrac{x^6}{x^2}\right) = 3x^4$, choice (C).

Remember to subtract exponents when dividing.

13. C

Go through the answer choices one at a time, and select the choice whose digits have a sum and product that are equal.

(A) 111. Product = (1)(1)(1) = 1.
Sum = 1 + 1 + 1 = 3. Eliminate.

(B) 220. Product = (2)(2)(0) = 0.
Sum = 2 + 2 + 0 = 4. Eliminate.

(C) 321. Product = (3)(2)(1) = 6.
Sum = 3 + 2 + 1 = 6.

Bingo! Choice (C) is correct.

14. D

If $x = \dfrac{1}{8}$, and we are asked to solve for y when $\dfrac{2}{x} = \dfrac{y}{4}$, begin by plugging in $\dfrac{1}{8}$ for x. $\dfrac{2}{\frac{1}{8}} = \dfrac{y}{4}$.

Cross-multiply and solve. $\dfrac{1}{8}y = 8$, so $y = 64$, (D).

15. D

When parallel lines are crossed by a transversal, all acute angles formed are equal, and all acute angles are supplementary to all obtuse angles. So in this diagram, obtuse angle y is supplementary to the acute angle of 55°. Angle x is an acute angle, so it is equal to 55°. Therefore, angle x is supplementary to angle y, and the two must sum to 180°.

16. A

If you're looking for a in terms of b, try to isolate the a on one side of the equation.

$$3ab = 6$$
$$ab = 2$$
$$a = \dfrac{2}{b}$$

(A) is correct.

17. C

Distribute the numbers outside the parentheses and solve for y.

$$4(y - 1) = 2(y + 2)$$
$$4y - 4 = 2y + 4$$
$$2y = 8$$
$$y = 4$$

(C) is correct.

18. B

Since RS and RT are equal, the angles opposite them must be equal. Therefore, angle T = angle S. Since the degree measures of the three interior angles of a triangle sum to 180, 70 + angle measure S + angle measure T = 180, and angle measure S + angle measure T = 110. Since the two angles, S and T, are equal, each must have angle measures half of 110, or 55.

19. B

When D is divided by 15, the result is 6 with a remainder of 2. That means that $D = 6(15) + 2$ or 92. When 92 is divided by 6, the remainder is 2. (B) is correct.

20. C

The average of 7 consecutive even numbers is 24. That means that 24 must be smack dab in the middle of the set of numbers. So the set must be {18, 20, 22, 24, 26, 28, 30}. The largest number is 30, choice (C).

21. D

The surface area of a rectangular solid is $2lw + 2lh + 2wh$. In this case that would be $(2 \times 2 \times 3) + (2 \times 2 \times 4) + (2 \times 3 \times 4) = 12 + 16 + 24 = 52$ square inches, choice (D).

22. A

If $100 \div x = 10n$, that can be rewritten as $\dfrac{100}{x} = 10n$. Cross-multiply and you get $100 = 10nx$. $nx = \dfrac{100}{10} = 10$. (A) is correct.

23. B

A circle contains 360°, so

$$(4x + 15) + (2x - 5) + (6x - 10) = 360$$
$$4x + 2x + 6x + 15 - 5 - 10 = 360$$
$$12x = 360$$
$$x = 30$$

24. C

$5! = 5 \times 4 \times 3 \times 2 \times 1 = 120$. Choice (C) is right.

25. A

If Melissa has $5n$ photographs, and she gives n photographs to each of three friends, she would have given away $3n$ photographs. $5n - 3n = 2n$. (A) is correct.

MECHANICAL COMPREHENSION ANSWERS AND EXPLANATIONS

1. A

Torque is a twisting force. This is very different from horsepower (the rate that work is done), or force (a push or pull).

2. D

Speed is very different from velocity, in that velocity (a vector quantity) implies both speed and direction.

3. B

The relationship between force, mass, and acceleration is described using the formula $F = ma$. If mass increases, more force is required to achieve the same acceleration rate.

4. A

Force is a vector quantity. This means that it expresses both magnitude and direction.

5. C

Objects at rest may still have many forces acting on them (gravity, to name just one). If so, the forces are all counteracted by equal and opposite forces, so the *net force* acting on these objects is zero.

6. D

A hockey puck has a coefficient of kinetic friction (however small) that causes it to lose velocity.

7. A

An astronaut's mass will be the same no matter where he or she is, but their weight will be less in outer space due to their increased distance from earth.

8. B

Weight is dependent on mass and acceleration due to gravity ($W = mg$).

9. D

The coefficient of static friction is always greater than the coefficient of kinetic friction. If a force is applied, but the box does not move, no work has been done ($W = Fd$). The nature of the surface the box rests on will define the coefficient of friction between the box and that surface.

10. D

It doesn't matter how many people are pushing on the car. If it doesn't move, no work has been done.

11. A

Newton's Third Law of Motion tells us that when the bullet is fired, the bullet exerts that same amount of force on the gun as the gun exerts on the bullet.

12. C

Torque (twisting force) can be increased by increasing the length of the wrench, or by increasing the force applied to the wrench.

13. D.

A vehicle traveling at a constant speed has no net forces acting on it, so its acceleration rate is zero.

14. C

The spaceship has a much greater mass than the astronaut, so it will accelerate, but at a much slower rate than the astronaut will.

15. B

Meters per second is a quantity that is related to speed. Acceleration and acceleration due to gravity are both measured in meters-per-second^2.

16. C

Vector quantities express both magnitude and direction. Examples of vector quantities include velocity and force.

17. C

Accelerating at the rate of $1\frac{m}{s^2}$ will result in a velocity of $10\frac{m}{s}$ at the end of ten seconds. The quantity $1\frac{m}{s^2}$ implies that acceleration is taking place at $1\frac{m}{s}$ each second.

18. C

Horsepower is a measure of the rate that work is done.

19. D

The energy of movement is known as kinetic energy.

20. A

Using the formula $W = F \times d$, it can be seen that 1 pound of force applied through a distance of 1 foot will result in 1 foot-pound of work being done.

21. B

The principle of conservation of energy tells us that the amount of energy in the universe is constant.

22. A

Using the formula $PE = mgh$, the potential energy (PE) of an object is determined by the mass of the object (m), acceleration due to gravity (g), and the height that the object is raised (h).

23. D

When gasoline is burned in an internal combustion engine, *chemical* energy is converted into heat energy.

24. C

A machine's efficiency is expressed as the percentage of the source energy that it converts into usable energy.

25. C.

The distance the ball travels will depend upon the impulse that was applied to it. Impulse is determined by multiplying the force by the amount of time that the force was applied.

ELECTRONICS INFORMATION ANSWERS AND EXPLANATIONS

1. B

Loads convert electrical energy into some other useful form of energy. Examples of loads include heating elements (heat), light bulbs (light), and solenoids (motion).

2. A.

Household appliances are made to operate on AC (alternating current), which is available at all the outlets in a residential wiring system.

3. D

Hertz is an expression of the frequency (cycles per second) of alternating current. One hertz (hz) is the same as one cycle per second.

4. B

Variable resistors come in two designs: the potentiometer and the rheostat. The potentiometer is a three-wire design, whereas the rheostat is a two-wire design. Rheostats are used for lamp dimmers and volume controls in stereos.

5. D

An earth ground is found outside a building, and normally utilizes conductors such as conduit or pipe that is already in the ground. All of the ground connectors in a residential wiring system will be attached to an earth ground, which is used to "funnel" away stray electricity in appliances and prevent it from causing electrical shock.

6. B

The ground system in an automobile makes it possible to have a "one-wire" electrical system, in which all electrical components on a vehicle are powered by only one wire from the battery. In these systems, the component's other connection will go to the chassis (ground). Negative-ground means that the negative post of the battery is connected to the chassis/frame of the vehicle.

7. A.

Whenever electrical current passes through a resistance, a voltage drop takes place. Areas of high resistance in an electrical circuit will cause a high voltage drop.

8. C

Kirchoff's voltage law tells us that the sum of the voltage drops in a circuit will equal the circuit's applied voltage.

9. B

A closed circuit will conduct electrical current. Therefore, it could not have infinite resistance, which would cause zero current to flow in the circuit.

10. A

Ohm's law tells us that $E = I \times R$. If voltage E stays constant, and resistance R rises, current I would have to drop.

11. A

Ohm's law tells us that $R = E \div I$. If resistance R stays constant, and voltage E rises, current I will also have to increase.

12. C

A switch that is turned "off" will not allow current to flow in the circuit. This means that the circuit is "open" and has infinite resistance.

13. B

A capacitor is made to block DC (direct current), but allow AC (alternating current) to flow. Capacitive reactance is a capacitor's "opposition" to the flow of current, and this tends to diminish as the frequency of alternating current increases.

14. **D**

A capacitor is made up of two conductors made of metal foil, with an insulator (dielectric) between them.

15. **D**

An electromagnet's magnetic field becomes stronger when more turns of wire are added to it, more current is passed through the coil, or an iron core is placed in the middle of the coil.

16. **C**

When current passes through a resistance, a voltage drop will take place. This represents an energy loss, and this energy is normally dissipated in the form of heat.

17. **A**

A zener diode acts like a regular diode up until a certain amount of reverse bias. It will "break down" at a specified threshold voltage and allow current to flow in both directions.

18. **B**

When current flows freely through a diode, this is known as "forward bias." When current reverses its direction, the diode will block this flow and its condition is known as "reverse bias."

19. **C**

A transistor has three connections: the base, the emitter, and the collector. The transistor is switched off and on by voltages applied to their base. When a voltage appears across the base-emitter junction, the transistor switches on and allows current to flow between the collector and emitter.

20. **B**

When capacitors are connected in parallel, their total capacitance increases. This is in contrast to resistors, which will decrease their total resistance as they are connected in parallel.

Part Two

AFQT REVIEW

CHAPTER TWO

Word Knowledge

INTRODUCTION

We know, we know, you hate vocabulary tests. Either they are an insult to your intelligence, or they manage to dredge up a word that's so obscure that it's hard to imagine ever using such a word in your military career or elsewhere. But let's face it, what legitimate test would really be complete without grading you on your verbal skills? The ASVAB is no different. And because the two verbal sections of the ASVAB figure heavily into your AFQT, the calculated score which helps to determine if and where you'll be placed if you want to enter the Armed Forces, you should take the verbal sections of the ASVAB seriously.

And, like it or not, it also makes sense for them to care. Because whether you plan on wiring jets, swabbing decks, or writing checks, word knowledge will come into play. That's why the ASVAB wants to see how your ability to understand vocabulary stacks up.

KNOW WHAT TO EXPECT

The ASVAB is fairly straightforward on its verbal test sections. The Word Knowledge section of the ASVAB will test, primarily, your ability to define words. Some of the words tested are less common than others and therefore more difficult. But very few of the words are what we'd call "SAT words"—meaning words that are by nature difficult and rarely used except on standardized tests.

On the Word Knowledge section you will be given 11 minutes to complete a total of 35 questions. Because the questions are short and sweet and generally fall into the either-you-know-it-or-you-don't category (although, as we shall discuss soon, you may know more than you think), most people don't have too much trouble finishing this section.

Nonetheless, you should be prepared, as on any ASVAB section, to guess on any questions you don't get to.

A little more than half the questions will be straight synonym questions. That's what we call the questions where you are simply given a word, and asked to choose the answer choice closest to it in meaning. Here's an example of this type of question.

EXAMPLE 1

1. <u>Gregarious</u> most nearly means

    (A) conspicuous
    (B) twisting
    (C) outgoing
    (D) deep

Unfortunately, these questions don't provide much in the way of context clues. But there are still techniques to that can help you find the answer when you aren't sure of the definition. We will look at these in a bit. If you were able to come up with (C), *outgoing*, as the closest synonym of gregarious, you may not have to rely on our techniques all that often. But it's still good to learn them for the occasional curve ball that gets thrown on this section.

IT'S NOT JUST A VOCABULARY TEST

Some Word Knowledge questions will provide you with context clues. Make sure to use those clues!

On the remaining questions, the word in question will appear in the context of a sentence. For that reason, we refer to these as in-context questions.

Here's an example of this question type.

EXAMPLE 2

2. <u>Nomadic</u> tribes often move their villages when the seasons change.

    (A) warlike
    (B) wandering
    (C) exclusive
    (D) hasty

On these questions, you almost always can use the clues in the sentence to help find the answer, even if you aren't familiar with the underlined word. Here, for instance, the sentence describes tribes that move around when the seasons change. What would you call such tribes? Warlike? Not necessarily. Exclusive? Probably not. Hasty? That doesn't quite follow. Oh wait, we skipped one. Wandering? Oh yes, that makes sense! They would be called wandering tribes if they move around with the change of seasons. Surprisingly often, only one answer choice will make sense in the context of the sentence on this question type. The correct answer here has to be (B), and nomadic does in fact mean *wandering* or *migrant*.

So, as you can see, you don't always have to know the vocabulary word to get the correct answer on Word Knowledge section. No doubt, people with an already strong vocabulary are at an advantage here. But even if you aren't a lexicographer, you can prepare yourself for doing your best when the underlined word is unfamiliar. We'll also take some time to help show you the best ways to increase your vocabulary quickly. This is not only a good preparation for this test, but it may also help you in your later studies.

So let's get started.

IMPROVING AND BUILDING YOUR VOCABULARY

While sitting around and reading the dictionary might help you learn vocabulary words, just as important, as we have seen, is the ability to cope with the unfamiliar words you encounter while reading. When you come across strange vocabulary in a book you are reading, do you always run to a dictionary to look up the word? Most likely you do not (although it's not a bad idea, especially when you're trying to improve your vocabulary). Often, however, you don't really need to look up the word because you can figure out its meaning by the way it's used in the sentence or paragraph. This is what we mean by understanding vocabulary through context and it's an essential critical reading skill. Our ASVAB strategies will show you how to squeeze the most out of these context clues.

But before we examine those strategies, let's look at how to improve your vocabulary.

You should note that there are two distinct types of tough ASVAB vocabulary words:

1. Unfamiliar words
2. Familiar words with unfamiliar secondary meanings

You may run across some words that are hard because you have never seen them used before, although for the most part, ASVAB Word Knowledge vocabulary tends not to be that obscure. Other words, such as *appropriate* and *flag*, can also trip you up because they seem easy at first but in fact have less commonly known secondary definitions. For instance, *flag* and *appropriate* both have meanings as verbs that differ from their more familiar meanings. On in-context questions in particular, you should be prepared to see familiar words used this way.

To get a sense of your vocabulary strength, take a few minutes to go through the following list of typical ASVAB vocabulary words and see how many you know. Write your definition to the right of each word, and then score yourself. Give yourself one point for every word you know. Answers and study advice based on your score follow the quiz.

resolute _____

terse _____

vanquish _____

cautious _____

lethargic _____

sullen _____

distraught _____

legible _____

fawn (v.) _____

jeer _____

adrift _____

query _____

impure _____

disinterested _____

pathetic _____

Here are the definitions:

resolute	determined
terse	short, abrupt
vanquish	to defeat or conquer in battle
cautious	careful in actions and behaviors
lethargic	sluggish, inactive, apathetic
sullen	depressed, gloomy
distraught	extremely troubled; agitated with anxiety
legible	possible to read or decipher
fawn (v.)	to brown-nose or act in a servile manner
jeer	taunt, ridicule
adrift	wandering aimlessly, afloat without direction
query	a question; to call into question
impure	lacking in purity, containing something unclean
disinterested	impartial; unbiased
pathetic	sad, pitiful, tending to arouse sympathy

If you got six definitions or fewer right, you should start working on building your vocabulary as soon as possible. The techniques and tools in this chapter will teach you ways to improve your vocabulary and help you to make the most out of what you already know about words.

If you got between seven and eleven definitions right, your vocabulary is about average. It's important for you to do well on ASVAB verbal questions in order to insure your AFQT score is on the level. We recommend using the techniques and tools discussed in this chapter to help you out.

If you got more than eleven definitions right, your vocabulary is above average. You can always polish it further, though. Even if your time is short, you should learn the strategies in the "Decoding Strange Words" section and concentrate on getting the best Word Knowledge score possible.

A Vocabulary-Building Plan

A great vocabulary can't be built overnight, but you can begin building a good ASVAB vocabulary with a little bit of time and effort. Here's our best advice on how to do that.

Learn Words Strategically

The best words to learn are those that often appear on tests like the ASVAB. We recommend that you begin your studies with a vocabulary-building book like Kaplan's *Word Power*. Try to learn ten new words a day by using the techniques discussed below. Keep reviewing those words until you're sure you've committed them to memory.

Study Word Roots and Prefixes

Many tricky vocabulary words are made up of prefixes and suffixes that can get you at least part way to the definition. Thankfully, on the ASVAB, part way is often far enough to get you the right answer. For instance, if you know that the prefix *bio* means "life", you might be able to decode the definition of *biography*, which means a life story or the history of an individual. Fortunately, many ASVAB word roots may already be familiar if you've studied a foreign language, particularly a Romance language such as French, Spanish, or Latin.

Think Like a Thesaurus

On the ASVAB it's better to know a little bit about a lot of words than to know a lot about a few words. In other words, it's better to think like a thesaurus than like a dictionary. For instance, instead of studying the dictionary definition of *lackluster*, you can study *lackluster* in a thesaurus along with words like the following: *drab, dull, flat, lifeless, lethargic, listless, sluggard, somnolent.* Instead of just learning one word, learn them together and you'll get 12 words for the price of one definition.

Personalize Your Vocabulary Study

Figure out a study method that works for you and stick to it. But realize that most students don't learn best by reading passively from lists. Here are some of our studying suggestions:

PERSONALIZE YOUR HOME STUDY

- Use flashcards.
- Make a vocabulary notebook.
- Make a vocabulary tape.
- Look for hooks or phrases that will lodge a new word in your mind.

Use flashcards. Write down new words or word groups and run through them whenever you have some spare time. Write the word or word group on one side of a 3 × 5 index card and a short definition on the other side.

Create a vocabulary notebook. List words in the left-hand column and their meanings in the right-hand column. Cover up or fold over the page to test yourself. See how many words you can define from memory.

Make a vocabulary tape. Record the unfamiliar word, pause for a moment, and then record its definition. Listen to the tape on your portable cassette player. Quiz yourself by defining the word in your head before you hear the answer. Play it when you're on the go, or whenever you have a few spare moments.

Try to come up with "mnemonics." That is, try to come up with hooks to lodge new words into your head. Create visual images, silly sentences, rhymes, whatever, to build associations between words and their definitions.

DECODING STRANGE WORDS ON THE TEST

You should also realize that even with the best preparation in the world, you might see unfamiliar words on test day. No matter how much time you spend with flashcards, word lists, and vocabulary tapes, you should be prepared for a surprise. Fortunately, there are ways of dealing with unfamiliar vocabulary on the ASVAB that don't involve cursing your fate and sighing loudly to the annoyance of your fellow test takers.

Trust Your Hunches

Vocabulary knowledge is not an all-or-nothing proposition. Don't write off a word you see on the ASVAB just because you can't recite its definition. There are many levels of vocabulary knowledge.

- Some words you know so well that you can rattle off their dictionary definitions.
- Some words you "sort of" know. You can't define them precisely and you probably wouldn't use them yourself, but you understand them when you see them in context.
- Some words you barely recognize. You know you've heard them before, but you're not sure where.
- Some words you've never, ever seen before.

If the word before you falls in the second or third categories, go with your hunch. The following techniques may help you to get a better fix on the word.

Try To Recall Where You've Heard the Word Before

If you can recall a phrase in which the word appears, that may help you locate the correct answer.

Take a look at the following example. Remember that you don't need to know the dictionary definition to solve a question like this one. A sense of where you've heard a word before may be sufficient.

EXAMPLE 3

3. After the school banned the controversial group, its members continued to hold <u>clandestine</u> meetings.

    (A) amicable
    (B) spirited
    (C) auspicious
    (D) secret

Looking at the underlined word, you may not have known the definition of *clandestine*, but you may have heard the word used in phrases like "*clandestine activity* " on the news or in spy films. In that case, you may have gotten a sense of the meaning, which is "covert" or "secret." This also makes complete sense in the context of this sentence. Choice (D) is the correct answer.

Think Positive/Negative

Sometimes just knowing the "charge" of a word—that is, whether a word has a positive or negative sense—will be enough to earn you points on the ASVAB. Take the word *auspicious*. Let's assume you don't know its dictionary definition. Ask yourself: Does *auspicious* sound positive or negative? How about *callow*? Negative words often just sound negative. Positive words, on the other hand, tend to sound more friendly. If you said that *auspicious* is positive, you're right. It means "favorable or hopeful." And if you thought that *callow* is negative, you're also right. It means "immature or unsophisticated."

You can also use prefixes to help determine a word's charge. *Mal-*, *de-*, *dis-*, *dys-*, *un-*, *in-*, *im-*, and *mis-* often indicate a negative, while *pro-*, *ben-*, *magn-*, and *eu-* are often positives.

Some words are neutral and don't have a charge. But if you can get a sense of the charge of a word, you can probably answer some questions on that basis alone.

In the example below, begin by getting a sense of the "charge" of the underlined word.

EXAMPLE 4

4. <u>Rankle</u> most nearly means

(A) exhort
(B) impress
(C) relieve
(D) irk

Word sense is a very subjective thing, but in this case, most people, even if they can't come up with an exact definition of *rankle*, can just tell by the sound of the word that it has some sort of negative connotation. And in this case, just having that sense should be enough for you to pick the correct answer.

Choices (B) and (C) are clearly too positive for either to be the right answer. And choice (A) is neither positive nor negative, which also can't be right if you're sure that the word in question is negative. *Rankle*, like *irk*, means to annoy or irritate. So you shouldn't become rankled if you don't know the exact definition of a word. Try to come up with the word charge instead. It may be enough to get you to the correct answer.

Now that we've talked about how to deal with ASVAB vocabulary, it's time to take a look at the Kaplan Method for handling Word Knowledge Questions.

KAPLAN'S 3-STEP METHOD FOR WORD KNOWLEDGE QUESTIONS

1. Predict a synonym for the underlined word.

On in-context questions, you can usually make a prediction based on the clues in the sentence, even if you are unfamiliar with the word. On synonym questions, you'll have to rely on word knowledge alone. In either case, if you can make an exact prediction, that's excellent. You may proceed to step 2. If not, skip ahead to step 3.

2. Scan the answer choices and pick the closest match.

You may find the very word you predicted among the answer choices, but if not, you should be able to find the closest match. Be somewhat careful here, because sometimes there are close seconds among the answer choices.

3. If you can't come up with an exact prediction, use decoding strategies on the word, and eliminate answer choices accordingly.

If you can not predict the meaning of the word, try using the decoding strategies we discussed earlier. Does the word contain word roots that can help you to ascertain the meaning? Have you heard the word used before in a phrase or sentence? Does the word have a positive or a negative charge?

You probably won't see too many words that are totally foreign to you on this test. So use whatever you can dredge up to get a sense of the word and eliminate answer choices that cannot be right. Then guess from the remaining answer choices. Never leave a question blank!

Now you can try this method out on the practice set that follows. Give yourself just 11 minutes to answer the following 35 questions.

WORD KNOWLEDGE PRACTICE SET

1. <u>Ghastly</u> most nearly means

    (A) fun
    (B) lazy
    (C) torrid
    (D) awful

2. The brothers ran away in <u>cowardice.</u>

    (A) pain
    (B) fear
    (C) hopelessness
    (D) temperance

3. <u>Resignation</u> most nearly means

    (A) losing
    (B) waste
    (C) acceptance
    (D) pride

4. He promised to <u>cooperate</u> with the authorities.

    (A) fight
    (B) talk
    (C) work with
    (D) placate

5. It is <u>imperative</u> that you go to college to get a good job these days.

    (A) sad
    (B) timely
    (C) open
    (D) crucial

6. Everyone says he lost the election due to lack of <u>initiative</u>.

    (A) satisfaction
    (B) irritation
    (C) money
    (D) ambition

7. The city council sought <u>reparations</u> for the oil spill.

    (A) compensation
    (B) sadness
    (C) thanks
    (D) antipathy

8. Many times, the older sibling holds <u>dominion</u> over his younger siblings.

    (A) authority
    (B) safety
    (C) ability
    (D) guilt

9. His professors made a point of acting <u>erudite</u>.

    (A) civil
    (B) progressive
    (C) scholarly
    (D) amoral

10. <u>Tangible</u> most nearly means

    (A) real
    (B) open
    (C) graphic
    (D) costly

11. <u>Feasible</u> most nearly means

    (A) workable
    (B) breakable
    (C) imperfect
    (D) evident

12. <u>Foolhardy</u> most nearly means

    (A) stubborn
    (B) vigorous
    (C) proud
    (D) reckless

13. <u>Truncate</u> most nearly means

(A) widen

(B) shorten

(C) pack

(D) join

14. The coat that I bought three years ago now looks <u>shabby</u>.

(A) fluffy

(B) heavy

(C) threadbare

(D) angry

15. <u>Seclude</u> most nearly means

(A) isolate

(B) tempt

(C) acquire

(D) emit

16. <u>Acquit</u> most nearly means

(A) surrender

(B) obtain

(C) appraise

(D) clear

17. <u>Simulate</u> most nearly means

(A) agitate

(B) review

(C) endure

(D) replicate

18. His explanation left me even more <u>befuddled</u> than before.

(A) mystified

(B) grubby

(C) satisfied

(D) gloomy

19. The suspect <u>eluded</u> the police.

(A) expected

(B) sidestepped

(C) insulted

(D) questioned

20. <u>Erroneous</u> most nearly means

(A) approximate

(B) unplanned

(C) mistaken

(D) sensual

21. <u>Incriminate</u> most nearly means

(A) frighten

(B) investigate

(C) absolve

(D) implicate

22. <u>Garbled</u> most nearly means

(A) rinsed

(B) pointed

(C) jumbled

(D) whispered

23. <u>Synthetic</u> most nearly means

(A) expensive

(B) unusual

(C) artificial

(D) unattractive

24. Jimmy's tavern was one of my favorite <u>haunts</u> during college.

(A) landmarks

(B) obsessions

(C) shelters

(D) hangouts

25. The dam <u>ruptured</u> during the heavy storm.

    (A) conducted
    (B) endured
    (C) broke
    (D) wobbled

26. <u>Opulent</u> most nearly means

    (A) luxurious
    (B) overweight
    (C) transparent
    (D) smelly

27. <u>Creep</u> most nearly means

    (A) squeak
    (B) move slowly
    (C) grip tightly
    (D) retreat

28. <u>Leverage</u> most nearly means

    (A) influence
    (B) height
    (C) mechanism
    (D) humor

29. <u>Viscous</u> most nearly means

    (A) treacherous
    (B) green
    (C) syrupy
    (D) wild

30. Stay away from the <u>feral</u> cats that live in the woods.

    (A) wild
    (B) furry
    (C) cuddly
    (D) captive

31. His spirit did not <u>flag</u> even during the city's darkest hour.

    (A) signal
    (B) rise
    (C) float
    (D) fall

32. <u>Benefactor</u> most nearly means

    (A) critic
    (B) recipient
    (C) supporter
    (D) mediator

33. <u>Prohibition</u> most nearly means

    (A) shyness
    (B) ban
    (C) agreement
    (D) display

34. <u>Hypocrite</u> most nearly means

    (A) poser
    (B) scholar
    (C) follower
    (D) dictator

35. The <u>ultimate</u> goal of his exercise regimen was to win the pentathlon.

    (A) first
    (B) secondary
    (C) legitimate
    (D) final

ANSWER KEY

1. D	8. A	15. A	22. C	29. C
2. B	9. C	16. D	23. C	30. A
3. C	10. A	17. D	24. D	31. D
4. C	11. A	18. A	25. C	32. C
5. D	12. D	19. B	26. A	33. B
6. D	13. B	20. C	27. B	34. A
7. A	14. C	21. D	28. A	35. D

ANSWERS AND EXPLANATIONS FOR
WORD KNOWLEDGE PRACTICE SET

1. D

Even if you didn't know that *ghastly* means "awful," if you had a sense that ghastly has a negative charge, you could have gotten the correct answer that way. *Torrid*, by the way, means hot or passionate, as in a "torrid love affair."

2. B

Most people know that *cowardice* means lack of courage, with the closest match here being *fear* (B), but the careless test taker might have chosen a "close second" answer choice from among the other negative words, such as *pain* or *hopelessness*. Don't be in that much of a rush!

3. C

Sometimes, if you are having trouble with a word, such as *resignation* here, try coming up with a different part of speech, and then working on a synonym from the related word. For instance, if you come up with *resigned*, you might be able to make an easier sentence, such as: He was *resigned* to defeat. And from this you figure out that resignation most nearly means *acceptance*.

4. C

Even if you weren't positive of the meaning of *cooperate* here, you could have gotten rid of *fight* (A) and *placate* (D), because these words make no sense in the context of the sentence. And you could also have used word roots to break the underlined word down: *co-* means "with" and *operate* means "work."

5. D

Here's another case, where you could get the correct answer just by the context of the sentence (unless you really do think that it is sad that you have to go to college to get a good job these days). *Imperative*, like *crucial*, means very important or essential.

6. D

Choices (A) and (B) clearly make no sense in the context of this sentence. And (C) is a distracter: while he could lose an election because of a lack of *money*, that's not what initiative means. A lack of *ambition* could plausibly explain why he lost the election. *Initiative* more precisely means "resourcefulness," but *ambition* is the closest match here.

7. A

Here none of the answer choices make sense in the context of the sentence except for the correct choice, (A), *compensation*. *Reparations*, like *compensation*, means damages, or repayment for loss suffered.

8. **A**

Here again, you should be able to get the correct answer just from the context of the sentence. Choices (B), (C), and (D) simply make no sense when read into the sentence. *Dominion* means "control," "sway," or "authority."

9. **C**

Choice (C) makes the most sense in the context of the sentence. How would you expect professors to behave. *Civil*? Possibly, but it's not part of the job description. *Progressive*? That describes some professors, but certainly not all of them. *Scholarly*? Why yes! Professors are expected to act like scholars! And as for choice (D), *amoral*, meaning unprincipled or lacking in ethics—let's not even bother going there.

10. **A**

Even if you only "sort of" know the meaning of *tangible*, you might have a sense that something *tangible* can be felt or seen, as oppose to intangible objects which cannot. From that, you should be able to pick *real* (A) as the closest match.

11. **A**

When the question doesn't provide a context, try to come up with your own. Maybe you've heard something like: "The plan is feasible." Which answer choice best describes a plan? *Feasible* does mean "workable" or "viable."

12. **D**

If you know that *foolhardy* has a negative charge, that alone will probably direct you to the correct answer, *reckless* (D). *Foolhardy* and *reckless* both mean "rash" or "overly bold."

13. **B**

Try to dredge up where you've heard *truncate* before. If that doesn't work, ask yourself whether *truncate* could possibly mean each of the various answer choices. Sometimes, even if you have only the vaguest sense of a word, you will still know what the word cannot mean. *Truncate* does in fact mean *shorten*.

14. **C**

This one should have been easy. Choices (A), (B), and (D) make no sense in the context of the sentence. *Shabby* and *threadbare* both mean "tattered" or "worn out."

15. **A**

Once again, when in doubt, dredge up a context clue. Haven't you ever heard of a "secluded island"? And which of the answer choices best describe such an island? Only (A), *isolate*, makes any sense. *Isolate* and *seclude* both mean "to separate or keep away from contact with others."

16. D

Come on! Surely you've watched Court TV! If you hear that the defendant was "acquitted of all charges," you should know that means that the defendant was *cleared* of all charges, and is now free to go.

17. D

Even if you've never heard the word *simulate* before and don't know that it means the same as *replicate*, both of which mean "to reproduce or imitate," you might be able to use word roots and associated words to find the correct answer. *Simulate* has the prefix *sim-*, meaning "same," and *replicate* is very close to *replica*, meaning "copy" or "facsimile."

18. A

You may not have needed them, but otherwise, use those clues! Read the sentence without the underlined word: "His explanation left me even more _____ than before." In other words, he tried to explain, but I was left even more ____ than ever. Clearly the word in question has to mean something like "confused," which is what both *befuddled* and *mystified* mean.

19. B

If you were a suspect, what would you do? Would you *expect* the police? Would you *insult* the police? Would you *question* the police? Or would you *elude*, or sidestep, the police? We know that you in fact are law-abiding and would probably turn yourself in to the police if you were ever a suspect, but you know what we mean.

20. C

Erroneous means mistaken. You should have had no problem with this question if you realized that *erroneous* has the same root as "error," meaning "mistake."

21. D

Here's another case where you might be able to come up with an in-context phrase, such as "incriminating evidence," to get a fix on what *incriminate* means. "Incriminating evidence" is evidence that points the finger of guilt at someone; in other word, it's evidence that *implicates* someone in a crime. *Incriminate* and *implicate* both mean "to cast guilt or suspicion on."

22. C

Garbled means "jumbled" or "all mixed up", as in a "garbled message," which is one that gets messed up during transfer so that it no longer makes any sense.

23. C

Synthetic means *artificial*, as in the synthetic fabric polyester, which is neither expensive, unusual, nor, despite what some people say, unattractive.

24. D

This is yet another case where only one answer choice makes sense in the sentence. A tavern, even during one's college days, is unlikely to function as a *landmark*, an *obsession*, or even a *shelter*. It could easily function as a *hangout*, however. A secondary definition of *haunt* is *hangout*, or habitually frequented place.

25. C

If a dam ruptures during a heavy storm, that's bad news! It does not mean that the dam *conducted*, *endured*, or even *wobbled*. A dam *ruptures*, it *breaks*!

26. A

Opulent means *luxurious*. It helps if you've seen the word used in a phrase before, such as "opulent palace." Otherwise, you'll have to make your best guess.

27. B

You can tell from the answer choices that *creep* is being used here as a verb, so if you are unsure of the definition, try to use creep as a verb in a sentence. You might come up with something like: "He crept up on me carefully so that I wouldn't hear him." As this sentence illustrates, the verb *creep* means "to move slowly or crawl quietly."

28. A

Leverage means *influence* or power. Try to use the word in a sentence: He used his *leverage* to convince skeptical allies. If you are not sure of the meaning, eliminate answer choices that you know don't make any sense.

29. C

Have you ever heard the phrase "viscous fluid?" Which of the answer choices could logically describe a fluid? Only (C), *syrupy*, makes any sense. And *viscous* literally means "thick or glutinous"—in other words, *syrupy*.

30. A

There's no excuse for getting this question wrong. Why would you stay away from cats for being *furry* or *cuddly*? And how could *captive* cats live in the woods? There is, however, a good reason to stay away from *wild*, or *feral*, cats, so choice (A) makes perfect sense.

31. D

Once again, even if you did not know the meaning of *flag* when used as a verb, you should have been able to pick up the meaning from the context of the sentence. If his spirit did not *flag* even during the city's darkest hour, clearly *flag* here means something like *fall* or *fade*. Choice (D) alone makes sense.

32. **C**

Word roots alone could have gotten you to the correct answer (if you would study those word roots). *Bene-* means "good," and *factor* means "doer," so *benefactor* means "someone who does good things." Of the answer choices, (C) makes the most sense. Specifically, a *benefactor* is one who gives aid, usually in the form of money.

33. **B**

By now you should have heard of the Prohibition, which was a constitutionally enacted ban on alcohol that the United States experimented with, unsuccessfully, in the early 20th century. A small "p" *prohibition* refers to any ban, much like *to prohibit* means "to forbid."

34. **A**

A *hypocrite* is someone who says one thing and does another. Perhaps you knew that, but weren't quite happy with the correct answer choice, (A) *poser*. But a *hypocrite* and a *poser* are both phonies, and none of the other answer choices make any sense. The best answer does not always have to be a perfect answer.

35. **D**

Aside from the context clues, you might have been able to decipher the meaning of *ultimate* if you've studied a foreign language. For instance, the Spanish word for final is *ultimo*. And *ultimate*, in fact, means "final" or "eventual."

CHAPTER THREE

Paragraph Comprehension

INTRODUCTION

The ASVAB, like almost every other test of general knowledge, has included a reading section among its several subtests. In some ways, the ASVAB Paragraph Comprehension section is like any test of reading skills that you have ever taken. It provides passages for you to read and then asks questions for you to answer based solely on your reading of the passage. But because you are given only 13 minutes to read approximately 13 or 14 passages and answer 15 questions—that's 51 seconds per question, including the time it takes to read the passage—the ASVAB requires you read differently from the way you are used to in your everyday life.

As a rule, in our normal reading we read with one or two simple goals: to learn something, and/or to pass the time pleasantly. Needless to say, neither of these has anything to do with how to read on the Paragraph Comprehension section! Probably more than any other section on the ASVAB, doing well on the Paragraph Comprehension section is all about beating the clock. It's not enough to be able to answer the questions correctly—you have to answer them quickly as well. This requires developing a new approach to reading the passages on this all-important question type.

Understanding how to approach this question type begins with knowing what to expect. So let's take a look at how this section is put together.

TIME IS OF THE ESSENCE

The ASVAB Paragraph Comprehension section is made up of brief passages followed by one or more questions. You will be given just 13 minutes to complete 15 questions!

KNOW WHAT TO EXPECT

The Passages

Paragraph Comprehension passages vary in length from 30 words to 120 words. The longer passages may be accompanied by two or three questions, but you are unlikely to see more than one or two of these longer passages on any ASVAB section. The passages are drawn from a wide variety of topics, everything from art and science to business, politics, sports, biography, and history.

HOW *NOT* TO READ

- Don't try to understand the passage thoroughly. It's a waste of time.

- Don't get caught up in the details.

- Don't treat every part of the passage the same. Search for the answer you are looking for.

Almost all Paragraph Comprehension passages, no matter what the length or subject matter, tend to share one important characteristic. Compared to typical reading material, Paragraph Comprehension passages are extremely dense with information. This is one reason why they can be so difficult to slog through when you apply your usual reading skills. Not only is it useless to try to absorb everything you read when you read a Paragraph Comprehension passage, but doing so is likely to slow you down and hurt your score.

Never forget that your goal in this section is to answer the questions correctly. You get absolutely no extra points for having an especially thorough understanding of the passage. To get the score you're targeting on this section, you need to develop a method for handling Paragraph Comprehension questions quickly without getting bogged down with your reading of the passages. In fact, you need to learn to spend less time reading the passages so that you can spend more time understanding the questions and finding the correct answers. Let's quickly take a look at the components of a typical Paragraph Comprehension question.

EXAMPLE 1

The Taj Mahal was built by the Mughal emperor Shah Jahan as a burial place for his favorite consort, Arjumand Banu Bagam. She was known as Mumtaz Mahal, "the Elect of the Palace." Construction began soon after her death in 1631. The Taj Mahal and the surrounding complex of buildings and gardens was completed by about 1653. The Taj Mahal is much more than an expression of love and loss, though. It's a breathtakingly symmetrical representation of heaven.

1. Which of the following best describes the main idea of the passage?
   (A) the Taj Mahal as an expression of love and loss
   (B) the history of the building of the Taj Mahal
   (C) the Taj Mahal as an architectural representation of heaven
   (D) the balance between the building and the gardens in the Taj Mahal complex

This passage is full of dates, names, and all sorts of other useless information. Useless, you say? It certainly is when you get down to answering the question! Let's take a look.

THE QUESTIONS AND THE ANSWER CHOICES

The great majority of the passages will accompanied by just one question. That's why we suggest the following:

Read the question first!
Which of the following best describes the main idea of the passage?

When you read the question first, you find out what it is you are supposed to be looking for as you skim through the passage. You may need to identify the main idea of the passage; you may need to ascertain the passage's tone or purpose; you may need to find a specific piece of information; or you may be asked to make an inference based on the passage. By reading the question first, you'll know where to focus your attention as you read quickly through the passage.

For instance, here you have a "main idea" question. So you just need to locate the main point of the entire passage. All those details about when the Taj Mahal was built and for whom are not going to answer that question. Instead, you are look for the author's "big idea"—his or her take on the Taj Mahal. And you don't get that until you reach the end of the passage. If you realize that you are looking for the main idea of the passage, you'll know to skim past the details and filler until you zero in on the author's big idea. We'll show you some tricks for finding the main idea later, but now let's turn our attention to the answer choices.

  (A) the Taj Mahal as an expression of love and loss
  (B) the history of the building of the Taj Mahal
  (C) the Taj Mahal as an architectural representation of heaven
  (D) the balance between the buildings and the gardens in the Taj Mahal complex

If you knew that you were looking for the main idea of the passage and skimmed past the details, you should have no problem answering this question. The very last sentence of the passage states the author's central point: "[The Taj Mahal is] a breathtakingly symmetrical representation of heaven." You may want to mentally rephrase the main idea in your own words, because the correct answer will almost always be a paraphrase of the answer you have found. In this case, answer choice (C) is the close paraphrase we are looking for.

Sometimes, as here, the correct answer choice will be obvious once you understand the question and have found the relevant information in the passage. Other times, however, the correct answer choice will be fairly inconspicuous, and you may have to proceed by eliminating wrong answer choices. Of the four answer choices, three will have something wrong with their wording that makes them definitely wrong. For instance, (A) here is clearly wrong because the passage explicitly states that "the Taj Mahal *is much more than* an expression of love and loss." We will discuss eliminating strategies for the different question types in a bit. But you already know the basics of the Kaplan Method for Paragraph Comprehension. Let's quickly review the steps involved.

KAPLAN'S 4-STEP METHOD FOR PARAGRAPH COMPREHENSION

1. Read the question first.

You should always read the question before you look at the passage, because *how* you read and attack the stimulus will vary depending upon the task. If you know what you're supposed to do to the passage, you'll be able to focus your reading on the task ahead.

2. Read the passage.

Once you know your task, read as much of the passage as necessary to answer the question, paraphrasing as you go. Many, but not all, Paragraph Comprehension questions will require you to understand the gist or main idea of the passage. The key is to read actively and skim past unessential information.

3. Try to predict an answer.

Sometimes, depending upon the question, you'll know the answer without even looking at the answer choices. Other times, you'll just have a general idea of the answer may say. Either way, you'll have an easier time finding the correct answer if you have a sense of what you're looking for.

4. Attack the answer choices.

If you were able to prephrase an answer, skim the choices looking for a match. If you couldn't come up with a prephrase, read and evaluate the answer choices. You can always eliminate answer choices that stray beyond the scope of the passage. Other eliminating strategies will vary depending upon the question that was asked. Once you've settled on an answer, you may want to reread the question quickly to confirm that you've answered the question that was asked.

PARAGRAPH COMPREHENSION QUESTION TYPES

Main Idea Questions

Nearly anyone who has written a paper for class has been told about *thesis statements*. If you recall, these are the main idea or focus of a written piece. One major type of ASVAB

Paragraph Comprehension question asks you to glean from the passage what the main idea, or *thesis*, is. Unlike the details within the paragraph, the thesis is generally less specific. For instance, a thesis might be "Gold is one of the most valuable metals in the world." This would most likely be followed by descriptions of why this is so, perhaps because "gold is scarce", or because "gold is the world's monetary standard." But these statements, alone or together, would only explain *why* gold is valuable. *That* gold is valuable is the main idea.

This, in fact, is one way to distinguish between the main idea and the supporting details. One method for separating the main idea from the rest of the passage is to realize that the supporting details and the main idea answer two different types of questions, as you can see:

This:	*Answers the question:*
Main Idea	What does the author believe?
Supporting Details	Why does the author believe this?

So if you're unsure about whether a particular statement is the main idea, ask yourself: Does this sentence express what the author believes? Or does it explain why the author believes it? Now try out the following Main Idea question for size:

EXAMPLE 2

Desert plants have evolved very special adaptations for living in very dry conditions. Most have small thick leaves, which limits water loss by reducing the surface area relative to volume. Some desert plants shed their leaves during the driest months. Others, such as cacti, survive dry spells by subsisting on water stored in the fleshy stamen during the rainy season. Still other plants have ways of actively protecting their water supplies. The creosote bush, for instance, produces a powerful poison that discourages the growth of competing root systems.

2. The passage is mainly about
   (A) the varieties of life found in the desert
   (B) how desert plants have adapted to survive
   (C) competition between plants in the desert
   (D) the shortage of water in the desert

We hope you were easily able to spot the thesis sentence in the above passage. Here the first sentence supplies the main idea of the passage, and everything that follows supports this thesis, which is that desert plants have found different ways to adapt to the arid desert environment. Choice (B) is an excellent paraphrase of this main idea. Choice (C) is a somewhat tempting distracter, but it only refers to the example of the creosote bush and not the other deserts plants discussed in the passage.

Unfortunately, sometimes the thesis will not be so clearly laid out for the reader, and the shrewd ASVAB test-taker must be prepared to dig out the thesis from the paragraph even if it isn't directly stated. Being able to extract meaning from a paragraph is one big key to scoring well on the Paragraph Comprehension section. Take a look:

EXAMPLE 3

Alchemy is the name given to the attempt to change lead, copper, and other metals into silver or gold. Today alchemy is regarded as a pseudoscience. It is associated with astrology and the occult in the modern mind, and the alchemist is viewed in retrospect as a charlatan obsessed with dreams of impossible wealth. But for many centuries, alchemy was a respected art. In the search for the elusive secret to making gold, alchemists helped to develop many of the apparatuses and procedures used in laboratories today, and the results of their experiments laid the basic conceptual basis for the modern science of chemistry.

3.   The central point of the passage is that
     (A) alchemy is a pseudoscience
     (B) alchemists tried, but failed, to make gold from other metals
     (C) many alchemists dreamt of becoming rich
     (D) modern chemistry evolved out of alchemy

Here, the main idea has not yet been directly stated by the author, but you should be able to see the where the passage is leading. Sure, we tend to look upon alchemy today as a pseudoscience, *but* once it was a widely respected art, and its methods and conclusions led directly to the development of the modern science of chemistry. Thus, the main idea, although not yet explicitly stated, is best expressed by (D), modern chemistry evolved out of alchemy.

By the way, one of the tricks to zeroing in on the main idea of the passage is to pay attention to structural clues such as the *but* above. Words such as *but*, *though*, *however*, *although*, *nonetheless*, and *yet* indicate that passage is changing directions. When a passage contains one of these contrast clues, the main idea almost invariably occurs after the switch in direction.

Finally, on Main Idea questions it is often easy to eliminate a few answer choices immediately. Wrong answers to Main Idea questions usually do one of the following:

•   They're too specific, dealing with just one small detail of the passage.
•   They're too general, going beyond the scope of the passage.
•   They contradict the passage.
•   They're too extreme.

Purpose Questions

Another general question that's closely related to the Main Idea question, but, luckily for you, is usually easier to answer, is the question that simply asks the purpose of the passage. The passage itself may be instructions on how to pick a certain type of laundry detergent or an appeal to better understand the importance of beans. Whatever the case, one of the most useful (and simplest) skills you'll be tested on is simply to identify "What is this passage trying to do?"

Take a look at what this type of question looks like.

> EXAMPLE 4
>
> The carrot is a popular vegetable that has become a staple food the world over. For over 2,000 years, carrots have been cherished for their ability to improve your health and for their high levels of key vitamin A. Because they are hearty, carrots are generally available year-round, and because of this they are a popular addition to almost any meal.
>
> 4. The purpose of this passage is to
>   (A) explain how to cook carrots
>   (B) describe how carrots differ from other vegetables
>   (C) detail the ways in which carrots are misunderstood
>   (D) give the reader information on why carrots are
>   popular

This is a good example of a Purpose question. Choices (A), (B), and (C) all stray beyond the scope of the passage—the passage does not explain how to cook carrots; nor does it compare carrots to other vegetables; and it never details the ways in which carrots are "misunderstood." Only answer choice (D) is successful, as it explains why the writer chose to write the piece.

Tone Questions

One final type of question that deals with the passage as a whole will ask you to identify the tone or mood of the author's words. This is sometimes easier said than done. Words are tricky, and sometimes when an author is being satirical, the tone may be hard to recognize at first. But the overall emotion of an ASVAB passage should be clear if you read and pay particular attention to the sort of descriptive language used in the passage.

Here's an example of this type of question.

EXAMPLE 5

On cold days, it took longer for her to light the old wood-burning stove. It was her job to get up before her brothers and sisters and gather wood from the shed out back and bring it in and get the fire started. It was a hard life, but the only one she knew. Later, when she had a home and a family of her own, she would always remember lighting the old, rattling stove in her youth.

5. The tone of this passage is
   (A) thoughtful
   (B) angry
   (C) mournful
   (D) excited

Here's another case where paying attention to the entire passage is the best strategy. While there are moments of hardship mentioned in the passage, the overall sense is that the character remembers her youth with a certain fondness even if it was hard. So (B) is too harsh. Choice (C) isn't really appropriate, and (D) is flat out wrong. Only choice (A) is correct based on the passage. Note also that the correct answers to tone questions on the ASVAB tend to be among the least extreme emotions of the various choices listed.

AVOID EXTREME MOODS

You can almost always get rid of a few extreme answer choices on tone questions. ASVAB reading passages tend to be fairly flat. So you can almost always eliminate words that are overly emotional—words like *angry, ecstatic, unhappy,* etc.—as unlikely answers to tone questions.

Detail Questions

Detail questions ask you to find specific information explicitly stated within the passage. On these questions, you do not have to read for the author's main idea. In fact, it is crucial on this type of question not to over-analyze or read too much into the question. You should also be somewhat suspicious of answer choices that use the same language as the given passage, because the correct answer to a detail question will almost always be a paraphrase of what you find in the passage.

Check out the following example.

EXAMPLE 6

Newton High School's basketball team is among the best in the state. With ten wins and only two losses, Newton is off to its best start in seven years. The season is only half over, but already Newton has beaten its arch-rival Calloway High.

6. Newton High has won
    (A) two games
    (B) the state tournament
    (C) ten games
    (D) twelve games

In this case, the correct answer is (C), ten games. This information is directly stated in the second sentence. The other answers could be tricky to someone who hasn't read the question carefully, but focusing on the question first should have helped you eliminate them.

Perhaps that was too easy an example, so let's try a slightly tougher detail question.

STRATEGY TIP

The correct answer to a detail question will almost always be paraphrase of information found in the passage.

EXAMPLE 7

The dancer and choreographer Martha Graham is regarded as one of the outstanding innovators in the history of dance. In a career that lasted over fifty years, Graham created more than 170 works ranging from solos to large-scale pieces, and danced in most of them herself. Trained in a variety of different international styles of dance, she began in the early 1920s to break away from the rigid traditions of classical ballet. She wanted to create a new dance form that would reflect the transformed atmosphere of the postwar period.

7. Martha Graham introduced new dance techniques in order to
    (A) break away from the traditions of classical ballet
    (B) attract attention to her dance troupe
    (C) express the changed mood of her time
    (D) emphasize the rigidity of conventional dance movement

Perhaps it seems unfair to have to answer a question about Martha Graham and modern dance on the ASVAB. But if that's how you feel, you'd better learn to suck it up now, or else you'll never make it through boot camp! Seriously, this question is slightly harder than the previous one because it's easier here to misread the question.

This question is asking *why* Martha Graham introduced new dance techniques. The answer to this question is found in the last sentence: "She wanted to create a new dance form that would reflect the changed atmosphere of the postwar period." The only answer choice that paraphrases this idea is (C).

In this case, choice (A) was a tempting distracter, because its wording can be found almost verbatim in the passage. But choice (A) describes *what* Martha Graham did, not *why* she did it. And of course, you know to be suspicious of answer choices that use the exact same wording as the passage.

In fact, you can almost always eliminate wrong answer choices to detail questions for one of the following reasons:

- They don't answer the question that's been asked.
- They use similar wording to the passage, but distort what was said.
- They contradict the passage.
- They go outside the scope of the passage, stating things that weren't said.
- They use extreme wording.

Inference Questions

Sometimes the ASVAB will ask you questions about the passage that are not directly stated, but are instead implied by the passage. Scanning the passage details that will allow you to prephrase the answer doesn't work so well on these questions. On these questions, it is often best to read through the entire passage, and then attack the answer choices, eliminating those that do not follow from the passage.

Another thing that makes it hard to prephrase an answer to an inference question is the way these questions tend to be worded. Here are just a few of the ways an inference question might be worded. As you can see, the wording doesn't point you to a specific part of the passage:

Which of the following is implied by the passage?

The author apparently feels that

According to the passage, the reader may conclude that

It can be inferred from the passage that

If the statements in the passage are true, it must also be true that

The answers to inference questions may relate to the main idea of the passage, but they may also follow from secondary details found in the passage. Here's what you need to know about how to approach this question type. The correct answer to an inference question is the one answer that must be true given what's stated in the passage. Consequently, wrong answer choices on inference questions are those that:

- Contradict the passage
- May or may not be true based on the passage
- Are too strongly worded
- Go beyond the scope of the passage, suggesting things that aren't discussed

Let's take a look.

EXAMPLE 8

Leaders are not born strong. They grow that way based on events early on in their lives. Taking a look at the early life of any great leader shows moments where great strength was required. These moments of greatness brought out extraordinary grace and courage. It was only later that such qualities were on display for everyone to see.

8. Based on the information given, one can say that
    (A) leaders are larger in stature than normal people
    (B) nonleaders are incapable of grace and courage
    (C) great leaders emerge from great circumstances
    (D) leaders are required for great moments

The correct answer to this question is (C). In this case, the inference is related to the main point of the paragraph, which is to discuss how great leaders are made. (A) is simply not discussed in the passage. (B) also is not stated in the passage. (D) is a statement that cannot really be judged based on the information available. Only (C) must be true based on the information in the passage.

Let's take a look another inference question, one that requires you to connect the dots.

DON'T INFER TOO MUCH!

ASVAB writers don't expect you to infer too much when they ask an inference question. While you may have to combine information from two parts of the passage or make a deduction, you don't want to read between the lines too much. In fact, sometimes the ASVAB writers will make a detail question look like an inference question by asking what the passage implies when the answer is, in fact, explicitly stated.

EXAMPLE 9

Dan and Sonya are married and have exactly three children—Betty, George, and Tara—and exactly three grandchildren. George sometimes babysits for Betty's twin daughters, but Tara never babysits for George's child.

9. If these statements are true, which of the following must be true?
    (A) All of Dan's grandchildren are female.
    (B) Tara has no children.
    (C) Tara sometimes babysits for Betty's children.
    (D) Sonya has at least one grandson.

Here's an instance where you actually do have to put together pieces of information from different parts of the passage. You are told, by inference, that Betty, George, and Tara have three children altogether. You are also told the Betty has two children and that George has one child. Therefore, it must be true that Tara has no children, choice (B). Note that all of the wrong answer choices *could* be true, but none of them has to be true based on the information in the passage.

One final type of inference question requires you to take a look at the passage as a whole and then complete the line of thought. It will ask you to take the stated facts into account and to make a conclusion based on them.

Here's an example of what we mean.

EXAMPLE 10

In each of the last three years, a court in this country has awarded a settlement in excess of $300 million. This is a travesty of justice, and it unfairly burdens the court system. To alleviate the strain on the nation's court system, _____.

10. Which of the following best completes the above passage?
    (A) there should be fewer lawsuits
    (B) lawsuits should name more than one defendant
    (C) courts should cease awarding excessive settlements
    (D) settlements should be awarded based solely on need

The correct answer here is choice (C). While the merits of answer choice (A) or (B) are debatable, they are not issues discussed in this passage. And choice (D) likewise is not discussed in the passage, and it's too strongly worded as well. The conclusion you are asked to draw is what should be done to alleviate the burden on the court system. If the gist of the argument is that awards are too big, it would seem logical that if courts stopped being excessive in awarding settlements, it would help alleviate the strain on the courts.

Correct Sequence Questions

There may be one or two questions on the ASVAB that ask you to identify the next step in a series of how-to steps based on a description given in the passage. For instance, the passage may explain the steps involved in changing a tire or building a birdhouse. Unless you have developed a deep, abiding fear of reading step-by-step instructions, based on bad experiences with do-it-yourself guides in the past, you should have little problem with these questions. Just take sufficient care to locate the correct step in the passage to answer the question.

Here's an example of what this type of question looks like.

EXAMPLE 11

To throw a good curveball, it's first necessary to "choke" the ball by wedging the ball down between your thumb and forefinger. Next, cock your wrist to the left. When you release the ball, the ball should snap down and to the right. The resulting pitch should drop and curve to the left.

11. After "choking" the ball, you should
 (A) cock your wrist to the left
 (B) release the ball to the left
 (C) wedge the ball between your finger and thumb
 (D) spin the ball counterclockwise

According to the passage, to throw a curve ball you must first "choke" the ball by wedging it between your thumb and forefinger. Next, you cock your wrist to the left. Once you release the ball, the spin should occur. The question merely asks you to identify the step immediately after "choking" the ball. Of the choices given, only (A) satisfies as an answer.

Vocabulary-in-Context Questions

One final type of question found of the Paragraph Comprehension section will ask you for the meaning of a word used in the paragraph. While a good vocabulary can't hurt you on this question type, these questions really test your ability to *read for context clues*. If you try to answer the question based solely on your vocabulary knowledge without reading how the word is being used in the paragraph, there's a good chance you'll get the question wrong, because several answer choices will contain possible definitions of the word in question. The good news is that you don't have to have a dictionary-depth familiarity with the word in question—you just have to be able to glean its meaning from the context in which it appears. The correct answer will be a word that can replace the word in question without altering the meaning of the sentence.

Here's how we suggest you handle this question type:

1. Read the sentence containing the word, looking for context clues.
2. Predict a word that could replace the vocabulary word.
3. Check the answer choices for a word that matches.
4. Plug your selection into the sentence to make sure it makes sense.

Try this method out on the following Vocabulary-in-Context question.

EXAMPLE 12

Sapphira and the Slave Girl was the last novel of Willa Cather's illustrious literary career. Begun in 1937 and finally completed in 1941, it is regarded by critics as one of her most personal works. Although the story takes place in 1856, well before Cather's own birth, she drew heavily on vivid childhood memories as well as tales handed down by older relatives to describe life in rural northern Virginia in the middle of the nineteenth century. She even went on an extended journey to the area to give the story a further ring of authenticity.

12. In this context, the word *extended* means
   (A) enlarged
   (B) postponed
   (C) stretched
   (D) prolonged

If you tried out our method for handling this question type, you might have predicted that *extended* in this context means "extensive" or "lengthy." By predicting a possible answer, you should have been able to zero in quickly on the closest match, which is (D), prolonged. And if you read that choice back into the sentence, it makes sense: "She even went on an *prolonged* journey to the area to give the story a further ring of authenticity."

Otherwise, you could have eliminated wrong-sounding answer choices. (A), enlarged, might seem related to a long trip, but it doesn't sound quite right in context. (B), postponed, is easy to eliminate; Cather's trip was not put off until a future time. (C), stretched, is a definition of *extended*, but not one that works here. Only choice (D) makes sense in this context.

Now that we've shown you with the ins and outs of Paragraph Comprehension, you should try out all the strategies we've discussed in this chapter on the practice set that follows. Make sure to give yourself just 13 minutes to try to answer all 15 questions!

PARAGRAPH COMPREHENSION PRACTICE SET

The presidential election in November 2000 showed once again how important it is for all Americans to take advantage of their right to vote. The election was so close that it took weeks to finalize the tally and the controversy surrounding chads, voting machines and the court system only served to reinforce the sentiment that each vote counts.

1. The main idea of the passage is that

    (A) voting machines are not adequate
    (B) the Supreme Court should decide who will be the president
    (C) voting is a right that can be taken away
    (D) every voter should exercise his or her right and vote

Four years ago, the governor came into office seeking to change the way politics were run in this state. Now, it appears he has been the victim of his own ambitious political philosophy. Trying to do too much has given him a reputation as being pushy, and the backlash in the state has let him accomplish little. He may very well lose in his reelection bid.

2. The governor's approach to politics was

    (A) business as usual
    (B) overly idealistic
    (C) careless and sloppy
    (D) undeterred by critics

Since its first official documentation by Sir George Everest in 1865, Mount Everest in Nepal has been the "Holy Grail" of mountaineers. Sir Edmund Hillary was the first man to successfully complete the ascent to the peak in May 1953. His feat won him international acclaim, not to mention knighthood. But much less celebrated is the first successful ascent of Everest by a woman, which did not take place until May 16, 1975. Junko Tabei of Japan was the first woman to reach the summit of the world's most famous single peak. The first American woman to scale its heights successfully was Stacy Allison of Portland in 1988.

3. Mount Everest was first conquered by

    (A) Sir George Everest
    (B) Junko Tabei
    (C) Sir Edmund Hillary
    (D) Stacy Allison

It is without question a travesty that our children are no longer given healthy, nutritious food options for lunch in our public schools. Hamburgers, pizza, and chocolate are not only giving our kids a bigger waistline, but these junk foods are also helping teach them poor eating habits. It is imperative that we change the mindset that any food is good food and start offering students better meals at the same prices. Otherwise, a new generation of obese Americans is a given.

4. According to the passage, over the past few years, school lunches have gotten

    (A) more expensive
    (B) more exotic
    (C) healthier
    (D) less nutritious

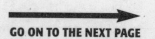

GO ON TO THE NEXT PAGE

Many times families choose to replace old furniture when just a minor amount of maintenance is all that is needed. To fix a wooden chair that is wobbly, follow these easy steps. First, check the joints of the chair to see if the chair is structurally sound. There should be small dowel rods and a corner block to keep the chair together. Next, use a ripping chisel to remove the corner block. Once the block is free from the chair, you should be able to glue the joints back together. Finally, once the glue looks dry, place the corner block back on the chair and gently mallet the block onto the dowels. In no time, you will have saved not only the chair, but also your hard-earned money!

5. After removing the corner block, you should

   (A) mallet the dowels into place
   (B) check the joints for damage
   (C) glue the joints tightly
   (D) replace the corner block

James felt the pulse of the crowd. There was a low murmur just under the house music. Backstage, his bandmates were tuning or drumming lightly on tabletops. In a few moments, the whole country would watch the band play. What a change from those dingy bars and clubs a few years ago. Maybe all the hard work had finally paid off. Looking down at his callused hands, he wondered if maybe this would be the break they had been working so hard for.

6. The tone of this passage is one of

   (A) sadness
   (B) anticipation
   (C) anger
   (D) ambivalence

Packaging on many popular foods is deceiving to consumers. Too often, the print is small and hard to read. And if you can read it, it's often confusing or intentionally vague. This is especially true on the nutrition label. The government really ought to do something about the nutrition labels on food because the existing laws just don't go far enough.

7. The author would probably support which of the following?

   (A) magazine advertisements for cigarettes
   (B) warning labels on compact discs
   (C) fine print on a contract
   (D) food ads in the Sunday paper

In an age where we have pills for depression, dysfunction, and aggression, not to mention headaches, it is important that we not forget that many drugs can have serious side effects. These may range from internal bleeding, vomiting, or soreness in the limbs to, in more extreme cases, loss of consciousness or even coma. If you experience unwanted side effects, it is important to get to a hospital immediately and seek treatment. Drinking alcohol or smoking cigarettes may also contribute to violent side effects.

8. One of the possible side effects of drugs is

   (A) drinking alcohol
   (B) dysfunction
   (C) internal bleeding
   (D) none of the above

GO ON TO THE NEXT PAGE

A character created at the height of atomic postwar paranoia, the Incredible Hulk is a fascinating look at the dual nature of human beings. On the one hand, he is a mild-mannered, bespectacled scientist. On the other, he is a rampaging beast whose strength is surpassed only by his potential for rage. More than a statement about nuclear dangers, the Hulk is a reflection of the two sides in each of us—the calm, logical human and the raging animal.

9. According to the author, the comic book character of the Hulk is

    (A) a reflection of humanity
    (B) really an animal
    (C) mild mannered
    (D) a protest about atomic power

Once considered the best high school player in the country, the onetime prodigy now spends his days working as a bricklayer for a local construction company. Asked if he is bitter about the way his life turned out, he replies "Not at all." In fact, he says, his only regret is that he didn't study hard enough and go to college. He still gets recognized on occasion, but an extra 80 pounds and bad knees keep him from reliving his former glory on the court.

10. The word *prodigy* in the passage most nearly means

    (A) depressed loser
    (B) shy scientist
    (C) gifted youngster
    (D) bitter malcontent

For most students of biology, Charles Darwin is considered the father of evolution. But few realize that he is but one of many theorists who noted that genetics and animals showed progression over time. Henri Bergson, for instance, formulated a theory that today is known more commonly as *theistic evolution*, or evolution from God. But Darwin's ability to articulate his theories in writing and to account for many diverse examples of evolutionary biology means that other theories are often seen as little more than offshoots of the original idea of Darwinian evolution.

11. According to the passage, Darwin's theory persists because

    (A) Bergson was right
    (B) Darwin accounted for many variations
    (C) genetics is an inexact science
    (D) evolution is not accepted by the mainstream

GO ON TO THE NEXT PAGE

Questions 12 and 13 refer to the following passage.

Diamond is the hardest known material and has long been used in various industrial shaping processes, such as cutting, grinding, and polishing. Diamond, sapphire, ruby (sapphire with chromium "impurities"), and garnet are increasingly important in various applications. For example, diamond is used in sensors, diaphragms for audio speakers, and coatings for optical materials. Sapphire is used in gallium nitride-based LEDs, ruby is used in check valves, and synthetic garnet is used in lasers intended in applications in medical products.

12. An appropriate title for this passage would be

    (A) The Timeless Allure of Precious Stones
    (B) Nontraditional Uses of Diamonds
    (C) Industrial Uses for Precious Stones
    (D) Gem Hardness and Utility

13. It can be inferred from this passage that

    (A) diamonds are more precious than sapphires
    (B) rubies come from the same type of stone as do sapphires
    (C) garnets are used in various industrial shaping processes
    (D) precious stones are more costly than ever

Questions 14 and 15 refer to the following passage.

Cats were first domesticated 4,000 years ago by the ancient Egyptians, who revered them as household gods. By the third century B.C., the domestic cat was widely distributed across Europe thanks to seafaring Greek merchants and colonizers who associated cats with the goddess Artemis and used them to protect their grain supplies.

After millions of the creatures were slaughtered alongside the hundreds of thousands of pagans, heretics, and Jews with whom they were associated during the Middle Ages, cats may have gotten their revenge. The absence of cats in Europe probably contributed to the spread and the severity of the bubonic plague that devastated the continent in the 14th century.

14. An appropriate title for this passage would be

    (A) Ancient Egyptian Deities
    (B) From Gods to Pariahs: The Early History of the Domestic Cat
    (C) Cats and the Bubonic Plague
    (D) Cats and Dogs from Antiquity through the Middle Ages

15. It can be inferred from this passage that

    (A) after cats were slaughtered in the Middle Ages, the rodent population in Europe rose
    (B) Greek merchants sold domestic cats for large sums of money
    (C) the bubonic plague could be spread through cats
    (D) cats were especially popular house pets among pagans, heretics, and Jews

ANSWER KEY

1. D	6. B	11. B
2. B	7. B	12. C
3. C	8. C	13. B
4. D	9. A	14. B
5. C	10. C	15. A

ANSWERS AND EXPLANATIONS FOR PARAGRAPH COMPREHENSION PRACTICE SET

1. D

From the first sentence to the very last, the reader should be able to glean that the author is vehemently in favor of the idea that "each vote counts." Choice (D) most clearly reflects this sentiment. You can also eliminate wrong answer choices (B) and (C) because they are never mentioned in the passage. And "voting machines," (A), are mentioned in the passage, but only to support the conclusion that every vote counts.

2. B

From the information given, you should have seen that the governor was very determined to get things done his way. So his approach could hardly be described as business as usual, choice (A). Nowhere in the passage is his approach described as careless and sloppy, choice (C). And given that the backlash has affected his capacity to succeed, his approach was not undeterred by critics, choice (D). Only (B) is addressed in the paragraph. Seeking to change the way politics are run indicates an idealistic approach to politics.

3. C

This detail question asks you for the first person to conquer Mount Everest. Researching the passage, you must be careful not to assume that the mountain is named for its conqueror. While Sir George Everest, (A), first documented and recorded the height of Everest in 1865, it was Sir Edmund Hillary who completed the first ascent to the peak in 1953. The question does not ask for the first woman, or the first American woman, to reach the summit, so (B), Junko Tabei, and (D), Stacy Allison, are out. The correct answer is (C).

4. D

The author feels strongly that meals in school cafeterias have become more and more similar to the junk food available at fast food joints. Choice (A) is not applicable, regardless of its validity, because it is not the central point of the passage. Choice (B) is nowhere indicated in the passage, and choice (C) is the opposite of what we are asked in the question. Of the answer choices given, only choice (D), less nutritious, correctly answers the question.

5. C

This is a "correct sequence" question, so your first task is to locate the step that discusses removing the corner block. Removing the corner block is finally mentioned in the fifth sentence. After using a ripping chisel to remove the block from the chair, the worker is free to glue the joints back together to tighten them, choice (C).

6. B

To correctly gauge the tone of a passage, you should pay attention not only to the details, but also to the language and description. In this passage, James is clearly waiting to go onstage. Words like *pulse*, *murmur* and even *maybe* invite the reader to feel excitement and nervousness as James does. Of the answer choices given, (D) is clearly wrong, as James definitely cares about what is going to happen. He seems wistful, but never sad, (A), or angry, (C). The only answer that successfully captures James's mood is choice (B), anticipation.

7. B

Judging from the irate tone of the author and the subject matter at hand, one can safely assume that the author is interested in public safety. Clearly small print is not going to be popular with this author, so choice (C) is out. Choice (D) doesn't make sense and choice (A) is not something thought of as good for public safety. Only choice (B), warning labels on compact discs, is likely to be supported by the author given his passion for consumer labels.

8. C

According to the details of the passage, one possible side effect from prescription drug usage is internal bleeding. Others may include vomiting, soreness of the limbs, loss of consciousness or even coma. Drinking alcohol. (A), can exacerbate side effects, but it is not a side effect itself, and dysfunction, (B), is discussed as one of the conditions treated by drugs, not as a side effect of drug use.

9. A

From the details of the passage, it is clear that the author sees the character of Hulk as a symbol. Of the answer choices, only (A) and (D) seem appropriate to readers familiar with Incredible Hulk comic books. And while choice (D) may or may not be true, in this passage, the author chooses to focus on the Hulk's reflection of the dual nature of humans.

10. C

According to the passage, the one-time star athlete is now a local bricklayer. There is nothing in the passage to indicate that the person in question was ever a depressed loner (A), shy scientist (B), or bitter malcontent (D), but it only makes sense that he was once a gifted youngster (C). The term *prodigy* refers to a person with natural ability, often at a young age.

11. B

The author, while maintaining that there were other scientists with competing ideas, notes towards the end that Darwin's eloquence and his ability "to account for many diverse examples" helped him establish his theories as the benchmark by which others stacked up. Thus, choice (B) is correct. None of the other choices are supported by the passage.

12. C

The passage here discusses industrial uses for precious stones, so the correct answer choice (C) should pretty much jump out at you. This passage is not about the "timeless allure" of these stones (A), and gem "hardness" is only mentioned in reference to diamonds, so (D) is out. (B) is wrong because the passage is not just about diamonds, not to mention that the industrial uses for diamonds that are mentioned are fairly traditional.

13. **B**

The passage notes parenthetically that a ruby is a sapphire with chromium "impurities," so one can logically infer that both gems come from the same kind of stone, choice (B). All the other answer choices are never mentioned anywhere in the passage.

14. **B**

The correct answer choice to this main idea question is (B). The passage briefly touches on the history of domestic cats, from the time of ancient Egypt when they were viewed as household gods, through to the Middle Ages when they were slaughtered by superstitious Christians along with pagans, heretics, and Jews. Thus the title, "From Gods to Pariahs (meaning outcasts): The Early History of the Domestic Cat." If the correct answer does not jump out at you, you can always eliminate wrong answer choices. (A) is wrong because the passage is clearly about domestic cats, not ancient Egyptian deities. Choice (C) is too narrow, given that the passage begins in ancient Egypt. And choice (D) is out because dogs are never mentioned in the passage.

15. **A**

This inference question requires a little more inferring than most. You are told that after cats were slaughtered in the Middle Age and that their absence probably contributed to the spread and the severity of the bubonic plague that devastated the continent. Why would this be the case? The logical inference is that the rodent population must have increased, and rodents helped to spread the bubonic plague. If this inference did not come to you, you could also have eliminated wrong answer choices. There's nothing in the passage to indicate that Greek merchants sold domestic cats "for large sums of money," (B). And it doesn't follow that the bubonic plague could be spread through cats, given that their absence, not their presence, precipitated the plague. Finally, just because cats were slaughtered along with pagans, heretics, and Jews, that does not necessarily mean that they were "especially popular house pets" with these groups, as (D) states.

CHAPTER FOUR

Math on the ASVAB

INTRODUCING ASVAB MATH

For some reason, not many people are neutral on the subject of mathematics. As a general rule, either you love or hate it. Either you derive a secret thrill out of doing a good math problem, or your third-grade math teacher traumatized you to the point where the very sight of numbers and math symbols induces nausea and blurred vision. Perhaps we exaggerate a bit, but you get the idea. On whichever side of the Great Math Divide you reside, we have some important news for you regarding math on the ASVAB.

First a word to the math crackerjacks out there. We probably shouldn't worry about you. You'll do okay on the ASVAB math sections with or without our help. But you should be acing the ASVAB math sections, and yet somehow a lot of good math students don't. Why not? Perhaps it's because they think that the same skills that reward success on other math tests necessarily translate to success on the ASVAB. They're wrong.

On other math tests, solving a problem the way you've been taught to in class is rewarded. On the ASVAB, solving problems the correct way can slow you down and/or get you into trouble. On other math tests, if you do the work but accidentally miss a step you'll still get partial credit. On the ASVAB you will not.

ASVAB math is not very tough, but it can be tricky. Turning a good ASVAB math score into a great ASVAB math score requires learning to avoid "careless" errors—and realizing that these errors are often the result of traps built into the questions. What we want to show you is a different approach to test taking, one that takes advantage of, instead of falling prey to, the nature of the ASVAB.

And now a word to the math haters out there. You should be viewing the math sections of the ASVAB as an opportunity. Here's where you can have your revenge on that math teacher who made your life miserable. After all, success is the best revenge. We'll show you how to avoid doing more math than is necessary on the ASVAB. By taking advantage of the standardized test format of the ASVAB, you too can get a very good ASVAB math score. But to do that first you need to understand the nature of the test.

KNOW WHAT TO EXPECT

There's a lot of math out there. Someday you may need to immerse yourself in the intricacies of number theory or multivariable calculus. However, for the purposes of the ASVAB, you only need to know a small subset of all of the math out there. The most commonly tested math concepts fall within the areas of arithmetic, algebra, and geometry. You may also possibly see some simple probability and statistics questions.

The two math sections on the ASVAB are called "Arithmetic Reasoning" and "Mathematical Knowledge." Because together they form the quantitative half of the Armed Forces Qualifying Test, you'll want to do well on these sections no matter what your ultimate vocational aim in the military is. So let's take a quick look at these sections now, how they differ and how they are similar.

The **Arithmetic Reasoning** section is a 36-minute, 30-question test of your ability to handle arithmetic word problems. It covers the types of arithmetic problems encountered in everyday life. This test is designed to measure your ability to apply reasoning to solve common problems involving math. Typical Arithmetic Reasoning questions include questions that involve tallying numbers, as well as questions about rates, percents, ratios, proportions, averages, unit conversions, and the like.

The **Mathematics Knowledge** section is a 24-minute, 25-question test of your understanding of a wide range of concepts in arithmetic, algebra, and geometry. This test is designed to measure general mathematical knowledge. You may still see the occasional word problem on the Mathematical Knowledge section of the ASVAB, but in general the questions, while drawn from a wider base of mathematical concepts, are more straightforward than the word problems found on the Arithmetic Reasoning section. For this reason, you are given slightly less time per question on this section than on the Arithmetic Reasoning section.

HOW TO APPROACH ASVAB MATH

Now that you know how the two sections differ, let's discuss what makes them similar. For the purposes of doing well on the ASVAB, the most important similarity between the two sections is that all of the questions in both sections are multiple choice, with four answer choices. As you will soon see, there are many ways to take advantage of this fact when you encounter a problem on either section that gives you trouble.

Look at it this way. You are given roughly one minute per math question (about 72 seconds per question on the Arithmetic Reasoning section and 58 seconds per question on the

Mathematical Knowledge section, but a minute is close enough) on the ASVAB. But given the tricky nature of some of the questions in the Arithmetic Reasoning and Mathematical Knowledge sections, those minutes can fly by quickly. To do your best on these sections, you need to develop an approach that's different from the way you handle most math tests.

How's that, you say? You've probably been exposed to the great majority of the math concepts tested on the ASVAB in high school math tests. This begs the question as to why you would need to approach ASVAB math any differently than you would any other math.

ASVAB MATH IS NOT A HIGH SCHOOL MATH TEST

No one is going to check your work. Choose the *fastest* method to solve the problem even if your math teacher would not approve.

The answer to this question is that you don't necessarily have to do the math *differently*; it's just that you have to do it very deliberately. Because you'll be under a lot of time pressure when you take the test, you'll want to use your time well. And sometimes the quickest route to answering the problem is not the way you were taught to do to problem back in math class. Ultimately, the best way to take control of your testing experience is to approach every ASVAB math problem the same way. This doesn't mean that you will solve every problem the same way. Rather, it means you will use the same process to decide how to solve—and whether to solve—each problem. And to accomplish this we have developed the Kaplan Three-Step Method for ASVAB Math.

KAPLAN'S 3-STEP METHOD FOR ASVAB MATH

Step 1: Read Through the Question.

Okay, this may seem a little too obvious. Of course, you're going to read through the question. How else can you solve the problem? In reality, this is not quite as obvious as it seems. The point here is that you need to read the entire question carefully *before* you start solving the problem. If you don't read the question carefully, it's incredibly easy to make careless mistakes. Consider the following problem:

EXAMPLE 1

1. At Blinky Burgers restaurant, two hamburgers and five orders of french fries cost the same as four hamburgers and two orders of french fries. If the restaurant charges $1.50 for a single order of french fries, how much does it charge for two hamburgers?

   (A) $2.25
   (B) $3.00
   (C) $4.50
   (D) $6.00

It's crucial that you pay close attention to precisely what the question is asking. This question contains a classic trap that's very easy to fall into if you don't read the question carefully. Can you spot the trap?

Notice that you're being asked to find the cost of two hamburgers, not one. Many students will get this question wrong by finding the price for one hamburger, and then forgetting to double it. It's a careless mistake to make, but it's easy to be careless when you're working quickly. That's why you always have to make sure you know what's being asked.

Step 2: Decide Whether to Do It Now

DON'T WORRY ABOUT ONES THAT GOT AWAY

Sure it feels good to try to answer every question on a given ASVAB math section. But if you end up not getting back to a question or two, don't feel bad. By spending more time on the questions you *can* answer, you're likely to get a great score even if you have to guess blindly at a few questions.

Another reason to read carefully before answering is that you probably shouldn't solve every problem on your first pass. A big part of taking control of your ASVAB test experience is deciding which problems to answer and which to save for later.

Before you try to solve the problem, decide whether you want to do it now. If you have no idea how to solve the problem, or if you think the problem will take a long time to solve, you should skip it for now and circle the question in your test booklet. Spend your time on the problems you can solve quickly, and then return to ones that give you trouble after you've finished the rest of the section.

Step 3: Look For the Fastest Way to Answer the Question

Once you've understood what the question asks and have decided to tackle it now, it's time to look for shortcuts. Sometimes the "obvious" way to solve the problem is the long way. For instance, in the previous example, the obvious way for many students would be to turn this word problem into two algebraic equations: $2H + 5F = 4H + 2F$, and $F = 1.50$. From there you could substitute 1.50 for F in the first equation, solve for H, and then multiply your answer by 2.

But if you think carefully, there's often an easier approach. Here, for instance, if two hamburgers and five orders of fries cost the same as four hamburgers and two orders of fries, take away all the items that are the same in the two orders and you're left with three orders of fries costing the same as two hamburgers. Since one order of fries costs $1.50, three orders cost $4.50, so $4.50 must also be the cost of two hamburgers. The correct answer is (C), and you didn't even have to set up any algebraic equations.

TEXTBOOK APPROACHES VERSUS BACKDOOR APPROACHES

Sometimes the textbook approach will be the best way to the answer on the ASVAB. Other times, however, as we've just seen, applying common sense and backdoor strategies will get you to the correct answer more quickly and easily. The key is to be open to creative approaches to problem solving. Often this involves taking advantage of the standardized test format of the ASVAB.

The 30 questions that make up the Arithmetic Reasoning section of the ASVAB are all word problems with four numbers, percents, or fractions in the answer choices. The 25 questions that make the Mathematical Knowledge section also have four answer choices, but because this section also tests algebra, sometimes the answer choices will contain variables. In either case, it's important to note that the answer is right in front of you—you just have to find it. Two methods in particular are extremely useful when you don't see—or would rather not use—the textbook approach to solving the question. We call these strategies *backsolving* and *picking numbers*. These strategies aren't always quicker than more traditional methods, but they're a great way to make confusing problems more concrete. And if you know how to apply these strategies, you're guaranteed to nail the correct answer every time you use them. Let's examine these strategies now.

Backsolving

Since almost all the Arithmetic Reasoning questions contain numbers in the answer choices, often you can use this to your advantage by "backsolving." What this means is that sometimes it's easiest to work backwards from the answer choices.

Here's how it works. When the answer choices are numbers, you can expect them to be arranged from small to large (or occasionally from large to small). The test maker is not very creative with the order of the answer choices. What you want to do is start with either choice (B) or (C). Choose whichever number is easier to work with. If that number works when you plug it into the problem, you're done. That's the answer, so move on. If it doesn't work, you can usually figure out whether to try a larger or smaller answer choice next. By backsolving strategically this way, you usually don't have to try out more than two answer choices before you zero in on the correct answer. If this seems confusing, check out the following problem and explanation.

EXAMPLE 2

2. In a certain school, the ratio of boys to girls is 3 to 7. If there are 84 more girls than boys, how many boys are there?

   (A) 48
   (B) 63
   (C) 72
   (D) 147

The correct answer should yield a ratio of boys to girls of 3 to 7, so let's try out choice (B).

If there are 63 boys, there are $63 + 84 = 147$ girls, so the ratio of boys to girls is $\dfrac{63}{147} = \dfrac{9}{21} = \dfrac{3}{7}$, which is just what we want. That means we're done.

Okay, so that was a bit easy. So the answer isn't always the first choice you pick. But usually, when you start with (B) or (C) and that answer doesn't work, you'll know which direction to go. Either (B) or (C) will be too big or too small, leaving you with only one or two answers that could possibly be correct.

Let's try another one, this time a geometry question from the Mathematical Reasoning section.

EXAMPLE 3

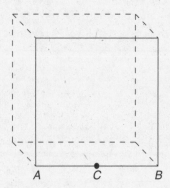

3. If the surface area of the cube above is 96, and *C* is the midpoint of *AB*, what is the length of *AC* ?

  (A) 2

  (B) 2.5

  (C) 3

  (D) 4

For some reason, when the problem involves geometry, many students completely forget that there are backdoor approaches to the answer. On a confusing geometry problem with numbers in the answer choices like this one, backsolving is definitely the way to go.

Again we'll start with B, $AC = 2.5$. If $AC = 2.5$, the edge length of the cube is 5, so each face of the cube is $5^2 = 25$ square inches. There are 6 faces to a cube, so the entire surface area would be $25 \times 6 = 150$ square inches.

This is too large so (C) and (D) are also out, and the answer is (A). If you were running short on time, you would just pick (A) and move on.

But let's just prove the answer is (A) to feel good about ourselves. If $AC = 2$, the edge length of the cube is 4, so each face of the cube is $4^2 = 16$ square inches. There are 6 faces to a cube, so the entire surface area would be $16 \times 6 = 96$ square inches.

So the answer is indeed (A).

Let's quickly recap the steps involved in backsolving:

1. Start with choice B or C.
2. Eliminate choices you know are too big or too small.
3. Keep going until you find the choice that works.

Now let's look at another backdoor strategy that comes in handy on a lot of Mathematical Knowledge questions, and also occasionally on Arithmetic Reasoning questions that involve fractions or percents.

Picking Numbers

Sometimes a math problem can seem more difficult than it actually is because it's general or abstract, particularly on the Mathematical Knowledge section. You can make a question like this more concrete—and easier—by substituting numbers for the variables. Here's what we mean by picking numbers to make an abstract problem concrete.

> EXAMPLE 4

4. When n is divided by 14 the remainder is 10. What is the remainder when n is divided by 7?

    (A) 2
    (B) 3
    (C) 4
    (D) 5

For starters, you might note that just because the question contains numbers in the answer choices, that doesn't mean that you can always backsolve. Here, backsolving doesn't make any sense. The problem is confusing because the question contains an annoying unknown value, n, rather than an actual number. So to make this abstract question concrete, you should pick a number for n that leaves a remainder of 10 when divided by 14. The easiest strategy is to pick $n = 24$ (because $14 + 10 = 24$). Now try your number out. $24 \div 7 = 3$ remainder 3. Thus, the answer is (B).

SPEED TIP

When picking a number on a remainder problem, add the remainder to the number you're dividing by.

Picking numbers works great on word problems that contain variables. This is great news, since these problems can be especially confusing on the ASVAB. Give the following example a try:

EXAMPLE 5

5. Four years from now, Ray will be twice as old as his sister will be then. If Ray is now R years old, how old is his sister?

    (A) $\dfrac{R-4}{2}$

    (B) $R - 4$

    (C) $\dfrac{R+4}{2}$

    (D) $R - 2$

Now maybe you just love to translate word problems into algebra equations. Fine then, do it your way. But keep in mind, picking numbers can be much, much easier and quicker on questions like this one. Here's how you do it. Begin by picking a number for R, Ray's age now. Make it a nice and simple round number such as $R = 10$. Now substitute 10 for R in the question and the answer choices, and you're left with the following, much simpler problem:

EXAMPLE 5

5. Four years from now, Ray will be twice as old as his sister will be then. If Ray is now 10 years old, how many years old is his sister?

    (A) $\dfrac{10-4}{2}$, or 3

    (B) $10 - 4$, or 6

    (C) $\dfrac{10+4}{2}$, or 7

    (D) $10 - 2$, or 8

Now let's see. Ray is now 10 years old, so in four years he'll be 14, which means his sister will be seven years old then. Since she'll be seven in four years, that means she must be three years old now. The correct answer must be (A).

As we've just seen, picking numbers on problems containing variables involves the following the steps.

1. Pick nice, easy numbers for the variables in your question.

2. Answer the question using the numbers you've picked. This answer is your target number.

3. Now substitute the numbers you picked for the variables in the answer choices. See which answer gives you your target number.

To be safe, you should always try out all the answer choices. If more than one answer choice gives you your target number, pick different numbers to eliminate the remaining wrong answers. Don't worry. This happens very rarely and it doesn't take much time to pick numbers twice.

Not only does picking numbers make the problems such as the above one easier to understand, but when you solve a problem by picking numbers, you can be sure you got the right answer. This is because you've already proven that your answer works with real numbers; thus there's no need to double-check your work.

The problem we just looked at contained variables in the answer choices, but there are two other great places to pick numbers, and these questions can occur in either ASVAB math section. These are word problems that contain unknown values and have percents or fractions in the answer choices. The key to solving these problems quickly lies in knowing how to pick good numbers. Let's take a look.

PICKING GOOD NUMBERS

Don't just pull a number out of a hat. Certain numbers work best on certain types of problems.

- *On percent problems, 100 is an easy number to work with.*

- *On fraction problems, pick the largest denominator in the answer choices.*

EXAMPLE 6

6. The value of a certain stock rose by 30 percent from March to April, and then decreased by 20 percent from April to May. The stock's value in May was what percent of its value in March?

(A) 90%

(B) 100%

(C) 104%

(D) 110%

Notice that even though the question involves the value of a certain stock, that value is never given. If we pick a number for the value of the stock, we can see much more easily what is going on. On percent problems you're almost always best off picking 100 for the unknown value. Let's say the stock originally cost $100. If it rose by 30 percent from March to April, its value in April would have been $130. If the value then decreased by 20 percent in May, 20 percent of $130 is $26, so the value drops to $104 in May. Since $104 is 104 percent of $100, the correct answer is (C).

That was easy. Now let's try a fraction word problem.

EXAMPLE 7

7. Keiko spent $\frac{1}{4}$ of her monthly salary on a television, and spent half of what was left to pay her rent and utility bills. If she spent $\frac{2}{3}$ of her remaining salary on other expenses, and put what was left into her savings account, what fraction of her monthly salary went into her savings account?

(A) $\frac{1}{6}$

(B) $\frac{1}{8}$

(C) $\frac{1}{12}$

(D) $\frac{1}{24}$

Our rule for picking numbers on fraction problems is to pick the largest number from among the denominators in the answer choices, so let's say that Keiko starts with $24. She spends $\frac{1}{4}$ of that, or 6 dollars, on a television. That leaves her with $18. She spends half of that on rent and utilities, so she's left with 9 dollars. She spends $\frac{2}{3}$ of that on other expenses, leaving her with 3 dollars. She puts that into her savings account, so she puts $\frac{3}{24} = \frac{1}{8}$ of her monthly salary into her savings account. So the correct answer must be (B).

STREAMLINE

Look for ways to avoid doing unnecessary work. Resist the temptation to check work that must be correct.

The rest of the math section of this book will deal with math content review. Some of this will be familiar, some may be less familiar. Take a look at all of it. But spend more time with the subjects that are less familiar. Even if you feel comfortable with a particular subject, make sure to do the practice sets. There's no harm in practicing extra problems.

CHAPTER FIVE

Arithmetic Reasoning

INTRODUCTION

As you should know by now, on the Arithmetic Reasoning Section of the ASVAB you are given 36 minutes to complete 30 arithmetic word problems. The most fearful aspect of this description for most students is the last part, that bit about "word problems." It's bad enough having to do arithmetic without the aid of a calculator. But having to weed through a tiny and generally boring story and then translate the English into math to come up with a solution is not most people's idea of a good time.

But when you get down to it, the math you do every day takes place in a narrative context. You go to a store and buy three bananas that cost 25 cents each and hand the clerk one dollar. Because there is a 4 percent sales tax on food items, you expect to get back (after some quick calculation) 22 cents in change.

Or perhaps you just trust the clerk when he tells you what you owe and accept whatever change he gives you. You probably won't get cheated all that often going through life that way, but it doesn't make for a good math test. Arithmetic Reasoning questions may be just a little tougher than the above story, but they invariably involve prosaic real-life stories like the one above dealing, for the most part, with addition, subtraction, division, and multiplication, as well as applied arithmetic concepts like rates, averages, percents, ratios, probability, and so on.

Because doing well on the Arithmetic Reasoning section of the ASVAB involves both understanding the arithmetic concepts involved and being able to translate English into math, this chapter begins with a review of all the arithmetic concepts that have been known to appear on the ASVAB, and then goes on to examine the specifics of handling word problems. You should know up front that many of the arithmetic concepts reviewed in this chapter are at least as likely to appear on the Mathematics Knowledge section of the ASVAB as on the Arithmetic Reasoning section. That's all the more reason to study them.

There are 25 exercise questions for you to try your hand at as you go through all the topics. Finally, this chapter concludes with a full-length practice set of 30 Arithmetic Reasoning questions for you to take under timed conditions.

So let's begin our review.

ARITHMETIC REVIEW

First, take a look at a few definitions

Number Type	Definition	Examples
Integers	Whole numbers, including 0 and negative whole numbers.	$-900, -3, 0, 1, 54$
Fractions	A **fraction** is a number that is written in the form $\frac{A}{B}$ where A is the numerator and B is the denominator.	$-\frac{5}{6}, -\frac{3}{17}, \frac{1}{2}, \frac{899}{901}$
	An **improper fraction** is a number that is greater than 1 (or less than -1) that is written in the form of a fraction. An improper fraction can be converted to a **mixed number**.	$-\frac{65}{64}, \frac{9}{8}, \frac{57}{10}$ $-1\frac{1}{64}, 1\frac{1}{8}, 5\frac{7}{10}$
Positive/Negative	Numbers greater than 0 are positive numbers; numbers less than 0 are negative. 0 is neither positive nor negative.	Positive: $\frac{7}{8}, 1, 5, 900$ Negative: $-64, -40, -11, -\frac{6}{13}$
Even/Odd	An even number is an integer that is a multiple of 2.	Even numbers: $-8, -2, 0, 4, 12, 188$
	An odd number is an integer that is not a multiple of 2.	Odd numbers: $-17, -1, 3, 9, 457$
Prime Number	An integer greater than 1 that has no factors other than 1 and itself. 2 is the only even prime number.	$2, 3, 5, 7, 11, 59, 83$
Consecutive Numbers	Numbers that follow one after another, in order, without skipping any.	Consecutive integers: 3, 4, 5, 6 Consecutive even integers: 2, 4, 6, 8, 10 Consecutive multiples of 9: 9, 18, 27, 36
Factor	A positive integer that divides evenly into a given number with no remainder.	The complete list of factors of 12: 1, 2, 3, 4, 6, 12
Multiple	A number that a given number will divide into with no remainder.	Some multiples of 12: 0, 12, 24, 60

Odds and Evens

EVEN + EVEN = EVEN	EVEN − EVEN = EVEN	EVEN × EVEN = EVEN
EVEN + ODD = ODD	EVEN − ODD = ODD	EVEN × ODD = EVEN
ODD + EVEN = ODD	ODD − EVEN = ODD	ODD × EVEN = EVEN
ODD + ODD = EVEN	ODD − ODD = EVEN	ODD × ODD = ODD

Positives and Negatives

There are few things to remember about positives and negatives. You will not see many problems that focus specifically on positives and negatives, but you must know the basics because these concepts will show up as part of harder problems.

Adding a negative number is basically subtraction.

> $6 + (−4)$ is really $6 − 4$ or 2.
> $4 + (−6)$ is really $4 − 6$ or $−2$.

Subtracting a negative number is basically addition.

> $6 − (−4)$ is really $6 + 4$ or 10.
> $−6 − (−4)$ is really $−6 + 4$ or $−2$.

DIVIDING POSITIVES AND NEGATIVES

Negative ÷ negative = positive

Positive ÷ negative = negative

Multiplying and **Dividing** positives and negatives is like all other multiplication and division, with one catch. To figure out whether your product is positive or negative, simply count the number of negatives you had to start. If you had an odd number of negatives, the product is negative. If you had an even number of negatives, the product is positive.

> $6 \times (−4) = −24$ (1 negative → negative product)
> $(−6) \times (−4) = 24$ (2 negatives → positive product)
> $(−1) \times (−6) \times (−4) = −24$ (3 negatives → negative product)

Similarly,

> $−24 \div 6 = −4$ (1 negative → negative quotient)
> $−24 \div (−4) = 6$ (2 negatives → positive quotient)

Factors and Multiples

To find the **prime factorization** of a number, keep breaking it down until you are left with only prime numbers.

To find the prime factorization of 168:

> $168 = 4 \times 42$
> $= 4 \times 6 \times 7$
> $= 2 \times 2 \times 2 \times 3 \times 7$

To find the **greatest common factor (GCF)** of two integers, break down both integers into their prime factorizations and multiply all prime factors they have in common.

If you're looking for the greatest common factor of 40 and 140, first identify the prime factors of each integer.

$$40 = 4 \times 10$$
$$= 2 \times 2 \times 2 \times 5$$
$$140 = 10 \times 14$$
$$= 2 \times 5 \times 2 \times 7$$
$$= 2 \times 2 \times 5 \times 7$$

Next, see what prime factors the two numbers have in common and then multiply these common factors.

Both integers share two 2s and a 5, so the GCF is $2 \times 2 \times 5$ or 20.

If you need to find a **common multiple** of two integers, you can always multiply them. However, you can use prime factors to find the **least common multiple (LCM)**. To do this, multiply all of the prime factors of each integer as many times as they appear. When a prime factor appears a different number of times in the integers, then that prime factor is to be multiplied the number of times that the prime factor appears in the integer containing the prime factor the greatest number of times. This may sound confusing, but is pretty clear once it's demonstrated. Take a look at the example to see how it works.

Common multiple of 20 and 16:

$$20 \times 16 = 320$$

320 is a common multiple of 20 and 16, but it is not the least common multiple.

Least common multiple of 20 and 16:

$$20 = 2 \times 2 \times 5$$
$$16 = 2 \times 2 \times 2 \times 2$$

Least common multiple = $2 \times 2 \times 2 \times 2 \times 5 = 80$

Notice that the prime factor 2 occurs 2 times in 20 and 4 times in 16, so when finding the least common multiple, we took 4 factors of the prime number 2.

REMEMBER *PEMDAS*

When performing multiple operations, remember PEMDAS: **P**arentheses, **E**xponents, **M**ultiplication and **D**ivision, **A**ddition and **S**ubtraction. You may find it easier to remember as *Please Excuse My Dear Aunt Sally*.

The Order of Operations

You need to remember the order in which arithmetic operations must be performed. PEMDAS (or *Please Excuse My Dear Aunt Sally*) may help you remember the order.

<u>P</u>lease = Parentheses
<u>E</u>xcuse = Exponents
<u>My</u> <u>D</u>ear = Multiplication and Division (from left to right)
<u>A</u>unt <u>S</u>ally = Addition and Subtraction (from left to right)

For example:

$$3^3 - 8(4 - 2) + 60 \div 4$$
$$= 3^3 - 8(2) + 60 \div 4$$
$$= 27 - 8(2) + 60 \div 4$$
$$= 27 - 16 + 15$$
$$= 11 + 15$$
$$= 26$$

Exercise

i. What are the prime factors of 330? _____

ii. What is the least common multiple of 18 and 24? _____

iii. $44 - 20 \div 4 \times 8 =$ _____

Divisibility Rules

Divisible by	The Rule	Example: 558
2	The last digit is even.	a multiple of 2 because 8 is even
3	The sum of the digits is a multiple of 3.	a multiple of 3 because $5 + 5 + 8 = 18$, which is a multiple of 3
4	The last 2 digits comprise a 2-digit multiple of 4.	NOT a multiple of 4 because 58 is not a multiple of 4
5	The last digit is 5 or 0.	NOT a multiple of 5 because it doesn't end in 5 or 0
6	The last digit is even AND the sum of the digits is a multiple of 3.	a multiple of 6 because it's a multiple of both 2 and 3
9	The sum of the digits is a multiple of 9.	a multiple of 9 because $5 + 5 + 8 = 18$, which is a multiple of 9
10	The last digit is 0.	not a multiple of 10 because it doesn't end in 0

Exercise

iv. What are the following numbers divisible by?

1,455 _____

50,022 _____

0 _____

Fractions and Decimals

Generally, it's a good idea to **reduce fractions** when solving math questions. To do this, simply, cancel all factors that the numerator and denominator have in common.

$$\frac{28}{36} = \frac{4 \times 7}{4 \times 9} = \frac{7}{9}$$

To **add fractions**, get a common denominator and then add the numerators.

$$\frac{1}{4} + \frac{1}{3} = \frac{3}{12} + \frac{4}{12} = \frac{3+4}{12} = \frac{7}{12}$$

To **subtract fractions**, get a common denominator and then subtract the numerators.

$$\frac{1}{4} - \frac{1}{3} = \frac{3}{12} - \frac{4}{12} = \frac{3-4}{12} = -\frac{1}{12}$$

To **multiply fractions**, multiply the numerators and multiply the denominators.

$$\frac{1}{4} \times \frac{1}{3} = \frac{1 \times 1}{4 \times 3} = \frac{1}{12}$$

To **divide fractions**, invert the second fraction and multiply. In other words, multiply the first fraction by the reciprocal of the second fraction.

$$\frac{1}{4} \div \frac{1}{3} = \frac{1}{4} \times \frac{3}{1} = \frac{1 \times 3}{4 \times 1} = \frac{3}{4}$$

To **compare fractions**, multiply the numerator of the first fraction by the denominator of the second fraction to get a product. Then, multiply the numerator of the second fraction by the denominator of the first fraction to get a second product. If the first product is greater, the first fraction is greater. If the second product is greater, the second fraction is greater.

Compare $\frac{2}{3}$ and $\frac{5}{8}$.

$$2 \times 8 = 16$$

$$5 \times 3 = 15$$

16 is greater than 15, so is $\frac{2}{3}$ is greater than $\frac{5}{8}$.

To **convert a fraction to a decimal**, divide the denominator into the numerator.

To convert $\frac{8}{25}$ to a decimal, divide 25 into 8.

$$\frac{8}{25} = 0.32$$

To **convert a decimal to a fraction**, first set the decimal over 1. Then, move the decimal over as many places as it takes until it is immediately to the right of the units digit. Count the number of places that you moved the decimal. Then add that many 0s to the 1 in the denominator.

$$0.3 = \frac{0.3}{1} = \frac{3.0}{10} \text{ or } \frac{3}{10}$$

$$0.32 = \frac{0.32}{1} = \frac{32.0}{100} \text{ or } \frac{8}{25}$$

Exercise

v. Reduce the following fractions and expressions to lowest terms:

$\frac{39}{72} =$ _____

$\frac{248}{504} =$ _____

$\frac{5}{9} + \frac{2}{6} =$ _____

$\frac{1}{2} - \frac{3}{7} =$ _____

vi. Convert the following fractions to decimals:

$\frac{11}{16} =$ _____

$\frac{5}{8} =$ _____

vii. Convert the following decimals to fractions:

$0.15 =$ _____

$0.64 =$ _____

Common Percent Equivalencies

Familiarity with the relationships among percents, decimals and fractions can save you time on test day. Don't worry about memorizing the following chart. Simply use it to refresh your recollection of relationships you already know (e.g., $50\% = 0.50 = \frac{1}{2}$) and to familiarize yourself with some that you might not already know. To convert a fraction or decimal to a percent, multiply by 100%. To convert a percent to a fraction or decimal, divide by 100%.

Fraction	Decimal	Percent	Fraction	Decimal	Percent
$\frac{1}{20}$	0.05	5%	$\frac{2}{5}$	0.40	40%
$\frac{1}{10}$	0.10	10%	$\frac{1}{2}$	0.50	50%
$\frac{1}{8}$	0.125	12.5%	$\frac{3}{5}$	0.60	60%
$\frac{1}{6}$	$0.16\overline{6}$	$16\frac{2}{3}\%$	$\frac{2}{3}$	$0.66\overline{6}$	$66\frac{2}{3}\%$
$\frac{1}{5}$	0.20	20%	$\frac{3}{4}$	0.75	75%
$\frac{1}{4}$	0.25	25%	$\frac{4}{5}$	0.80	80%
$\frac{1}{3}$	$0.33\overline{3}$	$33\frac{1}{3}\%$	$\frac{5}{6}$	$0.83\overline{3}$	$83\frac{1}{3}\%$
$\frac{3}{8}$	0.375	37.5%	$\frac{7}{8}$	0.875	87.5%

Decimal Division and Scientific Notation

One common type of arithmetic problem on the ASVAB involves dividing numbers that contain decimals. Take a look at what we mean.

$$7.2 \div 0.004 = ?$$

Having to keep track of all those decimal places complicates what would otherwise be a simple division problem. That's why we recommend that you get rid of the decimal places before you divide. Here's how you do it. First, turn the division problem into a fraction:

$$7.2 \div 0.004 = \frac{7.2}{0.004}$$

Then move the decimal points in the denominator and the numerator the same number of places to the right, adding zeros as necessary, until you have completely gotten rid of them.

$$\frac{7.2}{0.004} = \frac{7,200}{4}$$

Now you have that simple division problem you were looking for.

$$\frac{7,200}{4} = 1,800$$

There's also a chance you might see scientific notation on the ASVAB, a method of writing very large and very small numbers that also involves moving decimal points.

The exponent of a power of 10 indicates how many zeros the number would contain if it were written out. For example, $10^4 = 10,000$ (4 zeros) since the product of four factors of 10 is equal to 10,000.

When multiplying a number by a power of 10, move the decimal point to the right the same number of places as the number of zeros in that power of 10.

$$0.0123 \times 10^4 = 123$$

When dividing by a power of 10, move the decimal point to the left.

$$43.21 \div 10^3 = 0.04321$$

Multiplying by a number with a negative exponent is the same as dividing by a positive exponent. Therefore, when you multiply by a number with a positive exponent, move the decimal to the right. When you multiply by a number with a negative exponent, move the decimal to the left.

Exponents and Roots

Exponents are the small raised numbers written to the right of a variable or number. They indicate the number of times that variable or number is to be used as a factor. On the ASVAB, you'll usually deal with numbers or variables that are squared, but you could see a few other concepts involving exponents.

To **add** or **subtract** terms consisting of a coefficient (the number in front of the variable) multiplied by a power (a power is a base raised to an exponent), both the base and the exponent must be the same. As long as the base and the exponents are the same, you can add the coefficients.

$$x^2 + x^2 = 2x^2$$
$$3x^4 - 2x^4 = x^4$$
$$x^2 + x^3 \text{ cannot be combined.}$$

MULTIPLYING POWERS

To multiply powers with the same base, add exponents. To raise a power to an exponent, multiply exponents.

To **multiply** terms consisting of coefficients multiplied by powers having the same base, multiply the coefficients and add the exponents.

$$2x^5 \times 8x^7 = (2 \times 8)(x^{5\,+7}) = 16x^{12}$$

To **divide** terms consisting of coefficients multiplied by powers having the same base, divide the coefficients and subtract the exponents.

$$6x^7 \div 2x^5 = (6 \div 2)(x^{7-5}) = 3x^2$$

To **raise a power to an exponent**, multiply the exponents.

$$(x^2)^4 = x^{2 \times 4} = x^8$$

PERFECT SQUARE

Learn to recognize perfect squares.

A **square root** is a number that, when multiplied by itself, produces the given quantity. The radical sign "$\sqrt{}$" is used to represent the positive square root of a number, so $\sqrt{25} = 5$, since $5 \times 5 = 25$.

To **add** or **subtract** radicals, make sure the numbers under the radical sign are the same. If they are, you can add or subtract the coefficients outside the radical signs.

$$2\sqrt{2} + 3\sqrt{2} = 5\sqrt{2}$$

$\sqrt{2} + \sqrt{3}$ cannot be combined.

To **simplify** radicals, factor out the perfect squares under the radical, unsquare them, and put the result in front of the radical sign.

$$\sqrt{32} = \sqrt{16 \times 2} = 4\sqrt{2}$$

To **multiply** or **divide** radicals, multiply (or divide) the coefficients outside the radical. Multiply (or divide) the numbers inside the radicals.

$$\sqrt{x} \times \sqrt{y} = \sqrt{xy}$$

$$3\sqrt{2} \times 4\sqrt{5} = 12\sqrt{10}$$

$$\frac{\sqrt{x}}{\sqrt{y}} = \sqrt{\frac{x}{y}}$$

$$12\sqrt{10} \div 3\sqrt{2} = 4\sqrt{5}$$

To **take the square root of a fraction**, break the fraction into two separate roots and take the square root of the numerator and the denominator.

$$\sqrt{\frac{16}{25}} = \frac{\sqrt{16}}{\sqrt{25}} = \frac{4}{5}$$

Exercise

viii. Simplify the following expressions.

$$x^5 + 2x^5 = \underline{\hspace{2cm}}$$

$$2x(x^2 + 3y) = \underline{\hspace{2cm}}$$

$$(x^4)^3 = \underline{\hspace{2cm}}$$

$$\sqrt{49} - \sqrt{16} = \underline{\hspace{2cm}}$$

$$\sqrt{2} \times \sqrt{10} = \underline{\hspace{2cm}}$$

$$\sqrt{\frac{25}{64}} = \underline{\hspace{2cm}}$$

Factorials

On the ASVAB math sections, you may see an occasional "factorial" question. You'll know you're dealing with a factorial when you see an exclamation point (!) in a seemingly inappropriate place. For instance, when you see the following:

$$7! = ?$$

You are not supposed to read the question as:

7 (What a number!) = ?

The above question is actually asking you what "7 factorial" is, and the answer to that question is:

$$7! = 7 \times 6 \times 5 \times 4 \times 3 \times 2 \times 1 = 5{,}040$$

By the same token: $6! = 6 \times 5 \times 4 \times 3 \times 2 \times 1 = 720$

So you tell us. $5! = ?$

<u>Answer:</u> $5 \times 4 \times 3 \times 2 \times 1 = 120.$

You should also note that if you're ever given a fraction with factorials, there's always a lot of canceling that you can do before you try to multiply out the factorials.

APPLIED ARITHMETIC REVIEW

While the arithmetic concepts we've looked at so far could appear on the Arithmetic Reasoning section of the ASVAB, it's worth noting that due to the very nature of word problems, most of the questions in this section will involve some form of "applied arithmetic"—in other words, the arithmetic used to solve practical problems. Applied arithmetic includes subjects like percent problems, rates, averages, and probability.

It's also worth noting, as you look over the following pages, that almost every applied arithmetic concept involves what we at Kaplan like to call a "disguised" fraction. For instance, in a percent problem, the disguised fraction looks like this:

$$\text{Percent} = \frac{\text{Part}}{\text{Whole}}.$$

Whereas in a rate problem, the disguised fraction might look like this:

$$\text{Speed} = \frac{\text{Distance}}{\text{Time}}.$$

This should be good news. It means that if you can handle fractions, you should have no problem with the applied arithmetic concepts that appear on the ASVAB. Let's take a look.

Percent Problems

FROM FRACTION TO PERCENT

To change a fraction to a percent, multiply by 100%.

Remember this formula $\text{Percent} = \frac{\text{Part}}{\text{Whole}}$, which can also be written as $\text{Part} = \text{Percent} \times \text{Whole}$.

To find **part, percent,** or **whole,** plug the values you have into the equation and solve.

To convert the **English into math on a percent problem,** use the following conversion table.

English	Math Translation
%	/100 (or use decimal or fractional equivalent)
of	× (times)
what	*x* (or *n*, or any variable you like)
is	= (equals)

44% of 25 = 0.44 × 25 = 11

42 is what percent of 70?

$$42 = \frac{n}{100} \times 70$$

$$\frac{42}{70} = \frac{n}{100}$$

$$n = \frac{4200}{70}$$

$$n = 60\%$$

To **increase or decrease a number by a given percent,** take that percent of the original number and add it to or subtract it from the original number.

To increase 25 by 60%, first find 60% of 25.

$$25 \times 0.6 = 15.$$

Then add the result to the original number.

$$25 + 15 = 40.$$

To decrease 25 by the same percent, subtract the 15.

$$25 - 15 = 10.$$

The following formulas may also come in handy:

$$\text{Percent increase/greater} = \frac{\text{change}}{\text{original (smaller) number}}$$

$$\text{Percent decrease/less} = \frac{\text{change}}{\text{original (larger) number}}$$

A camera that originally cost $125 was sold on sale for $100. The sale price was what percent less than the original price?

Answer: Percent decrease $= \dfrac{\$25}{\$125} = \dfrac{1}{5} = 20\%$

SHORTCUT

A handy shortcut:

$x\%$ of $y = y\%$ of x.

Exercise

   ix. 16 of the 64 cookies on the tray are chocolate chip. What percent are NOT chocolate chip? ____

   x. 3% of 42 equals 42% of ____.

   xi. A school raised its monthly tuition from $200.00 per month to $275.00 per month. What was the percent increase in the monthly tuition?

Ratios, Proportions, and Rates

Ratios, like fractions, are another way of expressing **Part/Whole** relationships, although ratios often refer to **Part/Part** relationships as well. In either case, the setup remains the same:

Classic Ratio Setup: What is the ratio of $\dfrac{\text{(Part)}}{\text{to (Part or Whole)}}$

Look at the following example:

RATIOS CAN TAKE MANY FORMS

- There are 2 red marbles for every 3 marbles.

- The ratio of red marbles to green marbles is 2 : 3.

- The ratio of red marbles to green marbles is $\dfrac{2}{3}$.

   A class contains has 12 male students and 21 female students.

   The ratio of male students to female students $= \dfrac{12}{21} = \dfrac{4}{7}$.

   The ratio of male students to all the students in the class $= \dfrac{12}{12 + 21} = \dfrac{12}{33} = \dfrac{4}{11}$.

By the way, you always want to simplify ratios to their lowest terms.

A proportion is just a type of a ratio, one that shows the comparative relation between parts, things, or elements with respect to size, amount, or degree. Here's an example of a proportion question:

A picture that is 4 inches wide and 6 inches long is enlarged so that it is $7\frac{1}{2}$ inches long. What is the width of the enlarged picture?

To handle a proportion such as the one above, set it up as an equation of fractions (in this case, of width/length), and then cross-multiply to solve for the unknown value:

$$\frac{4}{6} = \frac{n}{7.5}$$

$$4 \times 7.5 = 6n$$

$$\frac{30}{6} = n$$

$$n = 5$$

So the enlarged picture is 5 inches wide.

Finally, a **rate** is simply a ratio that compares distance over time, or amount over time, or cost over units.

In other words: $\text{Rate} = \dfrac{\text{Distance}}{\text{Time}}$ or $\text{Rate} = \dfrac{\text{Amount}}{\text{Time}}$ or $\text{Rate} = \dfrac{\text{Cost}}{\text{Units}}$

Take a look at the following rate question.

A waitress serves 3 diners every 5 minutes. At this rate, how many customers will she serve in one hour?

The key to solving rate problems is to set them up as proportions, convert the units if necessary, and solve for the unknown value.

$$\frac{3 \text{ diners}}{5 \text{ minutes}} = \frac{x \text{ diners}}{1 \text{ hour}} \qquad \text{Set up a proportion.}$$

$$\frac{3 \text{ diners}}{5 \text{ minutes}} = \frac{x \text{ diners}}{60 \text{ minutes}} \qquad \text{Convert units.}$$

$$5x = 180 \qquad \text{Cross-multiply and solve.}$$

$$x = 36$$

Exercise

xii. There are 18 white marbles and 6 red marbles in a bag. What is the ratio of red marbles to white marbles? ____

xiii. $\frac{36}{8} = \frac{9}{y}$. What is the value of y ? _____

xiv. If it took Michael three hours to bike 48 miles, what was his average speed in miles per hour? ____

Averages and Probability

Averages, like ratios, proportions, and rates, are variations of fractions. Without further ado, we bring you the Average Formula:

$$\text{Average} = \frac{\text{Sum of the terms}}{\text{Number of terms}}$$

Whenever you are given two of the above pieces of information in an average question, you should go ahead and calculate the third. Take the following, for example:

What is the average of 3, 4 and 8?

Answer: The average is 5, because $\text{Average} = \frac{\text{Sum of the terms}}{\text{Number of terms}} = \frac{3 + 4 + 8}{3} = \frac{15}{3} = 5$.

Finally, a **probability** is the likelihood that a desired outcome will occur, which is once again expressed as a fraction between 0 and 1. The more likely it is that something is going to happen, the closer the probability is to 1.

To find the probability that something is going to happen:

$$\text{Probability} = \frac{\text{Number of favorable outcomes}}{\text{Number of possible outcomes}}$$

If there are 12 books on a shelf and 9 of them are mysteries, what is the probability of picking a mystery?

$\frac{9}{12} = \frac{3}{4}$. This probability can also be expressed as 0.75 or 75%.

To find the probability that **two events** will occur, find the probability that the first event occurs and multiply this by the probability that the second event occurs given that the first event occurs.

> If there are 12 books on a shelf and 9 of them are mysteries, what is the probability of picking a mystery first and a non-mystery second if exactly two books are selected?

PROBABILITY IS UNDER ONE

Probability is a part-to-whole ratio and can therefore never be greater than one.

Probability of picking a mystery: $\frac{9}{12} = \frac{3}{4}$.

Probability of picking a nonmystery: $\frac{3}{11}$. (Originally there were 9 mysteries and 3 nonmysteries. After the mystery is selected, there are 8 mysteries and 3 nonmysteries, i.e., 11 books remaining.)

Probability of picking both books: $\frac{3}{4} \times \frac{3}{11} = \frac{9}{44}$.

Exercise

xv. In a woodshop, one box contains 21 nails, another box contains 37 nails, and a third box contains 14 nails. What is the average (arithmetic mean) number of nails per box? _____

xvi. A basketball team scored an average (arithmetic mean) of 23 points per quarter in a certain game. What was the total number of points scored by the team during the game? _____

xvii. A bag contains 5 red jelly beans, 3 yellow jelly beans, 4 green jelly beans, and 8 black jelly beans. What is the probability that a jelly bean chosen at random will NOT be black? _____

xviii. If a fair coin is tossed three times, what is the probability that it will land on heads all three times? _____

ARITHMETIC WORD PROBLEMS

As you may have noticed, we already started sneaking word problems into the arithmetic review section you just completed. See? Word problems really aren't all that bad. You should find that ASVAB Arithmetic Reasoning words are pretty straightforward. Generally, all you have to do is translate the prose into math and solve. So let's take a look at how to do that.

Translation

Often, word problems seem tricky because it's hard to figure out precisely what they're asking. It can be difficult to translate English into math. The following table lists some common words and phrases that turn up in word problems, along with their mathematical translations.

When you see:	Think:
sum, plus, more than, added to, combined, total	+
minus, less than, difference between, decreased by	−
is, was, equals, is equivalent to, is the same as, adds up to	=
times, product, multiplied by, of, twice, double, triple	×
divided by, over, quotient, per, out of, into	÷
what, how much, how many, a number	x, n, etc.

Exercise

xix. Try translating the following sentences from English to math.

English	Math
Yolanda is 5 years older than Xavier.	
Ray has half as many baseball cards as Sal has.	
There are twice as many ostriches as penguins.	
The product of two numbers is 3 more than their sum.	

xx. In a certain class there are twice as many boys as girls. If the total number of students in the class is 36, how many boys are there?

(A) 12
(B) 18
(C) 24
(D) 27

xxi. Paul developed a roll of film containing 36 pictures. If he made 2 prints each of half of the pictures, and 1 print of each of the rest, how many prints did he make in all?

(A) 7
(B) 36
(C) 54
(D) 72

SIFT THROUGH THE FICTION— FIND THE MATH!

In some questions, the translation will be embedded within a "story." Don't be put off by the details of the scenario— it's the numbers that matter. Focus on the math and translate.

Word Problems with Formulas

Some of the more difficult word problems may involve translations with mathematical formulas. Since the ASVAB test does not provide formulas for you, you have to know these going in.

If a truck travels at 50 miles per hour for $6\frac{1}{2}$ hours, how far will the truck travel?

To answer this question, you need to remember the Distance Formula:

$$\text{Rate} = \frac{\text{Distance}}{\text{Time}} \text{ or Distance} = \text{Rate} \times \text{Time}$$

Once you note the formula, you can just plug in the numbers.

$D = 50 \times 6.5$
$D = 325$ miles

Now try a couple of these on your own.

Exercise

xxii. If the average (arithmetic mean) weight of a group of 6 children is 71 pounds, what is the total weight, in pounds, of the children?

(A) 348
(B) 366
(C) 396
(D) 426

xxiii. If a machine produces 150 widgets in 30 minutes, how many widgets will the machine produce in 4 hours?

(A) 600
(B) 750
(C) 900
(D) 1,200

Backdoor Strategies on Word Problems

Never forget that word problems are extremely susceptible to the backdoor strategies detailed in chapter 6. Here's a quick recap of **backsolving** and **picking numbers**.

Backsolving

When the problem is confusing and there are numbers in the answer choices, you may be able to backsolve your way to the answer by plugging the answer choices into the problem until you find one that works. Here's a review of the backsolving method.

- Start with choice (B) or (C).
- Eliminate choices you know are too big or too small.
- Keep going until you find the choice that works.

Try backsolving on the following problem.

Exercise

xxiv. Adam has 3 times as many Hawaiian shirts as Mike has. If Adam gives Mike 6 Hawaiian shirts, they would have an equal number of Hawaiian shirts. How many Hawaiian shirts does Mike have?

(A) 3
(B) 6
(C) 9
(D) 15

Picking Numbers

If the problem has percents or fractions and an unknown value, or if there are variables in the question and answer choices, picking numbers is backdoor strategy to apply. Here's a quick review of how to pick numbers:

- Pick nice, easy numbers for the variables or unknown values in your question.
- Answer the question using the numbers you've picked. This answer is your target number.
- Now substitute the numbers you picked for the variables in the answer choices. See which answer gives you your target number.

A few things to remember are:

- Pick easy numbers rather than realistic numbers. Keep the numbers small and manageable, but try to avoid 0 and 1.
- Don't pick the same number for more than one variable.
- When picking a number on a remainder problem, add the remainder to the number you are dividing by.
- Pick 100 on percent questions.
- Pick a common denominator in the answer choices on fraction questions.

Try picking numbers on the following problem.

Exercise

xxv. An antique dealer usually charges 20 percent more than his purchase price for any vase sold in his store. During a clearance sale, all items are marked 10 percent off. If the dealer sells a vase during the clearance sale, his profit on the vase (sale price minus purchase price) is what percent of the purchase price of the vase?

(A) 8%
(B) 9%
(C) 10%
(D) 12%

EXERCISE ANSWERS

i. $330 = 33 \times 10 = 3 \times 11 \times 2 \times 5$. The prime factors are 2, 3, 5 and 11.

ii. $18 = 2 \times 3 \times 3$. $24 = 2 \times 2 \times 2 \times 3$. So the least common multiple of 18 and 24 is $2 \times 2 \times 2 \times 3 \times 3 = 72$.

iii. $44 - 20 \div 4 \times 8 = 44 - 5 \times 8 = 44 - 40 = 4$.

iv. 1,455 is divisible by 3 and 5. 50,022 is divisible by 2, 3, 6, and 9. 0 is divisible by every non-zero integer.

v. $\dfrac{13}{24}, \dfrac{31}{63}, \dfrac{8}{9}, \dfrac{1}{14}$

vi. 0.6875, 0.625

vii. $\dfrac{3}{20}, \dfrac{16}{25}$

viii. $3x^5, 2x^3 + 6xy, x^{12}, 3, 2\sqrt{5}, \dfrac{5}{8}$

ix. $\dfrac{48}{64} = \dfrac{3}{4} = 75\%$

x.   3

xi. Percent increase $= \dfrac{\$75}{\$200} = \dfrac{3}{8} = 37.5\%$

xii. $1 : 3$

xiii. 2

xiv. 16 mph

xv. 24

xvi. 92

xvii. Probability $= \dfrac{12}{20} = \dfrac{3}{5}$

xviii. Probability $= \dfrac{1}{2} \times \dfrac{1}{2} \times \dfrac{1}{2} = \dfrac{1}{8}$

xix. $y = x + 5$, $r = \dfrac{s}{2}$, $o = 2p$, $a \times b = a + b + 3$ (Your variables may be different from ours.)

xx. **C**

You can either backsolve or do the algebra:

$$2g = b$$
$$g + b = 36$$
$$g + 2g = 36$$
$$3g = 36$$
$$g = 12$$
$$12 + b = 36$$
$$b = 24$$

xxi. **C**

$36 \div 2 = 18, (18 \times 2) + (18 \times 1) = 36 + 18 = 54$

xxii. **D**

Average $= \dfrac{\text{Sum of the terms}}{\text{Number of terms}}$, so $71 = \dfrac{x}{6}$ and $x = 71 \times 6 = 426$.

xxiii. **D**

You could set up a proportion and solve, or you could apply common sense. If the machine produces 150 widgets in 30 minutes, it must produce 300 widgets in an hour. Therefore, it must produce $4 \times 300 = 1,200$ widgets in 4 hours.

xxiv. **B**

Let's start with choice (B) and assume that Mike has 6 shirts. Adam has 3 times as many shirts as Mike, so that means he has 18 shirts. Thus if Adam were to give Mike 6 of his shirts, they would both have 12 shirts. This is what we want to happen, so the answer is choice (B), and you're done.

xxv. **A**

Let's pick 100 for the purchase price of the vase. The dealer pays \$100 for the vase, but usually charges 20 percent more, or \$120 for it. During the sale the vase's price is reduced 10 percent. 10 percent of \$120 is \$12, so the final sale price of the vase is \$108, meaning the dealer made a profit of $\dfrac{8}{100}$ or 8 percent on his original purchase price.

ARITHMETIC REASONING PRACTICE SET

1. Professor Jones bought a large carton of books. She gave 3 books to each student in her class and there were no books left over. Which of the following could be the number of books she distributed?

   (A) 133
   (B) 143
   (C) 252
   (D) 271

2. Two teams are having a contest, in which the prize is a box of candy that the members of the winning team will divide evenly. If team A wins, each player will get exactly 3 pieces of candy and if team B wins, each player will get exactly 5 pieces of candy. Which of the following could be the number of pieces of candy in the box?

   (A) 325
   (B) 353
   (C) 425
   (D) 555

3. Barry is four years older than his brother Cole, who is four years older than their sister Darcy. If the sum of their three ages is 60, how old is Barry?

   (A) 16
   (B) 20
   (C) 24
   (D) 28

4. Sheila cuts a 60-foot wire cable in equal strips of $\frac{4}{5}$ of a foot in length each. How many strips does she make?

   (A) 48
   (B) 60
   (C) 70
   (D) 75

5. Susie and Dennis are training for a marathon. On Monday, they both run 3.2 miles. On Tuesday, Susie runs $5\frac{1}{5}$ miles and Dennis runs 3.6 miles. On Wednesday, Susie runs 4.8 miles and Dennis runs $2\frac{2}{5}$ miles. During those 3 days, how many more miles does Susie run than Dennis?

   (A) 4.8
   (B) 4.0
   (C) 3.2
   (D) 3.0

6. If the number 9,899,399 is increased by 2,082, the result will be

   (A) 9,902,481
   (B) 9,901,481
   (C) 9,901,471
   (D) 9,891,481

7. Zim buys a calculator that is marked 30% off. If he pays $35, what was the original price?

    (A) $45.50
    (B) $47.00
    (C) $50.00
    (D) $62.50

8. Three lottery winners decide to split a cash prize in the ratio 1 : 2 : 3. If the cash prize is $12,000, what is the greatest amount earned by one of the three winners?

    (A) $2,000
    (B) $3,000
    (C) $4,000
    (D) $6,000

9. A copier can make 150 copies per minute. At this rate, how many minutes would it take to make 4,500 copies?

    (A) 20
    (B) 25
    (C) 30
    (D) 35

10. The average (arithmetic mean) age of the members in a five-person choir is 34. If the ages of four of the members are 47, 31, 27, and 36, what is the fifth member's age?

    (A) 29
    (B) 32
    (C) 34
    (D) 37

11. In a certain cookie jar containing only macaroons and gingersnaps, the ratio of macaroons to ginger snaps is 2 to 5. Which of the following could be the total number of cookies in the cookie jar?

    (A) 24
    (B) 35
    (C) 39
    (D) 48

Questions 12 and 13 refer to the following table.

LUNCHEON SPECIALS

Meal	Price
Hamburger	$3.00
Chicken	$2.75
Tuna Salad	$2.50
Pasta Salad	$2.25
Pizza	$1.50

12. If the table above represents the luncheon prices at a certain cafeteria, what is the average (arithmetic mean) price for a meal at this cafeteria?

    (A) $2.40
    (B) $2.50
    (C) $2.60
    (D) $2.70

13. If three people each ordered a different meal, which of the following could NOT be the total cost of the meals, excluding tax?

    (A) $7.00
    (B) $6.75
    (C) $6.25
    (D) $6.00

14. After the announcement of a sale, a bookstore sold $\frac{1}{2}$ of all its books in stock. On the following day, this bookstore sold 4,000 more books. Now only $\frac{1}{10}$ of the number of books in stock before the sale remain in the store. How many books were in stock before the announcement of the sale?

(A) 8,000
(B) 10,000
(C) 12,000
(D) 20,000

15. Brad bought a radio on sale at a 20% discount from its regular price of $118. If there is an 8% sales tax that is calculated on the sale price, how much did Brad pay for the radio?

(A) $86.85
(B) $94.40
(C) $101.95
(D) $127.44

16. Sheila charges $5.00 per haircut during the weekdays. On Saturday, she charges $7.50 per haircut. If Sheila has 6 customers each day of the week except Sunday, how much money does she earn in the five weekdays and Saturday?

(A) $175.00
(B) $180.00
(C) $195.00
(D) $210.00

17. The original price of a television decreases by 20 percent. By what percent must the price increase to reach its original value?

(A) 15%
(B) 20%
(C) 25%
(D) 30%

18. Team A had 4 times as many losses as it had ties in a season. If Team A won none of its games, which could be the total number of games it played that season?

(A) 15
(B) 18
(C) 21
(D) 24

19. Rose has finished $\frac{5}{6}$ of her novel after one week of reading. If she reads an additional tenth of the novel during the next 2 days, what part of the novel will she have read?

(A) $\frac{7}{15}$
(B) $\frac{4}{5}$
(C) $\frac{14}{15}$
(D) $\frac{29}{30}$

20. Joyce baked 42 biscuits for her 12 guests. If 6 biscuits remain uneaten, what is the average number of biscuits that the guests ate?

    (A) 2
    (B) 3
    (C) 4
    (D) 6

21. The average (arithmetic mean) weight of Jake, Ken, and Larry is 60 kilograms. If Jake and Ken both weigh 50 kilograms, how much, in kilograms, does Larry weigh?

    (A) 50
    (B) 60
    (C) 70
    (D) 80

22. A measuring cup contains $1\frac{2}{3}$ cups of water. It needs to be filled to the $3\frac{3}{4}$ cup mark. How much water must be added?

    (A) a little more than 1 cup
    (B) a little less than 2 cups
    (C) a little more than 2 cups
    (D) a little less than 3 cups

23. The user's manual for a stereo set includes a scale diagram in which 2 scaled inches represent 8 actual inches. If the speakers of the stereo set measure 6 inches in the diagram, how tall are they in reality?

    (A) 1 foot 6 inches
    (B) 1 foot 8 inches
    (C) 1 foot 10 inches
    (D) 2 feet

24. A bus carries 15 sixth graders, 18 seventh graders, and 12 eighth graders. If the bus contains only students from those three grades, what fraction of the total number of students on the bus is in the seventh grade?

    (A) $\frac{1}{5}$

    (B) $\frac{2}{7}$

    (C) $\frac{2}{5}$

    (D) $\frac{3}{7}$

25. A ferris wheel has 12 cars that can seat up to 3 people each. If every car on the ferris wheel is full except for 2 that contain 2 people and one that is empty, how many people are currently riding on the ferris wheel?

    (A) 31
    (B) 32
    (C) 34
    (D) 35

26. Which of the following represents 89,213 written in scientific notation?

    (A) 8.9213×10^2
    (B) 8.9213×10^3
    (C) 8.9213×10^4
    (D) 8.9213×10^5

27. A batch of salad dressing requires $1\frac{2}{3}$ cups of olive oil, $\frac{1}{2}$ cup of vinegar, and $\frac{3}{4}$ cup of water. How many cups of salad dressing will this recipe produce?

    (A) $1\frac{2}{3}$

    (B) $2\frac{5}{6}$

    (C) $2\frac{11}{12}$

    (D) $3\frac{7}{12}$

28. A tailor has 20 yards of shirt fabric How many shirts can she complete if each shirt requires $2\frac{2}{3}$ yards of fabric?

    (A) 7
    (B) 8
    (C) 9
    (D) 10

29. Carla drove her truck 414 miles on 18 gallons of gasoline. How many miles did she drive per gallon?

    (A) 18
    (B) 23
    (C) 74
    (D) 95

30. Douglas receives a 6% raise. If his old monthly salary was $2,250, what is his monthly salary now?

    (A) $2,256
    (B) $2,385
    (C) $2,400
    (D) $2,650

Answers and explanations appear on the following page.

ANSWER KEY

1. C	11. B	21. D
2. D	12. A	22. C
3. C	13. D	23. D
4. D	14. B	24. C
5. B	15. C	25. A
6. B	16. C	26. C
7. C	17. C	27. C
8. D	18. A	28. A
9. C	19. C	29. B
10. A	20. B	30. B

ANSWERS AND EXPLANATIONS FOR
ARITHMETIC REASONING PRACTICE SET

1. C

If Professor Jones was able to distribute all the books in groups of 3 without any left over, the number of books she started with was divisible by 3. Whichever choice is divisible by 3 must therefore be correct. For a number to be divisible by 3, the sum of its digits must also be divisible by 3. Only (C) fits this requirement: 2 + 5 + 2 = 9.

2. D

This problem tells you that the number of pieces of candy in the box can be divided evenly by 3 and 5. So the correct answer is the choice that has a 0 or 5 as its last digit, and the sum of whose digits is divisible by 3. Eliminate (B) because it doesn't end in either 0 or 5. Of the remaining choices, only (D) is also divisible by 3, since 5 + 5 + 5 = 15.

3. C

Use the answer choices to help find the solution. When backsolving you want to start with one of the middle numbers. We'll start here with (C), 24, for Barry's age. If Barry is 24, then his brother Cole is 20, and his sister is 16. Thus, the sum of their ages is 24 + 20 + 16 = 60, which is the sum we want. Choice (C) is it.

4. D

When you're asked how many strips $\frac{4}{5}$ of a foot in length can be cut from a 60-foot piece of wire, you are really being asked how many times $\frac{4}{5}$ goes into 60, or what is $60 \div \frac{4}{5}$. Before you even do the division, you can eliminate choices (A) and (B). This is because you know the answer has to be greater than 60, since $\frac{4}{5}$ is less than 1, which means it has to go into 60 more than 60 times. Now do the division. Dividing by a fraction is the same as multiplying by its inverse, so $60 \div \frac{4}{5} = 60 \times \frac{5}{4} = 15 \times 5 = 75$.

5. B

The simplest way to solve this problem is to convert the numbers so that they are all decimals. $5\frac{1}{5} = 5\frac{2}{10} = 5.2$. $2\frac{2}{5} = 2\frac{4}{10} = 2.4$. Now you can more easily compare the distances. On Monday, they ran the same number of miles. On Tuesday, Susie ran 5.2 miles and Dennis ran 3.6 miles. The difference between the two amounts is $5.2 - 3.6 = 1.6$, so on Tuesday Susie ran 1.6 more miles the Dennis did. On Wednesday, Susie ran 4.8 miles and Dennis ran 2.4 miles, so Susie ran $4.8 - 2.4 = 2.4$ more miles than Dennis did. The total difference for the three days is $1.6 + 2.4 = 4.0$ miles.

6. B

This question is simply asking for the sum of 9,899,399 and 2,082, which is 9,901,481, or choice (B).

7. C

You could backsolve on this question, but we'll go ahead and do it the straight way. Let's call the original price x. The price Zim paid is 70% of the original price (100% minus 30%). Thus $\frac{35}{x} = \frac{70}{100}$, so $70x = 3,500$ and $x = 50$.

8. D

The textbook approach is to come up with the ratio total by adding together the ratio parts:

$1 + 2 + 3 = 6$, so the $\frac{\text{Part}}{\text{Whole}}$ ratio for the biggest winner is $\frac{3}{6} = \frac{1}{2}$ the entire prize of $12,000, so he or she would earn $\frac{1}{2} \times \$12,000 = \$6,000$.

You could also backsolve with the answer choices, starting with one of the middle values, such as (B), $3,000. Assuming the greatest amount earned by one of the three winners is $3,000, the ratio of winnings is $1 : 2 : 3$, so the money would be divided $\$1,000 : \$2,000 : \$3,000$, for a total prize of $6,000. This is half the actual amount of $12,000, so it looks like $6,000 is the answer. But let's prove it: $1 : 2 : 3 = \$2,000 : \$4,000 : \$6,000$, for a total of $12,000, which works.

9. C

Set up a proportion: $\dfrac{150 \text{ copies}}{1 \text{ minute}} = \dfrac{4,500}{x \text{ minutes}}$

Now cross-multiply and solve: $150x = 4,500$, so $x = \dfrac{4,500}{150} = 30$.

10. **A**

Average = $\dfrac{\text{Sum of the terms}}{\text{Number of terms}}$, so here the average is $\dfrac{47 + 31 + 27 + 36 + n}{5}$.

Thus $34 = \dfrac{141 + n}{5}$, so by cross-multiplying you get $170 = 141 + n$.

So $n = 29$ and the answer is (A).

11. **B**

If the ratio of the parts is 2 : 5, then the total number of parts is $2 + 5 = 7$. Thus the actual total number of cookies must be a multiple of 7. The only answer choice that's a multiple of 7 is (B), 35.

12. **A**

To find the average price for a meal, use the formula:

$$\text{Average} = \frac{\text{Sum of the terms}}{\text{Number of terms}}$$
$$= \frac{\$3.00 + \$2.75 + \$2.50 + \$2.25 + \$1.50}{5}$$
$$= \frac{\$12.00}{5} = \$2.40.$$

13. **D**

The three lowest-priced meals—pizza at $1.50, pasta salad at $2.25, and tuna salad at $2.50—add up to $6.25. So it is not possible that a combination of three different meals could cost less than $6.25. Since choice (D), $6.00, is less than this, it could not be the total cost of three different meals.

14. **B**

You could backsolve here and get to the answer easily, but we'll solve this the old-fashioned way. After two days of the sale $\dfrac{1}{10}$ of the original number of books in stock is left. This means that altogether, $\dfrac{9}{10}$ of the original number of books have been sold. $\dfrac{1}{2}$ of the books were sold on the first day. $\dfrac{1}{2}$ can also be called $\dfrac{5}{10}$. If $\dfrac{9}{10}$ were sold in two days, and $\dfrac{5}{10}$ were sold on the first day, then on the second day $\dfrac{4}{10}$ must have been sold. You are told that 4,000 books were sold on the second day, so 4,000 must be $\dfrac{4}{10}$ of the original number of books. Now you need to determine what number 4,000 is $\dfrac{4}{10}$ of. $\dfrac{4}{10}n = 4,000$, so $n = \dfrac{10}{4} \times 4,000 = 10,000$.

15. **C**

This problem needs to be done in several steps. First find out what the sale price of the radio was. The discount was 20%, so the sale price was 80% of the original price.

Percent × Whole = Part

.80 × $118 = sale price

$94.40 = sale price

Now figure out how much tax Brad paid. The tax was 8% of the sale price.

Percent × Whole = Part

.08 × $94.40 = tax

$7.5520 = tax

$7.55 = tax

Now just add the tax to the sale price.

$94.40 + $7.55 = $101.95.

16. **C**

Each weekday Sheila earns:

$5.00 × 6 haircuts = $30 per weekday

Each Saturday Sheila earns:

$7.50 × 6 haircuts = $45 per Saturday

In 5 weekdays she earns 5 × $30 = $150.

In 1 Saturday she earns $45.

So in 5 weekdays plus 1 Saturday Sheila earns $150 + $45, or $195.

17. **C**

You have to realize here that while the value of the TV decreases and increases by the same *amount*, it doesn't increase and decrease by the same *percent*. That's why you want to pick numbers here. Let's pick $100 for the price of the television. If the price decreases by 20%, then since 20% of $100 is $20, the price decreases by $20. The new price is $100 − $20, or $80. For the new price to reach the original price ($100), it must be increased by $20. $20 is $\frac{1}{4}$ of 80, or 25% of $80. Thus the new price must be increased by 25%, choice (C).

18. **A**

Let the number of ties Team A had equal x. It lost 4 times as many games as it tied, or $4x$ games. It had no wins, so the total number of games played by Team A is $x + 4x = 5x$. So the number of games played must be a multiple of 5; the only choice that is a multiple of 5 is (A), 15.

19. C

Rose read $\dfrac{5}{6}$ of the novel and plans to read another $\dfrac{1}{10}$, which will result in her having read $\dfrac{5}{6} + \dfrac{1}{10}$ of the novel. Add these two fractions, using 30 as the common denominator:

$$\frac{5}{6} + \frac{1}{10} = \frac{25}{30} + \frac{3}{30} = \frac{28}{30} = \frac{14}{15}.$$

20. B

If 6 biscuits remained, $42 - 6 = 36$ were eaten by the 12 guests.

$\text{Average} = \dfrac{\text{Sum of the terms}}{\text{Number of terms}}$, so here the average is $\dfrac{36}{12} = 3$, choice (B).

21. D

$\text{Average} = \dfrac{\text{Sum of the terms}}{\text{Number of terms}}$, so if the average weight of the three men is 60 kg, the sum of their weights is $60 \times 3 = 180$ kg. This if Jake and Ken both weigh 50 kg, Larry must weigh $180 - (50 \times 2) = 80$ kilograms.

22. C

The question ask for "how much," but looking at the answer choices you'll note that you are not being asked for an exact amount. This is an estimation question. You need to compare the relative values of the two amounts. If the amount were simply 1 cup and 3 cups, it would clearly be 2 cups. But now you have to determine the relationship between $\dfrac{2}{3}$ and $\dfrac{3}{4}$. $\dfrac{3}{4}$ is just a little more than $\dfrac{2}{3}$. Thus, when you go from $1\dfrac{2}{3}$ cups to $3\dfrac{3}{4}$ cups, you are adding slightly more than 2 cups.

23. D

The best way to solve this one is to set up a proportion, solve it, and then convert the units:

$\dfrac{2}{8} = \dfrac{6}{n}$, so $2n = 6 \times 8$, and $n = \dfrac{48}{2} = 24$ inches, which is equal to 2 feet, choice (D).

24. **C**

The question asks you to identify the correct part-to-whole ratio from among the answer choices. In this case, the fraction will have the number of seventh graders, 18, as the numerator and the total number of students on the bus, $15 + 18 + 12 = 45$, as the denominator. Since $\dfrac{18}{45}$ is not an answer choice, it must be simplified:

$$\frac{18}{45} = \frac{18 \div 9}{45 \div 9} = \frac{2}{5}.$$

25. **A**

This question states that each seat of the ferris wheel can hold 3 people and that all but 3 of the 12 cars are full. Therefore, the 9 full cars containing 3 people each contain a total of 27 people. In addition, one of the remaining cars is empty and 2 cars contain 2 people each, adding 4 people to the 27 in the full cars for a total of 31 people on the ferris wheel.

26. **C**

Scientific notation is correctly represented as a number between 1 and 10 multiplied by a power of 10. To figure out what that power of 10 is, you have to carefully count out the number of decimal places you must move the decimal point of your original number until you reach a number between 1 and 10. To go from 89,213 to 8.9213 you must move the decimal point four places to the left, so that means you must multiply the number by 10 to the exponent 4. In other words, $89{,}213 = 8.9213 \times 10^4$.

27. **C**

You could try to estimate what the answer will be. If you do so, you will probably be able to get rid of (A) and (D), but (B) and (C) are so close that you are likely going to have to perform the addition. The easiest way to add these three amounts is to turn the mixed fractions into regular fractions, and then put all the fractions over the same denominator.

Here the least common denominator is 12, so let's convert those fractions: $1\dfrac{2}{3} = \dfrac{5}{3} = \dfrac{20}{12}$, $\dfrac{1}{2} = \dfrac{6}{12}$, and $\dfrac{3}{4} = \dfrac{9}{12}$. So the total amount of salad dressing that will be produced is $\dfrac{20}{12} + \dfrac{6}{12} + \dfrac{9}{12} = \dfrac{35}{12} = 2\dfrac{11}{12}$, choice (C).

28. A

This question is really asking you how many times $2\frac{2}{3}$ goes into 20, or what is $20 \div 2\frac{2}{3}$. To divide, first you'll want to turn the mixed fraction into a regular fraction. $2\frac{2}{3} = \frac{8}{3}$. Dividing by a fraction is the same a multiplying by its inverse, so $20 \div \frac{8}{3} = 20 \times \frac{3}{8} = \frac{60}{8} = \frac{15}{2} = 7\frac{1}{2}$.

Since you can't make half a shirt, the tailor can make a total of 7 shirts with this amount of fabric.

29. B

Miles per gallon $= \dfrac{\text{miles}}{\text{gallons}} = \dfrac{414}{18}$, so the answer is $414 \div 18$. But let's say that you would rather not divide 414 by 18. In that case you could now backsolve until you find an answer choice that when multiplied by 18 will give you 414. Let's start with (B), 23. Since $23 \times 18 = 414$, (B) is the answer.

30. B

First find 6% of $2,250. You could multiply $2,250 by 0.06, or you could look at it like this. 10 percent of $2,250 is $225, and 1 percent of $2,250 is $22.50. So 6% of $2,250 is $22.50 × 6 = $135. So Douglas's new monthly salary is $2,250 + $135 = $2,385, choice (B)

CHAPTER SIX

Mathematics Knowledge

INTRODUCTION

The Mathematics Knowledge section tends to be the more intimidating of the two ASVAB math sections for those whose enthusiasm for mathematics waned sometime before high school. We could point out that the Mathematics Knowledge section contains mostly straightforward math problems, unlike the Arithmetic Reasoning section, which presents all of its questions in the form of word problems. That doesn't matter, respond the whiners; what matters is the fact that the Mathematics Knowledge section covers a much wider range of topics—everything from arithmetic and geometry to the ins and outs of algebra!

To which we calmly respond that the breadth of knowledge covered by the Mathematics Knowledge section is not really so vast as it seems. In fact, if you've made it through the Arithmetic Reasoning chapter, you have already reviewed all of the arithmetic concepts that could appear on this section. For that reason, this chapter will pick up the math review with a look at the algebra and geometry concepts that may appear on this section of the ASVAB. We'll also show you ways to avoid doing algebra and geometry wherever possible, even if you can't avoid these subjects entirely.

We might also note that the Mathematics Knowledge section contains 25 questions, rather than the 30 questions found on the Arithmetic Reasoning section. And the fact that you are given 24 minutes to finish those questions, or slightly under a minute per question, as opposed to 72 seconds per question on the other section, indicates that the questions on the Mathematics Knowledge section usually take less time to answer than their Arithmetic Reasoning counterparts.

But probably the only real way for us to convince the skeptics out there that the Mathematics Knowledge section is one place on the ASVAB where even math haters can excel is by having those of you who fit this description go through this chapter and then take the practice set at the end of it. That'll show you!

ALGEBRA REVIEW

The difference between algebra and arithmetic is simply that algebra uses symbols called **variables**, such as x and y, to generalize arithmetic relationships. For some reason, many people have an irrational fear of variables, which are quite harmless in reality. If you have a problem with variables, we'll try to help you overcome this fear, or at least show you ways to avoid having to deal with them more than necessary.

Algebra problems on the ASVAB can appear in two forms: as straightforward math problems or as word problems. In fact, you may have noted that sometimes word problems on the Arithmetic Reasoning section involve unknown values, and so they can be treated as algebra problems, although often we find it easier to solve these questions using backdoor strategies such as picking numbers or backsolving. You will likewise find that algebra problems on the Mathematics Knowledge section are highly susceptible to these backdoor approaches. Nonetheless, on algebra questions on the ASVAB, the textbook approach is often the quicker approach. That's why we have kindly provided the following algebra review.

Expressions

An algebraic **expression** on the ASVAB test is likely to look something like this:

$$(11 + 3x) - (5 - 2x) =$$

It would, of course, be followed by four answer choices. In addition to algebra, this problem tests your knowledge of odds and evens and the order of operations (PEMDAS). It's not uncommon for algebra problems to contain elements of arithmetic, but there are certain algebraic concepts you need to know for the test.

The main thing that you need to remember about **expressions** on the ASVAB is that you can combine only "like terms."

For example, to combine monomials or polynomials, simply add or subtract the coefficients (the numbers that come before the variables) of terms that have the exact same variable. When completing the addition or subtraction, do not change the variables.

$$6a + 5a = 11a$$

$$8b - 2b = 6b$$

$$3a + 2b - 8a = 3a - 8a + 2b = -5a + 2b \text{ or } 2b - 5a$$

Remember, you cannot combine:

$$6a + 5a^2$$

or

$$3a + 2b$$

Now, try the following sample problem.

Exercise

i. $(11 + 3x) - (5 - 2x) =$

(A) $6 + x$

(B) $6 + 5x$

(C) $13 + 3x$

(D) $14 - 3x$

(E) $16 + 5x$

Multiplying and dividing monomials is a little different. In addition and subtraction, you can combine only like terms. With multiplication and division, you can multiply and divide terms that are different. When you multiply monomials, multiply the coefficients of each term. Add the exponents of like variables. Multiply different variables together.

$$(6a)(4b) =$$
$$= (6 \times 4)(a \times b)$$
$$= 24ab$$

$$(6a)(4ab) =$$
$$= (6 \times 4)(a \times a \times b)$$
$$= (6 \times 4)(a^{1+1} \times b)$$
$$= 24\,a^2b$$

WATCH OUT

Make sure you combine only like terms.

Use the FOIL method to multiply and divide binomials. FOIL stands for First, Outer, Inner, Last.

$$(y + 1)(y + 2) =$$
$$= (y \times y) + (y \times 2) + (1 \times y) + (1 \times 2)$$
$$= y^2 + 2y + y + 2$$
$$= y^2 + 3y + 2$$

By the way, the final expression above, $y^2 + 3y + 2$, is known as a **quadratic**. A quadratic expression or equation is one that is written in the form $ax^2 + bx + c$ or $ax^2 + bx + c = 0$ where $a \neq 0$ (of course, the x can be another variable, such as y in the expression above). Don't be scared here by the terminology. Just realize that you may occasionally be called upon to **factor** a quadratic expression or equation on the ASVAB. This simply involves being able to reverse-FOIL. Take a look.

MEMORIZE THE FOLLOWING:

$(x + y)(x - y) = x^2 - y^2$

$(x + y)^2 = x^2 + 2xy + y^2$

$(x - y)^2 = x^2 - 2xy + y^2$

If you see one side of any of the above equations on the on the ASVAB, rewrite it as the other side of the equation. This should make answering the question very easy.

Factor $x^2 - 4x - 21$

To begin, build parentheses: $(x \quad)(x \quad)$

Now think . . .

What **Last** terms will produce **−21**?

What **Outer** & **Inner** terms will produce **−4x**?

Consequently: $x - 4x - 21 = (x - 7)(x + 3)$

Exercise

   ii. $5a + 2b - 3(b + 3a) =$

   iii. $-3a - (-2a) =$

   iv. $6xy \div 2x =$

   v. $(n - 6)(n + 3) =$

   vi. Factor $x^2 + x - 6$

Equations

The key to **solving equations** is to do the same thing to both sides of the equation until you have your variable isolated on one side of the equation and all of the numbers on the other side of the equation. For instance, you could be asked for the value of a in the following equation.

$$12a + 8 = 23 - 3a$$

First, subtract 8 from each side so that the left side of the equation has only variables.

$$12a + 8 - 8 = 23 - 3a - 8$$

$$12a = 15 - 3a$$

DON'T FORGET

Always do the same thing to both sides to solve for a variable in an equation.

Then, add $3a$ to each side so that the right side of the equation has only numbers.

$$12a + 3a = 15 - 3a + 3a$$
$$15a = 15$$

Finally, divide both sides by 15 to isolate the variable.

$$\frac{15a}{15} = \frac{15}{15}$$
$$a = 1$$

Sometimes you are given an equation with two variables and asked to **solve for one variable in terms of the other**. This means that you must isolate the variable for which you are solving on one side of the equation and put everything else on the other side. In other words, when you're done, you'll have x (or whatever the variable is) on one side of the equation and an expression on the other side.

Solve $7x + 2y = 3x + 10y - 16$ for x in terms of y.

Since you want to isolate x on one side of the equation, begin by subtracting $2y$ from both sides.

$$7x + 2y - 2y = 3x + 10y - 16 - 2y$$
$$7x = 3x + 8y - 16$$

Then, subtract $3x$ from both sides to get all the x's on one side of the equation.

$$7x - 3x = 3x + 8y - 16 - 3x$$
$$4x = 8y - 16$$

Finally, divide both sides by 4 to isolate x.

$$\frac{4x}{4} = \frac{8y - 16}{4}$$
$$x = 2y - 4$$

Exercise

   vii $5a - 6 = -11$

   viii. $6y + 3 = y + 38$

   ix. $18 = -6x + 4(3x - 3)$

   x.   If $5a = b$, what is a in terms of b?

   xi   If $y \neq 0$ and $2xy = 8y$, what is x?

Substitution

If a problem gives you the value for a variable, just plug the value into the equation and solve. Make sure that you follow the rules of PEMDAS and are careful with your calculations.

If $x = 15$ and $y = 10$, what is the value of $4x(x - y)$?

Plug 15 in for x and 10 in for y.
$$4(15)(15 - 10) =$$

Then solve.
$$(60)(5) = 300$$

Picking Numbers on Algebra Problems

By now you should be familiar with Kaplan's backdoor method of **picking numbers**. You should remember that the picking numbers strategy is particularly helpful on algebra problems.

Some typical questions that can be solved by picking numbers are:
- Age stated in terms of variables
- Remainder problems
- Percentages or fractions of variables
- Even/odd variables calculations
- Questions with algebraic expressions as answers

We'd like to add one more category to this list: algebraic equations that you'd rather not solve the normal way. For instance, take a look at the following fairly nasty algebra question.

EXAMPLE 1

1. If $r = 3s$, $s = 5t$, $t = 2u$, and $u \neq 0$, then $\dfrac{rst}{u^3} =$
    (A) 60
    (B) 50
    (C) 300
    (D) 600

Now you could use the method of substitution that we just discussed, or you could substitute your own numbers for the variables in this question—in other words, you could pick numbers. The trick is knowing where to begin picking.

Here, because all the other variables build upon u, you can begin by picking an easy number for u, such as 2.

If $u = 2$, then $t = 2 \times 2 = 4$, so $s = 5 \times 4 = 20$, and $r = 3 \times 20 = 60$.

Thus, $\dfrac{rst}{u^3} = \dfrac{60 \times 20 \times 4}{2 \times 2 \times 2} = 30 \times 10 \times 2 = 600$. So the answer here is (D).

Of course, if you wanted to solve this problem by substitution, your work would look something like this:

$$t = 2u,$$
$$s = 5t = 5 \times 2u = 10u,$$
$$r = 3s = 3 \times 10u = 30u,$$
$$\text{so } \frac{rst}{u^3} = \frac{30\cancel{u} \times 10\cancel{u} \times 2\cancel{u}}{\cancel{u} \times \cancel{u} \times \cancel{u}} = 600.$$

Whichever method you prefer is fine by us.

Backsolving on Algebra Problems

Likewise, you can also rely on backsolving when you have a straightforward algebra equation with numbers in the answer choices that you can plug back into the equation. Once again, if your algebra skills are top-notch, you'll probably find it quicker to solve the problem the ordinary way. But still, it's nice to know that there are other ways to crack an algebra question when you are feeling the least bit confused about the algebra. Take a look at what we mean.

EXAMPLE 2

2. If $(6x)^2 = 324$, then $x =$

(A) 3
(B) 4
(C) 6
(D) 9

Here you could solve for x, or you could just try out the answer choices, starting with one of the choices in the middle, such as (B), $x = 4$. $(6 \times 4)^2 = (24)^2 = 576$, which is too large, so the answer has to be (A). But we'll go ahead and prove it: $(6 \times 3)^2 = (18)^2 = 324$. Voila!

Inequalities

Solve **inequalities** like you would any other equation. Isolate the variable that you are solving for on one side of the equation and everything else on the other side of the equation.

$$4a + 6 > 2a + 10$$
$$4a - 2a > 10 - 6$$
$$2a > 4$$
$$a > 2$$

The only difference here is that instead of finding a specific value for *a*, you get a range of values for *a*. The rest of the math is the same.

There is, however, one <u>crucial</u> difference between solving equations and inequalities. **When you multiply or divide an inequality by a <u>negative</u> number, you must change the direction of the sign.**

$$-5a > 10$$
$$a < -2$$

If this seems confusing, think about the logic. You're told that −5 times something is greater than 10. This is where your knowledge of positives and negatives comes into play. You know that negative × positive = negative and negative × negative = positive. Since −5 is negative and 10 is positive, −5 has to be multiplied by something negative to get a positive product. Therefore *a* has to be *less* than −2, not *greater* than it. If $a > -2$, then any value for *a* that is greater than −2 should make −5*a* less than 10. Say *a* is 20, −5*a* would be −100, which is certainly *not* greater than 10.

The point here is that, while it's a good idea to memorize that you need to flip the sign if you multiply or divide by a negative, the math makes sense if you think about it.

Exercise

xii.   Solve for *y* in each of the following inequalities.

$$y + 2 > 10$$
$$10 + 2a - 3 < 4 - a$$
$$6y < -20 + y$$
$$18 - 6y > 12$$
$$3(y + 10) - 4 > 2 + 5(2y - 3)$$

ALGEBRA WORD PROBLEMS

We have already covered our basic approach to handling word problems in the last chapter, and our basic techniques for translating English to math are exactly the same whether the word problem classifies as an algebra problem, an arithmetic problem, or some cross between the two.

But here are a few additional pointers that may help you to deal in particular with algebra word problems on the ASVAB:

1. Read through the whole question. Do this to get a sense of what's going on. You want to know the basic situation described, the type of information you've been given, and—most important of all—what exactly you are being asked.

2. Identify the different variables or unknowns and label them. For example, if the problem discusses Charlie's and Veronica's warts, you may wish to use "c" to represent Charlie's warts and "v" to represent Veronica's warts. Notice that we didn't use "x" and "y." If we had, we might later forget whether x represented Charlie's warts or Veronica's.

3. Translate the problem into math. This usually entails rewriting the English sentences into equations or statements. The sentence "Veronica has four fewer warts than Charlie has" would become: $v = c - 4$. Notice that the math terms are not in the same order as the English terms in the sentence. When you translate, you are translating the ideas. The idea here is "four fewer warts than Charlie." That means $c - 4$, not $4 - c$!

4. Tackle the math. Solve the equations. Be careful as you crunch the numbers. Make sure you've determined the value that the question is asking you for.

5. Check your work, if you have time.

Now you can try these pointers out on the following example.

EXAMPLE 3

3. On four successive days, a farmer picks exactly twice as many apples each day as on the previous day. If over the course of the four days he picks a total of 12,000 apples, how many apples does he pick on the second of the four days?
    (A) 1,200
    (B) 1,600
    (C) 2,000
    (D) 2,400

If you like to backsolve, you could undoubtedly solve this problem that way, but this time we'll translate the English into math and solve. If you solve for the number of apples picked on the first day, you could double that amount to get the number picked on the second day. Let x represent the number of apples that the farmer picks on the first day. Then on the second, third, and fourth days, the farmer picks $2x$, $4x$, and $8x$ apples, respectively. Since he picks a total of 12,000 apples, $12,000 = x + 2x + 4x + 8x$, so $12,000 = 15x$, and $x = \dfrac{12,000}{15} = 800$ apples. But that's for the first day. On the second day, he picks twice as many: $800 \times 2 = 1,600$.

And trust us, algebra word problems on the ASVAB never get tougher than this example.

GEOMETRY REVIEW

You will definitely see some geometry on the Mathematical Knowledge section of the ASVAB. Like the rest of the math on the ASVAB, geometry questions range from straightforward to somewhat tricky. You can count on seeing questions that test your knowledge of line and angles, triangles, circles, and other assorted geometric figures. Additionally, you may see a bit of solid geometry.

You will be expected to know certain geometry formulas on the ASVAB. Never forget that backdoor strategies such as picking numbers and backsolving work equally well on geometry problems. Now let's begin that review.

Lines and Angles

Line Segments

Some of the most basic geometry problems on the ASVAB deal with line segments. A **line segment** is a piece of a line, and it has an exact measurable length. Questions will give you a segment divided into several pieces, give you the measurements of some of these pieces, and ask you for the measurement of a particular piece.

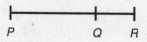

RULE TO REMEMBER

A straight angle contains 180°.

If $PR = 12$ and $QR = 4$, $PQ =$

$PQ = PR - QR$

$PQ = 12 - 4$

$PQ = 8$

The point exactly in the middle of a line segment, halfway between the endpoints, is called the **midpoint** of the line segment. To bisect means to cut in half, so the midpoint of a line segment bisects that line segment.

M is the midpoint of *AB*, so *AM* = *MB*.

Exercise

xiii. If points *A*, *D*, *B*, and *C* lie on a line in that order, *AB* = 8, *DC* = 16, and *D* is the midpoint of *AB*, then *AC* = ?

Angles

A **right angle** measures 90 degrees and is usually indicated in a diagram by a little box. The figure above is a right angle. Lines that intersect to form right angles are said to be **perpendicular.**

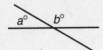

Angles that form a straight line add up to 180 degrees. In the figure above, *a* + *b* = **180.**

When two lines intersect, **adjacent angles are supplementary,** meaning they add up to 180 degrees. In the figure above, *a* + *b* = 180.

Angles around a point add up to 360 degrees. In the figure above,
$a + b + c + d + e = 360$.

When lines intersect, angles across the vertex from each other are called **vertical angles** and **are equal to each other.** Above, $a = c$ and $b = d$.

Exercise

In the following figures, find x:

   xiv.

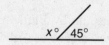

   xv.

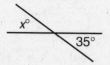

   xvi.

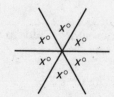

Parallel Lines

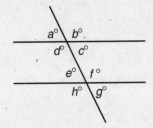

When parallel lines are crossed by another line:

- **Corresponding angles are equal (for example, $a = e$).**
- **Alternate interior angles are equal ($d = f$).**
- **Same side interior angles are supplementary ($c + f = 180$).**
- **All four acute angles are equal, as are all four obtuse angles.**

Triangles

Triangles in General

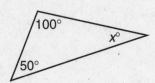

The three interior angles of any triangle **add up to 180°.** In this figure, $x + 50 + 100 = 180$, so $x = 30$.

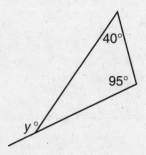

An exterior angle of a triangle is equal to the **sum of the remote interior angles.** In this figure, the exterior angle labeled $y°$ is equal to the sum of the remote angles: $y = 40 + 95 = 135$.

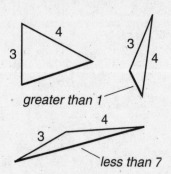

greater than 1

less than 7

The length of one side of a triangle must be **greater than the positive difference** and **less than the sum** of the lengths of the other two sides. For example, if it is given that the length of one side is 3 and the length of another side is 4, then you know that the length of the third side must be greater than $4 - 3 = 1$ and less than $4 + 3 = 7$.

Exercise

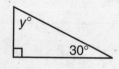

xvii. $y =$

xviii. If two sides of a triangle are 5 and 8, which of the following could be the length of its third side? (circle all that are possible)

$$3 \qquad 5 \qquad 9 \qquad 13 \qquad 15$$

Triangles—Area and Perimeter

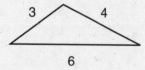

The **perimeter** of a triangle is the sum of the lengths of its sides.

The **perimeter** of the triangle in the figure above is:
$$3 + 4 + 6 = 13$$

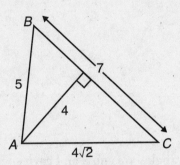

Area of triangle $= \frac{1}{2}$(base)(height)

The height is the perpendicular distance between the side that's chosen as the base and the opposite vertex. In this triangle, 4 is the height when the 7 is chosen as the base.

$$\text{Area} = \frac{1}{2}\,bh = \frac{1}{2}(7)(4) = 14$$

Exercise

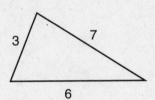

xix.   Perimeter =

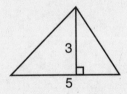

xx.   Area =

Similar Triangles

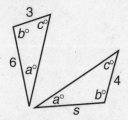

Similar triangles have the same shape: **corresponding angles are equal and corresponding sides are proportional**. These triangles are similar because they have the same angles. The 3 corresponds to the 4 and the 6 corresponds to the *s*.

$$\frac{3}{4} = \frac{6}{s}$$
$$3s = 24$$
$$s = 8$$

Special Triangles

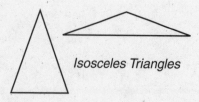

Isosceles Triangles

An isosceles triangle is a triangle that has **two equal sides**. Not only are two sides equal, but the angles opposite the equal sides, called base angles, are also equal.

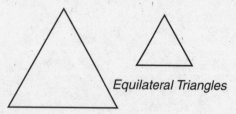

Equilateral Triangles

Equilateral triangles are triangles in which **all three sides are equal**. Since all the sides are equal, all the angles are also equal. All three angles in an equilateral triangle measure 60 degrees, regardless of the lengths of sides.

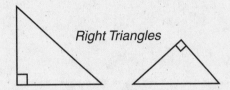

A right triangle is a triangle with a **right angle**. Every right triangle has exactly two acute angles. The sides opposite the acute angles are called the **legs**. The side opposite the right angle is called the hypotenuse. Since it's opposite the largest angle, the hypotenuse is the longest side of a right triangle.

Right Triangles

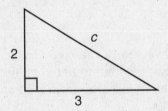

The Pythagorean Theorem:

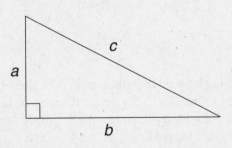

$$a^2 + b^2 = c^2$$

Note: *a* and *b* are the perpendicular sides, or *legs*, of a right triangle, and *c* is the longest side, or *hypotenuse*, of the triangle.

If one leg is 2 and the other leg is 3, then:

$$2^2 + 3^2 = c^2$$

$$c^2 = 4 + 9$$

$$c = \sqrt{13}$$

Exercise

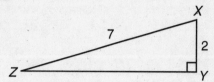

xxi. In right triangle *XYZ*, what is the length of *YZ*?

Pythagorean "Triplets"

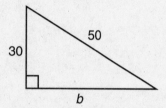

If a right triangle's leg-to-leg ratio is 3 : 4, or if the leg-to-hypotenuse ratio is 3 : 5 or 4 : 5, it's a 3-4-5 triangle and you don't need to use the Pythagorean theorem to find the third side. Just figure out what multiple of 3-4-5 it is. In this right triangle, one leg is 30 and the hypotenuse is 50. This is 10 times 3-4-5. The other leg is 40.

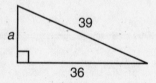

If a right triangle's leg-to-leg ratio is 5 : 12, or if the leg-to-hypotenuse ratio is 5 : 13 or 12 : 13, then it's a **5-12-13 triangle** and you don't need to use the Pythagorean theorem to find the third side. Just figure out what multiple of 5-12-13 it is. Here, one leg is 36 and the hypotenuse is 39. This is 3 times 5-12-13. The other leg is 15.

Exercise

Find the missing side in each of the following triangles:

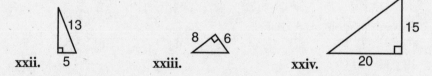

Quadrilaterals

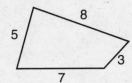

The **perimeter** of a polygon is the sum of the lengths of its sides.

The perimeter of the quadrilateral in the figure above is:
$5 + 8 + 3 + 7 = 23$

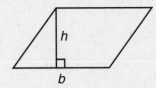

A parallelogram is a quadrilateral with two sets of parallel sides. Opposite sides are equal, as are opposite angles. The formula for the area of a parallelogram is:

Area = (base)(height)

In the diagram above, h = height and b = base, so Area = bh

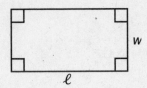

A **rectangle** is a parallelogram containing four right angles. Opposite sides are equal. The formula for the area of a rectangle is:

Area = (length)(width)

In the above diagram above, ℓ = length and w = width, so area = ℓw.

Perimeter = $2(\ell + w)$

A **square** is a rectangle with four equal sides.
The formula for the area of a square is:

Area = (side)^2

In the diagram above, s = the length of a side, so Area = s^2.

Perimeter = 4s

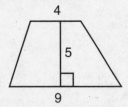

A **trapezoid** is a quadrilateral with one pair of parallel sides. The two parallel sides of a trapezoid are called the bases.

The formula for the area of a trapezoid is:

Area = $\frac{1}{2}$ (sum of the lengths of the bases)(height)

In the diagram above, the area of the trapezoid is $\frac{1}{2}$ (4 + 9)(5) = 32.5

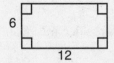

If two polygons are similar, then corresponding angles are equal and corresponding sides are in proportion.

In the figures above, the two rectangles are similar because all the angles are right angles, and each side of the larger rectangle is $1\frac{1}{2}$ times the corresponding side of the smaller rectangle.

Exercise

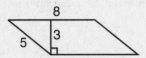

xxv. What is the area of the parallelogram above?

xxvi. What is the area of the trapezoid above?

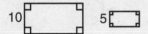

xxvii. The rectangles above are similar. If the area of the larger rectangle is 300, what is the area of the smaller rectangle?

Circles

A **circle** is a figure with each point an equal distance from its center. In the diagram, *O* is the center of the circle.

The **radius** of a circle is the straight line distance from its center to any point on the circle. All radii of one circle have equal lengths. In the figure above, *OA* is a radius of circle *O*.

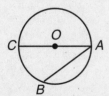

A **chord** is a line segment that connects any two points on a circle. Segments *AB* and *AC* are both chords. The largest chord that may be drawn in a circle will be a diameter of that circle.

A **diameter** of a circle is a chord that passes through the circle's center. All diameters are the same length and are equal to twice the radius. In the figure above, *AC* is a diameter of circle *O*.

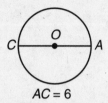

$$AC = 6$$

The **circumference** of a circle is the distance around it. It is equal to πd, or $2\pi r$. In this example: Circumference $= \pi d = 6\pi$

The **area** of a circle equals π times the square of the radius, or πr^2. In this example, since *AC* is the diameter, $r = \frac{6}{2} = 3$, and:

$$\text{Area} = \pi r^2 = \pi(3^2) = 9\pi$$

Exercise

xxviii. Radius = 3

Diameter =

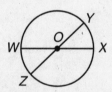

xxix. *OZ* = 4

WX =

OX =

xxx. Radius = 8

Circumference =

xxxi. Area = 16π

Radius =

Solid Geometry

The only solid geometry formulas that you are expected to know for the ASVAB concern rectangular solids, or boxes. If you are asked about any other solid on the ASVAB, the question will provide the relevant formula. Here are the two formulas that you may need to know:

Volume of a Rectangular Solid or Box = $\ell \times w \times h$

Surface Area of a Rectangular Solid or Box = $2\ell w + 2wh + 2\ell h$

Note: ℓ = length, w = width, h = height

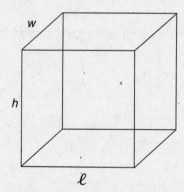

Exercise

xxxii. The length of an edge of a cube is 5. What is the volume of the cube?

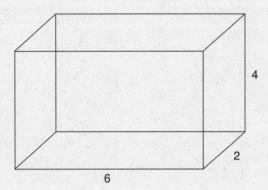

xxxiii. What is the surface area of the rectangular solid pictured above?

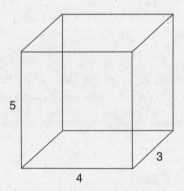

xxxiv. What is the volume of the rectangular solid pictured above?

xxxv. Find the height of a rectangular solid whose width is 7, whose length is 9, and whose volume is 504.

ANSWERS TO EXERCISES

i. **B** $(11 + 3x) - (5 - 2x) =$
$11 + 3x - 5 + 2x =$
$11 - 5 + 3x + 2x =$
$6 + 5x$

ii. $-4a - b$

iii. $-a$

iv. $3y$

v. $n^2 - 3n - 18$

vi. $x^2 + x - 6 = (x + 3)(x - 2)$

vii. $a = -1$

viii. $y = 7$

ix. $x = 5$

x. $a = \dfrac{b}{5}$

xi. $x = 4$

xii. $y > 8$
$a < -1$
$y < -4$
$y < 1$
$y < \dfrac{39}{7}$

xiii. $AC = 20$

xiv. $x = 135$

xv. $x = 35$

xvi. $x = 60$

xvii. $y = 60$

xviii. 5, 9 (The third side must be greater than 3 and less than 13.)

xix. 16

xx. $\dfrac{15}{2}$

xxi. $\sqrt{45}$ or $3\sqrt{5}$

xxii. 12

xxiii. 10

xxiv. 25

xxv. 24

xxvi. 24

xxvii. 75

xxviii. Diameter = 6

xxix. $WX = 8, OX = 4$

xxx. Circumference = 16π

xxxi. Radius = 4

xxxii. Volume = $5 \times 5 \times 5 = 125$

xxxiii. Surface area = $2(2 \times 4) + 2(2 \times 6) + 2(4 \times 6) = 88$

xxxiv. Volume = $3 \times 4 \times 5 = 60$

xxxv. Height = $\dfrac{504}{7 \times 9} = 8$

MATHEMATICS KNOWLEDGE PRACTICE SET

1. If the average of 5 consecutive odd numbers is 11, then the largest number is

   (A) 17
   (B) 15
   (C) 13
   (D) 11

2. The price of a newspaper rises from 5 cents to 15 cents. What is the percent increase in price?

   (A) 75%
   (B) 150%
   (C) 200%
   (D) 300%

3. If $x = \sqrt{3}$, $y = 2$, and $z = \frac{1}{2}$, then $x^2 - 5yz + y^2 =$

   (A) 1
   (B) 2
   (C) 4
   (D) 7

4. $\dfrac{15 \times 7 \times 3}{9 \times 5 \times 2} =$

   (A) $\dfrac{2}{7}$
   (B) $3\dfrac{1}{2}$
   (C) 7
   (D) $7\dfrac{1}{2}$

5. $(3d - 7) - (5 - 2d) =$

   (A) $d - 12$
   (B) $5d - 2$
   (C) $5d + 12$
   (D) $5d - 12$

6. Jim can run at a rate of 1 mile per 5 minutes and Rebecca can run at a rate of 1 mile per 8 minutes. If they both start at Point A at the same time and run in the same direction at their respective rates, how far ahead will Jim be from Rebecca in 40 minutes?

   (A) 3 miles
   (B) 5 miles
   (C) 8 miles
   (D) 15 miles

7. 64, 16, 4, 1. . .

   The next term in the above sequence is

   (A) $\dfrac{1}{4}$
   (B) 0
   (C) $-\dfrac{1}{4}$
   (D) -4

8. If the sales tax on the purchase of a certain item is 8% of the sticker price, and the sales tax comes to $120, what is the sticker price of the item?

   (A) $11.60
   (B) $1,000
   (C) $1,160
   (D) $1,500

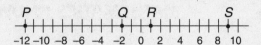

9. If the perimeter of the above square is 36, what is the circumference of the circle?

   (A) 6π
   (B) 9π
   (C) 12π
   (D) 18π

10. If x is an integer, which of the following expressions is always even?

   (A) $2x + 1$
   (B) $3x + 2$
   (C) $5x + 3$
   (D) $6x + 4$

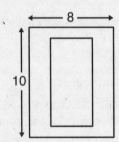

11. What is the area of the frame in the above diagram if the inside picture has a length of 8 and a width of 4?

   (A) 16
   (B) 24
   (C) 48
   (D) 56

12. What is the distance from the midpoint of $\overline{PQ}$ to the midpoint of $\overline{RS}$?

   (A) 12
   (B) 14
   (C) 16
   (D) 18

13. For all a, $(3a + 4)(3a - 4)$

   (A) $6a$
   (B) $3a^2 - 4$
   (C) $9a^2 - 4$
   (D) $9a^2 - 16$

14. If $s - t = 5$ what is the value of $3s - 3t + 3$?

   (A) 11
   (B) 12
   (C) 15
   (D) 18

15. Five less than 3 times a certain number is equal to the original number plus 7. What is the original number?

   (A) 2
   (B) 6
   (C) 11
   (D) 12

16. If $abc \neq 0$, then $\dfrac{a^2bc + ab^2c + abc^2}{abc} =$

   (A) $a + b + c$
   (B) abc
   (C) $a^3b^3c^3$
   (D) $a^2 + b^2 + c^2$

17. What is the complete factorization of $2x + 3x^2 + x^3$?

    (A) $x(x - 2)(x + 3)$
    (B) $x(x - 1)(x + 2)$
    (C) $x(x + 1)(x + 2)$
    (D) $x(x + 2)(x + 3)$

18. $\left(\sqrt{7}\right)^3 =$

    (A) 7
    (B) 14
    (C) $7\sqrt{7}$
    (D) $14\sqrt{7}$

19. $[(12 - 11) - (10 - 9)] - [(12 - 11 - 10) - 9] =$

    (A) -20
    (B) 0
    (C) 16
    (D) 18

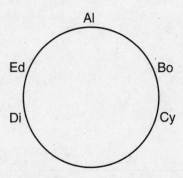

20. Five people are seated around a table as shown above. If 52 cards are dealt to the five people beginning with Al and continuing clockwise, who gets the last card?

    (A) Bo
    (B) Cy
    (C) Di
    (D) Ed

21. In quadrilateral *DEFG*, the degree measures of the four angles are in the ratio of 2:3:5:6. What is the difference in the degree measures between the largest and the smallest angles?

    (A) 135
    (B) 112.5
    (C) 90
    (D) 75

22. If $\frac{c}{d} = 3$ and $d = 1$, then $3c + d =$

    (A) 4
    (B) 7
    (C) 9
    (D) 10

23. If $3^{n-7} = 81$, then $n =$

    (A) 4
    (B) 9
    (C) 11
    (D) 18

24. If $3 = \frac{9b}{a}$, what is $\frac{a}{b}$ equal to?

    (A) $\frac{1}{3}$
    (B) 3
    (C) 9
    (D) 27

25. What is the volume of a cube with a surface area of 96?

    (A) 16
    (B) 27
    (C) 48
    (D) 64

ANSWER KEY

1. B	10. D	18. C
2. C	11. C	19. D
3. B	12. A	20. A
4. B	13. D	21. C
5. D	14. D	22. D
6. A	15. B	23. C
7. A	16. A	24. B
8. D	17. C	25. D
9. B		

ANSWERS AND EXPLANATIONS FOR
MATHEMATICS KNOWLEDGE PRACTICE SET

1. B.

One trick for dealing with consecutive numbers is to realize that the middle number in a group of consecutive numbers is equal to the average of the numbers. So of the five consecutive odd numbers, the middle or third number is 11, the fourth number is 13, and the fifth or final number is 15.

2. C

This question can be a bit tricky, but not if you know that percent increase = $\dfrac{\text{change}}{\text{original number}} \times 100\%$, so in this case, the percent increase equals $\dfrac{10}{5} \times 100\%$, or 200%.

3. B

You are given values for all the variables, so just plug those values into the equation you are given. $x^2 - 5yz + y^2 = (\sqrt{3})^2 - 5(2)\left(\dfrac{1}{2}\right) + (2)^2 = 3 - 5 + 4 = 2.$

4. B

$$\frac{15 \times 7 \times 3}{9 \times 5 \times 2} = \frac{\cancel{5} \times \cancel{3} \times 7 \times \cancel{3}}{\cancel{3} \times \cancel{3} \times \cancel{5} \times 2} = \frac{7}{2} = 3\frac{1}{2}$$

5. D

Eliminate the parentheses by distributing the minus operation over the second set of parentheses: $(3d - 7) - (5 - 2d) = 3d - 7 - 5 - (-2d) = 3d - 7 - 5 + 2d$. Now combine like terms and perform the additions and subtractions: $3d + 2d - 7 - 5 = 5d - 12$.

6. A

Jim runs 1 mile per 5 minutes, so in 40 minutes he will run 8 miles. Rebecca runs 1 mile per 8 minutes, so in 40 minutes she will run 5 miles. Thus, if they start out at the same point and run in the same direction, after 40 minutes Jim will be $8 - 5 = 3$ miles ahead of Rebecca.

7. A

Determine the relationship between the numbers in this sequence. 64 is 4 times 16, which is 4 times 4, which is 4 times 1. In other words, every term in the sequence is $\dfrac{1}{4}$ of the preceding term, so the next term in the sequence is $\dfrac{1}{4} \times 1$, or $\dfrac{1}{4}$.

8. D

The sales tax is 8% of the sticker price, so if the sales tax is \$120, and we call the sticker price x, then $\$120 = 0.08x$. So $x = \dfrac{\$120}{0.08} = \dfrac{\$12,000}{8} = \$1,500.$

9. B

If the perimeter of the square is 36, then each of the four sides equals 9. The side of the square is the same length as the diameter of the circle, so if the diameter of the circle is 9, the circumference is 9π.

10. D

You could either apply the rules of odds and evens, or you could pick even and odd numbers for x to see which answer choice always works. For instance if x is an odd integer, such as 1, then (A) and (B) add up to odd numbers, so they are out. Now if you pick an even number for x such as 2, then (C) is out because $5x + 3 = 5(2) + 3 = 13$, which is also odd. But choice (D) works in both cases. This only makes sense according to the rule of odds and evens, because $6x$ will always be even, since 6 is even and an even number times any number is even. So $6x + 4$ must be even because an even number plus an even number is always even.

11. C

The area of the frame is the area of the larger rectangle minus the area of the smaller rectangle, or $(8 \times 10) - (4 \times 8) = 80 - 32 = 48$.

12. A

To find the midpoint of a segment on the number line you can add the endpoints and the divide the sum by 2. So the midpoint of PQ is $\frac{(-12) + (-2)}{2} = \frac{-14}{2} = -7$. The midpoint of RS is $\frac{1 + 9}{2} = \frac{10}{2} = 5$. Thus the distance between the two points is the positive difference between their coordinates, or $5 - (-7) = 12$.

13. D

Apply FOIL:

$(3a + 4)(3a - 4) =$
$(3a)(3a) + (3a)(-4) + (3a)(4) + (4)(-4) =$
$9a^2 - 12a + 12a - 16 =$
$9a^2 - 16$

14. D

If $s - t = 5$, then if you multiply both sides by 3, you get $3s - 3t = 15$. Thus $3s - 3t + 3 = 15 + 3 = 18$.

15. B

Translate the English into math bit by bit. "Five less than 3 times a certain number" becomes "$3x - 5$;" "is equal to the original number plus 7" becomes "$= x + 7$." So altogether you have $3x - 5 = x + 7$.

Now solve for x:

$$3x - 5 = x + 7$$
$$3x - x = 7 + 5$$
$$2x = 12$$
$$x = 6$$

16. A

Every term in the fraction is a multiple of abc, so you can reduce accordingly:

$$\frac{a^2bc + ab^2c + abc^2}{abc} = \frac{a \times \cancel{abc}}{\cancel{abc}} + \frac{b \times \cancel{abc}}{\cancel{abc}} + \frac{c \times \cancel{abc}}{\cancel{abc}} = a + b + c$$

17. C

First factor out an x from each term, and then rearrange the terms and factor what's left:

$$2x + 3x^2 + x^3 = x(2 + 3x + x^2)$$
$$= x(x^2 + 3x + 2)$$
$$= x(x + 1)(x + 2)$$

18. C

When it comes to confusing exponents, the rule is: when in doubt, expand it out, like so:

$$(\sqrt{7})^3 = (\sqrt{7})(\sqrt{7})(\sqrt{7}) = 7(\sqrt{7}).$$

19. D

Follow PEMDAS:

$$[(12 - 11) - (10 - 9)] - [(12 - 11 - 10) - 9]$$
$$= [1 - 1] - [-9 - 9]$$
$$= 0 - (-18)$$
$$= 18$$

20. A

Five people are being dealt 52 cards, so we will divide 52 by 5. $52 \div 5 = 10$ remainder 2. Since we are starting with Al, after dealing 5 cards we will be ready to start with Al again. So after 50 cards, we will be ready to start with Al again. Al gets the 51st card and Bo gets the 52nd card, choice (A).

21. **C**

The sum of the degree measures of the angles of a quadrilateral is 360. Since the angles of quadrilateral *DEFG* are in a ratio of 2 : 3 : 5 : 6, you could set up an equation where x represents one part of the ratio:

$$2x + 3x + 5x + 6x = 360$$
$$6x = 360$$
$$x = 22.5$$

Now find the difference on the degree measures of the largest and smallest angles:

$$6x - 2x = 4x = 4(22.5) = 90$$

22. **D**

Since we told the value of d, we can plug it into the equation $\frac{c}{d} = 3$ to find the value of c. We are told that $d = 1$, so $\frac{c}{d} = 3$ can be rewritten as $\frac{c}{1} = 3$. Since $\frac{c}{1}$ is the same as c, we can rewrite the equation as $c = 3$. Now we can plug in the values of c and d into the expression:

$3(3) + 1 = 10$.

23. **C**

$81 = 3 \times 3 \times 3 \times 3 = 3^4$, so $3^{n-7} = 3^4$. Since the exponents are equivalent, that means $n - 7 = 4$, so $n = 7 + 4 = 11$, choice (C).

24. **B**

Begin by putting the numbers on one side of the equation:

$$3 = \frac{9b}{a}, \text{ so } \frac{b}{a} = \frac{3}{9} = \frac{1}{3}$$

Now you can flip the fractions on both sides of the equation (yes, you are allowed to do that):

$$\frac{b}{a} = \frac{1}{3}, \text{ so } \frac{a}{b} = \frac{3}{1} = 3$$

25. **D**

If the surface area of a cube is 96, that means that each of the six faces of the cube has an area one-sixth of 96, in other words, area of $a = \frac{96}{6} = 16$. And if each square face of the cube has an area of 16, then each edge of the cube has a length of $\sqrt{16}$, or 4. Thus the volume of the cube is $(\text{edge})^3 = 4^3 = 64$.

Part Three

REVIEW OF TECHNICAL ASVAB SUBTESTS

CHAPTER SEVEN

General Science

INTRODUCTION

The General Science section of the ASVAB covers a grab bag of topics that you may or may not have studied in high school or elsewhere. You'll be answering 25 questions in 11 minutes, so it's a good idea to know what to expect. Although the very breadth of topics covered can be somewhat intimidating—everything from health science and biology to astronomy, meteorology, geology, and even a bit of chemistry and physics—your understanding of these topics does not have to run very deep. For instance, in the area of chemistry you should have a rudimentary understanding of the composition of an atom and know a few things about the elements on the Periodic Table and some related terms and concepts. But you would never be expected to know how to balance a chemical equation, diagram a molecule, or anything that complicated.

BREADTH, NOT DEPTH

The General Science section of the ASVAB covers a lot of science topics, but you will never be expected to know too much about any one topic.

In fact, General Science questions on the ASVAB tend to emphasize pragmatic knowledge, the kinds of facts about the physical world that any military person would benefit from knowing. This is one reason why the single most common type of question on the General Science section asks about human nutrition. You will also be expected to know certain science terminology, everything from parts of the human body to the classification of living things and the geological time scale. But still and all, it's not that bad.

This review will cover the following broad areas:

- Life Science (health, nutrition, and biology)
- Earth Science (geology, meteorology, and astronomy)
- Physical Science (elementary physics and chemistry)

Let's get started.

LIFE SCIENCE

Health and Nutrition

Although nutritionists themselves don't always agree about what constitutes a healthy diet, certain facts are clear. A healthy diet requires a combination of protein, carbohydrates, fat, minerals, vitamins, and fiber. Proteins, carbohydrates, and fats (macronutrients) are necessary to provide energy. Minerals and vitamins (micronutrients), along with fiber, are necessary to maintain proper bodily functions.

Proteins are necessary for the body's maintenance, growth, and repair. Animal proteins are contained in meat, fish, eggs, and cheese. Vegetable proteins are found in peas, beans, nuts, and some grains.

Carbohydrates include both starches and sugars. They are major sources of energy for the body's metabolism. Starches are found in bread, cereal, rice, potatoes, and pasta. Sugars are found in fruits, cane sugar, and beets.

Fats also provide energy for metabolism. There are three types of fats: saturated, monounsaturated, and polyunsaturated. Those wishing to reduce the bad cholesterol levels in their blood should avoid saturated fats, although monounsaturated and polyunsaturated fats can actually decrease levels of bad cholesterol. Sources of saturated fats include meats, shellfish, eggs, milk, and milk products. Sources of monounsaturated fats include olives and olive oil, grapeseed oil, almonds, cashews, brazil nuts, and avocados. Sources of polyunsaturated fats include corn oil, flaxseed oil, pumpkinseed oil, safflower oil, soybean oil, and sunflower oil.

Minerals in small quantities are needed for a balanced diet. Some necessary minerals are iron, zinc, calcium, magnesium, and sodium chloride (salt).

Vitamins also help to regulate metabolism. Below is a table of the vitamins and minerals necessary to maintain good health.

Vitamin or Mineral	Sources	Results of Deficiency
A	Fish and liver, green and yellow fruits and vegetables	Night blindness, skin irritations, bad breath, depression, insomnia
B_1	Wheat germ, whole grain cereals, poultry, legumes, eggs, pasta	Loss of appetite, beriberi
B_2	Liver, milk, eggs, green vegetables, whole grains	Weakness, skin infections
B_{12}	Meat, eggs, dairy products, fish	Anemia
C	Citrus fruits, tomatoes, vegetables, strawberries	Scurvy, bleeding gums
D	Milk, eggs, cheese, fish	Rickets, brittle bones
E	Vegetable oils, whole grains, green vegetables, nuts and seeds	Sterility
K	Green vegetables, vegetable oils, pork, liver, egg yolks	Excessive bleeding, osteoporosis
Folic Acid	Beans, grains, green vegetables, organ meats	Sore tongue; birth defects
Calcium	Dairy foods, seafood, green vegetables, sea vegetables	Fragile bones, numbness
Chromium	Apples, liver, cheese, meat, whole grains, dried beans	Lack of energy, myopia
Copper	Nuts, beans, organ meats, raisins, seafood, legumes, green vegetables	Depression, fractures and bone deformities, weakness
Iron	Liver, eggs, clams, fish, meat, poultry, dark green leafy vegetables	Anemia, breathing difficulties, constipation
Magnesium	Dairy products, fish, meat, seafood	Aching muscles, anxiety, broken nails, disorientation
Zinc	Fish, meats, poultry, seafood, whole grains, nuts, beef liver, egg yolks, lima beans, mushrooms	Acne, brittle nails, eczema, fatigue, poor appetite

Fiber passes through the body unchanged but is part of a healthy diet. Fiber provides bulk, which allows the large intestine to carry away waste matter. Good sources of dietary fiber include leafy green vegetables, carrots, turnips, peas, beans, and potatoes, as well as raw and cooked fruits, cereals, and whole-grain foods.

KNOW WHAT TO EXPECT

You can expect to see at least one or two nutrition questions on the ASVAB, so learn your nutrition facts.

Water is also essential for survival. The body loses approximately four pints of water each day, which must be replenished. Most foods contain water, facilitating proper water maintenance.

The Human Body

As with any organism, the human body is composed of several systems that work together to absorb and distribute nutrients throughout the body, remove wastes, respond to stimuli in the environment, and reproduce. We'll review these systems separately, with a little comparative physiology thrown into the mix.

The Skeleton and Muscles

The skeleton and muscles are responsible for holding the body together. Without a skeleton you would be just a mass of organs, veins, and skin. That's totally gross. Such an arrangement might work for an octopus, but it's a no-go for a self-respecting land mammal. Some organisms, namely **arthropods** (a huge animal phylum that includes insects, spiders, and crustaceans), have **exoskeletons**, or external skeletons. **Vertebrate** animals, including man, have internal skeletons, or **endoskeletons**.

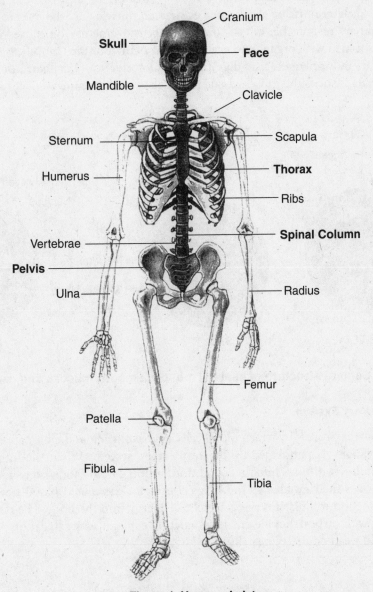

Figure 1. Human skeleton

The human skeleton contains both **bone** and **cartilage**. Bones provide the primary support, while cartilage, which is more flexible, is found at the end of all bones, at the joints, in the nose, and in the ears. Wiggle your nose and you will feel cartilage at the end of it. Bones not only provide structural support for the body and protect vital organs, but they also produce blood cells and store minerals such as calcium. Attaching the skeleton to muscles are **tendons**, tough fibrous cords made of connective tissue. And connecting bones to bones at joints such as the elbow, knee, fingers, and vertebral column are **ligaments**, which are also made of connective tissue.

Most muscles work in conjunction with the skeleton to support the body and allow movement. **Skeletal** muscles, also known as **striated** muscles, are the muscles attached to the skeleton that are responsible for all the voluntary movements you make. **Smooth** muscle, which is associated with organs and is also known as **involuntary** muscle, is the muscle used in involuntary movements such as digestion and reproduction. **Cardiac** muscle, which is only found in heart tissue is the muscle tissue that makes up the heart.

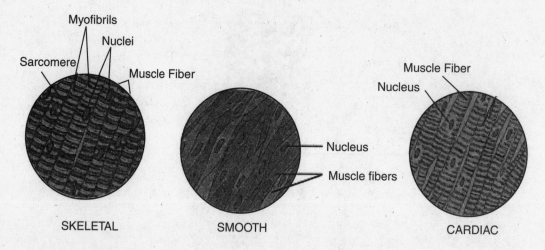

Figure 2. General structure of skeletal muscle, smooth muscle, and cardiac muscle

The Respiratory System

Respiration—the process by which blood cells absorb **oxygen** and eliminate **carbon dioxide** and **water vapor**—is performed by the **respiratory system**. When the lungs fill with air, oxygen from the air diffuses into the blood, and carbon dioxide and water vapor diffuses into the air, which is then exhaled as the lungs contract. Oxygenated blood flows through the body, allowing intracellular nutrients to release energy into the body. The removal of water vapor along with carbon dioxide during exhalation explains why exhalation produces visible steam in cold weather. Pretty neat, huh?

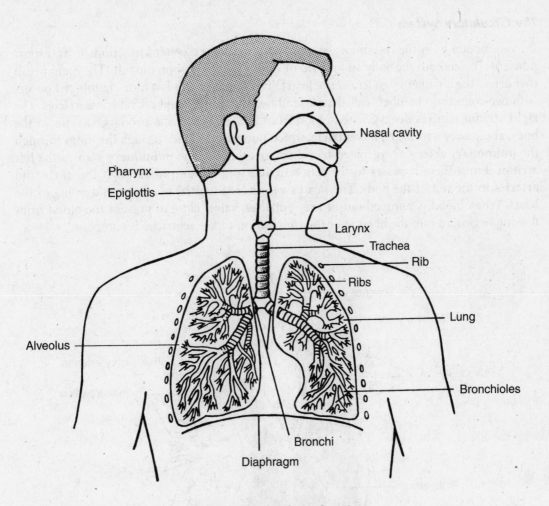

Pharynx

Epiglottis

Nasal cavity

Larynx

Trachea

Rib

Ribs

Lung

Alveolus

Bronchioles

Bronchi

Diaphragm

Figure 3. The respiratory system

When air enters through the **nose**, it passes through the **nasal cavity**, which filters, moistens, and warms air, and then through the **pharynx**, which further filters the air and aids in protection against infection. The air then passes through the open **epiglottis**, which closes when swallowing to prevent food from going down the wrong pipe, and into the **trachea**, which further cleanses the air. The trachea branches into the **left and right bronchi**, which are two tubes that lead to the **lungs**. There the bronchi further subdivide into smaller tubes called **bronchioles**. Each bronchiole ends in a small sac called an **alveolus**. It is in the alveolus that oxygen from the air enters into the bloodstream via capillaries. The **diaphragm**, as every opera singer knows, is a system of muscles that allow the lungs to expand and contract, drawing air in and out.

The Circulatory System

In conjunction with the respiratory system, the **circulatory system** functions to transport nutrients throughout the body and get rid of wastes such as carbon dioxide. The main organ that drives the circulatory system is the **heart**. The human heart is a four-chambered pump, with two collecting chambers called **atria**, and two pumping chambers called **ventricles**. The **right atrium** receives deoxygenated blood from the **vena cava**, the two largest veins in the body, and passes it to the **right ventricle**, which pumps the blood through the lungs through the **pulmonary artery**. Oxygenated blood returns through the **pulmonary vein** to the **left atrium**. From there it passes to the **left ventricle** and is pumped through the **aorta** and **arteries** to the rest of the body. The heart's **valves** are essential to efficient pumping of the heart. When blood is pumped out of the ventricles, valves close to prevent the blood from flowing backward into the heart after the contraction of the ventricles is complete.

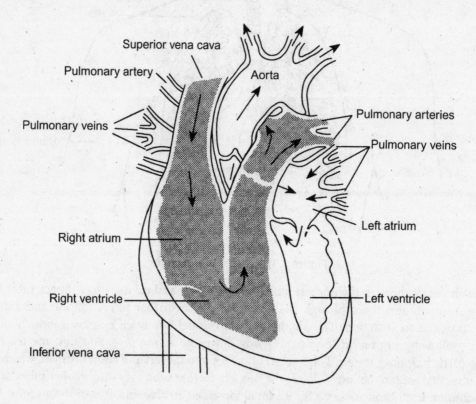

Figure 4. Human heart

The **arteries** carry blood from the heart to the tissues of the body. They repeatedly branch into smaller arteries (**arterioles**), which supply blood to the tissues via the capillaries. Arteries carry blood away from the heart, and for that reason are thick-walled, conducting oxygenated blood at high blood pressure. Only the pulmonary artery does not contain oxygenated blood, as it carries deoxygenated blood into the lungs.

Veins, on the other hand, carry blood back to the heart from the capillaries. Veins are relatively thin-walled, conduct blood at low pressure, and contain many valves to prevent backflow. Veins have no pulse and carry dark red, deoxygenated blood. The lone exception is the pulmonary vein, which carries freshly oxygenated blood from the lungs back into the heart.

Finally, **capillaries** are thin-walled vessels that are very small in diameter. Capillaries, not arteries or veins, permit exchange of materials between the blood and the body's cells (this is called **diffusion**).

Blood consists of **cells** suspended in **plasma**, the liquid component of blood. There are three types of cells found in blood: **red blood cells**, which are the oxygen-carrying cells; **white blood cells**, which fight infection by destroying foreign organisms; and **platelets**, which are cell fragments that allow blood to clot. All blood cells are created in the **bone marrow**, which is located in the center of bones.

Also note that blood comes in four different types: A, B, AB, and O. Type O is the **universal donor**, which means that type O blood can be given to anybody. Type AB is the **universal recipient**, which means that someone with type AB blood can receive any type of blood.

The Lymphatic System

The lymphatic system is a network of vessels and nodes that runs in parallel with the circulatory system. **Lymph vessels** follow the routes of blood vessels, collecting extracellular fluid (called **lymph**) and carrying it back into the circulatory system via the largest lymph vessel, called the **thoracic duct**, which sends the lymph back to the blood stream shortly before the blood enters the heart.

Another major function of the lymphatic system is to assist in immune surveillance. As the lymph moves through the lymphatic system, it passes through **lymph nodes**. The lymph nodes are bulges, found in the pelvic area, the neck, and the armpits, that contain **lymphocytes**, immune cells that help fight disease by filtering out bacteria, extracellular proteins, and cancerous cells. Because lymphocytes are so critical in fighting infections, lymph nodes often swell up when you are sick.

The Digestive and Excretory Systems

The digestive system is responsible for breaking down foods into material the body can use for energy and bodybuilding. The digestive tract is essentially a long and winding tube that begins at the mouth and ends at the anus.

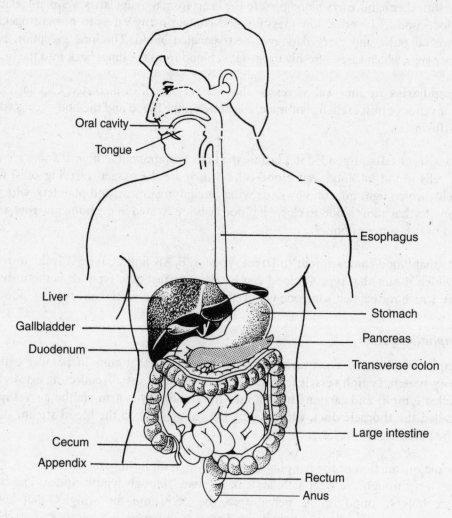

Figure 5. The digestive system

The process of digestion progresses as follows:

- In the mouth, the teeth and the tongue aid in mechanical digestion, while **salivary amylase** contained in the saliva begins to break down starch.

- From the mouth, the chewed food moves into the **esophagus**. Contractions push the food through the esophagus and into the stomach.

- In the **stomach**, food is mixed with **gastric acids** and **pepsin**, which acts on **protein**.

- In the **small intestine**, the bulk of digestion takes place. The small intestine is very long, about 23 feet on average. Food is broken down completely by enzymes produced in the walls of the small intestine, in the pancreas, and in the liver. The acids produced by the **pancreas** contain **lipase**, which changes fat to glycerol and fatty acids; **pancreatic amylase**, which breaks down complex carbohydrates into simple sugars; and **trypsin**, which converts polypeptides into amino acids. **Bile** produced by the **liver** aids in the physical digestion of emulsifying fat. All these digested substances, except for the fatty acids and glycerol, are then absorbed in the small intestine through capillaries that carry the blood into the liver and then throughout the rest of the body. The fatty acids and glycerol are absorbed and transported throughout the body by the lymphatic system.

THE SMALL INTESTINE IS NOT THAT SMALL!

In the average adult, the small intestine, if uncoiled, could easily measure 25 feet or longer, making it much larger than the large intestine (although, to be fair, the larger intestine does have a larger diameter). The small intestine is where the great bulk of digestion takes place.

- In the **large intestine**, water and minerals remaining in the waste matter are absorbed back into the body.

- In the **rectum**, solid waste matter is stored. In the **bladder**, liquid waste (urine) is stored.

- Solid waste matter is periodically released through the **anus**, and urine is released through the **urethra**.

The Nervous System

The nervous system consists of the **brain**, the **spinal cord**, and the network of billions of nerve cells called **neurons**. The nervous system controls the functions of the body and receives stimuli from the environment.

The nervous system consists of the **central nervous system**, which contains the neurons in the brain and spinal cord, and the **peripheral nervous system**, which contains all the other neurons found throughout the body.

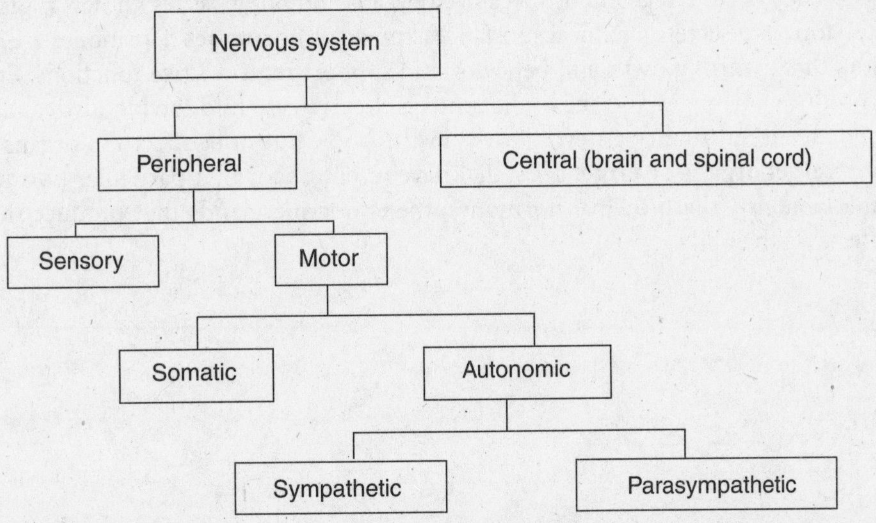

Figure 6. The nervous system

The main components of the central nervous system are as follows:

- The **cerebrum** is the major part of the brain. It is thought to be the **center of intelligence**, responsible for hearing, seeing, thinking, etc.

- The **cerebellum** is a big cluster of nerve tissue that forms the basis for the brain. It is concerned with **muscular coordination** and the coordination of impulses sent out from the cerebrum.

- The **medulla** or brain stem, is the connection between the brain and the spinal cord. It controls **involuntary actions** such as breathing, swallowing, and the beating of the heart.

- The **spinal cord** is the major connecting center between the brain and the network of nerves. It **carries impulses** between all organs and the brain and is also the control center from many **simple reflexes**.

- The peripheral nervous system can be subdivided into:

  - The **somatic nervous system**, which consists of peripheral nerve fibers that send sensory information to the central nervous system and control **voluntary actions**.

  - The **autonomic nervous system**, which regulates **involuntary activity** in the heart, stomach, and intestines.

The Endocrine System

The endocrine system is a group of specialized organs and body tissues known as **glands** that produce, store, and secrete chemical substances known as **hormones**. Hormones are chemical regulators that control growth and behavior and support reproductive functions. Endocrine glands produce hormones and the brain controls their release into the bloodstream. Once in the bloodstream, hormones go everywhere in the body, but only affect the organs or cells, known as **target organs** or **target cells**, that have receptors for that particular hormone. The following table lists the principal hormones, the endocrine glands that produce them, and their effects on the body.

Endocrine gland	Hormone	Effect
Anterior pituitary	Growth hormone	Stimulates muscle and bone growth
	FSH	Stimulates activity in ovaries and testes
	TSH	Stimulates the thyroid gland
	ACTH	Stimulates the adrenal cortex
	Prolactin	Causes milk secretion
Posterior pituitary	Oxytocin	Causes the uterus to contract
	Vasopressin	Causes the kidney to absorb water
Thyroid	Thyroxin	Regulates the rate of metabolism
Parathyroid	Parathyroid hormone	Increases the blood calcium concentration
Adrenal cortex	Aldosterone	Increases sodium and water absorption in kidney
Adrenal medulla	Epinephrine and norepinephrine (adrenaline)	Increases the blood sugar concentration; readies the body for strenuous activity
Pancreas	Insulin	Regulates and decreases the sugar content of blood
	Glucagon	Increases the sugar content of blood
Ovaries	Estrogen	Promotes female secondary sex characteristics
	Progesterone	Thickens endometrial lining
Testes	Testosterone	Promotes male secondary sex characteristics

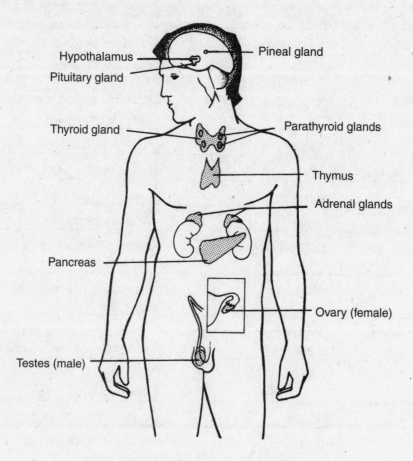

Figure 7. The endocrine system

The Reproductive System

The reproductive system involves two sets of organs, male reproductive organs and female reproductive organs. During human reproduction the male organ, or **penis**, ejaculates more than 250 million **sperm**, produced in the **testes**, into the **vagina**, some of which make their way to the uterus. During **ovulation**, which occurs approximately every 28 days, an egg, or **ovum**, is released from the **ovary** and begins to travel through the **oviduct (fallopian tube)** and into the **uterus**. At the same time, the **endometrial lining** of the uterus becomes prepared for implantation. If the sperm unites with the ovum, a fertilized egg, or **zygote**, is formed which implants in the uterus and eventually develops into a **fetus**. If the ovum fails to become fertilized, the uterine lining sloughs off during **menstruation**. From puberty to menopause, this menstrual cycle repeats monthly except for periods of pregnancy. After childbirth, **prolactin**, a hormone secreted by the pituitary, activates the production of milk.

Genetics

Genetics is the study of heredity, the process by which characteristics are passed from parents to offspring. The basic laws of genetics have been understood since the late eighteenth century, when they were first discovered by Gregor Mendel. What Mendel discovered was that in sexual reproduction, individual heredity traits separate in the reproductive cells, so that reproductive cells, known as **gametes**, have half as many **chromosomes** (large strings of hereditary units) as normal cells (which is why gametes are called **haploid**). Genetic traits are inherited independently of one another, and when different traits are crossed during the fertilization of an egg, often one trait is **dominant** and the other is **recessive**.

In human reproduction, the female gamete (ovum) combines with the male gamete (sperm), each of which contains 23 unpaired chromosomes, to produce a zygote, which contain 23 pairs of chromosomes, or a total of 46. **Meiosis** is the process by which gametes are created. Sexual reproduction by meiosis and fertilization results in a great deal of variation among offspring.

A **gene** is defined as a unit of inheritance. A gene consists of hereditory factors called **alleles**. Each of us has two **alleles** for every gene. These alleles may or may not be alike. If the alleles are alike, that person is **homozygous** for that particular gene. If the alleles are different, he or she is **heterozygous** for that particular gene.

A person's **genotype** is his or her genetic makeup, including both dominant and recessive alleles. A person's **phenotype** is simply how his or her genes express themselves in physical characteristics. Take eye color, for example. If a man has brown eyes, then brown eyes are part of his phenotype. But let's say that his mother has blue eyes. The allele for blue eye color (b) is recessive to the allele for brown eye color (B), as well all other eye colors. So this means two things, genotypically speaking: the mother is homozygous for blue eye color (bb) and the son is heterozygous for brown eye color (Bb). Now let's say that the son has a sister who has blue eyes like her mother. That means that the father must also be heterozygous for brown eye color (Bb).

This can all be understood more easily by drawing a diagram called a Punnett square, which is used to predict the genetic makeup of offspring:

	B	b
b	Bb	bb
b	Bb	bb

**Figure 8. Punnett square
(first generation)**

As you can see from this diagram, the parents had an even chance of having blue-eyed or brown-eyed children. Let's say, however, that the son marries someone else who is brown-eyed with a blue-eyed parent. To calculate the probability that their children will be either blue-eyed or brown-eyed, you would have to create a new Punnett square:

	B	b
B	BB	Bb
b	Bb	bb

**Figure 9. Punnett square
(second generation)**

Now you can see that this couple has a 75 percent probability of having brown-eyed children, and a 25 percent probability of having blue-eyed children.

The sex of babies is determined by the genes contained on the sex chromosome. In females, the two sex chromosomes are alike and are designated as XX. In males, the sex chromosomes are heterozygous and designated as XY.

Thus, during fertilization, the zygote necessarily receives an X chromosome from the mother, but may receive either an X or a Y chromosome from the father. If the father contributes an X chromosome, the baby will be female; if he contributes a Y chromosome, the baby will be a male. Thus we can see that Henry VIII was terribly in the wrong when he divorced or beheaded wives for producing female rather than male heirs.

The Classification of Living Things

You may know that as a human you belong to the species *Homo sapiens*, and that you are also a primate, a mammal, a vertebrate, and an animal. Thus, you already know quite a bit about the classification of living things, at least as it pertains to your own species. All living things fall into a careful classification scheme that goes from the broadest level of similarity—**kingdom**—to the narrowest—**species**. Let's begin by looking at the kingdoms, of which there are five in all.

The Kingdoms	
Monera	Includes bacteria, cyanobacteria (blue green algae), and primitive pathogens. Considered the most primitive kingdom, it represents prokaryotic (as opposed to eukaryotic) life forms—that is, the cells of Moneran organisms do not have distinct nuclei.
Protista	The simplest eukaryotes (cells have nuclei). Includes protozoa, unicellular and multicellular algae, and slime and water slime molds. Ancestor organisms to plants, animals, and fungi; many can move around by means of flagella.
Fungi	Includes mushrooms, bread molds, and yeasts. Fungi lack the ability to photosynthesize, they are called decomposers, breaking down and feeding on dead protoplasm (extracellular digestion).
Plantae	Have the ability to photosynthesize, so they are called producers. There are four major phyla, Bryophyta, or mosses, and Tracheophyta, which have vascular systems, gymnosperms, and angiosperms.
Animalia	Produce energy by consuming other organisms, so they are called consumers. Can be either vertebrates, phylum Chordata, or invertebrates such as mollusks, arthropods, sponges, coelenterates, worms, etc.

You should also note that **viruses** are a type of life form that scientists have difficulty in defining. (In fact, many scientists argue that viruses are not living organisms.) Viruses do not fit easily into any classification scheme because they do not have a true cell structure. Instead, they rely upon the cell structures of other organisms to reproduce. Thus, some scientists refer to viruses as nonliving things, even though they contain protein and nucleic acid. Many human diseases are caused by viruses, including polio, measles, influenza, AIDS, chickenpox, and herpes.

But let's get back to real living things. The classification scheme has seven different levels. They are:

    Kingdom—which contains several related *phyla*.

    Phylum—which contains several related *classes*.

    Class—which contains several related *orders*.

    Order—which contains several related *families*.

    Family—which contains several related *genera*.

    Genus—which contains several related *species*.

    Species—which contain organisms so similar that they can reproduce with one another to create viable fertile offspring.

So you may want to remember: **Kingdom Phylum Class Order Family Genus Species.**

Here's a mnemonic to help you: **King Philip's Class Ordered the Family-sized Gino's Special.**

A MUSHROOM IS NOT A PLANT (BUT IT'S SOMEWHAT LIKE AN ANT!)

Unlike plants, fungi, such as mushrooms, cannot photosynthesize, and instead feed by absorbing nutrients from the organic material in which they live. Most fungi build their cell walls out of chitin. This is the same material as the hard outer shells of insects and other arthropods. Plants do not make chitin.

Animal Phyla, Classes, and Orders

As noted above, animals can either be vertebrates, in which case they belong to the phylum Chordata, or invertebrates, in which case they could belong to any of several phyla. Let's take a closer look at those invertebrate phyla now.

Invertebrates

Phylum	Examples	Characteristics
Porifera	Sponge	Simplest animals; porous, lacking bony skeleton or tissues; mostly marine animals
Coelenterata	Jellies, hydra, sea anemone, coral	Marine animals with two layers of cells, hollow digestive cavity, and tentacles
Platyhelminthes	Marine flatworm, tape worm, liver fluke, planaria	Three layers of cells; flat with bilateral symmetry; many live as parasites in humans
Nematoda	Hookworm, ascaris, trichina	Digestive tract with a mouth and anus; most are parasitic
Annelida	Earthworm, leech, polychaete	Long segmented body; digestive system; closed circulatory systems
Echinodermata	Sea star, sea horse, sea urchin, sea cucumber	Aquatic animals with spiny skin, some of which have five or more arms that spread out in radial symmetry
Mollusca	Snail, clam, mussel, oyster, scallop, octopus, squid	Soft bodies, sometimes enclosed in univalve or bivalve shell; move by means of muscular foot or tentacles
Arthropoda	Insect, spider, crab, lobster, shrimp, centipede, millipede	Largest animal phylum; segmented bodies covered by exoskeleton; jointed appendages

Vertebrates, or the phylum Chordata, fall into five major classes. Let's take a quick look at those classes.

Vertebrates

Class	Examples	Characteristics
Fish (Osteichthyes and chondrichthyes)	Shark, bass, tuna, perch, mackerel, salmon, stingray, etc.	Marine species; cold-blooded; use internal gills for respiration; use fins for locomotion
Amphibians (Amphibia)	Frog, toad, caecilian, salamander, newt	Can live both in water and on land; cold-blooded; born with gills; develop lungs in the adult stage; lay soft eggs
Reptiles (Reptilia)	Lizard, snake, turtle, alligator, crocodile	Cold-blooded; breathe air through lungs; have scales; most (except snakes) have legs for movement; lay shell covered eggs
Birds (Aves)	Chicken, peacock, eagle, sparrow, robin, ostrich, etc.	Warm-blooded with feathers and wings; lay eggs with brittle shells; most can fly
Mammals (Mammalia)	Dolphin, kangaroo, mouse, beaver, cat, bear, ape, man, etc.	Warm-blooded with fur- or hair-covered bodies; newborns fed milk from mother's mammary glands

Finally, it's helpful to know some of the major orders of mammals. There are nineteen in all, but here are eight:

Mammals

Orders	Examples	Characteristics
Monotremes	Duck-billed platypus, echidna	Most primitive mammals, also known as protheria; lay eggs and have only one hole for both excretion and reproduction
Marsupials	Kangaroo, koala, opossum, wallaby	Also called metatheria; nonplacental, young born in a comparatively underdeveloped stage and develop in mother's pouch
Cetaceans	Dolphin, porpoise, whale	Marine mammals with forelimbs that have been modified into flippers; one of many orders of placental, or eutheria, mammals
Rodents	Beaver, mouse, rat, squirrel, skunk, rabbit, etc.	Relatively small, gnawing mammals that have in both jaws a single pair of incisors with a chisel-shaped edge
Artiodactyls	Giraffe, pig, deer, camel, sheep, cow, moose, etc.	Even-toed, hoofed, typically herbivorous, quadruped mammals with teeth adapted for grinding
Perissodactyls	Horse, donkey, zebra, tapir, rhinoceros	Odd-toed, hoofed, nonruminant, quadruped mammals with teeth adapted for grinding
Carnivores	Cat, dog, bear, fox, wolf, coyote, lion, etc.	Typically flesh-eating mammals with powerful jaws and sharp teeth and claws
Primates	Monkey, lemur, tarsier, ape, man	Typically omnivorous mammals that have the ability to grasp objects and can generally stand on two legs

Ecology

Ecology is the study of the interrelationships between organisms and their physical surroundings. Just as biologists classify organisms according to terminology that goes from the general to the specific, ecologists employ a similar set of terminology:

Biosphere: The zone of planet Earth where life naturally occurs, including land, water, and air, extending from the deep crust to the lower atmosphere.

Biome: A major life zone of interrelated species bound together by similar climate, vegetation, and animal life.

Ecosystem: A system made up of a community of animals, plants, and other organisms interrelated within its physical and chemical environment.

Community: The collection of all populations of a habitat.

Population: A group of organisms of the same species living in the same region.

There are at least seven distinct biomes. Let's take a look.

Biome	Description:
Tundra	Located in the high northern altitudes, this is the coldest of all biomes. The ground is permanently frozen, so no trees can grow there. Vegetation includes shrubs and grasses. Animal life includes polar bears, caribou, wolves, penguins, walruses, seals, as well as several types of insects.
Taiga	Just south of the tundra, the ground is warm enough to allow for the growth of conifers (evergreens). Its seasons are divided between short, moist, and moderately warm summers, and long, dry, and cold winters. Animals include moose, bears, elk, beavers, deer, squirrels, and rabbits.
Deciduous Forests	Closer to the equator than taigas, the climate here has distinct hot and cold seasons. Trees here are mostly deciduous, that is, they have broad leaves that shed annually. A wide variety of plants and animals can be found here.
Grasslands	Also called the prairie, the savanna in Africa, the steppe in central Asia, and the pampas in South America. Characterized by the dominance of grasses rather than trees or large shrubs due to insufficient rainfall. Summers are hot and winters cold. Animals include antelope, bison, zebra, giraffe, lions, elephants, snakes, lizards, kangaroo, and aardvarks.
Tropical Rain Forests	Located near the equator and characterized by heaviest rainfall anywhere on Earth and the largest variety of terrestrial animal and plant life. The trees here grow very tall, forming a thick canopy of leaves that prevents much light from reaching the ground. Animals include monkeys, birds, snakes, lizards, frogs, tapirs, spiders, and insects.
Deserts	The driest places on Earth. Can be either hot or cold. Plant and animal life is scarce and especially adapted to the arid environment. Plants are mostly cacti. Animals are mostly nocturnal and include addax, coyote, bats, lizards, jackrabbits, snakes, owls, camels, and small rodents.
Marine	By far the largest biome, comprising 75 percent of the Earth's surface. Many, many forms of marine plant life and algae grow here; animals include crabs, mussels, snails, starfish, sponges, coral, sea anemones, dolphins, whales, etc., and many, many varieties of fish. Oceanographers break the marine biome down into further, more precise, biomes.

Ecosystems, Communities, and Populations

The difference between biomes and ecosystems is that biomes need merely share similar characteristics, whereas ecosystems must be contiguous and contain organisms that actually interact together. An ecosystem can be large or small, and can include both pristine and highly developed areas. However, the word is rarely, if ever, applied to disjunct spaces: two similar mountaintops would ordinarily be considered similar ecosystems rather than a single ecosystem, unless the land mass between them is also included and the organisms on the one mountaintop interact with the organisms on the other.

An ecosystem contains a community, and this community may contain many populations of organisms. The various populations within a community fall into one of several roles in the food chain.

Producers (plant life): Also known as **autotrophs**, they make their own food via photosynthesis.

Decomposers (bacteria and fungi): Also known as **saprotrophs**, they break down organic matter and release minerals back into the soil.

Scavengers (many insects and certain vertebrates, such as vultures and jackals): Also known as **detrivores**, these are animals that function like decomposers, by consuming refuse and decaying organic matter, especially **carrion**, or decaying flesh.

Consumers (most animals): Also known as **heterotrophs**, refers to animals that consume other organisms to survive. Consumers are divided into three types:

Primary Consumers: Also known as **herbivores**, they subsist on plants. Examples include grasshoppers, deer, cows, squirrels, and rabbits.

Secondary consumers: Also known as **carnivores** or predators, they subsist mainly on primary consumers. Examples include lions, wolves, and sharks. Some secondary consumers are also **omnivores**, meaning they consume producers and consumers as well.

Tertiary consumers: Also known as **top carnivores**, they consume, at least to some extent, secondary consumers. Many tertiary consumers are also **omnivores**, meaning they consume producers and primary consumers as well. One example of a tertiary consumer is a polar bear, which consumes walrus, which in turn consumes clams and other shellfish. An example of an omnivore is man (although, on an individual basis, some people refrain from eating other consumers).

LIFE SCIENCE PRACTICE SET

1. A deficiency of which of the following can lead to beriberi?

   (A) Vitamin A
   (B) Vitamin B$_1$
   (C) Vitamin B$_{12}$
   (D) Vitamin D

2. Which of the following describes the proper pathway of blood through the heart?

   (A) vena cava → right atrium → right ventricle → pulmonary artery → pulmonary vein → left atrium → left ventricle → aorta
   (B) vena cava → right atrium → right ventricle → pulmonary vein → pulmonary artery → left atrium → left ventricle → aorta
   (C) vena cava → right atrium → left atrium → pulmonary artery → pulmonary vein → left atrium → left ventricle → aorta
   (D) vena cava → right atrium → left atrium → pulmonary vein → pulmonary artery → left atrium → left ventricle → aorta

3. Most human digestion takes place in the

   (A) esophagus
   (B) stomach
   (C) small intestine
   (D) large intestine

4. Which blood type can be donated to anyone?

   (A) A
   (B) B
   (C) O
   (D) AB

5. A typical human gamete contains

   (A) 2 chromosomes
   (B) 23 chromosomes
   (C) 46 chromosomes
   (D) 92 chromosomes

6. Color-blindness is a sex-linked recessive trait found on the X chromosome. If the incidence of color-blindness in a certain male population is 1 in 20, what would be the predicted incidence of color-blindness among females in the same population?

   (A) 1 in 20
   (B) 1 in 40
   (C) 1 in 200
   (D) 1 in 400

7. Which of the following belongs in the phylum Chordata?

   (A) sea horse
   (B) squid
   (C) eel
   (D) lobster

8. The order that includes man is called

   (A) Chordata
   (B) Mammalia
   (C) Primate
   (D) Homidae

9. Which of the following is an example of a primary consumer?

   (A) moss
   (B) mushroom
   (C) jackal
   (D) deer

10. One feature distinguishing the taiga biome from the tundra biome is the presence of

   (A) mammals
   (B) birds
   (C) shrubs
   (D) trees

[Answers found on page 258.]

EARTH SCIENCE

Earth science is the study of the Earth and the universe around it. For purposes of the ASVAB, it's helpful to know a few facts about our planet and the solar system in which it travels. Let's begin on terra firma with a look at geology.

Geology

Geology is the science that deals with the history and composition of the Earth and its life, especially as recorded in rocks. In part by studying rocks, scientists have been able to determine that the Earth is made up of three layers. The outermost layer, or **crust**, comprises roughly one percent of the total Earth's volume. It varies in thickness from 10 kilometers to as much as 80 kilometers. Beneath the crust lies the **mantle**, which comprises more than 75 percent of the Earth's volume. Roughly 3,500 kilometers thick, the mantle contains mostly iron, magnesium, and calcium, and is much hotter and denser than the Earth's surface because temperature and pressure inside the Earth increase with depth. It is this heat and pressure, among other things, that lead to interesting phenomena such as volcanoes on the surface of the Earth.

At the center of the Earth lies the **core**, which is nearly twice as dense as the mantle because its composition is metallic (iron-nickel alloy) rather than stony. The Earth's core contains two distinct parts: a 2,300-kilometer-thick liquid **outer core** and a 1,200-kilometer-radius solid **inner core**. As the Earth rotates, metallic fluid in the outer core revolves around the solid core, generating electric currents and creating the Earth's magnetic field.

MYSTERIES OF SCIENCE

About once every million years, the Earth's magnetic poles reverse their polarity (magnetic north becomes magnetic south, and vice versa). The last time they did so was about 700,000 years ago. Within a relatively short period of geologic time—probably less than 10,000 years—the existing magnetic field can reduce to a very small intensity and then reestablish itself with approximately equal intensity in exactly the opposite direction. Scientists still don't know why this happens.

Plate Tectonics

As noted, the interior of the Earth is quite hot, somewhere between 3,000° and 4,000° C. This heat is generally prevented from escaping thanks to the solid rock in the Earth's upper mantle and crust. The crust and rigid upper part of the mantle (the lithosphere) consist of approximately 30 separate pieces called **plates**. These plates actually move very slowly upon the more ductile mantle beneath (the asthenosphere), and this has caused the continental landmasses to drift slowly apart over the course of hundreds of millions of years.

Along the edges of these plates are **fault lines**. (Fault lines are simply places where the plates slide relative to each other.) When plates slide relative to each other along fault lines earthquakes can occur. In the United States, California gets more than its share of earthquakes because the San Andreas fault line runs up its coast. When an earthquake occurs, scientists use the **Richter scale** to measure its intensity. The Richter scale goes from 1 to 10, with each step representing a magnitude that is about 10 times greater than the preceding step. So a tremor that measures 1 represents a disturbance that can be detected only by instruments, while one that measures 7 (which would be 1,000,000 times as powerful) can cause major damage to buildings.

Types of Rocks

The Earth's rocks fall into three categories, based upon how they are formed.

Rock Type	How it was formed	Examples
Igneous	Formed from the hardening of molten rock, or magma, which is called lava when it reaches the surface of the Earth.	Granite, pumice, obsidian, basalt
Sedimentary	Formed by the sedimentation, or gradual depositing, of small bits of rock, clay and other materials. Over time this deposited material becomes cemented together. Most fossils are found in sedimentary rocks.	Shale, sandstone, gypsum, dolomite, coal
Metamorphic	Formed when other rock material is altered through temperature, pressure, or chemical processes.	Marble, slate, gneiss, quartzite

Geologic Time Scale

Most of what is known about the history of our planet has been learned by studying the fossil record found in sedimentary rock. By studying rocks, we now know that the Earth is approximately 4.6 billion years old, and that for most of that time, very few fossil traces were left. This is why the period from 4.6 billion years to 570 million years ago is called the **Precambrian Eon**, meaning the period before the fossil record began. It turns out, however, that early geologists who studied the Precambrian Eon were unable to recognize early, primitive fossils, and in fact life first appeared on Earth as early as 3.5 billion years ago! Here are some fun facts about the history of our planet as detailed on the geologic time scale.

Eon	Era	What happened ...
Precambrian (4.6 B to 544 M yrs. ago) The time of few fossils	**Hadean** (4.6–3.8 B yrs. ago)	"Hades-like" era. Oceans of liquid rock, boiling sulfur, and impact craters everywhere! Life doesn't stand a chance.
	Archaean (3.8–2.5 B yrs. ago)	"Ancient" era. Earth's crust cools and oceans form. Single-celled, prokaryotic blue-green algae appear in the ocean starting 3.5 B yrs. ago. There is as yet no life on land.
	Proterozoic (2.5 B–544 M yrs. ago)	"Early life" era. By 1.8 B yrs. ago the first eukaryotic life begins to appear. Oxygen begins to build up in the atmosphere.
Phanerozoic (544M yrs. ago to present) The time of evident life	**Paleozoic** (544-248 M yrs. ago)	"Old life" era. Dramatic explosion in multicellular life forms occurs. Animals, plants, and fungi take to the land, and insects take to the air. At end of the era, largest mass extinction ever wipes out 90 percent of all marine animal species.
	Mesozoic (248-65 M yrs. ago)	"Middle life" era. Beginning, middle, and end of the reign of the dinosaur, as well as other reptiles. Conifers and flowering plants make first appearance.
	Cenozoic (65 M yrs. ago-present)	"Recent life" era. Often called "the Age of Mammals," it's also the period when most bird, flowering plant, and insect species first appear.

We've only just scratched the surface of the geologic time scale, which has been further subdivided into shorter periods, ages, and epochs, each rich in fossil detail about the evolution of life on this planet. So there's a lot you can learn by looking at rocks. Now let's take a look at the weather.

Meteorology

Meteorology is not just the study of weather, but of the atmosphere and atmospheric phenomena in general. The first thing you should know is that there are several layers to the atmosphere, beginning here on the surface of the Earth and continuing up several thousand kilometers above us. Here they are.

Troposphere: The troposphere is where all weather takes place; it is the region of rising and falling packets of air. Depending on the latitude and the season, it can range from 6 to 17 kilometers thick. Most of the air surrounding the Earth, which is roughly 79 percent nitrogen and 21 percent oxygen, is found in the troposphere. There is a thin buffer zone, called the **tropopause**, between the troposphere and the next layer.

Stratosphere: Above the troposphere is the stratosphere, where airflow is mostly horizontal. The thin **ozone layer** in the upper stratosphere has a high concentration of ozone, a particularly reactive form of oxygen. This layer is primarily responsible for absorbing the ultraviolet radiation from the Sun. As you enter the stratosphere, the temperature is about −60° C. As you approach the upper boundary of the stratosphere, called the **stratopause**, which is about 50 kilometers above us, temperatures start to warm as a result of direct heat.

Mesosphere: Above the stratosphere is the mesosphere, which extends to about 90 kilometers above the Earth. As you enter the mesosphere, the temperature starts to drop again, to as low as −90° C degrees. This is where we see "falling stars," meteors that fall to the Earth and burn up in the atmosphere. As you approach the upper boundary of the mesosphere, called the **mesopause**, the temperature stabilizes.

Thermosphere: So called because the temperature continues to increase with the altitude, with recorded temperatures reaching as high as 2,000° C at its upper limits, which extends to several thousand kilometers above the Earth. The thermosphere is further divided into two regions, the **ionosphere** below and the **exosphere** above.

Ionosphere: Directly above the mesopause is the ionosphere, where many atoms become ionized, meaning they gain or lose electrons so that they have a net electrical charge. The ionosphere is where aurora (northern lights) take place, and is also responsible for absorbing the most energetic photons from the Sun, and for reflecting radio waves, thereby making long-distance radio communication possible. The ionosphere extends from 90 km to 640 kilometers above the Earth.

Exosphere: The exosphere is almost a complete vacuum, with extremely low densities of hydrogen and helium particles. This is the area where many satellites orbit the Earth. The exosphere extends for several thousand kilometers above the Earth.

Air Temperature, Density, Pressure, and Humidity

Almost half of the Sun's radiation that hits the Earth passes through the layers of the atmosphere and reaches the Earth's surface, where it is absorbed by the land and water in the oceans, which in turn warm the air above them. For various reasons discussed below, the Earth's surface does not absorb heat evenly, which causes differences in air temperature. These differences in air temperature also cause differences in air density, because air density decreases with an increase in temperature.

An increase in the air pressure, on the other hand, causes the air density to increase. The air's pressure is affected by the weight of air pressing down on the Earth, which can vary based on the varying thickness of the troposphere. Earth's gravity, of course, causes the downward force that we know as weight. Since the pressure depends on the amount of air above the point where you're measuring the pressure, the air pressure falls as you go higher. Air generally flows from high-pressure areas to low-pressure areas. This air movement is called wind.

Because heat transfer occurs more easily on land than on water, the air above land heats up more quickly than the air above the oceans during daylight hours, and at night, air over land cools down more quickly than air over water. Not only does the temperature of air vary depending on whether it is heated over land or water, but the humidity does too. Not surprisingly, air masses formed over land are dry, while those formed over oceans are humid, and air masses formed near the poles are cold, while those formed near the equator are warm.

Fronts

As noted, differences in air pressure cause wind and the movement of air masses of different temperatures towards each other. When a warm air mass overtakes a cold air mass, you have a **warm front**. As the warm air advances, it rides over the cold air ahead of it, which is heavier. As the warm air rises, the water vapor in it condenses into clouds that can produce rain, snow, sleet, or freezing rain—often all four.

When a cold air mass overtakes a warm air mass, you have a **cold front**. Most cold fronts are preceded by a line of precipitation as they roar across an area. However, some cold fronts produce very little or no precipitation as they move. The only sign that a front has moved through your area is a sudden change in winds and temperature.

Sometimes two air masses meet and neither is displaced. Instead, the two fronts push against each other in a stalemate. This is called a **stationary front**. Stationary fronts often cause cloudy, wet weather that can last a week or more.

Finally, an **occluded front** occurs when cold air replaces cool air quickly or vice versa at the surface, with warm air above. A cold occlusion occurs when cold air shoves its way under cool air at the surface. Warm air aloft is usually to the west of the surface front in mid-latitudes. A warm occlusion occurs when cool air rises over cold air. The warm-cold air boundary is often east of the surface front. Both types of fronts are usually associated with rain or snow and cumulus clouds. Temperature fluctuations are small and winds are gentle.

Clouds

Clouds come in different varieties based on their shape, size, and altitude. The three main types are:

Stratus clouds, which are low-hanging, broad, flat clouds that blanket the sky. The lowest of low clouds, when they occur on the ground they are called fog. Dark stratus clouds indicate that rain will soon occur.

Cumulus clouds, which are massive clouds that are puffy, like popcorn, with relatively flat bottoms and rounded tops. When cumulus clouds darken you can expect heavy rain.

Cirrus clouds, which are the thin, wispy clouds that occur much higher in the atmosphere, at elevations of 20,000 feet or more.

Also note that clouds can have mixed qualities, and these clouds are named accordingly. A cloud with qualities of both a cirrus and a cumulus cloud would be called a **cirrocumulus** cloud; one with qualities of both a stratus and a cumulus cloud would be called **stratocumulus**; and one with qualities of both a stratus and a cirrus cloud would be called **cirrostratus**. Finally, clouds that are pregnant with rain are called **nimbus** clouds, and depending on the shape of the rain cloud you could have a **nimbostratus** cloud or a **cumulonimbus** cloud.

Enough with terrestrial phenomena. Let's explore the solar system.

Our Solar System

As you probably know, our Sun is just one of billions of stars in our galaxy, and our galaxy is just one of billions of galaxies in the universe. Scientists can only guess at how many of the billions upon billions of stars out there might contain orbiting planets as our Sun does, and how many of those planets might contain the proper conditions to sustain life. But quite a bit is known about our own solar system, and some of these facts may make their way onto the ASVAB. So let's explore our solar system.

Our solar system consists of one star, which we call the Sun, nine planets and all their moons, several thousand minor planets called asteroids, and an equally large number of comets. The Sun's age is calculated to be around 4.7 billion years, which is only slightly older than the Earth itself. This only makes sense, given that scientists believe the Sun was formed from a cloud of hydrogen that swirled around and mixed with small amounts of substances that had been produced in the bodies of older stars. This parent cloud gave birth to the entire solar system. The dense, hot gas at the center of the cloud gave rise to the Sun; the outer regions of the cloud—cooler and less dense—gave birth to the planets and other phenomena.

The Sun

Our **Sun** is classified as a **G2V** star, or **yellow dwarf**. G2 stars are approximately 6,000° C at the surface, are yellow, and contain many neutrally charged metals such as iron, magnesium, and calcium. The "V" indicates that the Sun is a dwarf star, or fairly small by the standards of stars. This is a fortunate fact, because the longevity of a star is inversely proportional to its size. Large stars probably cannot exist long enough for life to occur on any planets that might form around them. Our own Sun probably has at least another 5 billion years in it before it burns out in a supernova. This should be fairly reassuring news.

Although a dwarf in comparison to other stars, the Sun contains almost 99.9 percent of the mass of our solar system. Like all stars, the Sun is a gigantic ball of superheated gas, kept hot by atomic reactions emanating from its center. In our Sun, these atomic reactions are in the form of **hydrogen fusion**: four hydrogen atoms combine to form one helium atom. The temperature at the core of our Sun is thought to be about 15,000,000° C; temperatures at the surface range between 4,000° and 15,000° C. The diameter of the Sun is about 1.4 million kilometers, or more than 100 times that of Earth, and its surface area is approximately 12,000 times that of Earth.

The Sun's **core** is surrounded by the **radiative zone**, where the energy created in the core radiates out via photons. The average temperature in the radiative zone is about 2,500,000° C. The outer 15 percent of the Sun's radius is called the **convective zone**, where the average temperature is about 1,000,000° C. Because of the lower temperature, energy here travels to the surface via bulk motions of gas in a process called convection. What appears to be the surface of the Sun is called the **photosphere**. The layer outside the photosphere is called the **chromosphere**, which extends several thousand kilometers beyond the photosphere. The chromosphere is in steady motion, with huge projections that can be seen to burst from it extending up to 170,000 kilometers into space. Outside the chromosphere is the **corona**, which consists of very tenuous gases (essentially hydrogen) that create a magnificent spectacle during a solar eclipse. Beyond the corona, heat from the Sun radiates through space, warming the rest of the solar system.

The Planets and Other Phenomena

The four planets closest to the Sun—**Mercury**, **Venus**, **Earth**, and **Mars**—are called **terrestrial planets**, meaning they are similar to our own planet in composition, with inner metal cores and surfaces of rock. Aside from the Earth, only Mars among the four terrestrial planets has moons of its own, although they are much smaller than our own Moon, and are probably asteroids captured in Mars's gravitational orbit. Earth is the largest of the terrestrial planets, although Venus is close to it in size. An interesting fact about Venus is that its rotation is "retrograde"—that is, although it has a counterclockwise orbit around the Sun, as do all the planets, its orbit around its own axis is clockwise. Moreover, its rotation around its own axis is quite slow, around 243 days, as

ALL IN A DAY'S WORK

A day is a measure of how long it takes a planet to make one full rotation around its axis. One day on Earth is 23 hours, 56 minutes, and 4.091 seconds.

Other planets have different lengths of day:

• Mercury: 59 days

• Venus: 243 days

• Mars: 24 hours, 37 minutes, 23 seconds

• Jupiter: 9 hours, 55 minutes

compared to its rotation around the Sun, which takes 225 days. So a Venusian day is longer than a Venusian year! Although none of the terrestrial planets aside from the Earth is thought to have conditions capable of sustaining life, polar icecaps have been spotted on both Mars and Mercury.

KNOW YOUR PLANETARY ORDER!

It can be helpful to know the order of the planets on the ASVAB. Here it is and here's a mnemonic to help you memorize it:

Mercury Venus Earth Mars Jupiter Saturn Uranus Neptune Pluto

Men Very Early Made Jars Stand Up Nearly Perfectly (And if you don't like our mnemonic, you can come up with your own!)

The five planets beyond Mars—**Jupiter**, **Saturn**, **Uranus**, **Neptune**, and **Pluto**—are referred to as the **outer planets**. The first four of these are also called **Jovian planets**, meaning they are similar in composition to Jupiter—that is, they are all **gas giants**. The outermost planet, Pluto, is also the smallest planet, only about two-thirds the size of Mercury, and has a solid surface like the terrestrial planets, only icier. It does have an orbiting moon almost half its size. Pluto also has the most eccentric orbit of all the planets, so that at certain periods during its orbit it is actually closer to the Sun than the next nearest planet, Neptune. When Pluto is near the Sun, it has a thin atmosphere, but when Pluto travels to the outer regions of its orbit, the atmosphere freezes and "collapses" to the planet's surface. In this regard, Pluto acts like a comet.

The Jovian planets are composed primarily of helium and hydrogen, much like the Sun. Jupiter is the largest of the Jovian planets, with a diameter 11.2 times that of the Earth and a volume approximately 1,300 times that of the Earth. All of the Jovian planets have multiple moons, anywhere from eight to more than 30. They also all have rings, most notably so on Saturn. The rings of Saturn, and most likely the other Jovian planets as well, are composed mostly of ice crystals.

In addition, the solar system contains thousands of small bodies such as **asteroids** and **comets**. Most of the asteroids orbit in a region between the orbits of Mars and Jupiter called the **main asteroid belt**. Asteroids are thought to be primordial objects left over from the formation of the solar system. They resemble rocks pocked with crater marks. While most asteroids are probably the about size of pebbles, some can be fairly large. The largest known asteroid is about the size of Texas. Asteroids are also known as **meteoroids**, and when they fall into the Earth's gravitational field, they are seen as "falling stars," called **meteors**, as they burn up in the Earth's mesosphere. Those meteors that make it to the Earth's surface are called **meteorites**.

The main home of comets lies far beyond the orbit of Pluto, in the **Oort Cloud**. Comets are sometimes called dirty snowballs or icy mudballs. They are a mixture of ices (both water and frozen gases) and dust that for some reason didn't get incorporated into planets when the solar system was formed. This makes them very interesting as samples of the early history of the solar system. Comets are invisible except when they are near the Sun. Most comets have highly eccentric orbits that take them far beyond the orbit of Pluto; these are seen once and then disappear for millennia. Only the short- and intermediate-period comets, such as **Halley's Comet**, stay within the orbit of Pluto for a significant fraction of their orbits. When they are near the Sun and active, comets have highly visible **tails**, up to several hundred million kilometers long, composed of plasma and laced with rays and streamers caused by interactions with the solar wind.

But by far the most important body in the solar system aside from the Sun, as it relates to life on Earth, is our own **Moon**. Because of the gravitational pull that exists between the Moon and Earth, we have **tides**. High tides occur twice a day, when the Moon is at the points closest to and furthest from the affected mass of water. It is suspected that life would never have evolved on land without the constant ebbing and flowing of the oceanic tides on coastal areas.

Eclipses

Another interesting fact about our Sun and Moon is that although the Sun is about 400 times the diameter of the Moon, it is also, on average, about 400 times as far away from the Earth as the Moon. We say "on average" because the Moon's orbit around the Earth is **elliptical**—that is, sometimes it is closer to the Earth and sometimes it is further away from the Earth. But on average, the relative size of the Sun and the Moon, as they appear to us on the Earth, appears the same. This allows for the fascinating phenomenon known as the **total solar eclipse**.

A solar eclipse occurs when the Moon falls directly between the path of the Sun and the Earth, blocking the light from the Sun and causing a shadow to be cast on a small area of the Earth. If a solar eclipse occurs when the Sun and Moon appear to be the exact same size, the Moon exactly covers the Sun and a total solar eclipse occurs. These are of special interest to astronomers because during total eclipses, outer layers of the Sun that are not usually visible, such as the spectacular corona, can be seen. The alignment of the Earth, Moon, and Sun has to be exact for a total eclipse to occur. Even when the alignment is exact, not everyone will see a total eclipse, because for the alignment to be correct for the Northern Hemisphere it must be slightly off in the Southern Hemisphere (and vice versa).

If you ever have the fortune to experience a total solar eclipse, you must be extremely careful not to stare at the eclipse directly (you can use a pinhole projector instead). This is because staring at the Sun directly at any time, including during a solar eclipse, can cause permanent damage to the eye's retina, even blindness.

If the alignment is not exact, a **partial eclipse** may occur. This occurs when the Moon only partially overlaps the Sun and blocks only part of it from our view. An **annular eclipse** occurs when the apparent size of the Moon is smaller than that of the Sun, and the Moon does not fully block the Sun from our view. An annular eclipse looks like a "bull's eye."

A **lunar eclipse** occurs when the Moon passes through the Earth's shadow—that is, the Earth passes directly between the Moon and the Sun. Because the Earth is much larger than the Moon, usually the entire Moon is eclipsed. Because the full phase can be seen from anywhere on the night side of the Earth, a lunar eclipse can be seen by more people than a solar eclipse. Since the Moon is moving through the Earth's shadow, and the size of the Earth is much greater than the size of the Moon, a lunar eclipse lasts for about 3.5 hours (as opposed to a solar eclipse, which lasts on the order of about 7.5 minutes).

EARTH SCIENCE PRACTICE SET

1. The ozone layer is found in the

   (A) troposphere
   (B) stratosphere
   (C) mesosphere
   (D) thermosphere

2. The feature most responsible for the earth's magnetic poles is the earth's

   (A) crust
   (B) mantle
   (C) core
   (D) water content

3. The clouds that occur at the highest altitudes are called

   (A) cirrus
   (B) cumulus
   (C) nimbus
   (D) stratus

4. Life on Earth has existed for approximately

   (A) 4.6 billion years
   (B) 3.8 billion years
   (C) 2.5 billion years
   (D) 544 million years

5. Which of the following is NOT a sedimentary rock?

   (A) shale
   (B) sandstone
   (C) slate
   (D) coal

6. The Sun comprises approximately what percent of the solar system's mass?

   (A) 50
   (B) 75
   (C) 95
   (D) 99

7. The smallest planet in the solar system is

   (A) Mars
   (B) Mercury
   (C) Venus
   (D) Pluto

8. Which of the following is most responsible for the oceanic tides?

   (A) the gravitational pull of the Sun on the Earth
   (B) the gravitational pull of the Moon on the Earth
   (C) the heat of the Sun
   (D) the magnetic pull of the poles

[Answers on p. 259]

PHYSICAL SCIENCE

Scientists would know very little about our solar system without an understanding of physics and chemistry, collectively known as the physical sciences. So let's take a quick look at these subjects, which have been known to appear on the ASVAB General Science section.

Before we delve into physics and chemistry, you should realize one thing. Real scientists don't muck with British measurements such as miles and gallons. Instead, real scientists use the metric system. We've already used the metric system throughout most of this chapter, but let's review it quickly.

Measurement

The standard unit of **length** is the **meter**, which is slightly more than three feet, or about 39.4 inches. One thousand meters is called a **kilometer**, which is approximately three-fifths of a mile. One one-hundredth of a meter is called a **centimeter**, and one one-thousandth of a meter is called a **millimeter**. If you want to talk really small, one ten-millionth of a millimeter is called an **ångstrom**.

Using a similar prefix scheme, **mass** is measured in **grams, kilograms, milligrams**, and so on. There are approximately 28.3 grams in an ounce, and a mass of one kilogram will have a weight of approximately 2.2 pounds (at the surface of the earth).

Volume is the measurement of three-dimensional space. One **cubic centimeter** can be called just that, or it can be called a **milliliter**. A milliliter is also one one-thousandth of a **liter**, which is equal to slightly more than a quart in liquid measure, or about 33.8 ounces. So a **kiloliter** is equal to 1,000 liters, or a **cubic meter**, if you prefer.

Finally, the metric system equivalent of temperature is the **Celsius scale**, also known as degrees centigrade. According to the **Fahrenheit scale**, which is more familiar to most people in the United States, water freezes at 32° F and boils at 212° F. On the Celsius scale, water freezes at 0° C and boils at 100° C. The general equations for converting from the Fahrenheit scale to the Celsius scale, or vice versa, are as follows:

$$F° = \frac{9}{5}C° + 32$$

$$C° = \frac{5}{9}(F° - 32)$$

Finally, there is one other temperature scale commonly used by scientists, known as the **Kelvin scale,** or the absolute zero scale. Absolute zero is the temperature at which matter has no heat and its molecules are completely still; in theory, absolute zero is the lowest temperature possible. On the Kelvin scale, absolute zero is set at 0° K, which is equal to −273° C. Otherwise, degrees Kelvin use the same increments as degrees Celsius, so that water freezes at 273° K and boils at 373° K.

Physics

Physics is the science dealing with the properties, changes, and interactions of matter and energy. There are many branches of physics, including mechanics, thermodynamics, magnetism, optics, and electricity. This review will cover only the physics that might appear on the General Science section of the ASVAB. Other chapters of this book will examine more thoroughly the physics that might appear on the Mechanical Comprehension and Electrical Information sections of the ASVAB.

Important Formulas and Definitions

In physics, words that are often used imprecisely in common parlance have very strict definitions. For example the words **mass** and **weight** are often used interchangeably, when in fact they have very different meanings. Mass is defined as the amount of matter that something has, whereas weight is defined as the force exerted on an objects mass by gravity. Weight depends upon how strong the force of gravity is where you are. For example in deep space far enough from any planets or stars, your weight would be effectively zero. But you would still have the same mass as you would on Earth. The amount of matter that you contain hasn't changed. So, let's say you put an object on a scale, the scale has both english and metric units, and it gives you measurements of 2.2 lb, and 1 kg in english and metric units respectively. Most people will tell you that the object weighs either 2.2 lb or 1 kg depending on the units. In fact pounds are a unit of weight, and kilograms are a unit of mass. They are not equivalent concepts. So what is happening here? What is the scale actually reading? Why are they using the units pounds and kilograms together if they don't mean the same thing?

Let's say we are using a spring scale. If so, then the scale uses the force of gravity to make a measurement. An object is placed on the scale. The force of gravity pushes the object into the scale causing the spring to compress. So in this case what we are measuring is clearly the weight of the object. A measurement of 2.2 pounds for example, which is the English system unit of the force of gravity, acting on the object would give us the weight of the object. If we tried to use the scale on the moon however, we would get a reading less than 2.2 pounds (actually 6 times smaller) due to the smaller gravity on the moon. What confuses the issue is that in some cases our spring scale will give us a reading in kilograms. This is a measurement of mass which is constant no matter where in the universe the object is. Yet the scale would not read 1 kg if I used it on the moon. This is because the scale is actually reading weight and not mass. However at the surface of the earth, because we know how strong the pull of gravity is, we also know that an object that has a 1 kg mass will weigh exactly 2.2 pounds there. So the scale is calibrated accordingly. (The metric unit of weight is actually the Newton, which is equal to the mass times the acceleration due to gravity.)

Velocity, Momentum, and Acceleration

Velocity is the rate at which an object changes position. **Velocity = displacement of an object ÷ time**. In physics, velocity is called a vector quantity, meaning it is fully described by both a magnitude and a direction.

Momentum is the tendency of an object to continue moving in the same direction. **Momentum = mass × velocity.**

Acceleration is the rate of change of velocity. **Acceleration = change in velocity ÷ change in time.**

Force, Work, and Power

Force is the push or pull that forces an object to change its speed or direction. **Weight** is just one example of a force, in this case the force of gravity. A unit of force is called a **newton**, which is the force required to impart an acceleration of one meter per second squared to a mass of one kilogram.

Work is defined as the force exerted on an object times the distance moved in the direction of the force. **Work = force × distance.** A unit of work is called a **newton-meter** or **joule**.

Power is the rate at which work is performed. **Power = work ÷ time**, or **Power = (force × distance) ÷ time.** A unit of power is called a **joule per second**, also known as a **watt**.

Newton's Laws

Sir Isaac Newton was an English physicist, mathematician, and certifiable genius. In the 17th century he came up some of our most important formulas for understanding the properties of motion and gravity. Here they are.

1. Newton's first law of motion. *An object at rest tends to stay at rest, and an object in motion tends to stay in motion at a constant speed in a straight line (constant velocity), unless acted upon by an unbalanced force.* An example of an unbalanced force—one that keeps objects in motion from staying in motion on Earth—is friction, the force that resists relative motion between two bodies in contact.

2. Newton's second law of motion. *When dealing with an object for which all existing forces are not balanced, the acceleration of that object, as produced by the net force, is in the same direction as the net force and directly proportional to the magnitude of the net force, and is inversely proportional to the object's mass.* Expressed mathematically, Newton's second law states the following: **Net force = mass × acceleration.** This law is also known as the **law of inertia**, because the greater the mass of an object, the greater the force needed to overcome its inertia (its reluctance to change velocity).

3. Newton's third law of motion. *For every action, there is an equal and opposite reaction.* In other words, when an object exerts a force on another object, the second object exerts a force of the same magnitude but in the opposite direction on the first object. For example, consider what happens when a gun is fired. A bullet fires and the gun recoils. The recoil is the result of action-reaction force pairs. As the gases from the gunpowder explosion expand, the gun pushes the bullet forwards and the bullet pushes the gun backwards. The acceleration of the recoiling gun is, however, smaller than the acceleration of the bullet, because acceleration is inversely proportional to mass, and the bullet, as a rule, has a smaller mass than the gun.

4. Newton's law of gravitation. *All objects in the universe attract each other with an equal force that varies directly as a product of their masses, and inversely as a square of their distance from each other. This force is known as* **gravity.** Take, for example, the gravitational force between the Sun and the Earth. According to Newton's law of gravitation:

- The force exerted on the Earth by the Sun is equal and opposite to the force exerted on the Sun by the Earth.

- If the mass of the Earth were doubled, the force on the Earth would double.

- If the mass of the Sun were doubled, the force on the Earth would double.

- If the Earth were twice as far away from the Sun, the force on the Earth would be a factor of four smaller.

Energy

Energy can be defined as the **capacity to do work**. It may be either **kinetic** or **potential**. **Kinetic energy** is the energy possessed by a moving object. **Potential energy** is the energy stored in an object as a result of its position, shape, or state. An example of kinetic energy is a boulder rolling down a hill. An example of potential energy is a boulder carefully poised at the top of a hill so with that with the slightest push it will roll down the hill and crush an unsuspecting enemy. Or, to use a less violent example, potential energy is the energy stored in a storage battery.

According to the law of conservation of energy, energy can neither be created nor destroyed. Instead, it changes from one form to another. For instance, getting back to the storage battery, when the battery is being drawn from, chemical energy is changed to electrical energy, which then may be changed to mechanical energy, and so on. Energy is found in many different forms, including:

chemical	light	solar
electrical	mechanical	sound
gravitational	nuclear	wind
heat		

Sound and light energy travel in waves (although it gets complicated in the case of light). So let's take a look at the properties of waves.

Sound Waves

Sound waves are produced when an object vibrates, disturbing the medium around it. These waves can travel through air, liquids, and solids, but they cannot be transmitted through a vacuum, or empty space. Sound waves transmitted through air do not travel as fast as those transmitted through water, and those transmitted through water do not travel as fast as those transmitted through metal or wood. This is why a person can hear an approaching train sooner by putting his or her ear to the tracks than by listening for the train in an upright position.

The pitch of sound is directly related to the frequency of the sound waves. Sound waves with a high frequency produce a high pitch. Sound waves with a very high pitch are inaudible to humans, although they can be heard by dogs and other creatures. Sometimes, a human (and probably a dog as well) will perceive a sound as being a different frequency than the actual frequency of the sound. This is due to the **Doppler effect**. The Doppler effect occurs when either the source of the sound waves, the listener, or both, are moving. For example, if you are that person listening for a train to pass, the sound of the train will appear to change as it approaches and then passes you. It will sound higher as it approaches and passes directly past you, and lower as it moves further away from you. This is because you are receiving the sound waves at a quicker rate as their source approaches you, and at a slower rate as their source is moving away from you. The higher frequency is perceived as a higher pitch. Try listening for the Doppler effect the next time an ambulance passes by you.

Because light waves also experience a Doppler effect, scientists use this effect to determine how quickly astral objects are moving towards or away from Earth. Since astral light sources are essentially constant, when they **blueshift**, or gradually appear bluer, they are moving closer to us, and when they **redshift**, or gradually appear redder, they are moving away from us. Astronomers use Doppler shifts to calculate precisely how fast stars and other astronomical objects are moving toward or away from Earth.

Electromagnetic Spectrum

While on the subject of light, you should realize that visible light makes up only one small part—the visible part—of the electromagnetic spectrum. The electromagnetic spectrum covers all the different wavelengths and frequencies of photon energy, radiant energy such as the energy we receive from the sun. Visible light waves fall in the middle of the electromagnetic spectrum. Starting with lowest frequency (and therefore the longest wavelength), the electromagnetic spectrum goes from **radio waves** to **microwaves** to **infrared waves** to **visible light** to **ultraviolet light** to **X-rays** and finally to **gamma rays**, the most active radiant energy known to exist.

Visible light breaks down into different colors as well, based upon the frequency of the waves. Red has the lowest frequency, which is why wavelengths just below the frequency of visible light are called infrared; likewise, violet has the highest frequency, so wavelengths just above the frequency of visible light are called ultraviolet.

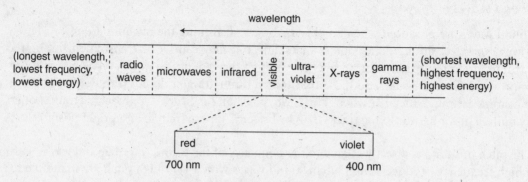

Figure 10. Electromagnetic spectrum

Optics

As noted above, light, as well as the entire electromagnetic spectrum, possesses properties of waves. However, unlike sound waves, which are mechanical, light waves are electromagnetic and can travel through empty space. They also travel at much higher speeds than do sound waves. The speed of light traveling through a vacuum is 299,792,458 meters per second (or roughly 300 million meters per second or 186,000 miles per second). This rate, although called the speed of light, also applies to the rest of the electromagnetic spectrum, from the speed of radio waves to the speed of gamma rays.

Refraction

It should be noted, however, that the speed of light can slow down, depending on the material through which the waves move; for example, light travels more slowly through water or glass than through a vacuum. The ratio by which light is slowed down is called the **refractive index** of that medium. For instance, the refractive index of a diamond is 2.4, which means that light travels 2.4 times faster when traveling through a vacuum than when traveling through a diamond.

Not only does the light change speeds as it travels through different transparent media, but it bends as well. This phenomenon is called refraction. If you put a straw in a clear glass of water, the straw appears to bend as it enters the water. This optical illusion is due to refraction.

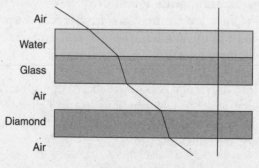

Figure 11. Refraction

As light travels from a less dense medium to a more dense medium, as from air to water, light bends toward the perpendicular, or **normal** in optical terms. As it then travels from a more dense to a less dense medium, as from water back to air, it bends away from the **normal**. The degree of bending is based on the differences in the refractive indexes of the two media.

It so happens that every color in the spectrum refracts a little differently from every other color. This is why white light separates into its component colors when it passes through a prism. The shorter wavelengths slow down and bend more than the longer wavelengths, so violet bends the most, and red the least.

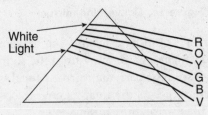

Figure 12. Prism

A diamond, because of its extremely high refractive index, will exaggerate this spreading of colors. The shorter wavelengths slow down and bend more than longer wavelengths. The larger index of refraction also means that the light will be internally reflected a greater number of times before emerging from one of the facets. The net result is greater color dispersion. A diamond will sparkle with a greater variety of colors than a piece of glass with the exact same shape. This is just one way that you can tell the difference between a fake rock and the genuine article.

Reflection

Any wave, including light, that bounces off a flat, smooth barrier follows the **law of reflection**, which states that the **angle of incidence** is equal to the **angle of reflection** as measured from a line normal to the barrier. In the case of light, this barrier is often a mirror.

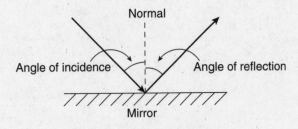

Figure 13. Law of reflection

Concave and Convex Mirrors and Lenses

Mirrors and lenses either can be flat, or they can be concave (curved in, like a cave) or convex (curved out, like a swelling). Because of the law of reflection, a **concave mirror** is also called a **converging mirror**, because the angles of incidence of rays of light parallel to the normal all converge upon a point.

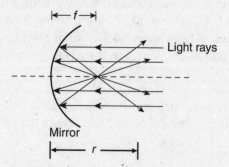

Figure 14. Converging mirror

An example of a concave mirror would be a magnifying makeup mirror, which magnifies images at close range. If you draw the mirror away from the source of the image, the image falls out of focus as the image source nears the mirror's **focal point**, the point where the mirror's angles of incidence converge. As the image source keeps moving beyond the focal point, the image reappears in the mirror, only upside down.

A **convex mirror**, on the other hand, is known a **diverging mirror** because it diverges the light waves that strike it. This type of mirror is commonly found behind the counter in convenience stores; the diverging lens reflects light rays from all over the store, allowing a clerk to keep an eye on activity throughout the store.

Lenses, unlike mirrors, operate on the principle of refraction. A **concave lens**—one that is thicker on the edges than it is in the middle—is also known as a **diverging lens** because it diverges the light waves that pass through it. In nearsightedness, light waves converge before they meet the retina. A nearsighted person sees objects close up but not far away. A concave lens placed before the eye bends light so that it converges further back in the eye, reaching the retina and correcting nearsightedness.

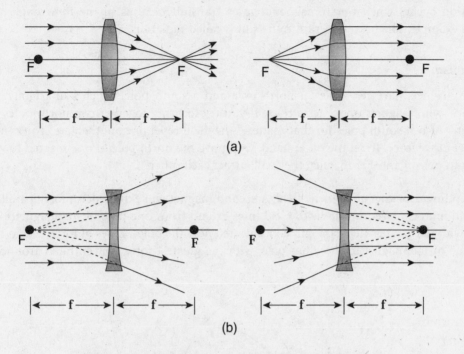

Figure 15. Converging lens (a) and diverging lens (b)

A **convex lens**—one that is thicker in the middle than on the edges—is also called a **converging lens** because it converges parallel waves that pass through it. This type of lens is used in reading glasses to correct farsightedness, as well as in magnifying glasses, cameras, telescopes, and microscopes. Children often use such lenses to concentrate sunlight and burn small pinholes in pieces of paper.

Heat

There are three means by which heat energy may be transferred from one object to another: **conduction**, **convection**, and **radiation**.

Conduction is the simplest method of heat transfer. It is accomplished by direct contact, such as placing your finger on a hot iron, which we recommend you not try at home. Metals are generally good **conductors** of heat. Other materials, such as wood, Styrofoam, and plastic, are poor conductors of heat, which makes them good **insulators**.

Convection is the transfer of heat unevenly in a liquid or gas, lowering the density of the heated liquid or gas, which causes it to rise and the cooler liquid or gas to fall. The resulting circulatory movement is termed convection. Hot air balloons operate on the principle of convection, because the hot gas in the balloon causes it to rise above the cooler air around it.

Radiation occurs when electromagnetic waves transmit heat, as in the foregoing paper-buring example. The heat we get from the sun is called radiation.

Magnetism

Simple magnets have two poles, a north pole and a south pole. Much like a Hollywood romance, with magnets opposites attract. If you try to bring together two north poles of a magnet—or two south poles for that matter—they will repel one another, and you can feel their repulsive force. If, on the other hand, you move the north pole of one magnet towards the south pole of another magnet, they will attract each other.

Surrounding a magnet a magnetic field. A second magnet will experience a force parallel to the field lines if placed in the field. Field lines extend from one pole of the magnet to the other, with the greatest field strength concentrated near the poles. Lines of force extend from one pole of the magnet to the other pole, with the greatest force concentrated around the poles.

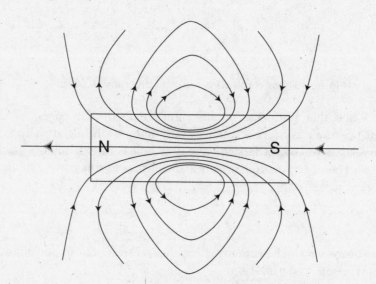

Figure 16. Magnetic field

Because the Earth itself is magnetized, with a North Pole and a South Pole, a magnetic compass, which contains a small, lightweight magnet balanced on a nearly frictionless, nonmagnetic surface, can be used to tell direction. The magnet, which is generally called a needle, has one end marked with an arrow and often the letter "N". This end of the needle is the magnet's south pole, which constantly orients itself to point toward the Earth's North Pole, allowing the person reading the compass to gain bearings from that direction.

In 1820, a Danish scientist named Hans Oersted discovered that an electrical current running through a wire produces a magnetic field. This caused other scientists to theorize that magnetism should be able to create electric currents. In 1831, an English scientist named

Michael Faraday provided the key to the practical generation of electricity: **electromagnetic induction**. Faraday discovered that a voltage could be generated across a length of wire if that wire were exposed to a perpendicular magnetic field flux of changing intensity. An easy way to create a magnetic field of changing intensity is to move a permanent magnet next to a wire or coil of wire. This discovery led to the development of **electric generators**, the means by which nearly all electric power is generated to this day.

To really understand how electricity works, you need to have a basic understanding of chemistry, which is what we'll look at now.

Chemistry

Chemistry is the science dealing with the composition and properties of substances, and with the reactions by which substances are produced from or converted into other substances. Matter is anything that has mass and occupies space, and any form of matter has certain chemical properties based upon its molecular composition. Let's start by going over some basic terms.

Element: A substance that cannot be separated into different substances by ordinary chemical methods. All matter is composed of elements, and all the known elements are listed on the Periodic Table of Elements (see figure 17).

Atom: The smallest component of an element that still retains the properties of the element. An atom may combine with similar particles of other elements to produce compounds. Atoms consist of a complex arrangement of electrons in motion about a positively charged nucleus containing protons and (except for hydrogen) neutrons.

Proton: A subatomic particle found in the atom's nucleus that carries a positive electric charge.

Neutron: A subatomic particle found in the atom's nucleus that does not have an electric charge and is therefore neutral.

Electron: A subatomic particle that orbits the nucleus of an atom. An electron carries a negative charge and has a miniscule mass. Ordinarily an atom has the same number of negative electrons around the nucleus as the number of positive protons in the nucleus.

Molecule: The smallest particle of an element or compound that can exist in the free state and still retain the characteristics of the element or compound. The molecules of elements consist of one atom or two or more similar atoms; those of compounds consist of two or more different atoms.

1 H 1.0																	2 He 4.0
3 Li 6.9	4 Be 9.0											5 B 10.8	6 C 12.0	7 N 14.0	8 O 16.0	9 F 19.0	10 Ne 20.2
11 Na 23.0	12 Mg 24.3											13 Al 27.0	14 Si 28.1	15 P 31.0	16 S 32.1	17 Cl 35.5	18 Ar 39.9
19 K 39.1	20 Ca 40.1	21 Sc 45.0	22 Ti 47.9	23 V 50.9	24 Cr 52.0	25 Mn 54.9	26 Fe 55.8	27 Co 58.9	28 Ni 58.7	29 Cu 63.5	30 Zn 65.4	31 Ga 69.7	32 Ge 72.6	33 As 74.9	34 Se 79.0	35 Br 79.9	36 Kr 83.8
37 Rb 85.5	38 Sr 87.6	39 Y 88.9	40 Zr 91.2	41 Nb 92.9	42 Mo 95.9	43 Tc (98)	44 Ru 101.1	45 Rh 102.9	46 Pd 106.4	47 Ag 107.9	48 Cd 112.4	49 In 114.8	50 Sn 118.7	51 Sb 121.8	52 Te 127.6	53 I 126.9	54 Xe 131.3
55 Cs 132.9	56 Ba 137.3	57 La* 138.9	72 Hf 178.5	73 Ta 180.9	74 W 183.9	75 Re 186.2	76 Os 190.2	77 Ir 192.2	78 Pt 195.1	79 Au 197.0	80 Hg 200.6	81 Tl 204.4	82 Pb 207.2	83 Bi 209.0	84 Po (209)	85 At (210)	86 Rn (222)
87 Fr (223)	88 Ra 226.0	89 Ac† 227.0	104 Unq (261)	105 Unp (262)	106 Unh (263)	107 Uns (262)	108 Uno (265)	109 Une (267)									

58 Ce 140.1	59 Pr 140.9	60 Nd 144.2	61 Pm (145)	62 Sm 150.4	63 Eu 152.0	64 Gd 157.3	65 Tb 158.9	66 Dy 162.5	67 Ho 164.9	68 Er 167.3	69 Tm 168.9	70 Yb 173.0	71 Lu 175.0
90 Th 232.0	91 Pa (231)	92 U 238.0	93 Np (237)	94 Pu (244)	95 Am (243)	96 Cm (247)	97 Bk (247)	98 Cf (251)	99 Es (252)	100 Fm (257)	101 Md (258)	102 No (259)	103 Lr (260)

Figure 17. Periodic Table of the Elements

In order to be able to read the Periodic Table of Elements, there are a few things you need to understand. For starters, elements are arranged in order of increasing **atomic number**, from left to right and from top to bottom. The different **rows** of elements are called **periods**. The periods correspond to the **shells**, or the different orbits that electrons occupy around atoms. As a rule, electrons will occupy the lowest shell they can, and move on to higher shells only after lower shells are occupied (although this rule is sometimes violated) so as to minimize the energy of the atom. Every element in the top row (the first period) has one shell for its electrons. Every element in the second row (the second period) has two shells for its electrons, and so on. At this time, the maximum number of shells is seven.

The Periodic Table has a special name for its columns too. The elements in a column are called a **group**. The elements in a group have the same number of electrons in their outer shell. It is the group that an element occupies, much more than the period, that determines its chemical properties. This is because the number of electrons needed to complete an element's outer shell shapes the way in which it reacts with other elements to form molecules. For instance, every element in the first column (Group I) has one electron in its outer shell. The elements in this group are called **alkali metals**, which describe soft, silvery metals that react strongly with water. The further down the group you go, the more violent this reaction is. These alkali metals are usually stored under oil to protect them from moisture and oxygen. You may be familiar with the alkali metal **sodium** (Na) and its highly reactive properties.

By the same token, every element on the second column (Group II) has two electrons in the outer shell. As you keep counting the columns, you'll know how many electrons are in the outer shell. Note that the far right-hand column is composed of a group called the **noble gases**, sometimes referred to as inert gases, because these elements generally don't react with other elements since their outer shell is completely filled.

HYDROGEN IS SPECIAL

Hydrogen has only one proton, and unlike every other element, has no neutrons. This is why the *atomic number* and the *atomic weight* of Hydrogen are almost identical (1 versus 1.007).

Now take a look at an individual element box within the Periodic Table. Here's **chlorine**.

```
┌──────────┐
│    17    │
│          │
│    Cl    │
│          │
│   35.5   │
└──────────┘
```

Figure 18. Chlorine

Chlorine is found on the column just to the left of the noble gases column of the periodic table (Group VIIA), which makes it a **halogen**, a term that describes the group of very reactive, nonmetallic chemical elements that are just one electron shy of having a complete outer shell. When it is in its pure form, chlorine is a greenish-yellow, poisonous gas with a disagreeable odor. Its **atomic number** is **17**, which is the number of protons in the nucleus of a chlorine atom, and also the number of electrons orbiting its shells. Its **atomic symbol**, Cl, is fairly close to its name, unlike the symbols of some other common elements, such as **Fe** (iron), **Au** (gold), **Ag** (silver), **W** (tungsten), or the aforementioned **Na** (sodium), symbols that derive from the elements' Latin names, rather than their familiar English names.

Finally, the **atomic weight** of chlorine is listed as **35.45**, which is the weight of one atom of chlorine expressed in atomic mass units: it is the average weight of all the **isotopes** of chlorine. Isotopes are different forms of an element that have different atomic weights because they have different numbers of neutrons. The atomic weight tells you how many neutrons, on average, an element has. Because electrons have a negligible mass, if you round off the atomic weight of an element and subtract its atomic number, you get the number of neutrons found on a typical atom of the element. So chlorine has, on average, about $35 - 17 = 18$ neutrons per atom, although a fairly common isotope of chlorine has 19 neutrons, which is why the atomic weight is 35.45.

Note that **metals** (sodium, copper, silver, gold, iron, etc.) generally have three or fewer electrons in the outermost energy level and tend to give up electrons readily. Metals tend to be shiny, malleable, and are good conductors of heat and electricity. Approximately 75 percent of the elements on the Periodic Table are metals or metalloids. **Nonmetals** have five or more electrons in their outer shells, and thus hold on to their electrons tightly (chlorine, nitrogen, oxygen, etc.). Nonmetals often occur as gases, although they can also occur as solids (sulfur, iodine, phosphorus, etc.), and even the occasional liquid (bromine).

Compounds

Unstable elements readily form into **compounds** with properties very distinct from the elements from which they are composed. For instance, the aforementioned sodium and chlorine, both of which are extremely unstable and noxious as elements, combine to form the stable and edible compound sodium chloride ($NaCl$), more commonly known as table salt. Table salt is called an **ionic compound** because each chlorine atom borrows an electron from each sodium atom and the atoms stick closely together to form a very tightly bound crystalline structure when salt is in solid form. When it is placed in solution, however, such as when table salt is poured in water, the atoms dissociate into sodium ions and chloride ions. An **ion** is an electrically charged atom; in this case each of the sodium atoms is positively charged because it has lent an electron to its corresponding chloride atom, and each of the chloride atoms is negatively charged for the same reason. Because of this ionic dissolution, salt water is an excellent electrical conductor, which is one good reason not to go swimming in the ocean during an electrical storm.

There are thousands of common compounds, including water (H_2O) and the many organic compounds, all of which contain carbon. An example of an organic compound is glucose ($C_6H_{12}O_6$), otherwise known as table sugar. Table sugar is an example of a **covalent compound**, which means, among other things, that it does not ionize when dissolved in water. In a covalent compound, the atoms in the molecule have covalent bonds; that is, they share electrons in pairs, so that each atom provides half the electrons.

Solutions and Concentrations

While on the subject of compounds dissolved in water, you should know that in the world of chemistry, the substance being dissolved in the water is called a **solute**, the water (or whatever liquid the solute is dissolved into) is called a **solvent**, and the resulting mixture is called a **solution**. Solutes may be solids, liquids, or gases. Solutions are often classified according to their **concentration**, or how much solute they contain. Solutions with a relatively small of amount of solute per solvent are termed **dilute**, while solutions with a relatively large amount of solute per solvent are termed **concentrated**. Moreover, solutions that can still dissolve more solvent without changing the temperature or pressure of the solution are called **unsaturated**.

Solutions that contain the maximum amount of solute that can be dissolved at a given temperature and pressure are called **saturated**. Finally, solutions that contain more solute than they can normally hold at a given temperature and pressure are called **supersaturated**.

Acids and Bases

An **acid** is a substance that gives up positively charged hydrogen ions (H^+) when dissolved in water. Acids corrode metals and generally have a sour taste (those that are potable, that is). Some common acidic solutions are vinegar (which has acetic acid) and lemon juice (which has citric acid). More potent acids include hydrochloric acid, nitric acid, battery acid, and sulfuric acid, all of which are extremely corrosive and must be handled with the utmost care.

A **base** is a substance that gives up negative charged hydroxyl ions (OH^-) when dissolved in water. Basic substances are may also be referred to as **alkaline**. Bases typically taste bitter. Some common basic substances found in a kitchen include baking soda, Phillip's Milk of Magnesia™, and soap. More potent bases include sodium hydroxide (lye), bleach, and Drano™. When acids and bases react (and they react together rather powerfully), the substances neutralize each other and turn into water and a salt.

The **pH** of a solution is a number from 0 to 14 that indicates how basic or acidic that solution is. According to the pH scale, solutions with a pH less than 7 are acidic, with the degree of acidity increasing tenfold with each declining number. For instance, black coffee has a pH of 5; vinegar, which is 100 times as acidic as coffee, has a pH of 3; and battery acid, which is 100 times as acidic as vinegar, has a pH of 1. A solution with a pH of 7 is neutral. Pure water has a pH of 7. Solutions with a pH greater than 7 are basic, with the degree of alkalinity once again increasing tenfold with each increasing number. Baking soda has a pH of 9, ammonia solution has a pH of 11, and bleach has a pH of 13, making it 10,000 times as basic as baking soda.

Physical versus Chemical Reactions

Matter may undergo either a **physical change** or a **chemical change**. The form, size, and shape of matter may be altered in a physical change, but the molecules remain unchanged. For instance H_2O may exist as a solid (ice), a liquid (water), or a gas (steam) as the temperature and pressure change. In fact, all substances have freezing points and boiling points, although the temperature and pressure needed to create these different states of matter may never occur in real-earth conditions. Another illustration of a physical change is table sugar being dissolved in water; the molecules ($C_6H_{12}O_6$) never change even as the sugar crystals dissolve and the sugar molecules mix in with the water molecules.

In a chemical change, molecules of new matter are formed that are different from the original molecules of matter. When molecules undergo a chemical change, the process is called a **chemical reaction**. The molecules that enter the reaction are called **reactants** and the molecules that result from the reaction are called **products**. Common examples of chemical reactions include the formation of rust on iron and the conversion of wood to charcoal in a fire.

You will never have to balance a chemical equation (a diagram of the reactants and products in a chemical reaction) on the ASVAB, but it is helpful to know that there are four different types of chemical reactions. Here they are.

Synthesis

Synthesis occurs when two or more elements or compounds combine to form a new compound. For example, hydrogen gas and oxygen gas may combine to form water. Here's what the chemical equation for this reaction looks like:

$$2H_2 + O_2 \rightarrow 2\ H_2O$$

Decomposition

In a **decomposition reaction**, one substance breaks down into two or more substances. A decomposition reaction is the reverse of a synthesis reaction. For example, water can break back down into hydrogen gas and oxygen gas. Here's what this chemical equation would look like:

$$2\ H_2O \rightarrow 2H_2 + O_2$$

Single Displacement

In a **single displacement reaction**, a single element replaces another element in a compound. Two reactants yield two products. For example, when zinc combines with hydrochloric acid, the zinc replaces hydrogen to form zinc chloride and hydrogen gas. The chemical equation for this single displacement reaction looks like this:

$$Zn + 2HCl \rightarrow ZnCl_2 + H_2$$

Double Displacement

In a **double displacement reaction**, parts of two compounds switch places with each other to form two new compounds. In a double displacement reaction, two reactants yield two products. For example, when silver nitrate combines with sodium chloride, two new compounds, silver chloride and sodium nitrate, are formed because the sodium and silver switch places. The chemical equation for this double replacement reaction looks like this:

$$AgNO_3 + NaCl \rightarrow AgCl + NaNO_3$$

And that covers all the science that could appear of the General Science section of the ASVAB. Finally! Once again, a quick quiz follows.

PHYSICAL SCIENCE PRACTICE SET

1. What is 77° F in degrees Celsius?

    (A) 25°
    (B) 32°
    (C) 37°
    (D) 5°

2. Which of the following best explains the recoil action of a shooting gun?

    (A) Newton's First Law of Motion
    (B) Newton's Second Law of Motion
    (C) Newton's Third Law of Motion
    (D) Newton's Law of Gravitation

3. If the Moon's orbit were to change so that it was twice as close to the Earth as is it presently is, its gravitational pull on the Earth would

    (A) increase two-fold
    (B) increase four-fold
    (C) remain the same
    (D) decrease two-fold

4. The most common element in the Earth's atmosphere is

    (A) helium
    (B) hydrogen
    (C) nitrogen
    (D) oxygen

5. Which of the following waves on the electromagnetic spectrum has the highest frequency?

    (A) microwaves
    (B) X-rays
    (C) visible light
    (D) radio waves

6. A straight pole placed at an angle in the water appears to bend as it enters the water. This optical illusion is caused by

    (A) deflection
    (B) diffraction
    (C) reflection
    (D) refraction

7. An element whose outer shell is only missing a few electrons is called a

    (A) metal
    (B) nonmetal
    (C) metalloid
    (D) noble gas

$$6H_2O + 6CO_2 \rightarrow C_6H_{12}O_6 + 6O_2$$

8. The process of photosynthesis, described in the chemical equation above, is an example of

    (A) synthesis
    (B) decomposition
    (C) single displacement
    (D) double displacement

[Answers on p. 259]

ANSWERS AND EXPLANATIONS FOR GENERAL SCIENCE PRACTICE SETS

Life Science Practice Set

1. **B.**

Beriberi is caused by a lack of Vitamin B_1, also known as thiamine.

2. **A**

The proper pathway of blood through the heart is as follows:

vena cava $\rightarrow$ right atrium $\rightarrow$ right ventricle $\rightarrow$ pulmonary artery $\rightarrow$ pulmonary vein $\rightarrow$ left atrium $\rightarrow$ left ventricle $\rightarrow$ aorta

3. **C**

Most digestion takes place in the small intestine.

4. **C**

Type O blood, also known as the "universal donor" type, can be donated to anyone.

5. **B**

A typical human gamete contains half the number of chromosomes as a normal cell, or 23.

6. **D.**

If color-blindness is a recessive sex-linked chromosome found on the X chromosome, the incidence of color-blindness among men indicates the incidence of the color-blindness gene, which is 1 in 20. Because females have two X chromosomes, for a female to be color-blind, both X chromosomes would have to contain the recessive gene. Thus the probability that a female in the population would be color-blind would be $\frac{1}{20} \times \frac{1}{20} = \frac{1}{400}$.

7. **C**

The eel is a type of fish, and therefore it belongs in the phylum Chordata.

8. **C**

The Primate order includes man, who also belongs to the phylum Chordata, the class Mammalia, and the family Homidae.

9. **D**

A deer is an example of a primary consumer, that is, an animal that consumes only vegetation.

10. **D**

The taiga differs from the tundra in that the ground is warm enough to allow conifers to grow.

Earth Science Practice Set

1. B

The ozone layer is found in the upper stratosphere.

2. C

The Earth's magnetic field is caused by the liquid outer core spinning around the solid inner core, which generates an electric current.

3. A

Cirrus clouds are found at the highest altitudes of all clouds.

4. B

Life on Earth has existed for approximately 3.8 billion years.

5. C

Slate is not a sedimentary rock, but is a metamorphic rock.

6. D

The Sun comprises 99 percent of the solar system's mass.

7. D

The smallest planet in the solar system is Pluto.

8. B

The oceanic tides are caused by the gravitational pull of the Moon on the Earth.

Physical Science Practice Set

1. A

To convert the temperature from degree Fahrenheit to degrees Celsius, first subtract 32, and then multiply by $\frac{5}{9}$. $77 - 32 = 45$. $45 \times \frac{5}{9} = 25$.

2. C

The recoil action of a shooting gun is explained by Newton's Third Law of Motion, that is, for every action there is an equal and opposite reaction.

3. B

Objects attract each other with a force that varies inversely as the square of their distance from each other. So if the Moon were twice as close to the Earth as it presently is, it would exert four times the gravitational pull.

4. C

Nitrogen accounts for about 77 percent of the composition of the atmosphere.

5. B

Of the wave states listed, X-rays have the highest frequency in the electromagnetic spectrum (gamma rays have an even higher frequency).

6. D

The optical illusion that makes straight objects appear to bend as they enter water is caused by refraction.

7. B

An element whose outer shell is only missing a few electrons is called a nonmetal.

8. C

A single element (carbon) detaches from 6 carbon dioxide molecules and attaches to 6 water molecules, to form a single sugar molecule and 6 oxygen molecules. Because only one element is making the switch, this is considered a single-displacement reaction.

CHAPTER EIGHT

Automotive Information

INTRODUCTION

Despite its appearance at times, the ASVAB is much more than just a military entrance exam. It is a collection of tests designed to record not only your abilities in math, science and language, but also to see if your interests and aptitudes may lie in other areas. One prominent area that they look at is automotive technology.

For some, this section will seem easy. You may spend your weekends fixing cars, or maybe you are just an auto enthusiast. For others, this review might as well be written in Greek. Knowing this, we have tried our best to design this chapter with both groups in mind: on the one hand, a review of basics for those in the know about the inner workings of cars, on the other, a primer for those who know that cars need gas and then they go forward and that's about it.

Take your time with this section, remembering that you can't possibly know everything in this review after one read. You should see it as a learning process whereby you can pick up a little about drive trains one day and a little about exhaust systems the next. We're confident that by the time you're done with this section, the ASVAB's auto questions will seem easier than an oil lube.

AUTOMOTIVE SYSTEMS

The modern automobile is a technological marvel. Thousands of parts are assembled to form the means that most of us use for our daily transportation. Space-age materials and advanced computer control systems are used extensively in its construction, but in spite of all this, the basic systems within the automobile still function the same as they always have.

Despite its size, any automobile is still only made up of many **parts**. Parts are the smallest pieces that are used in the construction of the automobile. Parts could include such items as bolts and screws, spark plugs, or accessory drive (fan) belts. The parts of the vehicle cannot be disassembled any further, so they form the foundation for the construction of the vehicle.

Parts are put together to form **assemblies**. An example of an assembly would be a vehicle's starter motor. A service technician may take apart an assembly and replace parts in it as part of the vehicle repair process. However, the trend is towards replacing assemblies in their entirety as opposed to servicing them. Assemblies are more complex and are important to the operation of the vehicle, but they cannot stand alone to perform useful work. In order to do this, groups of assemblies must be incorporated into vehicle systems.

Automobile **systems** are groups of assemblies that are put together to perform specific tasks. The vehicle's starting system would include the starter motor, but would also include critical components such as the battery, ignition switch, and associated cables and wiring. Put all together, these components can work to crank (turn) the engine for starting purposes.

The major automotive systems are:

Engine: generates power to drive the vehicle's wheels and various accessories.

Cooling system: removes excess heat from the engine.

Lubrication system: circulates motor oil through the engine to reduce friction and make the engine run smoothly.

Fuel system: ensures that correct amounts of air and fuel are available for efficient combustion in the engine.

Ignition system: generates and times the spark that initiates combustion.

Exhaust system: forms a "pipeline" for waste gases to be removed from the engine and then be dissipated to the open atmosphere.

Emission control system: helps limit toxic vehicle emissions.

Electrical system: includes starting, charging, lighting, and accessory systems.

Computer system: controls all aspects of vehicle operation, including engine, drive train, brakes, and suspension.

Drive train: transmits power from the engine to the vehicle's drive wheels.

Suspension and steering: controls the vehicle's ride quality and handling.

Brake system: stops the vehicle safely and predictably.

BASIC ENGINE THEORY

Engines used in most automobiles are known as **internal combustion engines**. Combustion is the rapid burning of an air/fuel mixture. Internal combustion means exactly that: fuel is burned *internally* and the resulting heat is used directly to power an engine. This is different from an external combustion engine, such as a steam engine, where the fuel is burned in a boiler and the heat is used to create steam, which is then piped to the cylinders where the actual work is done.

Internal combustion engines can be fueled with gasoline, diesel fuel, or other petroleum products such as propane or natural gas. Three things must be present before combustion can take place: air, fuel, and a heat source that can be used to ignite the air/fuel mixture. If any one of those three elements is missing, combustion stops and the engine will not run.

There are common components in all internal combustion engines. These components include:

Engine block: forms the framework for the engine cylinders and reciprocating assembly.

Piston: a cylindrically-shaped object with a solid crown (top) that moves up and down in the engine's cylinders. Hot gases from the combustion of the air-fuel mixture push on the piston to do the actual work.

Cylinder: forms a guide for the piston to move in; allows the piston to move up and down as the engine completes its cycle.

Piston rings: seal the piston to the cylinder and prevent combustion gases from leaking past. Oil rings prevent oil from the engine crankcase from making its way into the combustion chamber.

Wrist pin: connects the piston to the connecting rod, and forms a pivot point for the small end of the connecting rod to move on.

Connecting rod: connects the piston/wrist pin assembly to the engine's crankshaft. The large end of the connecting rod attaches to the crankshaft on the connecting rod journal.

Crankshaft: converts the linear (straight line) motion of the piston into rotary motion, which can then be used to power a vehicle or drive an accessory.

Cylinder head: located above the piston, it houses the combustion chamber, the intake and exhaust valves, and the intake and exhaust ports.

Combustion chamber: located in the cylinder head directly above the piston, it is where the actual combustion of the air-fuel mixture takes place.

Intake valve: allows air-fuel mixture to be drawn into the combustion chamber. When closed, it must seal the combustion chamber from the intake port.

Exhaust valve: allows waste gases to be removed from the combustion chamber. When closed, it must seal the combustion chamber from the exhaust port.

Camshaft: responsible for the opening and closing of the engine's intake and exhaust valves. The camshaft turns at one-half the speed of the engine's crankshaft.

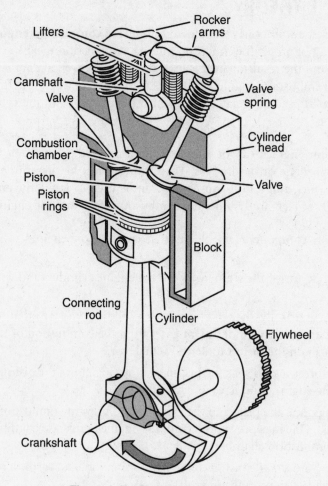

Figure 1. Basic engine components

The conversion of linear (straight line) motion into rotary motion as achieved by the piston-connecting rod-crankshaft combination is very similar to the leg of a bicycle rider. As the rider's upper leg moves up and down (piston), her lower leg (connecting rod), bicycle pedals, and sprocket (crankshaft) convert that straight line motion into rotary motion which then can be used to drive the wheels of the bicycle.

Most internal combustion engines are built to utilize a **four stroke-cycle**. This means that it takes four strokes of the piston to complete one cycle of events. A stroke of the piston is defined as the piston movement from the top of its travel in the cylinder (**TDC** or **Top Dead Center**) to the bottom of its travel (**BDC** or **Bottom Dead Center**) or vice versa. With the piston connected to the crankshaft through the connecting rod, one stroke of the piston generates one-half turn of the crankshaft. A four stroke-cycle engine thus requires *two complete revolutions* (or turns) of the crankshaft to complete one cycle of events.

The four stroke-cycle begins with the **intake stroke**. The piston is at TDC (Top Dead Center), and the intake valve is beginning to open. As the piston moves downward in the cylinder, a low-pressure area is created above the piston. This low-pressure area can also be described as a vacuum. Since the intake valve is open and is allowing atmospheric air to enter the combustion chamber, higher atmospheric air pressure pushes air through the engine's intake system and towards the low-pressure area above the piston. As the air is traveling through the intake system, fuel is injected into the air stream before it enters the combustion chamber. This allows the cylinder to fill with a fresh charge of air/fuel mixture. Once the piston reaches BDC (Bottom Dead Center), the intake valve is almost closed again and the engine is ready to begin the next phase of the combustion cycle.

The piston now starts on an upward stroke, and both of the engine's valves are closed. With the combustion chamber then sealed, the continued upward motion of the piston will compress the air-fuel mixture in the cylinder as the engine starts its **compression stroke**. The gases in the cylinder are forced into a progressively smaller space as the piston continues toward TDC. These gases become progressively hotter and the air/fuel mixture becomes more easily ignited as the particles of fuel get closer and closer together.

Just before the piston reaches TDC, the spark plug fires and ignites the air-fuel mixture, starting a flame that then travels across the combustion chamber. This flame further heats the gases in the combustion chamber and the resulting rapid expansion of these gases pushes on the piston as it passes TDC and then continues its downward stroke. This is known as the **power stroke** of the engine, and this is where all of the engine's power is generated. The piston continues its descent, with hot gases pushing it downwards towards BDC.

Just before the piston reaches BDC, the exhaust valve starts to open and the engine begins its fourth and final stroke, the **exhaust stroke**. The gases in the combustion chamber are now spent and must be purged from the engine. As the piston begins its upward movement, it pushes exhaust gases past the open exhaust valve and into the engine's exhaust system where it eventually is sent out to the open atmosphere. The piston continues its travel towards TDC, and at that point will have completed one complete cycle of events. This cycle then starts over as the intake stroke begins again.

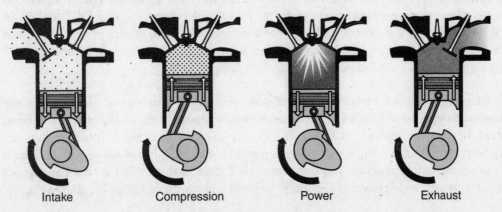

Intake   Compression   Power   Exhaust

Figure 2. Four-stroke cycle

Internal combustion engines do not create energy. Scientists tell us that energy cannot be created or destroyed; it can only be converted from one form into another. Internal combustion engines convert the **chemical energy** in the air/fuel mixture into **heat energy**, and this heat energy is then converted into **mechanical energy**. Because there are two energy conversions that take place in an internal combustion engine, there is a great amount of energy loss and consequently its efficiency is very low. Approximately one-third of the energy in the air/fuel mixture gets converted into useable power. The remainder is lost as waste heat, both through the exhaust and the engine's cooling system.

CYLINDER ARRANGEMENT

Automotive engines can be built in a number of different configurations, and these can most easily be classified in terms of the engine's **cylinder arrangement**. The most common numbers of cylinders in automobile engines are four, six, and eight, but there are a few designs that utilize three, five, ten, and even twelve cylinders.

The simplest cylinder arrangement is known as the **inline** design, in which all of the engine's cylinders are vertical and lined up in a row. This is a practical design for four and six-cylinder engines, but becomes very unwieldy with engines that utilize more than six cylinders. Inline four-cylinder engines are very popular in front-wheel drive cars with transverse (sideways) mounted engines. Inline engines are most often found in small to medium-sized vehicles.

Another variation of the inline engine is the **slant** version, and the most popular design here was the Slant-Six engine. This was basically an inline six-cylinder that was tilted to the side to fit better into engine compartments with lower hood lines. This now meant that engineers could build a long-stroke engine and install it into the compact cars that became popular in the early 60s. This design proved to be both durable and popular for decades.

There was a time when inline eight-cylinder engines were being built, but they were very heavy and required huge engine compartments to be designed around them. In order to work with body designers and make the front end of the car more pleasing to the eye, a **V-design** was introduced. This cut the length of the engine by half, and made the engine shorter, as now the cylinders were arranged in two banks that formed the shape of a "V." Now it was possible to fit a large-displacement engine into a smaller vehicle, so the era of the hot rod was ushered in. Engines with eight cylinders or more are now almost universally built in the "V" configuration, but the V-6 is also a very common design.

The last major cylinder arrangement that has been utilized by engine designers is the **horizontally opposed** or **flat** design. This has all of the cylinders lying on the horizontal plane, with half of the cylinders facing away from the other half and the crankshaft located between them. Some refer to this design as a "boxer" engine because the pistons move back and forth like a boxer throwing punches. The one major advantage to this design is that the engine's center of gravity is much lower so it is easier to build a more stable, better-handling vehicle.

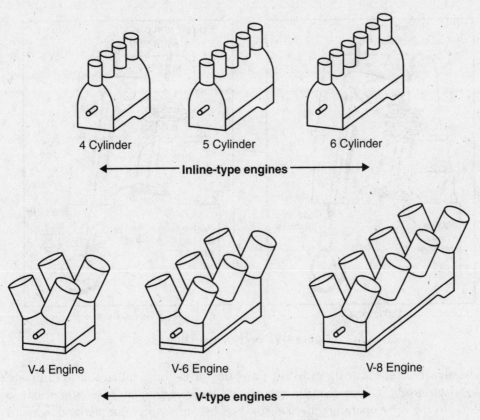

Figure 3. Cylinder arrangements

CAMSHAFT LOCATION

Another classification used to describe automotive engines is **camshaft location**. The camshaft is responsible for the opening and closing of the engine's valves, and it is driven by the crankshaft through a **timing chain** or **timing belt**. Most modern engines have the camshaft located in the engine block and the intake and exhaust valves located in the cylinder head. Engines built in this manner would be known as **overhead valve** or **OHV** engines.

If the camshaft is located in the engine block, it will operate the valves through lifters, pushrods, and rocker arms. Unfortunately, all these extra parts add a good deal of mass to the valve train (the mechanism that opens and closes the valves), and thus limits the speed of the engine. This is because the inertia of the valve train at high engine speeds can cause the valves to "float" and not get a chance to close completely between valve openings.

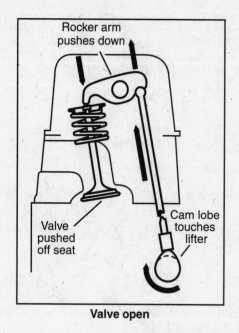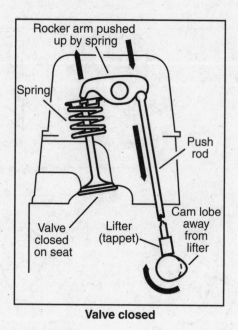

Figure 4. Valve train operation

Engine designers often locate the camshaft above the valves and are then able to eliminate the lifters and pushrods. The mechanism for driving the camshaft becomes somewhat more complex, but the valve operating mechanism itself becomes much simpler and lighter. Less mass in the valve train means that higher engine speeds can be attained. This design is known as **single overhead cam** or **SOHC**. In a V-type engine with two cylinder heads, there would be two camshafts, with one installed above each cylinder head.

One final step to make even higher engine speeds possible is to go to a **double overhead cam** or **DOHC** arrangement. This puts two camshafts into each cylinder head, and makes it so one cam operates the exhaust valves in that head, and the other operates all the intake valves. With this arrangement, it is possible to eliminate the rocker arms that are often used in SOHC engines and have the camshafts operate the valves directly through a follower. DOHC designs are most often used for racing engines. This is because their light valve trains allow for excellent valve control at high engine speeds, and the valves can be located in an optimum location for better air flow through the cylinder head.

MULTIPLE-VALVE CYLINDER HEADS

Engines may also be classified according to the number of valves used for each cylinder. The least expensive and most common arrangement is to use a **two-valve cylinder head**, with one intake valve and one exhaust valve per cylinder. To improve airflow through the engine and thus, engine performance, it is possible to design a multiple (more than two) valve cylinder head. Manufacturers have built cars that use three valves per cylinder, but now it is much more common to used a **four-valve** cylinder head in high performance applications. This arrangement has two intake valves and two exhaust valves for each cylinder.

ENGINE DISPLACEMENT

As pistons move up and down in their cylinders, they "sweep" out a certain volume. If one were to measure the volume that was displaced by each piston as it moved from BDC to TDC, that cylinder's **displacement** could be calculated.

Engine displacement is significant, because it gives an indication of how much air is moved through the engine during its cycle. Higher displacement engines move more air, thus more fuel can be burned and more horsepower generated. Also, higher displacement engines are physically larger because of their larger cylinder bores and longer strokes.

In order to calculate engine displacement, we must know the diameter of the cylinder bore, the stroke, and the number of cylinders in the engine. The cylinder **bore** is the diameter of the cylinder. The **stroke** is the total distance that the piston moves as it travels from TDC to BDC. Stroke is determined by the design of the crankshaft.

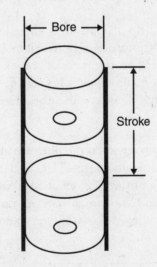

Figure 5. Engine displacement

The formula that can be used to calculate engine displacement is $\pi r^2 h$, where r is the radius of the cylinder bore (one-half the diameter) and h (height) is the stroke of the cylinder. For a V-8 engine with a bore of 4 inches and a stroke of 3.5 inches, the following calculation would be performed:

$$\pi (2 \text{ inches})^2 \times 3.5 \text{ inches} \times 8 \text{ cylinders} = 351.7 \text{ in}^3$$

Rounded off, this would be 350 cubic inches of displacement. Increasing either the engine's bore or stroke would result in an increase of displacement.

When measuring engine displacement using the SI (System International) or metric system, one would plug in bore and stroke measurements in centimeters. This would result in a displacement stated in **cubic centimeters** (**cc**). The convenience of the metric system is that it is easy to change units since the entire system is based on multiples of ten. In the case of engine displacements expressed in cubic centimeters, simply divide the number by 1,000 to change the units to liters (1 liter = 1,000 cc). For example, a 1,900 cc engine would be the same as a 1.9 liter engine.

Converting engine displacements from liters to cubic inches is also fairly easy, but a calculator might be required. Since 1 liter is roughly the same as 61 cubic inches, 1.9 liters could be converted by multiplying by 61. A 1.9 liter engine would have 116 cubic inches of displacement.

Compression Ratio

When the engine's piston moves from BDC to TDC on the compression stroke, the air/fuel mixture is squeezed and its temperature increases. The amount of "squeeze" that the engine places on the air/fuel mixture can be quantified in terms of its **compression ratio**.

A higher compression ratio will help increase an engine's overall efficiency. However, there is an upper limit as to how far the compression ratio can be increased before adverse effects on combustion are experienced. Higher compression ratios increase the temperature of the air/fuel mixture, and with lower quality fuel, it is possible to have the mixture "auto ignite" due to these higher temperatures. This would cause the engine to run roughly and could cause serious engine damage.

Measuring the volume in the cylinder when the piston is at BDC, and comparing that to the volume in the cylinder when the piston reaches TDC, will calculate the engine's compression ratio. For instance, if the volume of the cylinder at BDC were six times the volume at TDC, the compression ratio would be 6:1. Note that there are no units (such as inches or degrees) associated with compression ratio; it is strictly a ratio (comparison) of two volume measurements.

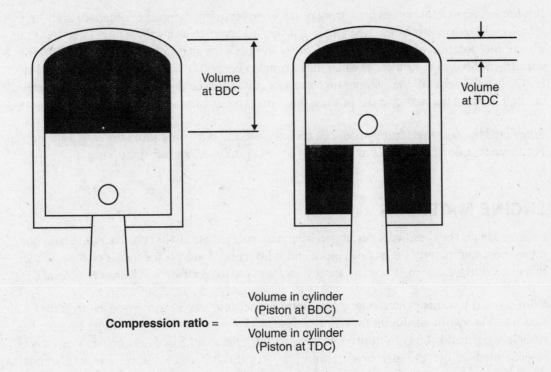

$$\text{Compression ratio} = \frac{\text{Volume in cylinder (Piston at BDC)}}{\text{Volume in cylinder (Piston at TDC)}}$$

Figure 6. Compression ratio

Most current gasoline engines use a compression ratio of around 9:1. Increasing the compression ratio past this level is risky due to the quality of the fuel available in most areas of the United States. It is possible to increase a gasoline engine's compression ratio to 12:1 if higher quality (octane) fuel is available.

FIRING ORDER

In multiple-cylinder engines, the power strokes of the cylinders will be evenly spaced over two revolutions of the crankshaft. Remember that it takes two revolutions of the crankshaft to complete one cycle of events in a four-stroke cycle engine. This means that all of the cylinders in the engine must complete a power stroke in two revolutions of the crankshaft. In the case of a four-cylinder engine, there would be one-half of a revolution of the crankshaft between power strokes. Two of the cylinders would fire during one revolution of the crankshaft, and the other two would fire during the second turn.

The order that the cylinders fire in is known as the **firing order**. A common firing order for four-cylinder engines is 1-3-4-2. This means that once the first cylinder fires, the crankshaft will make one-half turn, and then the third will fire and so on. Cylinders 1 and 3 will fire on the first turn of the crankshaft, and cylinders 4 and 2 will fire on the second turn of the crankshaft. In the case of a V-8 engine with a firing order of 1-8-4-3-6-5-7-2, cylinders 1, 8, 4, and 3 will fire on the first turn of the crankshaft, and 6, 5, 7, and 2 will fire during the second turn.

It is important to know an engine's firing order when servicing its ignition system or adjusting its valves. In older, distributor-type engines, it was necessary to know the firing order and the direction of rotation of the distributor in order to install the spark plug wires correctly. Valve adjustment becomes much easier when the technician knows the engine's firing order. The key is to adjust the valves of the cylinder that is at TDC and ready to fire, and then turn the engine enough to bring the next cylinder in the firing order to TDC and adjust its valves.

Many engines have their firing order cast directly into the intake manifold for easy reference. For those that don't, it is necessary to refer to the engine's service information.

ENGINE MATERIALS

Engines can also be classified according to what materials are used in its construction. Years ago, it was most common for the engine's block and cylinder head to be made from cast iron. While this was a durable design, it was also quite heavy and wasn't as efficient at transferring heat.

With a trend towards lighter engine assemblies, it became a common approach to utilize a cast-iron block with an aluminum cylinder head. Aluminum was a natural choice because of its light weight and ability to transfer heat easily. Since the majority of the engine's waste heat is generated at the cylinder head, aluminum fits the bill quite nicely. The one major drawback, however, is that an aluminum cylinder head is relatively fragile and is sensitive to overheating. Inline four-cylinder engines are often designed with a cast iron block and an aluminum cylinder head. High performance applications demand that the engine be as light as possible, so more exotic designs use aluminum blocks and cylinder heads. These engines are relatively rare and are also quite expensive.

DIESEL ENGINES

Another variation of the internal combustion engine is the diesel. **Diesel engines** are much simpler and more reliable than gasoline engines, mostly because they do not incorporate a spark-ignition system. Instead of using a spark to initiate combustion, diesel engines use a much higher compression ratio to generate sufficient **heat of compression** to ignite the air-fuel mixture. The compression ratio for a diesel engine can range anywhere from 16:1 to 22:1.

Another major difference between a diesel engine and most gasoline engines is that diesels inject their fuel directly into the combustion chamber. On the intake stroke, a diesel engine draws in only air, and it compresses this air during its compression stroke. Since the diesel's compression ratio is so high, a tremendous amount of heat is developed in the combustion chamber as the piston moves towards TDC. A high-pressure injection pump and a special nozzle are used to spray atomized fuel directly into the combustion chamber as the piston approaches TDC. The heat of compression is high enough to ignite this atomized fuel as it is injected, and the flame creates a controlled pressure rise to push the piston down on the power stroke and generate torque.

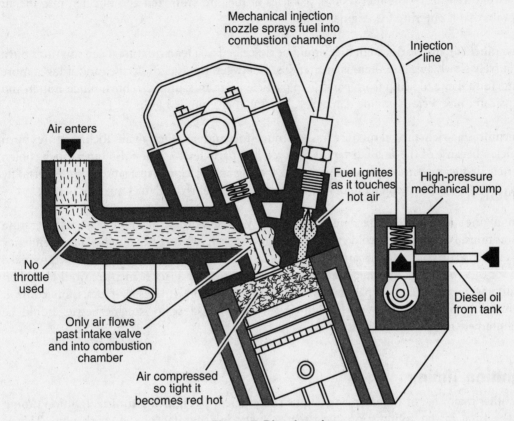

Mechanical injection
nozzle sprays fuel into
combustion chamber

Injection
line

Air enters

Fuel ignites
as it touches
hot air

High-pressure
mechanical pump

No
throttle
used

Diesel oil
from tank

Only air flows
past intake valve
and into combustion
chamber

Air compressed
so tight it
becomes red hot

Figure 7. Diesel engine

Diesel engines are most often utilized in medium to heavy-duty applications. This is because of their reliability and superior torque generation relative to a gasoline engine. Newer designs of diesel engines are more sophisticated, with electronic fuel system controls that make them burn cleaner with better power output.

ENGINE OPERATING CONDITIONS

Air-Fuel Mixture

For an engine to run efficiently, it is necessary to mix air and fuel in the correct amounts. Combustion suffers if there is too much fuel and not enough air, or if there is too much air and not enough fuel. The ideal ratio of air to fuel is known as **stoichiometric**, and it is the responsibility of the engine's fuel system to maintain that balance.

Air-fuel ratio is a comparison of the weight of the air relative to the weight of the fuel that has been mixed with it. The stoichiometric, or ideal, air-fuel ratio is 14.7:1. This means that 14.7 pounds of air is combined with 1 pound of fuel to create an ideal air-fuel mix. When fuel is mixed with air by the fuel system, particles of fuel are **atomized** and directed into the air stream that is entering the engine.

Too much air and not enough fuel would be described as a **lean** mixture. Lean mixtures burn relatively slowly because there is greater space between the fuel molecules and it takes more time for a flame to jump from particle to particle. Lean mixtures also burn much hotter, and thus can cause serious engine damage. A lean air-fuel ratio would be 17:1.

In contrast, a **rich** air fuel mixture has too much fuel and not enough air. Rich mixtures burn quicker because of the small distances between fuel particles, and they also burn much cooler. A rich air-fuel mixture can cause spark plug fouling and black exhaust smoke, but is certainly less threatening to an engine than lean mixtures. A typical rich air-fuel mixture is 10:1.

An engine's air-fuel mixture requirements will vary somewhat depending on its operating conditions. For instance, a cold engine will require a rich mixture because fuel has a tendency to condense on cold intake manifold runners and cylinder walls. Extra fuel is added to make up for this condition. Another condition that would require a richer mixture would be when full power is needed for passing on the highway. In the interests of emission control, drivability, and engine service life, an air-fuel mixture close to stoichiometric should be maintained as much as possible.

Ignition Timing

Another major factor in making an engine run efficiently is **ignition timing**. Ignition timing is the time in the combustion cycle that a spark is generated at the spark plug. This is described relative to the position of the engine's crankshaft. For instance, an ignition timing of five degrees **BTDC** would mean that the spark took place when the crankshaft was five degrees of rotation **before top dead center**.

The spark is most often timed so it will take place before the piston reaches top dead center on the compression stroke, because it takes time for the flame to move across the combustion chamber and to heat the gases in it. Once the heat starts expanding the gases in the combustion chamber, the piston is on its way down again and is ready to make an effective power stroke.

Regardless of how fast the engine is turning, it will take approximately the same amount of time for the flame to travel across the combustion chamber. This means that for higher engine speeds, the flame must be started earlier in order to generate the most effective downward push on the piston. This is known as **advancing the timing**. An example of an advanced timing would be 25 degrees BTDC. In this case, the spark takes place when the crankshaft is 25 degrees of rotation before top dead center.

In contrast, **retarding the timing** means that the spark is adjusted to take place later in the combustion cycle. Certain engine operating conditions might call for a retarded timing as part of normal engine operation. Ignition timing that is unnecessarily retarded, however, will have an adverse effect on engine performance. The most common symptoms of retarded timing are a lack of power and engine overheating. An engine with retarded timing will lack power because the flame has been started late and now the expanding gases are chasing the piston instead of pushing it. The engine can also overheat because the flame continues burning through the exhaust stroke, and burning gases are then pushed past the exhaust valve and into the cylinder head. The tremendous heat developed can then exceed the capacity of the cooling system, so engine temperature cannot be controlled effectively.

Combustion

Gasoline engine combustion is the rapid, thorough burning of a compressed air-fuel mixture, initiated by a spark from the engine's ignition system. It is a flame that starts at the spark plug and then moves rapidly across the combustion chamber, heating the gases and building pressure in an even, controlled manner.

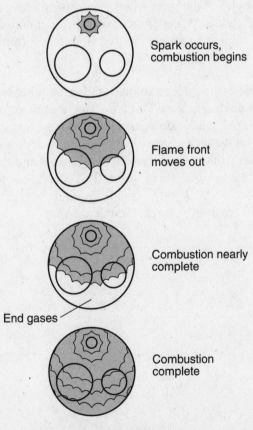

Figure 8. Normal combustion

Normal combustion does not involve an explosion, and it is always initiated by an electric arc at the spark plug. If combustion is started by something other than an electric arc at the spark plug, this is an abnormal condition known as **preignition**. Preignition takes place when combustion is started by a hot spot in the combustion chamber, such as a glowing spark plug electrode or a hot piece of carbon. Preignition is characterized by a "pinging" sound when the engine is under load. Basically, two independent flame fronts are developed in the combustion chamber, and the flame from the spark plug collides with the flame that started at the "hot spot." Preignition causes power loss, in part, because the combustion process finishes much earlier than if the flame had started at the spark plug and only advanced from there.

Normal combustion in an engine assembly is similar to pushing someone on a playground swing set. As the person on the swing moves backwards and approaches the top of their travel, the person pushing them gently slows them, and then pushes evenly but forcefully away to build the rider's momentum in a forward direction. Under these conditions, it could be expected that the rider and the person pushing them could maintain this activity for some time.

Now, consider putting a large board in the hands of the person that is pushing, and instructing that person to hit the rider with it in order to move them forward when they reach the top of their travel. Yes, the rider will move forward and gain some momentum in the process, but it is unlikely that this approach could be maintained for any length of time. This is similar to what happens to an engine that is suffering from a condition known as **detonation.**

Detonation is when an air-fuel mixture explodes, rather than burns. It can often take place when an engine's air-fuel mixture is lean. This is because lean mixtures burn very slowly, and as the flame moves across the combustion chamber, the unburned gases become heated due to the advancing flame and the increasing compression in the cylinder. If the temperature of these unburned gases rises sufficiently, they will "auto ignite" and the flame front from this explosion collides with the original flame front. The pressure spike from this abnormal combustion results in a brutal shock to the engine assembly, and can be heard as a "knock." Severe engine damage can result from unchecked detonation.

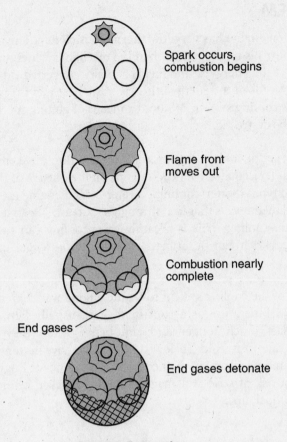

Spark occurs, combustion begins

Flame front moves out

Combustion nearly complete

End gases

End gases detonate

Figure 9. Detonation

Another possible cause of detonation is over-advanced timing. With a spark-initiated flame that is started too early in the combustion cycle, the piston is still compressing the remaining unburned gases before the flame can reach them. The temperature of the unburned gases rises rapidly, and can also detonate before being consumed by the flame. Most automotive computer control systems incorporate a "knock sensor" that monitors the engine for detonation, and will retard the ignition timing when it occurs in order to prevent engine damage.

COOLING SYSTEM

The internal combustion engine has very low **thermal efficiency**. This means that the heat content of the fuel it burns is much greater than the mechanical energy it generates. In fact, only about one-third of the energy in the fuel is actually converted into useful mechanical energy. The other two-thirds of the energy is lost as waste heat that is dissipated through the exhaust system and the **cooling system**. Without a means of getting rid of this waste heat, an engine would quickly be destroyed.

There are two major types of cooling systems in modern automotive engines. The first type is **air-cooling**, where air is circulated over cooling fins on the outside of the engine to remove excess heat. The second type is **water-cooling**. A water-cooled engine uses a liquid coolant to pick up excess heat and then rejects that heat through a radiator. The vast majority of vehicles built today utilize water-cooling. This is because water-cooling can maintain a consistent operating temperature, and it can be utilized to heat the passenger compartment of the vehicle.

It is the responsibility of the cooling system to let the engine warm up quickly, and then to maintain the engine's temperature at a consistent level, usually between 185° and 200° Fahrenheit. Engines last much longer and run better when they are kept at these temperatures. If they are run cold (below 180°), they have a tendency to build up contamination in their motor oil and in their combustion chambers. Engines that are run too hot (above 205°) are at risk of serious damage, including cracked cylinder heads and even possible engine seizure (lock up).

Coolant

The most critical component of the cooling system is the coolant itself. Engine coolant is normally made up of a 50/50 mix of antifreeze and water. The most common type of antifreeze is ethylene glycol, which has some exceptional properties which make it especially suited to be an automotive engine coolant. A 50/50 mix of ethylene glycol and water will not freeze until its temperature reaches –34° Fahrenheit. This is why it is called antifreeze. Frozen coolant can lead to serious engine damage (even a possible cracked block), so it is important that the coolant be freeze-protected. This same 50/50 mix will also raise the boiling point of the coolant. This is important in hot weather, because it makes the coolant that much more efficient at transferring heat.

Automotive antifreeze also contains corrosion inhibitors. This is extremely important, as without them the cooling system would corrode badly. Corrosion inside the cooling system can cause clogging, poor heat transfer, and leaks. It is good practice to replace the engine's coolant every two to three years, as these corrosion inhibitors deplete over time.

The latest engine coolant technology still utilizes ethylene glycol, but uses a very different corrosion inhibitor package. These new inhibitors have a much longer service life than the older, silicate-based formulas, so coolant replacement is only required every five years.

Components

The major components of a water-cooling system include:

Water pump: responsible for moving coolant through the cooling system in order to transfer and control heat.

Water jacket: hollow sections in the engine block and cylinder head that allow coolant to be transferred through them. These are the areas that the coolant must absorb heat from.

Thermostat: controls engine temperature by allowing coolant to flow into the radiator when the coolant temperature rises above a certain level.

Bypass tube: allows coolant to flow back into the water pump from the cylinder head when the thermostat is closed.

Radiator hoses: flexible hoses that allow hot coolant to flow between the engine and the vehicle's radiator.

Radiator: responsible for transferring heat from the coolant to the outside air.

Radiator cap: responsible for maintaining pressure in the system, and allowing coolant to transfer between the coolant reservoir and the radiator.

Coolant recovery bottle: forms a reservoir for coolant to flow in and out of the cooling system as the engine increases and decreases in temperature.

Operation

Coolant is circulated through the engine by a belt-driven water pump. The engine crankshaft drives the belt, so the water pump actually uses engine power to operate it. The water pump takes coolant in and pushes it into the engine block. The coolant then makes its way upward into the cylinder head, and then returns to the inlet of the water pump through the bypass tube. As long as the thermostat is closed (engine is below operating temperature), the coolant will continue to circulate in this manner.

When the thermostat opens, hot coolant moves past the thermostat into the upper radiator hose, and then the coolant enters the radiator itself. The radiator is made up of dozens of thin tubes that allow the coolant to flow through the inside, and cool air to move across the outside of the tubes. The cooler air absorbs the heat from the coolant, and the coolant then enters the lower radiator hose and returns to the inlet of the water pump. The coolant continues to take this path until its temperature drops to the point where the thermostat closes. At that point, the coolant returns to circulating through the engine alone until it reaches a high enough temperature to open the thermostat again.

Since automotive cooling systems operate at close to the boiling point of water (water boils at 212° F), it is important that steps be taken to raise the boiling point of the coolant to maintain cooling system efficiency. If the engine's coolant actually started to boil, the rate of heat transfer in the engine would drop as the water pump would not be able to move the coolant as well and the steam bubbles would not pick up heat from the internal surfaces of the engine.

Engine cold, thermostat closed

Coolant circulates through bypass to pump and
back to engine but does not go through radiator

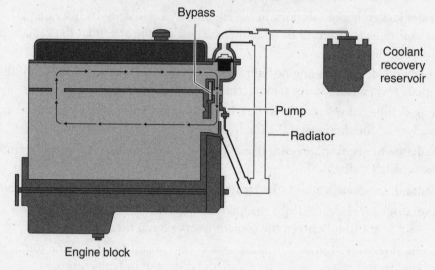

Engine warm, thermostat open

Coolant circulates through radiator

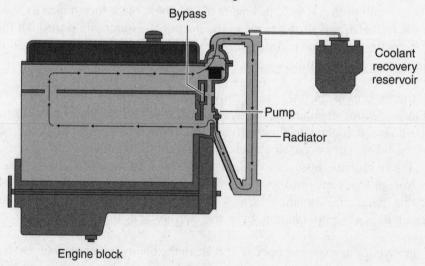

Figure 10

One of the methods used to raise the boiling point of the water has already been mentioned: using coolants made up of a 50/50 mix of ethylene glycol and water. The other method that can be utilized is raising the pressure in the cooling system. The **radiator cap** is responsible for this, and most are designed to maintain anywhere from 9 to 16 pounds per square inch (psi) of pressure in the cooling system. For every 1 psi of pressure that is placed on the cooling system, the boiling point of the coolant is raised approximately 3° F. A 15-psi radiator cap would then raise the boiling point of the coolant to 212° F to 260° F. This would make the cooling system better able to transfer heat than if it were not pressurized at all.

Radiator caps incorporate two separate valves: a pressure valve and a vacuum valve. As the engine warms up, the coolant in the cooling system will tend to expand. This expansion will raise the pressure in the cooling system, but when the pressure reaches the radiator cap's rating, the pressure valve in the radiator cap will lift and allow some coolant to flow from the radiator into the coolant recovery bottle. This flow will continue as the cooling system pressure exceeds the rating of the radiator cap. The coolant level in the recovery bottle will rise until the engine reaches operating temperature.

When the engine is shut down and begins to cool, the coolant will contract and create a low-pressure area inside the cooling system. If left unchecked, this low-pressure in the cooling system would cause the radiator hoses to collapse and can have an adverse effect on the cooling system at engine startup.

To prevent this, the radiator cap also has a vacuum valve built into it, and this will open when the engine is cooling to allow coolant to flow from the recovery bottle back into the cooling system. In one sense, the cooling system is "breathing" as the engine warms up and cools down, and this can be easily observed by the level of the coolant in the recovery bottle.

Maintenance

Cooling systems require maintenance in order to keep them operating at peak efficiency. Again, the coolant itself is absolutely critical and making sure to have this replaced every two to three years is a good maintenance practice. The strength of the coolant should be kept at a 50/50 mix of antifreeze and water. This will ensure that the coolant has sufficient freeze protection and corrosion resistance.

Other things to watch for are the condition of the belt driving the water pump, and that there are no leaks in the system. The level of the coolant in the recovery bottle when the engine is cold should be somewhere near the "cold" or "minimum" line. If this level drops over time, it will be necessary to determine where the coolant is disappearing.

Most often, a leak will be external and can be observed as it drips from hose connections or faulty cooling system components. It is possible, however, to have an internal leak in which the coolant is flowing into the engine's crankcase. If you notice that your coolant level is dropping and the oil is turning milky, see a qualified automotive technician immediately to determine the source of the leak.

A good safety practice is to never remove an engine's radiator cap when the engine is at operating temperature. Hot, pressurized coolant will be expelled from the system and this can cause severe burns. To check coolant level in the system, always look at the level of the coolant in the recovery bottle.

LUBRICATION SYSTEM

The next most critical system in terms of engine operation is the **lubrication system**. Without lubrication, the internal parts of the engine would develop enough friction to stop (seize) the engine completely. The lubrication system is responsible for the following functions:

Lubricates: puts an oil film between moving parts to reduce friction and smooth engine operation.

Cools: puts motor oil in contact with hot engine parts (such as the underside of the piston) and transfers heat to the oil pan, or the engine oil cooler if applicable.

Seals: motor oil acts as a sealer between the piston, the piston rings, and the engine cylinder walls. This helps seal combustion gases in the combustion chamber and makes the engine run more efficiently.

Cleans: additives in the motor oil cause contaminants to be suspended in the oil, so they can be filtered out by the engine's oil filter.

Quiets: motor oil dampens engine noise and makes the engine run quieter.

Motor Oil

Motor oil is the most critical component of the lubrication system. It is carefully engineered to provide peak performance under the toughest engine operating conditions, so choosing and using high quality motor oil is extremely important for the life of an engine.

Motor oil is made up of two main components: base oil, and an additive package. The base oil is most commonly refined from crude oil. Crude oil is made up of many components, so it is necessary to be able to separate the useful parts from the rest. Crude oil can be refined or **distilled** to take out all of the unwanted components and produce reasonably pure base oil. This base oil cannot function alone as motor oil, however, so petroleum engineers combine it with a chemical additive package that enhances the performance of the oil. Some of the additives that are combined with the base oil include foam suppressants, detergents, antioxidants, and viscosity improvers. The additive package will vary according to the conditions that the engine is expected to operate in.

Synthetic oils represent a step beyond base oil refining. Petroleum engineers enhance the molecular structure of the base oil to create motor oil with exceptional properties. Synthetic oil is engineered to withstand higher temperatures and pressures than ordinary motor oil, but can also cost two to three times as much. This additional cost is no object for those who wish to extend their engine's service life and keep it running at top performance.

One of the most important properties of motor oil is **viscosity**. Viscosity is resistance to flow, and is expressed as a number that is directly proportional to the thickness of the oil. The *Society of Automotive Engineers* or SAE is responsible for developing the standards concerning motor oil viscosity. Oil with a viscosity rating of SAE 5 would have a relatively low viscosity (low resistance to flow), whereas SAE 50 oil would have a high viscosity.

It is important to use oil that has a high enough viscosity to protect the engine at high temperatures, but not so high that it becomes very difficult to get that engine started in cold weather. For that reason, it is very common for engine manufacturers to specify the use of **multiviscosity** motor oil. An example of multiviscosity motor oil would be 5W-30. The "W" stands for winter, and this means that at 0° F, this motor oil will act like an SAE 5 for easy starting. The 30 refers to the oil's rating when it reaches 212° F, so this represents how the oil will act when the engine is at operating temperature. Multiviscosity motor oils are formulated to work effectively under a wide range of operating temperatures.

Another important motor oil rating system is the API quality rating. API is the *American Petroleum Institute*, and they are responsible for setting standards for motor oil quality. For a gasoline engine, this rating would have a prefix of "S," and then the next letter would identify the specific quality standard that the motor oil meets. The first gasoline motor oils produced had a quality rating of SA, but greater demands on motor oils led to ratings that currently exist at the SJ level. Today's engines would not last very long if they were operated with an SA motor oil.

A motor oil with a "C" prefix for its quality rating would be suited for diesel engine use (i.e., a CD rating). Motor oil that had both an "S" and a "C" rating would be suited for either gasoline or diesel engine use. An example of this would be motor oil with a rating of SJ/CD.

Components

The primary components of the lubrication system are as follows:

> **Oil pan:** forms the reservoir for the engine oil at the bottom of the engine.

> **Oil pickup tube and screen:** immersed in motor oil, this "screens out" large solids and directs oil into the oil pump.

> **Oil pump:** responsible for pumping the oil through the engine oil galleries. It is normally driven by the engine's camshaft.

> **Pressure relief valve:** prevents excessive pressure from building in the lubrication system.

> **Oil filter:** filters oil from the oil pump before it is sent to the various parts of the engine.

> **Oil galleries:** passages or "drillings" in the engine assembly that transport oil to critical components.

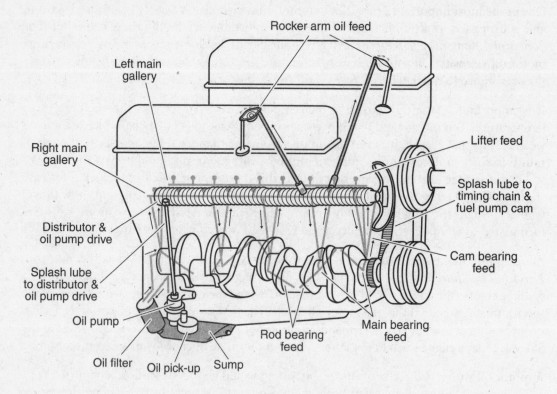

Figure 11. Lubrication system

Operation

The engine's oil reservoir is at the bottom of the engine, in the oil pan. All oil used in the engine drains to the oil pan, where it has an opportunity to cool. The oil pump draws oil from the oil pan into its inlet through the pickup tube and screen. The motor oil moves through the oil pump, and then is transferred under pressure to the engine's oil filter. The oil filter removes particulates from the oil, and sends the clean oil on to the main oil galleries.

When the engine is cold, the oil has a higher resistance to flow and thus requires a good deal more energy to pump it through the system. This also causes the engine's oil pressure to rise. If the oil pressure rises above the pressure relief valve's setting, the relief valve will open and allow some of the oil to drain back into the oil pan before it is pumped into the oil filter. This prevents engine oil pressure from rising to the point where it can damage components such as the oil filter.

Oil that is pumped into the engine's main oil galleries is directed to all areas that require oil for lubrication and cooling. The lubrication system is much like the circulation system in the human body. The heart (pump) forces blood (motor oil) into the arteries (main oil galleries), and from there the blood is transferred to progressively smaller blood vessels as it makes its way through the body.

The most critical area in the engine in terms of lubrication requirements is the engine's reciprocating assembly. The pistons, connecting rods, and crankshaft all require motor oil to lower friction and to remove heat. The largest oil galleries in the engine are used to move oil to these areas, and galleries are drilled directly through the crankshaft to provide oil under pressure to the connecting rod bearings. Oil that leaks off the connecting rod bearings is thrown onto the cylinder walls, where it helps lubricate and cool the pistons.

Other oil galleries take oil from the main oil gallery and direct it to the engine's valve train. This is where the camshaft, lifters, push rods, rocker arms, and valve stems get their lubrication. Other parts that may receive lubrication from this oil would be the camshaft drive, or timing chain and associated gear drives for the oil pump, ignition distributor, etc.

Oil that has circulated through the engine eventually drains back into the oil pan. The oil pan is located at the bottom of the engine and thus sits low in the engine compartment where cooler air typically resides. This cool outside air absorbs heat from the oil pan and helps cool the engine oil inside. At this point, the oil is ready to be picked up by the oil pump and to be circulated back into the lubrication system.

Maintenance

The key to lubrication system maintenance is to change the engine oil and filter on a regular basis, and to use top quality motor oil and filters. This is the cheapest and most effective maintenance that can be performed on a vehicle.

Oil change intervals are determined by the conditions that the vehicle is driven in. Short trips and cold operation are much harsher on an engine than long distance highway running. Check the owner's manual for service intervals; often there will be two different ones specified depending on the conditions that the vehicle is driven in. Harsher conditions mean that service intervals are shorter.

There is no substitute for quality when it comes to engine oil and filters. Purchase the best motor oil and filter that you can afford, and change them at the specified service intervals in order to enjoy the best service life from your vehicle's engine.

FUEL SYSTEM

The **fuel system** is responsible for maintaining the correct air-fuel mixture for efficient engine operation. If the air-fuel mixture is not adjusted correctly, drivability, emission control, fuel economy, and engine service life can suffer.

Up until about 20 years ago, it was most common for air-fuel mixture to be determined through mechanical means. This was accomplished through the use of a **carburetor**, which was very reliable but incapable of providing the precision required in modern fuel systems. Due mostly to the demands of emission control regulations, the carburetor has been made obsolete in favor of **electronic fuel injection**. This system is controlled by an onboard computer and incorporates a feedback function that gives it flexibility to adjust to changing engine conditions very quickly. Electronic fuel injection systems continue to evolve, as emission control laws get progressively tighter. The basic system, however, is simple and its operation easily understood.

Components

The following are the major components of an electronic fuel-injection system:

Electric fuel pump: located in the vehicle's fuel tank, the fuel pump supplies fuel under pressure to the fuel injectors.

Fuel filter: filters contaminants from the fuel before it reaches the fuel rail.

Fuel rail: a manifold that supplies fuel under pressure to the inlets of all the engine's fuel injectors.

Fuel pressure regulator: regulates pressure in the fuel rail according to intake manifold vacuum. Excess fuel is bled to the fuel return line, where it is sent back to the fuel tank.

Fuel injector: sprays fuel into the intake air stream as it receives electrical signals from the Powertrain Control Module (PCM). The location of the injector will determine the specific type of fuel injection system being used on the engine.

Powertrain Control Module (PCM): another name for the vehicle's central computer, it is responsible for control of all functions associated with the engine and transmission.

Intake manifold: distributes air to the intake ports on the cylinder heads.

Intake air filter: all air entering the engine passes through the air filter, which removes airborne contaminants that could damage internal engine parts.

Throttle body/throttle plate: the throttle plate, which is connected to the throttle pedal, controls engine speed and output torque.

Fuel Injection System Designs

When fuel injection systems first came into common use, they were designed to utilize either one or two injectors mounted in a **throttle body** that took the place of the carburetor. This is known as a **throttle body injection system** or **TBI**. While this system proved to be reliable, it was not capable of providing a high enough level of fuel control to meet emission control requirements. Most engines are now built with **multiport fuel injection**, which has an injector for each engine cylinder.

With multiport fuel injection, the injectors are located in the intake manifold, with their spray directed towards the intake valves. As air enters the intake manifold, it will flow all the way to the cylinder head before fuel is injected into it. This allows for much better air-fuel mixing and prevents fuel droplets from falling out on the intake manifold runners.

The newest fuel-injection system designs incorporate a fuel injector that sprays fuel directly into the combustion chamber. This is known as **direct injection**. Engineers are working to inject the fuel as close as possible to where the actual combustion takes place, in an effort to increase fuel control and create a cleaner burning, more efficient engine.

Multiport Injection System Operation

When the ignition key is turned to the "run" position, electric current is sent to the fuel pump and pressure is developed in the fuel rail. The fuel pump is located in the fuel tank, and its pickup tube is submerged in the fuel. While it is inconvenient to service a fuel pump that is located in the fuel tank, it should be noted that most pumps work better when they are asked to "push" rather than "pull." Having the pump located directly in the fuel tank makes its operation much more reliable and efficient.

The fuel pump forces fuel into the main fuel line, and then into the filter, which is normally located along the vehicle's frame. The filter removes contaminants in the fuel to prevent sticking and clogging of the fuel injectors and the pressure regulator. The filtered fuel is then sent to the fuel rail, where it can enter the fuel injectors.

Fuel pressure continues to build in the fuel rail, until it reaches the pressure regulator's relief pressure. The fuel pressure regulator will bleed fuel to the return line to prevent rail pressure from rising past this point. All of the injectors now have fuel pressure applied to their inlets, but will not inject fuel unless commanded to by the PCM.

When the ignition key is moved to the "start" position, the engine is cranked over and the cylinders that are on their intake stroke begin to draw air into their respective combustion chambers. Since fuel now must be added to the intake air, the PCM will direct an electrical pulse to the fuel injectors to open the injector and allow fuel to spray into the intake air stream. The moment the PCM stops the electrical pulse, the fuel injector closes and stops fuel from being injected into the air stream.

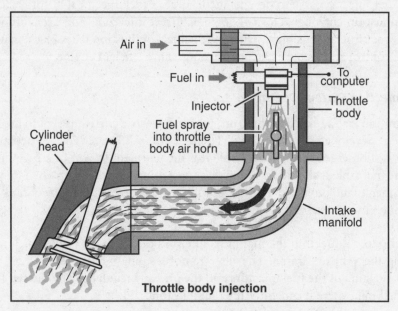

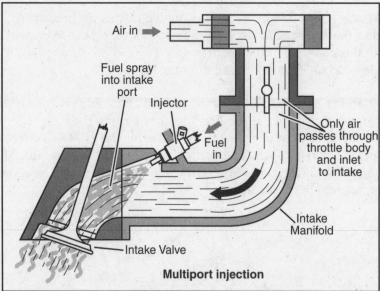

Figure 12. Fuel injection types

Engine speed and power are controlled by varying the amount of air entering the engine. This is accomplished through the use of a **throttle plate** in the intake air stream. The throttle plate is connected to the driver's throttle pedal. The driver can move the throttle plate to allow anywhere from a minimum amount of air (idle speed) up to a maximum amount of air (**WOT** or **Wide Open Throttle**) to enter the intake manifold. As more air enters the engine, more fuel must be injected to maintain the correct air-fuel mixture.

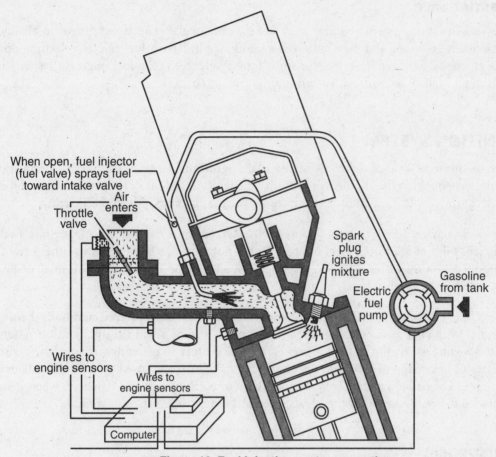

Figure 13. Fuel injection system operation

Since the fuel pressure at the injector stays within a narrow range, the way to increase the amount of fuel being injected is to increase the length of the electrical pulse being sent from the PCM. This is how the PCM richens or leans the mixture: by controlling the **pulse width** being sent to the injector.

When the engine is starting, a relatively long pulse width is sent to the injector to richen the air-fuel mixture. This pulse width becomes shorter, however, as the engine warms up and less fuel is needed to make the engine run smoothly. The pulse width at idle speed is relatively short, but becomes much longer as the throttle plate is opened and more air enters the engine's cylinders. Pulse width is measured in milliseconds, and this can be measured using special diagnostic equipment to help a technician pinpoint problems in the fuel system.

Maintenance

The fuel-injection system requires very little maintenance. The filters must be changed occasionally (both air and fuel), and it is a good idea to have a fuel injector cleaning done after an engine has been in service for some time. Aside from that, fuel injection systems are built to give reliable service with a minimum of maintenance.

IGNITION SYSTEM

One of the most critical vehicle systems is the **ignition system**. Without it, combustion cannot take place, so the engine will not run. The ignition system must generate high voltage sparks at the correct time in order to make the engine run smoothly and efficiently.

The earliest automotive ignition systems were operated by a magneto. A magneto is a self-sufficient form of ignition system because it does not require a battery or any other external components for operation. Magneto-style ignitions are still in common use on small engines that incorporate a pull-start.

As vehicle electrical systems became more refined, battery-powered ignitions became popular. With engines now using an electric start instead of a hand crank, ignition systems were designed to require electric current from the battery to generate a spark. The earliest versions of this design were built to operate on the standard 6 volts used by electrical systems of that time. The ignition system gained a new level of performance and reliability when it was upgraded to operate as part of the 12-volt electrical system that is still in use today.

Components

The ignition system can be divided into two distinct subsystems: the primary and the secondary. The primary is the low voltage part of the system, where the secondary is high voltage.

The following are the major components found in the **primary** of a basic electronic ignition system:

> **Battery**: supplies power to the ignition system for starting the engine.
>
> **Ignition switch**: turns the engine on and off by switching power to the ignition system.
>
> **Primary coil winding**: the low-voltage winding in the ignition coil. This is made up of several hundred turns of relatively heavy wire.
>
> **Ignition module**: a transistorized switch that turns the primary current on and off.
>
> **Reluctor and pickup coil**: responsible for generating a signal that operates the ignition module. The reluctor is mounted on the distributor shaft, and generates a signal in the stationary pickup coil as it rotates with the distributor.
>
> **Distributor**: driven by the engine's camshaft, the distributor is responsible for timing the spark and distributing it to the correct cylinder. Like the camshaft, the distributor turns at one-half the speed of the engine.

The following are the major components found in the **secondary** of a basic electronic ignition system.

Secondary coil winding: the high-voltage winding in the ignition coil. This is made up of several thousand turns of fine wire, wound around the primary coil winding.

Coil wire: transmits high voltage from the secondary coil winding to the distributor cap.

Distributor cap and rotor: directs high voltage from the coil wire to each cylinder in the firing order. This is a switching mechanism that allows one ignition coil to serve all the engine cylinders.

Spark plug wires: transmit high voltage from the distributor cap to each spark plug.

Spark plugs: threaded into the cylinder head, the spark plug protrudes into the combustion chamber and generates the spark to initiate combustion.

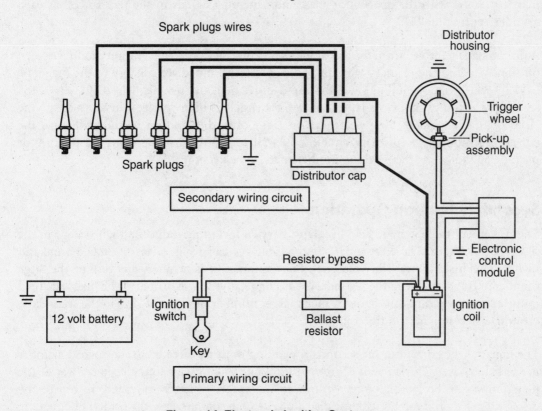

Figure 14. Electronic Ignition Systems

Primary Ignition Operation

When the driver turns the ignition switch to the "run" position, current is sent from the battery, through the ignition switch, and on to the primary coil winding. From the coil winding, that same current flows through the ignition module and back to the battery through the vehicle ground circuit. The low-voltage (primary) section of the ignition system is responsible for the control of the secondary, or high-voltage section. Whatever happens in the secondary system is in response to the events in the primary section.

The ignition system works because of a phenomenon known as **electromagnetic induction**. If a magnetic field moves across a stationary wire, voltage is induced in the wire. Another dimension of this principle is that electric current passing through a wire will produce a magnetic field around that wire. This means that electric current can be used to generate a magnetic field, and a magnetic field can be used to generate electric current.

The current that flows through the ignition primary winding builds a strong magnetic field that surrounds both it and the secondary coil winding. The ignition module allows this current to flow through the primary winding until it receives a signal from the pickup coil in the distributor, telling it to turn off this current. As the distributor turns with the engine, the reluctor rotates with the distributor shaft and generates signals in the pickup coil as each cylinder approaches TDC.

A timing signal received from the distributor's pickup coil causes the ignition module to turn off the current in the primary winding. This causes an immediate collapse of the magnetic field in the primary winding, and the rapid movement of the magnetic field across the secondary windings induces a large voltage in them. This high voltage is used to create the electric arc at the spark plug electrodes. At this point, the ignition module will turn the current back on in the primary circuit, and wait for another signal from the distributor pickup coil indicating the need for another spark to be generated.

Secondary Ignition Operation

The collapse of the magnetic field in the primary coil winding induces a high voltage in the secondary winding. These secondary system voltages can reach levels of 30,000 volts and higher. This huge increase in voltage in the ignition coil is achieved because of the large number of turns of wire in the secondary winding relative to the primary. The magnetic field in the primary winding cuts across a much larger number of turns of wire in the secondary, creating a **step-up** effect in the coil.

The high voltage current in the secondary winding must be directed to the correct cylinder in the firing order. This current is directed through the **coil wire** to the center tower of the **distributor cap**. From this point, it flows to the **rotor**, which is mounted on top of the distributor shaft and rotates with the distributor. As the engine turns, the rotor will direct the current to the appropriate cylinder and send it through the **spark plug wire** to the **spark plug**. The electric arc at the spark plug is used to initiate combustion.

Current Ignition System Design

The ignition system has been the focus of much of the refinement of the internal combustion engine in the past 30 years. There was a time that faulty ignition was responsible for 95 percent of engine failures. This percentage has decreased significantly as ignition systems are made simpler. The driving force behind this has been emission control regulations and a push for greater reliability.

The original battery-powered ignition systems used mechanical breaker points to turn the current on and off in the primary winding. This was a troublesome arrangement, as the breaker points were a high-maintenance item and were typically neglected by the average car owner.

The next big step in ignition design was to eliminate the breaker points in favor of a transistor-switched design. The distributor now had an electronic pickup inside it that sent signals to an ignition module that switched the current on and off. Fewer moving parts meant greater reliability.

Since engine performance relies heavily on accurate ignition timing, engineers began to look carefully at how to eliminate more moving parts from the ignition system. This led to the elimination of the distributor in a design that was named the **distributorless ignition system** or **DIS**. DIS systems use one ignition coil to operate two spark plugs, so a V-8 engine now required four separate coils instead of one. However, this system still utilized spark plug wires, which are another high-maintenance item.

The most recent ignition system designs have eliminated the spark plug wires, thus requiring an ignition coil for each cylinder. These are known as **coil-on-plug** ignitions. The ignition coils are mounted directly over the spark plugs on this design, and the coils are controlled by the vehicle computer system. While the incorporation of computer control has increased ignition system complexity, the elimination of moving and high-maintenance components has led to an accurate and reliable ignition system design that requires very little maintenance.

EXHAUST SYSTEM

The exhaust system is responsible for removing waste gases from the engine. It must do this so that it allows these gases to flow freely, deadens the sound of the exhaust, and keeps the gases and heat away from the vehicle cabin, and thus, the occupants.

Typical components found in an exhaust system include the following:

Exhaust manifolds: attached directly to the exhaust ports on the cylinder head. The majority of the exhaust heat and noise is focused on the exhaust manifolds. These are often made from cast-iron for durability under high heat conditions.

Catalytic converter: responsible for converting the toxic components of engine exhaust into relatively harmless compounds such as carbon dioxide and water.

Muffler: incorporates an expansion chamber to diminish loud exhaust noises.

Tailpipe: the exit point for exhaust gases as they enter the open atmosphere. The tailpipe normally exits at the rear of the vehicle.

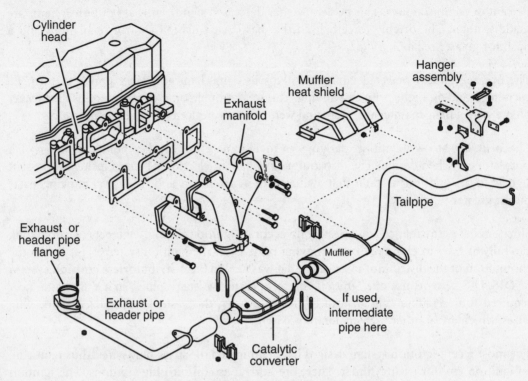

Figure 15. Exhaust system components

Operation

As gases flow from the exhaust ports of the engine, they are collected by the **exhaust manifold**. On a V-type engine there would be two exhaust manifolds, one for each cylinder head. These manifolds would then feed the gases into steel exhaust pipes, which connect the major components of the exhaust system.

The exhaust gases would then be sent into the **catalytic converter**. High heat is developed in the catalytic converter as it reduces the toxic components of the exhaust to less toxic gases. Some vehicles use two, and even three, catalytic converters in an effort to meet emission control regulations.

After leaving the catalytic converter, exhaust gases are directed into the **muffler**. The muffler has expansion chambers built into it that absorb the audio shock waves generated by the engine's exhaust. The muffler is normally located towards the rear of the car, somewhere between the catalytic converter and the tailpipe.

Engine exhaust is highly toxic. The most dangerous of the toxic gases emitted by the engine's exhaust is **carbon monoxide**, an odorless, colorless gas. It is extremely important that these gases be routed in such a way that they do not come into contact with the driver or passengers in the vehicle. This usually involves sending these gases to the rear of the vehicle where they are dissipated to the open air by the **tailpipe**.

The exhaust system must allow the engines exhaust gases to flow freely. If the exhaust system causes a restriction in the flow of gases, this will diminish the engine's performance. This is because engine output is determined by how much air and fuel it can burn to generate horsepower. Anything that restricts the flow of air into or out of the engine will cause horsepower loss.

Performance enthusiasts often install **header pipes** in the exhaust system. These take the place of the exhaust manifolds that originally came with the engine. The idea is to allow exhaust gases to flow more freely and allow the engine to breathe better. Header pipes are engineered to maximize the flow of exhaust gases from the engine. Increased performance is usually gained at the expense of durability, as header pipes are much more fragile than cast-iron exhaust manifolds.

Maintenance

Exhaust system maintenance is usually fairly straightforward. Inspect the system from time to time for physical damage; there should be no restrictions and no leaks. The system should also be tight in terms of its mounting brackets and clamps. Any damage should be repaired immediately.

The catalytic converter will enjoy a long service life if the vehicle's engine is kept in good running order. An engine that burns oil or has ignition or fuel system problems will punish the catalytic converter. Under no circumstances should a vehicle be run with the catalytic converter taken out of the exhaust system. Federal environmental laws specify fines for anyone that alters or removes vehicle emission control equipment. Many states will not issue registration for vehicles that do not meet emission control standards, so it is in the vehicle owner's best interests to maintain these systems and keep them in good operating condition.

EMISSION CONTROL SYSTEM

Control of vehicle emissions has been the most important influence on engine design for the past 30 years. Virtually all refinements of the internal combustion engine during this period have been made in an effort to comply with the Clean Air Act as formulated by the Environmental Protection Agency (EPA). This set of laws was enacted, in part, to combat a growing problem in America's urban areas: diminished air quality due to vehicle emissions.

Overall, it can be said that the program has worked. The number of vehicles on the road in the United States has increased exponentially, but air quality in the bigger cities has improved. The Clean Air Act is not static, however, as each year the vehicle manufacturers must comply with a tighter set of regulations that further restrict the amount of toxins put into the air by the cars they build.

Vehicle Emissions

Emissions are generated in three different places on the vehicle. The tailpipe accounts for the majority of that; approximately 60 percent of the toxins are in the exhaust gas stream. Of the remaining 40 percent, half comes from the vehicle's fuel system, and the other half comes from the engine crankcase. Measures must be taken to deal with the emissions from all three areas in order to make a vehicle meet emission control standards.

Not all of the emissions from an automobile are toxic. However, some that are not considered to be toxic do have an impact on the environment as they are classified as greenhouse gases, which have been linked to global warming.

The gases that are generated during vehicle operation include the following:

Hydrocarbons (HC): unburned fuel that is emitted from the tailpipe, or that evaporates from the vehicle's fuel system.

Carbon monoxide (CO): partially burned fuel that is emitted from the tailpipe. CO is odorless, colorless, and extremely toxic.

Oxides of nitrogen (NOx): high temperatures in the combustion chamber cause nitrogen to combine with oxygen. Nitrogen comprises over 70 percent of atmospheric air, but is normally inert. NOx is a primary contributor to photochemical smog, as it reacts with HC when exposed to sunlight.

Oxygen (O_2): a certain amount of oxygen is left over from the combustion process.

Carbon dioxide (CO_2): while not specifically toxic, carbon dioxide is considered to be a greenhouse gas.

Water vapor: a normal byproduct of combustion, water vapor is also considered to be a greenhouse gas.

There are many different ways to reduce vehicle emissions. For our purposes, four major subsystems of a vehicle's emission controls will be discussed.

Positive Crankcase Ventilation (PCV) System

One of the earliest emission controls that was incorporated into common use was the **positive crankcase ventilation (PCV) system**. Prior to 1960, it was common practice to allow crankcase gases to vent to the atmosphere through a **road draft tube**. Once it became clear that these gases represented 20 percent of a vehicle's emissions, engineers designed the PCV system to ventilate the crankcase without allowing the raw gases to be emitted to the open atmosphere.

The PCV system takes fresh filtered air and moves it through the engine crankcase, picking up oil fumes and gases that leak past the piston rings and drawing them into the intake manifold through the **PCV valve**. These gases are then burned in the engine's cylinders, preventing them from escaping to the atmosphere unprocessed.

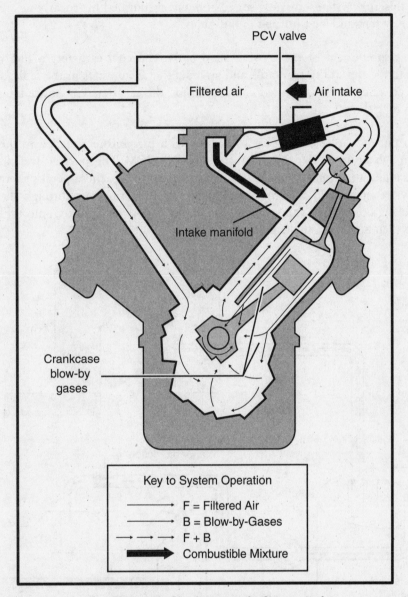

Figure 16. Crankcase emission control

One of the benefits of the PCV system is a cleaner crankcase. Since fresh air is always being drawn through the crankcase and the fumes are constantly being removed, engine oil lasts longer and the internal parts of the engine stay cleaner.

Fuel Evaporation Control (EVAP) System

Fuel evaporation is another major contributor to vehicle emissions. If vented to the open atmosphere, a vehicle's fuel tank and fuel system will allow hydrocarbons to evaporate into the outside air. This unburned fuel represents 20 percent of the total vehicle emissions. To counteract this, fuel systems are now sealed and any evaporated hydrocarbons are collected by the EVAP system and later burned in the engine.

The primary component of the EVAP system is the **charcoal canister**. A fuel vapor line connects it to the top of the fuel tank, and any fuel that evaporates in the tank follows this line and is collected in the activated charcoal inside the canister. The entire fuel system is sealed, including the gas cap.

In order to put the collected fuel to work, there is a **purge line** attached to the charcoal canister, through a **purge valve** that is controlled by the PCM. This purge valve is attached to the engine's intake manifold. Once the engine is running and reaches operating temperature, the purge valve opens and the intake manifold vacuum draws air through the charcoal canister, picking up any fuel vapors there. These fuel vapors are directed into the intake air stream, and then burned in the engine.

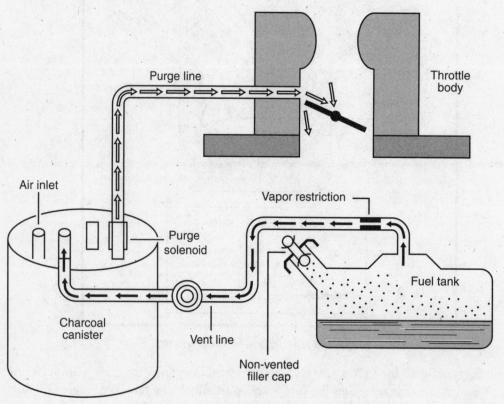

Figure 17. Evaporative emissions control system

A similar system is found at many gas stations in the United States. Rather than allowing fuel to evaporate into the open atmosphere, many gas pumps now have vapor recovery systems built in to their nozzles. All of the evaporated fuel from the nozzle and the vehicle's open fuel tank is then collected and sent back to the storage tanks in an effort to cut down on HC emissions at the gas pump.

Exhaust Gas Recirculation (EGR) Valve

Atmospheric air is made up of 75 percent nitrogen, 20 percent oxygen, and 5 percent of various other gases. Nitrogen is inert under most conditions, meaning it will not react chemically with other gases. However, if exposed to very high temperatures in an engine's combustion chamber, nitrogen will combine with oxygen to create NO_x. NO_x is not desirable, as it is a major contributor to photochemical smog. In order to reduce the amount of NO_x that is generated by an engine, the temperatures inside the combustion chamber must be reduced. This is where the exhaust gas recirculation valve goes to work.

The EGR valve forms a bridge between the engine's exhaust system and the intake manifold. Under most operating conditions, the EGR valve is closed and prevents exhaust gases from flowing. However, when the vehicle is under load, and combustion chamber temperatures are high, the EGR valve will open and allow a certain amount of exhaust gas to flow into the intake manifold.

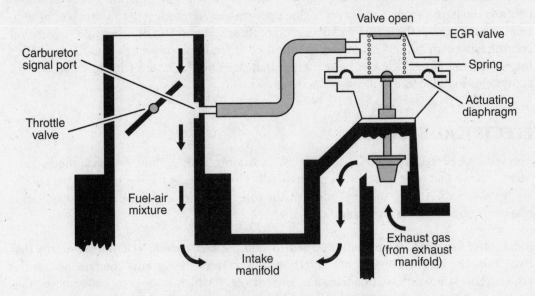

Figure 18. Exhaust gas recirculation

The net effect of diluting the air-fuel mixture with exhaust gases is that peak combustion temperatures are reduced and nitrogen is prevented from reacting with oxygen to produce NO_x. EGR valves are also very important for controlling detonation. Most engines now use a computer-controlled EGR system as part of its engine control strategy.

Catalytic Converter

Probably the best known of all the emission control subsystems is the catalytic converter. The catalytic converter is designed to reduce the emissions that come from the vehicle's tailpipe, so it is located in the exhaust system. All of the exhaust gases coming from the engine must pass through the catalytic converter before they are released to the open atmosphere.

Earlier designs of the catalytic converter were known as **two-way**, because they only dealt with HC and CO emissions. All modern catalytic converters are **three-way**, since they are built to reduce HC, CO, and NO_x emissions. Precious metals such as platinum, palladium, and rhodium are used in their construction, as these metals act as catalysts for chemical reactions. A catalyst is a material that encourages chemical reactions without being consumed by the reaction. The catalytic converter is built to encourage further burning of the exhaust gases to prevent unburned and partially burned fuel, as well as NO_x, from going out the tailpipe. All cars built for sale in the US will have at least one catalytic converter, but some have been designed with as many as three in an effort to meet tight environmental regulations.

Maintenance

The PCV system requires some maintenance, as the PCV valve and possibly its fresh air filter must be changed from time to time. Most of the other systems, however, are relatively maintenance-free and only require service when there is a malfunction. Faulty emission controls can have a major impact on engine performance, so automotive technicians need to be very familiar with the theory and operation of these systems. Disabling any of the emission control subsystems on a vehicle is a violation of federal law subject to fines and possible imprisonment. No vehicle can be registered that does not have all of its emission control subsystems installed and working properly.

ELECTRICAL SYSTEM

The vehicle's electrical system is growing in importance with each new vehicle model year. Many systems that were once driven mechanically are now being redesigned to be part of the electrical system. A basic understanding of the role and function of the electrical system is extremely important for any vehicle owner.

Automotive electrical systems are designed to utilize direct current (DC). This means that electrical current only flows in one direction as it powers the various components on the vehicle. This is in contrast to alternating current (AC), which is used to power household appliances. Alternating current changes the direction of its current flow many times per second.

The major subsystems of the electrical system include the following:

Battery: stores electrical energy in chemical form. Provides direct current (DC) for engine starting and accessory operation.

Starting system: responsible for cranking the engine to get it started. The battery and starter motor are the major components of the starting system.

Charging system: responsible for supplying electrical current to charge the battery, as well as for vehicle operation. The major component of the charging system is the alternator.

Lighting system: headlights, marker lights, brake lights, tail lights, etc.

Accessories: this includes the rear window defogger, windshield wipers, stereo, blower motors, and all other electrically powered accessories.

Battery

The battery is the foundation for the entire electrical system. It produces electrical current for starting the engine, provides current to the electrical system when the load exceeds the output of the alternator, and acts as an electrical "shock absorber," preventing voltage spikes.

An automobile battery is made up of lead plates immersed in an electrolyte made up of sulphuric acid and water. This is why this type of battery is known as a **lead-acid battery**. As the battery discharges, the sulphuric acid in the electrolyte is reduced to water, and the lead plates become lead sulphate. Charging the battery restores the chemical composition of the lead plates and the electrolyte.

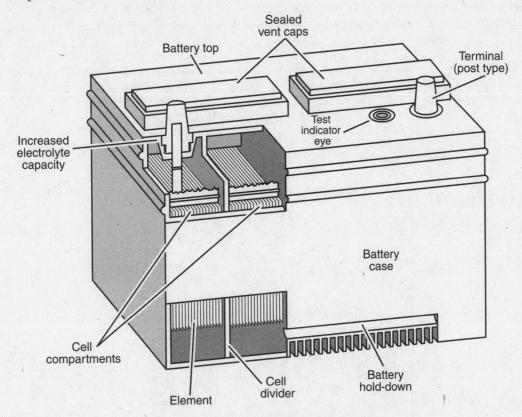

Figure 19. Battery construction

Each cell of a lead-acid battery produces approximately 2.1 volts. There are six cells in an automotive battery, so a fully charged lead-acid battery will measure 12.6 volts. A battery's voltage decreases as it is discharged. A battery that measures 12.4 volts is 75 percent charged, and at 12.2 volts, it is only 50 percent charged. When a 12-volt battery measures 12 volts, it only has 25 percent of its charge remaining.

A lead-acid battery gives off hydrogen gas when it is being charged. Hydrogen gas is highly volatile. It is extremely important not to create sparks around an automobile battery, because the hydrogen gas it produces could explode.

The electrolyte in a discharged battery is mostly water, so it can freeze in cold weather. Boosting a vehicle with a frozen battery is very dangerous as this can also cause a battery explosion. It is rare for a frozen battery to be brought back to serviceable condition, because the lead plates often suffer irreparable damage during the freezing and thawing process.

Starting System

In order to start the engine, an electrically operated starter motor is utilized. When the ignition switch is moved to the "start" position, an electrical current is sent to the starter solenoid, which engages the starter drive gear onto the engine's ring gear (located on the flywheel). When the drive is engaged, the solenoid connects the battery to the starter motor, which then turns the engine at sufficient speed to start it. Allowing the ignition switch to return to the "run" position causes the starter drive to disengage from the flywheel; the starter motor stops turning, and the engine now runs on its own.

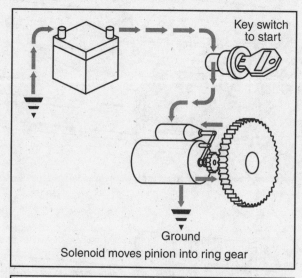

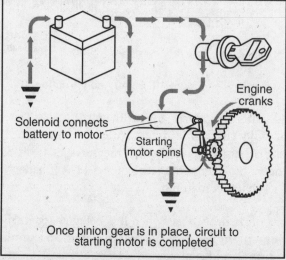

Figure 20. Starting motor operation

The starter drive gear has a small number of teeth, and the engine's ring gear has a large number of teeth. This is how the starter motor generates so much cranking power, through a speed reduction of approximately 18:1. This means that the starter motor turns 18 times faster than the engine, but it also means that it generates 18 times more torque to turn the engine.

Charging System

Once the engine is running, the charging system provides electrical current to recharge the battery and power the vehicle's electrical system. The main component of the charging system is the **alternator**. The alternator is belt-driven by the engine's crankshaft, and converts mechanical energy into electrical energy. The alternator produces alternating current (AC), which is then **rectified** by an internal set of diodes known as the **rectifier bridge**. The rectifier bridge converts AC to DC, which can be used to power the vehicle's electrical system.

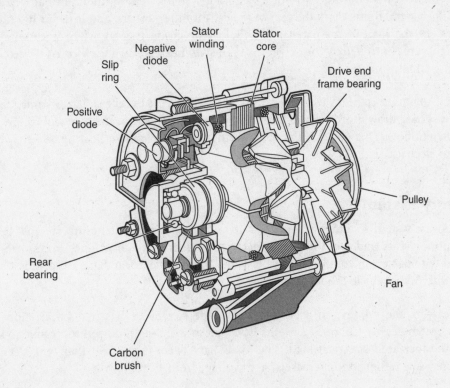

Figure 21. Alternator

A **voltage regulator** controls the output of the alternator. Normal system voltage during engine operation is around 14.5 volts. Turning on the headlights, heater motor, and other accessories on the vehicle increases the **load** on the electrical system and system voltage drops. The voltage regulator senses this decrease in system voltage and responds by increasing the alternator's output to compensate for it. As long as the alternator's output is able to match the load on the electrical system, the system voltage will remain close to 14.5 volts.

If the electrical load decreases (accessories are turned off), the system voltage will rise. The voltage regulator decreases the output of the alternator gradually as the system voltage gets closer and closer to 14.5 volts. The idea here is to prevent system voltage from rising past 14.5 volts. Voltages above this level will cause battery overcharging and can stress electrical system components.

Earlier charging system designs used an external voltage regulator. This meant that the voltage regulator was separate from the alternator itself. The next step was to install the voltage regulator in the alternator housing to simplify design and increase reliability. Late model charging systems control the alternator using the vehicle's onboard computer.

Lighting System

There are many lights built into a vehicle's lighting system. **Headlights** illuminate the road ahead of the car, **tail lights** mark the rear of the car for other drivers, and **interior lights** help the driver see the instrument panel and other areas inside the car when necessary. The various lights are controlled by the driver through **switches** that turn the electrical current to the lighting circuits on and off.

The vehicle's lighting circuits are protected by **fuses** or **circuit breakers**. If, for some reason, the circuit should draw more current than it has been designed for, the fuse will "blow" and cut off current flow. This protects the wires in the circuits from overheating and may even prevent an electrical fire.

Accessory System

The accessory system includes a wide variety of components, including stereos, heater motors, power seats and windows, and electric window defrosters. Since accessories are associated with passenger comfort, it is no wonder that the electrical demands of this system increase with every vehicle model year.

The increase in the number of accessories in modern vehicles has had implications for electrical system design. Charging systems have had to increase in output to be able to keep up with the increased electrical load. The loads have become so great that new electrical systems are being designed to increase system voltage from 12 to 42 volts.

Maintenance

The most important maintenance that should be done on the vehicle's electrical system relates to the battery. Over time, the battery top becomes dirty and its connections get corroded. A solution of warm water and baking soda can be poured over top of the battery to neutralize acids that have accumulated there. The battery should then be rinsed with water and dried off.

A battery terminal cleaner can be purchased at any auto parts store. Remove the battery terminals (negative connection first) and clean the inside of the cable connector and the battery posts. When reassembling the terminals, reconnect the negative cable last and use some high temperature grease on the outside of the connection to prevent corrosion.

COMPUTER SYSTEM

Computer control first came on to the automotive scene in the early '80s. Early automotive computers controlled only a few engine-related functions, but today it is rare to find an automotive component that is not a participant in the vehicle's overall computer control strategy.

Computer control systems work much like the human nervous system. **Sensors** provide data to the **computer**, which processes this information and sends signals to **actuators** to control vehicle functions. In the case of the human body, the eyes and ears send signals to the brain, which processes this information and send signals to the various muscles to control body movement.

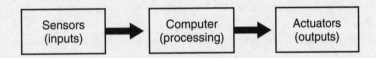

Figure 22. Computer system

The major components of the automotive computer system include the following:

Sensors: these generate signals based on rotational speed, temperature, pressure, and relative position. The sensors are the "eyes and ears" of the computer system. An example of a sensor would be an oxygen sensor, which is responsible for sending data to the computer concerning the oxygen content of the exhaust gases. This information is used by the computer to determine whether the engine's air-fuel mixture is rich or lean.

Computer: processes data from the sensors based on a preprogrammed strategy (software) and then generates outputs to control vehicle functions. The computer is the "brain" of the computer system. In today's vehicles, the computer is often referred to as the **Powertrain Control Module** or **PCM**.

Actuators: these receive output signals from the computer and control vehicle functions. An example of an actuator would be a fuel injector, because it responds to signals from the computer to inject a specific amount of fuel into the intake air stream.

There are very few vehicle systems that are not controlled by the PCM. Communication with the PCM is essential in order to troubleshoot problems and keep the vehicle running in top condition. Automotive technicians communicate with the PCM using a **scan tool**, which allows them to get information from the computer concerning the operation of the various vehicle systems. The scan tool is connected to the vehicle's computer system through a **diagnostic data link** that is located near the driver's seat.

DRIVE TRAIN SYSTEM

The engine can produce power to move the vehicle, but this energy must be processed and transmitted effectively in order to accelerate the vehicle smoothly and quickly. Transmitting power from the engine to the wheels is the responsibility of the vehicle's drive train.

The components used in the drive train will vary depending on vehicle design. For instance, a rear-wheel drive vehicle will have a different drive train configuration from a front-wheel drive vehicle. Four-wheel drive requires even more drive train components to get the job done.

An important part of any drive train is the **transmission**. The two main types of transmissions are the **automatic** and the **manual**. Drivers who like to have more control over the operation of the vehicle will often choose a manual transmission, because the driver is responsible for shifting the gears up and down. A car with an automatic transmission is much easier to operate because it does not use a **clutch** and does all of the gear shifting automatically.

While rear-wheel drive was the most common design in years past, front-wheel drive has become very popular, especially in small to medium-sized cars.

The typical components found in a front-wheel drive vehicle with a manual transmission include the following:

Clutch: transmits torque from the engine to the transmission. The clutch can be released and engaged to allow smooth starts and transmission shifting.

Transaxle: has several "gears" that are selected according to the speed of the vehicle and how fast the driver would like to accelerate. The transaxle is a combination of the transmission and the **drive axle**, which are normally two separate components in a rear-wheel drive vehicle.

Half-shaft: a short drive shaft that transmits power from the transaxle to the drive wheels. Used only in front-wheel drive vehicles, the half shafts must be able to apply power to the drive wheels while allowing them to move up and down and turn the vehicle. There are two half shafts, one for each drive wheel.

Constant-velocity (CV) joints: located at each end of a half-shaft, CV joints can transmit power through very steep angles. The inboard CV joint is located at the transaxle, while the outboard CV joint is located behind the vehicle wheel.

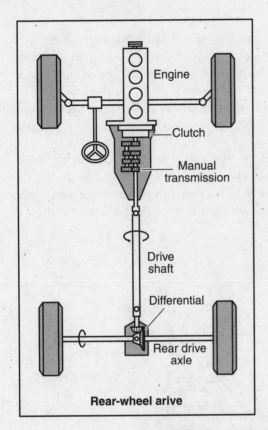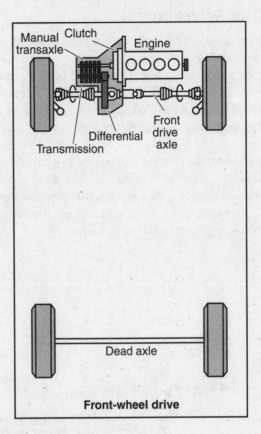

Figure 23. Rear- and front- wheel drive

Other drive train components that may be found in other vehicle designs include the following:

Transmission: used in rear and four-wheel drive vehicles, the transmission is responsible for matching engine speed to the desired speed of the vehicle.

Drive shaft: a longer version of the half-shaft, the drive shaft transmits torque from the transmission to the drive axle. The drive shaft is also required to allow up and down movement of the vehicle's wheels, but not to the same extent as the half-shaft in a front-wheel drive.

Universal joints: located at each end of the drive shaft, the universal joint allows the shaft to operate at an angle with the component that it is driving. Also known as **U-joints**.

Drive axle: transmits engine power through a 90 degree angle, and splits that power between the two drive wheels. The wheels are attached to the ends of the drive axle. The drive axle incorporates a **differential,** which allows the left and right wheel to turn at different speeds as the vehicle goes around a corner.

Transfer case: located between the transmission and the drive axles on a four-wheel drive vehicle. The transfer case splits the engine's power between the front and rear drive axle.

Gear Selection

Transmissions are built with several forward "speeds" or "gears." For instance, a four-speed transmission would have four forward gears and one reverse. A driver would typically start from a stop using **low (first) gear**. In this gear, the transmission would increase the **torque** from the engine sufficiently to be able to start the vehicle from a standstill. However, this would limit the vehicle's speed once it did start rolling, so the driver would then select **second gear** and so on as the vehicle continued to accelerate.

High (fourth) gear would be used to allow the vehicle to cruise on the highway. Engine speed would be moderate to low in this gear, allowing for maximum fuel economy and quiet running. To accelerate quickly, however, the driver would **downshift** to a lower gear in order to increase engine speed and torque. Proper gear selection is important when operating a vehicle with a manual transmission.

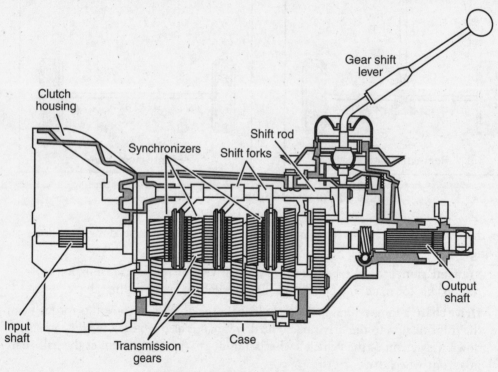

Figure 24. Manual Transmission

Automatic Transmissions

Automatic transmissions are much more complex than their manual counterparts, yet are much easier to operate. The reason that many drivers prefer them is that automatic transmissions don't use a clutch. Learning to start out from a stoplight and shift a manual transmission smoothly and effectively is problematic for many drivers. This is because the release and engagement of the clutch must be synchronized with the movement of the shift lever and the vehicle's throttle. Anyone can learn how to do this, but manual transmissions require extra patience on the part of the student.

Instead of using a clutch, automatics transmit engine torque from the engine to the transmission through a **torque converter**. The torque converter uses fluid to transmit power, and allows for a certain amount of slippage when the vehicle is stopped. It is essentially two fans facing each other, one being the drive fan and the other, the driven fan. However, instead of pushing air from one fan to the other, fluid is pumped between them. This fluid movement is what transmits the power across the torque converter.

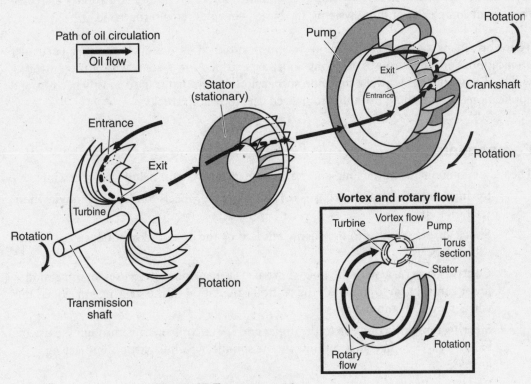

Figure 25. Torque converter

Automatic transmissions do all of the gear selection for the driver. This is done in the transmission using hydraulics and **planetary gear sets**. The newest automatic transmissions are controlled electronically by the vehicle's powertrain control module.

SUSPENSION AND STEERING SYSTEM

Of all the aspects of vehicle operation, two that are a high priority for most drivers is ride comfort and handling. Engineers continue to work on building a car that rides smooth on even the worst roads, and yet is able to corner easily at high speed.

The newest suspension and steering systems have incorporated computer control in an effort to achieve these high standards. While the sophistication of computer control has increased the overall complexity of these systems, the basic principles remain the same.

There are many types of suspension systems, and each is designed to fit a particular application. For our purposes, the long-short arm suspension system with linkage steering will be discussed. This is a very common suspension system that is used mostly in front-end applications in everything from medium-sized cars to pickup trucks.

Components

The major components of the long-short arm suspension system include the following:

Springs: hold the vehicle's chassis up and allow the wheels to move up and down in relation to it.

Shock absorbers: absorb the energy released by the up and down movement of the vehicle wheels.

Control arms (A-arms): the long-short arm suspension system uses an upper and lower control arm to maintain the vertical orientation of the steering knuckle as the wheel moves up and down.

Steering knuckle: connects to the upper and lower control arms through the use of ball-joints. The wheel hub mounts on the spindle, which is part of the steering knuckle.

Ball joints: "ball and socket" assemblies that allow the steering knuckle to turn and move up and down simultaneously.

Steering linkage: connects the steering wheel to the steering knuckle.

Wheel hub: forms the mounting point for the vehicles tire assembly.

Tire: makes contact with the road and provides a "footprint" to aid in vehicle stability and handling.

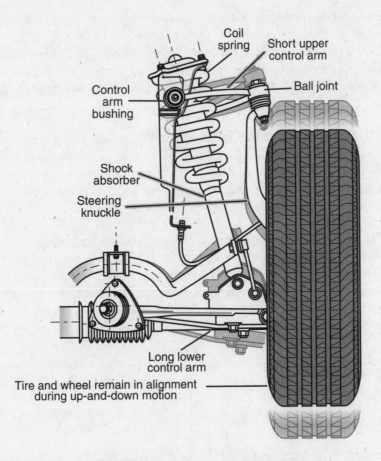

Coil spring
Short upper control arm
Ball joint
Control arm bushing
Shock absorber
Steering knuckle
Long lower control arm
Tire and wheel remain in alignment during up-and-down motion

Figure 26. Long-short arm suspension

Construction and Operation

In order to make a vehicle ride smoothly, the wheels must be able to move up and down while the vehicle chassis stays steady. This is the job of the vehicle **springs**; they must be able to allow this movement of the wheels without transmitting road shock. However, the springs absorb energy as this happens and must release this energy without bouncing the vehicle after encountering a bump. Springs are built in a number of different designs, including the coil spring, leaf spring, torsion bar, and air spring.

The **shock absorber** is installed between the chassis and a control arm to help absorb some of the energy as the spring is compressed (or **jounced**), and then absorbs energy from the spring as it **rebounds** afterwards. This prevents this extra energy from being transmitted to the chassis, and thus, the passengers. The shock absorber uses a piston and hydraulic oil to absorb the excess mechanical energy from the suspension system and then releases that same energy in the form of heat.

The **upper and lower control arms** form the supports for the steering knuckle. The control arms are attached to the chassis through the use of **control arm bushings**. The spring is placed between the chassis and one of the control arms. The spring can be installed on either the upper or lower control arm in a long-short arm suspension. The control arm with the spring on it becomes the load-bearing arm as the vehicle weight is supported through it on the way to the steering knuckle and tire assembly.

An **upper ball joint** and a **lower ball joint** are used to attach the steering knuckle to the control arms. Ball joints are built similar to a human hip joint, with a ball and stud rotating in a socket to allow a wide arc of movement. As the control arms move up and down, the ball joints allow the steering knuckle to move freely with them. They also allow the steering knuckle to turn left and right as it is moved by the steering linkage.

The **steering linkage** forms the connection between the steering wheel and the steering knuckle. There are two main designs in common use, the **linkage steering** and the **rack and pinion**. Long-short arm suspensions most commonly use linkage steering to connect the steering column to the **pitman arm**, **center link**, and **idler arm**. **Tie rods** are then used to make the final connection to the steering knuckles. Smaller vehicles most commonly use the rack-and-pinion steering system because it is the most compact of the two major steering systems.

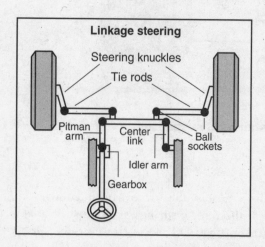 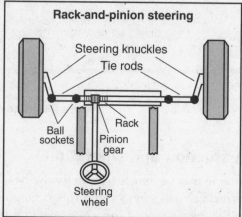

Figure 27. Steering system types

Tires

Tires are one of the most critical components of the suspension and steering system. They support the weight of the vehicle and make final contact with the road surface. The most common tire design is the **radial tire**, which is known for its stable footprint and low rolling resistance.

Tire construction begins with the **beads**. The bead is a circular piece of steel wire that is encased in rubber. The bead forms the mounting point for the tire on the **rim**. **Body plies** form the main body of the tire and run from bead-to-bead. All other parts of the tire attach to the body plies, including the **liner** (sealed surface inside the tire), the **sidewalls**, and the **tread**.

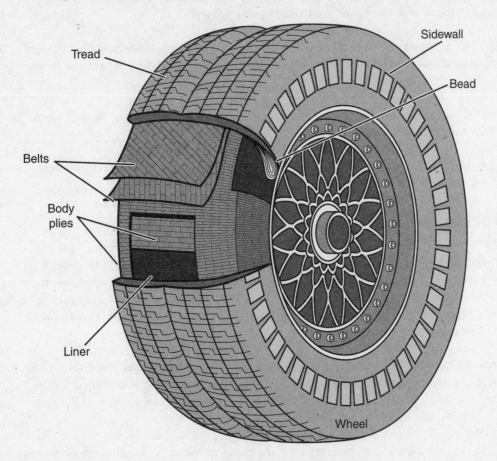

Figure 28. Tire construction

Belts are used between the plies and the tread to help stabilize the tire's footprint (where the tire makes contact with the road). A stable footprint means better traction under all road conditions, and makes the vehicle handle and brake better.

The load-carrying ability of a tire is determined by the number of body plies that are used in its construction. For example, a 2-ply tire would be for light loads, where a truck might use a 4 or 6-ply tire.

Tires are identified using a system known as **P-Metric**. This system gives the tire buyer a thorough understanding of the tire size and recommended use so the correct tires can be purchased for their vehicle.

An example of a P-Metric tire number would look like this: P215/75R-14.

The "P" tells us that this tire is designed for a passenger car. If this were an "LT," the tire would be especially suited for light trucks, and a "C" would be a commercial vehicle application.

The "215" indicates the **section width** in millimeters. Section width is a measurement of the width of the tire across its sidewalls.

The "75" is the **aspect ratio** of the tire. This is a comparison of the height of the tire (measured from the bead to the tread) relative to its section width. This tire's height is 75 percent of its width.

The "R" stands for radial. A radial tire is distinct because its plies run directly from bead-to-bead instead of diagonally like a bias-ply tire.

The "14" tells us that this tire is made for a 14", diameter rim. It is a measurement of the inside diameter of the tire.

Maintenance

The primary maintenance that should be performed on suspension and steering systems is lubrication of the ball joints, tie rod ends, and other components. This should be done with a hand-powered grease gun, and the amount of grease should be metered carefully. Too much grease makes a mess and can rupture "balloon" seals that are used on some components. A good rule of thumb is two strokes of the grease gun handle for each chassis grease fitting every time you change the oil and filter.

Suspension and steering systems require less maintenance in recent model years, due to the fact that many components that once required periodic lubrication are now "lubed for life." These components are sealed and do not have grease fittings on them, so they only require periodic inspection and ultimately, replacement if they are worn.

The most important part of tire maintenance is proper inflation. Low inflation pressures increase rolling resistance, and therefore increase fuel consumption. Also, a tire run at low pressures can fail prematurely due to overheating of the sidewalls. Look for a decal on the driver's door to get information on the tire size and inflation pressures that are recommended for your vehicle.

BRAKE SYSTEMS

Of all the systems on a car, the most important may well be the brake system. It is one thing to not be able to go; it is another thing again to not be able to stop. Anyone who has experienced a brake failure can testify to the helpless feeling inspired by a lack of response from the brake pedal.

Brake systems are energy conversion devices: they convert the kinetic (moving) energy of the vehicle into heat energy. A brake system becomes more powerful as it gains ability to increase friction and reject heat. Heavier vehicles and performance-oriented vehicles need to have more powerful brakes. If the weight of a vehicle is doubled, it will need twice as much braking power to stop it in the same amount of time. However, doubling the speed of a vehicle raises the braking requirement four times. Speed has a much greater effect on braking requirements than weight.

The major components found in any brake system include the following:

> **Brake pedal:** the mechanical connection between the driver's foot and the master cylinder.
>
> **Master cylinder:** located in the engine compartment just in front of the driver, the master cylinder generates the fluid pressure to operate the brake assemblies at the wheels.
>
> **Fluid reservoir:** provides fluid to the brake circuits. The fluid reservoir is located on top of the master cylinder.
>
> **Brake lines:** transmit fluid pressure from the master cylinder to the brake assemblies. These can be steel lines that run along the vehicle chassis or flex hoses that are used to connect the steel lines to the brake assemblies.

The two major types of brake assemblies are as follows:

> **Drum brakes:** expanding shoes make contact with a rotating drum to develop friction and slow the vehicle.
>
> **Disk brakes:** brake pads on either side of a rotating disk are "pinched" together to slow the vehicle.

Brake systems are **hydraulically operated**. A pumping piston, located in the **master cylinder**, is operated by the **brake pedal** and puts pressure on the system's **brake fluid**. Since fluids cannot be compressed, the brake fluid travels through the **brake lines** and moves the pistons in the **brake assemblies** to operate the brakes. The harder the driver presses on the brake pedal, the more fluid pressure is developed and more braking power is generated.

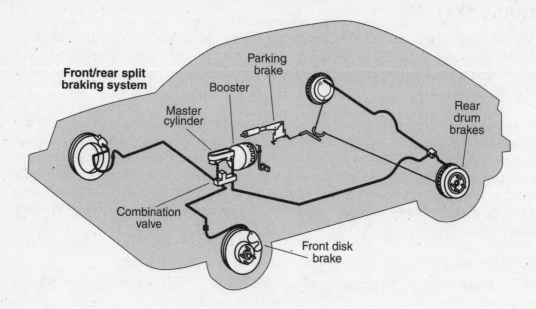

Figure 29. Dual hydraulic brake systems

Brake fluid is not made from oil. Most brake fluids are made from **glycol**. This is because glycol has a high boiling point, a low freeze point, and can absorb any moisture that makes its way into the brake system. Brake fluid makes an excellent paint stripper. If spilled onto a car's finish, be sure to pour or spray water on the spill to keep it from damaging the paint.

Drum Brakes

Drum brakes have been in use for many years. Although not as popular as they once were, they are still used on many vehicles, mostly due to their versatility. It is easy to incorporate a parking brake into a drum brake assembly, so this is one reason why drum brakes are still used on the rear wheels of many vehicles.

The parts that develop the friction in a drum brake are the **brake shoes**. There are two brake shoes in any drum brake assembly. The brake shoes are operated by a **wheel cylinder** that is located between the brake shoes. As hydraulic pressure is applied to the wheel cylinder, the pistons inside push apart and act against the brake shoes. The brake shoes push outwards against the brake drum, and the resulting friction slows the vehicle.

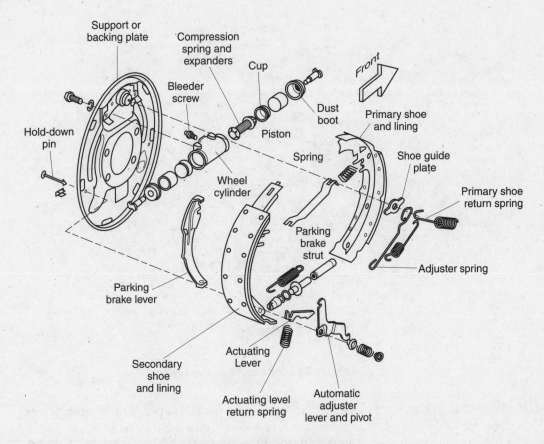

Figure 30. Drum brake assembly

When the driver releases the brake pedal, hydraulic pressure is released from the wheel cylinder, and the brakes shoes are pulled back by the return springs. The brake assembly is then able to rotate freely until the next brake application.

Disk Brakes

As the driver applies the brakes, the weight of the car tends to shift forward onto the front wheels. This means that the front brakes are required to do approximately two-thirds of the total braking. This is why it is very common to have disk brakes on the front of the car, and drum brakes on the rear.

Disk brakes are much more powerful than drums. The pistons used to actuate disk brakes are much larger, and can apply more force to the brake pads. Also, brake rotors used in disk brakes are more easily cooled, as they are better exposed to the cool air under the car and are often designed with air passages through them to enhance heat rejection. Better brake cooling means better braking power.

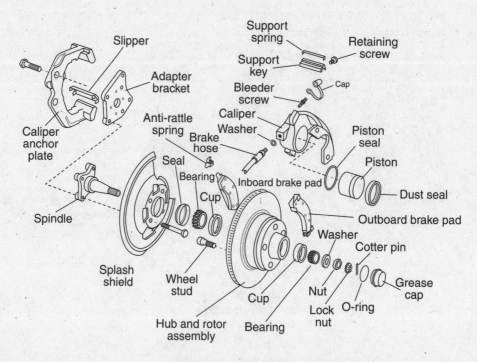

Figure 31. Disk brake assembly

The piston that operates a disk brake is housed in a **brake caliper**. This caliper "floats" laterally as the brake is applied and released, and makes it possible for one piston to operate the pads on both sides of the rotor. This makes the caliper operate similar to a "c-clamp." As the screw is tightened on one side, the entire assembly is drawn together and "pinches" tightly on the item being clamped.

Power Brakes

Braking pressure can be boosted using a **brake booster**. The brake booster is located between the brake pedal and the master cylinder. Engine intake manifold vacuum is utilized to generate greater force on the master cylinder, so higher hydraulic pressures can be generated in the brake system. Some brake booster systems use fluid pressure from the power steering system to increase braking power.

Antilock Brakes

Just like every other vehicle system, computer control is being incorporated into the brake system. Most cars now come equipped with **antilock brakes (ABS)**, which prevent wheel lock under hard braking conditions. This gives more control to the driver in slippery conditions and allows the vehicle to stop more predictably.

AUTOMOTIVE INFORMATION PRACTICE SET

1. How many revolutions of the crankshaft does it take to complete one cycle of events in a four stroke-cycle engine?

   (A) one-half
   (B) one
   (C) two
   (D) four

2. The _____ stroke takes place after the compression stroke.

   (A) intake
   (B) power
   (C) exhaust
   (D) ignition

3. The engine's crankshaft is connected to the piston through the

   (A) cylinder
   (B) intake valve
   (C) exhaust valve
   (D) connecting rod

4. Engine displacement can be increased by

   (A) increasing the diameter of the cylinder bore
   (B) increasing the length of the stroke
   (C) both A and B
   (D) neither A nor B

5. A material used in engine construction is

   (A) copper
   (B) aluminum
   (C) carbon
   (D) silver

6. A V8 engine will fire _____ cylinder(s) in one revolution of the crankshaft.

   (A) one
   (B) two
   (C) four
   (D) eight

7. A 12:1 air-fuel mixture would be a _____ mixture.

   (A) rich
   (B) lean
   (C) stoichiometric
   (D) none of the above

8. Normal combustion is characterized by _____.

   (A) an explosion in the combustion chamber
   (B) a flame starting at the spark plug and advancing quickly across the combustion chamber
   (C) a flame initiated by a "hot spot" in the combustion chamber
   (D) all of the above

9. Diesel engines utilize a _____.

   (A) high compression ratio
   (B) spark ignition system
   (C) low compression ratio
   (D) carburetor

10. The antifreeze in the engine's coolant will

    (A) lower the boiling point of the coolant
    (B) raise the boiling point of the coolant
    (C) raise the freeze point of the coolant
    (D) lower the corrosion resistance of the coolant

11. Normal flow for the engine's coolant would be

    (A) water pump outlet, radiator, cylinder head, engine block
    (B) water pump outlet, engine block, radiator, cylinder head
    (C) water pump outlet, cylinder head, radiator, engine block
    (D) water pump outlet, engine block, cylinder head, radiator

12. Which of the following statements concerning the cooling system is true?

    (A) The coolant stops flowing when the thermostat is closed.
    (B) The radiator always has coolant flowing through it.
    (C) As long as the engine is running, the water pump is pumping coolant.
    (D) The radiator cap prevents coolant from flowing back into the system.

13. Fuel injection is better than carburetion because it provides

    (A) more precise fuel control
    (B) better fuel economy
    (C) smoother engine operation
    (D) all of the above

14. Electronic fuel injectors are controlled by the

    (A) powertrain control module
    (B) fuel pressure regulator
    (C) electric fuel pump
    (D) ignition switch

15. Cold engines require _____ mixtures.

    (A) rich
    (B) lean
    (C) stoichiometric
    (D) none of the above

16. The PCM receives signals from the vehicle's _____.

    (A) sensors
    (B) diagnostic data link
    (C) actuators
    (D) scan tool

17. The PCM controls vehicle functions through the use of _____.

    (A) actuators
    (B) sensors
    (C) components
    (D) assemblies

18. Automotive technicians communicate with the PCM through the use of _____.

    (A) sensors
    (B) actuators
    (C) hand tools
    (D) a scan tool

19. Disk brakes are most often found on the _____ of the vehicle.

    (A) left side
    (B) front
    (C) right side
    (D) rear

20. The front brakes do _____ of the vehicle's braking.

    (A) $\dfrac{1}{4}$

    (B) $\dfrac{1}{3}$

    (C) $\dfrac{1}{2}$

    (D) $\dfrac{2}{3}$

21. What statement best describes how ABS brake systems work?

    (A) ABS prevents the wheels from locking at any time.
    (B) ABS prevents the wheels from locking only when the vehicle is stopped.
    (C) ABS prevents the wheels from locking when the brakes are applied at high speed.
    (D) ABS will lock the wheels during any brake application.

ANSWERS AND EXPLANATIONS FOR
AUTOMOTIVE INFORMATION PRACTICE SET

1. D

It takes four revolutions of the crankshaft to equal each four-stroke cycle.

2. B

The next stroke after the compression stroke is known as the power stroke. This is what generates the engine's power.

3. D

The connecting rod is what links the crankshaft to the piston and helps provide rotary motion, and therefore, power.

4. C

An increase to the diameter of both the cylinder bore and the length of the stroke is necessary to increase engine displacement. This enables for greater horsepower.

5. B

Aluminum, because of its light weight and malleability, is the material of choice for car-makers today.

6. C

V8 engines fire four cylinders in one crankshaft revolution. It takes two revolutions of the crankshaft to complete the cycle of events.

7. A

A 12:1 ratio of air to fuel would be a rich mixture, fast-burning and possibly producing black smoke.

8. B

In normal combustion, a flame goes from the spark plug across the combustion chamber, heating the gases and building pressure in an even, controlled manner.

9. A

Diesel engines operate with a high compression ratio. The compression ratio for a diesel engine can range anywhere from 16:1 to 22:1.

10. B

Antifreeze raises the boiling point of your coolant, thereby rendering it much more efficient at transferring heat.

11. D

The correct order of the coolant flow should be water pump outlet first, then the engine block, followed by the cylinder head, and finally the radiator.

12. C

If the water pump is operating correctly, then whenever the engine is in action, the pump is pumping coolant into the radiator.

13. D

The correct answer is that fuel injection gives you all of these: more precise fuel control, better fuel economy, and smoother engine operation. It also requires much less maintenance.

14. A

Of the items given, only the powertrain control module is in charge of firing and regulating electronic fuel injectors.

15. A

Rich mixtures are preferable for cold engines because as the engine warms up, less fuel is needed to make the engine run smoothly.

16. A

The "brain" of the car, it is the job of the PCM to gather signals from the car's sensors and generate outputs to control the vehicle's functions. The diagnostic data link, choice (B), connects a scan tool to the PCM ; the scan tool, (D), is what technicians use to read the PCM.

17. A

The PCM takes the information it gets from sensors and sends it along to actuators, which then perform the functions necessary to operate the car. Components and assemblies are general terms for different parts of a car.

18. D

Technicians, in order to read a car's PCM, use a scan tool to decode the PCM's information on vehicle operation.

19. B

As the driver applies the brakes, vehicle weight shifts forward, and onto the front wheels, meaning that front brakes bear the vast burden of the total braking. This is why it is very common to have disk brakes on the front, choice (B).

20. **D**

As weight is thrust toward the front of the vehicle, front brakes are asked to bear roughly $\frac{2}{3}$ of the load in total braking.

21. **C**

Anti-lock brakes (ABS) activate only once the driver applies the brakes. Therefore, answer choice (A) is incorrect. When the vehicle is stopped, no braking is necessary. Of the answer choices, only (C) is appropriate, as ABS brake systems operate at high speeds, making it so the wheels cannot lock and cause the car to lose control.

CHAPTER NINE

Shop Information

INTRODUCTION

One type of question on the ASVAB that many test-takers may find challenging relates to the identification of shop tools. Luckily, we have prepared for you a primer on the basics of tool identification and usage. Pay particular attention to the ways in which these individual tools are used, as the ASVAB covers not only what these tools are, but also *how* they are used.

Why does the ASVAB cover tools in such detail? Well, remember that this is a test not only of your verbal and quantitative abilities, but also a vocational test designed to help you identify your aptitudes in a variety of fields, including industrial and maintenance trades. In order to work effectively in any industrial or technical environment, a technician must be able to identify tools correctly and use them safely. Hand tools are the foundation of industry; very little work would get done without them. Even the largest piece of equipment would not run for very long if hand tools were not available for their maintenance and repair.

For instance, a powerful diesel engine can do vast amounts of work in a short period of time. This machine can do many times the amount of work that a person equipped with only hand tools could do. Yet, without simple hand tools to change the oil, tighten bolts and service the filters, this machine would soon stop running. And since workers of all trades rely on hand tools to get their jobs done, the purpose of this section is to familiarize you with many types of basic hand tools and to give you a better idea of how to use them safely.

Let's take a look at the sort of tools the ASVAB will be asking about. While no one can be expected to know every one of these tools by heart, including all their various sizes and uses, it is still useful to examine each section of this chapter in detail. Consider taking the time to look over each type of tool separately, noting how each differs. One day look at wrenches; the next, spend some time with screwdrivers. In a few weeks, you'll have a great grasp of ASVAB tools basics.

WRENCHES

Wrenches are among the most basic tools in a mechanic's tool box. Since machines are held together by bolts and other threaded fasteners, a good selection of wrenches is an absolute necessity.

There are two basic types of wrenches; the **open-end** and the **box-end**. The open-end wrench is made for speed. Since the end is open, it is easy to slide the wrench on and off a fastener, such as a cap screw. The downside to the open-end wrench is that it only makes contact with two sides of a six-sided (hex) bolt head. This means that it is easy to "round off" the edges of fasteners that are very tight, subsequently making them a real nuisance to remove.

To loosen tight fasteners, it is a good idea to use a box-end wrench. The box end wraps completely around the head of a bolt, and therefore makes greater surface contact. This added contact area makes it less likely that the technician could round off the bolt head, and makes it much easier to loosen tight or "frozen" fasteners. Box-end wrenches normally come in a 12-point configuration, but some are made as 6-point.

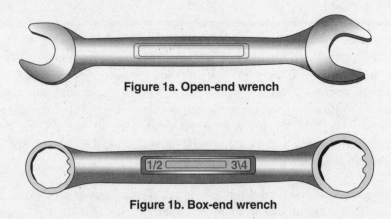

Figure 1a. Open-end wrench

Figure 1b. Box-end wrench

The most common wrench arrangement is the **combination wrench**. This design has an open-end and a box-end built into opposite ends of a wrench. Both ends are made to fit the same size fastener, but the technician can loosen the bolt with the box end, and then finish removing the bolt more quickly using the open end.

When the specific size wrench for a fastener is not available, an **adjustable wrench** (sometimes referred to as a **Crescent® wrench**) can be used. While the adjustable wrench is convenient, it is not recommended for other than emergency use as the adjustment loosens very easily and makes it more likely that the wrench will slip on the nut. Adjustable wrenches are specified according to their length.

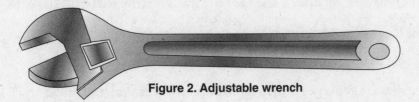

Figure 2. Adjustable wrench

Wrenches can be pulled or pushed, but it is much safer to pull them. This is because it is easier to control any sudden movements if the wrench is being pulled towards you. Pushing a wrench can easily result in skinned knuckles if the fastener suddenly comes loose. Also, keep in mind that tight fasteners can be more easily loosened with longer wrenches.

SOCKETS

Figure 3. Standard sockets

An alternative to using wrenches to loosen fasteners is the use of **sockets**. Like wrenches, sockets come in both **6 and 12-point designs**. Six-point is a stronger design, and is usually the mechanic's first choice in the smaller socket drive sizes. However, 12-point is definitely the most popular in large drive sizes, such as $\frac{3}{4}$ and above.

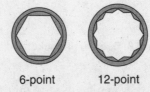

6-point   12-point

Figure 4. Six-point and twelve-point sockets

To determine the size of socket required for a job, simply measure the distance between two parallel sides of the bolt head. If the bolt head measures $\frac{9}{16}$" across two parallel sides, then a $\frac{9}{16}$" socket is required to loosen it.

Sockets come in a variety of **drive sizes**. The drive size is determined by the size of the opening that attaches to the **drive tool**. For instance, if the square end of a socket measures $\frac{3}{8}$" across, then that would be a $\frac{3}{8}$" drive socket. The most popular drive sizes are $\frac{1}{4}$", $\frac{3}{8}$", $\frac{1}{2}$", and $\frac{3}{4}$". Larger drive sizes are available for the very large fasteners used in heavy industry. Take a look at the diagram below.

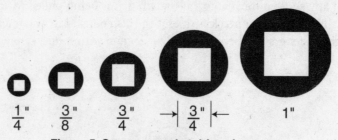

$\frac{1}{4}$" $\quad$ $\frac{3}{8}$" $\quad$ $\frac{3}{4}$" $\quad$ $\frac{3}{4}$" $\quad$ 1"

Figure 5. Common socket drive size range

Sometimes fasteners are located in areas that are difficult to get at with a regular socket, such as a nut that is threaded onto a long stud. In this situation, a technician would use a **deep socket** to reach over the stud and turn the nut. Deep sockets are just like regular sockets, except longer.

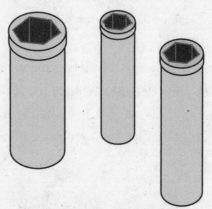

Figure 6. Deep-well sockets

Sockets are very versatile, because they can be used with a variety of drive tools. The most common drive tool for sockets is the **ratchet**, which turns the fastener in only one direction as the handle is moved back and forth through a narrow arc. Ratchets are reversible, so they can be set to tighten or loosen a fastener.

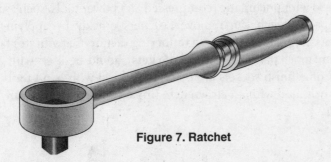

Figure 7. Ratchet

Sockets can also be attached to a ratchet through the use of an **extension**. This can be very useful when attempting to loosen bolts that are deep inside a hole or are otherwise difficult to get at. Further accessibility can be gained by using a **universal joint**, which can allow access to fasteners that are installed at angles.

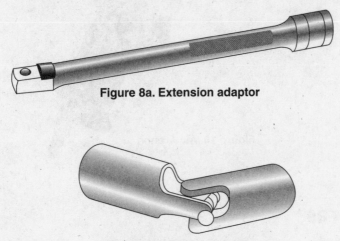

Figure 8a. Extension adaptor

Figure 8b. Universal joint

When attempting to loosen very tight fasteners, it is advisable to use a socket with a **breaker bar**. Breaker bars are also known as **flex handles** or **Johnson bars**. A long breaker bar attached to a socket can give enough twisting force to loosen very tight fasteners. Once the fastener is loose, then an ordinary ratchet can be attached to the socket to make for quick removal.

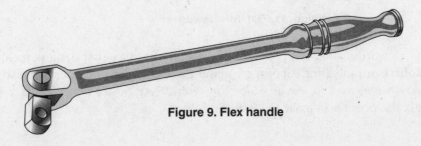

Figure 9. Flex handle

Sockets can also be used with pneumatic (compressed air) power tools, such as an **air impact wrench**. The air impact wrench can remove fasteners quickly by applying tremendous amounts of torque (twisting force) using a "hammering" action that vibrates fasteners loose. It is important to remember that only **impact sockets** should be used with an air impact wrench. Ordinary chrome finish sockets are made to be used with hand tools only and can be damaged very easily if used with an air wrench. Impact sockets can be easily identified by their dull black finish.

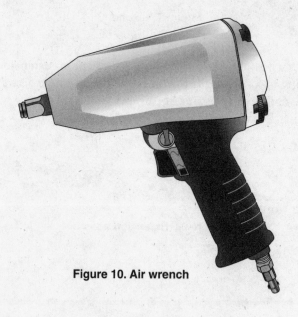

Figure 10. Air wrench

SCREWDRIVERS

Smaller fasteners (such as machine screws and wood screws) can often be removed and installed using a **screwdriver**. Screwdrivers come in many different sizes and configurations. The oldest screwdriver design is the **flat tip** type, which is basically a flat blade made to turn a screw with a single slot across the top of it.

Figure 11. Flat tip screwdriver

The flat tip screwdriver is far less popular now in light of some newer designs, including the **Phillips**, **Robertson**, and **Torx**. All of these newer designs grip the fastener better so they are much easier to remove and install. Since the screwdriver makes better contact with the fastener, it is also possible to make the fastener tighter.

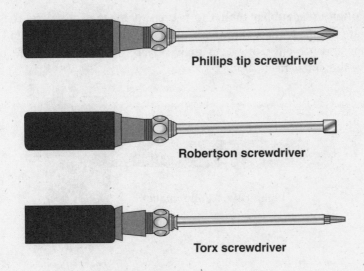

Phillips tip screwdriver

Robertson screwdriver

Torx screwdriver

Figure 12

Screwdrivers are now being designed with much more attention paid to the handle. The idea is to increase the contact that the technician's hand makes with the handle, and therefore increase the torque that can be applied to the fastener.

Of all the parts of the screwdriver, the tips take the most punishment during day-to-day use. It is important to inspect the tips of your screwdrivers regularly to determine which require replacement. In the case of the flat tip screwdriver, it is possible to grind the tip gently to true it up. Never use a screwdriver as a chisel or a prying tool. Be sure to use your hand tools only for the purpose they were designed.

HAMMERS

Striking objects in order to remove or install them is the job of the hammer. Almost every technician uses a hammer of some kind, whether it is used to drive a nail or to loosen pieces of an assembly. Hammers come in many designs and sizes according to their intended use.

The type most often used by metal workers and mechanics is known as a **ball-peen hammer**. This hammer is designed with a regular striking face like most hammers, but also has a rounded end that can be used for shaping metal and making gaskets.

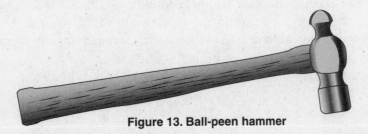

Figure 13. Ball-peen hammer

Mechanics will often use a **rubber mallet** to prevent damage to the parts they are striking. Rubber mallets are not made for maximum impact; they are designed to install delicate parts such as hub caps and prevent damage to their surface. A carpenter would use a **wooden mallet** to achieve the same effect.

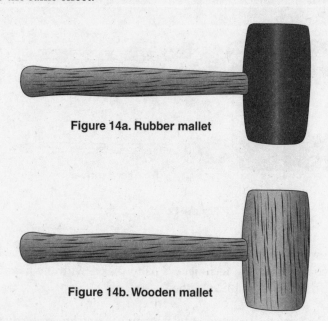

Figure 14a. Rubber mallet

Figure 14b. Wooden mallet

If more impact is desired, a **dead-blow hammer** can be used. The head of the dead blow is covered with plastic, but is also hollow and filled with lead shot or sand. The purpose of the lead shot is to prevent the hammer from rebounding as the object is being struck. This maximizes the impact on the object, without damaging the surface finish.

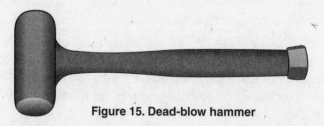

Figure 15. Dead-blow hammer

Carpenters often will use a **claw hammer**, which serves a dual purpose. The hammer head has two ends; one to drive nails and the other to remove nails. Claw hammers come in a variety of sizes, and these are determined by the weight of the hammer head. A general purpose claw hammer would have a 13 oz. head, while a rough framing hammer might be anywhere from 16 to 20 oz.

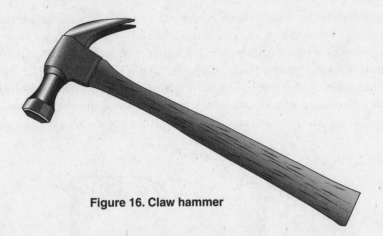

Figure 16. Claw hammer

Heavy jobs require the use of a **sledge hammer**. This is a long-handle hammer with a large steel head that typically requires both hands to operate. Probably the most famous use of sledge hammers was in the days of railway construction, when large spikes were driven into the railway ties to hold rails in place. Sledge hammers have very heavy heads, sometimes weighing up to several pounds.

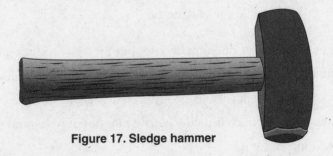

Figure 17. Sledge hammer

The most important maintenance item on a hammer is the tightness of the head on the handle. A loose hammer head can be extremely dangerous, as it could come off while in mid-swing. Loose hammer heads can be tightened by driving steel wedges into the head end of the handle. If this does not cure the problem, the old handle should be removed and replaced with a new one.

CHISELS, PUNCHES, AND DRIFTS

Hammers are often used in conjunction with a **chisel**, a **punch**, or a **drift**. A chisel normally has a long edge and is used for cutting, where a punch is narrow and is used for driving small fasteners and making layout marks. A drift is used for striking an object where it is important that the hammer itself not come in direct contact with the work.

The most common chisel is the **cold chisel,** which has a straight, sharp edge for cutting off bolt heads or separating two pieces of an assembly. Cold chisels get dull from time to time and must be resharpened on a bench grinder. It is important that the chisel be sharpened properly, as grinding too steep an angle can result in an edge that is easily dulled. The end that makes contact with the hammer (the beveled edge, or chamfer) can also get "mushroomed" as the metal gradually fatigues and spreads out. This should be dressed on a bench grinder to remove the excess metal, to prevent pieces from breaking off while the chisel is being struck.

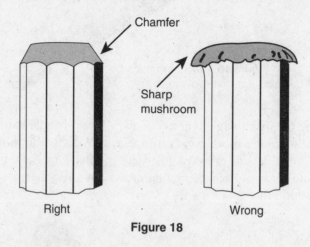

Figure 18

Punches are made in a number of different designs, but the most common ones are the **pin punch** and the **center punch**. Pin punches are straight and cylindrical in shape, and are used for driving roll pins. They come in various sizes, normally starting as small as $\frac{1}{16}''$ and going up to $\frac{1}{4}''$ in diameter. The pin punch is made to drive pins out of holes, and to follow the pin through the hole as it forces it out.

Figure 19. Pin punch

Center punches are used to make small indentations that serve as starting marks for drilling operations. Making a small indentation with a center punch can help the drill bit stay on target long enough to get a hole started. Attempting to drill a hole in metal without first marking it with a center punch can allow the drill bit to "walk" across the work and completely miss the original target.

Figure 20. Center punch

When using a hammer to drive parts in or out of an assembly, it is easy to damage the parts if they are struck directly by the hammer. The head of a ball-peen hammer is made from forged steel, and thus can easily damage parts that are made from softer materials. Placing a **drift** against the object and then striking the drift with a hammer prevents damage to the part that is being driven. Drifts are often made from soft metals such as mild steel, brass, and even aluminum.

Figure 21. Brass drift

SAWS

Cutting a material requires the use of a **saw**. Saws are used in many different trades, but are probably most utilized by carpenters. Carpenters saws include the **crosscut saw**, the **rip saw**, the **back saw**, and the **coping saw**.

The crosscut saw is designed to do what its name suggests: cut across the grain of the wood. Crosscut saw teeth are unique in that they cut like a knife. This is in contrast to a rip saw, that is made to cut with the grain of the wood and whose teeth are shaped like chisels. A rip saw's teeth are also set (bent) alternately from side to side to cut a relatively wide kerf (slot). This allows the rip saw to move freely as it cuts the wood.

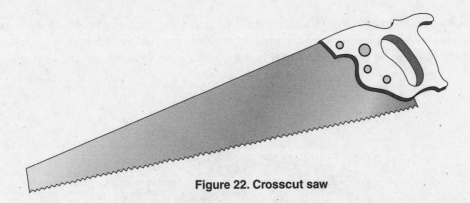

Figure 22. Crosscut saw

Saws made for rough work will have a fewer number of teeth per inch on the blade. For instance, a crosscut saw made for general use will have 8 teeth per inch, whereas a finishing saw would have either 10 or 11 teeth per inch. Rip saws can have as few as 5 teeth per inch, as it is less important for this saw to make a smooth cut.

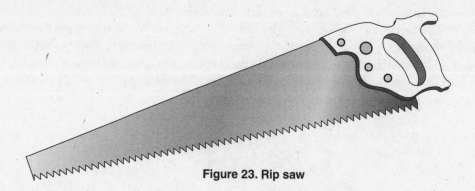

Figure 23. Rip saw

A coping saw is used to make fine, curving cuts. This saw uses a thin, flexible blade that is held tight on a wide frame. The blade can be rotated in the frame for further flexibility, making it easier to make difficult cuts on larger pieces of material.

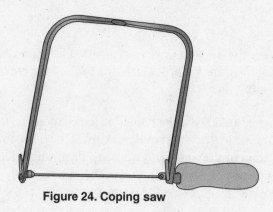

Figure 24. Coping saw

The **back saw** is also made from thin material, but has a rigid strip of steel on its top edge for reinforcement. A back saw is normally used for making fine cuts, so it has 14 to 16 teeth per inch. Back saws can be used with a **miter box** for making even cuts at specific angles.

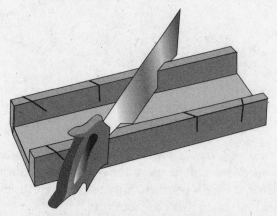

Figure 25. Miter box and back saw

The one saw that can be found in a mechanic's tool box is a **hacksaw**. Hacksaws are used for cutting metals such as steel, aluminum, or copper. The blades in a hacksaw are replaceable, and it is important to choose the right blade for the material that is going to be cut. This involves the material that the blade is made from, and the number of teeth per inch on the blade.

When selecting a hacksaw blade, keep in mind that larger numbers of teeth per inch help when cutting thinner materials. Also, remember that when installing a new blade, orient it so the teeth point away from the handle. This makes the hacksaw cut on the forward stroke, so let up on the downward pressure when pulling the hacksaw back.

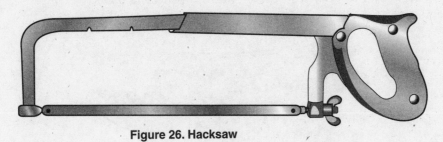

Figure 26. Hacksaw

Cutting Torches

Steel can be cut using an **oxyacetylene cutting torch**. This process involves the burning of oxygen and acetylene in a torch to produce a flame that is hot enough to melt steel. The oxygen is stored under tremendous pressure in a steel bottle, and this high pressure is reduced to working pressure (10–30 psi) using a **pressure regulator**. Acetylene is stored in a separate bottle and is also supplied to the torch through its own pressure regulator.

Special hoses connect the pressure regulators to the **torch assembly**. The torch will have valves for adjusting the flow of oxygen and acetylene, and also a handle to control the cutting process. The welder starts the flow of gases through the torch, and then uses a flint **striker** to get the flame started. Once the flame has started, the gas flow valves on the torch body can be used to adjust the flame.

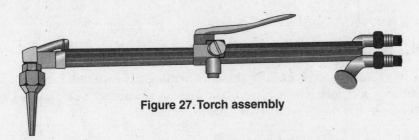

Figure 27. Torch assembly

Performing the actual cut is a two-step process. First, the steel must be heated until it is red-hot, then the handle on the torch assembly is pressed and the cutting process begins. Depressing the cutting handle allows an extra burst of oxygen to be sent through the torch tip, causing the red-hot metal to be rapidly "burned" away as the cut is made. Moving the torch forward as the handle is depressed will continue the cutting process.

Torch Safety

Safety is a major concern when cutting steel with an oxyacetylene torch. First, be sure to wear appropriate personal protective equipment such as cutting goggles, gloves, and leather boots when using the torch. Be absolutely sure not to roll up the cuffs of your pants. Any "pockets" created by pant cuffs will catch hot molten steel and likely catch your pants on fire. Be sure that any sparks or slag from the cut will roll off your pants and boots.

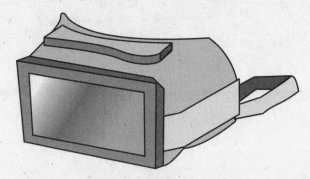

Figure 28. Cutting goggles

Look carefully at the shop area where you are about to cut. Remove any flammable materials and keep a fire extinguisher handy in case something does catch on fire. Keep an eye on things even after you are finished cutting, as sometimes "hot spots" remain that can cause problems.

Finally, be extremely careful when transporting bottled gases. Oxygen is stored at pressures up to 2,000 psi. If for some reason the hand valve gets knocked off the top of an oxygen bottle, the pressure release would turn the bottle into a projectile that can go through a shop wall. Check the cart carefully before moving a torch setup, making sure that the bottles are chained in properly.

DRILLING AND BORING TOOLS

Making small holes in wood or metal is done by **drilling** the material. Large holes can be made in wood or soft metals using a process known as **boring**. The two processes are essentially the same, but they use different tools to get the job done.

Drill bits are used for drilling holes. A carpenter would use drill bits up to $\frac{1}{4}$" in diameter, but a mechanic would commonly use drill bits as large as $\frac{1}{2}$". If larger holes than this must be made, special tools would be used to bore the hole.

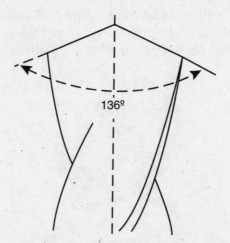

136º

Figure 29. Right-hand drill bit cutting edge

The vast majority of drill bits are made to cut while rotating in a clockwise direction (as viewed from above). These are known as **right-hand** drill bits. **Left-hand** drill bits are made to cut in the opposite direction. The most practical application for a left-hand drill bit is the removal of broken bolts from threaded holes. Drilling into the top of the broken fastener with To bore a large hole in wood, a carpenter would use either an **auger bit** or an **expansive bit**. An auger bit is shaped much like the stripes on a barber's pole, and is made to lift the sawdust out of the hole as the boring process continues. Common sizes for auger bits range from $\frac{3}{16}$" to 2". For holes larger than 2", an expansive bit can be utilized. Expansive bits are adjustable across a wide range of sizes and can be used for very large holes that are several inches in diameter. A left-hand drill bit will often grab the fastener and spin it up out of the hole, making the extraction process easy.

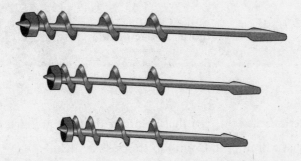

Figure 30. Auger bits

Hole saws can also be used for boring large holes. Hole saws are not adjustable, so each one is only capable of drilling one size of hole. However, it is possible to make them from tougher materials that can cut through anything from wood to soft metals.

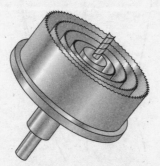

Figure 31. Hole saw

Today, it is rare for anyone to use hand-operated tools to drive drill bits and other boring tools. Instead, it is common practice to perform these operations using an **electric drill**. Electric drills can be identified by chuck size, reversibility, and whether they are designed to operate at a constant or variable speed.

Figure 32. Electric drill

The **chuck** of an electric drill is the part that holds the drill bit. A chuck is identified by the largest diameter bit that will fit in it. Common chuck sizes include $\frac{1"}{4}$, $\frac{3"}{8}$, and $\frac{1"}{2}$. Regular drill chucks can be tightened and loosened using a **chuck key**. Since it is easy to lose a chuck key, **keyless chucks** are becoming more popular. A keyless chuck makes it possible to tighten and loosen the chuck by hand.

Some drills can operate in both the clockwise and counter-clockwise directions. These are known as **reversible drills**. **Variable speed drills** are designed to operate over a range of speeds that can be determined by the position of the trigger.

As battery technology advances, it is getting more common for people to buy **cordless drills**. Longer times between battery recharges are just one of the reasons why these have become so popular. Most people like the idea of being able to do their work without being tied to extension cords and wall outlets. These products will only become more popular as their performance level increases.

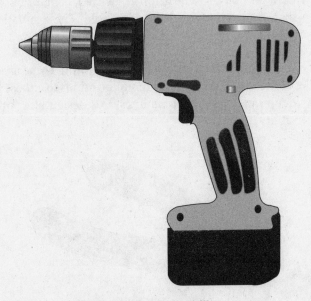

Figure 33. Cordless drill

The most important safety item to remember when using a drill is to use a sharp bit. Dull bits require more time and more pressure placed on the drill to get the job done. With smaller bits, this could result in bit breakage and damage to the surface of the material being drilled. Drill bits can be sharpened on a bench grinder using a special attachment. It is also possible to sharpen them on the bench grinder without the use of the special attachment. This does require some practice, as well as a good understanding of the cutting edge on the drill bit.

When using electric drills, it pays to take extra care when drilling larger ($\frac{1}{4}$" and above) holes in steel. Make sure to drill a small pilot hole first ($\frac{1}{8}$" works fine), then drill through this hole with the large bit. The most critical point is when the drill is just about to break through. It is a good idea to increase the speed of the drill at this point and let up on the pressure being placed on it. Otherwise, the bit can "grab" as it breaks through the steel, twisting the wrist and arm of the operator as the drill reacts to the sudden stoppage of the drill bit.

Before using electric power tools, always make sure that the electrical cord and the ground prong on the plug are in good condition. If these are damaged, it is possible for the operator to receive an electrical shock. These same guidelines apply to any extension cords being used. Electricity will always take the path of least resistance, so make sure that your body isn't going to be part of that path!

PLIERS

Repair operations often call for objects to be gripped, twisted, bent, or cut. Sometimes these objects are irregularly-shaped or otherwise difficult to hold. These situations are remedied best through the use of **pliers**.

The most common type of pliers is the **combination slip-joint**. These are adjustable at the joint of the two handles of the pliers. With two different positions to choose from, these pliers can grip objects in a wide range of sizes. Sometimes, this design also incorporates a wire cutter for increased versatility.

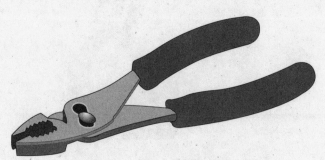

Figure 34. Combination slip-joint pliers

When large diameter objects must be gripped or twisted, a technician would use **adjustable joint pliers** to get the job done. These are adjustable over a large range of sizes, as they have multiple "arc-joints" that the pliers can be set into. The handles are also very long, which gives very good leverage and makes for maximum gripping power. These pliers are also commonly known as **water pump pliers** or **Channel-lock® pliers**.

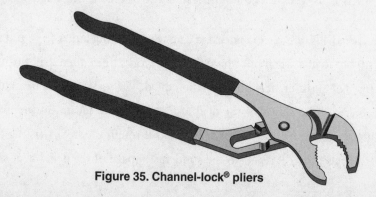

Figure 35. Channel-lock® pliers

Lineman pliers are used for cutting and bending heavy gauge wire. These are not size-adjustable, but are made for maximum leverage at the jaws to make the cutting process easier. This type of pliers would most often be used by electricians, but all trades utilize them at one time or another.

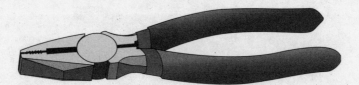

Figure 36. Lineman pliers

Diagonal cutters are pliers that are made exclusively for cutting. The two jaws are set at an angle (diagonally) to make it easier to cut wires straight across. Diagonal cutters are normally used for cutting wire and small cables. Some technicians refer to diagonal cutters as "dikes."

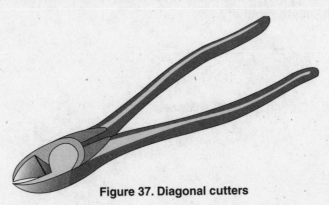

Figure 37. Diagonal cutters

For holding small objects in tight places, a pair of **needle nose pliers** could be used. These have very long, pointed jaws for maximum reach. Needle nose pliers are often used for intricate jobs like soldering circuit boards and small components, and they will most often have a wire cutter built into them at the base of the jaws.

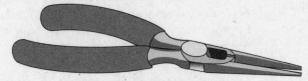

Figure 38. Needlenose pliers

Retaining-ring pliers are a specialized tool that are made to remove and install retaining (snap) rings. This involves gripping the rings and then compressing or expanding them, depending on their type. Some retaining ring pliers are convertible, meaning that they can be used for both internal and external snap rings.

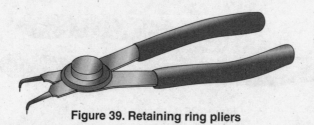

Figure 39. Retaining ring pliers

Locking pliers are used by technicians of all trades. Most people know them as **Vise-Grip®** pliers. They are adjustable, made in a large variety of jaw designs, and will lock tightly in place for holding or clamping objects together. Locking pliers often have wire cutters built into them as well for maximum versatility.

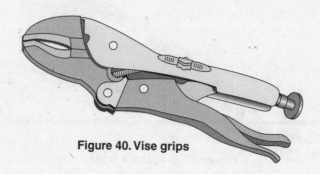

Figure 40. Vise grips

PLANING, SMOOTHING, AND SHAPING TOOLS

When working with wood, there are many occasions when it is necessary to remove a small amount of material to make a piece fit properly or to make a surface smooth. One tool that can be used for this purpose is a **plane**.

There are several different types of planes, but the one that would be best-suited for general purpose work is the **jack plane**. The jack plane has a smooth lower surface (plane bottom) and an adjustable-depth blade that protrudes slightly below this surface (through the mouth). This blade is set at an angle, similar to the blade in a disposable razor.

DON'T BE SURPRISED

While some of the tools in this chapter are probably more common to you from your own garage or in that of someone you know, be sure to pay special attention to some of the lesser known items as well, as the ASVAB may surprise you. Welding tools and tips and saws are known to have appeared on recent ASVAB tests.

When using a jack plane, the carpenter grasps the plane with both hands and moves it evenly across the surface of the work, "shaving" a thin layer of wood. If a heavier cut is desired, the blade can be adjusted to protrude further from the lower surface of the plane.

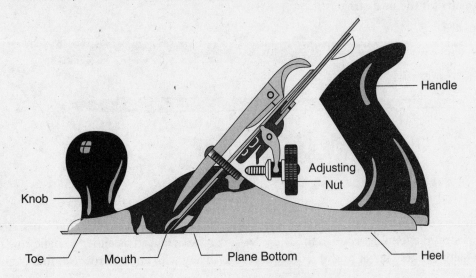

Figure 41. Jack plane

Wood chisels are used to shape wood as well as smooth a wood surface. Wood chisels come in a variety of widths, which can range from $\frac{1}{8}"$ to 2". A wood chisel is normally hand-operated, but when making deep cuts, a soft-faced mallet should be used to lightly tap the chisel through the work.

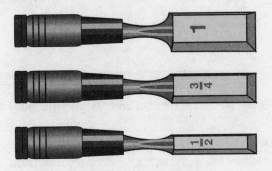

Figure 42. Wood chisels

Rasps are basically very coarse files that are used to trim, shape, and smooth wood. Round rasps are useful for cleaning up holes, whereas a flat rasp would be used to smooth flat surfaces. The cutting teeth on a rasp are coarse enough that it clears sawdust easily and is always ready for the next stroke.

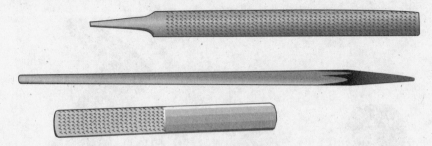

Figure 43. Rasps

Metalworkers use **files** to smooth, polish, and shape metal. Files are made from hardened steel and consist of diagonal rows of teeth. These teeth can be arranged as either a single row of parallel teeth (single-cut) or one row of teeth criss-crossing with another row (double-cut).

Files also are made in varying levels of coarseness. Files made for polishing would be known as **smooth files**, where one used for rough work would be called a **bastard** file. Files are made in flat, round, half-round, and triangular designs.

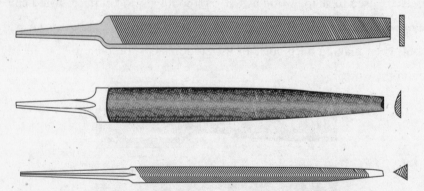

Figure 44. Flat file, half-round file, and triangular files

Most files do not come with handles. It is important to have a handle ready to attach to a file when it is put to use, as this will prevent the end of the file from being driven into the technician's hand. Remember that a file is made to cut only on the forward stroke, so it should be lifted slightly from the work when it is pulled back.

When doing sheet metal work, such as cutting flashing for a roof installation, it is useful to have a pair of **tin snips**. These are made like a pair of scissors, but have longer handles for greater cutting power and are made from forged steel for durability. Tin snips can also be used to cut other materials such as stainless steel shim stock, or asphalt shingles.

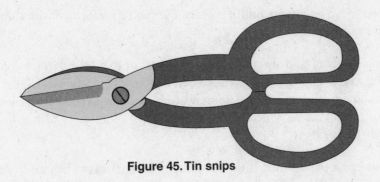

Figure 45. Tin snips

Sometimes you need a tool just to help with other tools. A **utility knife** can be used for cutting a wide variety of materials, including wood, plastics, and paper. Utility knives usually have replaceable blades, so it is easy to restore a sharp edge if it gets damaged. Some utility knives are made so that the damaged portion of the blade can be broken off and the blade extended to get a sharp edge.

Figure 46. Utility knife

Cutting and Filing Safety

In order to use all of these tools safely, it is extremely important to keep the cutting edges sharp. A sharp edge may sound more dangerous than a dull edge, but it will actually reduce the effort required to get the job done and make it less likely that operators will slip and hurt themselves.

When possible, be sure to protect the cutting edges of these tools when they are not being used. A file should be kept in its own sheath and not be allowed to rub against other files in a tool box. Utility knife blades should be retracted when not in use. Also, keep your tools dry to prevent rust that can damage cutting edges.

SOLDERING TOOLS

Soldering is a process that joins metals by bonding a metal alloy to their surfaces. This is different from welding, where the objects to be joined become one as their base metal melts together. Soldering is a low-temperature process that can be performed with simple tools and inexpensive materials.

Most solder is an alloy of lead and tin. The percentages of each metal in the solder will vary depending on the desired properties of the solder; i.e., melting point, etc. Higher percentages of lead will result in a lower melting point. However, high percentages of lead would be undesirable for pipes that carry drinking water, so often plumbers will use a solder that is made up mostly of tin.

The most critical part of soldering is the cleaning of the surfaces to be joined. Any oxides or other contaminants on the surface to be soldered will prevent a solid connection from being made. The best way to prepare a surface for soldering is to use a **flux** that will clean the surfaces with a chemical action. Electrical connections require a **rosin** flux, and solders made for this will have the flux contained in the core of the solder. This is known as **rosin-core solder**. Soldering sheet steel would require the use of an **acid-core solder**. Never use acid-core solder to make electrical connections.

There are a number of tools that can be used to generate the necessary heat to melt the solder, but in most cases a **soldering iron** will be used. Most soldering irons are electrically-powered, and can draw anywhere from 25 to 100 watts. Low-power irons would be used to solder electrical connections, whereas higher powered ones would be used in sheet metal work. Soldering irons are simple and inexpensive, but their main drawback is the amount of time that is required for them to warm up.

Tip   Power cord

Figure 47. Soldering iron

A tool that is often used for soldering electrical connections is the **soldering gun**. A soldering gun has a two-step trigger that allows the technician to quickly select a low or high heat setting. The main advantage to a soldering gun is the very rapid warm up cycle. When not being used, a soldering gun stays cold but will warm up to operating temperature very quickly when the trigger is pressed. A soldering gun also has a light built into it for illuminating the work.

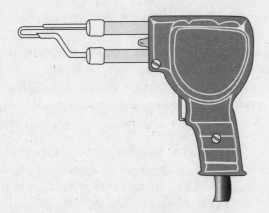

Figure 48. Soldering Gun

Soldering can also be accomplished through the use of a **torch**. Plumbers use hand-held propane torches for joining copper fittings and pipe, where small butane torches are available for electrical work. Technicians must be very careful when making electrical connections using a torch. Too much heat applied to the connection can damage the insulation on the wire.

Figure 49. Propane torch

When soldering, start by mechanically cleaning the materials to be joined. This may involve the use of a stainless steel brush or even sandpaper. If the pieces to be joined are large, it may pay to **tin** the surfaces before attempting to join them. Heat the surfaces gently while applying flux to them, and then add solder once the flux has thoroughly cleaned the material. Spread the solder thinly over the surface, making sure to heat thoroughly any area that is to be tinned. A stainless steel brush can be used to help spread the solder. Also, be sure to keep the soldering tip clean and "tinned" in order to make for the best heat transfer.

Before soldering an electrical connection, it is always a good idea to make a solid mechanical connection first. This will involve stripping insulation from wires and twisting them together. Keep in mind when soldering that the entire connection needs to be heated before applying solder to it. If only the solder is heated and it then is "melted" onto relatively cool wires, a "cold" solder joint is created that can exhibit unusual electrical properties.

Once the connection has been soldered, let the connection cool by itself without blowing on it or otherwise accelerating the cooling process. This will prevent crystallization of the solder and again, a cold solder joint. The finished product should be shiny with the solder reaching into the inner core of the connection. Be sure to protect the new connection with electrical tape or heat shrink tubing.

MEASURING INSTRUMENTS

A critical skill for any technician is the ability to make accurate measurements. This entails multiple tasks, including selecting the correct measuring instrument for the job, manipulating the instrument correctly during the measurement process, and then reading the instrument properly to get the final reading. Inability to perform these tasks sometimes results in very costly mistakes, so it is important to become familiar with measurement tools and how they are used.

Automotive technicians will sometimes use a **steel rule** or a **tape measure** to determine distances. These will measure in fractions of an inch as low as $\frac{1}{32}"$, but are ineffective when more accuracy is required. This is because the scale becomes too difficult to read with smaller measurements.

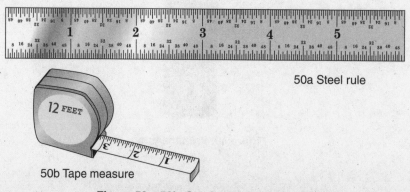

50a Steel rule

50b Tape measure

Figure 50a, 50b. Steel rule and tape measure

When accuracy down to one-thousandths of an inch is required, a **micrometer** is used. The most common type of micrometer is the **outside micrometer**. The outside micrometer is made to measure the outside diameter of cylindrically-shaped objects, as well as the thickness of flat objects. It is built similar to a c-clamp, where the **spindle** of the micrometer is rotated in and out to adjust the distance between it and the **anvil**. All measurements are taken between the spindle and the anvil.

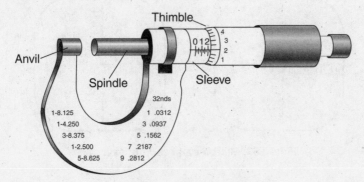

Figure 51. Outside micrometer

The **thimble** of the micrometer is attached directly to the spindle. The **sleeve** of the micrometer is stationary, and has markings on it indicating how far the spindle has been moved. As the thimble moves outward, it uncovers the graduations on the sleeve. The position of the thimble relative to the sleeve is what determines the micrometer reading.

Forty turns of the thimble will move the spindle exactly 1 inch. This means that each turn of the thimble moves the spindle $\frac{1}{40}$" or .025". The graduations on the sleeve are also marked every 0.025" to keep track of how many times the thimble has been turned. Each time the thimble completes one turn, another mark on the sleeve is uncovered. Four complete turns of the thimble move the spindle $\frac{1}{10}$ of an inch or 0.100", so this is marked with a large "1" on the sleeve. The mark at 0.200" is a "2", and so on.

The outside of the thimble has 25 evenly spaced graduations on it. Since a full turn of the thimble moves the spindle 0.025", this means that one of the graduations on the thimble is the equivalent of .001". In order to read a micrometer, it is simply a matter of adding the measurement on the sleeve to the number on the thimble that aligns with the longitudinal line on the sleeve.

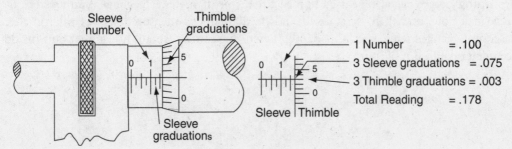

Figure 52. Reading a micrometer

If the markings on the sleeve of a 0–1" micrometer indicate 0.175" (7 full turns of the thimble), and the thimble reading is a 3, then 0.175" would be added to 0.003" to give a final measurement of 0.178". See the figure below for a micrometer reading exercise. The answers are on page 354.

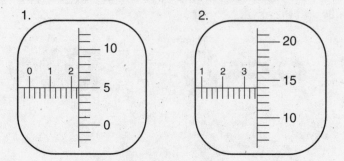

Figure 53. Micrometer reading exercise

Outside micrometers come in many sizes, as they are all made to measure a range of 1". Therefore, to measure a 2.356" diameter rod, the technician would select a 2–3" outside micrometer. To measure down to one ten-thousandths of an inch or 0.0001", a **vernier micrometer** would be used. Metric micrometers are also available that measure to 0.01 mm.

Another type of micrometer is the **inside micrometer**. The inside micrometer is made to measure the distance between two parallel surfaces, and also to measure the inside diameter of cylinders. Inside micrometers normally measure a range of 0.500", so there are spacers and different length rods included with it so that a wide range of measurements can be made.

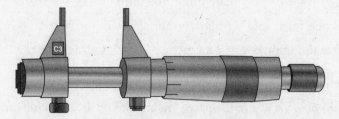

Figure 54. Inside micrometer

Telescoping gauges can also be used to measure inside diameter. The gauge is adjusted to fit snugly in a hole, and then is removed and its diameter is measured with a micrometer. Telescoping gauges are especially handy when measuring small holes that an inside micrometer could not fit into.

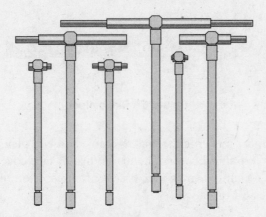

Figure 55. Telescoping gauges

A **depth micrometer** is used to measure the depth of holes and counter bores. Depth micrometers are different in that their sleeve graduations are backwards relative to an outside micrometer. Otherwise, they are read the same as other micrometers and can provide a high degree of accuracy when making these types of measurements.

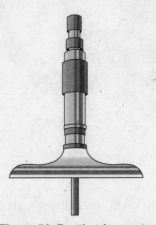

Figure 56. Depth micrometer

A measuring tool that can measure inside diameter, outside diameter, and depth down to 0.001" is the **vernier caliper**. This versatility comes at a price, however, as a vernier scale can be difficult to read, especially under poor light conditions. A more expensive alternative is a **dial caliper** that enhances the vernier scale with a large dial face and pointer that makes reading easy. If a technician was going to buy one precision measuring tool, a 0–6" dial caliper would be the best choice.

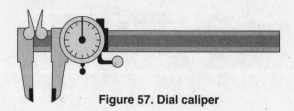

Figure 57. Dial caliper

Measurement of small linear movements, such as crankshaft end play or brake rotor runout, can be performed using a **dial indicator**. The dial indicator face covers 0–0.100″ graduated in 0.001″ increments. A c-clamp or magnetic base is often used to hold the dial indicator in place, making it versatile and easy to use.

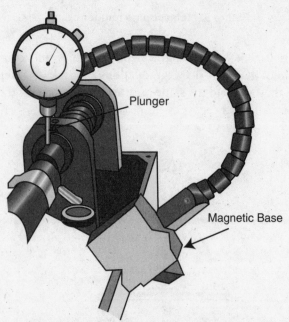

Plunger

Magnetic Base

Figure 58. Dial indicator and magnetic base

ANSWERS TO MICROMETER READING EXERCISE FROM PAGE 352.

1. 0.230″
2. 0.364″

In order to measure small gaps between two surfaces, a **feeler gauge** can be utilized. Feeler gauges are steel strips of specific thicknesses. Feeler gauges come in sets that cover a range of measurements. For instance, a common set of feeler gauges would start at 0.0015″, and work its way up to 0.030″, in 0.001″ increments. Feeler gauges can be used for measuring valve clearance and spark plug gaps (new plugs only).

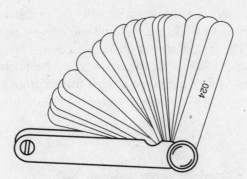

Figure 59. Feeler gauge set

To use a feeler gauge set, a technician would select a specific size of gauge and attempt to slide it into the gap that is to be measured. If that gauge slid in easily, the next size gauge would be selected and inserted into the gap. This process would continue until a gauge was found that fit snugly into the gap. The thickness of this gauge would then indicate the actual measurement. Just like with any other measuring tool, feeler gauges are available in metric units as well.

One variation of the feeler gauge is the **wire gauge**. The wire gauge is made up of a number of short pieces of calibrated wire. These can be used to measure the gap on used spark plugs, since the electrodes erode somewhat unevenly over time and make regular feeler gauges inaccurate when used for this purpose.

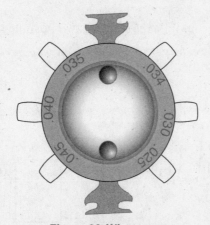

Figure 60. Wire gauge

FASTENERS

Most man-made assemblies are held together with **fasteners**. Building objects as one piece is often impractical; it is much easier to make a number of pieces and then assemble them. Fasteners hold these pieces together and make it easy to disassemble them for service.

FASTEN YOUR SEATBELT

Some of the most common types of tools to be tested on the ASVAB are fasteners (screws and bolts). It pays to review this wide range of tools.

The vast majority of fasteners are **threaded**. A bolt, for instance, has **external threads**, whereas a nut has **internal threads**. A threaded bolt can only be inserted into a nut or hole that has a similar thread. The type of thread that is placed on a fastener will vary according to the diameter of the fastener and the intended strength of the finished product. Threads are identified by their **pitch**, and this is measured using a **thread pitch gauge**.

Figure 61. Thread pitch gauge

Fractional-measurement fasteners (measured in fractions of inches) use threads that are identified by the number of threads per inch. There are two basic thread classifications within this group: **Unified National Coarse (UNC)**, and **Unified National Fine (UNF)**. A UNC or coarse thread would have relatively few threads per inch, where a UNF or fine thread would have a larger number of threads per inch.

A bolt that is $\frac{3''}{8}$ in diameter could, therefore, have two possible thread pitches. If it were a UNC bolt, it would have 16 threads per inch, where if it were a UNF bolt, it would have 24 threads per inch.

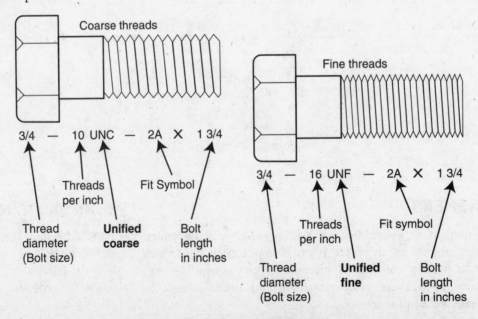

Figure 62. Bolt designation numbers

Metric fasteners use the *System Internationale (SI)* method of thread measurement, which designates the distance in millimeters between each thread. A metric bolt with a thread pitch of 2.0 would have threads that are 2.0 millimeters apart.

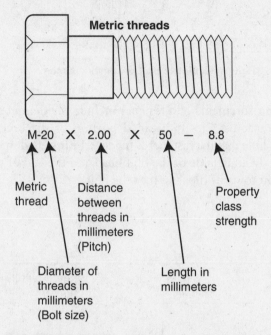

Figure 63. Metric bolt designation numbers

The strength of a bolt is determined by its **grade**. With fractional-measurement bolts, there are radial markings on the head that identify the grade. To determine the grade of the bolt, simply add 2 to the number of markings on its head. For instance, six markings would denote a grade 8 bolt. Three markings, however, would indicate that it is a grade 5 bolt. Grade 8 is considered to be a high strength bolt, where grade 5 is medium strength.

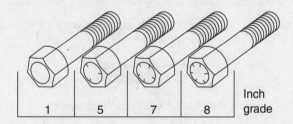

Figure 64. Bolt grades

Metric bolt strength is described by its **property class**. Property class is determined by a number that is marked on the head of the bolt. The quickest way to determine whether a bolt is metric or fractional is by the markings on the head. If the marking is a number, the bolt is probably metric. Radial markings, however, would indicate that this is a fractional-measurement bolt.

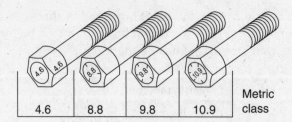

Figure 65. Metric bolt property classes

Two other important measurements of a fastener include the **diameter** and the **length**. The diameter is the distance across the unthreaded portion of the bolt. This would give an indication of the size of hole that the fastener is made to be installed in. The length of the bolt is the distance between the underside of the bolt head and the end of the bolt. Note that the bolt head does not count towards the length of the bolt.

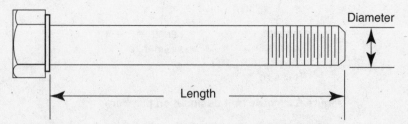

Figure 66. Fastener diameter and length

Generally speaking, threaded fasteners that are $\frac{1}{4}"$ in diameter and larger are known as **bolts**, where those that are smaller than $\frac{1}{4}"$ are known as **machine screws**. Machine screw size is identified using a number instead of a diameter measurement. Machine screw sizes range from 0 to 12. A 10–24 machine screw would have a #10 diameter with 24 threads per inch.

Figure 67. Round head machine screw

Nuts thread onto bolts or machine screws to clamp assemblies together. Nuts will have either a square head or a hexagonal head, and can be locked into position using several different methods. Regular hexagonal head nuts can be used with a **split lock washer** to prevent them from loosening. Split lock washers can be installed under the nut or under the head of the bolt or machine screw when a nut is not used.

Figure 68a. External tooth lock washer

Figure 68b. Split lock washer

Figure 68c. Internal tooth lock washer

Wing nuts are used when it is necessary to disassemble a component by hand. The two "wings" attached to the nut make it easy to tighten and loosen it without the aid of hand tools. In the past, a place where wing nuts were commonly used was on engine air cleaner housings. This made it easy to remove the housing cover to check the condition of the air cleaner.

Figure 69. Wing nut

A **castellated nut** uses a **cotter pin** to lock it into place, which must pass through a hole in the bolt or stud that the nut is threaded on.

Figure 70a. Castellated nut

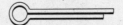

Figure 70b. Cotter pin

Lock nuts have a nylon insert incorporated into its threads that provides enough interference to prevent the nut from loosening.

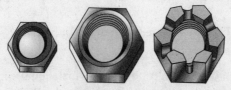

Figure 71. Lock nuts

When working with sheet metal, it is common practice to fasten the pieces together using **sheet metal screws**. A sheet metal screw is also known as a self-tapping screw because it is made to cut its own threads as it is screwed into the sheet metal. A starter hole is made with a punch or drill, and then the sheet metal screw is turned into the hole.

Figure 72. Sheet metal screw

Retaining rings (or **snap rings**) are used to prevent end-movement of cylindrical parts in bores or parts mounted on shafts. **External snap rings** are installed in grooves on shafts, whereas **internal snap rings** install in grooves inside a bore. Snap rings are installed and removed using snap ring pliers.

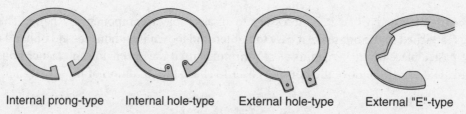

Internal prong-type   Internal hole-type   External hole-type   External "E"-type

Figure 73. Internal snap sings, external snap rings

Rivets can also be used to assemble parts. A rivet is simply a pin with a head at one end. A rivet is installed in a hole (the same diameter as the rivet) that is drilled through two pieces that are to be assembled. With the two pieces tightly clamped, the head of the rivet is placed on a hard surface, while the other end is formed into a head using a hammer or special riveting tool. This creates an assembly that is semipermanent, as the rivet must be drilled out to remove it.

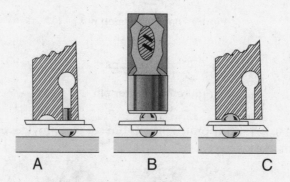

Figure 74. Installation of a regular rivet

A variation of the rivet is the **pop-rivet**. A pop rivet is installed using a **rivet gun,** which pulls part of the rivet out to expand the head on the other side. Pop rivets are very useful when access to one side of the assembly is limited.

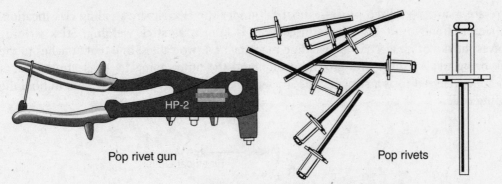

Pop rivet gun

Pop rivets

Figure 75. Pop rivet gun and pop rivets

WELDING TOOLS

The final section of ASVAB shop tool review relates to welding. When joining metals, the best way to achieve a high-strength joint is to use a **welding** process. Welding is very different from soldering in that it involves melting the base metal of the objects to be joined, a process that requires very high temperatures.

There are two major types of welding processes: **oxyacetylene welding** and **electric-arc welding**. Oxyacetylene welding involves the use of a torch that is fueled with oxygen and acetylene. Burning these two gases together creates an extremely hot flame; hot enough to melt steel and other ferrous (iron-based) materials. **Filler rod** is melted along with the base metal to produce a finished weld. Oxyacetylene welding has lost popularity over the years, as it is extremely slow and is relatively expensive because of its use of bottled gases.

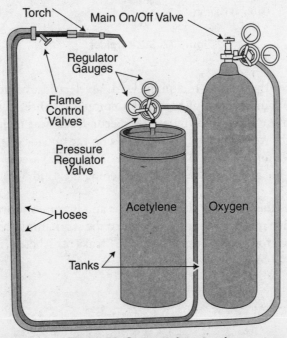

Figure 76. Oxyacetylene torch

There are many specialized processes that fall under the electric-arc welding classification. The simplest and most easily-recognized type is known as **stick welding**. Stick welding involves the use of an electric-arc welding machine and two cables: one that attaches to the work being welded through a ground clamp, and the other going to an electrode that is sometimes referred to as a **stinger**. The stinger is held by the welder and is used to hold the **welding rod**.

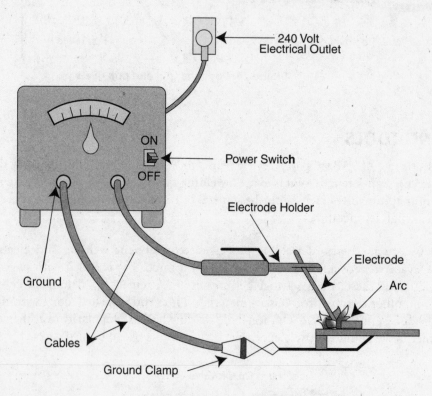

Figure 77. Stick welder

When the welder touches the welding rod on the work, an electric arc is formed. This electric arc generates a tremendous amount of heat and accomplishes three things. First, the heat melts the base metal of the material being welded. Second, the heat melts the electrode and deposits this metal in the weld as filler. Lastly, the **flux** on the outside of the electrodes burns and the generated gases form a "shield" around the weld. This gaseous shield prevents air from reacting with the hot metal and therefore weakening the weld.

As the welder continues the weld, the electrode burns and becomes shorter. The means that the welder must continue moving the stinger closer to the work until the electrode has been consumed. Once the electrode is used up, the welder "breaks off" the arc, and a new electrode is placed in the stinger to continue the weld.

If more heat is needed to perform the weld, the welder can increase the amount of electric current that is supplied by the welding machine. Generally speaking, the larger the pieces that are being welded or the larger the electrode that is being used, the greater the amount of current required to get the weld done.

The electric arc that is generated during this process gives off a very high intensity light. The ultraviolet light is so intense that it can "sunburn" exposed skin and burn the retinas of unprotected eyes. Welders must, therefore, cover all exposed skin with protective clothing (preferably leather) and wear face shields (helmets) with light filters. The filters are usually very dark, so the welder can view the welding process itself but nothing else.

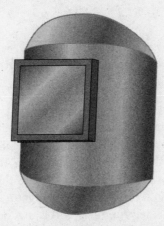

Figure 78. Welder's face shield

With older style welding helmets, the welder is required to keep the face shield raised until they are just about to strike the arc. At this point, the welder "flips" the face shield down over their face and touches the electrode on the work momentarily, starting the arc and beginning the weld process. Newer welding helmets have electronic filters that "sense" the ultraviolet light from an electric arc and switch from "clear" to "shaded" in a split second. This allows the welder to leave the helmet down while lining up the next weld, saving the time consumed with flipping the helmet up and down.

A completed stick weld leaves a covering of **slag** on the weld. This is the flux coating of the electrode that has been deposited over top of the weld to protect it while it cools. This slag is easily removed using a **chipping hammer** that has both a pointed edge and a chisel edge. Chipping the slag off and then brushing it with a wire brush allows the welder to inspect the weld for flaws before continuing the work.

Figure 79. Slag hammer

Another electric-arc welding process that continues to gain popularity is **MIG welding**. MIG welding is also known as **wire-feed welding** because the electrode used for the weld process is a wire that is automatically fed from a spool. MIG (Metal-Inert Gas) uses a bottled inert gas (such as argon) to shield the weld, and requires a relatively sophisticated welding machine. However, it is rapidly overtaking stick welding as the process of choice because it is relatively easy to master and isn't hobbled by having to always stop the arc to change electrodes. MIG welding is extremely popular with auto body shops and exhaust system fabricators because it works very well with sheet metal and thin pipe. MIG is also very effective for welding aluminum, so it is widely used in fabrication shops.

Figure 80. MIG Gun

SHOP INFORMATION PRACTICE SET

1. In order to make a bolt tighter, a
   _____ wrench should be used.

   (A) longer
   (B) shorter
   (C) heavier
   (D) shinier

2. A cotter pin is often used in
   conjunction with a _____.

   (A) lock nut
   (B) lock washer
   (C) castellated nut
   (D) machine screw

3. Adjustable joint pliers are also known
   as

   (A) water pump pliers
   (B) retaining ring pliers
   (C) Channel lock® pliers
   (D) A and C only

4. A $\frac{3}{8}"$ drill bit will fit into an electric
   drill with a _____ chuck.

   (A) $\frac{1}{4}"$

   (B) $\frac{3}{8}"$

   (C) $\frac{1}{2}"$

   (D) B and C only

5. The blade in a hacksaw should be
   installed with its teeth pointed

   (A) towards the handle
   (B) away from the handle
   (C) either A or B
   (D) neither A nor B

6. How is the length of a bolt measured?

   (A) Measure the length from end to
       end
   (B) Measure the length of the
       threaded portion only
   (C) Measure the length from the
       underside of the head to the end
       of the threads
   (D) None of the above

7. A bolt with a hexagonal head could
   be loosened using a(n)

   (A) open end wrench
   (B) box end wrench
   (C) 12-point socket and ratchet
   (D) all of the above

8. The tool shown above is used for

   (A) soldering electrical connections
   (B) stapling asphalt shingles
   (C) crimping electrical terminals
   (D) installing pop rivets

9. "Tinning" is a process that is related to

   (A) carpentry
   (B) roofing
   (C) soldering
   (D) welding

10. Soldering electrical connections requires the use of

    (A) rosin flux
    (B) acid flux
    (C) either rosin or acid flux
    (D) neither rosin or acid flux

11. Which tool would best be used for measuring the thickness of a steel shim?

    (A) steel rule
    (B) tape measure
    (C) inside micrometer
    (D) outside micrometer

12. The figure above is an example of a _____ screwdriver.

    (A) Flat tip
    (B) Phillips
    (C) Robertson
    (D) Torx

Answers and explanations appear on the following page.

ANSWERS AND EXPLANATIONS FOR SHOP INFORMATION PRACTICE SET

1. A

Fasteners can be tightened best with longer wrenches. Adding an extension or using an adjustable wrench (Crescent) may also improve tightening ability.

2. C

A castellated nut uses a cotter pin to lock it into place, which must pass through a hole in the bolt or stud that the nut is threaded on.

3. D

When large diameter objects must be gripped or twisted, a technician would use adjustable joint pliers to get the job done. These are adjustable over a large range of sizes, as they have multiple "arc-joints" that the pliers can be set into. The handles are also very long, which gives very good leverage and makes for maximum gripping power. These pliers are also commonly known as *water pump pliers* or *Channel-lock® pliers*. Since choice (D) allows for both choices (A) and (C), it is the correct answer.

4. D

The chuck of an electric drill is the part that holds the drill bit. A chuck is identified by the largest diameter bit that will fit in it. Common chuck sizes include $\frac{1"}{4}$, $\frac{3"}{8}$, and $\frac{1"}{2}$. A $\frac{3"}{8}$ drill bit will fit into a $\frac{3"}{8}$ or $\frac{1"}{2}$ chuck, answers (B) and (C) respectively. The correct answer, therefore, to what a $\frac{3"}{8}$ drill bit will fit into is (D).

5. B

When installing a new hacksaw blade, orient it so the teeth point away from the handle. This makes the hacksaw cut on the forward stroke, so let up on the downward pressure when pulling the hacksaw back.

6. C

One important measurement of a fastener is the length. The length of the bolt is the distance between the underside of the bolt head and the end of the bolt. Note that the bolt head does not count towards the length of the bolt. Therefore, the best answer is (C).

7. **D**

The two basic types of wrenches—the open end and the box end—are both acceptable for loosening a hexagonal bolt. The open-end wrench is easy to slide on and off a fastener. The downside to the open-end wrench is that it only makes contact with two sides of a six-sided (hex) bolt head. The box-end wraps completely around the head of a bolt, and therefore makes greater surface contact. Box-end wrenches normally come in a 12-point configuration, but some are made as 6-point. Used with a ratchet, the correct size socket is ideal for loosening fasteners such as hexagonal bolts. Thus, because all the choices are acceptable, answer choice (D) is the best answer.

8. **D**

The tool shown in this question is known as a pop rivet gun. A variation of the rivet, the pop rivet is installed using a rivet gun, which pulls part of the rivet out to expand the head on the other side. Pop rivets are very useful when access to one side of the assembly is limited.

9. **C**

If two pieces to be joined by soldering are large, it may pay to tin the surfaces before attempting to join them. Heating the surfaces gently while applying flux to them, and then adding solder once the flux has thoroughly cleaned the material will accomplish this. Since soldering is the process involved, the correct answer is (C).

10. **A**

The best way to prepare a surface for soldering is to use a flux that will clean the surfaces with a chemical action. Electrical connections require a rosin flux, and solders made for this will have the flux contained in the core of the solder. This is known as rosin-core solder.

11. **D**

Since a steel shim is such a thin piece to measure, one would need an instrument with the capability of accuracy down to one-thousandths of an inch. The most common type of micrometer is the outside micrometer. The outside micrometer is made to measure the outside diameter of cylindrically-shaped objects, as well as the thickness of flat objects. In this case, an outside micrometer is best because of the detail needed; if smaller measurements were needed, a vernier micrometer might be necessary. Another type of micrometer is the inside micrometer. But an inside micrometer is made to measure the distance between two parallel surfaces, and also to measure the inside diameter of cylinders, not a flat shim.

12. **D**

The tool in the illustration is known as a Torx screwdriver.

CHAPTER TEN

Mechanical Comprehension

INTRODUCTION

Welcome to what may be the trickiest section of the ASVAB: mechanical comprehension. Not to be confused with what an automotive guru might think of as "mechanics," here we refer to what is basic physics. But before you run screaming, remember that the ASVAB isn't a test of your genius potential. Best to consider it Physics 101. A lot of this information you probably already know or certainly have been exposed to—after all, physics is mostly the basic workings of existence (gravity, motion, energy, etc.)

We happen to think that you'll find it interesting to know why the world works the way it does. Why is it easier to lift something heavy with a lever? Why you can toss an apple into the air going sixty miles per hour and not have it fly off behind you? These and other mysteries explained by your good friends at Kaplan!

In order to understand how machines work, it is important to have a good grasp of **applied physics**. Physics is a science that deals with the fundamental laws that govern the physical universe. Over the centuries, scientists have observed various natural phenomena that led them to wonder whether a physical principle was behind the behavior. This wonderment and natural curiosity led to discoveries that became the **laws of physics**. These laws are descriptions of how the universe behaves, and help us explain much of what used to be inexplicable.

Applied physics is the practical application of the laws of physics. In other words, it is the practice of making things work. All trades people practice applied physics of some kind, so it is of the utmost importance that those entering the trades as a career have a solid understanding of physical laws. The purpose of this chapter is to give you a greater understanding of basic mechanics, simple machines, and fluid power.

Let's get started.

FORCE

Force is a push or a pull. Forces are acting all around us, whether we know it or not. Some are fairly obvious, such as a tractor pulling a plow, or a baseball being hit into the stands. Other invisible forces are often taken for granted, such as gravity. Gravity is a force that keeps us standing on the ground instead of floating around in midair. The chair you are likely sitting in right now is applying a force on your body to hold you up, which counteracts the downward force of your body's weight. Since force has a magnitude and a direction that it is applied in, it is known as a **vector quantity.**

Without force being applied to them, objects would not move (or, if they were already in motion, they would remain in motion). Objects with a great deal of **mass** (such as a freight train) require a large force to move them. Large masses also require large forces to slow them down if they are already moving.

Keep in mind that mass is quite different from **weight**. Weight can vary, as it is related to the force of gravity. If for some reason gravity is diminished, weight will also diminish. Mass, on the other hand, will not vary from location to location. Mass is an amount, with no particular direction related to it, so it is described as a **scalar quantity**.

Isaac Newton (1642–1727) laid the foundation for an area of physics called **mechanics** with his discovery of three laws of motion. These three laws help us understand what causes objects to change their motion.

NEWTON'S FIRST LAW OF MOTION

An object continues in a state of rest or in a state of motion at a constant speed along a straight line, unless compelled to change that state by a net force.

Newton's First Law of Motion

An object continues in a state of rest or in a state of motion at a constant speed along a straight line, unless compelled to change that state by a net force.

An object at rest has no **net** force acting on it. There are forces acting on it, but they are equal and opposite in direction, so they effectively "cancel" each other. Likewise, an object that is in motion will continue in a straight line at a constant speed if no net force acts on it. A bullet flying through the air would continue in a straight line at a constant speed forever, if forces such as gravity or wind resistance did not act on it. Gravity generates a force that causes the bullet to move towards the earth, whereas wind resistance creates a **drag** (also a force) that causes the bullet to slow down.

Newton's first law of motion is also referred to as the **law of inertia**. Inertia is directly related to the mass of an object, and it is described as "the natural tendency of an object to remain at rest or in motion at a constant speed over a straight line." Objects with greater mass are much harder to get moving, or slow down once they are moving, so they have greater inertia.

Newton's Second Law of Motion

When a net force F acts on an object of mass m, the acceleration a that results is directly proportional to the net force and has a magnitude that is inversely proportional to the mass. The direction of the acceleration is the same as the direction of the net force.

Newton's second law can be summarized by the formula

$$F = ma$$

NEWTON'S SECOND LAW OF MOTION

When a net force F acts on an object of mass m, the acceleration a that results is directly proportional to the net force and has a magnitude that is inversely proportional to the mass. The direction of the acceleration is the same as the direction of the net force.

where m is measured in kilograms (kg), a is in meters per second^2 $\left(\frac{m}{s^2}\right)$, and F is in newtons (N). These are all SI (System Internationale) measurements. Note that ma actually means mass $\times$ acceleration (mass multiplied by acceleration).

Acceleration occurs when the velocity of an object changes (increases or decreases). An acceleration of $1\frac{m}{s^2}$ means that the velocity of the object is increasing 1 meter per second each second. Starting from a standstill, an object with an acceleration rate of $1\frac{m}{s^2}$ will achieve a velocity of $5\frac{m}{s}$ in a period of 5 seconds.

Velocity is different from **speed**. Speed indicates how fast an object is moving, but gives no indication of the direction of movement. Velocity gives an indication of both speed and direction, so it is known as a vector quantity.

When a net force acts on an object, the object will accelerate in the direction of the net force. However, the acceleration will be less if the mass of the object is greater. For instance, if a net force of 100 N is applied to a 100 kg block, the block will accelerate in the direction of the force at a rate of $1\frac{m}{s^2}$. However, if the size of the block is increased to 200 kg, the acceleration rate will be only $0.5\frac{m}{s^2}$. Either increasing the force or decreasing the mass will cause the acceleration rate to increase.

Newton's first law is simply an extension of his second law. Using $F = ma$, inserting zero in F requires that zero also be inserted in a. If the net force acting on a mass is zero, the acceleration of that mass will also be zero. Objects that travel at a constant velocity have an acceleration rate of zero, so the net force acting on them is zero. Objects that are at rest are also experiencing zero acceleration, as their velocity is not changing.

Newton's Third Law of Motion

Whenever one body exerts a force on a second body, the second body exerts an oppositely directed force of equal magnitude on the first body.

NEWTON'S THIRD LAW OF MOTION

Whenever one body exerts a force on a second body, the second body exerts an oppositely directed force of equal magnitude on the first body.

Newton's third law is summarized by the oft-used phrase, "for every action (force), there is an equal and opposite reaction." An illustration of this is a hand gun being fired. The bullet will exert an equal force on the gun to the one the gun exerts on the bullet. The force on the bullet causes it to accelerate rapidly, as it has very little mass. The gun and the shooter, however, have a great deal more mass than the bullet, so they will accelerate (recoil) at a much slower rate in the opposite direction.

This law also explains how a car is able to move. As it accelerates, the wheels of a car will "push-off" and exert a certain amount of force on the earth. The earth, in turn, will exert the same amount of force on the wheels of the car, but in the opposite direction. The earth accelerates backwards, while the car accelerates forward.

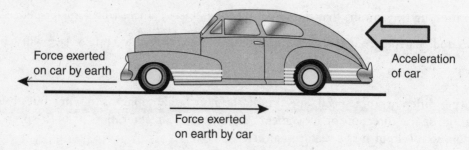

Force exerted on car by earth

Acceleration of car

Force exerted on earth by car

Figure 1. Car accelerating, with forces drawn

Remember that the mass of the earth is huge relative to the mass of the car. Keeping Newton's second law in mind ($F = ma$), we see that because the earth's mass is so large, its acceleration due to the force of the car's wheels would be imperceptible. The mass of the car is much smaller, so its acceleration rate will be greater.

WEIGHT

As seen previously, weight is different from mass. Mass is an intrinsic property of matter, whereas weight is dependent on the force of gravity. Gravity is the downward pull that the earth exerts on bodies outside of itself.

Isaac Newton discovered that every particle in the universe is attracted to every other particle. This concept became a physical law known as **Newton's Law of Universal Gravitation**. The gravitational force that each body exerts on the other grows stronger as the bodies get closer. The force also increases as the mass of the bodies increase.

This explains why a man standing on the moon weighs $\frac{1}{6}$ of what he would weigh on the surface of the earth. While the radius of the moon is smaller than the earth, the mass of the moon is a fraction of the earth's mass. Since the mass of the moon is so much less than that of the earth, it exerts significantly less gravitational pull on other bodies around it.

Since gravity exerts a force on bodies that pulls them together, this force causes an **acceleration due to gravity**, which is represented by the symbol *g*. For bodies near the earth's surface, *g* is calculated to be 9.80 $\frac{m}{s^2}$. This can be used to find the weight of an object using the formula

$$W = mg$$

Where *W* is weight in newtons (N), *m* is mass in kilograms (kg), and *g* is acceleration due to gravity.

FRICTION

When moving an object across a surface, **friction** will oppose the movement. An example of this would be a hockey puck sliding along an ice surface. While ice has much less friction than most surfaces, it will still exert a **sliding frictional force** on the puck that eventually causes it to stop moving.

When an object is not moving, a force that attempts to slide it across a surface will encounter a different type of friction. Attempting to push a stationary box across a concrete floor will require the worker to overcome the **static frictional force** that opposes the movement.

According to Newton's third law, for every action there is an equal but opposite reaction. As an object sits on a table, its weight generates a downward force acting on the table. This force is counteracted by an equal upward force generated by the table back on the object. This upward reactive force is called the **normal force**, and is represented by F_N. Normal force has an impact on the frictional force developed by an object. The higher the normal force of an object, the more friction it will develop with the surface it is resting on. In short, the heavier the object, the more friction it will develop.

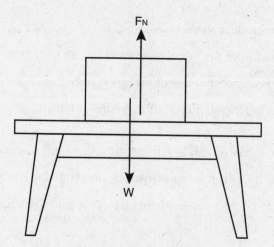

Figure 2. Normal force

In order to calculate frictional forces, the **coefficient of static friction** must be known. This number has no units associated with it, but represents the magnitude of the friction between the object and the surface it rests on. Smooth surfaces may have a coefficient of static friction of 0.01, whereas a rough surface may be as high as 1.5. Multiplying the coefficient of static friction by the normal force yields the **maximum static frictional force**, shown by the formula

$$f_s^{MAX} = \mu s F_N$$

where μs is the coefficient of static friction, F_N is the normal force in newtons (N), and f_s^{MAX} is the maximum static frictional force in newtons (N). The maximum static frictional force is the amount of force that must be applied to a static (non-moving) object to start it moving.

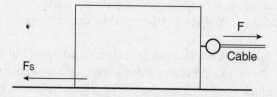

Figure 3. Sliding an object

Once the maximum static frictional force f_s^{MAX} has been overcome and the object is moving, the **coefficient of kinetic friction** comes into play. The coefficient of kinetic (moving) friction is usually less than the coefficient of static friction. It usually takes less effort to keep an object sliding than it does to get it to slide in the first place. The kinetic frictional force can be calculated using the formula

$$f_k = \mu_k F_N$$

where **μk** is the coefficient of kinetic friction, **F_N** is the normal force in newtons (N), and f_k is the kinetic frictional force in newtons (N).

TENSION

When cables are used to pull an object, forces exerted through the cable result in a force being applied to the object being pulled. This results in **tension** in the cable (the cable is being pulled from both directions) as an object will exert an opposing force to the force being applied by the cable.

An interesting question arises when a net force is applied to an object through a cable. Is the tension in the cable equal at both ends? To answer this question, the mass of the cable itself must be taken into account.

The net force applied to the object will cause it to accelerate, but the object by itself will require less force to accelerate it than the combination of the object and the cable. In other words, more force must be applied to the other end of the cable than what is actually applied to the object. This is why a cable is more likely to break at the end where the force is applied rather than where it connects to the object being moved.

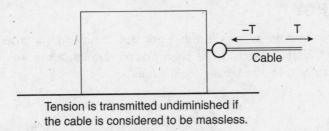

Tension is transmitted undiminished if
the cable is considered to be massless.

Figure 4. Tension in a cable

When solving most physics problems involving tension in a rope or cable, it is nearly always assumed that the cable is massless. While this is not the way it is in real life, it simplifies matters because tension is then considered to be the same in all parts of the cable under all conditions.

WORK

Work is accomplished when force is applied against an object. This is summarized by the formula

$$W = Fd$$

where F is force in newtons (N), d is distance in meters (m), and W is work in joules (J). These units are also part of the SI system of measurement.

If a force of 100 N is applied to a car, and the car is moved 10 meters, then a total of 1,000 joules of work has been done.

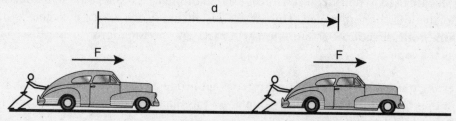

Work is done if force F is applied over distance d

If force is applied to the car, but the car does not move, no work has been done. This can be seen in the formula $W = F \times d$, where zero distance (d) results in work (W) being zero as well. No matter how much force is applied, no movement results in zero work being accomplished.

KINETIC ENERGY

When work is done to move an object, this work will result in an increase in the **kinetic energy** of the object. Kinetic energy is the energy of movement. When an object is moving, its kinetic energy can be calculated using the formula

$$KE = \frac{1}{2}mv^2$$

Where m is mass in kilograms (kg), v is speed in meters per second $\left(\frac{m}{s}\right)$, and KE is kinetic energy in joules (J). Note that work and kinetic energy are both measured in joules. This is not a coincidence, as any work that is done to accelerate an object at rest to speed v will be converted into the kinetic energy of that object. This principle is known as the **work-energy theorem**.

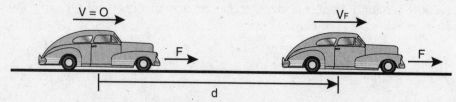

Figure 6. Car accelerating from a standstill to speed V_F

An example of work being done to increase the kinetic energy of an object is an arrow being shot from a bow. Remember that work can be calculated using the formula $W = Fd$. The bowstring exerts a force F over a distance d as the arrow is accelerated, and this work becomes the kinetic energy of the arrow as its mass m is accelerated to a speed v.

According to this theorem, the reverse is also true. An object with kinetic energy is also able to do work, if it pushes or pulls another object. The amount of work it can do is limited to the amount of kinetic energy it has.

GRAVITATIONAL POTENTIAL ENERGY

To raise an object to a certain height h, work must be done. This work then becomes the **gravitational potential energy** of the object. An object's potential energy (PE) can be calculated using the formula

$$PE = mgh$$

Where m is mass in kilograms (kg), g is acceleration due to gravity $\left(9.8 \frac{m}{s^2}\right)$, h is the height of the object in meters (m), and PE is gravitational potential energy measured in joules (J). The higher the object is raised (h), the greater the potential energy of the object. Increasing the mass (m) of the raised object will also increase it potential energy.

A falling object has its potential energy (PE) converted into kinetic energy (KE) as it falls. Conversely, an object that is thrown straight up into the air will reach its highest point, and the potential energy it has at this point can be no greater than the kinetic energy it had when it was first thrown.

Another example of this is a gymnast on the high bar. The gymnast will have the highest kinetic energy at the bottom of their swing, and this is converted into gravitational potential energy as he or she swings upwards. Remember that the gymnast typically moves the slowest at the very top of the swing. At this point, their kinetic energy is at a minimum, while the potential energy has peaked.

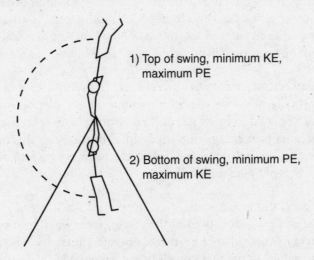

Figure 7. Gymnast on high bar

This effect is explained best by the **principle of conservation of mechanical energy**, which states that the total mechanical energy ($PE + KE$) of an object remains constant as the object moves as long as no external work is done on the object, and the object does no work on its surroundings. (In other words, in a closed system.)

POWER

Power is the **rate** that work is done. Consider the example of a man pushing a small car over a distance of 100 meters. If the man pushes with a force of 100 N to move the car, then using $W = F \times d$, we see that $100 \text{ N} \times 100m = 10,000$ joules of work has been done. If another man can do the same amount of work in one-half the time, then that man has twice as much power as the first man.

If it takes 1,000 seconds for the first man to do 10,000 joules of work, then work has been done at the rate of 10 joules per second. If the second man can do 20,000 joules of work in the same amount of time, then this man has done the work at the rate of 20 joules per second. In other words, the second man is twice as powerful as the first man.

Performing work at the rate of 1 joule per second is the same as expending 1 watt of power. The watt is named in honor of James Watt (1736–1819), the inventor of the steam engine. The unit of power that most people in the United States are familiar with is **horsepower**, as this is the unit that is used to rate internal combustion engines. Horsepower uses a different system of measurement, as it is defined as 550 foot-pounds per second of work being done. One horsepower is the equivalent of 746 watts.

CONSERVATION OF ENERGY

Work is done as energy is used to move objects. Energy is multifaceted, as it comes packaged in many different forms. Electrical energy is used to run motors and power appliances. Heat energy warms our homes and dries our clothes. Chemical energy is what makes a battery work, and is the way that fuels such as gasoline and diesel fuel store energy. Other forms of energy that are part of our everyday lives include mechanical, light, and nuclear energy.

All forms of energy can be converted into other forms. An example of this is nuclear energy. By itself, it is not particularly useful. However, nuclear energy can be converted into heat energy, which then can be used to make steam. This steam can be sent into a steam turbine, which converts the steam's heat energy into mechanical energy, and this mechanical energy can be used to power an electrical generator. This is the process by which much electricity is generated here in the United States and in Europe.

An electrical power generation plant cannot create energy. All it can do is convert energy from one form into another. The fuel used by the power plant, whether it be coal, diesel fuel, or nuclear, is the **energy source** that it needs to generate electricity. The job of the power plant is to convert the energy of the fuel into electrical energy. Many of the machines that we use from day to day are built to convert energy from one form into another more useful form.

Scientists tell us that there is a finite amount of energy in the universe, and that the total amount of energy in the universe never changes. Energy, therefore, cannot be created or destroyed; it can only be converted from one form into another. This is known as the **principle of conservation of energy**.

While energy is converted from one form into another relatively easily, it is often done very inefficiently. For example, an automobile engine uses gasoline to generate the mechanical energy necessary to move the vehicle. This is done with a great deal of energy being lost in the form of heat. Two-thirds of the heat energy generated by the combustion of the gasoline is lost out the cooling and exhaust systems. This leaves only one-third of the heat energy to be converted into mechanical energy to move the car.

In the example above, all of the chemical energy in the gasoline is converted into another form of energy. No energy is created or destroyed. However, only one-third of that chemical energy gets converted into a type of energy that can be used, making an automobile engine only thirty-three percent efficient. One of today's major engineering challenges is to make machines more efficient, turning more of the source energy into useful energy.

MOMENTUM

If a hockey player takes a "slap-shot," the player's stick will apply a force to the puck for a specific amount of time. A harder shot would mean that a higher average force was applied to the puck for a longer period of time. The product of the average force and the time it is applied to an object is known as the **impulse** of the force. Impulse is a vector quantity and is in the same direction as the force that is applied. Impulse can be calculated using the formula

$$\text{Impulse} = F\Delta t$$

where F is the average force in newtons (N), and Δt is the time interval that the force acts. Impulse is thus measured in newton-seconds (N · s).

As a result of the impulse, the puck will leave the player's stick at a certain velocity. If the puck had a greater mass, the velocity would be lower. The reverse is also true. A golfer strikes a golf ball (with a much smaller mass than a hockey puck) and the impulse sends the ball up to several hundred yards. Mass and velocity are both factors in a mechanical concept known as **linear momentum**. Linear momentum can be calculated using the formula

$$p = mv$$

where m is mass in kilograms (kg), v is velocity in meters per second $\left(\frac{m}{s}\right)$, and p is the linear momentum of an object in kilogram-meters per second $\left(\text{kg} \cdot \frac{m}{s}\right)$. Since velocity involves both magnitude and direction, this makes momentum a vector quantity as well.

The relationship between impulse and momentum is described by the **impulse-momentum theorem**, which states "when a net force F acts on an object, the impulse of the net force is equal to the change in momentum of the object." Using a golf analogy, the harder the golf ball is hit, and the longer the club makes contact with the ball, the greater the change in momentum of the ball.

Conservation of Linear Momentum

When objects collide or "push off" from each other, total linear momentum of the system (the objects involved) remains constant. This effect is known as the **principle of conservation of linear momentum**.

Imagine two skaters standing still and facing each other. This system (the two skaters) will have a total momentum of zero, since neither one of the skaters is moving. Suddenly, they "push off" from each other and each moves backwards away from the other skater. Assuming that friction is negligible, the total momentum of the system will remain at zero.

Figure 8. Skaters "pushing off" from each other

At first glance, this may not make sense, because each of the skaters is moving and both have mass and velocity. Remember, however, that momentum is a vector quantity, so it has both magnitude and direction. When the skaters push off from each other, the momentum of the one skater is negative, while the other is positive since they are moving in opposite directions. The momentum of each skater is the same magnitude, but opposite in direction, so the total of the two is still zero.

Which of the skaters will be moving the fastest after pushing off? Using the formula $p = mv$, it can be seen that if the magnitude of p is equal for both skaters, then the skater with the greatest mass will have the least velocity. The skater with the least mass will move faster from the point of origin.

Now, consider two freight cars on a section of track. Both are moving in the same direction, with one moving faster and closing with the other. Again neglecting friction, it is possible to calculate the momentum of each of the freight cars, and add these to derive the total momentum of the system.

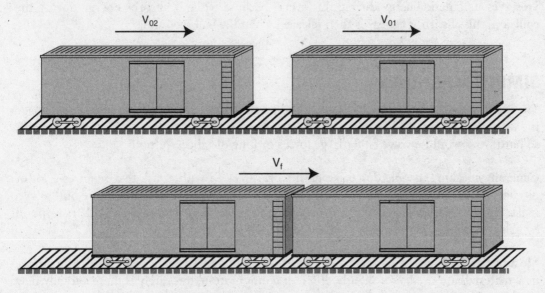

Figure 9. Two freight cars on the same track

As the freight cars get closer, they eventually "couple" together and move as one. Using the principle of conservation of linear momentum, the momentum of the coupled units (now acting as one mass) will be the same as the total momentum of the freight cars when they were moving separately. Mathematically speaking, it can be said that

$$m_1 v_1 + m_2 v_2 = (m_1 + m_2)\, v_f$$

where v_f is the final velocity of the "coupled" freight cars.

COLLISIONS

When two objects collide, total linear momentum of the system is conserved. Total kinetic energy, however, may be less after the collision, depending on the nature of the event. For instance, a car crash is a collision, but much damage takes place during that collision. Since it requires energy to damage the car (i.e.; crushing steel panels), a good deal of kinetic energy is absorbed during the collision. This is an example of an **inelastic collision**.

Completely inelastic collisions are when the objects stick together after colliding. This type of collision loses a greater amount of kinetic energy than inelastic collisions. An example of an inelastic collision is a bullet being fired into a piece of wood, and lodging there.

Collisions that preserve the total kinetic energy of the system are known as **elastic collisions**. An example of an elastic collision is a rubber ball being bounced off the floor. The ball preserves its kinetic energy during this event, because while it absorbs energy during the collision, this absorbed energy is then released when the ball rebounds.

SIMPLE MACHINES

The idea behind the invention of many of the machines we use today is to reduce or manage the work that we do. We have already seen that work is defined as force $\times$ distance ($w = fd$), so hard work would involve either large forces or long distances, or both.

Generally speaking, people don't like hard work. If faced with a task that requires a lot of physical effort, the worker often spends at least part of their time trying to figure out how to make the work easier. For many, this involves getting someone else to do it. Others respond by using machines that can ease the burden.

Most of the machines being built today are simply refinements of age-old ideas. Sometimes new materials are used, or a slightly different configuration, but rarely is there a totally new machine that is introduced. For trade people, understanding how these simple machines work is essential in order to diagnose and service machinery effectively.

Mechanical Advantage

What makes work difficult is often the amount of force that must be applied to get the job done. Heavy objects need to be lifted, parts need to be pushed together or apart, and large machines need to be moved. Often, it is difficult or impossible for a human being to apply enough force to get the job done.

In order to increase the available force to a much larger one, **mechanical advantage** is used. Mechanical advantage is defined as "the advantage gained by the use of a mechanism in transmitting force." Using the proper equipment, it is possible to increase or even multiply force many times over what is initially applied.

Simple machines such as the inclined plane, wedge, screw, lever, pulley, and wheel and axle can be used to increase applied force. Other more sophisticated methods such as hydraulics work exceptionally well for this purpose, but have greater potential for failure as they utilize more moving parts.

It is important to remember that there is no free lunch when it comes to work. While mechanical advantage can be used to amplify force, this is done at the expense of distance. In other words, the work put out can never exceed the work put into one of these machines. The good news, however, is that they make hard work easier by breaking it down into smaller, more manageable pieces.

Inclined Plane

One of the simplest ways of managing lifting tasks is through the use of the **inclined plane**. Imagine attempting to lift a 100 kg (about 220 pound) box from ground level to the bed of a pickup truck. This is a difficult, if not impossible task for one man. This can go much easier if an inclined plane (or ramp) is placed between the ground and the bed of the truck.

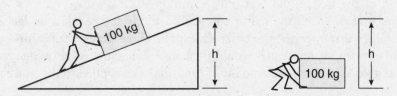

Figure 10. Lifting a box, or pushing up a ramp to height h

Remember that the work that is done to lift the box will be the same as the final gravitational potential energy of the box ($PE = mgh$). Therefore, the same amount of work will be done whether the box is pushed up the ramp (assuming no friction), or if it is lifted into the truck directly. The difference with the ramp is that a much smaller force can be applied to load the box into the truck. This force must be applied over a longer distance, but it will give some mechanical advantage to make the task easier.

To make the task easier yet, the ramp can be made longer. This results in the slope leading to the truck bed being less steep, so less force is required to move the box up the ramp. However, the smaller force would have to be applied over a longer distance to get the job done.

Wedge

The **wedge** is a variation of the inclined plane, in that it is made to move whereas the inclined plane stays stationary. It can be used for many purposes, including lifting, splitting, and tightening. The mechanical advantage that can be gained with a wedge is determined by the ratio of its length to its height.

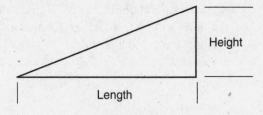

Figure 11. Wedge

A wedge that is constructed with the same length and height will offer no mechanical advantage. This is because it will lift the same distance as it is pushed horizontally. When the distance of the lift is the same as the distance the initial force travels, the force in will equal the force out.

Making the wedge longer relative to its height (less slope) will change this by decreasing the amount of lift that takes place as the wedge is moved horizontally. This increases the amount of force that can be generated by the wedge and makes it easier to lift heavy objects. Remember that if force is increased by the wedge, then the distance it will lift will be less than the distance it moved horizontally.

An application of the wedge that was once common in heavy duty vehicles was wedge-operated drum brakes. When the driver stepped on the brake pedal, a wedge was forced between two rollers that operated the brake shoes. The brake shoes would thus expand and act against the moving drum, which would then slow the vehicle. The wedge had a small slope, so it was able to increase the amount of force that was applied to the brake shoes.

Other common applications of the wedge include knives, chisels, log splitters, and securing hammer heads on their handles.

Screws

The concept of the inclined plane is also utilized in the design of the **screw**. A screw is a solid shaft with an inclined plane (threads) wrapped around it much like a spiral staircase. As a screw is turned into a threaded hole, the threads cause it to move forwards or backwards, depending on the type of thread and the direction of rotation. The screw is thus able to convert rotary motion into linear (straight line) motion.

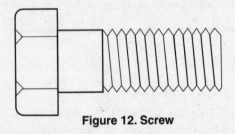

Figure 12. Screw

Screws can be used as fasteners or to change force and motion. A bench vise is an example of a machine that utilizes a screw to generate a clamping force. Tightening the vise handle with a circular motion causes the vise jaws to clamp together. Common household items that utilize the screw are the base of a light bulb, and a jar lid.

Levers

Another simple machine that can be used to amplify force or distance, as well as change direction, is the **lever**. There are three basic types of levers, so this machine lends itself to many different applications.

The **first class lever** is used to increase force or distance, and to change the direction of the force. An example of a first class lever is a child's teeter-totter.

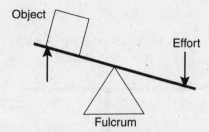

Figure 13. First class lever

The **fulcrum** is the point that the lever pivots on. When effort is applied to one end of the lever, it changes direction at the other end. The position of the fulcrum will define whether any mechanical advantage is gained. If the fulcrum is closer to the object being lifted, less effort is required to do the work. However, the end that the effort is applied to must move further to get the job done.

The opposite effect takes place when the fulcrum is moved closer to where the effort is applied. Now the distance the object can be moved is amplified, but the force is diminished.

A **second class lever** is used to increase force only. An excellent example of a second class lever is a wheelbarrow.

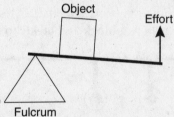

Figure 14. Second class lever

The mechanical advantage of the second class lever increases as the object is moved closer to the fulcrum. This can also be accomplished by increasing the length of the lever. As the lever is lifted, the distance that the object is lifted is always less, so lifting force increases.

The **third class lever** is used to increase distance. It is similar to the second class lever in that the fulcrum is at one end. The object, however, is at the other end of the lever, with the effort being applied somewhere in between. An example of a third class lever is a fishing pole.

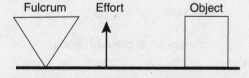

Figure 15. Third class lever

Since distance moved is increased with a third class lever, force is therefore diminished. This effect magnifies as the effort is applied closer to the fulcrum.

Pulleys

Applying force to an object is sometimes best accomplished through the use of a **pulley**. A pulley is a wheel that carries a flexible rope, belt, or chain.

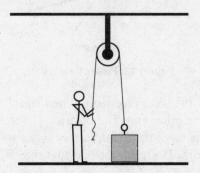

Figure 16. Person pulling a rope through a pulley to lift an object

Block and Tackle

It is relatively uncommon for one pulley to be used by itself. More often, two or more pulleys will be used in an arrangement known as a **block and tackle** to increase lifting force.

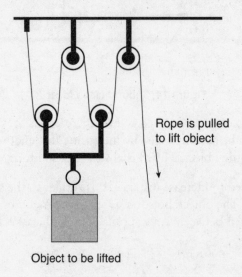

Rope is pulled to lift object

Object to be lifted

Figure 17. Block and tackle

The block and tackle shown here has four pulleys; two are attached to a stationary object (such as the ceiling or wall of a building) and the other two are attached to the lower block (connected to the load). As the rope is pulled, the lower block moves towards the stationary pulleys. Note that in order to lift the load 1 foot, it is necessary to pull the rope a total of 4 feet. This is because each of the four rope links must shorten by 1 foot to get the lower block to move 1 foot. Neglecting friction, this gives a total mechanical advantage of 4:1, so if 4 pounds of force are required to lift a load, only 1 pound needs to be applied to the rope.

Wheel and Axle

Another variation of the pulley concept is the **wheel and axle**. Like the block and tackle, the wheel and axle can be used to increase mechanical advantage. It uses two wheels mounted on a shaft, with one wheel having a larger diameter than the other. An example of a wheel and axle is the steering wheel of a car.

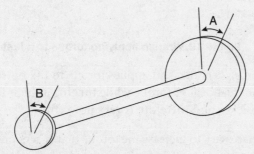

Movement at A becomes smaller than movement at B —
force is increased at B

Figure 18. Wheel and axle

The large diameter wheel will usually be the one that has the effort applied to it. Large movements of the large wheel result in small movements of the small wheel. Since a large movement (or distance) is being translated into a small movement, the force is then being increased.

The exact amount of mechanical advantage is determined by the ratio of the radius of the wheels. If the large wheel is 20 inches in diameter, and the small wheel is 10 inches in diameter, the total mechanical advantage is 2:1. This means that force can be doubled across this assembly, but distance at the small wheel will be one-half of the movement of the large wheel.

Gears and Gear Ratios

While **gears** are not included in the list of classic simple machines, they are of fundamental importance to an understanding of how machines work. Gears can be used anywhere that force is being transmitted between two points, and are excellent for gaining mechanical advantage. In order to understand how gears work, however, a technician must have a thorough understanding of **torque** and its relationship with speed.

Torque is **twisting force**. When a bolt is being tightened, torque is being applied to the bolt. When tightening a fastener, if one uses a wrench that is 1 foot long, and applies a force of 100 pounds to the end of the wrench, 100 foot-pounds (ft-lb) of torque is being applied. Simply multiply the applied force by the length of the wrench to determine the torque.

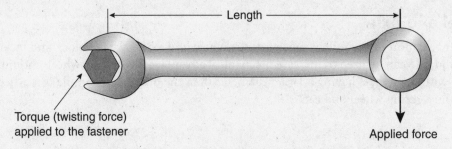

Figure 19. Wrench applying torque to a fastener

As an engine moves a vehicle, its crankshaft applies torque to the power train of the vehicle. If an engine can generate a great deal of torque while turning at high RPMs (revolutions per minute), it can do work quickly, and therefore is very powerful.

There are times when it is necessary to increase the torque that is generated by an engine. These times usually occur when vehicle speed is low and the driver wishes to accelerate quickly. Pulling away from a stop light is an example of a time when more torque is required than speed, since what is required to get the vehicle moving is a large twisting force at the wheels.

Gears can be used to change the speed and torque of an engine. The gears are located in the vehicle's power train (transmission and drive axle) and the **overall gear ratio** will determine how fast the vehicle can go and how much torque is applied to the drive wheels.

If a small gear drives a large gear, a **speed reduction** takes place. The large gear will turn slower than the small gear and the speed of the output will be slower. However, there will also be an associated **torque multiplication** (increase) that takes place and now the torque output of the large gear will be greater than what was applied to the small gear. A speed decrease means that torque will increase.

Consider "Torque" and "Speed" to be two boys on a teeter-totter. Whenever "Torque" goes up, "Speed" goes down, and vice versa. A mathematician would describe these two quantities to be **inversely proportional**.

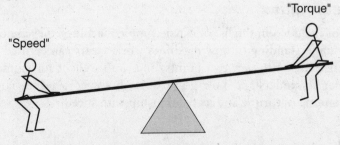

Figure 20. Relationship between torque and speed

If the drive gear had 20 teeth, and the driven gear had 40 teeth, a speed reduction would take place and the gear ratio would be 2:1. This means that the driven gear would turn at half the speed of the drive gear. Keep in mind that *smaller gears always turn faster*. If 100 foot-pounds of torque were applied to the drive gear, we could expect that since the speed was reduced by one-half, the torque output would double. The output torque would then be 200 foot-pounds.

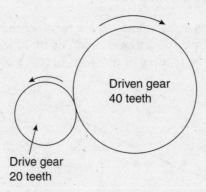

Figure 21. Gearset with 2:1 ratio

If the drive gear had the same number of teeth as the driven gear, this would represent a 1:1 gear ratio and would be known as a **direct drive**. No speed change across this gear set would mean that torque would remain the same as well.

A large gear driving a small gear would be described as an **overdrive**. There would be a speed increase across this gear set, and a proportional torque decrease. Transmission designers sometimes utilize an overdrive to lower engine RPM at highway speed and increase fuel economy. However, when the driver wishes to pass another motorist, they will select a gear ratio that allows a torque increase to help the vehicle accelerate faster.

Keep in mind that two gears meshed together will turn in opposite directions. In order to make the driven gear turn in the same direction as the drive gear, an **idler gear** must be placed between them. The idler gear will not alter the gear ratio between the drive and driven gears, no matter what size it is.

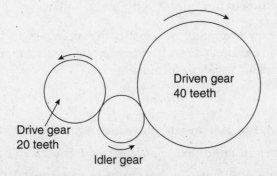

Figure 22. Drive, idler, and driven gear set (2:1 ratio)

Pulleys and Speed Ratios

The same principles that define how gears and gear ratios work apply to a two-pulley set with a drive belt between them. The one big difference between a pulley-belt combination and a gear set is that both pulleys will rotate in the same direction, whereas two gears meshed together will rotate in opposite directions.

The speed ratio between pulleys is determined by the radius of the pulleys. If a drive pulley has a radius of 5 inches, and the driven pulley has a radius of 10 inches, the speed ratio will be 2:1. This means that the speed will be reduced by one-half, and the torque output will double.

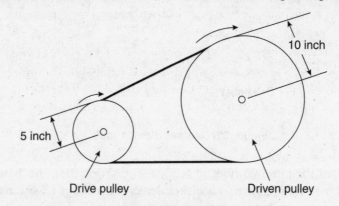

Figure 23. Pulley-belt set

As with gear sets, remember that *smaller pulleys always turn faster*. In the example above, the small pulley will turn at twice the speed of the large pulley, because it takes two turns of the small pulley to generate one turn in the large one.

FLUID POWER: HYDRAULICS

Fluid power can also be used to gain mechanical advantage. While the classic simple machines are effective and reliable, they are limited in the sense that force only can be amplified in their immediate area. When more versatility is required, **hydraulics** can be used. Hydraulics is the transmission of force through the use of liquids.

In order to understand how hydraulics works, it is first necessary to have a grasp of the concept of **pressure**. If force is applied evenly over a certain area, then pressure is applied to that area. Pressure is calculated using the formula

$$P = \frac{F}{A}$$

Where F is force in pounds (lb), A is area in square inches (in^2), and P is pressure in pounds per square inch (psi). Keep in mind that $\frac{F}{A}$ means that F is divided by A. A force of 100 pounds applied over an area of 10 square inches results in a pressure of 10 pounds per square inch (psi) being developed.

Using the formula for pressure, we can derive $F = PA$, which is useful for calculating the amount of force that is developed when pressure P is applied to area A.

There are three major principles that make hydraulics work:

1. The **first principle** is that **liquids are effectively incompressible**. Even when extremely high pressure is applied to a liquid, the volume of the liquid will decrease only a very small amount. This property makes liquids very effective for transmitting force.

2. The **second principle** of hydraulics is that **liquids conform themselves to the shape of their container**. Whether in a pipe or a pump, liquids will always change their shape to fill the space completely.

3. The **third principle** was discovered in 1650 by a French scientist named Blaise Pascal. Pascal observed that **when pressure is applied to a completely enclosed fluid, this pressure is transmitted undiminished to all parts of the fluid and the enclosing walls**. This observation became **Pascal's Law**, which can be used to explain how force can be amplified in a hydraulic system.

Note the diagram below with two hydraulic cylinders connected by a pipe. The cylinders each have sealed pistons that can move up and down in the cylinders. If the piston in one cylinder moves down, it will force liquid through the pipe to the other cylinder and cause that cylinder to rise.

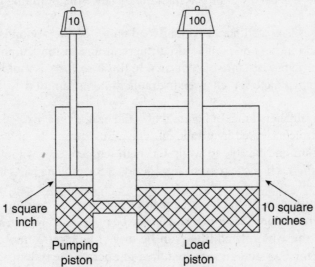

Figure 24. Connected hydraulic cylinders

The key to amplifying force with two hydraulic cylinders is the difference in the diameter of their pistons. Note that one piston is much smaller than the other. The smaller piston is known as the **pumping piston**, and this is the piston that the effort is applied to. The surface area of the pumping piston that makes contact with the liquid is only a fraction of the size of the **load piston**, which is the piston that will raise the load.

If a load of 100 pounds is to be raised by the load piston, how much force will have to be applied to the pumping piston? To answer this question, the first step is to calculate the fluid pressure that will be required to develop 100 pounds of force on the load piston.

Note that the load piston has a total surface area of 10 square inches. Using the formula $P = \dfrac{F}{A}$, 100 pounds ÷ 10 square inches = 10 pounds per square inch (psi) of pressure that should be applied to the load piston.

Knowing that the pumping piston must develop 10 psi of pressure, and that this piston has a surface area of 1 square inch, the formula $F = PA$ can be used to calculate the force that must be applied to the pumping piston. 10 psi × 1 square inch = 10 pounds of force that must be applied to the pumping piston.

Note that the force applied to the pumping piston is $\dfrac{1}{10}$ of the force that is developed at the load piston. The mechanical advantage gained with a system such as this is determined by the ratio of the surface areas of the pistons.

It is not possible to get more work out of a machine than what is put in. Since work is defined as force × distance $(W = fd)$, it is clear that if force is amplified with a hydraulic system, then the distance the load is moved will be less than the distance the pumping piston moves.

If the load piston rises 1 inch with a 100 pound load on it, 100 inch-pounds of work will have been done. To do 100 inch-pounds of work at the pumping piston, 10 pounds of force will have to be moved through a distance of 10 inches. In this case, force is multiplied ten-fold, but distance is decreased by a factor of ten. Even hydraulic systems cannot defy the laws of physics.

While there are many different kinds of liquids that could be used in a hydraulic system, the most common type is petroleum-based **hydraulic oil**. The oil used must be able to flow under low temperature conditions and be able to withstand high temperatures without breaking down. Since oil is a lubricant, this helps to prevent wear between the moving parts in the system.

The pumping of fluid in a hydraulic system does not have to be done with a hydraulic cylinder and pumping piston. This function can also be performed with gear or **vane pumps**. Since these pumps must be rotated, they can be driven by electric motors or even diesel engines to generate the flow and pressure required to operate the system's actuators.

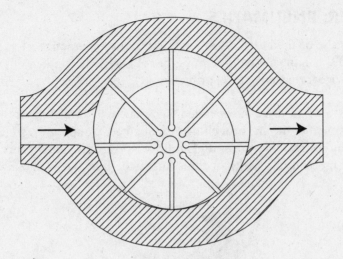

Figure 25. Vane pump

When hydraulic cylinders are used to do work, they are known as **linear actuators**. This is because they produce movement in a straight line and apply force in mechanical systems. Work can also be performed in a hydraulic system through the use of **rotary actuators**, such as a hydraulic motor. A hydraulic motor (gear or vane type) converts flow and pressure into rotary motion, producing torque.

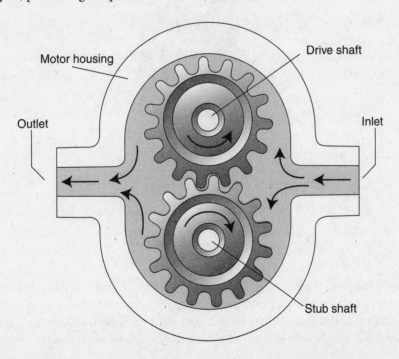

Figure 26. Gear-type hydraulic motor

FLUID POWER: PNEUMATICS

Air movement can also be used to perform work. The term **pneumatics** refers to a branch of mechanics that deals with the mechanical properties of gases. Air, wind, or other gases can be used to operate devices or generate force or pressure.

Compressed air is used to drive air-operated tools, such as an air impact wrench or air ratchet. Energy is stored in the air through the use of an **air compressor**, which reduces the volume of the air and increases its pressure. The air compressor is another energy conversion device, converting mechanical energy of the compressor into the potential energy of the compressed air.

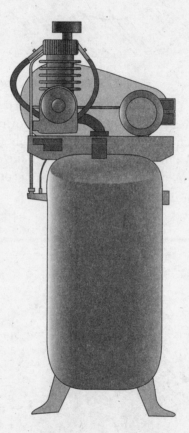

Figure 27. Air compressor

The air compressor pumps air into a storage tank, and continues pumping until the tank is filled to a certain pressure. Most air compressors are built to maintain pressure in the tank at 90–120 pounds per square inch. When compressed air is released from the tank, the pressure drops and eventually reaches the point where the air compressor starts and fills the tank again.

An air line is connected to the storage tank and the appropriate tool is connected to the other end of this line. When the tool is turned on, compressed air travels through the line and its energy is converted into mechanical energy at the tool. Spent air is then exhausted from the tool, making a loud noise that is the trademark of all air tools.

The key to making air tools work well is ensuring that a sufficient volume of air is supplied to the tool. When an air tool is turned off and no air is moving through the line, air pressure will be the same through all parts of the system. This changes, however, when a large volume of air moves from the tank and through the line to the air tool. If the air line is either too long or too small a diameter, this will restrict the flow of air. Flow restrictions will cause a large pressure drop in the line, resulting in poor performance of the air tool.

The effect of lowering air pressure through a restriction can be used constructively in a device known as a **venturi tube**. The venturi tube was invented by an Italian scientist named G.B. Venturi (1746–1822), who noted that fluid pressure dropped as it passed through a constricted channel.

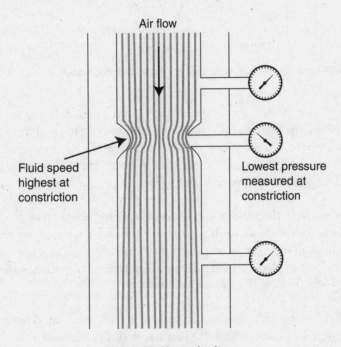

Figure 28. Venturi tube

The venturi tube is utilized in many different devices, the best-known being the automobile carburetor. A carburetor is responsible for mixing air and fuel in the correct ratio for combustion purposes in an engine. The major component of the carburetor is a venturi, and air entering the engine is first directed through the venturi on its way to the intake manifold. The open end of a siphon tube is placed in the venturi constriction, with the lower end of the tube immersed in gasoline that is contained in the carburetor's float bowl.

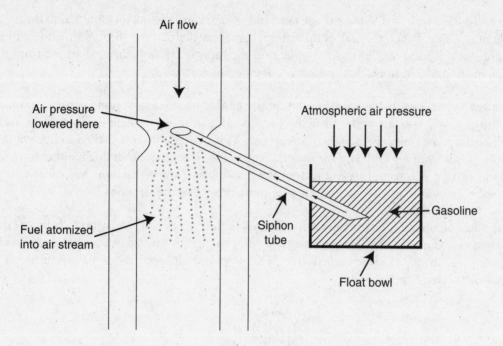

Figure 29. Venturi with siphon tube and float bowl

As air flows through the venturi, its pressure drops in proportion to the volume of air. This pressure drop results in the higher atmospheric air pressure forcing fuel through the tube and into the air stream, where it is atomized. As the volume of air increases, the pressure in the constriction decreases and allows more gasoline to enter the air stream. This is how the carburetor regulates the air-fuel ratio for the engine.

The drop in air pressure in the venturi is directly related to the speed of the fluid. Note that in order for the same volume of air to move through the constriction, it will have to speed up in order to move through the narrow constriction at the same rate as it does in the rest of the tube. This effect is best explained using **Bernoulli's Theorem**, which states that the total mechanical energy of a flowing fluid remains constant.

The total mechanical energy of a fluid is comprised of its gravitational potential energy, the energy associated with its pressure, and its kinetic (moving) energy. If a fluid is flowing on a horizontal plane, then its gravitational potential energy does not vary. However, if a constriction causes the fluid's kinetic energy to increase, Bernoulli's theorem tells us that its pressure must decrease in order for its total mechanical energy to remain constant.

Bernoulli's theorem explains why aircraft can fly. An aircraft wing is designed so that its top surface is longer than its lower surface. As air moves over the wing, the air that moves over the top surface must travel faster than the air on the underside. This results in air pressure on the top of the wing being lowered, and since the pressure is greater on the lower surface, **lift** is achieved.

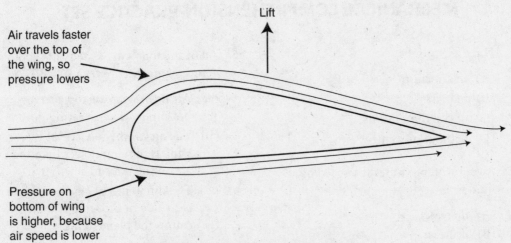

Figure 30. Airflow over an aircraft wing

Instrumentation relies heavily on Bernoulli's theorem and the venturi effect. The rate of fluid flow can be measured by passing the fluid through a venturi, then measuring the corresponding pressure at the constriction. As the rate of flow increases, the pressure in the constriction will decrease proportionately. A chart can be created that matches flow rate with the corresponding pressure, and this can be used to calibrate the instrument. Fluid flow indicators are only one example of instruments that utilize this principle.

MECHANICAL COMPREHENSION PRACTICE SET

1. Force exists only

   (A) in a vacuum
   (B) in pairs
   (C) in two dimensions
   (D) without movement

2. A venturi tube causes the speed of a fluid to

   (A) increase
   (B) decrease
   (C) stay the same
   (D) vary

3. The energy source for pneumatic tools is

   (A) atmospheric air
   (B) compressed air
   (C) compressed oxygen
   (D) electric wall outlets

4. A carburetor uses a venturi tube to meter gasoline into an engine's intake air stream. What actually *pushes* the fuel into the venturi tube, however, is

   (A) fuel pump pressure
   (B) intake manifold vacuum
   (C) atmospheric air pressure
   (D) cylinder compression

5. All of the following statements about aerodynamic lift are true EXCEPT

   (A) Air flows over the top and the bottom sides of the wing.
   (B) The air on the top side of the wing is moving slower than the air on the bottom side.
   (C) The difference in air pressure on each side of the wing is what causes the plane to lift.
   (D) Air pressure is greater on the bottom side of the wing.

6. In a certain gear position, the input shaft of a manual transmission is turning at the same speed as the output shaft. This gear ratio is known as

   (A) a speed reduction
   (B) a direct drive
   (C) an overdrive
   (D) none of the above

7. One foot-pound of torque is equivalent to

   (A) 12 inch-pounds
   (B) 10 inch-pounds
   (C) 1 newton-meter
   (D) 12 newton-meters

8. In using a wrench to loosen a bolt, to apply the maximum possible torque, a force should be applied

   (A) perpendicular to the wrench, halfway up the handle.
   (B) parallel to the wrench, at the end of the handle.
   (C) perpendicular to the wrench, at the end of the handle.
   (D) at an angle between parallel and perpendicular, at the end of the handle.

9. Increasing the inside diameter of a hydraulic line would cause fluid speed to

   (A) increase
   (B) stay the same
   (C) decrease
   (D) none of the above

10. Greater mechanical advantage would be realized in a hydraulic system if one pump were changed to another with

    (A) higher displacement
    (B) lower displacement
    (C) a lower gallons-per-minute output
    (D) Both B and C are correct.

11. The design of a kitchen knife is based on which of the following simple machines?

    (A) first-class lever
    (B) inclined plane
    (C) pulley
    (D) wedge

12. Hydraulic oil can be pumped with

    (A) gear pumps
    (B) piston pumps
    (C) vane pumps
    (D) all of the above

13. A small-diameter hydraulic cylinder pumps oil into a large-diameter hydraulic cylinder. With this arrangement, _____ will be amplified.

    (A) force
    (B) distance
    (C) temperature
    (D) Both A and B are correct.

14. Which of the following factors would increase the restriction to fluid flow in a hydraulic line?

    (A) decreased inside diameter
    (B) increased length
    (C) fewer sharp angles in the line
    (D) Both A and B are correct.

15. Increasing the speed of a fluid will cause its _____ to rise.

    (A) temperature
    (B) viscosity
    (C) pressure
    (D) force

ANSWERS AND EXPLANATIONS FOR MECHANICAL COMPREHENSION PRACTICE SET

1. B

According to Newton's Third Law, a force acting on a body always elicits an equal, opposite force acting against it and the opposite force acts back on the object that is exerting the force on the body. Thus, force always acts *in pairs*.

2. A

According to Bernoulli's Theorem, the drop in air pressure in a venturi tube is directly related to the speed of the fluid. In order for the same volume of air to move through the constriction, it will have to speed up in order to move through the narrow constriction at the same rate as it does in the rest of the tube. The total mechanical energy of a flowing fluid remains constant. Thus, a venturi tube causes the speed of the fluid to *increase*, choice (A).

3. B

Compressed air gives pneumatic tools the pressure they need to function effectively.

4. C

Air pressure drops within a venturi tube in proportion to the volume of air. This pressure drop results in higher atmospheric air pressure forcing fuel through the tube and into the air stream. As the volume of air increases, the pressure in the constriction decreases and allows more gasoline to enter the air stream.

5. B

Again referring to Bernoulli's Theorem, a wing is designed so that its top surface is longer than its lower surface. The air moves over the top of the wing faster than the air on the underside. This results in *lift*. Choice (B) misstates this theorem, therefore it is the correct choice.

6. B

If the drive gear and the driven gear have the same number of teeth, a 1:1 gear ratio appears. This type of ratio is known as a *direct drive*.

7. A

One foot-pound is directly equal to twelve inch-pounds.

8. C

Torque is maximized the further away the force is applied from the axis of rotation, and when force is applied perpendicular to the line of the wrench, choice (C).

9. **C**

Increasing the inside diameter of a hydraulic line would mean decreasing the pressure exerted on the fluid flowing through that line. Thus, a decrease in pressure means a *decrease* in the speed of the fluid in the line.

10. **D**

In this case, a new pump with both a lower displacement and a lower gallons-per-minute output would achieve a greater mechanical advantage in a hydraulic system.

11. **D**

A kitchen knife is a simple machine whose design is based on the physics of a wedge.

12. **D**

Hydraulic oil can be pumped through a hydraulic cylinder with a pumping piston or can be pumped with gear or vane pumps. Since these pumps must be rotated, they can be driven by electric motors. Since (A), (B), and (C) are correct, choice (D) is the answer.

13. **A**

In the case where a small-diameter hydraulic cylinder pumps into a large-diameter hydraulic cylinder, force is what will be amplified. This is because the pressure, in terms of force per area, has increased due to an increase in area.

14. **D**

Changing the length or the diameter of a fluid line would decrease the pressure inside the line, thereby increasing the restriction. Since answer choices (A) and (B) are both correct, choice (D) is the answer.

15. **C**

Increased speed when applied to fluid means increased pressure.

CHAPTER ELEVEN

Electronics Information

INTRODUCTION

Basic electrical and electronics knowledge grows more valuable with each passing day. Many devices that were once controlled by mechanical means have now become part of the electronic domain. Electronics has breathed new life into many machines that have been around for a long time, as well as bringing new machines into existence that never would have been possible with older technology.

Virtually every aspect of our lives has been changed by electronics. Entertainment and communications are just two examples of industries that have been revolutionized by this technology. While the field of electronics is often highly sophisticated, it still starts with fundamental electrical theory. This chapter has been written to give the reader a greater understanding of what electricity is, how it works, and how it can be controlled to perform many useful functions.

The ASVAB test-makers recognize the importance of electronics knowledge as well. This is why the electronics section of the ASVAB is an important one. The section that follows introduces you to basic electronics and familiarity with circuitry. For some of you who already dabble in fixing appliances or building simple circuits, this stuff might seem easy. For those of you who can't program their VCR, you better get started!

THE ATOM

A solid understanding of electricity begins at the atomic level. Matter is composed of **atoms**, which are the smallest particles that elements can be broken into and still retain the properties of that element. For instance, copper is an element. Copper is listed in the **Periodic Table of the Elements** (see below) as **Cu**, with an atomic number of 29. The smallest particle that copper can be broken into and still be copper is a copper atom.

PERIODIC TABLE OF THE ELEMENTS

1 H 1.0																	2 He 4.0
3 Li 6.9	4 Be 9.0											5 B 10.8	6 C 12.0	7 N 14.0	8 O 16.0	9 F 19.0	10 Ne 20.2
11 Na 23.0	12 Mg 24.3											13 Al 27.0	14 Si 28.1	15 P 31.0	16 S 32.1	17 Cl 35.5	18 Ar 39.9
19 K 39.1	20 Ca 40.1	21 Sc 45.0	22 Ti 47.9	23 V 50.9	24 Cr 52.0	25 Mn 54.9	26 Fe 55.8	27 Co 58.9	28 Ni 58.7	29 Cu 63.5	30 Zn 65.4	31 Ga 69.7	32 Ge 72.6	33 As 74.9	34 Se 79.0	35 Br 79.9	36 Kr 83.8
37 Rb 85.5	38 Sr 87.6	39 Y 88.9	40 Zr 91.2	41 Nb 92.9	42 Mo 95.9	43 Tc (98)	44 Ru 101.1	45 Rh 102.9	46 Pd 106.4	47 Ag 107.9	48 Cd 112.4	49 In 114.8	50 Sn 118.7	51 Sb 121.8	52 Te 127.6	53 I 126.9	54 Xe 131.3
55 Cs 132.9	56 Ba 137.3	57 La* 138.9	72 Hf 178.5	73 Ta 180.9	74 W 183.9	75 Re 186.2	76 Os 190.2	77 Ir 192.2	78 Pt 195.1	79 Au 197.0	80 Hg 200.6	81 Tl 204.4	82 Pb 207.2	83 Bi 209.0	84 Po (209)	85 At (210)	86 Rn (222)
87 Fr (223)	88 Ra 226.0	89 Ac† 227.0	104 Unq (261)	105 Unp (262)	106 Unh (263)	107 Uns (262)	108 Uno (265)	109 Une (267)									

	58 Ce 140.1	59 Pr 140.9	60 Nd 144.2	61 Pm (145)	62 Sm 150.4	63 Eu 152.0	64 Gd 157.3	65 Tb 158.9	66 Dy 162.5	67 Ho 164.9	68 Er 167.3	69 Tm 168.9	70 Yb 173.0	71 Lu 175.0
*														
†	90 Th 232.0	91 Pa (231)	92 U 238.0	93 Np (237)	94 Pu (244)	95 Am (243)	96 Cm (247)	97 Bk (247)	98 Cf (251)	99 Es (252)	100 Fm (257)	101 Md (258)	102 No (259)	103 Lr (260)

Figure 1. Periodic Table of Elements

A copper atom is composed of a **nucleus** and **electrons** that are in motion around the nucleus. Two types of particles are found within the nucleus: **protons** and **neutrons**. Protons have a positive charge, and neutrons are neutrally charged. The nucleus is the heaviest part of the atom and accounts for the majority of the atom's mass. Electrons that are in motion around the nucleus have a negative charge, and there is one electron for each proton that resides in the nucleus. (While early models of the atom proposed that the electrons move around the nucleus much like planets orbit the sun, their actual motion is much more difficult to describe.)

Since a copper atom has an equal number of protons and electrons, the atom is neutrally charged. This means that the atom is stable and does not seek to gain or lose electrons. There are 29 protons in the nucleus, so 29 electrons reside in orbit around the nucleus. The various orbits that the electrons occupy around the nucleus are known as **shells**, and these shells are thought to look much like our solar system. The sun would represent the nucleus, and the electrons move in shells that are similar to the orbits that planets travel in.

The shells are thought to be limited in their capacity to hold electrons. The first shell that is closest to the nucleus can hold a maximum of two electrons. If an atom has more than two electrons, this first shell would be filled and then the remaining atoms would occupy the second shell. The second shell can hold a maximum of eight electrons, so an atom with more than ten electrons would fill the first two shells and then any remaining electrons would go into the third shell.

The third shell can hold up to 18 electrons. A copper atom has 29 electrons, so it would fill the first three shells completely and have one electron left to begin a fourth shell. The outer shell of an atom is known as its **valence shell**, and this shell plays a major role in determining the electrical properties of an element.

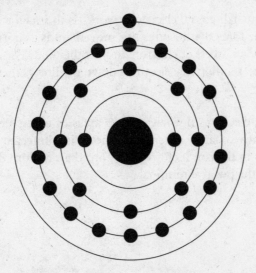

Figure 2. Copper Atom (29 electrons)

The number of electrons that reside in the valence shell are what determines whether an element is a **conductor**, a **semiconductor**, or an **insulator**. A conductor is an element that freely conducts electricity, whereas an insulator does not conduct electricity at all. A semiconductor is neither a good conductor nor insulator, but has some remarkable properties that make it very useful for making electronic components.

If the valence shell of an atom has less than four electrons, that element is said to be a conductor. This is because there is a weaker bond between the positively-charged nucleus and the few electrons in this shell, so it is easy to "free" these electrons and move them from atom to atom. Copper has one electron in its valence shell, so it is a conductor. Another example of a conductor from the periodic table is aluminum (symbol **Al**, atomic number 13). Aluminum has a total of three shells, with the valence shell having three electrons.

Increasing the number of electrons in the valence shell results in stronger bonds with the nucleus, and makes it very difficult to break these electrons free. More than four electrons in the valence shell means that the element is an insulator. Insulators do not conduct electricity, and therefore are useful for creating electrical barriers. Examples of insulators are rubber and plastic.

Semiconductors exist in the "no man's land" between conductors and insulators. Semiconductors have exactly four electrons in their valence shell, and are neither good conductors nor good insulators. A good example of a semiconductor is carbon (symbol **C**, atomic number 6). The carbon atom will have two electrons in the first shell, and four electrons in its valence shell. A better-known semiconductor is silicon (symbol **Si**, atomic number 14). Silicon is the foundation upon which transistors and computer chips are built.

ELECTRON FLOW THEORY

A convenient way of visualizing how electricity works is to imagine it as electrons flowing through a conductor. The force that inspires this movement is a shortage of electrons at one end of the conductor, and an excess of electrons at the other end. The atoms of the conductor act like a "bucket brigade," sending free electrons down the line as they pick up free electrons from upstream.

In **electron flow theory**, electrons flow away from areas of excess negative charge, to those with a deficiency of negative charge. When a conductor is connected across the terminals of the battery, the electrons in the conductor will be forced away from the negative terminal of the battery and towards the positive terminal.

It was once thought that electricity was made up of positive charges moving through a conductor. This was the basis for conventional current flow theory in which it was thought that it is positive charges that are in motion rather than the electrons. While this theory has lost importance in light of electron flow theory, it can still be very useful and is sometimes more convenient for diagnostic purposes. In practice, it makes no difference which theory is used, as long as one or the other is used consistently.

VOLTAGE

In order to make electrons move through a conductor, there must be a force that causes them to move. Water will move from a high-pressure area in a pipe towards a lower-pressure area, but if the pressure is equal at both ends, no movement takes place. Electricity is no different, as there must be electrical "pressure" applied to a conductor to cause electrons to move.

Electrical pressure is known as **voltage**, and it is measured in volts (symbolized by the letter **V**). The higher the voltage that is applied to a conductor, the greater the electrical pressure. Voltage is also known as **electrical potential**, or **electromotive force**. A technician would measure voltage using a **voltmeter**.

CURRENT

The rate of flow of electrons through a conductor is known as **current**. Current is measured in **amperes**, and an ampere is defined as one **coulomb** of electrical charge flowing past a point in one second. The symbol used for amperes is **A**.

One coulomb is the amount of charge in 6.25×10^{18} electrons. This is the same as 6,250,000,000,000,000,000 electrons. If this many electrons flow past a point in a conductor in one second, one ampere of current is flowing. Current is measured using an **ammeter**.

AC versus DC

There are two types of electrical current: **direct current** and **alternating current**. Direct current (**DC**) means that current only flows one way in a conductor. This is the type of current that is delivered by a battery. Alternating current (**AC**) is when the current flowing in a conductor changes direction (moves back and forth) many times in a second. Household electrical outlets deliver alternating current.

Here in North America, alternating current is always delivered at **60 cycles per second**. This is also known as **60 hertz** (**hz**). One cycle would be voltage starting at zero, increasing to a maximum level in one direction, then decreasing to zero, increasing to a maximum level in the reverse direction, then returning to zero again. 60 hertz means that 60 complete voltage cycles like the one just described take place in one second.

In European countries, the standard is 50 hertz, so many US-made appliances and electronic devices need a special converter to operate on the electrical power available there.

RESISTANCE

Opposition to the flow of current is known as **resistance**. Resistance is measured in **ohms**, and one ohm is the amount of resistance that will allow one ampere of current to flow if one volt of electrical pressure is placed on a conductor. The symbol for the ohm is Ω (omega), and resistance can be measured using an **ohmmeter**.

All conductors have a certain amount of resistance, with some having more than others. Three materials that are most often used as conductors are silver, copper, and aluminum. Of these three, silver is the best conductor as it exhibits the lowest resistance. Unfortunately, silver is relatively expensive, so the next best choice is copper. Copper has only a slightly higher resistance than silver, but is much less expensive. Most cable and wire is currently made from copper. Aluminum has a higher resistance than copper, and exhibits some other characteristics that make it even less than desirable as a conductor. While aluminum was used extensively in residential wiring at one time, it is now used only in a few select applications.

As resistance in a conductor increases, current flow decreases. This means that current and resistance are **inversely proportional**. Voltage and current, on the other hand, are **directly proportional**. Anytime voltage increases, current will also increase.

A good way to visualize the relationship between voltage, resistance, and current is to compare them to a garden hose and nozzle that are connected to a household water faucet. Consider the water pressure in the hose to be voltage, the nozzle to be the resistance, and the hose to be the conductor. When full water pressure is delivered to the hose with the nozzle closed, there is no water flow. Water pressure (voltage) has been applied to the hose (conductor), but no water (current) flows because the nozzle is closed (high resistance).

Now imagine what happens when the nozzle is opened. The resistance has now been lowered and water flows from the hose. Resistance decreases, and current increases. If the nozzle is opened up completely, this results in a large flow of water from the hose. Also, imagine what happens if the household water pressure increases. More pressure applied to the hose would also result in more water flow.

OHM'S LAW

The relationship between voltage, current, and resistance is summed up in **Ohm's Law**. Ohm's law states that voltage in volts is equal to the current in amperes multiplied by the resistance in ohms, or

$$E = I \times R$$

The letters used in the formula can be confusing, but it's important to be familiar with them since this is the way that Ohm's law is most often stated. **E** represents voltage. This is best remembered as **E**lectromotive force, which is another word for voltage. **I** represents current. Current is the rate of flow of electrons, or the **I**ntensity of the flow. (Specifically, **I** is the rate of charge flow.) Finally, **R** represents **R**esistance.

The key to using Ohm's law is to remember that whenever two of the quantities are available, the third can always be calculated. This might require some juggling of the basic formula to arrive at a solution. For instance, if resistance and current are known, voltage can be calculated using $E = I \times R$. However, if voltage and resistance are known, then current can be calculated using $I = E \div R$. Finally, when current and voltage are known, then resistance can be calculated using $R = E \div I$.

An easy way to remember these three formulas is to start by drawing the pie chart shown below. If you want to know voltage, cover the E with your hand. This leaves I and R uncovered, and you will note that they are next to each other, so they would be multiplied. The formula to use is $E = I \times R$.

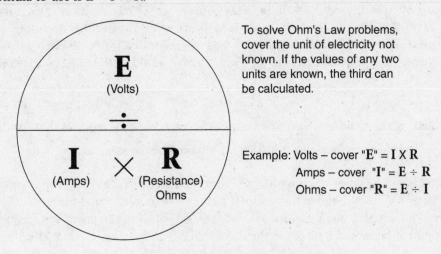

To solve Ohm's Law problems, cover the unit of electricity not known. If the values of any two units are known, the third can be calculated.

Example: Volts – cover "**E**" = **I X R**
Amps – cover "**I**" = **E ÷ R**
Ohms – cover "**R**" = **E ÷ I**

Figure 3. Ohm's Law pie chart

If you want to know resistance, you would cover the R with your hand. This leaves E on top of I. The formula to use to determine resistance is $R = E \div I$.

Finally, the formula used to calculate current is found by covering I with your hand, leaving the E on top of the R. The formula to use is then $I = E \div R$. Divide E in volts by R in ohms to determine I in amperes.

As an example, when voltage is 12 volts, and resistance is 4 ohms, current can be calculated using $I = E \div R$. 12 volts is divided by 4 ohms to get 3 amperes. The current flowing in this circuit is 3 amperes.

UNITS

When using Ohm's law, it is important to keep in mind that the quantities used must be expressed in ohms, amperes, and volts. If any of these quantities are given in other units, these should be converted before making calculations with them.

For instance, current is often expressed in **milliamperes**. A milliampere (**mA**) is $\frac{1}{1,000}$ of an ampere. Milliamperes can be converted to amperes by moving the decimal point three places to the left. So, 500 mA would be the same as 0.5 A.

Resistance is often expressed as **kilohms** (**KΩ**) or megohms (**MΩ**). A KΩ is 1,000 ohms, and a MΩ is 1,000,000 ohms. To convert kilohms to ohms, move the decimal point three places to the right. 6 KΩ would then become 6,000 Ω. Megohms can be converted to ohms by moving the decimal point six places to the right. 10 MΩ would be the same as 10,000,000 Ω.

Voltage can be given in a number of different units. Small voltages are expressed as **millivolts** (**mV**), which are the same as $\frac{1}{1,000}$ of a volt. Converting mV to V requires that the decimal point be moved three places to the left. 1,000 mV would be the same as 1 V.

Large voltages can be given in **kilovolts** (**KV**) or even **megavolts** (**MV**). A KV is 1000 volts, so converting KV to V requires the decimal point to be moved three places to the right. Therefore, 3 KV equals 3,000 V. Since a MV is 1,000,000 volts, converting to volts requires the decimal point to be moved 6 places to the right. 6 MV then becomes 6,000,000 V.

ELECTRICAL POWER

Electrical power is a term that refers to the actual rate at which energy is provided to and consumed by an electric circuit. Power is expressed in **watts**, and can be calculated by multiplying the voltage (in volts) applied to the circuit by the current (in amperes) that flows in the circuit.

$$P = I \times E$$

For example, a household light bulb that has 120 volts applied to it and draws 0.5 A of current would be a 60 watt bulb. As with Ohm's law, if any two of the quantities are known, the third can be calculated. Keep in mind that all units should be in watts, volts, and amperes when using this formula.

BASIC CIRCUITS

In order for electric current to flow, there must be a **circuit** for it to follow. There are three essential components of an electrical circuit: a voltage source, a **load**, and conductors to connect the load to the voltage source. When these three components are connected so that current can flow, we have a **closed circuit**.

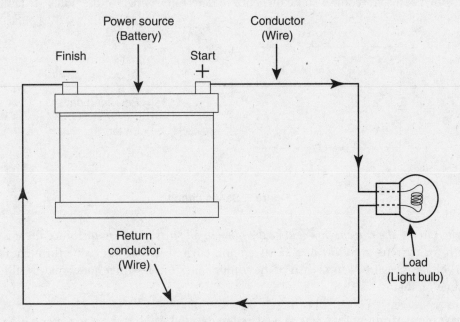

Figure 4. Simple circuit

A load is basically a resistance that converts electrical energy into some other energy form. For instance, a light bulb is a load. It is a resistance and it converts electrical energy into light energy and heat. Other examples of loads are electric motors, heating elements, and solenoids.

If a load's resistance were to decrease, the current flowing in the circuit would increase. However, if the circuit were broken, as in a wire (conductor) being disconnected, no current would flow. This would be called an **open circuit**, and the circuit's resistance would be described as infinite. Infinite resistance causes no current flow; low resistance causes high current flow.

An example of an open circuit is a burned-out light bulb. The filament in the bulb is broken or melted, so there is no longer a circuit for current to follow. This represents an infinite resistance in the circuit, so no current flows. The same effect takes place when the light switch is turned "off." The contacts in the switch are separated, which creates an open circuit, and current flow stops.

MAKE THE CIRCUIT

The building block of modern electronics is the circuit. Pay attention to the following sections on circuits to get the best possible score on the ASVAB.

Series, Parallel, and Series-Parallel Circuits

An electrical circuit that has only one path for current to flow is known as a **series circuit.** A break (opening) at any point in the circuit will cause current to stop flowing in all parts of the circuit. An excellent example of a series circuit is a string of miniature Christmas lights, in which one burned-out bulb will put all of the lights out. This arrangement can be exasperating to deal with, because it requires some diligence to determine which of the bulbs are faulty.

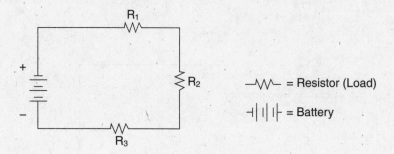

Figure 5. Series circuit

In a series circuit, *the current flow will be the same in all parts of the circuit.* Since there is only one path for current to follow in a series circuit, current will be the same throughout the circuit. Voltage measured across each of the components, on the other hand, may be different depending on their resistance.

It is much more common for loads to be wired in **parallel**. With this arrangement, each load is wired "across" the other loads, instead of in-line with them. If any one of the loads were to fail (turn into an open circuit), this would have no impact on the operation of the other loads. In the case of Christmas tree lights wired in parallel, one burned-out bulb might go out, but all of the others would stay lit. It is easy to determine which of the bulbs is faulty, and the remainder of the lights continue burning.

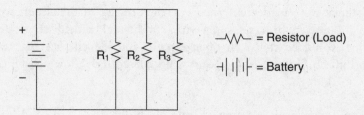

Figure 6. Parallel circuit

Parallel circuits are the exact opposite of series circuits in that *voltage is the same throughout each parallel branch of the circuit*, while current flow varies. All components in a parallel circuit will have the same voltage applied to them, but the current flow through each of these components will vary depending on the resistance of the component.

The most popular arrangement is the **series-parallel circuit**. This would have some components, such as an on/off switch, wired in series with a number of loads that are connected in parallel. An example of this would be the tail light circuit in a car. There is a switch on the dash that controls all of the tail lights, so it is wired in series with the lights. The lights themselves, however, are wired in parallel. If the switch is turned off, this will turn off all of the lights. However, if the switch is on and one of the lights were to fail, all of the other lights would continue burning.

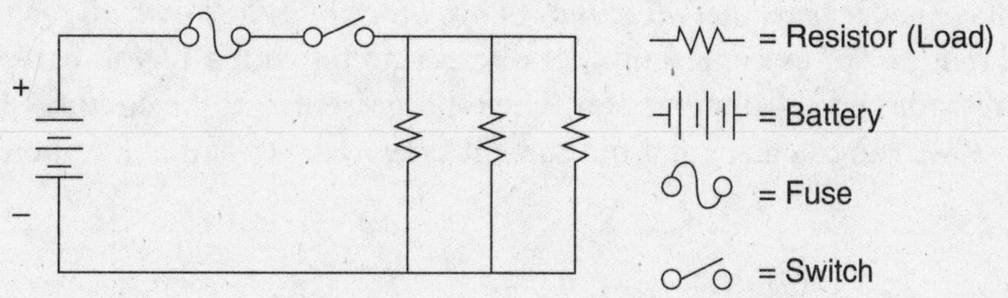

Figure 7. Series-parallel circuit

Most residential wiring circuits are series-parallel. Wall outlets are wired in parallel, but are all fed from a circuit breaker that is wired in series. Switching off the circuit breaker will turn off power to all of the outlets. However, if the circuit breaker is on, voltage is provided to all of the outlets whether there are loads plugged into them or not.

Total Circuit Resistance

When a number of loads are connected together, it is useful to be able to calculate total circuit resistance in order to determine how much current will flow through the circuit when a specified voltage is applied.

Calculating total resistance in series circuits is simply a matter of adding all of the resistances together. Expressed in terms of a formula, we get

$$R_{Total} = R_1 + R_2 + R_3 \ldots$$

In the case of a 6 ohm, a 5 ohm, and a 4 ohm resistor connected in series, the total resistance would be 6 + 5 + 4 = 15 ohms.

When three or more resistors are connected in parallel, the following formula should be used:

$$\frac{1}{R_{Total}} = \frac{1}{R_1} + \frac{1}{R_2} + \frac{1}{R_3} \ldots$$

Kirchoff's Voltage Law

As current passes through a resistance (no matter how small), there is always a **voltage drop** that takes place across that resistance. Higher resistance results in a higher voltage drop. A technician can measure this voltage drop using a voltmeter connected in parallel with a component that has power applied to it.

In order to calculate total resistance in parallel circuits, two different formulas can be used depending on how many resistors are in the circuit. In the case of two resistors in parallel, we can use

$$R_{Total} = (R_1 \times R_2) \div (R_1 + R_2)$$

We saw earlier that a series circuit has only one path for current to flow, so the current flow is the same at all points in the circuit. The voltages across the components (loads) in the circuit will vary, however, depending on the resistance of each individual component.

The voltage drop across a component can be calculated if its resistance and the current flowing through it are known. Using $E = I \times R$, a 20-ohm load with 0.5 amperes flowing through it will have a voltage drop of 20 ohms $\times$ 0.5 amperes = 10 volts across it.

Kirchoff's voltage law tells us that *all of the voltage drops in a closed-circuit loop must add up to the applied voltage.* For example, consider a series circuit with a 12 volt battery connected to an 8-ohm resistor and a 4-ohm resistor. The total resistance of the circuit is 12 ohms, and using $R = E \div I$, we can calculate that the current flow in the circuit is 1 ampere.

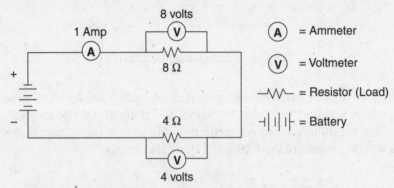

Figure 8. Circuit with voltmeters across the resistors
(Kirchoff's Voltage Law)

Since the current is the same throughout a series circuit, this means that 1 ampere is flowing through both the 8-ohm resistor and the 4-ohm resistor. Knowing the resistance and the current flow, we can now calculate the voltage drop across each of these resistors. Using $E = I \times R$, the voltage drop across the 8 ohm resistor is 1 ampere $\times$ 8 ohms = 8 volts. In the case of the 4-ohm resistor, 1 ampere $\times$ 4 ohms = 4 volts. Adding these two voltage drops together gives us 12 volts, which is the same as the applied voltage.

Kirchoff's voltage law is most useful when dealing with series circuits. It tells us that if there are large voltage drops taking place in the circuit's conductors, there will be less voltage available for the loads. In a circuit with a 12-volt battery powering a 12-volt light bulb, the light bulb will burn brightly if there are 12 volts applied to it. Keep in mind that if the conductors develop high resistance (due to poor connections or damage to the wire), they will develop higher voltage drops. Higher voltage drops at the conductors result in less voltage available for the bulb, so it will burn less brightly.

Another good example of this is the starting system of a car. The engine's starting motor functions well if there is sufficient voltage applied to it. The battery must be strong for this to take place, but even a strong battery cannot overcome high voltage drops in the battery cables. Poor connections at the battery or where the cables attach to the starter or engine block will result in voltage drops that lower the available voltage for the starter. Lower available voltage will result in slow cranking, and in this case it is neither the starter nor the battery that is at fault. When troubleshooting poor performance of an electrical component, be absolutely sure that the component is receiving the proper voltage before condemning it!

Kirchoff's Current Law

Parallel circuits are unique in that voltages throughout the circuit remain the same, but the current flowing through the loads will vary, depending on their resistance. A parallel circuit is a series of junctions, and as current is supplied to a junction, it must branch off in two or more directions.

Kirchoff's current law tells us that *the total current directed into a junction equals the total current leaving the junction*. In other words, what goes in, must come out. This law is useful when calculating total current consumed by a parallel circuit. Consider a 12-volt battery supplying power to three 12-ohm resistors connected in parallel.

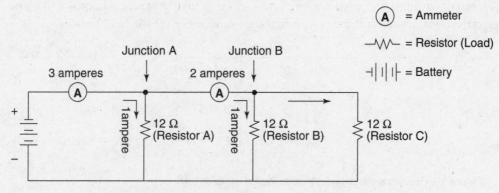

Figure 9. 12-volt battery and three 12-ohm resistors in parallel (Kirchoff's Current Law)

Using Ohm's law, we know that each of the 12-ohm resistors will draw 1 ampere of current, since 12 volts is applied to each of the resistors. Kirchoff's current law would then say that since there are three resistors that each draw 1 ampere, the total current drawn by the circuit would be 3 amperes. At Junction A, 3 amperes will flow into the junction, while 1 ampere would flow down into Resistor A and 2 amperes would flow on to Junction B. At Junction B, the 2 amperes flowing in will split into 1 ampere into Resistor B and 1 ampere into Resistor C.

When another load is connected to a parallel circuit, the circuit's total resistance drops and more current is drawn. This explains why a circuit breaker "kicks out" when too many electrical appliances are plugged in to a single circuit. As each new appliance is plugged in, more current is being drawn through the breaker until it exceeds the breaker's preset limit.

Adding more loads also increases the wattage that must be supplied to the circuit. In the example above, each of the 12-ohm resistors draws 1 ampere of current with 12 volts applied to it. Using P = I x E, we calculate that each of these resistors draws 12 volts x 1 ampere = 12 watts, and the total power consumption of the three resistors will be 12 x 3 = 36 watts. If another 12-ohm resistor was connected in parallel, the total power requirement would increase to 48 watts, and so forth.

Ground

When electrical circuits are constructed, it is often useful to build them on a chassis that can act as a conductor. This permits common connections in the circuit to be joined at the chassis, which simplifies the wiring immensely. When this common connection represents the zero voltage point of the system, it is known as the circuit's **ground**.

An excellent illustration of ground is the chassis of an automobile. All of the electrical components on the vehicle would normally require two wires to power them: one to the battery positive and one to the battery negative. Half of the wiring can be eliminated by connecting the battery negative post to the chassis of the vehicle, which turns the chassis into the negative conductor for every circuit. Now, only one wire must run to the component from the battery positive, and the component's negative wire is connected to the chassis. This is known as a **one-wire electrical system**, and it is the system that is used on every vehicle built today.

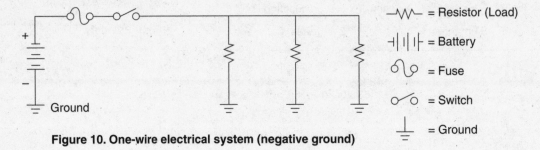

Figure 10. One-wire electrical system (negative ground)

A vehicle's ground is the zero-voltage point in the system. The remainder of the system operates at a voltage that is above ground. Since all vehicles being built today have the negative post of the battery connected to the chassis, these are all known as **negative ground systems**. There was a time when some vehicles were built with positive ground systems, but negative ground became the eventual standard for all car manufacturers.

In residential wiring, ground is a common connection throughout the wiring system that protects from electrical shock. All of the wiring grounds are connected to an **earth ground** (such as a copper rod driven into the ground or buried conduit) and this is used to guide electrical current away from panels and equipment should an internal short-circuit take place.

The ground wire in an electrical cord is connected to the chassis (frame) of the equipment. Since earth ground is a zero voltage point, all "stray" electricity will go to it by following the path of least resistance through the copper ground conductor. This system can only work if the ground prong is intact on the plug of the appliance's electrical cord. Do not use any piece of electrical equipment that does not have an intact ground prong on its plug!

Resistance, Current, and Heat

Whenever current passes through a resistance, a voltage drop takes place. This represents an energy loss, and this energy is normally dissipated in the form of heat. An electric heating element takes full advantage of this principle. Heating elements are normally made of a wire with higher than normal resistance. When electric current passes through it, heat is generated. These types of elements can be found in stoves, electric dryers, and toasters.

Poor electrical connections can get hot due to high resistance. Sometimes this will appear as a burnt connector or switch where the poor connection is located. Conductors that are too small for the amount of current they are carrying can also get hot. It is important to keep electrical connections clean and tight, and to use the proper gauge of wire for the expected current flow in order to prevent electrical failures.

Now that we've spent some time with electrical theory, let's see how that theory is put into practice.

ELECTRICAL COMPONENTS

Resistors

Not all components within an electrical circuit require the same voltage. There are also times when it is useful to be able to raise or limit current in a circuit in order to control certain functions (i.e., volume in a stereo). A component that can be utilized to limit current and/or voltage is a **resistor**.

A resistor does what its name suggests: it creates a specific amount of resistance that generates a voltage drop when current passes through it. As mentioned before, this voltage drop represents an energy loss that is dissipated in the form of heat. Resistors are rated according to the number of watts of power they can safely dissipate. If this power rating is exceeded, the resistor will overheat and eventually fail.

It is important to note that resistors present the same opposition to AC current flow as they do to DC current flow. This is in contrast to inductors and capacitors, two electrical components that will be discussed later in this section.

> There are two major types of resistors used today: the **fixed resistor** and the **variable resistor**.

Fixed resistors have specific resistance values and are rated in ohms. Carbon-based fixed resistors are cylindrical in shape and have colored bands on them to identify their resistance value. The physical size of the resistor is related to its power rating, which is measured in watts. The larger the resistor, the higher its power rating. Carbon-based resistors are generally used in low-current applications, because of their lower power ratings (typically between $\frac{1}{10}$ watt and 2 watts).

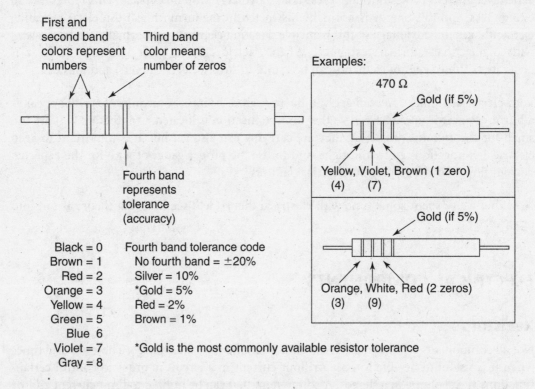

First and second band colors represent numbers

Third band color means number of zeros

Fourth band represents tolerance (accuracy)

Black = 0
Brown = 1
Red = 2
Orange = 3
Yellow = 4
Green = 5
Blue 6
Violet = 7
Gray = 8

Fourth band tolerance code
No fourth band = ±20%
Silver = 10%
*Gold = 5%
Red = 2%
Brown = 1%

*Gold is the most commonly available resistor tolerance

Examples:

470 Ω
Gold (if 5%)
Yellow, Violet, Brown (1 zero)
(4)   (7)

Gold (if 5%)
Orange, White, Red (2 zeros)
(3)   (9)

For high current applications, it is more common to use wire-wound fixed resistors. These utilize a high resistance wire that is cut to a specific length. These are normally encased in a high-temperature ceramic and are better able to dissipate heat.

Variable resistors come in two types; the **rheostat** and the **potentiometer**. These are both built with movable arms that "wipe" across a resistive surface, thus varying the resistance presented to the circuit it is connected to. The primary difference between them is that a potentiometer utilizes three terminals, where the rheostat uses only two.

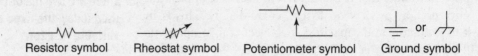

Resistor symbol   Rheostat symbol   Potentiometer symbol   Ground symbol

Figure 12

In a potentiometer, the majority of the current passes through the resistor itself with a small amount of current being "tapped" by the movable arm. A potentiometer is most often used to generate an output voltage based on the position of the movable arm. A rheostat, in contrast, has only two terminals, so all of the current passes through the movable arm. Rheostats are used to control current through a load, such as instrument panel lights or a radio volume control.

Capacitors

Capacitors (also known as **condensers**) are electrical storage units. They are constructed as two metal foil conducting plates with a very thin insulator (known as a **dielectric**) between them. Because of the very close proximity of the two foil conducting plates, it is possible to connect a DC voltage source across a capacitor and store an electrical charge.

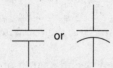

Figure 13. Capacitor symbol

A capacitor can store an electrical charge because the DC voltage source creates an excess of electrons on the negative plate and a shortage of electrons on the positive plate. The electrostatic attraction between the positive and negative charges keeps the charge intact in the capacitor, even when the voltage source is removed. The capacitor will discharge itself if a conductor is connected across it, as a path is then created for electrons to flow from the negative plate to the positive plate.

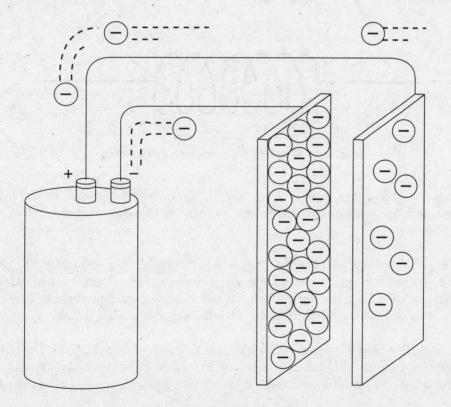

Figure 14. Simple condenser

Since the capacitor can charge and discharge easily, it will allow AC (alternating current) to flow across it, but will block DC (direct current). As the frequency (cycles per second) of alternating current increases, a capacitor's opposition to the flow of that current decreases. A capacitor's opposition to the flow of current is known as **capacitive reactance**, and this is measured in ohms.

The electrical storage ability of a capacitor allows it to act as an electrical "shock absorber," soaking up surges and voltage spikes. It is also able to smooth out voltage ripples that generate radio frequency interference, making the capacitor useful as a noise filter.

Capacitance is represented by the symbol **C**, and its unit of measurement is the **farad**. A farad is sufficient capacitance to store one coulomb of electrons with an electrical potential of one volt applied. The farad is a very large amount of capacitance, so most capacitors are normally rated in microfarads (one millionth of a farad).

Inductors

As electric current passes through a wire, a magnetic field is generated around the wire. The magnetic field can be made stronger by winding the wire into a coil. This then generates a magnetic field similar to the diagram below.

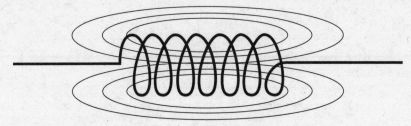

Figure 15. Magnetic field around a coil winding

If the coil is wound onto a ferrous (iron) core, the magnetic field around the coil becomes even stronger. This is because magnetic lines of force travel more easily through iron than through air.

Just as electricity can be used to create magnetism, magnetism can also be used to generate electricity. If a magnetic field is moved across a conductor at right angles, a voltage is **induced** in the conductor. This is the principle that makes power generation possible. Moving the magnetic field across the conductor faster will induce an even higher voltage.

When current first flows through a coil, the magnetic field builds relatively slowly. This is because the expanding magnetic field generates a voltage in the coil that opposes the original current flow. This is known as **counter-emf**, and it is produced by a process known as **self-induction**.

When the current is cut off, the magnetic field then collapses, and this collapsing magnetic field generates a voltage in the coil that keeps the current flowing.

This effect was observed by the Russian physicist Heinrich Lenz (1804-1865), and was formulated into Lenz's law. Lenz's law states that an induced current is in such a direction that its magnetic effect opposes the change by which the current is induced.

Electrical components that exhibit the property of self-induction are known as **inductors**. Inductors resist change in current flow. If current is increasing, the inductor opposes the increase by generating a voltage that moves against the applied current. If current decreases, the inductor uses the magnetic energy in the coil to oppose the decrease and to keep the current flowing.

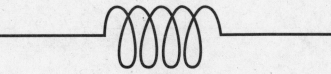

Figure 16. Inductor symbol

The symbol used to represent induction is **L**. Induction is measured in **henries**, but since this is a very large unit, it is more common for inductors to be rated in millihenries ($\frac{1}{1000}$ of a henry) or microhenries ($\frac{1}{1,000,000}$ of a henry).

Inductors work exactly opposite to capacitors, in the sense that they allow DC to pass easily, but resist the flow of AC. This is known as **inductive reactance**, and it will rise in direct proportion to the frequency of the current flowing through the inductor. Higher frequencies mean higher inductive reactance or opposition to the flow of current. Like capacitive reactance, inductive reactance is measured in ohms.

Electric motors, solenoids, and electromagnetic clutches are all examples of components that are not inductors per se, but exhibit self-inductive properties due to the fact that they have coil windings in them. Measures are often taken to "short circuit" the voltage spikes that are generated when current to these components is cut off. This usually involves the installation of a **clamping diode** across the coil.

Inductors are used extensively in electronics, especially in radio communications. They are often paired with variable capacitors to make tuning devices and oscillator circuits for radio receivers and transmitters.

Impedance

Electronic circuits that utilize resistors along with capacitors and inductors (RCL circuits) will exhibit a property known as **impedance**. Impedance is the total opposition to the flow of electrical charge. Current flow in such a circuit will inspire reactance on the part of the inductor and the capacitor. High-frequency current will increase the inductive reactance, where low-frequency current will cause capacitive reactance to rise. The resistor, on the other hand, is frequency-independent and will always present the same opposition to the current flow, whether it is AC or DC.

A series circuit of a capacitor, resistor, and inductor will vary in its impedance depending on the frequency of the current flowing in the circuit. DC current will not flow through a capacitor, so the capacitive reactance is high and thus circuit impedance is high. High frequency AC will not flow through an inductor, so inductive reactance is high and circuit impedance is high.

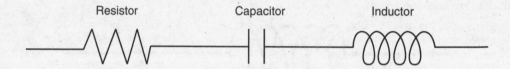

Figure 17. Series RCL circuit

Somewhere between these two extremes lies a point called the **resonance frequency**. This is the AC signal frequency at which the inductive and capacitive reactance of the circuit cancel, leaving only the circuit resistance to impede the flow of current. This is the principle by which radio tuners work. An inductor/capacitor combination will have a resonance frequency that allows signals of that same frequency to pass easily, but will present high impedance to frequencies outside of that.

Semiconductors

The term **semiconductor** refers to an element that has four electrons in its valence shell. Since the bonds between these four electrons and the nucleus are somewhat strong, these elements are neither good conductors nor good insulators. Elements that are widely recognized as semiconductors are **silicon** and **germanium**.

In their pure form, silicon and germanium are not particularly useful. However, when impurities are added to their crystalline structure in a process called **doping**, a whole new world of possibilities spring forth.

The crystalline structure of pure silicon is very stable. The four valence electrons in each silicon atom bond with the valence electrons in the atoms around it, so no free electrons exist to allow current flow. This can be changed by "doping" the silicon's crystal structure with either phosphorous, arsenic, or antimony. Since these elements all have five electrons in their valence shell, they will bond themselves to the other silicon atoms, but leave one free electron that is able to migrate throughout the crystal. This changes the silicon crystal into an **N-type** material. This new material is still electrically neutral, but is able to conduct electricity due to the presence of free electrons.

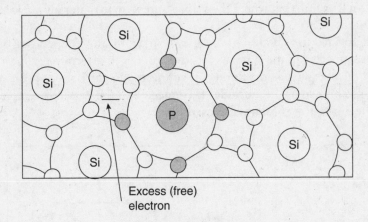

Excess (free) electron

Figure 18. N-type material

If silicon is doped with elements that have three electrons in their valence shells (such as boron or indium), the result is a "**hole**" being left where an electron would normally reside in the crystalline structure. These holes can also migrate throughout the crystal. This takes place as an electron moves into a hole, thus creating a hole in the spot it previously occupied. As electrons flow in one direction, holes will flow in the opposite direction. **P-type** material is thus noted for its ability to conduct current by the movement of holes.

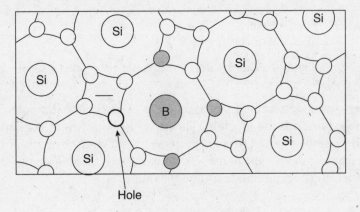

Hole

Figure 19. P-type material

Diodes

P-type and N-type materials can do little by themselves. When they are joined together in **junctions**, however, the real magic begins. When a P-type material is joined with an N-type material, a **diode** is created. A diode is an electrical one-way valve. Current can pass easily in one direction, but is blocked in the opposite direction. The reason this happens is because of what takes place at the junction where the P-type and N-type materials are joined.

If a battery is connected to a diode, current may or may not flow, depending on which ends of the diode are connected to the battery's positive and negative terminals. For instance, if the P-type material (also known as the **anode***)* is connected to the battery positive and the N-type material (also known as the **cathode**) is connected to the battery negative, current will flow through the diode as it is **forward-biased**.

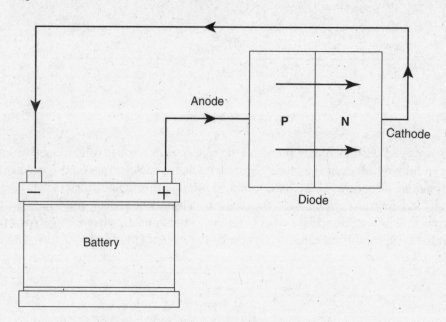

Figure 20. Current flow through a diode (forward bias)

Since the battery's positive terminal has a shortage of electrons, the holes in the P-type material are repelled towards the junction. The excess of electrons at the battery's negative terminal repels the free electrons in the N-type material and sends them towards the junction as well. The electrons in the N-type material then cross over the junction to fill the holes in the P-type material, and current flows through the diode.

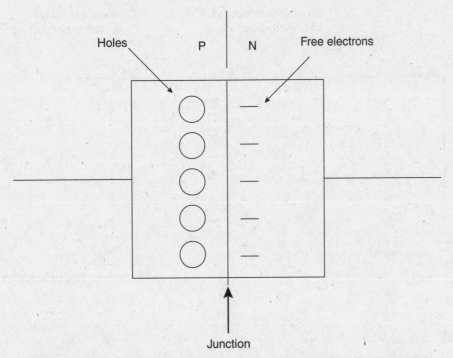

Figure 21. Electrons and holes move towards the junction (forward bias)

Reversing the diode's connection to the battery creates a new set of conditions. Connecting the P-type material to the battery negative will cause the holes to move away from the junction, as they are attracted to the excess electrons at the negative terminal. The N-type material's free electrons also move away from the junction, since they are attracted to the opposite charge on the battery's positive terminal. Since the holes and electrons have both moved away from the junction, no electron transfer takes place there and current flow stops. The diode is now in a **reverse-bias** condition.

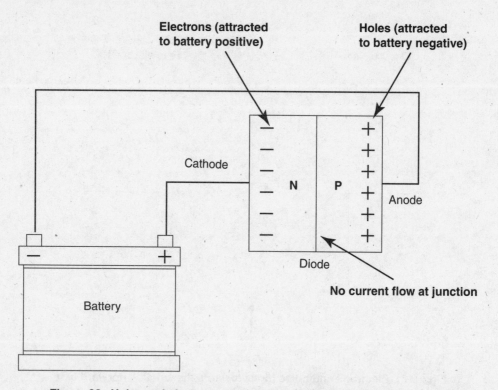

Figure 22. Holes and electrons moving away from the junction (reverse bias)

The most common application for diodes is **rectification**. Rectification is the conversion of AC into DC. Four diodes can be connected in a diamond configuration to create a **full-wave rectifier**, which is the foundation for most DC power supplies. Diodes are also used for rectification in automotive alternators, where generated AC is converted into DC to be used in the vehicle electrical system.

Zener Diodes

Diodes are rated according to the maximum amount of current that can flow in the forward-bias direction without damaging them. They also are rated according to their **peak inverse voltage** (**PIV**), which is the maximum amount of voltage that can be withstood in the reverse-bias direction. If this peak inverse voltage rating is exceeded, the diode can be permanently damaged.

Zener diodes are made to operate with a reverse bias current whose voltage exceeds the rating of the diode. In other words, reverse bias current will not flow through a zener diode until it reaches a certain threshold voltage. At that point, the zener diode "breaks down" and allows current to flow in the reverse direction, without damage to the diode. Once the voltage drops below the zener's rating, it will go back to normal diode operation and prevent reverse-bias current from flowing.

Figure 23. Zener diode symbol

Zener diodes are often used for voltage regulation, as well as for controlling high voltage spikes that can damage delicate electronic equipment.

Transistors

The transistor is one of the most important inventions of all time. A transistor is versatile, as it can be used as an electrical switch, an amplifier, or a current regulator. Since there are no moving parts in a transistor and it is made from solid silicon, it is known as a **solid state device**, which makes it very reliable. It is also very compact in its design, as thousands of transistors can fit into a single **integrated circuit** (**IC**).

Prior to the introduction of the transistor, much of its work was performed by **vacuum tubes**. Tubes, as they were called, were bulky and consumed a lot of energy as they gave off tremendous amounts of heat. They were also very slow to warm up, so it would often be several minutes before a tube-type radio or TV was in operation after it had been switched on.

The transistor has made all but the highest power applications of vacuum tubes obsolete, save for one. **CRT** (**cathode ray tube**) computer and TV screens are based on vacuum tube technology and are still in common use. The CRT is rapidly becoming obsolete as well as it is being replaced by flat displays utilizing **LCD** (**liquid crystal display**) technology.

Transistors are constructed in a similar fashion to diodes in that they are made up of junctions of P-type and N-type material. However, they are slightly more complex than a diode because they are made up of three separate pieces of semiconductor material that are joined to create two junctions inside the transistor.

There are two types of transistors: an **NPN transistor**, and a **PNP transistor**. An NPN transistor is made up of a thin piece of P-type material sandwiched between two pieces of N-type material. A PNP transistor is the opposite: two pieces of P-type material that have a piece of N-type material between them.

Follow the Arrows

The key to remembering which symbol identifies which kind of transistor is that the arrow always points to the N-type material.

Inside the transistor, wires connect to the three pieces of semiconductor material. Each piece is given a name. The middle piece is always called the **base**; the two outside pieces are called the **collector** and the **emitter**. The symbol for the transistor has an arrow that identifies the emitter. The direction of the arrow tells us what type of transistor it is. The key to remembering which symbol identifies which type of transistor is that the arrow always points in the direction of the N-type material.

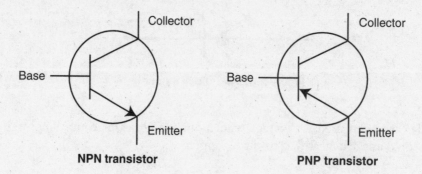

NPN transistor   **PNP transistor**

Figure 24. Symbols for NPN and PNP transistors

The transistor works by using a small amount of current to control a large amount of current. In the case of an NPN transistor, a positive voltage applied to the base will "turn on" the transistor and allow a relatively large current to flow from the collector to the emitter. The moment the positive voltage is removed from the base, the transistor turns off and stops the current flow.

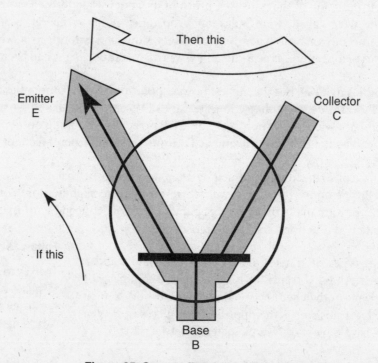

Figure 25. Current flow in an NPN transistor

PNP transistors work in an opposite way than do NPN transistors. A PNP transistor requires a negative voltage at the base to turn it on, and the current then flows from the emitter to the collector (conventional current theory).

If the signal applied to the base is rapidly switching on and off, the transistor can "mirror" this signal with a much larger current flow between the collector and emitter. This makes a transistor very useful for handling **digital signals**, which are "on-off" type signals.

A constantly varying signal can also be **amplified** by most transistors. As current flow increases between the base and the emitter, current flow will also increase between the collector and emitter, up to a point called **saturation**. The **gain** of the transistor is the ratio between the collector-emitter current and the base-emitter current. A high-gain transistor is one that amplifies a signal to a greater degree. It is common for transistors to exhibit gains of anywhere between 100 and 200.

For increased gain, two transistors can be connected in a configuration called a **Darlington pair**, named after its inventor, Sidney Darlington. This allows a very small current to control a very large current. This type of circuit is very common in automotive and other electronic applications.

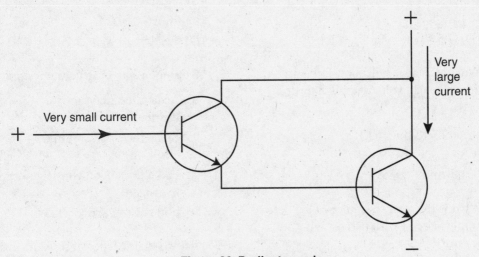

Figure 26. Darlington pair

There is a small amount of voltage drop that takes place across a diode or transistor, so heat is generated by these components. In small current applications, this heat is kept to a minimum so no special measures need to be taken to cool them. As current increases, however, more heat is generated and can reach the point where it will damage the junctions between the N-type and P-type materials. In these applications, transistors are kept cool using **heat sinks**, which are constructed to increase the surface area of the transistor case and enhance heat dissipation. Heat sinks are normally made from aluminum, which has excellent heat transfer properties.

In places where the size of the heat sink is limited, a cooling fan is often utilized. Nowhere is this more critical than in a CPU (central processing unit) of a personal computer. Without heat sinks and cooling fans, computer chips would soon self-destruct due to excessive heat build up.

ELECTRONICS INFORMATION PRACTICE SET

1. How much current will flow in a circuit that has 60 mV applied to a 15 KΩ resistance?

   (A) 0.004 mA
   (B) 0.9 A
   (C) 4.0 A
   (D) 900 A

2. What voltage is required for 30 A to flow through a 60 KΩ resistance?

   (A) 1800 V
   (B) 1.8 KV
   (C) 18 KV
   (D) 1.8 MV

3. What resistance will allow 2 mA to flow when 25 volts is applied to it?

   (A) 12.5 Ω
   (B) 12.5 KΩ
   (C) 12,500 Ω
   (D) B and C are correct

4. What is the total resistance of a parallel circuit with two 6-ohm resistors?

   (A) 1 ohm
   (B) 2 ohms
   (C) 3 ohms
   (D) 12 ohms

5. What is the total resistance of a parallel circuit with three 6-ohm resistors?

   (A) 1 ohm
   (B) 2 ohms
   (C) 3 ohms
   (D) 18 ohms

6. What is the total resistance of a parallel circuit with two 6-ohm resistors and a 12-ohm resistor?

   (A) 1 ohm
   (B) 2 ohms
   (C) 2.4 ohms
   (D) 24 ohms

7. A circuit with flowing current in it is considered

   (A) open
   (B) closed
   (C) short
   (D) dead

8. "Doping" a silicon structure is done to

   (A) make the silicon into another element
   (B) make the silicon conduct electricity
   (C) make the silicon cling tighter to hydrogen
   (D) none of the above

9. The two major types of resistors today are the fixed resistor and

   (A) the neutral resistor
   (B) the passive resistor
   (C) the diode resistor
   (D) the variable resistor

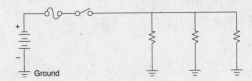

Ground

10. The electrical system pictured above is known as a

    (A) coil-wrought electrical system
    (B) one-wire electrical system
    (C) parallel-series
    (D) none of the above

11. Direct current (DC) flows _____ in a conductor.

    (A) two ways
    (B) backwards
    (C) one way
    (D) answers B and C only

ANSWERS AND EXPLANATIONS FOR ELECTRONICS INFORMATION PRACTICE SET

1. A

To solve this problem, the first step is to convert 60 mV to V. Moving the decimal point three places to the left, this yields 0.060 V. Next, convert 15 KΩ to Ω. When the decimal point is moved three places to the right, this becomes 15,000 Ω. Since current is the unknown, the formula needed to finish the calculation is $I = E \div R$. Dividing 0.060 by 15,000 gives 0.000004 amperes. This can be converted to 0.004 mA.

2. D

Like the last problem, this one requires you to first convert the given measurements. Take the resistance and move the decimal. 60 KΩ becomes 60,000 Ω. Using our formula for calculating voltage, $E = I \times R$, we get 30 A × 60,000 Ω = 1,800,000 V, or 1.8 MV.

3. D

Calculating resistance is easy if you know the formula ($R = E \div I$) and can easily convert the factors in your equation. In this case, 2 mA should be converted to .002 A. The resistance comes out to be 25 V divided by .002 A, or 12,500 Ω of resistance. Note that the answer is tricky, as answer (B), 12.5KΩ, is just a shortened way of saying 12,500Ω. (B) and (C) are both correct, and the answer is therefore (D).

4. C

You must use the formula $R_{Total} = (R_1 \times R_2) \div (R_1 + R_2)$ to correctly calculate total resistance. If you have two 6-ohm resistors in a parallel circuit, then you have (6 × 6) divided by (6 + 6), which equals 3. The total resistance is 3 ohms.

5. B

Using the formula for finding total resistance of parallel circuits with three resistors, $\frac{1}{R_{Total}} = \frac{1}{R_1} + \frac{1}{R_2} + \frac{1}{R_3}$, you see that $\frac{1}{6} + \frac{1}{6} + \frac{1}{6} = \frac{3}{6}$ or $\frac{1}{2} = \frac{1}{R}$, therefore R=2.

6. C

The same formula rules apply for multiple resistor parallel circuits. $\frac{1}{R_{Total}} = \frac{1}{R_1} + \frac{1}{R_2} + \frac{1}{R_3}$ becomes $\frac{1}{R} = \frac{1}{6} + \frac{1}{6} + \frac{1}{12}$ or $\frac{5}{12}$. Since $\frac{1}{R} = \frac{5}{12}$, R = 2.4. Thus, the total resistance in this case is 2.4 ohms.

7. B

A closed circuit has continuity, and will allow current to flow in it.

8. B

The crystalline structure of pure silicon is very stable. The four valence electrons in each silicon atom bond with the valence electrons in the atoms around it, so no free electrons exist to allow current flow. This can be changed by "doping" the silicon's crystal structure with either phosphorous, arsenic, or antimony. Since these elements all have five electrons in their valence shell, they will bond themselves to the other silicon atoms, but leave one free electron that is able to migrate throughout the crystal. This allows the silicon to conduct current. Thus, the correct answer is (B).

9. D

The two major types of resistors used today are the fixed resistor and the variable resistor.

10. B

In the illustration, only one wire must run to the component from the battery positive, and the component's negative wire is connected to the chassis. This is known as a *one-wire electrical system*, and it is the system that is used on every vehicle built today.

11. C

Direct current (DC) means that current only flows one way in a conductor. This is the type of current in circuits powered by batteries.

CHAPTER TWELVE

Assembling Objects

INTRODUCTION

After sticking with same basic format for many years, the ASVAB has undergone several key changes recently. In addition to removing two previously used sections (Coding Speed, Numerical Operations) from all versions of the ASVAB, the test-makers also decided to introduce a new test section called Assembling Objects.

Unlike most of the other sections on the ASVAB, this is not a test of skills that you can really learn in advance. If it seems a bit like a psychological test (like a Rorschach ink blot test), that's because it is supposed to. While some tests are meant to measure someone's aptitude in concrete, quantifiable skills (such as algebra or vocabulary), others, like Assembling Objects, attempt to measure one's spatial and problem-solving abilities. This section is ultimately designed to see whether you can construct or reconstruct a series of objects based solely on eyeing the material.

Don't stress about it, though. Just as those verbal whizzes get through the math sections and the masters of algebra make it past word knowledge, everyone will get through the ASVAB Assembling Objects section by getting more familiar with the questions and their solutions.

WHAT WE KNOW

The makers of the ASVAB are fairly tight-lipped about their tests, but we know a few things about the new Assembling Objects section. There will be 16 questions total and you will have 9 minutes to complete them all. While this section is currently only required on the CAT (computer) version of the ASVAB, it is likely that it will appear on the paper-and-pencil version in the not too distant future.

There Are Two Distinct Types of Assembling Objects Questions: Shapes and Connectors

Shapes questions give you a series of seemingly incongruent shapes and ask you to configure them mentally into a single, unified shape. These are really just glorified puzzles. If you are good at geometry, you'll most likely be good at these questions, too. For some people, spatial questions are a breeze. For these people, shapes and arrangements just appear logically. But not everyone will find these questions quite so easy, especially when they are timed.

Let's take a look at an example to get a feel for what Shapes questions are like.

Shapes Questions

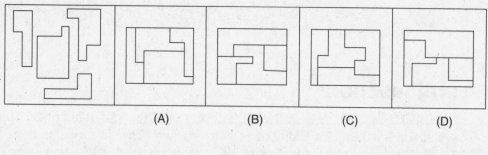

(A)   (B)   (C)   (D)

Sample 1

You can see that all four answer choices at first glance look pretty similar. Your best bet is to pick one shape from the initial box and to compare it quickly to the four choices to see if you can quickly eliminate a choice. The shape in the middle, which looks a bit like the state of Utah, is a good one. Quickly scanning all four answer choices, only (A) and (D) have this shape present. Therefore you can easily dismiss two of the choices. Next, just do the same with another shape. Picking the smallest shape at the bottom, you can see that only the shapes in (A) correspond to the original given shapes. Thus, (A) is the correct answer choice.

Not too bad, right?

Or maybe it didn't seem this easy to you. Maybe your brain is wired for different types of questions. So, how to approach this sort of strange looking question? Try to think of it as a game.

First, think about real objects with these shapes and how they fit together. Two halves of a square sandwich cut diagonally make triangles, right? Or think about the way a pizza is cut by straight lines, leaving smaller, individual round-edged triangles. Even a pyramid can be broken up into several smaller triangles. Keep these sorts of real life images in your head because Shapes questions are easily solved if you just think creatively.

Connectors Questions

Connectors objects questions work more like the directions to the gas grill your uncle tried to put together. The questions show you two shapes and a straight line with labeled points on them. Your job is to imagine how the line correctly connects the two shapes. Take a look at the sample below.

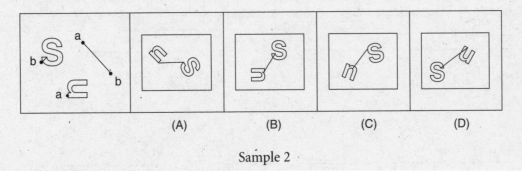

Sample 2

Pretty straightforward, right?

All you really have to do is pay attention to the placement of the various points and don't get caught up in how the shapes move around. The real key to the answer—B in this case—lies in the placement of the points and their relationship to the line given.

No Reason to Fear

There is no reason to fear ASVAB Assembling Objects. Just familiarize yourself as much as possible with the way these odd questions look and practice the skills above as much as possible. Try your hand at a few practice questions and then check the answers to see how you did. Remember, there is no real way to study for the Assembling Objects portion of the ASVAB. All you can do is prepare yourself for how the questions look so that you'll never be surprised.

ASSEMBLING OBJECTS PRACTICE SET

1.

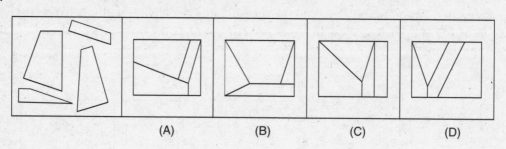

             (A)   (B)   (C)   (D)

2.

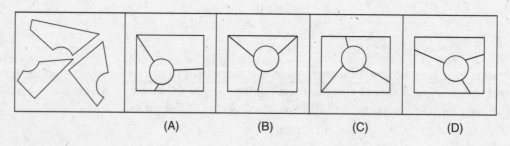

             (A)   (B)   (C)   (D)

3.

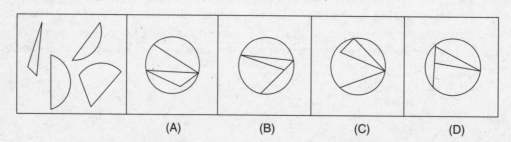

             (A)   (B)   (C)   (D)

4.

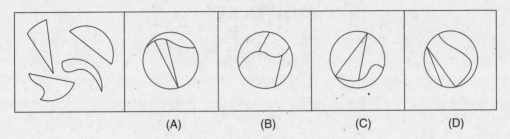

5.

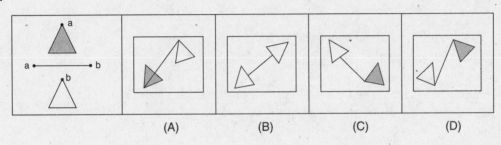

ASSEMBLING OBJECTS PRACTICE SET
ANSWER KEY

1. A

2. C

3. B

4. C

5. D

Part Four

ASVAB PRACTICE TESTS

ASVAB Practice Test II

ANSWER SHEET

Part 1: General Science (GS)

1 Ⓐ Ⓑ Ⓒ Ⓓ	6 Ⓐ Ⓑ Ⓒ Ⓓ	11 Ⓐ Ⓑ Ⓒ Ⓓ	16 Ⓐ Ⓑ Ⓒ Ⓓ	21 Ⓐ Ⓑ Ⓒ Ⓓ
2 Ⓐ Ⓑ Ⓒ Ⓓ	7 Ⓐ Ⓑ Ⓒ Ⓓ	12 Ⓐ Ⓑ Ⓒ Ⓓ	17 Ⓐ Ⓑ Ⓒ Ⓓ	22 Ⓐ Ⓑ Ⓒ Ⓓ
3 Ⓐ Ⓑ Ⓒ Ⓓ	8 Ⓐ Ⓑ Ⓒ Ⓓ	13 Ⓐ Ⓑ Ⓒ Ⓓ	18 Ⓐ Ⓑ Ⓒ Ⓓ	23 Ⓐ Ⓑ Ⓒ Ⓓ
4 Ⓐ Ⓑ Ⓒ Ⓓ	9 Ⓐ Ⓑ Ⓒ Ⓓ	14 Ⓐ Ⓑ Ⓒ Ⓓ	19 Ⓐ Ⓑ Ⓒ Ⓓ	24 Ⓐ Ⓑ Ⓒ Ⓓ
5 Ⓐ Ⓑ Ⓒ Ⓓ	10 Ⓐ Ⓑ Ⓒ Ⓓ	15 Ⓐ Ⓑ Ⓒ Ⓓ	20 Ⓐ Ⓑ Ⓒ Ⓓ	25 Ⓐ Ⓑ Ⓒ Ⓓ

Part 2: Arithmetic Reasoning (AR)

1 Ⓐ Ⓑ Ⓒ Ⓓ	7 Ⓐ Ⓑ Ⓒ Ⓓ	13 Ⓐ Ⓑ Ⓒ Ⓓ	19 Ⓐ Ⓑ Ⓒ Ⓓ	25 Ⓐ Ⓑ Ⓒ Ⓓ
2 Ⓐ Ⓑ Ⓒ Ⓓ	8 Ⓐ Ⓑ Ⓒ Ⓓ	14 Ⓐ Ⓑ Ⓒ Ⓓ	20 Ⓐ Ⓑ Ⓒ Ⓓ	26 Ⓐ Ⓑ Ⓒ Ⓓ
3 Ⓐ Ⓑ Ⓒ Ⓓ	9 Ⓐ Ⓑ Ⓒ Ⓓ	15 Ⓐ Ⓑ Ⓒ Ⓓ	21 Ⓐ Ⓑ Ⓒ Ⓓ	27 Ⓐ Ⓑ Ⓒ Ⓓ
4 Ⓐ Ⓑ Ⓒ Ⓓ	10 Ⓐ Ⓑ Ⓒ Ⓓ	16 Ⓐ Ⓑ Ⓒ Ⓓ	22 Ⓐ Ⓑ Ⓒ Ⓓ	28 Ⓐ Ⓑ Ⓒ Ⓓ
5 Ⓐ Ⓑ Ⓒ Ⓓ	11 Ⓐ Ⓑ Ⓒ Ⓓ	17 Ⓐ Ⓑ Ⓒ Ⓓ	23 Ⓐ Ⓑ Ⓒ Ⓓ	29 Ⓐ Ⓑ Ⓒ Ⓓ
6 Ⓐ Ⓑ Ⓒ Ⓓ	12 Ⓐ Ⓑ Ⓒ Ⓓ	18 Ⓐ Ⓑ Ⓒ Ⓓ	24 Ⓐ Ⓑ Ⓒ Ⓓ	30 Ⓐ Ⓑ Ⓒ Ⓓ

Part 3: Word Knowledge (WK)

1 Ⓐ Ⓑ Ⓒ Ⓓ	8 Ⓐ Ⓑ Ⓒ Ⓓ	15 Ⓐ Ⓑ Ⓒ Ⓓ	22 Ⓐ Ⓑ Ⓒ Ⓓ	29 Ⓐ Ⓑ Ⓒ Ⓓ
2 Ⓐ Ⓑ Ⓒ Ⓓ	9 Ⓐ Ⓑ Ⓒ Ⓓ	16 Ⓐ Ⓑ Ⓒ Ⓓ	23 Ⓐ Ⓑ Ⓒ Ⓓ	30 Ⓐ Ⓑ Ⓒ Ⓓ
3 Ⓐ Ⓑ Ⓒ Ⓓ	10 Ⓐ Ⓑ Ⓒ Ⓓ	17 Ⓐ Ⓑ Ⓒ Ⓓ	24 Ⓐ Ⓑ Ⓒ Ⓓ	31 Ⓐ Ⓑ Ⓒ Ⓓ
4 Ⓐ Ⓑ Ⓒ Ⓓ	11 Ⓐ Ⓑ Ⓒ Ⓓ	18 Ⓐ Ⓑ Ⓒ Ⓓ	25 Ⓐ Ⓑ Ⓒ Ⓓ	32 Ⓐ Ⓑ Ⓒ Ⓓ
5 Ⓐ Ⓑ Ⓒ Ⓓ	12 Ⓐ Ⓑ Ⓒ Ⓓ	19 Ⓐ Ⓑ Ⓒ Ⓓ	26 Ⓐ Ⓑ Ⓒ Ⓓ	33 Ⓐ Ⓑ Ⓒ Ⓓ
6 Ⓐ Ⓑ Ⓒ Ⓓ	13 Ⓐ Ⓑ Ⓒ Ⓓ	20 Ⓐ Ⓑ Ⓒ Ⓓ	27 Ⓐ Ⓑ Ⓒ Ⓓ	34 Ⓐ Ⓑ Ⓒ Ⓓ
7 Ⓐ Ⓑ Ⓒ Ⓓ	14 Ⓐ Ⓑ Ⓒ Ⓓ	21 Ⓐ Ⓑ Ⓒ Ⓓ	28 Ⓐ Ⓑ Ⓒ Ⓓ	35 Ⓐ Ⓑ Ⓒ Ⓓ

Part 4: Paragraph Comprehension (PC)

1 Ⓐ Ⓑ Ⓒ Ⓓ	4 Ⓐ Ⓑ Ⓒ Ⓓ	7 Ⓐ Ⓑ Ⓒ Ⓓ	10 Ⓐ Ⓑ Ⓒ Ⓓ	13 Ⓐ Ⓑ Ⓒ Ⓓ
2 Ⓐ Ⓑ Ⓒ Ⓓ	5 Ⓐ Ⓑ Ⓒ Ⓓ	8 Ⓐ Ⓑ Ⓒ Ⓓ	11 Ⓐ Ⓑ Ⓒ Ⓓ	14 Ⓐ Ⓑ Ⓒ Ⓓ
3 Ⓐ Ⓑ Ⓒ Ⓓ	6 Ⓐ Ⓑ Ⓒ Ⓓ	9 Ⓐ Ⓑ Ⓒ Ⓓ	12 Ⓐ Ⓑ Ⓒ Ⓓ	15 Ⓐ Ⓑ Ⓒ Ⓓ

Part 5: Automotive and Shop Information (AS)

1 Ⓐ Ⓑ Ⓒ Ⓓ	6 Ⓐ Ⓑ Ⓒ Ⓓ	11 Ⓐ Ⓑ Ⓒ Ⓓ	16 Ⓐ Ⓑ Ⓒ Ⓓ	21 Ⓐ Ⓑ Ⓒ Ⓓ
2 Ⓐ Ⓑ Ⓒ Ⓓ	7 Ⓐ Ⓑ Ⓒ Ⓓ	12 Ⓐ Ⓑ Ⓒ Ⓓ	17 Ⓐ Ⓑ Ⓒ Ⓓ	22 Ⓐ Ⓑ Ⓒ Ⓓ
3 Ⓐ Ⓑ Ⓒ Ⓓ	8 Ⓐ Ⓑ Ⓒ Ⓓ	13 Ⓐ Ⓑ Ⓒ Ⓓ	18 Ⓐ Ⓑ Ⓒ Ⓓ	23 Ⓐ Ⓑ Ⓒ Ⓓ
4 Ⓐ Ⓑ Ⓒ Ⓓ	9 Ⓐ Ⓑ Ⓒ Ⓓ	14 Ⓐ Ⓑ Ⓒ Ⓓ	19 Ⓐ Ⓑ Ⓒ Ⓓ	24 Ⓐ Ⓑ Ⓒ Ⓓ
5 Ⓐ Ⓑ Ⓒ Ⓓ	10 Ⓐ Ⓑ Ⓒ Ⓓ	15 Ⓐ Ⓑ Ⓒ Ⓓ	20 Ⓐ Ⓑ Ⓒ Ⓓ	25 Ⓐ Ⓑ Ⓒ Ⓓ

ANSWER SHEET

Part 6: Mathematics Knowledge (MK)

1 Ⓐ Ⓑ Ⓒ Ⓓ	6 Ⓐ Ⓑ Ⓒ Ⓓ	11 Ⓐ Ⓑ Ⓒ Ⓓ	16 Ⓐ Ⓑ Ⓒ Ⓓ	21 Ⓐ Ⓑ Ⓒ Ⓓ
2 Ⓐ Ⓑ Ⓒ Ⓓ	7 Ⓐ Ⓑ Ⓒ Ⓓ	12 Ⓐ Ⓑ Ⓒ Ⓓ	17 Ⓐ Ⓑ Ⓒ Ⓓ	22 Ⓐ Ⓑ Ⓒ Ⓓ
3 Ⓐ Ⓑ Ⓒ Ⓓ	8 Ⓐ Ⓑ Ⓒ Ⓓ	13 Ⓐ Ⓑ Ⓒ Ⓓ	18 Ⓐ Ⓑ Ⓒ Ⓓ	23 Ⓐ Ⓑ Ⓒ Ⓓ
4 Ⓐ Ⓑ Ⓒ Ⓓ	9 Ⓐ Ⓑ Ⓒ Ⓓ	14 Ⓐ Ⓑ Ⓒ Ⓓ	19 Ⓐ Ⓑ Ⓒ Ⓓ	24 Ⓐ Ⓑ Ⓒ Ⓓ
5 Ⓐ Ⓑ Ⓒ Ⓓ	10 Ⓐ Ⓑ Ⓒ Ⓓ	15 Ⓐ Ⓑ Ⓒ Ⓓ	20 Ⓐ Ⓑ Ⓒ Ⓓ	25 Ⓐ Ⓑ Ⓒ Ⓓ

Part 7: Mechanical Comprehension (MC)

1 Ⓐ Ⓑ Ⓒ Ⓓ	6 Ⓐ Ⓑ Ⓒ Ⓓ	11 Ⓐ Ⓑ Ⓒ Ⓓ	16 Ⓐ Ⓑ Ⓒ Ⓓ	21 Ⓐ Ⓑ Ⓒ Ⓓ
2 Ⓐ Ⓑ Ⓒ Ⓓ	7 Ⓐ Ⓑ Ⓒ Ⓓ	12 Ⓐ Ⓑ Ⓒ Ⓓ	17 Ⓐ Ⓑ Ⓒ Ⓓ	22 Ⓐ Ⓑ Ⓒ Ⓓ
3 Ⓐ Ⓑ Ⓒ Ⓓ	8 Ⓐ Ⓑ Ⓒ Ⓓ	13 Ⓐ Ⓑ Ⓒ Ⓓ	18 Ⓐ Ⓑ Ⓒ Ⓓ	23 Ⓐ Ⓑ Ⓒ Ⓓ
4 Ⓐ Ⓑ Ⓒ Ⓓ	9 Ⓐ Ⓑ Ⓒ Ⓓ	14 Ⓐ Ⓑ Ⓒ Ⓓ	19 Ⓐ Ⓑ Ⓒ Ⓓ	24 Ⓐ Ⓑ Ⓒ Ⓓ
5 Ⓐ Ⓑ Ⓒ Ⓓ	10 Ⓐ Ⓑ Ⓒ Ⓓ	15 Ⓐ Ⓑ Ⓒ Ⓓ	20 Ⓐ Ⓑ Ⓒ Ⓓ	25 Ⓐ Ⓑ Ⓒ Ⓓ

Part 8: Electronics Information (EI)

1 Ⓐ Ⓑ Ⓒ Ⓓ	5 Ⓐ Ⓑ Ⓒ Ⓓ	9 Ⓐ Ⓑ Ⓒ Ⓓ	13 Ⓐ Ⓑ Ⓒ Ⓓ	17 Ⓐ Ⓑ Ⓒ Ⓓ
2 Ⓐ Ⓑ Ⓒ Ⓓ	6 Ⓐ Ⓑ Ⓒ Ⓓ	10 Ⓐ Ⓑ Ⓒ Ⓓ	14 Ⓐ Ⓑ Ⓒ Ⓓ	18 Ⓐ Ⓑ Ⓒ Ⓓ
3 Ⓐ Ⓑ Ⓒ Ⓓ	7 Ⓐ Ⓑ Ⓒ Ⓓ	11 Ⓐ Ⓑ Ⓒ Ⓓ	15 Ⓐ Ⓑ Ⓒ Ⓓ	19 Ⓐ Ⓑ Ⓒ Ⓓ
4 Ⓐ Ⓑ Ⓒ Ⓓ	8 Ⓐ Ⓑ Ⓒ Ⓓ	12 Ⓐ Ⓑ Ⓒ Ⓓ	16 Ⓐ Ⓑ Ⓒ Ⓓ	20 Ⓐ Ⓑ Ⓒ Ⓓ

Part 9: Assembling Objects (AO)

1 Ⓐ Ⓑ Ⓒ Ⓓ	5 Ⓐ Ⓑ Ⓒ Ⓓ	9 Ⓐ Ⓑ Ⓒ Ⓓ	13 Ⓐ Ⓑ Ⓒ Ⓓ
2 Ⓐ Ⓑ Ⓒ Ⓓ	6 Ⓐ Ⓑ Ⓒ Ⓓ	10 Ⓐ Ⓑ Ⓒ Ⓓ	14 Ⓐ Ⓑ Ⓒ Ⓓ
3 Ⓐ Ⓑ Ⓒ Ⓓ	7 Ⓐ Ⓑ Ⓒ Ⓓ	11 Ⓐ Ⓑ Ⓒ Ⓓ	15 Ⓐ Ⓑ Ⓒ Ⓓ
4 Ⓐ Ⓑ Ⓒ Ⓓ	8 Ⓐ Ⓑ Ⓒ Ⓓ	12 Ⓐ Ⓑ Ⓒ Ⓓ	16 Ⓐ Ⓑ Ⓒ Ⓓ

PART 1: GENERAL SCIENCE (GS)

Time: 11 minutes; 25 questions

<u>Directions</u>: In this section, you will be tested on your knowledge of concepts in science generally reviewed in high school. For each question, select the best answer and mark the corresponding oval on your answer sheet.

1. Which of the following vitamins is considered essential to the promotion of good eyesight?

    (A) Vitamin A
    (B) Vitamin B
    (C) Vitamin C
    (D) Vitamin D

2. Orbiting around the nucleus of an atom are

    (A) anions
    (B) electrons
    (C) positrons
    (D) photons

3. Air is warmed and filtered first in the

    (A) trachea
    (B) pharynx
    (C) oral cavity
    (D) nasal cavity

4. Which of the following is an example of a tertiary consumer?

    (A) antelope
    (B) house cat
    (C) polar bear
    (D) vulture

5. Which material is a substance?

    (A) air
    (B) water
    (C) fire
    (D) earth

6. The moon's mass is about one-sixth of the earth's mass. Compared to the gravitational force the earth exerts on the moon, the gravitational force the moon exerts on the earth is

    (A) one-sixth as much
    (B) one-half as much
    (C) the same
    (D) six times as much

7. Fungi are organisms that break down dead matter and return the organic material back into the environment for reuse. They are examples of

    (A) producers
    (B) decomposers
    (C) consumers
    (D) mutualism

8. In degrees Kelvin, the freezing pointing of water is

    (A) −273°
    (B) 0°
    (C) 100°
    (D) 273°

9. Tough elastic tissues found in the joints that connect bones to bones are called

    (A) ligaments
    (B) tendons
    (C) cartilage
    (D) muscles

10. Stress, a poor diet, cigarette smoking, and heredity factors all contribute to individual's developing

    (A) diarrhea
    (B) high blood pressure
    (C) gall stones
    (D) anemia

11. A straw placed in a glass of water appears to be bent or broken. The property of light responsible for the straw appearing to be bent is called

    (A) refraction
    (B) diffraction
    (C) reflection
    (D) interference

12. Fossils are most likely to be found in which of the following types of rock?

    (A) igneous
    (B) metamorphic
    (C) sedimentary
    (D) volcanic

13. Animals that consume plants are called

    (A) saprophytes
    (B) herbivores
    (C) carnivores
    (D) omnivores

14. Which of the following provides the worst insulating material?

    (A) aluminum
    (B) wood
    (C) rubber
    (D) porcelain

15. Marsupial mammals differ from placental mammals in that

    (A) marsupials lay eggs
    (B) marsupial eggs contain very little yolk matter
    (C) marsupial umbilical cords do not contain blood vessels
    (D) marsupials bear premature embryos which complete development in their mothers' pouches

16. Rods and cones are light-sensitive cells inside the eye's

    (A) cornea
    (B) iris
    (C) pupil
    (D) retina

17. A boulder that begins to roll down a hill is an example of an energy conversion from

    (A) potential to thermal
    (B) potential to kinetic
    (C) kinetic to thermal
    (D) kinetic to potential

18. The lowest layer of the earth's atmosphere is called the

    (A) ionosphere
    (B) mesosphere
    (C) stratosphere
    (D) troposphere

19. At high altitudes, the boiling point of water

    (A) is higher than at sea level
    (B) is lower than at sea level
    (C) is the same as at sea level
    (D) cannot be determined

GO ON TO THE NEXT PAGE

20. As an ambulance passes, its pitch seems to change. This perception is best explained by

    (A) convection
    (B) refraction
    (C) the Doppler effect
    (D) momentum

21. All of the following are examples of vertebrates EXCEPT

    (A) turtle
    (B) shark
    (C) ostrich
    (D) octopus

22. Which of the following muscles are controlled by conscious thought?

    (A) smooth
    (B) striated (skeletal)
    (C) cardiac
    (D) all of the above

23. Which of the following is most responsible for oceanic tides?

    (A) the orbit of the earth around its own axis
    (B) the magnetic polarity of the earth
    (C) the orbit of the moon around the earth
    (D) the orbit of the earth around the sun

24. A substance that hastens a chemical reaction without undergoing chemical change itself is called a

    (A) bromide
    (B) catalyst
    (C) oxidizing agent
    (D) reactant

25. Lack of iron is associated with which of the following diseases?

    (A) anemia
    (B) hemophilia
    (C) goiter
    (D) rickets

STOP. IF YOU FINISH BEFORE THE TIME IS UP, YOU MAY CHECK OVER YOUR WORK ON THIS PART ONLY.

PART 2: ARITHMETIC REASONING (AR)

Time: 36 minutes; 30 questions

<u>Directions</u>: In this section, you are tested on your ability to use arithmetic. For each question, select the best answer and mark the corresponding oval on your answer sheet.

1. Three apples cost as much a 4 pears. Three pears cost as much as 2 oranges. How many apples cost as much as 72 oranges?

   (A) 36
   (B) 48
   (C) 64
   (D) 81

2. If 48 of the 60 seats on a bus were occupied, what percent of the seats were not occupied?

   (A) 12%
   (B) 15%
   (C) 20%
   (D) 25%

3. Effin sings for $1,000 an hour. Her rate increases by 50% after midnight. If she sings one night from 8:30 P.M. until 1:00 A.M., how much should she be paid?

   (A) $4,500
   (B) $5,000
   (C) $5,500
   (D) $6,000

4. Fran has a drawer containing 4 black t-shirts, 3 orange t-shirts, and 5 blue t-shirts. If she picks one t-shirt at random from the drawer, what are the chances that it will <u>not</u> be orange?

   (A) $\frac{1}{4}$

   (B) $\frac{1}{3}$

   (C) $\frac{2}{3}$

   (D) $\frac{3}{4}$

5. After a 5-hour flight from Newark, Harry arrives in Denver at 2:30 P.M. If the time in Newark is 2 hours later than the time in Denver, what was the time in Newark when Harry began the flight?

   (A) 10:30 A.M.
   (B) 11:30 A.M.
   (C) 3:30 P.M.
   (D) 5:30 P.M.

6. A full box contains 24 pieces of chocolate. If Doris starts out with 198 pieces of chocolate, how many pieces will she have left over if she fills as many boxes as she can?

   (A) 3
   (B) 6
   (C) 8
   (D) 10

7. If 75 percent of x is 150, what is the value of x?

   (A) 150
   (B) 175
   (C) 200
   (D) 250

8. Rachel's average score after 6 tests is 83. If Rachel earns a score of 97 on the 7th test, what is her new average?

   (A) 85
   (B) 86
   (C) 87
   (D) 88

GO ON TO THE NEXT PAGE

9. A delivery service charges $25.00 per pound for making a delivery. If there is an additional 8% sales tax, what is the cost of delivering an item that weighs $\frac{4}{5}$ of a pound?

(A) $20.00
(B) $21.60
(C) $22.60
(D) $24.00

10. A cake recipe requires $\frac{3}{5}$ of an ounce of vanilla extract. How many cakes can be made using a package containing 60 ounces of vanilla extract?

(A) 48
(B) 80
(C) 96
(D) 100

11. Ed has 100 more dollars than Robert. After Ed spends 20 dollars on groceries, he now has 5 times as much money as Robert. How much money does Robert have?

(A) $16
(B) $20
(C) $24
(D) $30

12. 587 people are traveling by bus for a field trip. If each bus seats 48 people and all of the buses but one are filled to capacity, how many people sit in the unfilled bus?

(A) 37
(B) 36
(C) 12
(D) 11

13. Riley brings 100 cookies to school for her class party. If there are 15 students in the class, including Riley, and there are 25 cookies left after the party, what is the average number of cookies that Riley and her classmates ate?

A. $1\frac{2}{3}$
B. 4
C. 5
D. 6

14. A person 4 feet tall casts a 9-foot shadow at the same time that a nearby tree casts a 21-foot shadow. What is the height of this tree?

(A) 7
(B) $8\frac{1}{2}$
(C) $9\frac{1}{3}$
(D) 10

15. In a group of 25 students, 16 are female. What percent of the group is female?

(A) 16%
(B) 40%
(C) 60%
(D) 64%

16. Phil is making a 40-kilometer canoe trip. If he travels at 30 kilometers per hour for the first 10 kilometers, and then at 15 kilometers per hour for the rest of the trip, how many minutes more will it take him than if he travels the entire trip at 20 kilometers per hour?

(A) 20
(B) 24
(C) 30
(D) 40

GO ON TO THE NEXT PAGE

17. In a certain class, 3 out of 24 students are in student organizations. What is the ratio of students in student organizations to students not in student organizations?

    (A) $\dfrac{1}{8}$

    (B) $\dfrac{1}{7}$

    (C) $\dfrac{1}{6}$

    (D) $\dfrac{1}{4}$

18. In a certain baseball league, each team plays 160 games. After playing half of their games, Team A has won 60 games and team B has won 49 games. If Team A wins half of its remaining games, how many of its remaining games must Team B win to have the same number of wins as Team A at the end of the season?

    (A) 51
    (B) 59
    (C) 60
    (D) 61

19. A vendor bought 10 crates of oranges for a total cost of $80. If he lost 2 of the crates, at what price would he have to sell the remaining crates in order to earn a total profit of 25 percent of the total cost?

    (A) $8.00
    (B) $10.00
    (C) $12.50
    (D) $15.00

20. A machine labels 150 bottles in 20 minutes. At this rate, how many minutes does it take to label 60 bottles?

    (A) 2
    (B) 4
    (C) 6
    (D) 8

21. What is the number of rectangular tiles, each 12 centimeters by 18 centimeters, needed to completely cover four flat rectangular surfaces, each 60 centimeters by 180 centimeters?

    (A) 50
    (B) 100
    (C) 200
    (D) 400

22. If a kilogram is equal to approximately 2.2 pounds, which of the following is the best approximation of the number of kilograms in one pound?

    (A) $\dfrac{5}{11}$

    (B) $\dfrac{3}{7}$

    (C) $\dfrac{3}{8}$

    (D) $\dfrac{1}{3}$

23. Two hot dogs and a soda cost $3.25. If three hot dogs and a soda cost $4.50, what is the cost of two sodas?

    (A) $0.75
    (B) $1.25
    (C) $1.50
    (D) $2.50

24. Danielle drives from her home to the store at an average speed of 40 miles per hour. She returns home along the same route at an average speed of 60 miles per hour. What is her average speed, in miles per hour, for the entire trip?

    (A) 48
    (B) 50
    (C) 52
    (D) 55

GO ON TO THE NEXT PAGE

25. At a certain school the ratio of teachers to students is 1 to 10. Which of the following could be the total number of teachers and students?

    (A) 100
    (B) 121
    (C) 222
    (D) 1,011

26. The average of two numbers is equal to twice the positive difference between the two numbers. If the larger number is 35, what is the smaller number?

    (A) 9
    (B) 15
    (C) 21
    (D) 27

27. Each of seven runners on a relay team must run a distance of 1.27 kilometers. Approximately what is the total combined number of kilometers run by the team in the race?

    (A) 11
    (B) 10
    (C) 9
    (D) 8

28. A certain room measures 18 feet by 24 feet. What is the square yardage of a wall-to-wall carpet that covers the floor of the room?

    (A) 24 square yards
    (B) 32 square yards
    (C) 42 square yards
    (D) 48 square yards

29. An employee's net pay is equal to gross pay minus total deductions. A certain employee's gross pay is $1,769.23 and his deductions are as follows: FICA, $218.99; Social Security, $107.05; Medicare, $25.03; state tax, $68.65; municipal tax, $42.75. What is the employee's net pay?

    (A) $1,306.76
    (B) $1,306.66
    (C) $1,305.76
    (D) $1,305.66

30. A carpenter is cutting wood to make a new bookcase with a board that is 12 feet long. If the carpenter cuts off 3 pieces, each of which is 17 inches long, how many inches long is the remaining board?

    (A) 36
    (B) 51
    (C) 93
    (D) 108

STOP. IF YOU FINISH BEFORE THE TIME IS UP, YOU MAY CHECK OVER YOUR WORK ON THIS PART ONLY.

PART 3. WORD KNOWLEDGE (WK)

Time: 11 minutes; 35 questions

<u>Directions</u>: In this section, you are tested on the meaning of words. Each of the following questions has an underlined word. Select the answer that most nearly means the same as the underlined word and mark the corresponding oval on your answer sheet.

1. <u>Impose</u> most nearly means

   (A) create
   (B) force
   (C) damage
   (D) trade

2. <u>Stunted</u> most nearly means

   (A) halted
   (B) daring
   (C) loose
   (D) blatant

3. A <u>sturdy</u> home can withstand nearly any disaster.

   (A) huge
   (B) strong
   (C) cold
   (D) cautious

4. He was <u>undeterred</u> in his quest to find her.

   (A) surprised
   (B) determined
   (C) careless
   (D) brazen

5. <u>Ennui</u> most nearly means

   (A) patient
   (B) gloating
   (C) annoyance
   (D) tasteful

6. <u>Mutable</u> most nearly means

   (A) changing
   (B) silent
   (C) big-hearted
   (D) calm

7. It was gross how they <u>squandered</u> the money.

   (A) gathered
   (B) presented
   (C) wasted
   (D) owned

8. The handwriting was nearly <u>illegible</u>.

   (A) unreadable
   (B) unethical
   (C) creative
   (D) dangerous

9. <u>Infinite</u> most nearly means

   (A) costly
   (B) unending
   (C) babyish
   (D) daily

10. <u>Longevity</u> most nearly means

    (A) training
    (B) lifetime
    (C) girth
    (D) lifestyle

GO ON TO THE NEXT PAGE

11. Kids always fall for that <u>ruse</u>.

    (A) trick
    (B) joke
    (C) story
    (D) backtalk

12. The president <u>proclaimed</u> it a national holiday.

    (A) suggested
    (B) renamed
    (C) announced
    (D) unmade

13. Even the most <u>rudimentary</u> details are crucial to understanding it.

    (A) basic
    (B) ecstatic
    (C) illogical
    (D) fancy

14. <u>Rout</u> most nearly means

    (A) careful
    (B) defeat
    (C) blatant
    (D) open

15. His <u>rogue</u> attitude was bad for team morale.

    (A) aggressive
    (B) sad
    (C) maverick
    (D) low-brow

16. Her decision didn't <u>resonate</u> very well with some.

    (A) state
    (B) goad
    (C) harmonize
    (D) condone

17. Duplicating steps is far too <u>redundant</u> at this late stage.

    (A) repetitive
    (B) upsetting
    (C) colorful
    (D) wishy-washy

18. Far be it from me to <u>prescribe</u> how to raise one's own children.

    (A) predict
    (B) dictate
    (C) expect
    (D) decide

19. <u>Logical</u> most nearly means

    (A) cognizant
    (B) easy
    (C) rowdy
    (D) sensible

20. <u>Prerequisite</u> most nearly means

    (A) required
    (B) tiny
    (C) gleeful
    (D) tasteful

21. It seems like loud people tend to <u>gravitate</u> towards other loud people.

    (A) stay away
    (B) break
    (C) move towards
    (D) close in on

22. The police felt it was best to be <u>cautious</u> when approaching the house.

    (A) excited
    (B) apathetic
    (C) dodgy
    (D) careful

23. <u>Braggart</u> most nearly means

    (A) clown
    (B) leader
    (C) showoff
    (D) deputy

24. Basing his opinions on <u>hearsay</u> doomed the case.

    (A) rumor
    (B) samples
    (C) truth
    (D) belief

25. <u>Taunt</u> most nearly means

    (A) grade
    (B) relate
    (C) ridicule
    (D) party

26. Most respond well to <u>constructive</u> criticism.

    (A) damaging
    (B) productive
    (C) lost
    (D) flattering

27. <u>Quantifiable</u> most nearly means

    (A) laughable
    (B) standard
    (C) countable
    (D) breakable

28. The least <u>effective</u> way of dealing with children is yelling.

    (A) tantalizing
    (B) creative
    (C) useful
    (D) positive

29. <u>Apathy</u> most nearly means

    (A) greatness
    (B) laziness
    (C) boredom
    (D) passion

30. It left a glaring <u>blemish</u> on his permanent record.

    (A) impact
    (B) defect
    (C) hesitancy
    (D) compliment

31. It will take a <u>consensus</u> to get this measure passed.

    (A) agreement
    (B) discussion
    (C) fight
    (D) reprimand

32. No coach can handle <u>dissent</u> from his players for long.

    (A) discussion
    (B) laughter
    (C) thought
    (D) insubordination

GO ON TO THE NEXT PAGE

33. <u>Tempo</u> most nearly means

    (A) hearty
    (B) safety
    (C) modernity
    (D) speed

34. She can take <u>solace</u> in the fact that it couldn't get much worse.

    (A) protection
    (B) comfort
    (C) glee
    (D) depth

35. Many <u>pitfalls</u> await the inexperienced climber.

    (A) joys
    (B) traps
    (C) ropes
    (D) talents

STOP. IF YOU FINISH BEFORE THE TIME IS UP, YOU MAY CHECK OVER YOUR WORK ON THIS PART ONLY.

PART 4. PARAGRAPH COMPREHENSION (PC)

Time: 13 minutes; 15 questions

<u>Directions</u>: This section contains paragraphs followed by incomplete statements or questions. Read the paragraph and select the answer that best completes the statements or answers the questions that follow, and mark the corresponding oval on your answer sheet.

Questions 1 and 2 refer to the following passage.

In modern society, a new form of folk tale has emerged: the urban legend. These stories persist both for their entertainment value and for the transmission of popular values and beliefs. Urban legends are stories we all have heard; they are supposed to have really happened, but they cannot be verified. It turns out that the people involved can never be found. Researchers of urban legends call the elusive participant in these supposedly "real-life" events a "FOAF:" a friend of a friend.

One classic urban legend involves alligators in the sewer systems of major metropolitan areas. According to the story, before alligators were a protected species, people vacationing in Florida purchased baby alligators to take home as souvenirs. After the novelty of having a pet alligator wore off, people would flush their souvenirs down the toilet. The baby alligators found a perfect growing environment in city sewer systems, where to this day they thrive on an ample supply of rats.

1. The passage suggests the real-life participants of urban legends

    (A) can be difficult to track down
    (B) are usually known, but only barely, by the teller
    (C) seem believable, but do not in fact exist
    (D) are the original tellers of the stories

2. According to the passage, the successful urban legend contains all of the following characteristics EXCEPT

    (A) the capacity to entertain
    (B) messages that conform to popular values
    (C) qualities of a folk tale
    (D) a basis in reality

When Babe Ruth was sold from the Boston Red Sox to the New York Yankees in 1920 for $100,000, most thought it was a bad trade. But few could have predicted that the Yankees, who had never before won a World Series, would go on to become the most successful franchise in sports history, or that the Red Sox, who had won the World Series five times before the Ruth trade, would never again win a World Series title. This turn of luck, now often called "The Curse of the Bambino," is one of baseball's most colorful stories, and one which is bound to continue until the Red Sox break the curse and win their first World Series title in over 80 years.

3. According to the passage, the Red Sox have won how many World Series titles?

    (A) five
    (B) seven
    (C) one
    (D) none

GO ON TO THE NEXT PAGE

Local elementary schools have changed considerably over the past 50 years. Where once we had schools in every small town, now students bus for miles to attend larger, more advanced schools. While most parents see this as a positive step for progress and education, some worry about their children losing touch with the simple things around them. A few have even decided to home school their children instead of sending them to nearby towns.

4. The author's tone in this passage is

   (A) embittered
   (B) informative
   (C) biased
   (D) ambivalent

Questions 5 and 6 refer to the following passage.

Most life is fundamentally dependent on photosynthetic organisms that store radiant energy from the sun. In almost all the world's ecosystems and food chains, photosynthetic organisms such as plants and algae are eaten by other organisms, which are then consumed by still others. The existence of organisms that are not dependent on the sun's light has long been established, but until recently they were regarded as anomalies.

Over the last twenty years, however, research in deep sea areas has revealed the existence of entire ecosystems in which the primary producers are chemosynthetic bacteria that are dependent on energy from within the earth itself. Indeed, the growing evidence suggests that these sub-sea ecosystems model the way in which life first came about on this planet.

5. The passage suggests that most life is ultimately dependent on what?

   (A) photosynthetic algae
   (B) the world's oceans
   (C) bacterial microorganisms
   (D) light from the sun

6. Which of the following conclusions about photosynthetic and chemosynthetic organisms is supported by this passage?

   (A) Both perform similar functions in different food chains.
   (B) Both are known to support communities of higher organisms at great ocean depths.
   (C) Sunlight is the basic source of energy for both.
   (D) Chemosynthetic organisms are less nourishing than photosynthetic organisms.

Halley's Comet has been known since at least 240 BC and possibly since 1059 BC. Its most famous appearance was in 1066 AD when it appeared right before the Battle of Hastings. It was named after the astronomer Edmund Halley, who calculated its orbit. He determined that the comets seen in 1530 and 1606 were the same object following a 76-year orbit. Unfortunately, Halley died in 1742, never living to see his prediction come true when the comet returned on Christmas Eve 1758.

7. It can be inferred from the passage that the last sighting of the Haley's Comet recorded before the death of Edmund Halley took place in

   (A) 1066
   (B) 1530
   (C) 1606
   (D) 1682

GO ON TO THE NEXT PAGE

Both alligators and crocodiles can be found in southern Florida, particularly in the Everglades National Park. Alligators and crocodiles do look similar but there are several physical characteristics that differentiate the two giant reptiles. The most easily observed difference between alligators and crocodiles is the shape of the head. The crocodile's skull and jaws are longer and narrower than the alligator's. When an alligator closes its mouth, those long teeth slip into sockets in the upper jaw and disappear. When a crocodile closes its mouth, the long teeth remain visible, protruding outside the upper jaw. In general, if you can still see a lot of teeth even when the animal's mouth is closed, you are looking at a crocodile.

8. One can distinguish a crocodile from an alligator

   (A) only when the animal's mouth is closed
   (B) by the location in Florida where the animal is found
   (C) by its thick, heavily armored skin
   (D) by the narrower snout found on a crocodile

A talent agent analyzed her company's records in an attempt to determine why it was placing so few actors in roles. She attributed the company's poor performance to the fact that often the actors sent to an audition were completely inappropriate for the role.

9. It can be inferred from the passage that the agent believes that

   (A) certain actors are inappropriate for certain roles
   (B) the actors her company represents are not very good
   (C) it is difficult to predict how appropriate an actor will be for a role
   (D) her company does not send enough actors to audition for major roles

One of the most commonly used of all meters is iambic pentameter. An iamb is the name for a word or words with two syllables with the stress on the second syllable. Pentameter refers to the number of feet, or groupings of syllables. In this case, the foot is an iamb. William Shakespeare is perhaps the most famous writer of the iambic pentameter, having composed hundred of poems in this meter, popularizing it for the masses.

10. According to the passage, a *foot* is

    (A) a grouping of syllables
    (B) similar to a meter
    (C) named after William Shakespeare
    (D) none of the above

It is often said that American involvement in World War I would not have begun in earnest were it not for the German sinking of the passenger ship the Lusitania on February 18th, 1915. Preferring prior to then to stay neutral in the war, America was until that time offering only financial and tactical support for Britain and France against Germany and Austria-Hungary. The sinking of the huge passenger ship, however, altered public opinion about U.S. involvement and subsequently led to military escalation, truly making the war a matter for the whole world.

11. The main idea of the passage is that

    (A) the Germans sank the *Lusitania* because of America's financial and tactical support for Britain and France
    (B) Austria-Hungary and Germany were allies in World War I
    (C) American involvement in World War I was minimal
    (D) the sinking of the *Lusitania* prompted increased American involvement in WWI

GO ON TO THE NEXT PAGE

When a movie panned by most film critics is a popular success, this is often seen as a sign of poor taste of the part of general audiences. But film critics belong to a fairly homogeneous class, and their preferences are often rooted in the prejudices of that class. Their opinions are no more likely to be an unerring guide to quality than those of the average moviegoer.

12. The passage above best supports which of the following conclusions?

    (A) Judgments of film quality by professional film critics are usually wrong.
    (B) Judgments of quality applied to movies are meaningless.
    (C) Film critics usually consider popular movies to be of poor quality.
    (D) When critics and general audiences disagree about a movie's quality, the critics' opinion is not necessarily more accurate.

The tomato originated in the new world. It was first domesticated around 700 AD by the Aztec and Incan civilizations. In the 16th century European explorers were so appreciative of the tomato that they introduced it to the rest of Europe. Although the French, Spanish, and Italians quickly began to adapt their recipes to the tomato, the English considered it poisonous. This myth continued into the American colonial period and it wasn't until the middle 1800s that the tomato began to gain acceptance in the U.S.

13. According to the passage, Americans did not start using the tomato until the mid-nineteenth century because

    (A) it was unavailable in the new world
    (B) they lacked recipes for using it
    (C) they believed it to be poisonous
    (D) it was viewed as a Mediterranean food

It was without a sense of humor that the foreign ambassador responded to allegations that his driver had over 2,000 unpaid parking tickets. For a moment it seemed as if he would perhaps go item by item to discount the allegation. Not only did he demand an apology for the way the story had been handled by the press, but he also insinuated that the incident might actually affect the two Countries' relations in the future. One thing that was never addressed, however, was the fact that the tickets have still not been paid.

14. The foreign ambassador would be most likely to

    (A) support a resolution to grant diplomats immunity from parking tickets
    (B) support a call for more police on the beat
    (C) admit involvement in parking scams around the city
    (D) return to his country if the tickets were paid.

Professional basketball will soon overtake Major League Baseball as America's favorite sport. While baseball salaries skyrocket because of owners' willingness to overpay for top players, NBA salaries follow a system of paying players based on the number of years they have been in the league. This system rewards veterans and keeps players happy. And the most recent infusion of international talent to the NBA has only broadened its marketability overseas, opening previously untapped markets in places as far away as China, Japan, Russia, and Australia, thus giving NBA players even more room at the bargaining tables.

15. According to the passage, the NBA's marketability will increase because

   (A) players are getting more money from owners
   (B) Major League Baseball is losing fans
   (C) international markets are opening up to the game
   (D) its system of rewarding veteran players is superior

STOP. IF YOU FINISH BEFORE THE TIME IS UP, YOU MAY CHECK OVER YOUR WORK ON THIS PART ONLY.

PART 5. AUTOMOTIVE AND SHOP INFORMATION (AS)

Time: 11 minutes; 25 questions

<u>Directions</u>: In this section, you will be tested on your knowledge of automotive and shop basics. For each question, select the best answer and mark the corresponding oval on your answer sheet.

1. Wood can be shaped using all of the following tools EXCEPT
   - (A) jack plane
   - (B) wood chisel
   - (C) flat rasp
   - (D) miter box

2. Ride quality is the job of the vehicle's _____ system.
   - (A) steering
   - (B) suspension
   - (C) charging
   - (D) brake

3. The cut in the wood left behind by a saw is known as the
   - (A) gap
   - (B) line
   - (C) trace
   - (D) kerf

4. A four-wheel drive vehicle uses a _____ to distribute power to the front and rear drive axles.
   - (A) transmission
   - (B) drive shaft
   - (C) torque converter
   - (D) transfer case

5. Crosscut saws are made to
   - (A) cut with the grain of the wood
   - (B) cut across the grain of the wood
   - (C) cut plywood only
   - (D) cut steel only

6. Rear-wheel drive power trains stretch
   - (A) from the engine front
   - (B) outward from the chassis
   - (C) from the engine back
   - (D) to the torque converter

7. Thread pitch of a metric fastener is determined by
   - (A) measuring the distance in millimeters between threads
   - (B) measuring the distance in inches between threads
   - (C) counting the number of threads per millimeter
   - (D) counting the number of threads per inch

8. On a P215/75R-14 tire, the 75 stands for
   - (A) the tire diameter in millimeters
   - (B) the tire width in millimeters
   - (C) the ratio of the tire's height to its width
   - (D) the diameter of the rim in millimeters

9. All of the following are parts of the vehicle's steering system EXCEPT:
   - (A) coil spring
   - (B) steering knuckle
   - (C) tie rod end
   - (D) idler arm

10. Engine valve timing is controlled by the
    - (A) crankshaft
    - (B) push rods
    - (C) lifters
    - (D) camshaft

GO ON TO THE NEXT PAGE

11. On a fuel-injected engine, the fuel pump is normally located

    (A) on the engine
    (B) on the vehicle frame
    (C) near the rear bumper
    (D) in the fuel tank

12. UNC fasteners have _____ threads per inch when compared to UNF fasteners of the same diameter.

    (A) more
    (B) less
    (C) the same number of
    (D) none of the above

13. In power brake systems, braking pressures are increased using

    (A) engine intake manifold vacuum
    (B) fluid pressure from the power steering system
    (C) Both A and B are correct.
    (D) Neither A nor B are correct.

14. All of the following are parts of the ignition primary system EXCEPT:

    (A) battery
    (B) ignition switch
    (C) reluctor and pickup
    (D) rotor

15. "Stoichiometric" is a term that describes

    (A) the ideal air-fuel mixture in a gasoline engine
    (B) the voltage required to generate a spark
    (C) the engine's breathing efficiency
    (D) theoretical horsepower

16. An oil's resistance to flow is known as its

    (A) quality rating
    (B) pumpability
    (C) lubricity
    (D) viscosity

17. All cars are currently being built with _____ electrical systems.

    (A) direct current
    (B) alternating current
    (C) negative ground
    (D) both A and C are correct

18. When arc-welding, the ground clamp should be connected to the

    (A) floor
    (B) welding rod
    (C) electrical outlet
    (D) work

19. A five-speed transmission

    (A) is a manual transmission
    (B) has four forward speeds and one reverse speed
    (C) has five forward speeds and one reverse speed
    (D) both A and C are correct

20. PCV stands for

    (A) periodic camshaft variation
    (B) positive crankcase ventilation
    (C) periodic crankcase ventilation
    (D) positive camshaft ventilation

21. Measuring the gap on used spark plugs is best accomplished using a

    (A) wire gauge
    (B) dial caliper
    (C) feeler gauge
    (D) inside micrometer

22. Air entering an engine's combustion chamber must pass through the

    (A) air filter
    (B) intake manifold
    (C) intake port in the cylinder head
    (D) all of the above

23. Which tool would be best suited for loosening a very tight nut?

    (A) open-end wrench
    (B) 12-point socket and breaker bar
    (C) 6-point socket and ratchet
    (D) 6-point socket and breaker bar

24. Vernier micrometers are made to measure to

    (A) 0.1 inch
    (B) 0.01 inch
    (C) 0.001 inch
    (D) 0.0001 inch

25. As lead-acid batteries discharge, their electrolyte gradually turns to

    (A) sulphuric acid
    (B) water
    (C) lead peroxide
    (D) none of the above

STOP. IF YOU FINISH BEFORE THE TIME IS UP, YOU MAY CHECK OVER YOUR WORK ON THIS PART ONLY.

PART 6: MATHEMATICS KNOWLEDGE (MK)

Time: 24 minutes; 25 questions

<u>Directions</u>: In this section, you will be tested on your knowledge of basic mathematics. For each question, select the best answer and mark the corresponding oval on your answer sheet.

1. For all x, $(3x + 4)(4x - 3) =$

    (A) $7x - 12$

    (B) $12x^2 - 12$

    (C) $12x^2 - 25x - 12$

    (D) $12x^2 + 7x - 12$

2. If a tree grew 5 feet in n years, what was the average rate at which the tree grew, in inches per year?

    (A) $\dfrac{60}{n}$

    (B) $\dfrac{5}{12n}$

    (C) $\dfrac{12n}{5}$

    (D) $\dfrac{n}{60}$

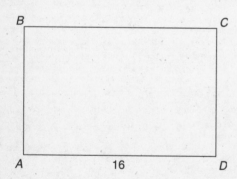

3. In the figure above, if the perimeter of rectangle $ABCD$ is 56, and the length of AD is 16, what is the area of $ABCD$?

    (A) 40

    (B) 64

    (C) 160

    (D) 192

4. If the sum of three different prime numbers is an even number, what is the smallest of the three?

    (A) 2

    (B) 3

    (C) 5

    (D) It cannot be determined from the information given.

5. If $a < b$ and $b < c$, which of the following must be true?

    (A) $b + c < 2a$

    (B) $a + b < c$

    (C) $a - b < b - c$

    (D) $a + b < 2c$

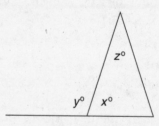

6. In the figure above, $x = 2z$ and $y = 3z$. and What is the value of z ?

    (A) 24

    (B) 30

    (C) 36

    (D) 54

GO ON TO THE NEXT PAGE

7. If the minute hand of a properly functioning clock moves 45 degrees, how many minutes have passed?

 (A) 6
 (B) 7.5
 (C) 12
 (D) 15

8. If $5^n > 10,000$ and n is an integer, what is the smallest possible value of n ?

 (A) 8
 (B) 7
 (C) 6
 (D) 5

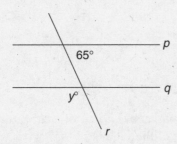

9. In the figure above, if line p is parallel to line q, what is the value of y ?

 (A) 65
 (B) 115
 (C) 125
 (D) 130

10. 15 percent of 15 percent of 200 is

 (A) 4.5
 (B) 6
 (C) 45
 (D) 60

11. What is the average (arithmetic mean) of $\frac{1}{20}$ and $\frac{1}{30}$?

 (A) $\frac{1}{25}$
 (B) $\frac{1}{24}$
 (C) $\frac{2}{25}$
 (D) $\frac{1}{12}$

12. If an angle measures y^o, what will its supplement measure in terms of y?

 (A) $90 - y$
 (B) $90 + y$
 (C) $180 - y$
 (D) $180 + y$

13. Diane painted $\frac{1}{3}$ of her room with $2\frac{1}{2}$ cans of paint. How many more cans of paint will she need to finish painting her room?

 (A) 2
 (B) 5
 (C) $7\frac{1}{2}$
 (D) 10

14. If $13 + a = 25 + b$, then $b - a =$

 (A) 38
 (B) 12
 (C) 8
 (D) −12

15. For all x, $3x^2 \times 5x^3 =$

    (A) $8x^5$

    (B) $8x^6$

    (C) $15x^5$

    (D) $15x^6$

16. If the sides of a square increase in length by 10%, the area of the square increases by

    (A) 10%

    (B) 15%

    (C) 20%

    (D) 21%

17. If $\dfrac{m}{2} = 15$, then $\dfrac{m}{3} =$

    (A) 7.5

    (B) 10

    (C) 22.5

    (D) 30

18. Which of the following is a polynomial factor of $6x^2 - 13x + 6$?

    (A) $2x + 2$

    (B) $2x + 3$

    (C) $3x - 2$

    (D) $3x - 3$

19. If the product of 3 and x is equal to 2 less than y, which of the following must be true?

    (A) $\dfrac{3x - 2}{y} = 0$

    (B) $3x - y - 2 = 0$

    (C) $3x + y - 2 = 0$

    (D) $3x - y + 2 = 0$

20. If $x > 1$ and $\dfrac{a}{b} = 1 - \dfrac{1}{x}$, then $\dfrac{b}{a} =$

    (A) $\dfrac{x}{x - 1}$

    (B) $\dfrac{x - 1}{x}$

    (C) $x - 1$

    (D) $\dfrac{1}{x} - 1$

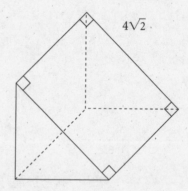

21. If the solid above is half of a cube, then the volume of the solid is

    (A) 16

    (B) $16\sqrt{2}$

    (C) 32

    (D) 64

22. When 7.6 is divided by 0.019, the quotient is

    (A) 4,000

    (B) 400

    (C) 40

    (D) 4

GO ON TO THE NEXT PAGE

23. What is the area of a circle with a circumference of 8 ?

    (A) $\dfrac{16}{\pi}$

    (B) 4π

    (C) 16

    (D) 16π

24. 36 percent of 18 is 18 percent of what number?

    (A) 9

    (B) 36

    (C) 72

    (D) 200

25. $\sqrt{104{,}906}$ is between

    (A) 100 and 200

    (B) 200 and 300

    (C) 300 and 400

    (D) 400 and 500

STOP. IF YOU FINISH BEFORE THE TIME IS UP, YOU MAY CHECK OVER YOUR WORK ON THIS PART ONLY.

PART 7: MECHANICAL COMPREHENSION (MC)

Time: 19 minutes; 25 questions

Directions: In this section, you will be tested on your knowledge of mechanics and basic physics. Select the best answer for each question and mark the corresponding oval on your answer sheet.

1. A car rolls down a hill. It travels progressively faster because

   (A) its potential energy is being converted into kinetic energy
   (B) the car's total mechanical energy remains constant as it moves
   (C) Both A and B are correct.
   (D) Neither A nor B are correct.

2. When a ball is thrown into the air, it has its maximum potential energy when

   (A) it leaves the hand of the person throwing it
   (B) it reaches the highest point in its travel
   (C) its velocity is zero
   (D) Both B and C are correct.

3. Objects that require more force to get them moving have greater

   (A) momentum
   (B) inertia
   (C) Both A and B are correct.
   (D) Neither A nor B are correct.

4. When two objects collide, total _____ of the system is conserved.

   (A) kinetic energy
   (B) potential energy
   (C) linear momentum
   (D) all of the above

5. Less force is required to push an object up a ramp when the ramp is made

   (A) less steep
   (B) more steep
   (C) so friction is reduced
   (D) Both A and C are correct.

6. Lifting a heavy box directly from ground level up to the top of a ramp is doing _____ pushing the box up the ramp (neglecting friction).

   (A) less work than
   (B) more work than
   (C) the same amount of work as
   (D) none of the above

7. All of the following statements about work are true EXCEPT

   (A) force is a component of work
   (B) it is possible to get more work out of a machine than what is put in
   (C) to do work, an object must be moved
   (D) work can be measured in foot-pounds

8. A chisel is an example of

   (A) a wedge
   (B) a first class lever
   (C) an inclined plane
   (D) a wheel and axle

GO ON TO THE NEXT PAGE

9. The difference between a wedge and an inclined plane is

    (A) a wedge has a steeper slope than an inclined plane
    (B) a wedge is made to move, where an inclined plane stays stationary
    (C) a wedge offers greater mechanical advantage than an inclined plane
    (D) none of the above

10. The design of a screw is based on which of the following simple machines?

    (A) inclined plane
    (B) wheel and axle
    (C) second class lever
    (D) pulley

11. As a screw is turned, it converts rotary motion into _____ motion.

    (A) reciprocating
    (B) spiral
    (C) linear
    (D) vertical

12. The design of a screwdriver is based on which of the following simple machines?

    (A) inclined plane
    (B) wheel and axle
    (C) first class lever
    (D) pulley

13. An increase in force accomplished through mechanical advantage is always accompanied by _____ in distance moved.

    (A) an increase
    (B) a decrease
    (C) no change
    (D) none of the above

14. The design of a prybar is based on which of the following simple machines?

    (A) first-class lever
    (B) second-class lever
    (C) third-class lever
    (D) inclined plane

15. A wheelbarrow is a second-class lever. The fulcrum of this design is located at the

    (A) wheel
    (B) handles
    (C) bucket
    (D) none of the above

16. In order to increase force with a first class lever, the fulcrum should be

    (A) moved towards where the effort is applied
    (B) kept in the same position
    (C) moved towards where the object is moved
    (D) removed altogether

17. The primary purpose of a third-class lever is to

    (A) increase force
    (B) increase distance moved
    (C) change the direction of motion
    (D) Both A and C are correct.

18. A _____ is a pulley with a grooved rim.

    (A) barrel
    (B) wheel
    (C) cylinder
    (D) sheave

19. A block-and-tackle utilizes

    (A) one pulley
    (B) more than one pulley
    (C) a flexible rope, belt, or chain
    (D) Both B and C are correct.

20. If a block-and-tackle offers a 10:1 mechanical advantage, the rope will have to be pulled _____ in order to move the load 10 inches.

    (A) 1 inch
    (B) 10 inches
    (C) 100 inches
    (D) 10 feet

21. The design of a doorknob is based on which of the following simple machines?

    (A) inclined plane
    (B) wheel and axle
    (C) first class lever
    (D) pulley

22. An automobile transmission can be used to

    (A) increase speed
    (B) increase torque
    (C) decrease speed
    (D) all of the above

23. A gear set that is used to increase speed is known as

    (A) a reduction
    (B) a direct drive
    (C) an overdrive
    (D) none of the above

24. A small gear with 10 teeth drives a large gear with 40 teeth. All of the following statements about this gear set are true EXCEPT:

    (A) the driven gear will rotate opposite to the drive gear
    (B) the gear ratio of this gear set is 4:1
    (C) torque output will be $\frac{1}{4}$ of the torque input
    (D) the small gear will turn faster than the large gear

25. A drive gear connects to the driven gear through an idler that has 10 teeth. If the idler gear is replaced with a gear having 20 teeth, how will this affect the operation of the gear set?

    (A) the torque output will increase
    (B) the speed output will increase
    (C) the driven gear will change direction
    (D) the operation of the gear set will not be altered

STOP. IF YOU FINISH BEFORE THE TIME IS UP, YOU MAY CHECK OVER YOUR WORK ON THIS PART ONLY.

PART 8: ELECTRONICS INFORMATION (EI)

Time: 9 minutes; 20 questions

<u>Directions</u>: In this section, you will be tested on your knowledge of electronics basics. For each question, select the best answer and mark the corresponding oval on your answer sheet.

1. Resistance is measured in

   (A) amperes
   (B) ohms
   (C) Ω
   (D) B and C are correct.

2. If current and amperage are known, power can be calculated using

   (A) $E = I \times R$
   (B) $P = I \times E$
   (C) $R = E \div I$
   (D) $P = I \div E$

3. The total resistance of three 15-ohm resistors in parallel is

   (A) $\frac{1}{5}$ ohm
   (B) 5 ohms
   (C) 10 ohms
   (D) 45 ohms

4. A circuit with current flowing in it is known as an

   (A) open circuit
   (B) closed circuit
   (C) short circuit
   (D) dead circuit

5. The symbol above represents a

   (A) resistor
   (B) capacitor
   (C) inductor
   (D) diode

6. The P-type material in a diode is also known as the

   (A) electrode
   (B) cathode
   (C) base
   (D) anode

7. Introducing impurities into the crystal structure of silicon is also known as

   (A) tinning
   (B) enhancing
   (C) processing
   (D) doping

8. Inductance is measured in

    (A) ohms

    (B) henries

    (C) millihenries

    (D) B and C are correct.

9. Capacitive reactance is measured in

    (A) ohms

    (B) farads

    (C) microfarads

    (D) B and C are correct.

10. All of the following statements about transistors are true EXCEPT:

    (A) N-type material has free electrons.

    (B) NPN transistors require a positive voltage at the base to turn them on.

    (C) The arrow in the transistor symbol is always placed on the collector.

    (D) P-type material conducts current through the movement of holes.

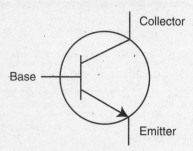

11. The symbol above represents

    (A) a PNP transistor

    (B) a zener diode

    (C) an NPN transistor

    (D) a diode

12. PIV stands for

    (A) proton is visible

    (B) peak inverse voltage

    (C) peak independent voltage

    (D) power infused voltage

13. Capacitors will allow _____ to pass, but will block the flow of _____.

    (A) protons : electrons

    (B) atoms : molecules

    (C) DC : AC

    (D) AC : DC

14. What is a heat sink?

    (A) a means of rejecting heat from electronic components

    (B) a component used to help warm up electronic equipment quickly

    (C) a tool used to solder electrical connections

    (D) none of the above

15. A typical gain specification for a transistor would be

    (A) 200 volts

    (B) 10

    (C) 150

    (D) 1000

16. A material that will not conduct electricity is known as

    (A) a conductor

    (B) a semiconductor

    (C) an insulator

    (D) none of the above

GO ON TO THE NEXT PAGE

17. All of the following materials are conductors EXCEPT

    (A) rubber
    (B) silver
    (C) copper
    (D) aluminum

18. A circuit with four 6-ohm resistors wired in series has 12 volts applied to it. What current flows through this circuit?

    (A) 5 mA
    (B) 50 mA
    (C) 500 mA
    (D) 5 A

19. A 120-volt light bulb rated at 100 watts would have how much current flowing through it?

    (A) 8.3 A
    (B) 0.833 mA
    (C) 833 mA
    (D) Both A and B are correct.

20. Adding more loads to a series circuit will cause the current flow in the circuit to

    (A) increase
    (B) decrease
    (C) stay the same
    (D) none of the above

STOP. IF YOU FINISH BEFORE THE TIME IS UP, YOU MAY CHECK OVER YOUR WORK ON THIS PART ONLY.

PART 9. ASSEMBLING OBJECTS (AO)

Time: 9 minutes; 16 questions

<u>Directions</u>: In this section, you will be tested on your ability to construct or connect a series of objects. For each question, select the best answer and mark the corresponding oval on your answer sheet.

1.

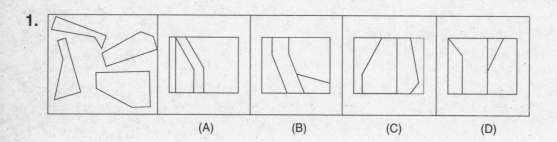

              (A)   (B)   (C)   (D)

2.

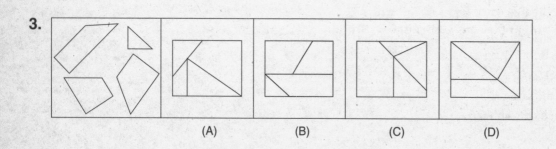

              (A)   (B)   (C)   (D)

3.

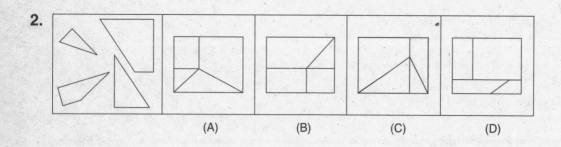

              (A)   (B)   (C)   (D)

4.

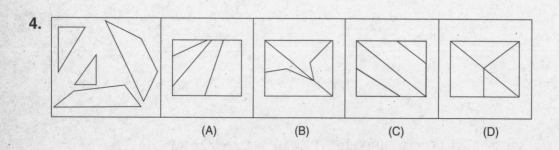

              (A)   (B)   (C)   (D)

GO ON TO THE NEXT PAGE

5.

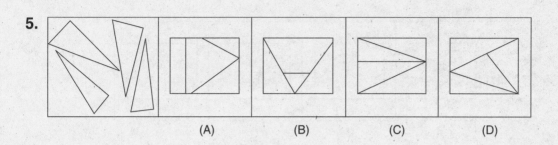

(A)   (B)   (C)   (D)

6.

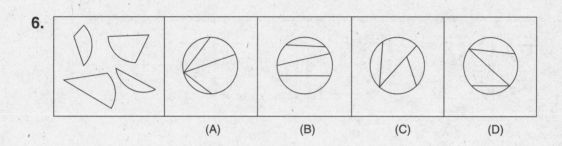

(A)   (B)   (C)   (D)

7.

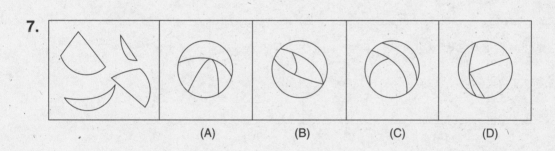

(A)   (B)   (C)   (D)

8.

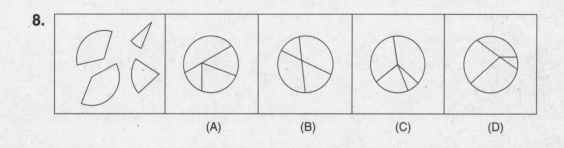

(A)   (B)   (C)   (D)

GO ON TO THE NEXT PAGE

9.

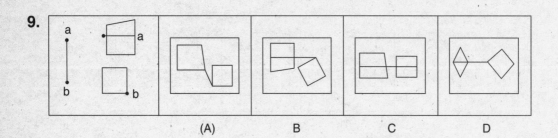

(A)   B   C   D

10.

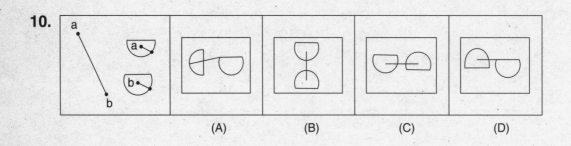

(A)   (B)   (C)   (D)

11.

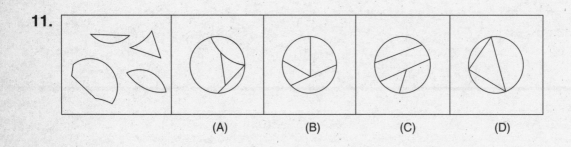

(A)   (B)   (C)   (D)

12.

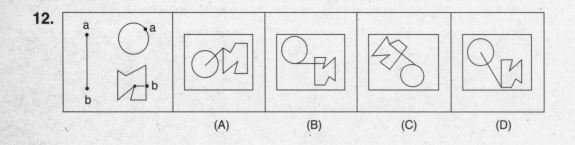

(A)   (B)   (C)   (D)

GO ON TO THE NEXT PAGE

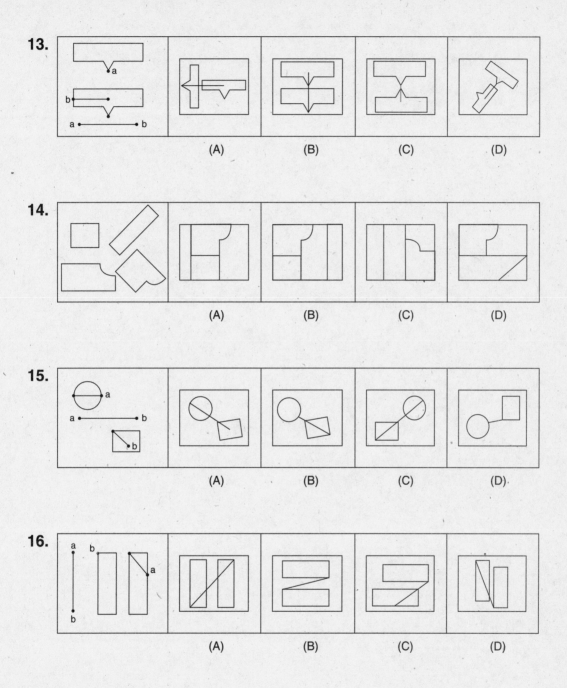

13. (A) (B) (C) (D)

14. (A) (B) (C) (D)

15. (A) (B) (C) (D)

16. (A) (B) (C) (D)

STOP! END OF TEST.

ASVAB Practice Test II
Answers and
Explanations

ANSWER KEY

General Science	Arithmetic Reasoning	Word Knowledge	Paragraph Comprehension	Auto and Shop Information
1. A	1. D	1. B	1. C	1. D
2. B	2. C	2. A	2. D	2. B
3. D	3. B	3. B	3. A	3. D
4. C	4. D	4. B	4. B	4. D
5. A	5. B	5. C	5. D	5. B
6. C	6. B	6. A	6. A	6. C
7. B	7. C	7. C	7. D	7. A
8. D	8. A	8. A	8. D	8. C
9. A	9. B	9. B	9. A	9. A
10. B	10. D	10. B	10. A	10. D
11. A	11. B	11. A	11. D	11. D
12. C	12. D	12. C	12. D	12. B
13. B	13. C	13. A	13. C	13. C
14. A	14. C	14. B	14. A	14. D
15. D	15. D	15. C	15. C	15. A
16. D	16. A	16. C		16. D
17. B	17. B	17. A		17. D
18. D	18. A	18. B		18. D
19. B	19. C	19. D		19. D
20. C	20. D	20. A		20. B
21. D	21. C	21. C		21. A
22. B	22. A	22. D		22. D
23. C	23. C	23. C		23. D
24. B	24. A	24. A		24. D
25. A	25. B	25. C		25. B
	26. C	26. B		
	27. C	27. C		
	28. D	28. C		
	29. A	29. C		
	30. C	30. B		
		31. A		
		32. D		
		33. D		
		34. B		
		35. B		

ANSWER KEY

Mathematics Knowledge	Mechanical Comprehension	Electronics Information	Assembling Objects
1. D	1. C	1. D	1. C
2. A	2. D	2. B	2. C
3. D	3. B	3. A	3. B
4. A	4. C	4. B	4. C
5. D	5. D	5. B	5. C
6. C	6. C	6. D	6. C
7. B	7. B	7. D	7. D
8. C	8. A	8. D	8. C
9. B	9. B	9. A	9. B
10. A	10. A	10. C	10. C
11. B	11. C	11. C	11. A
12. C	12. B	12. B	12. B
13. B	13. B	13. D	13. D
14. D	14. A	14. A	14. B
15. C	15. A	15. C	15. A
16. D	16. C	16. C	16. C
17. B	17. B	17. A	
18. C	18. D	18. C	
19. D	19. D	19. C	
20. A	20. C	20. B	
21. C	21. B		
22. B	22. D		
23. A	23. C		
24. B	24. C		
25. C	25. D		

GENERAL SCIENCE ANSWERS AND EXPLANATIONS

1. A

Vitamin A is considered essential to the promotion of good eyesight.

2. B

Orbiting around the nucleus of an atom are electrons.

3. D

Air is warmed and filtered first in the nasal cavity.

4. C

A polar bear is an example of a tertiary consumer, which is an animal that consumes secondary consumers, or other carnivores. The polar bear consumes animals, such as walruses, that also consume other animals, such as fish.

5. A

Chemically speaking, a substance is matter of particular or definite chemical composition. Water is considered a substance (H_2O), while air, fire, and earth can have variable chemical composition.

6. C

The gravitational force the moon exerts on the earth is the same as the gravitational force the earth exerts on the moon. According to Newton's third law, when the earth exerts its gravitational force on an object, such as the moon, that object exerts an equal and opposite force on the earth.

7. B

Fungi are decomposers (also known as saprophytes), returning the organic material from dead matter such as leaves, trees, and animal remains back into the environment. Producers make their own food, consumers must eat to gain energy, and mutualism is the type of symbiosis whereby organisms living together benefit.

8. D

In degrees Kelvin, the freezing pointing of water is 273°. In the Kelvin temperature scale absolute zero, which is −273° Celsius, is set at 0°, and any temperature in degrees Celsius is 273 degrees less than the same temperature as read in degrees Kelvin. Since the freezing point of water in degrees Celsius is 0°, in degrees Kelvin it is 273°.

9. A

Tough elastic tissues found in the joints that connect bones to bones are called ligaments. Tendons are connective tissue that unite a muscle with some other part, such as a bone. Cartilage is a somewhat elastic tissue (unlike bone) that in adults is found in some joints, respiratory passages, and the external ear. Finally, muscles are body tissue consisting of long cells that contract when stimulated to produce motion.

10. B

Stress, a poor diet, cigarette smoking, and heredity factors all contribute to individual's developing high blood pressure.

11. A

The property of light that causes a straw placed in a glass of water to appear bent is called refraction. Refraction is the deflection from a straight path undergone by a light ray or energy wave when passing obliquely from one medium (such as air) into another (such as water) in which its velocity is different.

12. C

Fossils are most likely to be found in sedimentary rock such as shale, which is a fissile rock formed by the sedimentation of clay, mud, or silt, and is composed of minerals and other matter, such as animal remains.

13. **B**

Animals that consume plants are called herbivores.

14. **A**

Aluminum is a poor insulating material, but a good conducting material. Wood, rubber, and porcelain are all comparatively good insulators.

15. **D**

Marsupial mammals differ from placental mammals in that marsupials bear premature embryos which complete development in their mothers' pouches.

16. **D**

Rods and cones are light sensitive cells inside the eye's retina.

17. **B**

A boulder that begins to roll down a hill is an example of an energy conversion from potential energy to kinetic energy.

18. **D**

The lowest layer of the earth's atmosphere is called the troposphere. This layer extends from the surface to the bottom of the stratosphere. Most weather changes occur here and the temperature generally decreases rapidly with altitude.

19. **B**

At high altitudes, the boiling point of water is lower than at sea level, because air pressure decreases as altitude increases.

20. **C**

As an ambulance passes, its pitch seems to change. This perception is best explained by the Doppler effect. As the ambulance approaches, the sound waves from its siren are compressed towards the observer. The intervals between waves diminish, which translates into an increase in frequency or pitch. As the ambulance recedes, the sound waves are stretched relative to the observer, causing the siren's pitch to decrease. By the change in pitch of the siren, one can determine if the ambulance is coming nearer or speeding away.

21. **D**

The octopus is an example of the phylum Mullusca. The ostrich, shark, and turtle are all vertebrates and thus belong to the phylum Chordata.

22. **B**

Striated muscles, also known as skeletal muscles, are controlled by conscious thought, unlike cardiac muscles or the smooth muscles of the digestive system, which are controlled by the autonomic nervous system.

23. **C**

The orbit of the moon around the earth, which exerts a gravitational pull on the ocean's waters, is the phenomenon most responsible for oceanic tides.

24. **B**

A substance that hastens a chemical reaction without undergoing chemical change itself is called a catalyst.

25. **A**

Lack of iron is associated with anemia.

ARITHMETIC REASONING ANSWERS AND EXPLANATIONS

1. D

Pick a number for the cost of one apple. Let's say each apple costs 4 cents. Then 3 apples cost 12 cents. The first sentence says that 3 apples cost as much as 4 pears, so 4 pears also cost 12 cents. How much would three pears cost? We know 4 pears cost 12 cents, so 1 pear must cost 3 cents, and 3 pears must cost 9 cents. Since 3 pears cost as much as 2 oranges, 2 oranges must also cost 9 cents. Since 36 × 2 = 72, 72 oranges cost the same as 36 × the cost of 2 oranges, or 36 × 9 cents, which is $3.24. Now we have to figure out how many apples cost $3.24. If one apple costs four cents, we just have to figure out how many times 4 cents goes into $3.24. It goes in 81 times, so 81 apples cost as much as 72 oranges, making (D) the correct answer.

2. C

If 48 of 60 seats are occupied, then 12 of 60 seats are unoccupied (since 60 − 48 = 12). What percent of the seats are unoccupied?

$$\text{Percent} = \frac{\text{Part}}{\text{Whole}} \times 100\% = \frac{12}{60} \times 100\% = \frac{1}{5} \times 100\% = 20\%, \text{ choice (C)}.$$

3. B

Let's break this question down into pieces. Before midnight, Effin gets paid $1,000 an hour. If she starts singing at 8:30 P.M., then she sings for $3\frac{1}{2}$ hours before midnight. Her earnings for that time are $3\frac{1}{2}$ times $1,000, or $3,500. Now let's find out how much she earns after midnight. Her rate increases 50% after midnight, so her hourly rate after midnight is $1,000 + 50% of $1,000. 50% of $1,000 is $500, so her rate per hour after midnight is $1,000 + $500 = $1,500. So she earns $1,500 for the hour she sings after midnight. For the last step, we add that to the amount she earns before midnight, so her total pay is $3,500 + $1,500 = $5,000, answer choice (B).

4. D

The probability of an event occurring is a fraction: the number of possible outcomes in which the event can occur divided by the total number of possible outcomes. Fran is going to pick one shirt and we want to figure out the probability that it will not be orange. In other words, what is the probability of picking a non-orange shirt? Aside from the orange shirts, there are 4 black shirts and 5 blue shirts, so altogether there are 9 non-orange shirts. So there are nine possible successful outcomes. The total number of shirts to choose from, including the orange shirts, is 12, so there are 12 possible outcomes. So the probability of Fran picking a non-orange shirt is $\frac{9}{12}$, which can be reduced to $\frac{3}{4}$, answer choice (D).

5. B

Draw a chart or table to help organize the information. Newark is two hours later than Denver, so if the time in Denver when Harry arrives is 2:30 P.M., then the time in Newark when he arrives in Denver is 4:30 P.M. The flight takes 5 hours, so the time he began in Newark is 5 hours earlier than 4:30 P.M., or 11:30 A.M., choice (B).

6. B

How many times does 24 go into 198? 198 ÷ 24 = 8 with a remainder of 6, so Doris will have 6 pieces of chocolate left over.

7. C

If 75% of x is 150, then $0.75(x) = 150$ or $\frac{3}{4}(x) = 150$. Multiply both sides by $\frac{4}{3}$ and you find that $x = 200$, choice (C). You could also work backwards from the answer choices. Only choice (C), 200, works. If $x = 200$, then $0.75(x) = 150$ since $0.75(200) = 150$.

8. A

The average formula is

$$\text{Average} = \frac{\text{Sum of the terms}}{\text{Number of terms}}$$

Don't just average the old average and the last test score—that would give the last score as much weight as all the other scores combined. The best way to deal with changing averages is to use the sums. Use the old average to figure out the total of the first 6 scores:

$$\text{Sum of first 6 scores} = (83)(6) = 498$$

Then add the 7th score and divide:

$$\frac{498 + 97}{7} = \frac{595}{7} = 85.$$

9. B

If the charge for one pound is $25.00, then the charge for $\frac{4}{5}$ of a pound would be $\frac{4}{5} \times \$25.00 = \$20.00$ plus 8% sales tax. 8% of $20.00 = $0.08(\$20.00) = \$1.60$. $\$20.00 + \$1.60 = \$21.60$, choice (B).

10. D

To answer this question we just have to figure out how many times $\frac{3}{5}$ goes into 60. We know that it will be more than 60, so right away we can eliminate (A). $60 \times \frac{3}{5} = \frac{60}{1} \times \frac{5}{3}$. This is easier to multiply if we do some canceling. 3 goes into 60 twenty times, so we can replace the 3 with a 1, and replace the 60 with a 20. So now we have $\frac{20}{1} \times \frac{5}{1}$, which equals 20×5, or 100, choice (D).

11. B

Solve a question like this using algebra if it's a strong area for you. Otherwise, work backwards from the answer choices. To solve this question using algebra, we'll need to set up equations and solve for R which is Robert's money. We're told that Ed has 100 more dollars than Robert.

$$E = R + 100.$$

Ed then spends 20 dollars and has five times as much money as Robert.

$$E - 20 = 5R.$$

Substitute $R + 100$ for E and solve. So:

$$R + 80 = 5R.$$
$$80 = 4R. \quad R = \$20, \text{ choice (B).}$$

If you were to backsolve, choose a value like $20 or $24 for Robert's money. Then see which value would work for all the information we're given in the question. Only choice (B), $20, works.

12. D

This question is actually a remainder question in disguise. If 587 people are to be divided among a number of buses that each seat 48 people, we need to divide 587 by 48 to see how many buses we would fill completely. The remainder would be the number of people in the unfilled bus. $587 \div 48 = 12$ and the remainder is 11, so (D) is correct.

13. C

Riley brought 100 cookies, and 25 are left over. That means that Riley and her classmates ate 75 cookies. So:

$$\text{Average} = \frac{\text{Sum of the terms}}{\text{Number of terms}} = \frac{75 \text{ cookies}}{15 \text{ students}}$$

$$= 5 \text{ cookies for each student.}$$

(C) is correct

14. C

This is a proportion question.

$$\frac{4 \text{ ft object}}{9 \text{ ft shadow}} = \frac{x \text{ ft object}}{21 \text{ ft shadow}}.$$

Cross-multiply to solve.

$$4 \times 21 = 9x$$
$$\frac{84}{9} = \frac{9x}{9}$$
$$x = 9\frac{1}{3}$$

Choice (C) is correct.

15. D

Percent times Whole equals Part:

$$\text{Percent} \times 25 = 16$$

$$\text{Percent} = \frac{16}{25} = \frac{16}{25} \times 100\% = 64\%$$

16. A

First find how long the trip takes him at each of the two different rates, using the formula

$$\text{Time} = \frac{\text{Distance}}{\text{Rate}}$$

He travels the first 10 km at 30 km per hour, so he takes $\frac{10}{30} = \frac{1}{3}$ hour for this portion of the journey.

He travels the remaining 30 km at 15 km per hour, so he takes $\frac{30}{15} = 2$ hours for this portion of the journey.

So the whole journey takes him $2 + \frac{1}{3} = 2\frac{1}{3}$ hours. Now we need to compare this to the amount of time it would take to make the same trip at a constant rate of 20 km per hour. If he traveled the whole 40 km at 20 km per hour, it would take $\frac{40}{20} = 2$ hours. Now $2\frac{1}{3}$ hours is more than 2 hours by $\frac{1}{3}$ hour, or 20 minutes.

17. B

Since 3 out of 24 students are in student organizations, the remaining $24 - 3$, or 21, students are not in student organizations. Therefore, the ratio of students in organizations to students not in organizations is $\frac{3}{21} = \frac{1}{7}$.

18. **A**

Begin by determining how many games each team has won and lost by mid-season. Team A had won 60 and lost 20 by mid-season. Team B had won 49 and lost 31 by mid-season. Over the remaining 80 games, Team A won 40 and lost 40. That means that Team A wound up with 60 + 40 = 100 wins. To win 100 games, Team B would have to win 100 − 49 = 51 games over the remainder of the season. (A) is correct.

19. **C**

A vendor bought 10 crates for a total cost of $80. He wants to make a total profit of 25% over the total cost. So the total sale would have to equal $80 + (0.25)($80) = $80 + $20 = $100. He lost 2 crates, so he would need to sell the remaining 10 − 2 = 8 crates for $100 to make the required profit. $\dfrac{\$100}{8 \text{ crates}}$ = $12.50 per crate; (C) is correct.

20. **D**

Set up a simple proportion on questions like this one:

$$\frac{150 \text{ bottles}}{20 \text{ minutes}} = \frac{60 \text{ bottles}}{x \text{ minutes}}.$$

$$150x = 1,200$$

Divide both sides by 150:

$$x = \frac{1,200}{150} = 8$$

(D) is correct.

21. **C**

This one's tricky since it's asking for the number of rectangular tiles, each 12 centimeters by 18 centimeters, needed to cover *four* flat rectangular surfaces, each 60 centimeters by 180 centimeters. To determine the number of smaller tiles needed, divide the total area of the four bigger rectangles by the area of one of the smaller rectangles.

$$\frac{4 \times 60 \times 180}{12 \times 18} = 4 \times 5 \times 10 = 200, \text{ and choice}$$

(C) is correct.

22. **A**

If one kilogram is approximately 2.2 pounds, then you would need to divide one pound by 2.2 pounds to determine how many pounds were in one kilogram:

$$\frac{1 \text{ pound}}{2.2 \text{ pounds}} = \frac{10}{22} = \frac{5}{11}, \text{ choice (A)}$$

23. **C**

Take your time and work through a problem like this one one step at a time. If two hot dogs and a soda cost $3.25 and three hot dogs and a soda cost $4.50, then the difference between the two prices would be the price of a single hot dog. A single hot dog costs $4.50 − $3.25 = $1.25. Now that we know the price of a single hot dog, we can solve for the price of a soda.

$$2(\$1.25) + a \text{ soda} = \$3.25$$
$$\$2.50 + a \text{ soda} = \$3.25$$
$$a \text{ soda} = \$0.75$$

Remember, we're looking for the cost of two sodas, so 2($0.75) = $1.50, choice (C).

24. **A**

This is a classic trap question. Intuitively, you'd assume that the average of 40 mph and 60 mph would be 50 mph. Unfortunately, your intuition would be wrong here. Keep in mind that you spend more time traveling at a slower speed, so your average for the entire trip will be closer to the slower speed. A quick way to solve a question like this one is to pick a convenient distance for the entire trip. Since we're dealing with 40 and 60 as rates, let's say the trip is 120 miles long because 120 is a multiple of both 40 and 60. The total average for the trip will be the total distance divided by the total time. Carefully line up your distances and times to solve:

$$120 \text{ miles at } 40 \text{ mph} = 3 \text{ hours}$$
$$120 \text{ miles at } 60 \text{ mph} = 2 \text{ hours}$$

Total distance = 240 miles. Total time = 5 hours.

$$\text{Average speed} = \frac{\text{Total distance}}{\text{Total time}} = \frac{240 \text{ miles}}{5 \text{ hours}} = 48 \text{ mph.}$$

Choice (A) is correct.

25. B

Call the number of teachers n. Then the number of students is $10n$. The total number of teachers and students is $n + 10n = 11n$.

Since you can't have a fraction of a student, n must be an integer, so that means the total number of teachers and students must be a multiple of 11. Scan the answer choices and locate (B), 11×11, as the correct answer.

26. C

Work backwards from your answer choices on this one. Begin with choice (C). If the smaller number is 21 (and the larger number is 35), does the math from the question make sense? If (C) is correct, then the average of 21 and 35 is equal to twice the positive difference between the two numbers. The average of 21 and 35 $= \dfrac{21 + 35}{2} = \dfrac{56}{2} = 28$. The positive difference between 21 and 35 is 14. Twice the positive difference would be 2(14) or 28. As we've already seen, this is also the average of the numbers, so (C) is correct.

We can also solve this question algebraically: Call the smaller number y. The average of the two numbers is $\dfrac{35 + y}{2}$. Twice the positive difference of the two numbers is $2(35 - y)$. The average is equal to twice the positive difference, so $\dfrac{35 + y}{2} = 2(35 - y)$. Solve:

$$\frac{35 + y}{2} = 2(35 - y)$$
$$35 + y = 4(35 - y)$$
$$35 + y = 140 - 4y$$
$$5y = 105$$
$$y = 21$$

27. C

Approximate on questions like this one. If each of seven runners is running a little more than 1.25 kilometers, the total distance run would be a little more than $7(1.25) = 8.75$ or close to 9 kilometers. Choice (C) is correct.

28. D

Be careful with units of measure on this one. You're given feet as units of length and width, but then are asked for square yardage rather than square footage in your answer choices. One easy way to handle this question is to begin by converting feet into yards. 18 feet by 24 feet is the same as 6 yards by 8 yards. If the length and width are 6×8, then the area of the room would be $6 \times 8 = 48$ square yards, choice (D).

29. A

This is a pure arithmetic computation question. That means that if you're careful, you should have no problems banking a correct answer here. Your computations should look something like this:

Add up all your deductions:
$218.99 + 107.05 + 25.03 + 68.65 + 42.75 = 462.47$

Now subtract total deductions from gross pay:
$1,729.23 - 462.47 = 1,306.76$, choice (A) is correct.

30. C

Be careful with the units again. Change 12 feet into inches. $12 \times 12 = 144$ inches. If you subtract 3×17 inch pieces from 144, that will give you the length of the remaining board. $144 - 3(17) = 144 - 51 = 93$. Choice (C) is correct.

WORD KNOWLEDGE ANSWERS AND EXPLANATIONS

1. B

Impose as a verb means to *establish by authority*. Of the answer choices given, only one seems to imply one person dictating to another. *Force* as a verb can be construed as *imposing*. Thus, answer choice (B) is correct.

2. A

Stunted means *stopped short* or *cancelled abruptly*. Answer choice (A), *halted*, also means stopped short.

3. B

While a *sturdy* home might be huge, it does not by nature have to be. Something sturdy, however, would be considered *strong*. Choice (B) is the most accurate answer.

4. B

Undeterred uses the prefix "un-", meaning *opposite of*, with the root word "deter." To deter something is to stop or hinder it. So something *undeterred* would be something unhindered or *determined*.

5. C

Ennui is a French word meaning *annoyed, bored*. Choice (C) is correct.

6. A

Mutable means *prone to change*. Choice (A), *changing*, is the best answer.

7. C

To *squander* is to *waste* or *fritter away* something. Of the choices given, only (C), *wasted*, satisfies as an answer.

8. A

Legible means *able to be read*. Here, the word given is *illegible*, or "not readable." Choice (A) is correct.

9. B

The word *infinite* means *lasting forever* or *unending*.

10. B

Longevity means *length of life*, so choice (B), *lifetime*, is correct.

11. A

Kids fall for lots of things, but even the phrasing of the question gives away the answer a little. Try to remember where you have heard "to fall for" used before. One "falls for" a trick. Answer (A) is correct.

12. C

To *proclaim* is to *announce or decree*, especially in regards to a prominent figure like a president. Answer (C), *announced*, is a synonym for the given word.

13. A

Rudimentary means *simple or easy*. Of the answer choices given, only (A), *basic* applies to something simple or rudimentary.

14. B

The word *rout* means *to defeat soundly* in battle or competition. Answer choice (B) is correct.

15. C

A *rogue* is someone who does not play by the rules. Thus, of the answer choices given, while a rogue may be aggressive or sad or low-brow, he or she is always a *maverick*, which also means someone who ignores the rules. Answer choice (C) is correct.

16. C

To *resonate* means *to sound appropriate* or hit the right note. Knowing a little musical terminology helps here, as *harmonizing* also refers to sounds mixing well together. Choice (C) is the best answer.

17. A

Redundant starts with the prefix "re-," or "again." The first choice you have available is *repetitive*, which means again and again. Answer choice (A) is correct.

18. B

Prescribe looks like a lot of words you know. It means *to lay down a rule or idea as law*. Think of prescriptions that doctors give which tell you what medicines to take and how. Of the words given as choices, (A) and (B) both seem possible. But given the meaning of *prescribe (as in prescription)*, it is logical that (B), *dictate,* is the correct answer.

19. D

Logical means based on logic or *sensible*. Answer choice (D) is correct.

20. A

Note that choice (A) is the word *required*, which has the same root as the given word. In this case, those roots are the same. Answer choice (A) is correct.

21. C

Gravitate is based on what the word it most looks like: gravity. So even if you didn't know that gravitate means *moving towards*, you might be able to make a guess based on your knowledge that the force of gravity pulls things closer together. Choice (C) is correct.

22. D

Cautious means *careful*. Answer choice (D) is correct.

23. C

The meaning of *braggart* is as simple as *someone who brags*. So while many leaders do brag, the correct answer choice here is (C), *showoff*.

24. A

Hearsay is a term often used in law. It means *unfounded stories*. A *rumor* is a story without proof. Choice (A) is correct.

25. C

To *taunt* is to *ridicule* or *tease*. Answer choice (C) is most correct.

26. B

The term *constructive criticism* refers to criticism that constructs or *builds up* the listener rather than destroying him or her. While *flattery* might build some people up, the correct answer here is choice (B), *productive*.

27. C

To *quantify* something is to *be able to count* it. Therefore, (C) is correct.

28. C

Something *effective* is useful, efficient, or productive. *Useful* is an answer choice, so choice (C) is correct.

29. C

Apathy means the state of not caring or *boredom*. Choice (C) is correct.

30. B

A *blemish* is a *glaring problem or defect.*

31. A

Consensus has a root of "con-" meaning *with* (don't confuse this with "con-" meaning *not*). Only answer choice (A) invites togetherness. Another way of tackling this question is to read the sentence carefully and glean that to get a measure passed, one would need *agreement*, not fighting. (A) is the correct answer.

32. D

Dissent has a negative connotation due to the root "dis-," meaning *not*. Answer choice (D) is the only negative choice. *Insubordination*, choice (D), is the correct response.

33. D

Tempo means *the speed of something*. Choice (D) is the right answer.

34. B

Try to fit some of the words into the sentence given to test their context. *Glee* and *protection* are both possible, but neither really seems appropriate to helping her feel better when times are bad. Glee is too happy and protection isn't enough. But *comfort*, (B), would make her feel better.

35. B

Pitfalls are *traps and problems that await*. Answer choice (B) is correct.

PARAGRAPH COMPREHENSION ANSWERS AND EXPLANATIONS

1. C

This is an inference question, so the correct answer may be implied but not spelled out directly. The first paragraph talks about the participants of urban legends. It turns out that they can never be found. In other words, the elusive participant in these supposedly "real-life" events does not actually exist, choice (C). Once you realize that urban legends are fictional, choices (A), (B), and (D) cannot be correct.

2. D

This is an EXCEPT question, so you are looking for the one answer choice that does not characterize successful urban legends. Here again, if you were able to glean that urban legends are fictional, the correct answer choice (D), a basis in reality, is clearly the correct answer. Otherwise, you could use the process of elimination on the wrong answer choices. The passage states that urban legends "persist both for their entertainment value and for the transmission of popular values and beliefs," so choices (A) and (B), which paraphrase this, are wrong. Finally, the very first sentence describes urban legends as a new form of folk tale, so (C) is out.

3. A

This is a very straightforward detail question, so just be careful to locate the information to answer the question. The question asks how many World Series titles have been won by the Red Sox, and the passage states that before the Ruth trade the Red Sox had won that series five times, but afterwards it never won another title. So the Red Sox won a total of five World Series titles, choice (A).

4. B

Remember that in tone questions the answers tend to be from the less extreme of the choices. Choice (B) is correct because the passage merely conveys relevant facts about an issue. While the author does describe two opposing reactions that parents have had to the changes that have taken place in elementary schools, no preference is implied. Therefore choices (A) and (C) are incorrect. Be cautious with choices such as these that use extreme language.

5. D

Although the wording of this question indicates that this is an inference question, the correct answer choice (D) can be gleaned directly from the first sentence. If most life is "dependent on organisms that store radiant energy from the sun," it doesn't take much to infer that most life is ultimately dependent on light from the sun. Remember that on inference questions you are looking for the one answer that must be true based on what is stated in the passage.

6. A

The first paragraph describes ecosystems that are dependent on photosynthetic organisms, while the second paragraph describes ecosystems that are dependent on chemosynthetic organisms. In both cases, the organisms serve similar functions as primary producers within their different food chains, so choice (A) is correct. Choice (B) is wrong because only chemosynthetic organisms are described in the passage as supporting higher organisms "at great ocean depths." (C) is clearly wrong because chemosynthetic organisms do not rely on sunlight for their basic source of energy. Choice (D) is never discussed in the passage.

7. D

This is a slightly tricky inference question, because a lot of dates are mentioned in the passage. Nonetheless, the passage states that Halley determined that the comet followed a 76-year orbit. He never lived to see the comet that appeared in 1758, so it follows that the last time the comet appeared before his death took place 76 years earlier, or in 1758 − 76 = 1682, choice (D).

8. D

The passage discusses a few ways to distinguish a crocodile from an alligator. The first and most easily observed of these is the fact that the crocodile's head and jaws are longer and narrower; in other words, it has a narrower snout, choice (D). (A) is out, because the animals' mouths do not necessarily have to be closed to distinguish one from the other. Choice (B) is out because both animals can be found in the Everglades National Park, and (C) is never discussed as one of the ways to distinguish one giant reptile from the other.

9. A

On this question you are asked to infer what the agent believes. Clearly she must assume that certain actors are inappropriate for certain parts, because if she didn't believe this her conclusion would make no sense; it wouldn't be possible for an actor to audition for an inappropriate part. The actors' talent (B) isn't questioned by the agent; she focuses on the types of roles. The possibility that an actor's appropriateness for the part may be difficult to predict (C) is never assumed by the agent; in fact, if anything, such an belief would weaken her conclusion. Major roles (D) are never discussed in the passage.

10. A

To answer this detail question, scan the passage for a reference to foot or feet. The first such mention is in the third sentence, which states: "Pentameter refers to the number of feet, or groupings of syllables." So clearly, a foot is just that, a grouping of syllables, choice (A).

11. D

This is a main idea question, so reading the passage for details is not necessary, although paying attention to the overall effect of those details is. The author notes that public opinion on the war was swayed when the Lusitania was attacked, prompting increased military involvement from the US. Choice (D) is a paraphrase of this main idea. Of the wrong answer choices, (A) is out because it distorts a detail found in the passage, implying a causal link between America's support for Britain and France and Germany's sinking of the Lusitania that is not supported by the passage. Choice (B) refers to a minor detail in the passage, and choice (C) is simply not true according to the passage, particularly after the sinking of the Lusitania.

12. D

In this inference question, you are asked to supply a conclusion that is best supported by the passage. The author seems to believe that critics' opinions aren't necessarily more significant than those of the average Joe, so (D), which restates this main idea, is easy to conclude. Though the author says the critics' opinions aren't more correct than those of average moviegoers, he doesn't imply (A) that they are usually incorrect. Choice (B) is out because it's not that judgments are meaningless, but that critics don't always make the right judgments. And we don't know how frequently critics dislike popular movies (C), only that when they do, they may not be right.

13. **C**

This detail question asks why Americans did not start using the tomato until the mid-nineteenth century. So what does the passage say? According to the passage, the English considered the tomato poisonous, and this myth continued to hold sway in America until the mid-nineteenth century; in other words, they too believed it to be poisonous, choice (C). None of the other answer choices are supported by the statements in the passage.

14. **A**

This question asks you to infer what the foreign ambassador might do in a given situation. From the details given, one can see the ambassador as a man who expects certain favors and protests loudly when those favors are not granted. Thus, of the choices given, choice (A) makes the most sense, as the ambassador clearly does not feel parking tickets should apply to diplomats.

15. **C**

Don't try to over-analyze on a detail question. They are straightforward and to find the answer you need only to check the text, which says that "the recent infusion of international talent has . . . broadened its marketability overseas," paraphrased in choice (C). While (A) and (D) are mentioned in the passage, they are used as evidence for the assertion that basketball will overtake baseball as America's favorite sport. (B) is not mentioned.

AUTO AND SHOP INFORMATION ANSWERS AND EXPLANATIONS

1. D

A bit of a trick question, because while a *miter box* might be used with a back saw to make even cuts in wood at specific angles, by itself, it is not capable of shaping wood. All of the other choices are tools capable of making cuts or smoothing edges on wood. The correct answer is (D).

2. B

Of all the aspects of vehicle operation, two that are a high priority for most drivers are ride comfort and handling. The suspension system, choice (B), is responsible for the ride quality of the vehicle.

3. D

The cut or slot left by a saw in a piece of wood is also know as a *kerf,* choice (D).

4. D

The *transfer case* is located between the transmission and the drive axles on a four-wheel drive vehicle and is the piece that splits the engine's power between the front and rear drive axle. The correct answer is (D).

5. B

The crosscut saw is designed to do what its name suggests: cut across the grain of the wood. Crosscut saw teeth are unique in that they cut like a knife, in contrast to a rip saw, which is made to cut with the grain of the wood. The correct answer here is (B).

6. C

Though rear-wheel drive trains are increasingly rare, they still show up from time to time. As the name suggests, *rear-wheel* drive trains focus on the back axle. They move from the engine to the back axle. Thus, answer choice (C) is the correct answer.

7. A

Be sure to note that the question asks for the thread pitch of a *metric fastener.* Metric fasteners use the *System Internationale (SI)* method of thread measurement, which designates the distance in millimeters between each thread. For instance a metric bolt with a thread pitch of 4.0 would have threads that are 4.0 millimeters apart.

8. C

Tires are identified using a system known as *P-Metric.* This system gives the tire buyer a thorough understanding of the tire size. The "75" in question is the *aspect ratio* of the tire. This is a comparison of the height of the tire (measured from the bead to the tread) relative to its section width. This tire's height is thus 75% of its width. The correct answer is (C).

9. A

Of the answer choices given, only (A), *coil spring,* is not a part associated with the steering system. Coil springs are what aid the wheels in moving up and down while the vehicle chassis stays steady. The other pieces listed—steering knuckle, tie rod end, and idler arm—are all parts of the steering system.

10. D

The *camshaft* is responsible for the opening and closing of the engine's intake and exhaust valves. The camshaft turns at one half the speed of the engine's crankshaft. The right answer here is (D).

11. D

In fuel-injected engines, the electric fuel pump is located in the vehicle's fuel tank and is what supplies fuel under pressure to the fuel injectors.

12. B

The two basic thread classifications—*Unified National Coarse (UNC),* and *Unified National Fine (UNF)*—have different numbers of threads per inch. A UNC or coarse thread would have relatively few threads per inch, where a UNF or fine thread would have a larger number of threads per inch. Thus, the answer to this question is (B), less.

13. C

Power brake systems use both the engine intake manifold vacuum and fluid pressure from the power steering system to increase pressure. Engine intake manifold vacuum is utilized to generate greater force on the master cylinder, so higher hydraulic pressures can be generated in the brake system. Some brake booster systems use fluid pressure from the power steering system to increase braking power. The answer is (C), both of these.

14. D

The primary is the low voltage part of the system and contains a battery, an ignition switch, a primary coil winding, an ignition module, a reluctor and pickup coil, and a distributor. A rotor is not a part of the ignition primary system. Thus, the correct answer is (D).

15. A

S*toichiometric* is the ideal ratio of air to fuel in the engine and it is the responsibility of the engine's fuel system to maintain this balance.

16. D

Viscosity is resistance to flow, and is expressed as a number that is directly proportional to the thickness of the oil.

17. D

Because they serve different purposes within an automobile, both negative ground current and direct current electrical systems are being built. Alternating current is used primarily for household appliances.

18. D

Stick welding involves the use of an electric arc welding machine and two cables: one that attaches to the work being welded through a *ground clamp,* and the other going to an electrode that is sometimes referred to as a *stinger.* For safety reasons, always clamp to the work. The correct answer is (D).

19. D

A modern five-speed transmission is a manual transmission and it has five forward speeds and one reverse speed. This is in contrast to automatic transmissions, which may have a different number of forward speeds.

20. B

The PCV (positive crankcase ventilation) system takes fresh filtered air and moves it through the engine crankcase, picking up oil fumes and gases that leak past the piston rings and drawing them into the intake manifold through the *PCV valve.* The correct answer is (B).

21. A

The correct answer is (A), wire gauge. The *wire gauge* is made up of a number of short pieces of calibrated wire. These can be used to measure gap on used spark plugs, since the electrodes erode somewhat unevenly over time and make regular feeler gauges inaccurate when used for this purpose.

22. D

Any air passing through to the car's combustion chamber must naturally pass through the intake port in the cylinder head, the intake manifold, and the air filter. All of these are correct. Since the intake valve is open and is allowing atmospheric air to enter the combustion chamber, higher atmospheric air pressure pushes air through the engine's intake system and towards the low-pressure area above the piston. As the air is traveling through the intake system, fuel is injected into the air stream before it enters the combustion chamber. The correct answer is (D).

23. D

Since most nuts are smaller sized, and because the *6-point* is a stronger design, it is usually the mechanic's first choice in the smaller socket drive sizes. And a *breaker bar* attached to a socket can give enough twisting force to loosen very tight fasteners. Thus, the best choice is answer choice (D).

24. D

Vernier micrometers, used when an outside micrometer is too large, are designed to read down to one ten-thousandths (0.0001) of an inch. Choice (D) is correct.

25. B

In lead-acid batteries, as the battery discharges, the sulphuric acid in the electrolyte is reduced to water, and the lead plates become lead sulphate. Answer choice (B) is the right answer.

MATHEMATICS KNOWLEDGE ANSWERS AND EXPLANATIONS

1. D

Use FOIL to solve:

$(3x + 4)(4x - 3)$
$= (3x)(4x) + (3x)(-3) + (4)(4x) + (4)(-3)$
$= 12x^2 - 9x + 16x - 12 = 12x^2 + 7x - 12.$

2. A

Pick numbers to solve this one. Let's say that $n = 2$. That means the tree grew 5 feet, or 60 inches, in 2 years, which means it grew at a rate of 30 inches per year. Plug in 2 for n into the answer choices, and only (A) gives the answer of 30 that you are looking for.

3. D

If the perimeter of *ABCD* is 56, then half that, or 28, is the sum of the length and the width, since the perimeter of a rectangle = 2(length + width). So if $AD = 16$, then $AB = 28 - 16 = 12$, and the area of *ABCD* must be $16 \times 12 = 192$.

4. A

The key to answering this question is realizing that 2 is the only even prime number. Since at least two of the three numbers will be odd, the sum of those two numbers will be even (Odd + Odd = Even), which means that the third number must be even for the sum of the three numbers to be even (Even + Even = Even). Therefore one of the numbers must be 2, which also happens to be the smallest prime number, so the answer is (A).

5. D

We're given two inequalities here: $a < b$ and $b < c$, which we can combine into one, $a < b < c$. We need to go through the answer choices to see which *must* be true. Choice (D): $a + b < 2c$. We know that $a < c$ and $b < c$. If we add the corresponding sides of these inequalities we'll get $a + b < c + c$, or $a + b < 2c$. This statement is *always* true, so it must be the correct answer.

6. C

Since the angle marked $x°$ and the angle marked $y°$ together form a straight angle, their measures must sum to 180°. Substitute in $2z$ for x and $3z$ for y, and solve for z.

$x + y = 180$
$2z + 3z = 180$
$5z = 180$
$z = 36.$

7. B

There are 360 degrees in a circle and 60 minutes in an hour, so you could solve this question by setting up a proportion. $\dfrac{45}{360} = \dfrac{n}{60}$, where n is the number of minutes. $n = \dfrac{45 \times 60}{360} = 7.5$, so the answer is (B).

8. C

$5 \times 5 \times 5 = 125$, and $125 \times 125 = 15,675$, which is the smallest power of 5 that's greater than 10,000. So $(5 \times 5 \times 5) \times (5 \times 5 \times 5)$, or $5^6 = 5^n$, and $n = 6$.

9. B

Since lines p and q are parallel, we can use the rule about alternate interior angles to fill in the following:

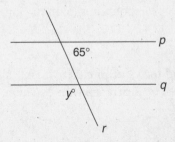

Since the angle marked $y°$ is adjacent and supplementary to a 65° angle, $y = 180 - 65 = 115$.

10. A

You could either turn the percents into decimals and multiply: $0.15 \times 0.15 \times 200 = 0.15 \times 30 = 4.5$, so the answer is (A), or you could take it one step at a time. 15 percent of 200 is $\frac{15}{100} \times 200 = 15 \times 2 = 30$. 15 percent of 30 is $\frac{15}{100} \times 30 = \frac{3}{20} \times 30 = \frac{3}{2} \times 3 = \frac{9}{2} = 4.5$, so the answer is (A).

11. B

Don't fall for the answer choice trap and assume that the average of $\frac{1}{20}$ and $\frac{1}{30}$ is $\frac{1}{25}$. Instead, use the average formula: Average $= \frac{\text{Sum of the terms}}{\text{Number of terms}}$. So, in this case, Average $= \frac{\frac{1}{20} + \frac{1}{30}}{2} = \frac{\frac{3}{60} + \frac{2}{60}}{2} = \frac{\frac{5}{60}}{2} = \frac{5}{120} = \frac{1}{24}$.

12. C

This question is just testing your knowledge of definitions. The *supplement* of an angle is the angle that when added to the original angle equals 180°. So if an angle measures $y°$, its supplement is $180 - y$.

13. B

If Diane has $\frac{2}{3}$ of her room still to paint, she'll need $2 \times 2\frac{1}{2}$ or 5 more cans to do the job.

14. D

You can't find the value of either variable alone, but you don't need to. Rearranging the equation, you get:

$$13 + a = 25 + b$$
$$13 = 25 + b - a$$
$$13 - 25 = b - a$$
$$b - a = -12$$

15. C

When you multiply terms that have exponents over the same base, you add the exponents and multiply the coefficients, so in this case you get:

$$3x^2 \times 5x^3 = (3 \times 5)x^{2+3} = 15x^5.$$

16. D

You can pick numbers to make sense of this geometry problem. You are asked to increase the sides of a square by 10 percent, so you want to pick a number for the original sides of the square of which it's easy to take 10 percent. For instance, you could say that the original square is 10 by 10. 10 percent of 10 is 1, so the dimensions of the increased square are 11 by 11. In this case, the area of the original square is 100, and the area of the new square is 121, which represents a 21 percent increase, choice (D).

17. B

If $\frac{m}{2} = 15$, then $m = 15 \times 2 = 30$, so $\frac{m}{3} = \frac{30}{3} = 10$.

18. C

To factor $6x^2 - 13x + 6$, you need a pair of binomials whose "first" terms will give you a product of $6x^2$ and whose "last" terms will give you a product of 6. And since the middle term of the result is negative, the two last terms must both be negative. You know that one of the factors is among the answer choices, so you can use them in your trial-and-error effort to factor. You know you're looking for a factor with a minus sign in it, so the answer's either (C) or (D).

Try (C) first: Its first term is $3x$, so the other factor's first term would have to be $2x$ (to get that $6x^2$ in the product). (C)'s last term is -2, so the other factor's last term would have to be -3. Check to see if $(3x - 2)(2x - 3)$ works:

$$(3x - 2)(2x - 3)$$
$$= (3x)(2x) + 3x(-3) + (-2)(2x) + (-2)(-3)$$
$$= 6x^2 - 9x - 4x + 6$$
$$= 6x^2 - 13x + 6$$

It works. There's no need to check (D).

19. D

Just be careful and translate the English into math: "the product of 3 and x is equal to 2 less than y" becomes $3x = y - 2$. But all of the equations in the answer choices set the right side of the equation to zero, so let's do that to our equation:

$$3x = y - 2$$
$$3x - y = -2$$
$$3x - y + 2 = 0.$$

20. A

Since $\dfrac{b}{a}$ is the reciprocal of $\dfrac{a}{b}$, $\dfrac{b}{a}$ must be the reciprocal of $1 - \dfrac{1}{x}$ as well. Combine the terms in $1 - \dfrac{1}{x}$ and then find its reciprocal.

$$\frac{a}{b} = 1 - \frac{1}{x} = \frac{x}{x} - \frac{1}{x} = \frac{x-1}{x}$$

Therefore, $\dfrac{b}{a} = \dfrac{x}{x-1}$.

21. C

This figure is an unfamiliar solid, so we shouldn't try to calculate the volume directly. We are told that the solid in question is half of a cube. We can imagine the other half lying on top of the solid, forming a complete cube.

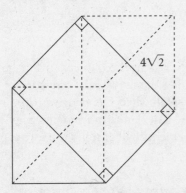

Notice that the diagonal with length $4\sqrt{2}$ and two of the cube's edges form an isosceles right triangle. In an isosceles right triangle, the hypotenuse is $\sqrt{2}$ times the length of a leg. Here the hypotenuse has length $4\sqrt{2}$, so the legs have length 4. Thus, the edges of the cube have a length of 4. The volume of a cube is the length of an edge cubed. So the volume of the whole cube is $4 \times 4 \times 4$, or 64. The volume of the solid in question is $\dfrac{1}{2}$ of this, or 32.

22. B

Begin by writing the division problem as a fraction: $\dfrac{7.6}{0.019} = x$. Now move the decimal points on the top and the bottom of the fraction the same number of places to the right until you are dealing with whole numbers: $\dfrac{7.6}{0.019} = \dfrac{7,600}{19}$. Now go ahead and divide: $\dfrac{7,600}{19} = 400.$

23. A

The circumference of a circle $= 2\pi(\text{radius})$, so the radius of a circle with a circumference of 8 is $\dfrac{8}{2\pi} = \dfrac{4}{\pi}$. The area of a circle $= \pi(\text{radius})^2$, so the area of a circle with a radius of $\dfrac{4}{\pi}$ is $\pi\left(\dfrac{4}{\pi}\right)^2 = \pi\left(\dfrac{16}{\pi^2}\right) = \dfrac{16}{\pi}$, choice (A).

24. B

You could translate the English into math to get : $.36 \times 18 = .18 \times n$, so $n = \dfrac{.36 \times 18}{.18} = 2 \times 18 = 36$. Of course, you don't have to go through all that work if you realize that x percent of $y = y$ percent of x.

25. C

Here you're looking for an extremely rough approximation (the answer choices all have a range of 100), so you could square the upper bounds of the ranges in the answer choices, until you find the range that encompasses 104,906. For instance, starting with the upper bound of (A), $(200)^2 = 40,000$, which is less than 104,906. Now try (B): $(300)^2 = 90,000$, which is still too low. Now check (C): $(400)^2 = 160,000$. 104,906 is between 90,000 and 160,000, so (C) is the answer.

MECHANICAL COMPREHENSION ANSWERS AND EXPLANATIONS

1. C

The principle of conservation of mechanical energy tells us that the total mechanical energy of an object (PE + KE) remains constant as an object moves. As the car rolls down the hill, its speed increases because its potential energy (PE) is being converted into kinetic energy (KE).

2. D

When a ball is thrown straight up, it has its maximum kinetic energy when it leaves the thrower's hand. This kinetic energy is converted into potential energy as it rises. Maximum potential energy (PE) occurs when the ball stops rising, and this is where its velocity is zero.

3. B

Inertia is a function of an object's mass. A large mass will require a large amount of force to cause it to accelerate. The larger the mass, the greater the inertia of the object.

4. C.

When two objects collide, total linear momentum of the system is conserved. Linear momentum is calculated using the formula p = mv.

5. D

It requires less force to push objects up ramps that are less steep. Even less force is required when the friction between the ramp and the object is reduced.

6. C.

Work is defined as force times distance. Lifting a box straight up to the top of a ramp will require the same amount of work as pushing the box up the ramp (neglecting friction). The end result is the same in both cases (the box is at the top of the ramp), so the work done is also the same.

7. B

It is not possible to get more work out of a machine than what is put in. Machines do not reduce the work we do, they simply manage it and make it easier by diminishing the amount of force that is required.

8. A

A chisel is an example of a wedge.

9. B

The wedge is a variation of the inclined plane, but is made to move where the inclined plane stays stationary.

10. A

A screw is based on the design of the inclined plane. The threads are wrapped around the screw much like a spiral staircase.

11. C

Rotating a screw results in its moving forward or backward, depending on the direction of rotation. This converts rotary motion into straight line, or linear motion.

12. B

A screwdriver gains mechanical advantage through the use of a large wheel (screwdriver handle) rotating a small wheel (screwdriver tip), much like a wheel and axle. Large movements converted into small movements will amplify the force applied.

13. B

Any time that force is increased through mechanical advantage, there will always be a proportional decrease in the distance moved.

14. A

A prybar can increase mechanical advantage, and can change the direction of motion, so it is a first class lever.

15. A

A second class lever is made to increase force, but not to change direction of the force. The fulcrum is thus located at the extreme end of the lever. In the case of the wheelbarrow, the wheel represents the pivot point (fulcrum).

16. C

Moving the fulcrum towards the object will increase the force applied to the object, but decrease the distance that the object can be moved.

17. B

A third class lever is made to increase the distance moved, with a proportional decrease in the force applied. A good example of a third class lever is a fishing pole.

18. D

A pulley with a grooved rim is called a *sheave* (pronounced "shiv").

19. D

A block-and-tackle requires a minimum of two pulleys, with a rope, belt, or chain used to operate them.

20. C

A 10:1 mechanical advantage implies that force will be multiplied ten times, but the distance moved by decrease by a factor of ten. This means that to lift a load 10 inches, the rope will have to be pulled 10 times that distance, or 100 inches.

21. B

A doorknob is similar to a wheel and axle in that a large wheel (the doorknob or handle) is used to operate a small wheel (the latch mechanism).

22. D

An automobile transmission has multiple speed ranges, which make it capable of increasing torque and decreasing speed (speed reduction), or increasing speed and decreasing torque (overdrive).

23. C

An overdrive is made to increase speed across the gear set, but will decrease torque output proportionately.

24. C

The torque output of this gear set will be four times the torque input.

25. D

The size of the idler gear will have no impact on the operation of the gear set.

ELECTRONICS INFORMATION ANSWERS AND EXPLANATIONS

1. D

Resistance is measured in ohms, and the symbol for an ohm is Ω (omega).

2. B

Power (in watts) is calculated by multiplying applied voltage (in volts) by current flow (in amperes).

3. A

Total resistance in a parallel circuit can be calculated using the formula $\frac{1}{R_T} = \frac{1}{R_1} + \frac{1}{R_2} + \frac{1}{R_3}$, etc. In this case, $\frac{1}{15} + \frac{1}{15} + \frac{1}{15} = \frac{3}{15}$, or $\frac{1}{5}$, $\frac{1}{5} = \frac{1}{R}$, so R = 5 Ω, answer choice (B).

4. B

A closed circuit has continuity, and will allow current to flow in it.

5. B

This symbol represents a capacitor.

6. D

The P-type material in a diode is the anode, and the N-type material is known as the cathode.

7. D

Pure silicon must be doped in order to generate holes or free electrons. This process creates the P and N materials needed to make diodes and transistors.

8. D

Inductance is measured in henries, but one henry (1 H) represents a very large amount of inductance. It is much more common to rate inductors using millihenries (mH).

9. A

A capacitor's capacitance is measured in farads, or microfarads. Its capacitive reactance, however, is measured in ohms.

10. C

The arrow in a transistor symbol is always placed on the emitter, and the arrow always points towards the N-type material at that junction.

11. C

This symbol represents an NPN transistor. Note that the base is made of P-type material, and the arrow always points towards the N-type material (in this case, at the emitter).

12. B

PIV stands for peak inverse voltage, which is the maximum voltage a diode can withstand when reverse-biased.

13. D

A capacitor is made to allow AC (alternating current) to pass, but it will block the flow of DC (direct current).

14. A

A heat sink is a component that is used to help cool solid-state devices such as transistors and diodes. They are often made of aluminum and have fins to increase their heat-rejection capacity.

15. C

A transistor can be used as an amplifier, and the output of the average transistor is 150 times the input signal. This is known as a transistor's *gain*.

16. **C**

An insulator is a material that does not conduct electricity.

17. **A**

Rubber is an example of an insulator. All of the other examples in this question are conductors.

18. **C**

Four 6-ohm resistors wired in series will have a total resistance of 24 ohms. Using $I = E \div R$, a total of 0.5 A will flow in this circuit. 0.5 A is the same as 500 mA.

19. **C**

Using the formula $I = P \div E$, 100 watts divided by 120 volts equals 0.833 A. This is the equivalent of 833 mA.

20. **B**

Adding more loads to a series circuit will result in an increase in the total circuit resistance. Whenever total resistance increases (and voltage stays the same), total current flow in the circuit will decrease.

ASVAB Practice Test III

ANSWER SHEET

Part 1: General Science (GS)

1 Ⓐ Ⓑ Ⓒ Ⓓ	6 Ⓐ Ⓑ Ⓒ Ⓓ	11 Ⓐ Ⓑ Ⓒ Ⓓ	16 Ⓐ Ⓑ Ⓒ Ⓓ	21 Ⓐ Ⓑ Ⓒ Ⓓ
2 Ⓐ Ⓑ Ⓒ Ⓓ	7 Ⓐ Ⓑ Ⓒ Ⓓ	12 Ⓐ Ⓑ Ⓒ Ⓓ	17 Ⓐ Ⓑ Ⓒ Ⓓ	22 Ⓐ Ⓑ Ⓒ Ⓓ
3 Ⓐ Ⓑ Ⓒ Ⓓ	8 Ⓐ Ⓑ Ⓒ Ⓓ	13 Ⓐ Ⓑ Ⓒ Ⓓ	18 Ⓐ Ⓑ Ⓒ Ⓓ	23 Ⓐ Ⓑ Ⓒ Ⓓ
4 Ⓐ Ⓑ Ⓒ Ⓓ	9 Ⓐ Ⓑ Ⓒ Ⓓ	14 Ⓐ Ⓑ Ⓒ Ⓓ	19 Ⓐ Ⓑ Ⓒ Ⓓ	24 Ⓐ Ⓑ Ⓒ Ⓓ
5 Ⓐ Ⓑ Ⓒ Ⓓ	10 Ⓐ Ⓑ Ⓒ Ⓓ	15 Ⓐ Ⓑ Ⓒ Ⓓ	20 Ⓐ Ⓑ Ⓒ Ⓓ	25 Ⓐ Ⓑ Ⓒ Ⓓ

Part 2: Arithmetic Reasoning (AR)

1 Ⓐ Ⓑ Ⓒ Ⓓ	7 Ⓐ Ⓑ Ⓒ Ⓓ	13 Ⓐ Ⓑ Ⓒ Ⓓ	19 Ⓐ Ⓑ Ⓒ Ⓓ	25 Ⓐ Ⓑ Ⓒ Ⓓ
2 Ⓐ Ⓑ Ⓒ Ⓓ	8 Ⓐ Ⓑ Ⓒ Ⓓ	14 Ⓐ Ⓑ Ⓒ Ⓓ	20 Ⓐ Ⓑ Ⓒ Ⓓ	26 Ⓐ Ⓑ Ⓒ Ⓓ
3 Ⓐ Ⓑ Ⓒ Ⓓ	9 Ⓐ Ⓑ Ⓒ Ⓓ	15 Ⓐ Ⓑ Ⓒ Ⓓ	21 Ⓐ Ⓑ Ⓒ Ⓓ	27 Ⓐ Ⓑ Ⓒ Ⓓ
4 Ⓐ Ⓑ Ⓒ Ⓓ	10 Ⓐ Ⓑ Ⓒ Ⓓ	16 Ⓐ Ⓑ Ⓒ Ⓓ	22 Ⓐ Ⓑ Ⓒ Ⓓ	28 Ⓐ Ⓑ Ⓒ Ⓓ
5 Ⓐ Ⓑ Ⓒ Ⓓ	11 Ⓐ Ⓑ Ⓒ Ⓓ	17 Ⓐ Ⓑ Ⓒ Ⓓ	23 Ⓐ Ⓑ Ⓒ Ⓓ	29 Ⓐ Ⓑ Ⓒ Ⓓ
6 Ⓐ Ⓑ Ⓒ Ⓓ	12 Ⓐ Ⓑ Ⓒ Ⓓ	18 Ⓐ Ⓑ Ⓒ Ⓓ	24 Ⓐ Ⓑ Ⓒ Ⓓ	30 Ⓐ Ⓑ Ⓒ Ⓓ

Part 3: Word Knowledge (WK)

1 Ⓐ Ⓑ Ⓒ Ⓓ	8 Ⓐ Ⓑ Ⓒ Ⓓ	15 Ⓐ Ⓑ Ⓒ Ⓓ	22 Ⓐ Ⓑ Ⓒ Ⓓ	29 Ⓐ Ⓑ Ⓒ Ⓓ
2 Ⓐ Ⓑ Ⓒ Ⓓ	9 Ⓐ Ⓑ Ⓒ Ⓓ	16 Ⓐ Ⓑ Ⓒ Ⓓ	23 Ⓐ Ⓑ Ⓒ Ⓓ	30 Ⓐ Ⓑ Ⓒ Ⓓ
3 Ⓐ Ⓑ Ⓒ Ⓓ	10 Ⓐ Ⓑ Ⓒ Ⓓ	17 Ⓐ Ⓑ Ⓒ Ⓓ	24 Ⓐ Ⓑ Ⓒ Ⓓ	31 Ⓐ Ⓑ Ⓒ Ⓓ
4 Ⓐ Ⓑ Ⓒ Ⓓ	11 Ⓐ Ⓑ Ⓒ Ⓓ	18 Ⓐ Ⓑ Ⓒ Ⓓ	25 Ⓐ Ⓑ Ⓒ Ⓓ	32 Ⓐ Ⓑ Ⓒ Ⓓ
5 Ⓐ Ⓑ Ⓒ Ⓓ	12 Ⓐ Ⓑ Ⓒ Ⓓ	19 Ⓐ Ⓑ Ⓒ Ⓓ	26 Ⓐ Ⓑ Ⓒ Ⓓ	33 Ⓐ Ⓑ Ⓒ Ⓓ
6 Ⓐ Ⓑ Ⓒ Ⓓ	13 Ⓐ Ⓑ Ⓒ Ⓓ	20 Ⓐ Ⓑ Ⓒ Ⓓ	27 Ⓐ Ⓑ Ⓒ Ⓓ	34 Ⓐ Ⓑ Ⓒ Ⓓ
7 Ⓐ Ⓑ Ⓒ Ⓓ	14 Ⓐ Ⓑ Ⓒ Ⓓ	21 Ⓐ Ⓑ Ⓒ Ⓓ	28 Ⓐ Ⓑ Ⓒ Ⓓ	35 Ⓐ Ⓑ Ⓒ Ⓓ

Part 4: Paragraph Comprehension (PC)

1 Ⓐ Ⓑ Ⓒ Ⓓ	4 Ⓐ Ⓑ Ⓒ Ⓓ	7 Ⓐ Ⓑ Ⓒ Ⓓ	10 Ⓐ Ⓑ Ⓒ Ⓓ	13 Ⓐ Ⓑ Ⓒ Ⓓ
2 Ⓐ Ⓑ Ⓒ Ⓓ	5 Ⓐ Ⓑ Ⓒ Ⓓ	8 Ⓐ Ⓑ Ⓒ Ⓓ	11 Ⓐ Ⓑ Ⓒ Ⓓ	14 Ⓐ Ⓑ Ⓒ Ⓓ
3 Ⓐ Ⓑ Ⓒ Ⓓ	6 Ⓐ Ⓑ Ⓒ Ⓓ	9 Ⓐ Ⓑ Ⓒ Ⓓ	12 Ⓐ Ⓑ Ⓒ Ⓓ	15 Ⓐ Ⓑ Ⓒ Ⓓ

Part 5: Automotive and Shop Information (AS)

1 Ⓐ Ⓑ Ⓒ Ⓓ	6 Ⓐ Ⓑ Ⓒ Ⓓ	11 Ⓐ Ⓑ Ⓒ Ⓓ	16 Ⓐ Ⓑ Ⓒ Ⓓ	21 Ⓐ Ⓑ Ⓒ Ⓓ
2 Ⓐ Ⓑ Ⓒ Ⓓ	7 Ⓐ Ⓑ Ⓒ Ⓓ	12 Ⓐ Ⓑ Ⓒ Ⓓ	17 Ⓐ Ⓑ Ⓒ Ⓓ	22 Ⓐ Ⓑ Ⓒ Ⓓ
3 Ⓐ Ⓑ Ⓒ Ⓓ	8 Ⓐ Ⓑ Ⓒ Ⓓ	13 Ⓐ Ⓑ Ⓒ Ⓓ	18 Ⓐ Ⓑ Ⓒ Ⓓ	23 Ⓐ Ⓑ Ⓒ Ⓓ
4 Ⓐ Ⓑ Ⓒ Ⓓ	9 Ⓐ Ⓑ Ⓒ Ⓓ	14 Ⓐ Ⓑ Ⓒ Ⓓ	19 Ⓐ Ⓑ Ⓒ Ⓓ	24 Ⓐ Ⓑ Ⓒ Ⓓ
5 Ⓐ Ⓑ Ⓒ Ⓓ	10 Ⓐ Ⓑ Ⓒ Ⓓ	15 Ⓐ Ⓑ Ⓒ Ⓓ	20 Ⓐ Ⓑ Ⓒ Ⓓ	25 Ⓐ Ⓑ Ⓒ Ⓓ

ANSWER SHEET

Part 6: Mathematics Knowledge (MK)

1 (A)(B)(C)(D) 6 (A)(B)(C)(D) 11 (A)(B)(C)(D) 16 (A)(B)(C)(D) 21 (A)(B)(C)(D)
2 (A)(B)(C)(D) 7 (A)(B)(C)(D) 12 (A)(B)(C)(D) 17 (A)(B)(C)(D) 22 (A)(B)(C)(D)
3 (A)(B)(C)(D) 8 (A)(B)(C)(D) 13 (A)(B)(C)(D) 18 (A)(B)(C)(D) 23 (A)(B)(C)(D)
4 (A)(B)(C)(D) 9 (A)(B)(C)(D) 14 (A)(B)(C)(D) 19 (A)(B)(C)(D) 24 (A)(B)(C)(D)
5 (A)(B)(C)(D) 10 (A)(B)(C)(D) 15 (A)(B)(C)(D) 20 (A)(B)(C)(D) 25 (A)(B)(C)(D)

Part 7: Mechanical Comprehension (MC)

1 (A)(B)(C)(D) 6 (A)(B)(C)(D) 11 (A)(B)(C)(D) 16 (A)(B)(C)(D) 21 (A)(B)(C)(D)
2 (A)(B)(C)(D) 7 (A)(B)(C)(D) 12 (A)(B)(C)(D) 17 (A)(B)(C)(D) 22 (A)(B)(C)(D)
3 (A)(B)(C)(D) 8 (A)(B)(C)(D) 13 (A)(B)(C)(D) 18 (A)(B)(C)(D) 23 (A)(B)(C)(D)
4 (A)(B)(C)(D) 9 (A)(B)(C)(D) 14 (A)(B)(C)(D) 19 (A)(B)(C)(D) 24 (A)(B)(C)(D)
5 (A)(B)(C)(D) 10 (A)(B)(C)(D) 15 (A)(B)(C)(D) 20 (A)(B)(C)(D) 25 (A)(B)(C)(D)

Part 8: Electronics Information (EI)

1 (A)(B)(C)(D) 5 (A)(B)(C)(D) 9 (A)(B)(C)(D) 13 (A)(B)(C)(D) 17 (A)(B)(C)(D)
2 (A)(B)(C)(D) 6 (A)(B)(C)(D) 10 (A)(B)(C)(D) 14 (A)(B)(C)(D) 18 (A)(B)(C)(D)
3 (A)(B)(C)(D) 7 (A)(B)(C)(D) 11 (A)(B)(C)(D) 15 (A)(B)(C)(D) 19 (A)(B)(C)(D)
4 (A)(B)(C)(D) 8 (A)(B)(C)(D) 12 (A)(B)(C)(D) 16 (A)(B)(C)(D) 20 (A)(B)(C)(D)

Part 9: Assembling Objects (AO)

1 (A)(B)(C)(D) 4 (A)(B)(C)(D) 7 (A)(B)(C)(D) 10 (A)(B)(C)(D) 13 (A)(B)(C)(D)
2 (A)(B)(C)(D) 5 (A)(B)(C)(D) 8 (A)(B)(C)(D) 11 (A)(B)(C)(D) 14 (A)(B)(C)(D)
3 (A)(B)(C)(D) 6 (A)(B)(C)(D) 9 (A)(B)(C)(D) 12 (A)(B)(C)(D) 15 (A)(B)(C)(D)
                                                              16 (A)(B)(C)(D)

PART 1: GENERAL SCIENCE (GS)

Time: 11 minutes; 25 questions

<u>Directions</u>: In this section, you will be tested on your knowledge of concepts in science generally reviewed in high school. For each question, select the best answer and mark the corresponding oval on your answer sheet.

1. Those wishing to consume a low-cholesterol diet should limit their intake of

    (A) nuts
    (B) avocados
    (C) bread
    (D) organ meats

2. Water at sea level boils at what temperature?

    (A) 100° F
    (B) 180° F
    (C) 212° C
    (D) 373° K

3. Which of the following subatomic particles has the largest mass?

    (A) proton
    (B) electron
    (C) positron
    (D) neutrino

4. Which of the following is an example of an autotroph?

    (A) a vulture
    (B) an apple tree
    (C) a toadstool
    (D) a sea anemone

5. Which of the following came first?

    (A) Cenozoic era
    (B) Mesozoic era
    (C) Paleozoic era
    (D) Precambrian era

6. Which of the following planets is larger than Earth?

    (A) Mars
    (B) Pluto
    (C) Uranus
    (D) Venus

7. An inorganic compound essential to the survival of animals is

    (A) glucose
    (B) salt
    (C) maltase
    (D) cellulose

8. The study of interactions between organisms and their interrelationships with the physical environment is known as

    (A) cytology
    (B) ecology
    (C) physiology
    (D) embryology

9. Most of the nutrients in food are absorbed in the body's

    (A) stomach
    (B) pylorus
    (C) small intestine
    (D) large intestine

GO ON TO THE NEXT PAGE

10. The gene for color blindness is X-linked. If normal parents have a color-blind son, what is the probability that he inherited the gene for color blindness from his mother?

    (A) 0%
    (B) 25%
    (C) 50%
    (D) 100%

11. Which of the following animals has the highest metabolic rate?

    (A) dog
    (B) horse
    (C) mouse
    (D) rabbit

12. Which of the following states of electromagnetic radiation has the longest wavelength and lowest frequency?

    (A) radio waves
    (B) microwaves
    (C) gamma rays
    (D) visible light

13. A lack of vitamin D can cause

    (A) anemia
    (B) night blindness
    (C) scurvy
    (D) rickets

14. Which of the following has the highest pH?

    (A) vinegar
    (B) water
    (C) baking soda
    (D) cranberry juice

15. Carbohydrates include

    (A) starches
    (B) sugars
    (C) Both A and B are correct.
    (D) Neither A nor B are correct.

16. Members of an order are more alike than members of a

    (A) class
    (B) family
    (C) genus
    (D) species

17. A major asteroid belt can be found in our solar system between

    (A) Venus and Earth
    (B) Earth and Mars
    (C) Mars and Jupiter
    (D) Jupiter and Saturn

18. Animals with chitinous exoskeletons and jointed appendages are classified as

    (A) arthropods
    (B) annelids
    (C) coelenterates
    (D) chordates

19. The atom of an element with an atomic number of 17 must have

    (A) 17 electrons
    (B) 17 protons
    (C) 17 neutrons
    (D) an atomic mass of 17

GO ON TO THE NEXT PAGE

20. Because mushrooms absorb nutrients from decaying leaves, they are classified as

    (A) autotrophs
    (B) anaerobes
    (C) saprophytes
    (D) protozoans

21. The vessel with the LEAST oxygenated blood is the

    (A) pulmonary artery
    (B) aorta
    (C) pulmonary vein
    (D) superior vena cava

22. Saliva in the mouth begins the process of breaking down

    (A) starch
    (B) fat
    (C) protein
    (D) all of the above

23. In which of the following kingdoms do cells lack nuclei?

    (A) Fungi
    (B) Monera
    (C) Plantae
    (D) Protista

24. An atom that is not electrically neutral is called

    (A) an isotope
    (B) a positron
    (C) an ion
    (D) an allotrope

25. Which of the following is an example of a metamorphic rock?

    (A) granite
    (B) marble
    (C) limestone
    (D) shale

STOP. IF YOU FINISH BEFORE THE TIME IS UP, YOU MAY CHECK OVER YOUR WORK ON THIS PART ONLY.

PART 2: ARITHMETIC REASONING (AR)

Time: 36 minutes; 30 questions

Directions: In this section, you are tested on your ability to use arithmetic. For each question, select the best answer and mark the corresponding oval on your answer sheet.

1. A certain machine caps 5 bottles every 2 seconds. At this rate, how many bottles will be capped in 1 minute?

   (A) 75
   (B) 150
   (C) 225
   (D) 300

2. Jonah traveled 650 miles on his most recent trip and averaged 25 miles to the gallon. If gasoline cost $1.30 per gallon, how much did he spend on his trip?

   (A) $26.00
   (B) $27.30
   (C) $32.50
   (D) $33.80

3. If there are approximately 3.86 liters in a gallon, and gasoline costs $1.54 per gallon, to the nearest penny what is the cost of a liter of gasoline?

   (A) $0.35
   (B) $0.40
   (C) $0.44
   (D) $0.47

4. How many minutes are there in one week?

   (A) 3,600
   (B) 7,200
   (C) 10,080
   (D) 86,400

5. Pat deposited 15 percent of last week's take-home pay into a savings account. If she deposited $37.50, what was last week's take-home pay?

   (A) $56.25
   (B) $112.50
   (C) $225.00
   (D) $250.00

6. If the ratio of males to females in a group of students is 3:5, which of the following could be the total number of students in the group?

   (A) 148
   (B) 150
   (C) 152
   (D) 154

7. A car travels 288 miles in 6 hours. At that rate, how many miles will it travel in 8 hours?

   (A) 360
   (B) 368
   (C) 376
   (D) 384

8. Martin's average score after 4 tests is 89. What score on the 5th test would bring Martin's average up to exactly 90?

   (A) 91
   (B) 92
   (C) 93
   (D) 94

GO ON TO THE NEXT PAGE

9. In 2000, the population of Town A was 9,400 and the population of Town B was 7,600. Since then, each year the population of Town A has decreased by 100 and the population of Town B has increased by 100. Assuming that in each case the rate continues, in what year will the two populations be equal?

   (A) 2009
   (B) 2010
   (C) 2017
   (D) 2018

10. One number is 5 times another number and their sum is −60. What is the lesser of the two numbers?

    (A) −10
    (B) −12
    (C) −48
    (D) −50

11. John gets paid $6.00 for each of the first 40 toy cars he makes in a week. For any additional toy cars beyond 40 his pay increases by 50%. How much does John get paid in a week in which he makes 48 toy cars?

    (A) $288
    (B) $300
    (C) $312
    (D) $321

12. If a bora = 2 fedis, and a fedi = 3 glecks, how many boras are equal to 48 glecks?

    (A) 8
    (B) 16
    (C) 32
    (D) 96

13. Nine temperature readings were taken, one reading every four hours, with the first reading taken at 12 P.M. What will be the time when the final reading is taken?

    (A) 4 P.M.
    (B) 8 P.M.
    (C) 12 A.M.
    (D) 4 A.M.

14. A school raised month tuition payments from $225.00 per month to $300.00 per month. The percent of the tuition increase is which of the following?

    (A) 25 percent
    (B) $33\frac{1}{3}$ percent
    (C) $66\frac{1}{2}$ percent
    (D) 75 percent

15. A truck going at a rate of 20 miles per hour takes 6 hours to complete a trip. How many fewer hours would the trip have taken if the truck were traveling at a rate of 30 miles per hour?

    (A) 4
    (B) 3
    (C) 2
    (D) 1

16. If a barrel has the capacity to hold 75 gallons, how many gallons does it contain when it is $\frac{3}{5}$ full?

    (A) 45
    (B) 48
    (C) 54
    (D) 60

GO ON TO THE NEXT PAGE

17. If a salary of $45,000 is subject to a 40 percent deduction, the new salary is

    (A) $18,000
    (B) $27,000
    (C) $30,000
    (D) $36,000

18. If pound of lawn fertilizer will cover 10 square yards, how many pounds will be needed to cover 450 square feet?

    (A) 4.5
    (B) 5
    (C) 9
    (D) 15

19. Fifteen people chip in $40 dollars each to throw a birthday bash for a mutual friend. If 35 percent of the money is spent on a group gift and the rest is spent on the party, how much was spent just on the party?

    (A) $210
    (B) $300
    (C) $350
    (D) $390

20. If an employee worked a total of $33\frac{1}{2}$ hours over five days, what was the average amount of time that the employee worked each day?

    (A) 6 hours, 35 minutes
    (B) 6 hours, 40 minutes
    (C) 6 hours, 42 minutes
    (D) 6 hours, 45 minutes

21. If a train starting out at Point A travels 180 miles at a rate of 60 miles per hour and then 150 miles at a rate of 75 miles per hour before arriving at Point B, what was the average rate, in miles per hour, for the entire trip?

    (A) 66
    (B) 67.5
    (C) 68.5
    (D) 70

22. After being discounted by 20 percent, a bicycle sells for $140.00. What was the original price of the bicycle?

    (A) $155.00
    (B) $162.00
    (C) $175.00
    (D) $180.00

23. A checking account has a balance of $1,162.76. After a check for $352.68 is deposited into the account and three checks are drawn from the account for the amounts of $152.45, $82.85, and $255.50, what is the new balance for the checking account?

    (A) $1,024.54
    (B) $1,024.64
    (C) $1,025.54
    (D) $1,025.64

24. Harold works 4.5 hours a day, 3 days each week after school. He is paid $4.25 per hour. How much is his weekly pay rounded to the next highest cent?

    (A) $13.50
    (B) $19.13
    (C) $54.00
    (D) $57.38

GO ON TO THE NEXT PAGE

Color of Chip	Number of Chips
orange	2
red	4
yellow	3
green	1
blue	6

25. The table above shows the number of chips of each color in an urn. Which color has a probability of 1 out of 8 of being chosen if 1 chip is chosen at random from the urn?

(A) orange

(B) red

(C) yellow

(D) green

26. What is the total cost of 4 sheets of 23¢ stamps, 2 sheets of 37¢ stamps, and 3 sheets of 60¢ stamps if each sheet has 100 stamps?

(A) $336

(B) $346

(C) $356

(D) $366

27. The Pacific Standard Time (PST) in Los Angeles is 3 hours earlier than the Eastern Standard Time (EST) in New York. A plane leaves Los Angeles at 5:30 P.M. PST and arrives in New York City at 12:45 A.M. EST. How long did the flight take?

(A) 4 hours, 15 minutes

(B) 4 hours, 45 minutes

(C) 6 hours, 45 minutes

(D) 7 hours, 15 minutes

28. After the price of a digital camera is discounted 25 percent, the camera sells for $120. What was the original price of the camera?

(A) $145

(B) $150

(C) $160

(D) $180

29. How many slices of bread, each weighing 1.5 ounces, are found in a loaf of sliced bread that weighs 1 pound, 11 ounces?

(A) 9

(B) 13

(C) 17

(D) 18

30. If it takes 20 minutes to type 5 pages, how long will it take to type a 162-page document?

(A) 10 hours, 12 minutes

(B) 10 hours, 36 minutes

(C) 10 hours, 45 minutes

(D) 10 hours, 48 minutes

STOP. IF YOU FINISH BEFORE THE TIME IS UP, YOU MAY CHECK OVER YOUR WORK ON THIS PART ONLY.

PART 3. WORD KNOWLEDGE (WK)

Time: 11 minutes; 35 questions

<u>Directions</u>: In this section, you are tested on the meaning of words. Each of the following questions has an underlined word. Select the answer that most nearly means the same as the underlined word and mark the corresponding oval on your answer sheet.

1. <u>Listless</u> most nearly means

   (A) capable
   (B) directionless
   (C) talkative
   (D) bungled

2. His ability to <u>comprehend</u> complex ideas made him a great teacher.

   (A) create
   (B) loosen
   (C) understand
   (D) compute

3. Whichever one shows first will be the <u>victor.</u>

   (A) singer
   (B) manufacturer
   (C) best
   (D) winner

4. <u>Lackadaisical</u> most nearly means

   (A) talented
   (B) relaxed
   (C) actual
   (D) personable

5. It was his <u>contention</u> that more money should be spent on education.

   (A) celebration
   (B) position
   (C) ideal
   (D) sacrifice

6. The arrest wasn't even <u>newsworthy</u>.

   (A) notable
   (B) defaming
   (C) incredulous
   (D) safe

7. His attendance in class was, if anything, <u>sporadic</u>.

   (A) latent
   (B) calming
   (C) irregular
   (D) common

8. <u>Potential</u> most nearly means

   (A) scary
   (B) trustable
   (C) telling
   (D) possible

9. <u>Blacklisted</u> most nearly means

   (A) sacred
   (B) barred
   (C) old-fashioned
   (D) barren

10. It is <u>presumptuous</u> to expect too many volunteers for such a tough task.

    (A) exciting
    (B) predictable
    (C) satisfying
    (D) overly assuming

GO ON TO THE NEXT PAGE

11. A <u>memento</u> can provide a way to remember your vacation once you are home.

    (A) sacrifice
    (B) emblem
    (C) souvenir
    (D) symbol

12. The school's president is far too concerned with his <u>legacy</u>.

    (A) memory
    (B) salary
    (C) tension
    (D) grace

13. The economy has some parents worried that their children's future is in <u>jeopardy</u>.

    (A) limbo
    (B) danger
    (C) custody
    (D) salvation

14. <u>Integrity</u> most nearly means

    (A) ability
    (B) coercion
    (C) togetherness
    (D) sincerity

15. He was punished harshly for such a minor <u>infraction</u>.

    (A) aptitude
    (B) belief
    (C) gift
    (D) violation

16. <u>Collective</u> most nearly means

    (A) group
    (B) rare
    (C) soft
    (D) free

17. *The War of the Worlds* was early radio's biggest <u>hoax</u>.

    (A) trick
    (B) story
    (C) treat
    (D) complication

18. The <u>genesis</u> of the idea was scribbled on a napkin.

    (A) cancellation
    (B) detail
    (C) origin
    (D) craft

19. The brothers' <u>feud</u> goes back to their childhood days.

    (A) love
    (B) dispute
    (C) sensitivity
    (D) belief

20. <u>Fraud</u> most nearly means

    (A) pretty
    (B) fake
    (C) disgusting
    (D) sanitary

21. <u>Adept</u> most nearly means

    (A) older
    (B) talkative
    (C) cautious
    (D) skilled

22. She is an <u>ardent</u> supporter of families' rights.

    (A) vocal
    (B) testy
    (C) unaffiliated
    (D) tired

GO ON TO THE NEXT PAGE

23. The town suffered from <u>rampant</u> overcrowding and crime.

    (A) overstated
    (B) widespread
    (C) old
    (D) predictable

24. Such a <u>puny</u> fence stands no chance with that big dog.

    (A) satisfying
    (B) colorful
    (C) ghastly
    (D) weak

25. <u>Sinister</u> most nearly means

    (A) brotherhood
    (B) believable
    (C) gaudy
    (D) evil

26. <u>Witty</u> most nearly means

    (A) sulking
    (B) bloody
    (C) clever
    (D) careless

27. The witness's <u>vivid</u> account of the crime certainly opened the jury's eyes.

    (A) clear
    (B) unobstructed
    (C) false
    (D) condescending

28. <u>Relinquish</u> most nearly means

    (A) concede
    (B) color
    (C) trick
    (D) berate

29. I can only hope that these good times <u>recur</u>.

    (A) disappear
    (B) satiate
    (C) return
    (D) let go

30. <u>Incite</u> most nearly means

    (A) induce
    (B) intrigue
    (C) blow
    (D) react

31. It was wise to <u>implement</u> such a bold strategy while his critics were distracted.

    (A) introduce
    (B) suggest
    (C) trivialize
    (D) guess

32. <u>Query</u> most nearly means

    (A) telling
    (B) question
    (C) bogus
    (D) captive

GO ON TO THE NEXT PAGE

33. No one should be in awe of such a <u>timid</u> animal.

    (A) crazy
    (B) fearful
    (C) dangerous
    (D) salty

34. <u>Colleague</u> most nearly means

    (A) enemy
    (B) savior
    (C) peer
    (D) pedant

35. His opponent proved to be a <u>potent</u> mixture of tough and smart.

    (A) costly
    (B) derelict
    (C) sad
    (D) powerful

STOP. IF YOU FINISH BEFORE THE TIME IS UP, YOU MAY CHECK OVER YOUR WORK ON THIS PART ONLY.

PART 4. PARAGRAPH COMPREHENSION (PC)

Time: 13 minutes; 15 questions

<u>Directions</u>: This section contains paragraphs followed by incomplete statements or questions. Read the paragraph and select the answer that best completes the statements or answers the questions that follow, and mark the corresponding oval on your answer sheet.

The character of Sherlock Holmes illustrates author Arthur Conan Doyle's admiration for the logical mind. In each case that Holmes investigates, he is able to use the most seemingly insignificant evidence to track down his opponent. In fact, Holmes' painstaking attention to detail often reminds the reader of Charles Darwin's *On the Origin of the Species*, published some twenty years earlier.

1. The author compares Sherlock Holmes to Charles Darwin to

   (A) show Holmes's educational background
   (B) explain evolution
   (C) show how both were logical and meticulous
   (D) praise Darwin for his research skills

The climate of a major city is often very different from the climate of the surrounding areas. However, the geographic differences between the city and the country do not have to be dramatic to show major climatic differences. Even between the center of a city and its suburbs, there are often differences in air temperature, humidity, wind speed, and direction. Tall buildings, paved streets, and parking lots affect such patterns as wind flow and water runoff.

2. According to the passage, the relationship between cities and climate

   (A) is based on pollution controls
   (B) is based on urban structures and the environment
   (C) is based on city politics
   (D) is drastically different than in rural areas

Marianne had seen it all on television—the Cuban Missile Crisis, man's first steps on the moon, the fall of the Berlin Wall, even the economic boom of the 1990s. So when she won the lottery and the news vans started gathering outside her house, it didn't yet dawn on her just how much her life would be changed. A little attention doesn't hurt you, she thought. But when she stepped outside to an army of eager young reporters, however, she began to wonder if there weren't bigger events somewhere in need of coverage.

3. The character in the passage would probably do which of the following?

   (A) wear revealing clothing
   (B) donate money anonymously
   (C) dye her hair bright colors
   (D) refuse the money publicly

GO ON TO THE NEXT PAGE

In the "Gunpowder Plot" of 1605, a group of conspirators planned to blow up the English King and Parliament. The conspirators were a group of English Catholics who objected to the government's religious policies and who decided to carry out a daring assassination. They rented a cellar under the Palace of Westminster and hid twenty barrels of gunpowder there, intending to explode the gunpowder when the King and Parliament met. However, the conspirators were unable to keep the plot secret and their infamous plan was foiled.

4. The word *infamous* most nearly means

   (A) heroic
   (B) funny
   (C) obscene
   (D) notorious

Just as Johnny hit yet another red light, his cell phone began to ring. He looked at his watch and saw that he was already 20 minutes late to what might be the most important meeting of his career. Reaching for his phone, he knocked over his drink, spilling piping hot coffee all over his lap. He screamed loudly in his car, and though it looked like no one could hear him, a woman nearby ran away from the edge of the car quickly.

5. The tone of this passage is

   (A) perturbed
   (B) tender
   (C) exciting
   (D) snooty

The presence or absence of water can have a dramatic effect on the plants in a given environment. The desert, for example, is a biologically complex area where rain is often violent and unpredictable. Since desert plants are dependent on the occasional rain for survival, they must act quickly to make the most of it when it appears. Many desert plants, as a result, can complete an entire life cycle in a matter of months or even weeks. The more barren a desert is, and thus the less rain, the more rare and astounding these life cycles and the blooms that accompany them will be.

6. According to the passage, the life cycle of desert plants

   (A) is unrelated to rain levels
   (B) is directly related to their color
   (C) is akin to that of local wildlife
   (D) may be short and dynamic

It is a common belief among writers that great art is born from experience. However, some of the greatest writers in literary history have been people with a very limited knowledge of the world. Novelist Jane Austen, for example, didn't venture far beyond her circle of family and friends. And yet, just by observing the people around her, she was able to write acclaimed comedies about love and marriage. Similarly, Robert Louis Stevenson, the author of classic adventures such as *Treasure Island* and *Kidnapped*, was an invalid who was stuck in his bed for much of his life. Their achievements illustrate that if you have a good imagination, you can write a novel, no matter how unadventurous your life may seem.

7. Based on the information in the passage, a writer should

   (A) always write about people and their social scenes
   (B) write only adventure stories
   (C) rely on imagination and not just experience
   (D) get advice from close family and friends

GO ON TO THE NEXT PAGE

Tania is an extremely versatile actress. In a recent series of plays, she played a schoolteacher, two divorcees, three best friends, and a stepmother. She played a divorcee throughout the first play, but in subsequent plays she often played more than one part. Who would have suspected her acting prowess a few years ago when she ran crying off the stage with a terrible case of stage fright?

8. The word *prowess* most nearly means

    (A) knowledge
    (B) disaster
    (C) talent
    (D) bias

Many people dream about living on a coral island, but probably few of us would be able to describe one with any accuracy. Popular books and films create a romantic image of these islands, and it is not always as nice if seen from the land. Beneath the waves, however, the coral island is a fantastic and very beautiful world, depending entirely upon a complex web of interrelationships between plants and animals. The environment of the coral reef is formed over thousands of years by the life cycle of vast numbers of animals.

9. One logical conclusion to draw from this passage is

    (A) coral animals are more colorful than other animals
    (B) the true beauty of coral islands is underwater
    (C) all coral islands are tropical paradises
    (D) coral islands are formed mostly by volcanos

Questions 10 and 11 both refer to the passage below.

Few of the immigrants of the period just before the turn of the century found life in America easy. Many of those who lacked professional skills and did not speak English found themselves living in slum conditions in the busy cities of the northeast, exploited by their employers and trapped at poverty level. Around the turn of the century a number of different organizations made efforts to help these newly arrived immigrants adapt to American life. While many groups emerged as leaders in these efforts to aid immigration, one organization preached a much colder answer to adapting to America.

A conservative group called the Daughters of the American Revolution approached immigrants with the expectation that newcomers should completely adopt American customs and culture. Consequently, they supported laws that required immigrants to take oaths of loyalty and to pass English language tests. They also tried to discourage the use of languages other than English in the schools.

10. Which of the following best tells what this passage is about?

    (A) the history of immigration in the United States
    (B) the cultural contributions offered by immigrants
    (C) how some sought to assimilate immigrants into America
    (D) how immigrant life affected U.S. cities

11. The author seems to imply that the Daughters of the American Revolution

    (A) understood the difficulties facing new immigrants
    (B) were ruthless in their intentions towards immigrants
    (C) preached fitting in, not standing out
    (D) believed that immigrants would not survive in America

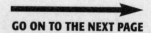

GO ON TO THE NEXT PAGE

Some animals use coloring to safeguard themselves from predators. In certain cases an animal adapts in color, shape, and behavior in order to blend into its environment. The camouflage of the pale green tree frog is a good example of this. The tree frog blends so perfectly into its surroundings that when it sits motionless it is all but invisible against a background of leaves. Another type of camouflage, shown by zebras and leopards, is a pattern that diverts the eye from the outline of the animal. The chameleon, even more versatile than these, changes color in just a few minutes to match whatever surface it happens to be lying on or clinging to.

12. According to the passage, a reason that animals use camouflage is

    (A) to divert the eye from the animal's outline

    (B) to make nesting more safe

    (C) so that frogs' and chameleons' habitats remain protected

    (D) to insure predatory dominance

Perhaps the biggest surprise of the Voyager mission was the discovery on the moons of Jupiter of intense volcanic activity. First seen on the moon Io, the eruptions were recognized as plumes of dust and gas and were immediately noticeable on the Voyager photographs. Further inspection revealed at least seven such events occurring all at once on Io's otherwise frigid surface. At other points, scientists detected three hot spots believed to be ponds of molten lava, sulfur, or sodium. The largest of these hot lakes was estimated to have a greater surface area than the state of Hawaii.

13. What was the most unexpected fact to emerge from the Voyager photographs?

    (A) the size of Io's molten lakes

    (B) the disappearance of impact sites on Europa

    (C) the discovery of volcanic activity on Io

    (D) the evidence of asteroid bombardment on all four moons.

GO ON TO THE NEXT PAGE

Questions 14 and 15 both refer to the passage below.

Most people think that the Hula Hoop was a fad born in the 1950s, but in fact people were doing much the same thing with circular hoops made from grape vines and stiff grasses all over the ancient world. More than three thousand years ago, children in Egypt played with large hoops of dried grapevines. The toy was propelled along the ground with a stick or swung around at the waist. During the fourteenth century, a "hooping" craze swept England, and was as popular among adults as kids.

The word hula became associated with the toy in the early 1800s when British sailors visited the Hawaiian Islands and noted the similarity between hooping and hula dancing. In 1957, an Australian company began making wood rings for sale in retail stores. The item attracted the attention of Wham-O, a fledgling California toy manufacturer. The plastic Hula Hoop was introduced in 1958 and was an instant hit.

14. According to the passage, all of the following statements are true EXCEPT

(A) most people do not appreciate the origins of the Hula Hoop

(B) the earliest prototypes of the Hula Hoop were made of grape leaves and stiff grasses

(C) early precursors Hula Hoop were primarily children's toys

(D) the Hula Hoop was an early success for the toy maker Wham-O

15. The author's primary purpose in this passage is to

(A) describe the way that fads like the Hula Hoop come and go

(B) discuss the origins of the Hula Hoop

(C) explain how the Hula Hoop got its name

(D) question the reasons for the Hula Hoop's popularity

STOP. IF YOU FINISH BEFORE THE TIME IS UP, YOU MAY CHECK OVER YOUR WORK ON THIS PART ONLY.

PART 5. AUTOMOTIVE AND SHOP INFORMATION (AS)

Time: 11 minutes; 25 questions

<u>Directions</u>: In this section, you will be tested on your knowledge of automotive and shop basics. For each question, select the best answer and mark the corresponding oval on your answer sheet.

1. In multi-port fuel injection, there is a fuel injector for every

    (A) cylinder
    (B) two cylinders
    (C) four cylinders
    (D) none of the above

2. The ignition _____ coil generates the high voltage for the spark plugs.

    (A) primary
    (B) preliminary
    (C) secondary
    (D) tertiary

3. In the firing order, the purpose of a distributor cap and rotor is to

    (A) create a link between the PCM and the rest of the car
    (B) undermine the spark plugs' voltage
    (C) direct high voltage from the coil wire to each cylinder
    (D) turn the primary current on and off

4. It takes concrete about _____ to cure completely.

    (A) 2 months
    (B) 1 day
    (C) 30 days
    (D) 1 year

5. The above illustration is of a

    (A) vise grips
    (B) pipe wrench
    (C) awl
    (D) ratchet

6. Running on _____ tires can cause the tire's sidewalls to overheat.

    (A) properly inflated
    (B) underinflated
    (C) overinflated
    (D) none of the above

7. Proper tire inflation is important for

    (A) vehicle stability
    (B) maximum tire contact with the road
    (C) maximum fuel economy
    (D) all of the above

8. A general purpose claw hammer would have a _____ oz. head.

    (A) 7
    (B) 13
    (C) 40
    (D) 212

9. A center punch would be used to

    (A) stop a rotating motor
    (B) start a hole for drilling
    (C) make a new belt loop on your jeans
    (D) stabilize a car jack

10. A 12-volt automotive battery has _____ cells.

    (A) 2
    (B) 4
    (C) 6
    (D) 8

11. Automatic transmissions use _____ to create speed ratios and transmit torque.

    (A) planetary gear sets
    (B) idler gears
    (C) spur gears
    (D) countershaft gears

12. The brake system is _____ operated.

    (A) hydraulically
    (B) cable
    (C) electrically
    (D) none of the above

13. To protect gears operating at high speeds, use

    (A) an air filter
    (B) roller bearings
    (C) a torque converter
    (D) a U-shaped yoke

14. MIG welding is also known as

    (A) Russian welding
    (B) coaxle welding
    (C) electric-bit welding
    (D) wire-feed welding

15. A bolt has

    (A) external threads
    (B) internal threads
    (C) topical threads
    (D) none of the above

16. Contact points would be found in _____ ignition systems.

    (A) coil-on-plug
    (B) distributorless
    (C) electronic
    (D) none of the above

17. To remove a small sliver of wood in order to create a better fit, use

    (A) a plane
    (B) a flat file
    (C) needle-nosed pliers
    (D) Johnson bars

18. The _____ connects the steering box to the steering linkage.

    (A) center link
    (B) idler arm
    (C) tie rod end
    (D) pitman arm

19. The catalytic converter is part of the vehicle's _____ system.

    (A) exhaust
    (B) emission control
    (C) Both A and B are correct.
    (D) Neither A nor B are correct.

GO ON TO THE NEXT PAGE

20. Which of the following additions often increases the versatility of slip-joint pliers?

    (A) ratchet head
    (B) extension capability
    (C) wire cutter
    (D) variable speeds

21. Advancing the ignition timing means that the spark takes place _____ in the combustion cycle.

    (A) earlier
    (B) later
    (C) at the same time
    (D) none of the above

22. The illustration above can be identified as which of the following?

    (A) auger bit
    (B) diode
    (C) rasp
    (D) tin snips

23. Long-short arm suspensions use

    (A) ball joints
    (B) upper control arms
    (C) lower control arms
    (D) all of the above

24. To cut off a bolt head, you would most likely use which of the following?

    (A) miter box
    (B) pin punch
    (C) coping saw
    (D) cold chisel

25. A loss of compression in an engine cylinder can be caused by all of the following, EXCEPT:

    (A) worn engine bearings
    (B) worn piston rings/cylinder wall
    (C) burned valves
    (D) blown head gasket

STOP. IF YOU FINISH BEFORE THE TIME IS UP, YOU MAY CHECK OVER YOUR WORK ON THIS PART ONLY.

PART 6: MATHEMATICS KNOWLEDGE (MK)

Time: 24 minutes; 25 questions

<u>Directions</u>: In this section, you will be tested on your knowledge of basic mathematics. For each question, select the best answer and mark the corresponding oval on your answer sheet.

1. If $\frac{3}{4} + 1\frac{1}{3} = \frac{5}{6} - x$, then $x =$

   (A) $-2\frac{11}{12}$

   (B) $-1\frac{1}{4}$

   (C) $\frac{1}{6}$

   (D) $1\frac{1}{4}$

2. For all a, $(3a + 4)(4a - 3) =$

   (A) $3a^2 - 4$

   (B) $9a^2 - 4$

   (C) $12a^2 + 7a - 12$

   (D) $9a^2 - 16$

3. If $2m > 24$ and $3m < 48$, which of the following could NOT be a possible value for m?

   (A) 13

   (B) 14

   (C) 15

   (D) 16

4. $\sqrt{75} + \sqrt{108} =$

   (A) $11\sqrt{3}$

   (B) $6\sqrt{5}$

   (C) $5\sqrt{6}$

   (D) $\sqrt{183}$

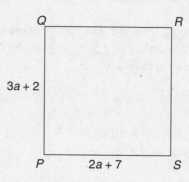

5. In the figure above, if *PQRS* is a square, what is the value of a?

   (A) $\frac{9}{2}$

   (B) 5

   (C) 7

   (D) 9

6. In triangle *ABC*, the degree measures of the three interior angles are in the ratio of 1:2:3. What is the difference in the degree measures between the largest and the smallest angles?

   (A) 30

   (B) 60

   (C) 90

   (D) 120

7. What is the perimeter of a right triangle with perpendicular sides of lengths 3 and 6?

   (A) $9 + 3\sqrt{5}$

   (B) $9 + 5\sqrt{3}$

   (C) $12 + 3\sqrt{3}$

   (D) 18

GO ON TO THE NEXT PAGE

8. In the diagram above, if $AD = BE = 6$, AE = 8 and $CD = 3(BC)$, then $BC =$

(A) 4
(B) 3
(C) 2
(D) 1

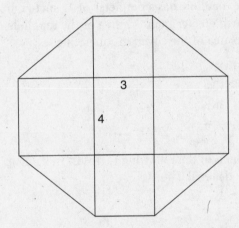

9. The figure above is composed of nine regions: four squares, four triangles, and one rectangle. If the rectangle has sides length 4 and width 3, what is the perimeter of the entire figure?

(A) 30
(B) 34
(C) 40
(D) 48

10. If $\dfrac{\sqrt{n}}{3}$ is an even integer, which of the following could be the value of n ?

(A) 27
(B) 48
(C) 81
(D) 144

11. Gheri is n years old. Carl is 6 years younger than Gheri and 2 years older than Jean. What is the sum of the ages of all three?

(A) $3n + 4$
(B) $3n - 4$
(C) $3n - 8$
(D) $3n - 14$

12. Which of the following is not a prime number?

(A) 2
(B) 37
(C) 51
(D) 67

13. What is the area of a circle whose circumference is 2π?

(A) $\dfrac{n}{2}$
(B) π
(C) 2π
(D) 4π

14. A high school band is composed of 13 freshmen, 20 sophomores, 16 juniors, and 15 seniors. What is the probability that a band member chosen at random will be a sophomore?

(A) $\dfrac{2}{5}$
(B) $\dfrac{1}{3}$
(C) $\dfrac{4}{13}$
(D) $\dfrac{5}{16}$

GO ON TO THE NEXT PAGE

15. If $k - 3 = -\dfrac{5}{3}$, then $3 - k =$

    (A) $-\dfrac{5}{3}$

    (B) $-\dfrac{3}{5}$

    (C) $\dfrac{5}{3}$

    (D) $\dfrac{3}{5}$

16. If $x \neq 0$ and $\dfrac{3x}{5} = 3x^2$, then $x =$

    (A) $\dfrac{1}{5}$

    (B) $\dfrac{3}{5}$

    (C) 3

    (D) 5

17. For all positive values a, b, c, and d, $a = 2b$, $\dfrac{1}{2}b = c$, and $4c = 3d$. What is the value of $\dfrac{d}{a}$?

    (A) $\dfrac{1}{3}$

    (B) $\dfrac{3}{4}$

    (C) $\dfrac{4}{3}$

    (D) 3

18. How many rectangular tiles with dimensions of 3 inches by 4 inches are needed to cover a rectangular area with dimensions of 2 feet and 3 feet?

    (A) 60
    (B) 72
    (C) 120
    (D) 144

19. For how many integer values of x will $\dfrac{7}{x}$ be greater than $\dfrac{1}{4}$ and less than $\dfrac{1}{3}$?

    (A) 6
    (B) 7
    (C) 12
    (D) 28

20. A circular manhole is covered by a circular cover which has a diameter of 14 inches. If the manhole has a diameter of 12 inches, how much greater than the area of the manhole is the area of the cover, in square inches?

    (A) π
    (B) 13π
    (C) 36π
    (D) 52π

21. Which of the following is closest in value to the decimal 0.40?

    (A) $\dfrac{1}{3}$

    (B) $\dfrac{4}{7}$

    (C) $\dfrac{3}{8}$

    (D) $\dfrac{1}{2}$

22. If x oranges cost the same as y peaches, peaches cost 39 cents each, and the cost of each orange is the same, how many dollars does each orange cost?

    (A) $\dfrac{39y}{100x}$

    (B) $\dfrac{39x}{100y}$

    (C) $\dfrac{3,900}{xy}$

    (D) $\dfrac{39x}{y}$

GO ON TO THE NEXT PAGE

23. A class of 40 students is to be divided into smaller groups. If each group is to contain 3, 4, or 5 people, what is the largest number of groups possible?

    (A) 10
    (B) 12
    (C) 13
    (D) 14

24. If the area of a triangle is 36 and its base is 9, what is the length of the altitude to that base?

    (A) 4
    (B) 6
    (C) 8
    (D) 12

25. If $x = -5$, then $2x^2 - 6x + 5 =$

    (A) 15
    (B) 25
    (C) 85
    (D) 135

STOP. IF YOU FINISH BEFORE THE TIME IS UP, YOU MAY CHECK OVER YOUR WORK ON THIS PART ONLY.

PART 7: MECHANICAL COMPREHENSION (MC)

Time: 19 minutes; 25 questions

<u>Directions</u>: In this section, you will be tested on your knowledge of mechanics and basic physics. Select the best answer for each question and mark the corresponding oval on your answer sheet.

1. A gear set has a ratio of 3:1. If the driven gear has 21 teeth, the drive gear will have

   (A) 7 teeth
   (B) 21 teeth
   (C) 24 teeth
   (D) 63 teeth

2. A gear ratio of 0.75:1 would mean that

   (A) the driven gear turns faster than the drive gear
   (B) the torque output is less than the input
   (C) the gear set is an overdrive
   (D) All of the above are correct.

3. A small pulley drives a large pulley with a belt. Which of the following statements about this arrangement are true?

   (A) the pulleys turn in opposite directions
   (B) the smaller pulley turns faster
   (C) speed output is greater than the input
   (D) A and C only are correct.

4. The speed ratio of a pulley drive is determined by

   (A) the radius of the pulleys
   (B) the length of the belt
   (C) the distance between the pulleys
   (D) the thickness of the belt

5. 100 foot-pounds of torque is applied to a gear set with a ratio of 4:1. The output torque would be

   (A) 25 foot-pounds
   (B) 75 foot-pounds
   (C) 100 foot-pounds
   (D) 400 foot-pounds

6. All of the following statements about liquids are true EXCEPT:

   (A) liquids are practically incompressible
   (B) liquids can be used to transmit force
   (C) all liquids are good lubricants
   (D) liquids conform to the shape of their container

7. All of the following pressure formulas are true EXCEPT:

   (A) $\text{pressure} = \dfrac{\text{force}}{\text{area}}$

   (B) $\text{force} = \text{pressure} \times \text{area}$

   (C) $\text{force} = \dfrac{\text{area}}{\text{pressure}}$

   (D) $\text{area} = \dfrac{\text{force}}{\text{pressure}}$

8. If 100 pounds of force are applied over an area of 2 square inches, the pressure would be

   (A) 50 pounds per square inch
   (B) 50 psi
   (C) 200 pounds per square inch
   (D) Both A and B are correct.

GO ON TO THE NEXT PAGE

9. A hydraulic cylinder

    (A) is a linear actuator
    (B) has a sealed piston
    (C) uses oil pressure to generate force
    (D) all of the above

10. Hydraulic fluid is normally

    (A) an oil
    (B) petroleum-based
    (C) Both A and B are correct.
    (D) Neither A nor B are correct.

11. In order to generate more force, a hydraulic cylinder with a _____ piston must be used.

    (A) thicker
    (B) larger diameter
    (C) smaller diameter
    (D) none of the above

12. When a net force acts on an object,

    (A) the object will slow to a stop
    (B) the force will give the object a cumulative force
    (C) the object will accelerate in the direction of the net force
    (D) constant velocity is impossible

13. Smaller pulleys always turn _____ than larger ones within the same system.

    (A) slower
    (B) the same
    (C) faster
    (D) with more friction

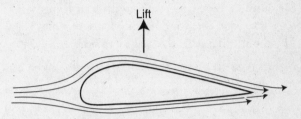

14. To achieve lift, the air pressure on the top of the wing (pictured above) must be _____ than the air pressure on the bottom side of the wing.

    (A) lower
    (B) higher
    (C) none of the above
    (D) cannot calculate air pressure

Questions 15 and 16 apply to the following formula for calculating pressure:

$$P = \frac{F}{A}$$

15. A load piston has a total surface area of 10 square inches and wants to raise 100 pounds. How much force will have to be applied?

    (A) 1,000 psi
    (B) 50.5 psi
    (C) 10 psi
    (D) cannot calculate with the information given

16. In the equation above, the ratio of the surface area of the pistons to the load piston is

    (A) 1:1
    (B) 1:10
    (C) 1:50
    (D) 1:100

GO ON TO THE NEXT PAGE

17. Given a block and tackle with four ropes to lift a load one foot, barring friction, what is the mechanical advantage gained?

    (A) 24:1

    (B) 10:1

    (C) 8:1

    (D) 4:1

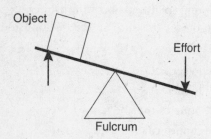

18. The lever shown above is an example of which kind of lever?

    (A) first class

    (B) second class

    (C) third class

    (D) none of the above

19. A puck slides across frozen ice. The puck will eventually slow to a stop because of

    (A) wind drag

    (B) gravity

    (C) sliding frictional force

    (D) inertia

20. When a bolt is being tightened, _____ is being applied to the bolt.

    (A) torque

    (B) friction

    (C) kinetic energy

    (D) gear ratio

21. Which of the following is an energy conversion device?

    (A) welding torch

    (B) air compressor

    (C) pumping piston

    (D) load piston

22. The equation $f_s^{MAX} = \mu_s F_N$ is used to find

    (A) the amount of kinetic energy

    (B) the cost of building a pulley

    (C) the force of gravity on objects

    (D) maximum static frictional force

GO ON TO THE NEXT PAGE

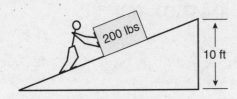

23. If the box above, weighing 200 lbs, will be moved 10 feet with a force of 100 N, assuming no friction, how much work will have been done once the box is moved?

    (A) 10 joules
    (B) 100 joules
    (C) 1,000 joules
    (D) 1 million joules

24. The symbol *g* in Newton's formula for the Second Law of Motion stands for

    (A) acceleration due to gravity
    (B) mass, in grams
    (C) the earth's surface
    (D) none of the above

25. If a gear and pinion have a ratio of 2:1 and the gear is rotating at 100 revolutions per minute, the pinion's speed is closest to

    (A) 200
    (B) 400
    (C) 800
    (D) 1,000

STOP. IF YOU FINISH BEFORE THE TIME IS UP, YOU MAY CHECK OVER YOUR WORK ON THIS PART ONLY.

PART 8: ELECTRONICS INFORMATION (EI)

Time: 9 minutes; 20 questions

<u>Directions</u>: In this section, you will be tested on your knowledge of electronics basics. For each question, select the best answer and mark the corresponding oval on your answer sheet.

1. _____ is the total opposition to the flow of electrical charge.

    (A) resistor
    (B) impedance
    (C) series circuit
    (D) valence

2. To increase the magnetic field of a current passing through a wire,

    (A) make the wire longer
    (B) place the wire underwater
    (C) wrap the wire around a nail
    (D) wrap the wire into a coil

3. Voltage can be expressed by all of the following units EXCEPT

    (A) millivolts
    (B) gigabolts
    (C) megavolts
    (D) kilovolts

Questions 4 and 5 refer to the following diagram.

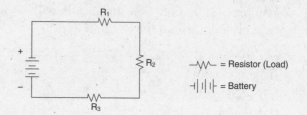

4. The circuit above is known as a _____ circuit.

    (A) closed
    (B) parallel
    (C) series
    (D) none of the above

5. In a circuit as pictured above, current flow

    (A) will change as it moves through the circuit
    (B) will remain unchanged as it moves through the circuit
    (C) is released from the circuit at a higher voltage
    (D) Both A and C are correct.

6. Wireless signals are transmitted via

    (A) DC signals
    (B) infinite resistance
    (C) sinusoidal waves
    (D) none of the above

GO ON TO THE NEXT PAGE

7. What resistance will allow 5 mA to flow when 50 volts is applied to it?

   (A) 10 Ω
   (B) 10 KΩ
   (C) 10,500 Ω
   (D) Both A and C are correct.

8. Stranded wires are _____ conductors than standard wires.

   (A) stronger
   (B) more flexible
   (C) weaker
   (D) worse

9. Diodes are rated based on

   (A) current flow in forward-bias direction
   (B) current flow in reverse-bias direction
   (C) current flow away from the center of the diode
   (D) Both A and B are correct.

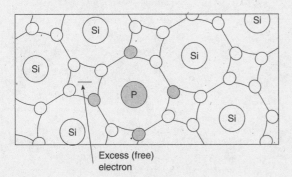

N-type material

10. The diagram above is an example of N-type material. N-type material can conduct electricity because of

    (A) silicon's unique structure
    (B) a free electron outside the valence shell
    (C) the presence of boron
    (D) none of the above

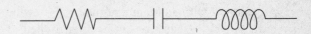

11. The circuit above is known as a

    (A) clamping diode
    (B) Zener diode
    (C) series RCL circuit
    (D) simple condenser

12. An example of a series circuit in everyday life would be

    (A) car taillights
    (B) neon sign
    (C) refrigerator light
    (D) Christmas lights

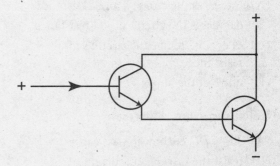

Darlington pair

13. The Darlington pair shown in the diagram above is used to

    (A) allow a small current to control a larger one
    (B) build a PNP transistor to carry more current
    (C) allow current to flow in all directions
    (D) allow valence shells to carry extra electrons

GO ON TO THE NEXT PAGE

14. An element with an atomic number of 10 will have _____ electrons in its valence shell.

    (A) 0
    (B) 2
    (C) 8
    (D) 10

15. An element with five electrons in its valence shell is an

    (A) conductor
    (B) semiconductor
    (C) insulator
    (D) none of the above

16. Adding more loads to a parallel circuit

    (A) increases the circuit's total resistance
    (B) decreases the circuit's total resistance
    (C) does not change the circuit's total resistance
    (D) none of the above

17. Unlike capacitors, inductors

    (A) allow DC current to pass easily
    (B) resist the flow of AC current
    (C) turn DC power around to increase power
    (D) Both A and B are correct.

18. In an automotive negative ground system, the ground is attached to

    (A) the steering column
    (B) the chassis
    (C) the engine block
    (D) the crankshaft

19. E is the symbol for

    (A) voltage
    (B) electromotive force
    (C) electrical pressure
    (D) all of the above

20. All of the following statements about series circuits are true, EXCEPT:

    (A) current flow is the same throughout
    (B) there is only one path for current to follow
    (C) current flow varies throughout the circuit
    (D) voltage drops across the loads depend on their resistance

STOP. IF YOU FINISH BEFORE THE TIME IS UP, YOU MAY CHECK OVER YOUR WORK ON THIS PART ONLY.

PART 9. ASSEMBLING OBJECTS (AO)

Time: 9 minutes; 16 questions

<u>Directions</u>: In this section, you will be tested on your ability to construct or connect a series of objects. For each question, select the best answer and mark the corresponding oval on your answer sheet.

1.

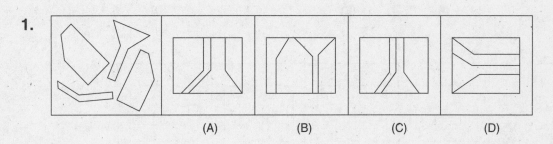

(A)   (B)   (C)   (D)

2.

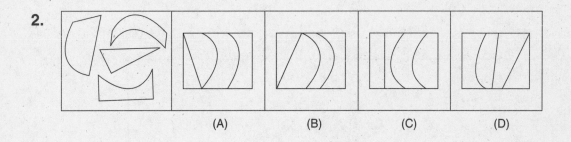

(A)   (B)   (C)   (D)

3.

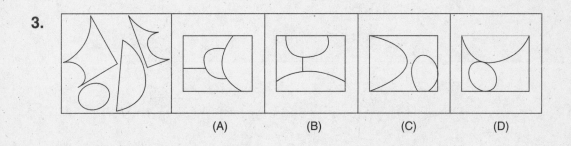

(A)   (B)   (C)   (D)

4.

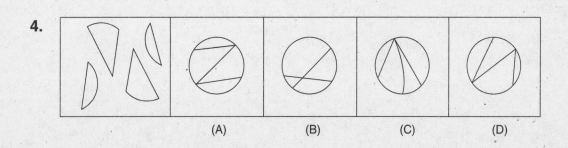

(A)   (B)   (C)   (D)

GO ON TO THE NEXT PAGE

5.

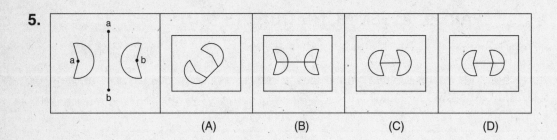

(A)   (B)   (C)   (D)

6.

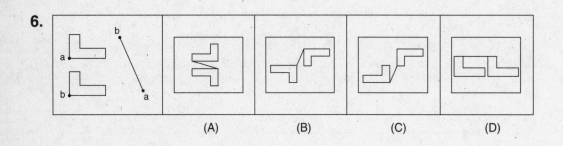

(A)   (B)   (C)   (D)

7.

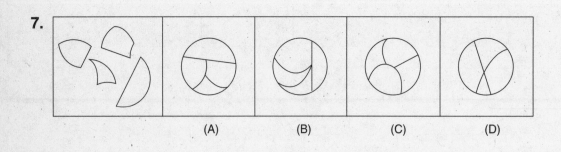

(A)   (B)   (C)   (D)

8.

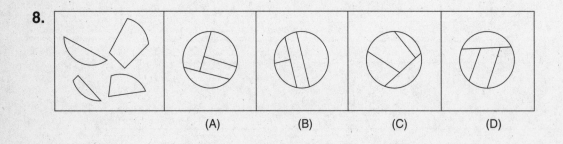

(A)   (B)   (C)   (D)

GO ON TO THE NEXT PAGE

9.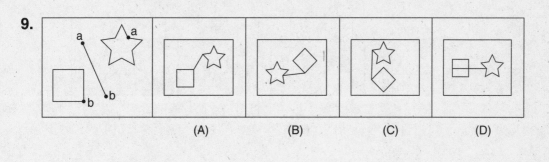

                (A)   (B)   (C)   (D)

10.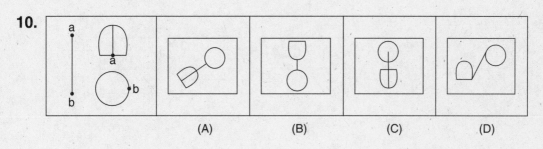

                (A)   (B)   (C)   (D)

11.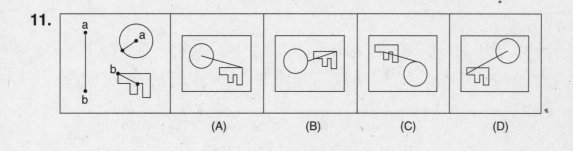

                (A)   (B)   (C)   (D)

12.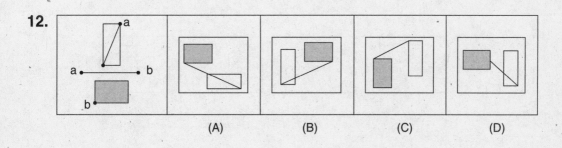

                (A)   (B)   (C)   (D)

GO ON TO THE NEXT PAGE

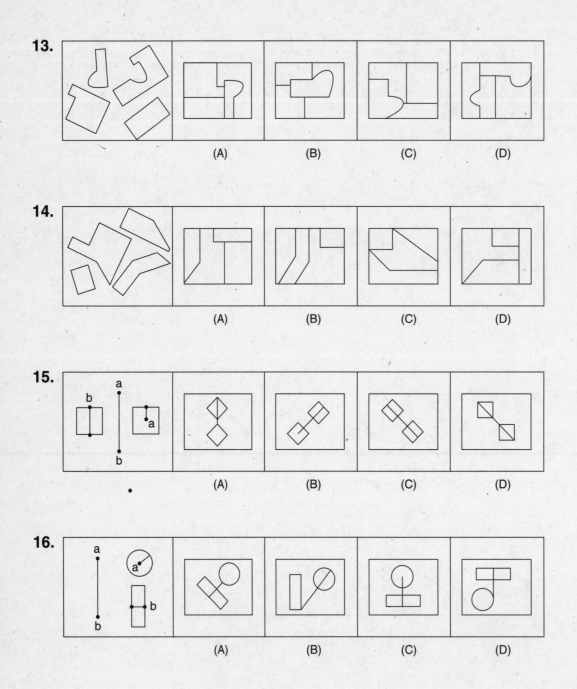

13.   (A)   (B)   (C)   (D)

14.   (A)   (B)   (C)   (D)

15.   (A)   (B)   (C)   (D)

16.   (A)   (B)   (C)   (D)

STOP! END OF TEST.

ASVAB Practice Test III
Answers and
Explanations

ANSWER KEY

General Science	Arithmetic Reasoning	Word Knowledge	Paragraph Comprehension	Auto and Shop Information
1. D	1. B	1. B	1. C	1. A
2. D	2. D	2. C	2. B	2. C
3. A	3. B	3. D	3. B	3. C
4. B	4. C	4. B	4. D	4. C
5. D	5. D	5. B	5. A	5. D
6. C	6. C	6. A	6. D	6. B
7. B	7. D	7. C	7. C	7. D
8. B	8. D	8. D	8. C	8. B
9. C	9. A	9. B	9. B	9. B
10. D	10. D	10. D	10. C	10. C
11. C	11. C	11. C	11. C	11. A
12. A	12. A	12. A	12. A	12. A
13. D	13. B	13. B	13. C	13. B
14. C	14. B	14. D	14. C	14. D
15. C	15. C	15. D	15. B	15. A
16. A	16. A	16. A		16. D
17. C	17. B	17. A		17. A
18. A	18. B	18. C		18. D
19. B	19. D	19. B		19. C
20. C	20. C	20. B		20. C
21. A	21. A	21. D		21. A
22. A	22. C	22. A		22. A
23. B	23. B	23. B		23. D
24. C	24. D	24. D		24. D
25. B	25. A	25. D		25. A
	26. B	26. C		
	27. A	27. A		
	28. C	28. A		
	29. D	29. C		
	30. D	30. A		
		31. A		
		32. B		
		33. B		
		34. C		
		35. D		

ANSWER KEY

Mathematics Knowledge	Mechanical Comprehension	Electronics Information	Assembling Objects
1. B	1. A	1. B	1. C
2. C	2. D	2. D	2. B
3. D	3. B	3. B	3. D
4. A	4. A	4. C	4. A
5. B	5. D	5. B	5. C
6. B	6. C	6. C	6. B
7. A	7. C	7. B	7. A
8. D	8. D	8. B	8. C
9. B	9. D	9. D	9. B
10. D	10. C	10. B	10. A
11. D	11. B	11. C	11. D
12. C	12. C	12. D	12. A
13. B	13. C	13. A	13. A
14. D	14. A	14. C	14. B
15. C	15. C	15. C	15. B
16. A	16. B	16. B	16. C
17. A	17. D	17. D	
18. B	18. A	18. B	
19. A	19. C	19. D	
20. B	20. A	20. D	
21. C	21. B		
22. A	22. D		
23. C	23. C		
24. C	24. A		
25. C	25. A		

GENERAL SCIENCE ANSWERS AND EXPLANATIONS

1. D

Those wishing to consume a low-cholesterol diet should limit their intake of organ meats. The cholesterol a person consumes (as distinguished from the cholesterol a person produces) comes only from animal fats, such as egg yolks, organ meats, and butter. Nuts and avocados, while high in fat, have no cholesterol in themselves, and bread is high in carbohydrates, but generally low in fat, cholesterol or otherwise.

2. D

Water at sea level boils at 212° F, 100° C, or 373° K.

3. A

Of the subatomic particles listed, the proton has the largest mass. Among subatomic particles, protons and neutrons have the most mass. Electrons, positrons, and neutrinos all have negligible masses relative to protons and neutrons.

4. B

An apple tree is an example of an autotroph. An autotroph is an organism capable of synthesizing its own organic substances from inorganic compounds, as through photosynthesis. Another term for an autotroph is a producer.

5. D

The Precambrian era, which began with the formation of the earth (about 4.6 billion years ago) and ended about 570 million years ago when the fossil record became clear, is the oldest of the earth's geologic time periods. It was followed by the Paleozoic era, which lasted until about 245 million years ago and was characterized by the appearance of a great variety of plant and animal species. Next came the Mesozoic era, which lasted until about 65 million years ago and was characterized by the rise and fall of the dinosaurs. Finally there was the Cenozoic era, which continues to the present, and has been characterized by the flourishing of a wide range of bird and mammal species, including, most recently, humans.

6. C

Mercury, Venus, Mars, and Pluto are all smaller than Earth. Of the planets listed, only Uranus is larger than Earth.

7. B

Salt is an inorganic compound considered essential to the survival of animals. Glucose, maltase, and cellulose are all organic compounds.

8. B

The study of interactions between organisms and their interrelationships with the physical environment is known as ecology. Cytology is the study of cells, physiology is the study of the organism, and embryology is the study of embryos and their development.

9. C

Most of the nutrients in food are absorbed in the body's small intestine.

10. D

If normal parents have a color-blind son, the probability that the son inherited the gene for color blindness from his mother is 100%. This is because color blindness is a sex-linked trait that is found on the X chromosome, which is inherited from the mother, as opposed to the Y chromosome, which is inherited from the father. Thus a male can only inherit the gene for color blindness from his mother.

11. C

The smaller the body mass of an animal, the higher its metabolic rate. Thus, of the animals listed, the mouse has the highest metabolic rate.

12. **A**

Of the states of electromagnetic radiation listed, radio waves have the longest wavelength and lowest frequency.

13. **D**

A lack of vitamin D can cause rickets

14. **C**

A high pH indicates a substance that is basic rather than acidic. Of the food products listed, baking soda is the most basic and has the highest pH.

15. **C**

Carbohydrates include both starches and sugars, which makes choice (C), both (A) and (B), correct.

16. **A**

Members of an order are more alike than members of a class.

17. **C**

A major asteroid belt can be found in our solar system between Mars and Jupiter.

18. **A**

Animals with chitinous exoskeletons and jointed appendages are classified as arthropods.

19. **B**

The atom of an element with an atomic number of 17 must have 17 protons.

20. **C**

Because mushrooms absorb nutrients from decaying leaves, they are classified as saprophytes. Another term for a plant living on dead or decaying organic matter is decomposer.

21. **A**

The vessel with the LEAST oxygenated blood is the pulmonary artery, which sends oxygen-depleted blood from the heart into the lungs to be oxygenated.

22. **A**

Saliva in the mouth often begins the process of breaking down starch. Fats and proteins begin breaking down later in the digestive process.

23. **B**

The Moneran kingdom is composed of prokaryotic organisms, that is, organisms with cells that lack nuclei.

24. **C**

An atom that is not electrically neutral is called an ion. An isotope is any of two or more species of atoms of a element that have the same atomic number and nearly identical chemical behavior but differ in atomic mass or mass number and other physical properties. A positron is a positively charged particle having the same mass and magnitude of charge as the electron and constituting the antiparticle of the electron. An allotrope is an element that has two or more different forms (as of crystals) usually in the same phase; an example of allotropy is carbon, which can exist in such different forms as graphite and diamonds.

25. **B**

A metamorphic rock is a rock that has undergone a pronounced change effected by pressure, heat, and water, resulting in a more compact and more highly crystalline condition. Marble is one example of a metamorphic rock.

ARITHMETIC REASONING ANSWERS AND EXPLANATIONS

1. B

If a machine caps 5 bottles every 2 seconds, then it would cap 30 times as many bottles in one minute (since a minute is 60 seconds). $5 \times 30 = 150$ bottles per minute, choice (B).

2. D

Jonah traveled 650 miles at 25 miles per gallon. To determine how many gallons he used, divide 650 by 25. $650 \div 25 = 26$ gallons. Each gallon costs \$1.30, so his cost for the trip would be $26 \times \$1.30 = \$33.80$, choice (D).

3. B

On a problem like this, which involves annoying calculations (they can't really expect us to do long division, can they?), often the best way to go is to backsolve from the answer choices. You can start with either (B) or (C). Since (B), \$0.40 is the easier number, we'll start there: If there are 3.86 liters in a gallon, and a liter of gasoline costs \$0.40, a gallon of gasoline costs $3.86 \times \$0.40 = \$1.544$, or roughly \$1.54 a gallon, which is the answer we want.

4. C

To determine the number of minutes in a week, begin with the number of minutes in an hour and work your way up from there. 60 minutes per hour. 24 hours per day, so there are $60 \times 24 = 1,440$ minutes per day. There are 7 days per week, so there are $1440 \times 7 = 10,080$ minutes per week. (C) is correct.

5. D

We know that 15% of take home pay = \$37.50. So $0.15(x) = \$37.50$. $x = \dfrac{37.5}{0.15} = \dfrac{3,750}{15} = 250$, so choice (D) is correct. You could also work backwards from the answer choices. $0.15 \times \$250 = \$37.50$. Either way you solve it, (D) is correct.

6. C

If the ratio of males to females is 3:5, then there are 8 parts total in the ratio. The total number of students must be a multiple of 8. Only choice (C), 152, is a multiple of 8.

7. D

A car travels 288 miles in 6 hours. Divide 288 by 6 to find the rate in miles per hour. $288 \div 6 = 48$ miles per hour. Then (48 miles per hour) $\times$ (8 hours) = 384 miles, choice (D).

8. D

If Martin's average score after 4 tests is 89, then the sum for his 4 tests would be $4 \times 89 = 356$. To average 90 on 5 tests, you would have to reach a sum of 450 for the 5 tests.

$450 - 356 = 94$, choice (D).

9. A

If the first year begins with Town A at 9,400 and Town B at 7,600, the populations are $9,400 - 7,600 = 1,800$ apart. Each year after 2000 beginning in 2001, the gap will close by 200. So it would take 9 more years for the gap to close entirely. So by 2009, the populations will be equal, choice (A).

10. D

One number is 5 times another number, and their sum is –60. You could rewrite that sentence as two equations and solve:

$$x = 5y$$
$$x + y = -60$$
$$5y + y = -60$$
$$6y = -60, \text{ and } y = -10$$

If $y = -10$, $x = 5y = 5(-10) = -50$. –50 is less than –10 , so (D) is correct.

11. C

First, you must see that there are two rates by which John gets paid: one for the first 40 cars ($6 per car) and a different rate for all other cars after those first 40 ($6 per hour plus 50% of $6, which is $6 + $3, or $9 per car). Since he makes 48 cars, he gets paid $6 × 40 cars ($240) plus 8 extra cars at $9 per car ($72) which totals $312, choice (C).

12. A

48 glecks at 3 glecks per fedi would equal $\frac{48}{3} = 16$ fedi. 16 fedi at 2 fedis per bora would equal $\frac{16}{2} = 8$ bora, choice (A).

13. B

Work through the clock systematically: First reading at 12 P.M. , second at 4 P.M., third at 8 P.M., fourth at midnight, fifth at 4 A.M., sixth at 8 A.M., 7th at 12 P.M., eighth at 4 P.M., ninth and final reading at 8 P.M., choice (B).

14. B

If tuition payments were raised from $225 to $300, you can use the percent increase formula to determine how much the tuition went up.

$$\text{Percent Increase} = \frac{\text{New} - \text{Old}}{\text{Old}} \times 100\%$$
$$= \frac{300 - 225}{225} \times 100\%$$
$$= \frac{75}{225} \times 100\%$$
$$= 33\frac{1}{3}\%, \text{ choice (B).}$$

15. C

If a truck takes 6 hours to complete a trip at 20 miles per hour, the total distance for the trip must be 6 × 20 = 120 miles. When traveling 120 miles at a rate of 30 miles per hour, the truck would take $\frac{120}{30} = 4$ hours. So instead of taking 6 hours, the truck took 4 hours. That saves 2 hours, so choice (C) is correct.

16. A

If a full barrel can hold 75 gallons, when it is $\frac{3}{5}$ full it will hold $\frac{3}{5}$ of 75 gallons. $\frac{3}{5} \times 75 = 3 \times 15$ or 45 gallons, choice (A).

17. B

A salary of $45,000 is reduced by 40 percent; that is like reducing it by $\frac{2}{5}$. $\frac{1}{5}$ of $45,000 is $9,000, so $\frac{2}{5}$ would be $18,000. $45,000 − $18,000 = $27,000 for a new salary, choice (B).

18. B

Remember that 10 square yards is 90 square feet since 1 square yards is 3 feet × 3 feet = 9 square feet. So a pound of lawn fertilizer covers 90 square feet. To cover 450 square feet, you would need $\frac{450}{90} = 5$ pounds of lawn fertilizer, choice (B).

19. D

If fifteen people contribute $40 each, that would amount to 15 × $40 = $600. Thirty-five percent of the money is spent on a group gift, so the remaining 65% of the money is spent on the party. 0.65($600) = $390, choice (D)

20. C

$\text{Average} = \dfrac{\text{Sum of the terms}}{\text{Number of terms}}$. In this question, an employee works for a sum total of 33.5 hours over 5 days. The average hours worked per day would be determined as follows:

$$\text{Average} = \frac{\text{Sum of the terms}}{\text{Number of terms}} =$$
$$\frac{33.5}{5} = 6 + \frac{3.5}{5} \text{ hours.}$$

We're not done, though. All the answers appear as minutes, not hours. So we need to convert 0.7 hours into minutes. There are 60 minutes in an hour, so 0.7 hours = 60(0.7) = 42 minutes. So the average amount of time worked on a given day is 6 hours and 42 minutes, choice (C).

21. A

To find the average speed for an entire trip, divide the total distance by the total time. If a train travels 180 miles at an average speed of 60 miles per hour, that leg of the journey must have taken $\frac{180}{60} = 3$ hours. The second leg of 150 miles at an average speed of 75 miles per hour would take $\frac{150}{75} = 2$ hours.

$$\text{Average Speed} = \frac{\text{Total distance}}{\text{Total time}}$$

$$= \frac{180 + 150}{3 + 2}$$

$$= \frac{330}{5} = 66 \text{ mph}.$$

So choice (A) is correct.

22. C

Try backsolving on a question like this one. Start with choice (C). If a bicycle sells for $175.00 and is discounted 20%, its price would be reduced by (0.20)($175) = $35. So the new price would be $175 − $35 = $140. That's the discount price we're looking for, so (C) is the correct answer.

23. B

This is purely an addition/subtraction question. Be careful, and double check your work, and you should be fine here.

Begin by adding the deposit to the balance:
$$1,162.76 + 352.68 = 1,515.44.$$

Then sum up the withdrawals:
$$152.45 + 82.85 + 255.50 = 490.80.$$

Then find your answer by subtracting the sum of the withdrawals from the balance:
$$1,515.44 - 490.80 = 1,024.64.$$
Choice (B) is correct.

24. D

If Harold works 4.5 hours per day for 3 days, then he works $4.5 \times 3 = 13.5$ hours at $4.25 per hour. He earns $13.5 \times \$4.25 = \$57.375$. That rounds up to $57.38, choice (D).

25. A

To determine probability, remember this handy formula:
$$\text{Probability} = \frac{\text{Number of desired outcomes}}{\text{Number of possible outcomes}}$$

In this case, we're looking for the color chip that would result in a probability of $\frac{1}{8}$. There are 16 chips total, so there are 16 possible outcomes. We can return to the probability formula to determine which chip would have the number of desired outcomes we're looking for:

$$\frac{1}{8} = \frac{x}{16} = \frac{2}{16}$$

So we want to choose the color chip of which there are 2. In this case, that is orange, choice (A).

26. B

Once again, you're up against a tricky computation question here. You can save yourself time if you realize that there are 100 stamps per sheet, which means that each sheet of 100 23-cent stamps would cost $23, each sheet of 37-cent stamps would cost $37, and each sheet of 60-cent stamps would cost $60. So your calculations should look something like this:

$(4 \times \$23) + (2 \times \$37) + (3 \times \$60) =$
$\$92 + \$74 + \$180 = \$346$, choice (B).

27. A

Keep in mind that Pacific time is three hours behind Eastern time. So if a plane leaves Los Angeles at 5:30 P.M. PST, it leaves at 8:30 P.M. EST. So if it arrives in New York at 12:45 A.M. EST, the total time of the flight would be 4 hours, 15 minutes, choice (A).

28. C

Try backsolving here. Start with choice (C). If the original cost of the camera was $160, and it was reduced by 25% or $\frac{1}{4}$, the new cost would be $160 − 0.25($160) = $160 − $40 = $120. That's the value we're looking for, so (C) is the correct answer.

29. D

Begin by converting all of your units to ounces. That means that 1 pound, 11 ounces equals 16 ounces + 11 ounces = 27 ounces. We want to determine how many 1.5 ounce slices make up the 27-ounce loaf. $\frac{27}{1.5} = \frac{270}{15} = 18$, choice (D).

30. D

If it takes 20 minutes to type 5 pages, then we can think of the 162-page document as a group of 5-page chunks, each taking 20 minutes to complete. That means there are $\frac{162}{5} = 32.4$ five page chunks to the document. Each chunk takes 20 minutes to type. So the total document takes $32.4(20) = 648$ minutes to type. 600 minutes is 10 hours, so 648 minutes is 10 hours and 48 minutes. (D) is correct.

WORD KNOWLEDGE ANSWERS AND EXPLANATIONS

1. B

Listless means *without aim or direction*, thus *directionless*, (B), is the correct answer.

2. C

Comprehend means *to grasp the nature or meaning of*, and *understand*, (C), is the answer closest to the original word.

3. D

A *victor* is defined as *one that defeats or vanquishes a foe*, so (D), *winner*, is the best answer.

4. B

Lackadaisical can't be understood from context, but something *lacking* means "missing," so taking a quick look at the other answers, the only answer missing anything is (B), *relaxed*, which is the lack of stress or action. Sure enough, the textbook definition of lackadaisical is *lacking life, spirit, or zest*.

5. B

A *contention* is defined as a *point advanced in a debate or argument*, so the answer (B), *position*, is closest in meaning to the given word.

6. A

Newsworthy is an adjective meaning *interesting enough to warrant coverage*, so (C) and (D) are out. While the arrest might make the arrested incredulous, answer (A), *notable*, is clearly the closest in meaning.

7. C

Something *sporadic* is something that is *occurring occasionally*. Thus answer choice (D) is wrong. Only answer choice (C), *irregular*, truly gets at the same meaning as the given word.

8. D

Potential means *possible or conceivable*, so answer (D) is the correct choice.

9. B

The odd word *blacklisted* refers to an old way of keeping out undesired people by creating a list of banned individuals. Thus, answer (B) is the only true answer, as banned and *barred* are similar words.

10. D

Presumptuous means *taking liberties* with what's given. Similarly, it also means *overly assuming*.

11. C

A *memento* is defined as *something that serves to warn or remind*, and the answer choice (C), *souvenir*, fits this definition perfectly.

12. A

Someone's *legacy* is the effect they leave behind once they are finished or departed. In this case, the school president is concerned about his *memory*, answer (A).

13. B

Something put in *jeopardy* is placed at a point of peril or danger. Thus, answer choice (B), *danger*, is the clear choice.

14. D

Integrity means having *especially moral or artistic values*, so while togetherness is a fine thing, someone having *sincerity* is most likely to be described as having *integrity*.

15. D

The noun *infraction* means to *break a rule or code*. Therefore, among the answer choices, answer (D), *violation*, comes closest to the meaning of the given word.

16. A

A *collective* is a body of people with like-minded goals or values, so only choice (A), *group*, makes sense.

17. A

Identifying the meaning of this kind of word in context is a good strategy here. A *hoax* is a *trick by convincing someone what is false is true*. *War of the Worlds* was a radio show in which Martians attacked the Earth. Clearly, convincing anyone that this was true was a *hoax*. Thus, answer (A) is correct. Even if you didn't know the true definition, you could probably have made a guess based on context clues.

18. C

From Latin, the word *genesis* means the *origin or coming into being* of something. From this, you can see that choice (C) is the only logical choice.

19. B

A *feud* is defined as a *quarrel that is often prolonged*, so of the answer choices given, only choice (B) seems to fulfill that definition.

20. B

Fraud is the *act of deceiving or misrepresenting*, so while something may be a deception and still be pretty, the true answer is choice (B), *fake*.

21. D

An *adept* person is someone highly skilled or well-trained, and while this person may be talkative, older, or cautious, the only correct answer is (D), *skilled*.

22. A

Ardent is the state of being *intense in feeling*, in other words outspoken, as in an *ardent champion* of a cause. *Testy* can be seen as argumentative or loudmouthed, but the best answer to this question is (A), *vocal*.

23. B

The word *rampant* implies an excess, or *without restraint*. Something *widespread* can be considered as having no boundaries. Also, given the context of the sentence, one can see that crime is out of control or at least very prevalent. Thus, choice (B) is the best answer.

24. D

Puny means *weak or without strength*, and *weak* is one of your answer choices, therefore choice (D) is correct.

25. D

Sinister is defined as *wicked or devious behavior*, and *evil* is another word for wicked. No other answer choice really fits the meaning of the given word.

26. C

The adjective *witty* is used to describe someone *characterized by cleverness*, definitely not someone sulking or careless. Only *clever* among the choices fits the definition.

27. A

An account said to "open the jury's eyes" would imply that it clarified or illuminated a situation. Thus, the last two choices are not appropriate, as they are negative responses. Of the other two, only choice (A) truly fits the definition as given by the context of the sentence.

28. A

To *relinquish* something is to *give it up*, so of the answer choices, only (A), *concede*, really fits.

29. C

Here's another good context question. The root of the given word *recur* is the prefix "re-," which means "again."

30. **A**

Incite means *to move to action*, and of the choices given, only (A), *induce*, gets that meaning across.

31. **A**

Similar to incite, the verb *implement* refers to *setting into motion or beginning*. While to *suggest* something might be to start a process, answer (A), *introduce*, can mean taking an action.

32. **B**

A *query* is a *question*. Therefore, answer choice (B) is correct.

33. **B**

Timid means *shy or lacking in courage*. While an animal that is scared may be dangerous if provoked, the correct answer choice is (B), *fearful*.

34. **C**

One's *colleague* is an *equal* or a *coworker*. Of the choices given, only *peer* is an acceptable answer. Choice (C) is correct.

35. **D**

Potent means *having or wielding authority or influence*. Another word for wielding influence would be *power*. Scanning the answer choices, only (D) is a possible answer.

PARAGRAPH COMPREHENSION ANSWERS AND EXPLANATIONS

1. C

The question asks you to read the passage with an eye towards its use of examples. Here, the author very clearly sets up the theme that Conan Doyle's character Holmes is a logical character. To illustrate that, he brings up a recognized scientific contemporary. Choices (A) and (B) have no bearing on the paragraph. Choice (D) brings up the idea of Darwin's meticulous research abilities, but does not reference the main focus of the paragraph (Holmes). Only choice (C) includes both men.

2. B

This detail question asks you to focus on the specific relationship between cities and climate as illustrated in the text. Looking back, we see that the paragraph introduces its subject first, and then gives some description of the changes that might take place. The last sentence in the paragraph finally gives us the information we need. Structures and man-made items affect the weather. Of the answer choices, choice (B) is the clearest paraphrase of that sentence.

3. B

This question asks you to make assumptions and predictions based on information given to you in the paragraph. From the tone of the passage, you can tell that Marianne is a generally quiet woman thrust into a high-profile situation. We can't really know what she's thinking exactly, but we can make an assumption based on the tone of the piece that she is overwhelmed by the attention given to her newfound wealth. Choices (A) and (C) seem to highlight the idea that she is a gaudy or flamboyant person, an assumption that seems all wrong given what we're told in the final sentence. Choice (D) is not reflected in the passage. Only answer choice (B) seems a fair assessment for Marianne's future behavior.

4. D

Here all you have to do is head back to the original text and find the word in question. Examining closely the context within which the word *infamous* is found, we find the group was plotting to blow up the King and the Parliament but were foiled. The gist of the paragraph is that the conspirators were up to no good, quite the opposite of heroes, choice (A). Choices (B) and (C) make no sense whatsoever. Only choice (D), *notorious*, accurately describes the sentiment the author meant.

5. A

Here's a nice easy one for you! All you have to do is judge the tone of the paragraph. Simple, right? Not so fast. Take a second to look at the language choices used: *screamed, knocked, ran*. Now take a close look at the answer choices, too. Choice (A) makes sense, since the action is so vivid and aggressive. Looks good, but let's save it and check out all the choices first. Answer (B) seems totally wrong for our purposes. Nothing here is tender. Choice (C) seems possible, but the sense of the paragraph is not so much exciting as dangerous. Choice (D) is wrong. Looking back at (C) and (A), choice (A) seems like the more appropriate choice.

6. D

Eliminate answers that either disagree with the passage, or that may or may not be true based on the passage. Choice (A) cannot be correct because it contradicts the passage: The life cycle is a direct result of the rain levels. (B) may or may not be true: although the passage mentions "astounding" blooms, it doesn't say anything about their color specifically. Wildlife, (C), isn't mentioned in the passage at all. (D) is a near-paraphrase of what the passage says about desert plant life cycles, so it is the correct answer.

7. C

The passage argues that many famous writers had narrow life experiences, but vivid imaginations, so look for an answer choice that makes a specific contrast between the need for imagination and experience in a writer's life. (C) makes that contrast. (A) contradicts the example of Robert Louis Stevenson, who wrote about things outside of his social scene. (B) similarly contradicts the example of Jane Austen, who did not write adventure stories. Friends and family (D) are mentioned in the passage, but not advice from friends or family.

8. C

The passage tells us that Tania was a good actress and gives examples of her variety of roles, so acting *prowess* describes a quality of good actors that she possesses. (C) suggests the positive quality of her versatility. Eliminate (B) and (D) because they are negative words, whereas you're looking for a positive quality. Knowledge, (A), is positive, but is not necessarily related to acting versatility.

9. B

Eliminate any answer choices that do not have to be true based on the passage. The color of coral animals (A) is not mentioned in the passage at all. (B) is practically a paraphrase of sentence two, "Beneath the waves . . . is a fantastic and very beautiful world," so (B) is the correct answer. (C) may or may not be true based on the passage. (D) is contradicted by the last sentence, which says that vast numbers of animals—not volcanoes—form coral islands.

10. C

In a question about the passage as a whole, the wrong answers will often be either too broad or too narrow, or will mention subjects that aren't in the passage. Eliminate answer choices that don't fit the scope of the passage. (A) is too broad: The passage is about groups of immigrants in a particular area and time, not the whole history of immigration. (B) can't be right because cultural contributions aren't mentioned in the passage. (C) is the correct answer: The idea of assimilation is referred to throughout the passage. (D) is too narrow: the effect on cities is only mentioned in one sentence.

11. C

The passage says that the DAR thought that immigrants should "completely adopt American culture and customs." The rest of the paragraph about the DAR just gives examples of what they did to support that belief, so we're looking for an answer choice that describes how they thought immigrants should conform. (C) matches that idea most closely. Notice that, while other answer choices may or may not be true, they don't fit specifically with what the author is saying about the DAR in the passage.

12. A

In the second sentence, the passage says that an animal adapts "color, shape and behavior in order to blend into its environment." The rest of the paragraph is a list of examples about how different animals become "all but invisible" with camouflage, so we're looking for an answer that says camouflage makes animals hard to see. (A) matches that idea. The passage says nothing about nesting (B) or habitats (C), and most of the animals mentioned are prey animals, not predators (D).

13. C

The key to this question is in the first sentence: " . . . the biggest surprise . . . was the discovery . . . of intense volcanic activity." Choice (C), the correct answer, is a paraphrase of the sentence about surprise. Don't be distracted by the rest of the details listed in the paragraph or by the other answer choices. The key idea here is the observers' surprise.

14. **C**

In an "all are true EXCEPT" question, concentrate on eliminating any answer choices that are true according to the passage. Eliminate choice (A) because it is true according to the first sentence. The second sentence says that choice (B) is true, so eliminate it too. Sentence four says that adults enjoyed the early Hula Hoops, so (C) must be false. (C) is the correct answer. The last two sentences of the passage show how (D) must be true since they describe how the Hula Hoop was a hit for the "fledgling" toy company.

15. **B**

Eliminate answer choices that are too broad, too narrow, or not mentioned in the passage. (A) is too broad: the passage doesn't include any information on fads besides the Hula Hoop. (B) is the correct answer: The passage starts with the earliest origins of the hoop toy and ends up with the popularization of the Hula Hoop. (C) is too narrow: only one sentence in the passage explains how the name came about. The passage says that the Hula Hoop is popular, (D), but doesn't address why.

AUTOMOTIVE AND SHOP INFORMATION ANSWERS AND EXPLANATIONS

1. A
There is a fuel injector for each cylinder. When the ignition key is moved to the "start" position, the engine is cranked over and the cylinders that are on their intake stroke begin to draw air into their respective combustion chambers. The PCM directs an electrical pulse to the fuel injectors to open the injector and allow fuel to spray into the intake air stream, and therefore into the cylinder.

2. C
The current that flows through the ignition primary winding builds a strong magnetic field that surrounds both it and the *secondary coil winding*. This is the device that creates high voltage for the spark plugs.

3. C
This is a switching mechanism that allows one ignition coil to serve all the engine cylinders.

4. C
It takes about one month, or *30 days*, for concrete to completely cure. The correct answer is (C).

5. D
The instrument pictured is a *ratchet*, used mostly for loosening or tightening bolts.

6. B
A tire that is run at low pressures can fail prematurely due to overheating of the sidewalls.

7. D
Not only do underinflated tires cause damage to the sidewalls, but vehicle stability, fuel economy and steering can all be affected as well. Thus the correct answer here is (D), all of the above.

8. B
Carpenters often will use a *claw hammer*, which serves a dual-purpose. The hammer head has two ends: one to drive nails and the other to remove nails. Claw hammers come in a variety of sizes, and these are determined by the weight of the hammer head. A general purpose claw hammer would have a 13 oz. head.

9. B
Center punches are used to make small indentations that serve as starting marks for drilling operations. Making a small indentation with a center punch can help the drill bit stay on target long enough to get a hole started.

10. C
There are six cells in an automotive battery.

11. A
Automatic transmissions do all of the gear selection for the driver. This is done in the transmission using hydraulics and *planetary gear sets*. The newest automatic transmissions are controlled electronically by the vehicle's powertrain control module.

12. A
Brake systems are *hydraulically operated*. A pumping piston, located in the master cylinder, is operated by the brake pedal and puts pressure on the system's brake fluid.

13. B
The best way to protect gears operating at high speeds and under high strain is via *roller bearings*. These alleviate stress on the gears in your engine.

14. D

MIG welding is also known as *wire-feed welding* because the electrode used for the weld process is a wire that is automatically fed from a spool.

15. A

The vast majority of fasteners are *threaded*. A bolt, for instance, has *external threads*, where a nut has *internal threads*.

16. D

None of the ignition systems listed would utilize contact points. Only older cars with breaker points would have contact points.

17. A

When working with wood, there are many occasions when it is necessary to remove a small amount of material to make a piece fit properly or to make a surface smooth. One tool that can be used for this purpose is a *plane*.

18. D

The *pitman arm* is a short lever arm connected to the steering gear which transmits the steering force from the cross shaft to the steering linkage system. Long-short arm suspensions most commonly use linkage steering to connect the steering column to the pitman arm, center link, and idler arm.

19. C

The catalytic converter is responsible for converting the toxic components of engine exhaust into relatively harmless compounds such as carbon dioxide and water and is, thus, part of both (A), the exhaust system, and (B), the emission control system.

20. C

The most common type of pliers is the *combination slip-joint*. These are adjustable at the joint of the two handles of the pliers. With two different positions to choose from, these pliers can grip objects in a wide range of sizes. Sometimes, this design also incorporates *a wire cutter* for increased versatility.

21. A

For higher engine speeds, the flame must be started *earlier* (A) in order to generate the most effective downward push on the piston. This is known as *advancing* the timing.

22. A

The piece shown is called an *auger bit*. It's job is to bore a large hole in wood and it is shaped much like the stripes on a barber's pole to lift the sawdust out of the hole as the boring process continues.

23. D

A common type of suspension system, long-short arm suspension systems include *ball joints*, *upper control arms* and *lower control arms*, among other components.

24. D

The most common chisel is the *cold chisel*, which has a straight, sharp edge for cutting off bolt heads or separating two pieces of an assembly.

25. A

Of the given choices, only (A), worn engine bearings, would not be the cause of a loss of compression, as the engine bearings do not weigh in on compression issues.

MATHEMATICS KNOWLEDGE ANSWERS AND EXPLANATIONS

1. B

In order to render this equation manageable, first turn the mixed number into an improper fraction, and then multiply both sides of the equation by 12 to clear the denominators:

$$\frac{3}{4} + 1\frac{1}{3} = \frac{5}{6} - x$$

$$\frac{3}{4} + \frac{4}{3} = \frac{5}{6} - x$$

$$12\left(\frac{3}{4} + \frac{4}{3}\right) = 12\left(\frac{5}{6} - x\right)$$

$$9 + 16 = 10 - 12x$$

$$12x = 10 - 9 - 16$$

$$12x = -15$$

$$x = -\frac{15}{12} = -\frac{5}{4} = -1\frac{1}{4}$$

2. C

Use FOIL:

$$(3a + 4)(4a - 3)$$

$$(3a \times 4a) + [3a \times (-3)] + (4 \times 4a) + [4 \times (-3)]$$

$$= 12a^2 - 9a + 16a - 12$$

$$= 12a^2 + 7a - 12.$$

3. D

If $2m > 24$, then $m > 12$. But so are all the answer choices, so check out the other inequality. If $3m < 48$, then $m < 16$. Thus, (D), 16, could not be a possible value for m.

4. A

For starters, (D) is out. When you add square roots, you can't simply combine the sums under the radical sign, as (D) does. But what you can do is factor out perfect squares from the number under the radical signs, like so:

$$\sqrt{75} + \sqrt{108} =$$

$$\sqrt{25 \times 3} + \sqrt{36 \times 3} =$$

$$\sqrt{25} \times \sqrt{3} + \sqrt{36} \times \sqrt{3} =$$

$$5\sqrt{3} + 6\sqrt{3} = 11\sqrt{3}.$$

5. B

Since the lengths of each side of a square are the same, $PQ = PS$. Therefore:

$$3a + 2 = 2a + 7$$
$$a = 5.$$

So choice (B) is correct.

6. B

The three interior angles of any triangle add up to 180°, and the parts of the ratio here add up to $1 + 2 + 3 = 6$. So to know what to multiply the ratio part numbers by to get numbers that add up to 180, divide 180 by 6, which gives you 30. Now you know that the three angles have degree measures of $1 \times 30 = 30$, $2 \times 30 = 60$, and $3 \times 30 = 90$. So the difference in the degree measures between the largest and the smallest angles is $90 - 30 = 60$.

7. A

The Pythagorean theorem states that in a right triangle, $a^2 + b^2 = c^2$, where a and b are the two perpendicular side lengths, called the legs, and c is the length of the hypotenuse. To figure out the perimeter of this triangle, we need the length of the hypotenuse, so let's apply the Pythagorean theorem:

$$(3)^2 + (6)^2 = c^2$$
$$9 + 36 = c^2$$
$$45 = c^2$$
$$c = \sqrt{45} = \sqrt{9} \times \sqrt{5} = 3\sqrt{5}$$

So now you can add together the sides to get the perimeter: $3 + 6 + 3\sqrt{5} = 9 + 3\sqrt{5}$.

8. D

Since AE is a line segment, all the lengths are additive, so $AE = AD + DE$. We're told that $AD = 6$ and $AE = 8$. So $DE = AE - AD = 8 - 6 = 2$. We're also told that $BE = 6$. So $BD = BE - DE = 6 - 2 = 4$. We have the length of BD, but still need the length of BC. Since $CD = 3(BC)$, the situation looks like this:

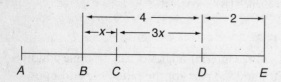

Here x stands for the length of BC. Since $BD = 4$, we can write:

$$x + 3x = 4$$
$$4x = 4$$
$$x = 1$$

So $BC = 1$, answer choice (D).

9. B

The central rectangle shares a side with each of the four squares, and the four squares form the legs of the four right triangles. Two of the rectangle's sides have a length of 4, so the two squares that share these sides must also have sides of length 4. The other two sides of the rectangle have a length of 3, so the other two squares, which share these sides, must also have sides of length 3. Each triangle shares a side with a small square and a side with a large square, so the legs of each triangle have lengths of 3 and 4, respectively.

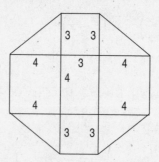

Since the legs are of length 3 and 4, the hypotenuse of each triangle must have a length of 5. The perimeter is the sum of the hypotenuses of the triangles and a side from each square:

$$\text{Perimeter} = 4(5) + 2(4) + 2(3)$$
$$= 20 + 8 + 6$$
$$= 34.$$

10. D

If $\dfrac{\sqrt{n}}{3}$ is an even integer, then $\dfrac{\sqrt{n}}{3} = 2k$, where k is an integer because any even integer is equal to 2 multiplied by an integer. Since $\dfrac{\sqrt{n}}{3} = 2k$, $\sqrt{n} = 6k$. Squaring both sides of $\sqrt{n} = 6k$, we have $(\sqrt{n})^2 = (6k)^2$, and $n = 36k^2$. So n must be a multiple of 36. Only choice (D), 144, is a multiple of 36. $144 = 4 \times 36$. Checking choice (D), $\dfrac{\sqrt{144}}{3} = \dfrac{12}{3} = 4$ and 4 is an even integer. Choice (D) is correct.

11. D

Here's a good opportunity to pick numbers. For instance, you could pick 10 for n, so that Gheri is 10 years old. In that case, Carl is 4 years old and Jean is 2 years old. So the sum of their ages is $10 + 4 + 2 = 16$. Now, if you plug 10 in for n into the answer choices, you get:

$3n + 4 = 3 \times 10 + 4 = 34$.   Too big.

$3n - 4 = 3 \times 10 - 4 = 26$.   No good.

$3n - 8 = 3 \times 10 - 8 = 22$.   Still too big.

$3n - 14 = 3 \times 10 - 14 = 16$.   That's more like it!

12. C

We hope you are comfortable with basic mathematical definitions. 2, 19, 37 and 67 are all prime. $51 = 3 \times 17$, so it is not prime. Knowing the *rules of divisibility* can help you when dealing with problems involving prime numbers, multiples, or factors. For instance, here one should be able to see quickly that 51 is divisible by 3, because its digits—5 and 1—add up to 6, which is a multiple of 3. (C) is correct.

13. B

The circumference of a circle $= 2\pi(\text{radius})$, so a circle with a circumference of 2π has a radius of 1. The area of a circle $= \pi(\text{radius})^2$ so the area of a circle with a radius of 1 is $\pi(1)^2 = \pi$.

14. D

To figure out the probability that a band member chosen at random will be a sophomore, you just have to apply the probability formula:

$$\text{Probability} = \frac{\text{Number of favorable outcomes}}{\text{Number of possible outcomes}},$$

or in this case,

$$\text{Probability} = \frac{\text{Number of sophomores}}{\text{Number of band members}}$$

$$= \frac{20}{13 + 20 + 16 + 15} = \frac{20}{64} = \frac{5}{16}.$$

Thus the correct answer is (D).

15. C

The key here is to realize that $a - b = -(b - a)$. So if $k - 3 = -\frac{5}{3}$, then $3 - k = -\left(-\frac{5}{3}\right) = \frac{5}{3}$.

16. A

Solve the equation $\frac{3x}{5} = 3x^2$ for x. Since $x \neq 0$, we can divide both sides by x. Then $\frac{3}{5} = 3x$. Dividing both sides by 3, we have $\frac{1}{5} = x$. Thus, $x = \frac{1}{5}$.

17. A

Here's another situation where you could pick numbers (otherwise you could use substitution). The key to picking numbers here is to know where to begin picking. Here the best place to start is with c and d. You're told that $4c = 3d$, so you make $c = 3$ and $d = 4$. So if $c = 3$ and $\frac{1}{2}b = c$, then $b = 6$. And if $b = 6$ and $a = 2b$, then $a = 12$. Therefore, using the numbers we picked $\frac{d}{a} = \frac{4}{12} = \frac{1}{3}$, choice (A).

18. B

Begin by converting the dimensions of the rectangular area to be covered to inches: 2 feet by 3 feet = 24 inches by 36 inches. 3 inches go into 24 inches 8 times, and 4 inches go into 36 inches 9 times, so to cover the area $8 \times 9 = 72$ tiles are needed.

19. A

$\frac{1}{4} = \frac{7}{28}$ and $\frac{1}{3} = \frac{7}{21}$, so the integer values for which $\frac{7}{x}$ will be greater than $\frac{1}{4}$ and less than $\frac{1}{3}$ are all the integers between 21 and 28. Play it safe and list them out: 22, 23, 24, 25, 26, 27, for a total of 6, choice (A).

20. **B**

The manhole cover has a diameter of 14 inches, so its radius is 7 inches and its area is $\pi(7)^2 = 49\pi$ square inches. The diameter of the hole is 12 square inches, so its radius is 6 inches and its area is $\pi(6)^2 = 36\pi$ square inches. Thus, the cover is $49\pi - 36\pi = 13\pi$ square inches greater than the area of the manhole.

21. **C**

Some answer choices you should be able to eliminate straight off the bat. $\frac{4}{7}$ is greater than $\frac{1}{2}$, so that's out, as is, for that matter, $\frac{1}{2}$. So you're left with $\frac{1}{3}$, which is about 0.333, and $\frac{3}{8}$, which is 0.375. Choice (C) is closest.

22. **A**

Since the question asks for the answer in dollars, start by converting cents to dollars. There are 100 cents in a dollar, so 39 cents $= \frac{39}{100}$ dollars. Since each peach costs $\frac{39}{100}$ dollars, y peaches cost $\frac{39}{100}y$ dollars. If x oranges cost as much as y peaches, x oranges also cost $\frac{39}{100}y$ dollars or $\frac{39y}{100}$ dollars. Then one orange costs $\frac{1}{x}$ as much, or $\frac{39y}{100x}$ dollars.

This is an ideal problem to solve by picking numbers. Let's say that 5 oranges and 10 peaches cost the same; that is $x = 5$ and $y = 10$. If peaches are 39 cents each, 10 of them will cost \$3.90, so that's the cost of 5 oranges. That means each orange costs $\frac{\$3.90}{5}$ or \$0.78. We try our numbers in each answer choice:

Choice (A): $\frac{(39)(10)}{(100)(5)} = \frac{390}{500} = \frac{39}{50} = 0.78$. This may be our answer.

Choice (B): $\frac{(39)(5)}{(100)(10)} = \frac{195}{1,000}$. Discard.

Choice (C): $\frac{3,900}{(5)(10)} = \frac{3,900}{50} = 78$. This is 78 dollars, not 78 cents. Discard.

Choice (D): $\frac{(39)(5)}{10} = \frac{195}{10} = 19.5$. Again, discard

Choice (A) it is!

23. **C**

To come up with the largest number of groups, you should minimize the number of students in each group. Each group must contain at least three students, so that means you could have a total of 12 groups with 3 students in them, and one final group with 4 students in it, for a total of 13 groups, choice (C).

24. **C**

The altitude to the base of the triangle is the same thing as the height of the triangle, and the area of a triangle $= \frac{1}{2}$(base)(height). So if the area of the triangle is 36 and its base is 9, the altitude is found as follows: $36 = \frac{1}{2}(9)$(altitude), so altitude $= \frac{36}{9} \times 2 = 4 \times 2 = 8$.

25. **C**

Just plug in -5 for x into the equation and solve:
$$2(-5)^2 - 6(-5) + 5 = 2(25) + 30 + 5 = 85.$$

MECHANICAL COMPREHENSION ANSWERS AND EXPLANATIONS

1. A

If, as stated, a gear set has a ratio of 3:1, and if the driven gear has 21 teeth, the drive gear will have 7 teeth. The correct answer is (A).

2. D

Having a gear ratio of 0.75:1 would mean that the driven gear turns faster than the drive gear because it is smaller. It also means that the torque output is less than the input and that, by name, the gear set is an overdrive gear set. So since all the given answers are correct, the correct response is (D).

3. B

Since the question asks which of the following are true, and since we always remember that smaller gears *always* turn faster, the answer is (B).

4. A

The speed ratio between pulleys is determined by the radius of the pulleys. For instance, if a drive pulley has a radius of 5 inches, and the driven pulley has a radius of 10 inches, the speed ratio will be 2:1.

5. D

Here, you are calculating the output torque when 100 foot-pounds of torque is applied to a gear set with a ratio of 4:1. The output torque for the 100-foot pounds, given that the ratio is 4:1 would be 400 foot-pounds of output torque. The correct answer is (D).

6. C

There are several properties of liquids that are unchanging. First, they are effectively incompressible. Even when extremely high pressure is applied to a liquid, the volume of the liquid will decrease only a very small amount. This property makes liquids very effective for transmitting force. And the second overarching principle of hydraulics

is that liquids conform themselves to the shape of their container. Whether in a pipe or a pump, liquids will always change their shape to fill the space completely. But not all liquids are by nature good lubricants. Here, the correct answer is (C).

7. C

Since answer choices (B) and (C) are similar, you know that one of these is most likely not true. The correct formula for calculating force is Force = Pressure × Area. The other answer choices are all derivatives of this formula except for (C).

8. D

This one's just to see if you are paying attention. Using the formula for pressure $\left(P = \dfrac{F}{A}\right)$, if 100 pounds of force are applied over an area of 2 square inches, then the resulting pressure is 50 pounds per square inch. Another way of shortening this answer is to say it is 50 *psi*. So technically, (D) is the answer, as both (A) and (B) are correct.

9. D

The truth is that a hydraulic cylinder is a linear actuator, does have a sealed piston, and also uses oil pressure to generate force. This is the main purpose of hydraulic cylinders. Consequently, (D) is the correct answer.

10. C

Hydraulic fluid is normally a petroleum-based oil.

11. B

The key to amplifying force with hydraulic cylinders is the difference in the diameter of their pistons. If one piston is much smaller than the other, the smaller piston is known as the *pumping piston*, and this is the piston that the effort is applied to. The surface area of the pumping piston that makes contact with the liquid is only a fraction of the size of the *load piston*, which is the piston that will raise the load. The correct answer to generate more force is to *increase* the diameter of the load piston.

12. C

According to Newton's Second Law of Motion, when a net force acts on an object, the object will accelerate in the direction of the net force. The acceleration will be less if the mass of the object is greater.

13. C

The speed ratio between pulleys is determined by the radius of the pulleys, with increased speed directly related to smaller diameter. Smaller pulleys *always* turn faster than larger ones. The correct answer is (C).

14. A

According to the rules of Bernoulli's theorem, as air moves over the wing, the air that moves over the top surface must travel faster than the air on the underside. This results in air pressure on the top of the wing being *lowered*, and since the pressure is greater on the lower surface, *lift* is achieved. The correct answer is (A).

15. C

The load piston has a total surface area of 10 square inches. Using the formula $P = \dfrac{F}{A}$, 100 pounds ÷ 10 square inches = 10 pounds per square inch (psi) of pressure that should be applied to the load piston.

16. B

The force applied to the pumping piston is $\dfrac{1}{10}$ of the force that is developed at the load piston. The mechanical advantage gained with a system such as this is determined by the ratio of the surface areas of the pistons.

17. D

Note that in order to lift the load 1 foot, it is necessary to pull the rope a total of 4 feet. This is because each of the four rope links must shorten by 1 foot to get the lower block to move 1 foot. Neglecting friction, this gives a total mechanical advantage of 4:1, so if 4 pounds of force are required to lift a load, only 1 pound needs to be applied to the rope.

18. A

The lever shown is an example of a first class lever with fulcrum, effort, and object.

19. C

In the example of the hockey puck sliding along an ice surface, while ice has much less friction than most surfaces, it will still exert a sliding frictional force on the puck that eventually causes it to stop moving.

20. A

Torque is *twisting force*. When a bolt is being tightened, torque is being applied to the bolt. For example, when tightening a fastener, if one uses a wrench that is one foot long, and applies a force of 100 pounds to the end of the wrench in a direction perpendiculsr to the wrench, 100 foot-pounds (ft-lb) of torque is being applied.

21. B

The air compressor is an energy conversion device, converting the mechanical energy of the compressor into the potential energy of the compressed air.

22. D

Multiplying the coefficient of static friction by the normal force yields the maximum static frictional force, shown by the formula $f_s^{MAX} = \mu_s F_N$ where μ_s is the coefficient of static friction, F_N is the normal force in newtons (N), and f_s^{MAX} is the maximum static frictional force in newtons *(N)*. The maximum static frictional force is the amount of force that must be applied to a static (nonmoving) object to start it moving.

23. C

Work is accomplished when force is applied against an object in motion. This is summarized by the formula

$$W = Fd$$

where F is force in newtons (N), d is distance in meters (m), and W is work in joules (J). These units are also part of the SI system of measurement. If a force of 100 N is applied to the box, and the box is moved 10 meters, then a total of 1,000 joules of work has been done.

24. A

According to Newton's Gravitational Law, since gravity exerts a force on bodies that pulls them together, this force causes an acceleration due to gravity, which is represented by the symbol *g*.

25. A

Due to the ratio of the gear to the pinion, the pinion rotates 100×2 times for each rotation of the gear.

ELECTRONICS INFORMATION ANSWERS AND EXPLANATIONS

1. B

Impedance is the total opposition to the flow of electrical charge.

2. D

As electric current passes through a wire, a magnetic field is generated around the wire. The magnetic field can be made stronger by winding the wire into a coil.

3. B

Voltage can be given in a number of different units. Small voltages are expressed as millivolts (mV), which are the same as $\frac{1}{1000}$ of a volt. Large voltages can be given in kilovolts (KV) or even megavolts (MV).

4. C

The circuit pictured is a *series* circuit.

5. B

In a series circuit, *the current flow will be the same in all parts of the circuit*. The current that leaves the voltage source must return to the voltage source, and since there is only one path for current to follow in a series circuit, current will be the same throughout the circuit.

6. C

A sinusoidal wave, or carrier wave, is used to transmit other high-frequency waves and wireless signals.

7. B

Calculating resistance is easy if you know the formula (R = E ÷ I) and can easily convert the factors in your equation. In this case, 5 mA should be made to be .005 A. The resistance comes out to be 50 V divided by .005 A, or 10,000 Ω of resistance. Remember to place your answer in the same form that the answer choices are given to you. Answer choice (B) is just a shortened way of saying 10,000 Ω.

8. B

Stranding wires makes them less brittle or capable of snapping by making them more flexible than standard, even insulated, wires. However, it has little effect on their ability to conduct or on their tensile strength. Answer choice (B) is correct.

9. D

Since diodes are rated according to the maximum amount of current that can flow in the forward-bias direction without damaging them and are also rated according to their peak inverse voltage (PIV), the maximum amount of voltage that can be withstood in the reverse-bias direction, the answer is (D), both (A) and (B).

10. B

The crystalline structure of pure silicon is very stable. The four valence electrons in each silicon atom bond with the valence electrons in the atoms around it, so no free electrons exist to allow current flow. This can be changed by "doping" the silicon's crystal structure with either phosphorous, arsenic, or antimony. Since these elements all have five electrons in their valence shell, they will bond themselves to the other silicon atoms, but leave one free electron that is able to migrate throughout the crystal. This changes the silicon crystal into an N-type material. This new material is still electrically neutral, but is able to conduct electricity due to the presence of free electrons. The correct answer is (B).

11. C

Electronic circuits that utilize resistors along with capacitors and inductors are known as *RCL* circuits.

12. D

An electrical circuit that has only one path for current to flow is known as a series circuit. A break (opening) at any point in the circuit will cause current to stop flowing in all parts of the circuit. An excellent example of a series circuit is a string of miniature Christmas lights.

13. A

For increased gain, two transistors can be connected in a configuration called a *Darlington pair*, named after its inventor, Sidney Darlington. This allows a very small current to control a very large current. This type of circuit is very common in automotive and other electronic applications. The correct answer is (A).

14. C

Taking a quick look at the periodic chart will tell you that there are always two electrons in an element's inner shell and that the remaining electrons reside in what is called the valence shell. An element with an atomic number of 10, therefore, will have eight electrons in its valence shell. The correct answer is (C).

15. C

More than four electrons in the valence shell means that the element is an insulator. Insulators do not conduct electricity, and therefore are useful for creating electrical barriers. Examples of insulators are rubber and plastic. Thus, an element with five electrons in its valence shell is (C), an insulator.

16. B

Based on the formula for finding total resistance, $\frac{1}{R_{Total}} = \frac{1}{R_1} + \frac{1}{R_2} + \frac{1}{R_3}$, one can see that adding loads to a parallel circuit is going to *decrease* the total resistance as you go. Thinking in non-mathematical terms, the added loads will decrease resistance within a parallel circuit. The correct answer is (B).

17. D

Inductors work exactly opposite to capacitors, in the sense that they allow DC to pass easily, but resist the flow of AC. This is known as *inductive reactance*, and it will rise in direct proportion to the frequency of the current flowing through the inductor. Since both A and B are correct, the best answer choice is (D), (A) and (B) only.

18. B

A vehicle's ground is the zero-voltage point in the system. The remainder of the system operates at a voltage that is above ground. Since all vehicles being built today have the negative post of the battery connected to the chassis, these are all known as *negative ground systems*. There was a time when some vehicles were built with positive ground systems, but negative ground became the eventual standard that all car manufacturers built to. The correct answer is (B).

19. D

The symbol E stands for voltage in Ohm's law. Electromotive force and electrical pressure are both simply other names for voltage. Thus, the correct answer is (D), all of the above.

20. D

Of the statements given about series circuits, only choice (D), voltage drops across the loads depend on their resistance, is not true of series circuits. In a series circuit, *the current flow will be the same in all parts of the circuit*. The current that leaves the voltage source must return to the voltage source, and since there is only one path for current to follow in a series circuit, current will be the same throughout the circuit. Voltage measured across each of the components, on the other hand, may be different depending on their resistance.

HOW TO READ YOUR ASVAB SCORES

Your real ASVAB scores will come in a variety of styles, ranging from raw score (right versus wrong) to composite scores (certain sections paired and taken separately). All of the scores matter, though some matter more than others.

Let's take a look.

How Is the Test Scored?

The **ASVAB** is scored in more ways than you can shake a stick at.

First, you receive a score for each of the eight subtests, and you will also receive a score for three "composite areas:"

- Verbal Ability Composite = Word Knowledge Score + Paragraph Comprehension Score
- Math Ability Composite = Arithmetic Reasoning Score + Mathematics Knowledge Score
- Academic Ability Composite = Verbal Ability Composite + Math Ability Composite

Second, your raw score is computed with this formula:

(Word Knowledge Score × 2) + (Paragraph Comprehension Score × 2) + (Arithmetic Reasoning Score) + (Mathematics Knowledge Score) = Raw Score

So for example, if you score 30 on Word Knowledge, 15 on Paragraph Comprehension, 25 on Arithmetic Reasoning, and 25 on Mathematics Knowledge, your raw score would be 140.

The raw score is then converted into a percentile score. If you score in the 70th percentile, for example, you scored higher than 69 percent of the people who took the test. This is the score that recruiters look at when determining if you're eligible to enlist.

Finally, you'll get a Military Careers Score, which combines the Academic Ability Composite score with the Mechanical Comprehension and Electronics Information scores. The score range is 140 to 240 (200 is the average). When you receive your scores, you will also receive the book *Military Careers*, which describes military jobs, and includes a graph that shows your chances of landing them based on the Military Careers Score. For example, your chances of qualifying for a certain job are 90 percent if you have a Military Careers Score of 220, but only 20 percent if you score 180 or lower.

Your scores from the General Science and Auto and Shop Information subtests are not included in the above, but they are used by recruiters to identify other career areas that you might have an aptitude for. The first and most important thing is to get a good Academic Ability Composite, otherwise you won't qualify for enlistment.

AFQT

For more detailed information on the general makeup of the ASVAB AFQT score, you should review the information included in the introductory chapter to this book. But it is also important to know how you're scored and what your AFQT score qualifies you to do.

The AFQT score you receive is, quite simply, the determining factor in your acceptance into any branch of the armed forces.

2 × [Word Knowledge + Paragraph Comprehension]

+

[Arithmetic Reasoning + Mathematical Knowledge]

= AFQT RAW SCORE

The AFQT raw score you receive is then translated into a percentile score (see explanation of percentile scores above) to determine your eligibility for the Armed Forces.

AFQT Percentile	AFQT Category
93–99	I
65–92	II
50–64	III-A
31–49	III-B
10–30	IV
1–9	V

The AFQT score has its cutoffs. No one under a score of 10 (Category V) is allowed to continue processing or enlist in the Armed Forces. Those with a score in Category IV (10-30) may continue processing at MEPS, but are ineligible for immediate enlistment. Acceptance of each other category percentile is done in accordance with Congressionally mandated standards.

No enlistees may come from the lowest 10 percentiles—CAT V—and no more than 25 percent of enlistees can have scores between the 9th and 31st percentiles—CAT IV. Operational standards for recruiting often differ but do not fall below these legal standards. Operational standards vary over time to reflect the needs of the service, the ease or difficulty of recruiting due to labor market conditions, or other factors. For example, operational standards might require that all enlistees have a high school diploma or that recruits be restricted to CAT I–IIIB. In addition, recruiter incentives are designed in a way that will influence the mix of recruits. For instance, the incentives are often designed to encourage recruiters to enlist "high-quality" recruits.

Each branch has set its own cut score for entry (given in percentiles). High enough AFQT scores give recruits the options of attractive occupational placements.

Air Force recruits must score at least **40** on the AFQT (non-HS diploma holders must score 50)

Marine Corps recruits must score at least **32** on the AFQT (GED holders must score at least 50)

Navy recruits must score at least **31** on the AFQT

Army recruits must score at least **31** on the AFQT (GED holders must score at least 50)

Bonuses and job choices are based on your score and the availability of each.

So you can see now why it is imperative that ASVAB takers with any interest in military enlistment pay particular attention to the math and verbal sections of the ASVAB, as they help determine not only eligibility for general enlistment, but also for job placement and for overall military branch acceptance.

NOTES

NOTES

Introducing a smarter way to learn.

- · Focused, practice-based learning
- · Concepts for everyday life
- · Recognition and recall exercises
- · Quizzes throughout

Available wherever books are sold.

www.kaptest.com
www.simonsays.com